Yearbook on

International

Communist Affairs

1980

Yearbook on

International

Communist Affairs

1980

EDITOR: Richard F. Staar

Associate Area Editors:

Eastern Europe and the Soviet Union	Milorad M. Drachkovitch
Western Europe	Dennis L. Bark
Asia and the Pacific	Ramon H. Myers
The Americas	William E. Ratliff
Africa and the Middle East	Lewis H. Gann
International Communist Front Organizations	Alex N. Dragnich

HOOVER INSTITUTION PRESS
STANFORD UNIVERSITY, STANFORD, CALIFORNIA

Hoover Institution Publication 235

CONTENTS

Asia and the Pacific

The Americas

Africa and the Middle East

International Communist Front Organizations

Biographies

Introduction

The purpose of the 1980 *Yearbook on International Communist Affairs*, the fourteenth consecutive volume in this series, is to provide basic data concerning organizational and personnel changes, attitudes toward domestic and foreign policies, and activities of communist parties and international front organizations throughout the world. Much of the information comes from primary source materials in the native languages. The profile on each party includes founding date, legal or proscribed status, membership, electoral and parliamentary (if any) strength, leadership, auxiliary organizations, domestic activities, ideological orientation, views on international issues, attitude toward the Sino-Soviet dispute, and principal news media. Identity as a Marxist-Leninist party remains the criterion for inclusion, and hence pro-Soviet, pro-Chinese, pro-Castroite, Trotskyist, and other rival communist movements are treated whenever possible.

Excluded from the *Yearbook* are a broad range of Marxist-oriented "liberation movements," such as the African National Congress, the Zimbabwe African People's Union, or the South West African People's Organization, even though all these bodies follow a pro-Soviet course. The *Yearbook* also omits a variety of Marxist-Leninist ruling parties that have a "socialist orientation." According to the Soviet party organ *Pravda* (3 February), several are on the road to a "revolutionary transformation." But they do not yet describe themselves, or are not alluded to in Soviet publications, as orthodox communist-ruled parties, and hence they do not merit inclusion in the *Yearbook*. Such is the case with the Parti congolais du travail, the ruling movement in the People's Republic of the Congo, whose Marxist-Leninist credentials for the moment are more rhetorical than actual. Moreover, movements such as the Frente de Libertação de Mocambique (FRELIMO) and Movimento Popular de Libertacão de Angola (MPLA) for the present may be described as Afro-Marxist rather than communist. Although the former rules in Mozambique, it still lacks the discipline, ideological solidarity, and organizational coherence down to the local level usually associated with orthodox communist movements. Similarly, the MPLA may consider itself Marxist, but it derives support from Soviet and East German advisers as well as from Cuban armed forces in a continuing struggle against opposition.

Omitted also, because of insufficient data, are such groups as the communist parties of Benin, the Faroe Islands, Hong Kong, Nigeria (the Socialist Workers' and Farmers' Party), and Saudi Arabia, even though their Marxist-Leninist orthodoxy may not be in dispute.

The following parties held congresses during 1979:

Country	*Date*
Australia	15–18 June
Belgium	30 March–1 April
Bolivia	20–24 April
Dominican Republic	17–19 March

El Salvador	May
France	9–13 May
Great Britain	10–13 November
Guadeloupe	January
Guyana	4–6 August
Haiti	early 1979?
Ireland	23–25 February
Italy	30 March–3 April
Kampuchea (KNUFNS)	29 September
Laos (conference)	16–20 February
Lebanon	May
Malta	16–18 February
Morocco	23–26 February
New Zealand	26–28 January
Norway (conference)	9–11 June
Peru	31 October–4 November
Portugal	1–3 June
Puerto Rico	– –
Romania	19–23 November
Senegal	16–17 February
Thailand	October or December?
United States	22–26 August

Membership. The number of parties recognized as orthodox by the Communist Party of the Soviet Union (CPSU) remained at 99, of which 17 held power. Only 27 were proscribed (legal status came in El Salvador, Bangladesh, and Iran; Argentina forced the party to go underground again). By geographic region, one-third, or nine, of these operated clandestinely in Africa and the Middle East.

Total world membership has been estimated at 75 million, compared with approximately 71 million in 1978, an increase of just over 5 percent. Modest additions were claimed by all East European ruling parties, except for those in Albania and Bulgaria, which did not release any new figures. Among the most important movements in Western Europe, only the French and Portuguese registered an increase; the Italian declined slightly.

In Asia and the Pacific, the ruling party of Afghanistan claims to have doubled its membership, which is impossible to substantiate. A new estimate for the Communist Party of India, based on information from that country, gives that party more than 500,000 members. Other figures remain more or less constant. The Chinese claimed an increase of 2 million members, however.

Latin American movements registered various changes, with large increases in Bolivia, the Dominican Republic, Ecuador, Guyana, Jamaica, Nicaragua, and Venezuela, indicating rising activity in these countries. New estimates are given for Chile and Haiti. The figures for Africa and the Middle East are the same as in 1978 because more recent information remains unavailable.

Three of the international communist front organizations registered changes. The World Federation of Scientific Workers claims approximately 450,000 members, most of whom reside in party-ruled states, according to a Bulgarian source. This represents a 50-percent increase over the old figures. Radio Moscow reported a membership of 190 million for the World Federation of Trade

Unions, a 44-million growth since the last release some years ago. Finally, the World Peace Council supposedly maintains affiliates in 130 countries, i.e., ten more than previously claimed.

The accompanying tables provide an overview of the 99 communist movements and ten front organizations, including either estimated or claimed figures on membership for both categories. Results of the latest elections, both for ruling and nonruling parties, and finally, the position of each party on the Sino-Soviet dispute are given.

Communist Party of the Soviet Union (CPSU). The phenomenon of an aging leadership in the Soviet Union was dramatized several times during the past year. Changes in General Secretary Leonid I. Brezhnev's health more than once resulted in alterations of his official schedule, and the failure of Prime Minister Aleksei N. Kosygin to appear on important occasions may help to explain the promotion of his top deputy, 74-year-old Nikolai A. Tikhonov, to full membership in the ruling Politburo (*Pravda*, 28 November). At the same time the CPSU secretary for agriculture, Mikhail S. Gorbachev, became a candidate member of the Politburo. A number of other reshuffles in party and government posts at various levels, especially in the republic of Georgia, occurred.

Domestically, the main CPSU concern seemed to center on the economy, where many failures were cited. At the end of November, it was officially admitted to a Central Committee plenum that there were serious shortfalls in both industry and agriculture (grain production was 47 million tons short of target), which led Brezhnev to criticize at least six government ministries. Concern with energy matters (petroleum production did not attain its goal either) was reflected in several official pronouncements and the appointment of a high-level commission to deal with the threatening crisis. At the earlier midyear meeting of the Council for Mutual Economic Assistance in Moscow, the Russians warned their partners to save energy because they would have to begin cutting deliveries (*CSM*, 20 July).

During the year, attention was frequently called to another shortcoming: the failure of the party's ideological effort to combat anticommunist influences ranging from apathy to religion. Moreover, Soviet citizens were warned over a year in advance against succumbing to ideological contamination from the many foreign visitors expected during the 1980 summer Olympic games (*Moskovskaya pravda*, 8 May).

The crackdown on dissidents continued, but repressive measures were applied with less publicity than in past years. Jewish emigration reached record levels (some 50,000 departed during 1979), but this did not foreshadow liberalization of the regime's policies. The attempt to publish an independent literary journal entitled *Metropol* resulted in its suppression and the expulsion of several members from the Soviet Writers' Union. A few issues of another publication entitled *Searches*, some of whose articles defended the Russian Orthodox church, private enterprise, and Eurocommunism, resulted in official action against the editors. In another sphere, persecution of workers who had attempted to organize an independent labor movement continued. Similarly, an effort to run some independent candidates for the USSR Supreme Soviet (among others, Roy Medvedev) was quashed by the electoral commission.

The centennial of I. V. Stalin's birth (21 December) resulted in a *Novosti* press agency release and an article in *Kommunist*, both of which charged that the enemies of the USSR had chosen this occasion to attack the CPSU and the Soviet state. However, the "Fighting Man's Calendar for 1979" (Kalendar' voina na 1979 god) included an article based on the official encyclopedia but omitted its negative assessment of Stalin.

The most dramatic foreign policy event was the Carter-Brezhnev meeting in Vienna during mid-June to sign the SALT II agreement, which the USSR promptly ratified. While propagandizing in support of the treaty at every opportunity, the Russians nevertheless continued their day-to-day criticism of the United States, exhibiting particular concern over the projected installation of

CHECKLIST OF COMMUNIST PARTIES AND FRONTS

Eastern Europe and the Soviet Union (9)

Area	Population (est.)	Communist party membership	Percent of vote; seats in legislature	Status	Sino-Soviet dispute
Albania	2,626,000	101,500 claim	99.9 (1978); all 250 Democratic Front	in power	independent
Bulgaria	8,892,000	817,000 claim	99.9 (1976); 272 of 400 Fatherland Front	in power	pro-Moscow
Czechoslovakia	15,239,000	1,473,000 claim	99.7 (1976); all 350 National Front	in power	pro-Moscow
East Germany (GDR)	16,793,000	2,127,413 claim	99.9 (1976); 127 of 500 National Front	in power	pro-Moscow
Hungary	10,735,000	797,000 claim	99.6 (1975); all 352 Patriotic People's Front	in power	pro-Moscow
Poland	35,391,000	3,080,000 claim	99.4 (1976); 262 of 460 Front of National Unity	in power	pro-Moscow
*Romania	22,057,000	2,930,000 claim	99.9 (1975); all 349 Front of Socialist Unity	in power	neutral
USSR	263,818,000	16,630,000 claim	99.9 (1979); all 1,500 CPSU-approved	in power	—
*Yugoslavia	22,074,000	1,855,638 claim	— (1978); all 308 Socialist Alliance	in power	independent
Total	397,625,000	29,811,551 claim			

Western Europe (24)

Area	Population (est.)	Communist party membership	Percent of vote; seats in legislature	Status	Sino-Soviet dispute
*Austria	7,498,000	25,000 est.	0.96 (1979); none	legal	pro-Moscow
*Belgium	9,841,000	10,000 est.	3.25 (1978); 4 of 212	legal	pro-Moscow
Cyprus	640,000	12,000 est.	30.0 (1976); 9 of 35 Greek Cypriot seats	legal	pro-Moscow
*Denmark	5,130,000	8,000 est.	1.9 (1979); none	legal	pro-Moscow
*Faroe Islands	43,000	insignificant	— (1977); none	allowed	split
*Finland	4,771,000	45,000 est.	17.9 (1979); 35 of 200	legal	pro-Moscow
*France	53,451,000	700,000 claim	20.6 (1978); 86 of 491	legal	pro-Moscow
*Germany (FRG)	61,181,000	42,000 est.	0.3 (1976); none	legal	pro-Moscow
West Berlin	2,100,000	7,500 est.	1.1 (1979); none	legal	pro-Moscow
*Great Britain	55,822,000	20,599 claim	0.05 (1979); none	legal	pro-Moscow
*Greece	9,390,000	29,300 est.	9.3 (1977); 11 of 300	legal	pro-Moscow
*Iceland	225,000	3,000 est.	19.7 (1979); 11 of 60	legal	split (3)
Ireland	3,267,000	600 est.	— (1977); none	legal	independent
*Italy	56,924,000	1,790,450 claim	30.4 (1979); 201 of 630	legal	pro-Moscow
*Luxembourg	358,000	600 est.	4.8 (1979); 2 of 59	legal	pro-Moscow
*Malta	343,000	100 est.	— (1976); none	legal	pro-Moscow
*Netherlands	14,015,000	15,000 est.	1.7 (1977); 2 of 150	legal	pro-Moscow
*Norway	4,077,000	2,000 est.	5.2 (1977); 2 of 155	legal	independent
*Portugal	9,866,000	164,000 claim	19.0 (1979); 47 of 250	legal	pro-Moscow
*San Marino	20,000	300 est.	21.1 (1978); 16 of 60	legal	pro-Moscow
*Spain	37,551,000	200,000 claim	10.5 (1979); 23 of 350	legal	independent
*Sweden	8,273,000	17,000 est.	5.6 (1979); 20 of 349	legal	independent
*Switzerland	6,333,000	5,000 est.	1.5 (1979); 3 of 200	legal	pro-Moscow
Turkey	44,236,000	2,000 est.	— (1977)	proscribed	pro-Moscow
Total	395,355,000	3,099,449			

Asia and the Pacific (22)

Area	Population (est.)	Communist party membership	Percent of vote; seats in legislature	Status	Sino-Soviet dispute
Afghanistan	14,702,000	100,000 claim	no elections scheduled	in power	pro-Moscow
*Australia	14,400,000	5,000 est.	-- (1977); none	legal	split (3)
*Bangladesh	88,092,000	2,500 est.	-- (1979); 1 of 300	legal	split
*Burma	33,517,000	7,000 est. (ca. 10,000 guerrillas)	-- (1978)	proscribed	pro-Beijing
China	958,030,000	37,000,000 claim	indirect elections (1978)	in power	--
*Hong Kong	4,693,000	2,000 est.	city council (1977)	legal	pro-Beijing
*India	669,785,000	100,000 CPM est. 546,000 CPI claim	4.3 (1977); 22 of 244	legal	neutral
*Indonesia	148,085,000	1,000 est.	-- (1977)	proscribed	pro-Moscow
*Japan	116,051,000	400,000 est.	10.4 (1979); 39 of 511	legal	split
*Kampuchea	4,500,000	unknown	no elections scheduled	in power	pro-Moscow
*Korea (DPRK)	18,717,000	2,000,000 est.	100.0 (1977); all 579	in power	pro-Moscow
*Laos	3,630,000	15,000 est.	no elections scheduled	in power	neutral
*Malaysia	12,280,000	3,150 est.	-- (1978)	proscribed	pro-Moscow
Mongolia	1,639,000	67,000 claim	99.9 (1977); all 354	in power	split
Nepal	14,028,000	5,000 est.	-- (1959)	proscribed	pro-Moscow
*New Zealand	3,119,000	500 est.	0.2 (1978); none	legal	split
Pakistan	80,171,000	few hundred est.	1979 elections postponed	proscribed	neutral
*Philippines	46,893,000	4,250 est.	-- (1978)	proscribed	split
Singapore	2,361,000	500 est.	-- (1976)	proscribed	split
*Sri Lanka	14,502,000	6,000 est.	1.9 (1977); none	legal	pro-Beijing
*Thailand	46,350,000	1,200 est.	-- (1979)	proscribed	split
*Vietnam	52,558,000	1,533,000 claim (plus 10,500 guerrillas)	99.0 (1976); all 492	in power	pro-Moscow
Total	2,348,103,000	41,799,100			

The Americas (27)

Area	Population (est.)	Communist party membership	Percent of vote; seats in legislature	Status	Sino-Soviet dispute
*Argentina	26,829,000	70,000 est.	no elections scheduled	proscribed	pro-Moscow
*Bolivia	5,216,000	2,500 est.	-- (1979)	proscribed	split
Brazil	124,428,000	4,000 est.	-- (1978)	proscribed	split
*Canada	23,755,000	2,500 est.	0.2 (1979); none	legal	split
*Chile	10,850,000	75,000 est.	elections promised	proscribed	split
*Colombia	26,115,000	12,000 est.	1.9 (1978); 3 of 311	legal	split
Costa Rica	2,168,000	3,000 est.	2.7 (1978); 3 of 57	legal	pro-Moscow
Cuba	9,900,000	200,000 est.	91.7(1976); 441 of 481	in power	pro-Moscow
*Dominican Republic	5,539,000	5,000 est.	-- (1978); none	legal	factions
Ecuador	7,781,000	2,000 est.	3.2 (1979); none	legal	split
El Salvador	4,600,000	225 est.	-- (1976)	legal	pro-Moscow
*Guadeloupe	318,000	3,000 est.	-- (1979); 7 of 36	legal	pro-Moscow
Guatemala	6,817,000	750 est.	-- (1974);	proscribed	pro-Moscow
Guyana	850,000	500 est.	26.0 (1973); 14 of 53	legal	pro-Moscow
*Haiti	5,500,000	250 est.	-- (1973)	proscribed	pro-Moscow
*Honduras	3,639,000	650 est.	promised 1979/80	proscribed	split
Jamaica	2,233,000	400 est.	-- (1976); none	allowed	pro-Moscow
Martinique	315,000	1,000 est.	-- (1979); 3 of 36	legal	pro-Moscow
Mexico	68,506,000	25,000 est. (100,000 claim)	5.0 (1979); 18 of 300 directly elected	legal	pro-Moscow
*Nicaragua	2,485,000	410 est. (1,200 claim)	-- (1974)	uncertain	split
Panama	1,862,000	550 est.	-- (1972); none	allowed	pro-Moscow
Paraguay	3,100,000	3,500 est.	-- (1973)	proscribed	split
*Peru	17,257,000	4,700 est.	5.9 (1978); 6 of 100	legal	split
Puerto Rico	3,300,000	125 est.	-- (1976); none	legal	pro-Moscow
*United States	220,232,000	15-20,000 claim	0.2 (1976); none	legal	pro-Moscow
*Uruguay	2,900,000	8,000 est.	elections promised by 1981	proscribed	pro-Moscow
*Venezuela	14,534,000	10,000 est.	9.0 (1978); 22 of 195	legal	factions (3)
Total	601,029,000	450,060			

Africa and the Middle East (17)

Area	Population (est.)	Communist party membership	Percent of vote; seats in legislature	Status	Sino-Soviet dispute
*Egypt	40,948,000	500 est.	— (1979)	proscribed	pro-Moscow
Iran	37,582,000	1,500 est.	— (1975)	legal	pro-Moscow
Iraq	12,907,000	2,000 est.	no elections since 1958	allowed	pro-Moscow
Israel	3,802,000	1,500 est.	4.6 (1977); 5 of 120 ("Democratic Front")	legal	pro-Moscow
Jordan	3,055,000	500 est.	no elections since 1967	proscribed	pro-Moscow
Lebanon	2,943,000	2,500 est.	— (1972); none	legal	pro-Moscow
Lesotho	1,306,000	negligible		proscribed	pro-Moscow
The Maghreb					
Algeria	18,249,000	400 est.	— (1976)	proscribed	pro-Moscow
Morocco	19,751,000	700 est.	— (1977); none	allowed	pro-Moscow
Tunisia	6,412,000	100 est.	— (1974)	proscribed	pro-Moscow
Nigeria	74,604,000	unknown	— (1976)	proscribed	pro-Moscow
*Réunion	503,000	2,000 est.	32.8 (1978); none in Paris	legal	independent
Saudi Arabia	8,103,000	negligible	no elections scheduled	proscribed	pro-Moscow
Senegal	5,519,000	2,000 est.	0.32 (1978); none	legal	pro-Moscow
South Africa	28,094,000	unknown	— (1977)	proscribed	pro-Moscow
Sudan	20,941,000	3,500 est.	— (1978)	proscribed	pro-Moscow
Syria	8,395,000	5,000 est.	— (1977); 6 of 195	allowed	pro-Moscow
Total	293,114,000	22,200			
Grand Total	4,035,236,000	75,182,360			

Note: *Based on fraternal greetings sent to the most recent communist party congress in Beijing, these 54 political units or countries either have pro-Chinese splinter groups or ruling movements that are at least neutral in the Sino-Soviet dispute. Many of them have more than one organization, e.g., Indonesia, North Kalimantan, and Surinam. Not listed above are communist parties (Marxist-Leninist) in Macao and South Korea.

International Communist Front Organizations (10)

	Claimed Membership	Headquarters
Afro-Asian People's Solidarity Organization	no data[a]	Cairo
Christian Peace Conference	no data	Prague
International Association of Democratic Lawyers	25,000	Brussels
International Organization of Journalists	150,000	Prague
International Union of Students	ca. 10,000,000[b]	Prague
Women's International Democratic Federation	over 200,000,000[c]	East Berlin
World Federation of Democratic Youth	ca. 150,000,000[d]	Budapest
World Federation of Scientific Workers	450,000[e]	London
World Federation of Trade Unions	ca. 190,000,000[f]	Prague
World Peace Council	(affiliates in 130 countries)[g]	Helsinki

Sources: Official figures on membership claimed during 1979 are from party newspapers or journals; estimates are from Central Intelligence Agency, *National Basic Intelligence Factbook* (Washington, D.C., July 1979).

Notes: [a] AAPSO-affiliated committees exist in most countries of Asia and Africa.
[b] The bulk of membership comes from communist-ruled states.
[c] Figures for 1966; none issued since then. Affiliates in over 100 countries, but most of membership is in Soviet Bloc.
[d] Most members live in party-ruled countries; others generally represent small groups attached to local communist parties.
[e] Bulgarian Telegraph Agency, Sofia, 19 February; the bulk of membership is from communist-ruled states.
[f] Radio Moscow, 3 October 1978. Some 90 percent live in party-ruled states, including 107 million from the USSR. Communist China is not a member. The Italian CGIL, with over 4 million members, withdrew in 1978 from the WFTU.
[g] *The World Peace Council: What It Is and What It Does* (Helsinki: WPC, 1978), p. 5.

Pershing-2 intermediate range and land-based cruise missiles with nuclear warheads in Western Europe. Tensions between Moscow and Washington were aggravated by the presence of a Soviet combat brigade in Cuba, the killing of American Ambassador Adolph Dubs in Kabul, the establishment of U.S. diplomatic relations with Beijing, and the massive invasion of Afghanistan that installed a Soviet puppet regime in that country. In a 31 December interview with ABC, President Carter admitted that Brezhnev had misled him about the Soviet action.

Relations with Western Europe were highlighted by arguments over Eurocommunism. Boris Ponomarev, CPSU secretary for liaison with nonruling parties, delivered a direct attack on this doctrine and asserted that Eurocommunism pits a particular model of socialism against that of "real socialism" and creates impediments for the international communist movement. Therefore, he said, the CPSU must engage in a "determined struggle" against all attempts to revise Marxist-Leninist doctrine (Radio Moscow, 17 October). The Italian, French, and Spanish parties reacted promptly. The first emphasized that Soviet newspapers did not print that part of Ponomarev's speech that dealt with Eurocommunism, suggesting that there might be a division on the subject in the Kremlin (*L'Unità*, 19 October). The French response seemed even more forthright. A statement the next day by Maxime Gremetz, the Political Bureau member responsible for interparty relations, maintained that Eurocommunism represented the "wave of the future." Moreover, he denied that Eurocommunism could hinder the development of international solidarity. (*L'Humanité*, 20 October.) The Spanish response was quoted in a dispatch from Madrid that cited an official source as saying that if the Ponomarev statement were not denied, it would constitute a radical contradiction of principles "necessary for normal development of relations between communist parties" (Radio Belgrade, 21 October).

The new conflict between the Soviet bloc and the Eurocommunists stemmed in part from the trial and conviction of several prominent Czechoslovak human rights activists (*CSM*, 23 October). Most of the East European regimes are disturbed by the dissidents. The international publicity given their actions has resulted in similar demands throughout the bloc, except in Albania and Bulgaria where quiet prevails.

Soviet relations with China continued to be strained. Pursuant to a June agreement, talks between the two countries were conducted in Moscow over a period of two months (29 September–30 November), but were adjourned after agreement to resume them in 1980 at Beijing. Soviet leaders were displeased with the visits by both Chinese party Chairman Hua Guofeng and Foreign Minister Huang Hua to several West European capitals in late fall and the latter's subsequent trip to Yugoslavia and Romania, which were accompanied by thinly veiled criticisms of the Soviet Union.

In Southeast Asia, the Russians were able to consolidate their foothold in part because of their support for Vietnam's invasion and as yet incomplete occupation of Kampuchea (Cambodia) as well as their support for the new Heng Samrin regime in Phnom Penh. Moreover, they also seemed to gain from China's less than decisive punishment of Vietnam. In addition, after a fifteen-year breach in relations, the CPSU and the Japanese Communist Party issued a communiqué on 25 December condemning China's attack against Vietnam as "an act of hegemony."

The USSR strengthened its position in the Middle East by signing a twenty-year friendship treaty with the People's Democratic Republic of Yemen (Radio Moscow, 25 October). Soviet officers reportedly control the Yemeni armed forces. The ongoing rebellion against the communist regime in Afghanistan brought additional Soviet military involvement, the first such action in the Third World. An estimated 45,000 to 100,000 USSR combat troops were fighting Muslim insurgents at the end of the year, following the installation of Babrak Karmal as the Soviet puppet ruler in Kabul on 30 December. His predecessor was overthrown on 27 December.

Also late in the year, a reliable source indicated that Iraq had concluded a new defense agreement for arms deliveries from the USSR, as well as an arrangement with Vietnam for the latter to train Iraqi combat pilots (*Foreign Report*, London, 3 October). A few weeks later, the USSR agreed to augment arms deliveries to Syria (ibid., 24 October).

Moscow continued to strengthen its ties with other less developed countries. New agreements were signed with the African regimes in Angola, Mozambique, and Ethiopia. The Soviets were, however, ordered to reduce their advisers from 40 to 5 in Nigeria (*NYT*, 22 August) and lost a base on Bioko Island in Equatorial Guinea when their six-year agreement expired on 31 December. In Latin America, the USSR exploited the meeting of the "nonaligned" countries during 3–9 September in Havana to demonstrate its continuing interest in the Western hemisphere (for the final declaration of this conference, see *Review of International Affairs*, Belgrade, 20 September, pp. 18–78).

Ruling Parties in Eastern Europe. The orthodox Stalinist regime in Albania remained both anti-Soviet and anti-Chinese, accusing both of having sold out to American imperialism. Radio Tirana (21 July) accused USSR "social imperialists" of pressuring and blackmailing their vassal states in Eastern Europe. Washington and Beijing were charged with plotting to dominate the world. On the centenary of Stalin's birth, Albanian leader Enver Hoxha published a book about his five meetings between 1947 and 1952 with the Soviet dictator (*The Times*, London, 21 December) and described him as a "giant."

Some major changes were made in the educational system of Bulgaria, but the most important developments took place in the economic field. Introduction of quasi-market mechanisms appeared to represent an effort to encourage productivity and to phase out subsidies to less efficient organizations. Moreover, there were hints that the regulations on foreign investment would be liberalized. Three new Politburo members were elected on 17 July, including the daughter of party leader Todor Zhivkov. Official price increases were announced for many commodities in order to assist exports (Radio Sofia, 16 November). In foreign affairs, close relations with the Soviet Union continued, with trade turnover during 1976–1980 scheduled to reach 24.5 as compared with 13.9 billion rubles over the previous five-year period. Brezhnev protégé and CPSU Politburo member Konstantin U. Chernenko received the Georgi Dimitrov order "for strengthening fraternal relations" (ibid., 3 December).

In Czechoslovakia the period under review witnessed continued activity by what has come to be known as the Charter 77 group. The regime's response has been to arrest and imprison more dissidents. Six members of the Committee for the Defense of Unjustly Persecuted Persons were sentenced to prison for allegedly bringing disrepute to Czechoslovakia abroad. This action evoked criticism by West European communists, notably those in France. About 350 Catholics signed a letter to Pope John Paul II, complaining about persecution by the government in Prague (Radio Vatican, 18 November). The poor performance of the economy was aggravated by the oil crisis, resulting in an imbalance in foreign exchange. The regime unswervingly supported all Soviet foreign policy positions. Several high-ranking party officials visited revolutionary rulers in African states. An exchange of 1.3 million party membership cards took place during the year; new credentials were to be issued in January 1980.

In East Germany, a further crackdown on dissidents occured through direct action as well as through new penal laws that made contacts with non-bloc citizens more difficult and impeded the work of Western journalists. At the same time, intensification of ideological indoctrination work among youth took place. Close ties with the Soviet Union were emphasized by Brezhnev's presence at the celebration of East Germany's 30th anniversary in early October. Among bloc leaders, only Ceauşescu did not attend. Contacts were expanded with revolutionary regimes in the Third World to which East Germany provides military, technical, and other assistance. Following the Soviet example, East German party leader Erich Honecker signed a friendship treaty with South Yemen at Aden after having visited Ethiopia (Radio East Berlin, 19 November). A month later, it was announced that a review (purge) of all communist party members would take place between 1 March and 30 April 1980.

Economic hardships overshadowed other developments in Hungary, leading to some protests, notably at the industrial center on Csepel island, where a statue of Lenin was found one morning dressed in rags. Prices for certain basic commodities rose sharply during January and again in July. The regime simultaneously issued a proclamation dealing with austerity and labor discipline and stipulating that wage increases would be related to enterprise productivity. Close ties with the USSR included a Brezhnev visit to Budapest between 30 May and 1 June. At the end of June it was decided to convene the next Hungarian communist party congress on 24 March 1980. As in the other bloc states, Hungary's leaders increased their contacts with Third World countries, especially with the recently established revolutionary regimes in Angola, Ethiopia, and South Yemen.

Perhaps the most important event of the year for Poland was the visit of Pope John Paul II (formerly Karol Cardinal Wojtyla) in early June, which stimulated national pride and interest in human rights. Television stations devoted only a few minutes each day to reporting the pope's travels. A new religious association for west and central Poland, called the Social Self-Defense Club, surfaced at this time. A new dissident group, the Confederation for an Independent Poland, announced its establishment early in the year. In foreign affairs, servicing of the U.S. $15 billion debt to the West absorbs more than two-thirds of all foreign exchange earnings. Most difficult for the regime was the problem of dealing with such mounting economic difficulties. The next congress of the Polish United Workers' (communist) Party will convene in February 1980 and attempt to solve some of these problems.

During the year, Romania alone among the Soviet bloc countries denounced the Vietnamese invasion of Kampuchea on 10 January. The strengthening of communist leader Nicolae Ceausescu's position and that of his wife Elena was confirmed by the party congress during 19–24 November. Both are members of the Permanent Bureau. Beginning in January 1980, there was to be an exchange of party cards, which means a membership review and purge. Economic performance was considerably below planned targets. It was announced that oil had been discovered in the Black Sea, but its extent has not been revealed. Romania's foreign policy remained assertively independent. Relations with the USSR were cool but correct; yet other East European countries were angered when the Romanians asked tourists to pay for gasoline in hard currency. High-ranking leaders visited several Middle East countries, and Ceausescu made a marathon tour of Africa (9–25 April), during which he signed a variety of agreements. On 1 August he belatedly received the Order of Lenin from Brezhnev in the Crimea even though it had been awarded on his 60th birthday (26 January 1978).

In January Yugoslavia, not a bloc member, also condemned Vietnam's invasion of Kampuchea (repeated in September in three newspapers). At the same time, it offered Albania "all-round cooperation." Edward Kardelj, heir apparent to Tito, died of cancer in February. Kardelj's protégé, Stane Dolanc, had been removed after eight years as executive secretary of the ruling party's Presidium shortly before, Tito visited Moscow in mid-May. Both sides admitted to differences, which later surfaced during the nonaligned conference in Havana. Belgrade hosted about 600 of the world's leading bankers in early October at the annual meeting of the International Monetary Fund (IMF) and the World Bank. In Yugoslavia, the inflation rate approached 30 percent and imports were $6 billion higher than exports. (Some 700,000 tons of wheat will be imported during 1979–1980). The IMF and other international organizations again were asked for help. Servicing of the foreign debt took $1.9 billion in 1979 and will rise to $2.9 billion in 1981 (*Frankfurter Allgemeine Zeitung*, 25 September).

The Council for Mutual Economic Assistance (CMEA) celebrated its 30th anniversary in Moscow at the end of June. Plans for bloc economic integration were advanced through fourteen new implementing agreements. While stressing an optimistic note, the meeting discussed a number of problems, notably energy. The Soviet Union continued to hold an advantageous position in an unequal partnership; during 1979 it supplied its East European client states with 75 to 80 percent of their iron ore and 70 to 75 percent of their petroleum requirements at prices one-fifth below OPEC levels. A CMEA planning session took place in Moscow on work to be done in 1980–1981 (*Pravda*, 6 December).

The Warsaw Treaty Organization (WTO) conducted "Friendship 79" war games on Czechoslovak territory in early February, with other exercises along Poland's seacoast the following month. Quadripartite maneuvers, code-named "Shield 79," took place during 16–19 May in Hungary. Romanian staff officers but no troop units participated. In a speech in East Berlin on 6 October, Soviet leader Brezhnev pledged to withdraw 20,000 of the 400,000 Soviet military as well as 1,000 of the 7,000 Soviet tanks and other unspecified equipment from East Germany over the next twelve months if new American missiles were not installed. NATO voted in mid-December to accept Pershing-2 and land-based cruise missiles from the United States.

Communist Parties of Western Europe. Over the past year, the same two principal themes continued to be stressed by Western Europe's 24 communist movements in their domestic and foreign polcies—"unity of the left" and détente, or peaceful coexistence, between the Soviet bloc and other states. The appeal for unity is directed at leftist organizations that oppose capitalism, a Europe of multinationals, and nuclear power in general and an independent Western European nuclear missile force in particular. At the same time, these communist parties ostensibly endorse stable government and world peace.

In contrast with 1978, however, communist activities in Western Europe have not continued to attract world attention, probably for several reasons: (1) no significant electoral victories were scored by these parties in the 10 June elections to the European parliament; (2) neither did any national election produce a shift toward significant communist representation; (3) congresses were held in Belgium, France, Great Britain, Ireland, Italy, Malta, Norway (conference), and Portugal, but neither leadership changes nor party splits occurred; (4) the previous momentum had disappeared as a result of electoral defeats in 1978 for the French party and in 1979 for the Italian party; and (5) although the slogan "unity of the left" continued to receive endorsement, virtually all of Western Europe's communist parties stressed the necessity of pursuing their own independent paths toward the goal of replacing capitalism with "socialism."

During 1979 16 of Western Europe's 24 parties continued to enjoy parliamentary representation: Belgium, Cyprus, Denmark, Finland, France, Greece, Iceland, Italy, Luxembourg, Netherlands, Norway, Portugal, San Marino, Spain, Sweden, and Switzerland. In contrast, Austria, the Faroe Islands, the Federal Republic of Germany, Great Britain, Ireland, Malta, Turkey, and West Berlin have no communist representatives in their legislatures.

National elections were held by eleven West European states during the year. Eight communist parties (those in Austria, Denmark, Finland, Great Britain, West Berlin, Italy, Luxembourg, and Switzerland) lost votes. Gains were registered in Portugal, Spain, and Sweden. Of the sixteen parties with elected representatives, representation continues to be largest in Italy, where the party has slightly less than one-third of the parliamentary seats (201 out of 630). Among the remaining fifteen parties, the one in San Marino had the next highest percentage of parliamentary seats (26.7), folllowed by Cyprus (25.7), Iceland (23.3), Portugal (18.8), France (17.5), and Finland (17.5). None of the remaining parties held more than 6.7 percent (Spain) of the parliamentary seats.

Communist strength, as indicated in part by these statistics, remained strongest in Italy, France, Cyprus, San Marino, and Iceland. However, the influence of the movements in Spain, Finland, Greece, and Portugal is significant. The Italian, French, and Spanish parties previously had endorsed Eurocommunism as a means, allegedly independent of Moscow, to achieve power. Since this did not produce sufficient votes for major victories, the year was marked by an absence of claims about communist party strength. The decline in votes received by eight movements in their respective national elections during the year suggests that 1980 will not bring any substantial gains to Western Europe's communist parties.

The relatively less attention devoted to Eurocommunism may have been due to its failure to become a cohesive political force. Thus, divergent strategies have been developed by the three main parties (those in France, Italy, and Spain). For several years it had appeared that "their lines were converging, emphasizing in varying degrees a claim of independence from Moscow, a will to share power in their own countries through the political process, a proclaimed acceptance of the basic theses of constitutional democracy and civil liberties" (*NYT*, 15 April).

However, during the year the French Communist Party (PCF) began "a shrill new campaign featuring nationalism, in the place of conciliation, as its main appeal for non–card-carrying voters, and tightened the ranks for members. It responded to what seemed an incipient crisis of identity with a resurgence of nostalgia for solidarity with Moscow and a return to what some French commentators call its 'ghetto mentality.' " (Ibid.) This was evident at the 23rd Congress, held 9–13 May. It left open the possibility of a new united front with the Socialists prior to the 1981 presidential elections but stressed the PCF claim of being the "sole and authentic representative of the working class."

The picture presented by French Communists at the end of the year was one of stagnation, as they attempted to re-establish a unity of the left on a new basis. This produced such anomalies as the PCF effort to solicit support from French farming interests by opposing Spanish membership in the European Economic Community, contrary to the position of Spanish communists. However, party leader Georges Marchais sent a letter to the president of France, proposing a Franco-Soviet mutual security treaty (*L'Humanité*, 11 December).

One consequence of developments in France involved a setback for Italian communists, who proclaim that their ideology differs from that of the Soviet bloc. Because their French comrades had broken with the Socialists, the Italian Communist Party (PCI) encountered greater difficulty in justifying continued support for the "historic compromise" with the Christian Democrats.

The major reason for this criticism was that the PCI began sharing the blame for the country's problems without having an opportunity to participate in the government. This in turn generated attacks by the radical left in Italy. Thus, at the PCI congress held 30 March–3 April, the delegates decided "to proclaim the creed of Marxism-Leninism optional for the party faithful," yet avoided any far-reaching doctrinal debate. Attention, instead, was focused on the upcoming parliamentary election, emphasizing "the third path" to socialism through "transformation" rather than "revolution," based on lessons learned from Soviet experience and from "the vicissitudes of social democracy." (*L'Unità*, 3 April.) The immediate consequences were defeat in the June national elections. The PCI lost 27 seats (attaining 11.6 percent fewer than previously) in parliament. Although these results had been predicted by public opinion polls, they represented the first time that support for the PCI declined in the postwar period.

In early 1980 the PCI will be confronted with the dilemma of reconciling its role as the parliamentary opposition with its contention that participating in the national legislature will contribute to restoring electoral strength in the regional and local elections scheduled for spring 1980. The movement thus has been placed in a precarious position, reflected in its support for the concept for Eurocommunism. This doctrine is defined as "the meeting point of original formulations by the various national parties, all of which identify with one essential objective: the building of socialism in Western Europe along a road that differs from the road pursued by countries in which socialism has been created" (ibid., 30 May). Party leader Enrico Berlinguer met with his Spanish counterpart in Madrid on 8 October to review tactics and strategy.

In 1977 the Communist Party of Spain (PCE) emerged as the first advocate of Eurocommunism. By the end of the following year, there were strong indications of more public support for the PCE. The movement continued to cultivate its image as a legitimate participant in political life, which produced positive results in the March 1979 national elections. The PCE increased its parliamentary strength by 14 percent, gained 3 additional seats, and now has 23 of the 350 in the Cortes. At the same time, the party experienced an internal dispute concerning criticism of leader Santiago Carrillo's support for a government of national unity, i.e., cooperation with all parties of the left.

The PCE remained critical of the Soviet Union (Spanish socialists claim the PCE receives money from the CPSU; *NYT*, 27 December) and continued to support Eurocommunism. Carrillo did recognize, however, that Eurocommunism was undergoing a serious crisis and attributed this to the disunity of the socialist movement in Western Europe. Toward the end of the year, after two weeks in China, a delegation of Spanish communists reported that both parties wanted to re-establish relations (*Mundo Obrero*, 14–21 November).

Views and positions taken by other communist movements in Western Europe were not without significance, but their activities generally reflected the momentum lost by the PCF and the PCI. In Portugal, where the party (PCP) opposes Eurocommunism, it continues to play an important role. Although PCP membership allegedly grew by 43 percent over the past three years and the PCP gained 7 (47 out of 250) seats in the parliament on 2 December, no communist occupies a cabinet post. At local levels it elected 50 out of 305 mayors (16.4 percent) and 299 of 4,042 presidents of parish councils (7.4 percent) two weeks later. The fourth largest communist movement in Western Europe, the PCP has not exerted any major or decisive influence on the government in Lisbon. This is due probably to Álvaro Cunhal's support for the CPSU as the leader of the international communist movement and his defense of USSR domestic policies, which have resulted in the PCP's being identified as a Stalinist movement.

In Turkey, Greece, Cyprus, and Malta, the activities of communist parties did not produce any significant impact on political life. Proscribed in Turkey, the movement in Greece remains split. The Greek Communist Party (Exterior) occupies 11 of the 300 seats in parliament, but the decisive influence on the left is the Pan-Hellenic Socialist Movement. Marxist in orientation, it won 92 parliamentary representatives. On Cyprus, the communist party never has held a cabinet post and plays a small role in island politics. It is, however, the oldest and best-organized political movement in that country and has one-fourth of all Greek seats in the legislature. The few communists on Malta held their first legal congress during 16–18 February and elected an eleven-member Central Committee.

Neither in Great Britain nor in Ireland does the party play a major role. The British party has not won a seat in Parliament during the past thirty years and received only 0.05 percent of the vote in the May national elections. The party does have one member in the upper house (Lord Milford) and elected its first mayor in 1979 (Rhondda, South Wales). Although small, its impact can be seen in extensive penetration by members of virtually all trade unions. These connections are significant since almost two-fifths of all Labour Party funds derive from trade union contributions. Approximately 88 percent of the votes at the annual Labour Party conference are cast by trade unions. At the 1979 conference, this situation was described by the general secretary of the Clerical Workers' Union as a "grotesque picture of members of other parties directing votes that may change the Labour Party."

No major developments occurred within the communist movements of Belgium, Denmark, the Netherlands, and Luxembourg. The same also applied, to some degree, in the Scandinavian countries. These northern parties held a conference in Stockholm to coordinate foreign policy stands (*IB*, no. 4). The Marxist party left in Norway is divided into three factions, which compete primarily against one another for electoral support and whose influence on general politics is negligible. In Iceland the party won just over one-sixth of all seats (11 out of 60, a loss of 3) in parliament. In Finland, it received just under 18 percent of the votes in March. The Swedish party, however, polled less than 6 percent in September. Although this more than doubled what the communists had received three years before, the nonsocialist parties won a small majority. Therefore, the twenty communists in parliament(out of 349 representatives) have been excluded from all committees.

The influence on national affairs exercised by the Austrian and Swiss communist parties is minor. The former received less than 1 percent of the vote in May, while the latter won only 1.5 percent in October. West Berlin voters gave the communists slightly more than 1 percent of their support for the city legislature in a March election.

In the Federal Republic of Germany, the party (DKP) continues to articulate its views in preparation for the 1980 national elections. The DKP receives its primary financial support from the East German party and maintains close ties with it. Active involvement in trade unions can be seen from the 85 percent of DKP members who also belong to one of these organizations. The domestic policy of the party focuses on "unity of action" among communists, social democrats, and Christian workers but strongly opposes the idea of Eurocommunism. The movement plays an insignificant role in West German electoral politics, and yet it devotes a major effort to ideological indoctrination of its younger members.

Communist Parties of Asia. The year 1979 appeared to bring substantial gains for the Soviet Union, which expanded its sphere of influence into West, East, and Southeast Asia. The USSR has clearly increased its capabilities to influence the foreign relations of other countries and to alter the course of domestic developments in certain Asian states.

Such was the case with Afghanistan, whose government signed a twenty-year treaty of friendship and cooperation with the Soviet Union (text broadcast over Radio Moscow, 5 December 1978). Immediately thereafter the regime at Kabul began receiving ever larger quantities of military equipment from the USSR. However, a power struggle within the ruling communist People's Democratic Party culminated in late September when Prime Minister Hafizullah Amin seized power and killed former leader Nur Mohammad Taraki. The new administration continued unsuccessful attempts to bring Muslim tribes outside the few cities under its control. The USSR airlifted 5,000 combat troops into Kabul, overthrew Amin, and installed a new leader, Babrak Karmal, who had lived in Czechoslovakia and the Soviet Union for the preceding fifteen months (*NYT*, 26 December). Refugees from Afghanistan totaled 300,000 at the end of 1979.

In Northeast Asia, North Korea again seemed to tilt toward the Soviet Union. Pyongyang reportedly has stationed more troops along its border with China, although both countries still conduct normal diplomatic relations. More important, during 1979 the North Koreans increased their trade with the USSR, were planning construction of a steel complex and a nuclear power plant with Soviet technical assistance, and allowed the Russian navy to use the port of Rajin. Strategically located in northern waters, with excellent railroad connections to Vladivostok, this port can be used for year-round navigation. Soviet technicians operate many of the facilities.

This tilt toward the USSR and the expansion of its influence should perhaps be interpreted as placing the Chinese on notice that other options exist for the North Koreans. Pyongyang obviously was worried by Beijing's punitive February military strike into Vietnam. During the spring, it appeared that North Korea might soften its long-standing rigid stance toward the United States, but attitudes again hardened in the summer and fall. Since the assassination of President Park Chunghee in late October in Seoul, the North is probably waiting to see what happens in South Korea and what the United States will do.

Perhaps of greater significance were the developments during the year in Indochina. Trends and patterns in that geopolitical region suggest that the Soviet Union has increased its influence substantially. The North Vietnamese expanded their hold on Laos, simultaneously increasing economic and political control over southern Vietnam as well as Kampuchea (Cambodia). Opposing them in the latter country is not only Pol Pot and his 25,000 Khmer Rouge guerrillas but also the nationalist leader Son Sann, former prime minister under Sihanouk, whose 5,000 men are supported by the Chinese (*NYT*, 24 December).

All of Southeast Asia seemed caught by surprise when Vietnam invaded Kampuchea, resulting in the limited Chinese reaction and the masses of refugees who found themselves in neighboring countries or on the high seas. For example, several hundred thousand Kampucheans have crossed into Thailand. Analysts estimated that as many as 750,000 refugees might end up in that country (*Far Eastern Economic Review*, 16 November). This would occur if, as predicted, the North Vietnamese launch an all-out offensive to crush the remaining opposition early in 1980.

It was within the context of these events that Soviet leaders decided to play the Indochina card. By the end of 1979, the USSR reportedly had sent more than 12,000 military advisers and technicians to assist the Vietnamese. A regular airlift moved vast quantities of food and materiel into Hanoi and Saigon. Russian ships with food docked at the Kampuchean port of Kompong Som, which had been restored by Soviet divers.

In the People's Republic of China (PRC), the 30th anniversary of power celebrated in October seemed a time for rejoicing and reflection. The top Chinese leaders were confident that they were following the right path. Although the contributions of Mao Zedong are acknowledged and praised, there is no attempt to hide his mistakes. Despite occasional speculation about a split between Chairman Hua Guofeng and Deng Xiaoping, the two appear to cooperate. The latter and his technocrats may have pushed the four modernizations too fast, however. By midyear, the government announced a modification of its economic plan. In some instances the Chinese were forced to renege on prior commitments involving foreign investments and capital, and some observers believe that they may have overextended themselves. In order to obtain as much as $2.5 billion in foreign exchange per year, there are indications that up to 1 million workers may be exported for labor abroad (*WP*, 4 December).

Aside from a crackdown on dissidents late in 1979, liberalizing trends in domestic affairs seemed to prevail. Former landlords, rich peasants, and their descendants were reclassified as members of people's communes, placing them in the same category as other people. Bank deposits and properties that had been confiscated from the middle class were returned. Workers received wage increases. Legality and predictability in law enforcement were stressed, culminating in the enactment of seven new laws in mid-1979. More political victims from past campaigns have been rehabilitated and even appointed to important government posts. The most famous case involved Peng Zhen. Moreover, in an issue of the party's ideological journal *Red Flag*, former President Liu Shaoqi was referred to as "comrade" and praised by noted writer and purge victim Ding Ling (*Hongqi*, December). This suggests that Liu's name may officially be cleared in the near future. The "gang of four" was to be tried in secret some time during 1980, according to a PRC spokesman.

On the international front, the most important event of 1979 was China's invasion of Vietnam in February. Ostensibly, this was to show the latter that it could not harass or shame citizens of Chinese extraction with impunity. However, the action may have been intended as a blow against the "strategic encirclement" of China by the Soviet Union. Casualties were high on both sides. Beijing probably felt that it had at least scored a moral victory over Hanoi by "teaching it a lesson." However, 57 communist parties throughout the world condemned China and not Vietnam (*Asian Wall Street Journal*, 13 March).

Sino-Soviet relations deteriorated following the Chinese invasion of Vietnam. Moreover, China announced that it would not renew the 30-year friendship treaty with the USSR, due to expire in February 1980, thus offending the Russians (*Beijing Review*, 6 April). Nevertheless, in early April Chinese leaders took the initiative of suggesting talks with Moscow (see above).

On the other hand, the Chinese leaders (the six members of the Standing Committee average nearly 71 years of age) had reason to view 1979 as a good year because of the long-awaited normalization of Sino-American relations that occurred in January. At the end of that month, Vice-Premier Deng Xiaoping's goodwill trip to the United States ostensibly generated even more good feeling toward Washington, D.C. The latter reciprocated with visits by its own political dignitaries. With the problems of frozen assets and immigration solved, the Carter administration proposed that the U.S. Congress grant most-favored-nation trading status to China. Some considered this discriminatory vis-à-vis the Soviet Union and a victory for the Chinese. Others believed that close ties between Washington and Beijing could be detrimental to the latter's aspirations for Third World leadership.

Significant developments in 1979 for Vietnam included the campaign to install a different communist regime in Kampuchea and the subsequent seventeen-day border war with China. Out of its half-million men under arms, Hanoi is using some 200,000 against opposing guerrilla forces throughout Kampuchea. Soviet support for Vietnam has been vocal.

Some disarray occurred in the Hanoi leadership, with a number of defections to China (including former Politburo member Hoang Van Hoan). Reportedly about 160,000 members were purged from party rolls. Fiscal chaos, failure of some aid programs to materialize, and food and other shortages precipitated a resort to forced labor. An all-out agricultural collectivization drive continued in the south, meeting with passive resistance and a consequent drop in production. Among the refugees, estimated during 1979 at more than 300,000, some two-thirds left Vietnam by boat. In addition, approximately 2 million ethnic Chinese have been expelled from the country. The Chinese population of Hanoi, for example, dropped from about 1,750,000 to 10,000.

The most important development of the year for the Japanese Communist Party (JCP) involved reconciliation with the CPSU. At the same time, the JCP lost governorships in a number of prefectures (including the large ones of Tokyo, Osaka, Kyoto, and Okinawa). It also lost several mayoralty races but gained in local assembly elections. Moreover, the JCP won 39 seats out of 511 in the Diet during the October national elections, even though the percentage of its popular vote did not increase. The results seem attributable to at least two factors: selective JCP priorities in support of candidates, and a low voter turnout because of typhoon-force rains on election day.

Discord between the Communist Party of India (CPI) and the Communist Party of India–Marxist (CPM) continued, but the two agreed to cooperate in the January 1980 parliamentary elections (*Pravda*, 27 November). The latter, with a smaller membership, exercises greater influence in India's politics by virtue of its strength throughout Kerala and West Bengal. For a time, it supported the Desai cabinet, but subsequently joined the opposition to oust it in July. Although independent for the most part, the CPM was critical of China's attack against Vietnam. The pro-Soviet CPI experienced internal difficulties, which culminated in the resignation of its 80-year-old chairman, Shriped Amrit Dange (*WP*, 27 November), effective after India's general elections. Dange, who held the chairmanship for seventeen years, has presumably left the way open for a return should the party do poorly in the balloting under the leadership of his challenger, General Secretary Rajeswara Rao. A third group, the Communist Party of India (Marxist-Leninist), a small amalgam of contending factions, takes a generally pro-Chinese line.

In Bangladesh, the party received legal status but made a poor showing in the 1979 elections, winning only 1 of the 300 seats in parliament. Of interest for the future is the establishment of the Democratic Front, led by the pro-Beijing communist party and composed of five groups, some of which are Marxist.

Communist Parties in the Americas. The Sandinist National Liberation Front (FSLN) overthrew Anastasio Somoza in Nicaragua during July after a protracted armed struggle that had been launched by the late Carlos Fonseca Amador eighteen years ago. During its campaign, the FSLN (reportedly almost 20,000 strong by the time of victory) received equipment from Cuba, volunteers from neighboring Central American countries, and the use of sanctuaries in Costa Rica. The Marxist orientation of the new government became immediately apparent, although it maintained a relatively low political profile. Fidel Castro announced that the first group of Cuban advisers, 530 teachers, would leave for Nicaragua (*Granma*, 11 November).

Leftist guerrillas and terrorists were active in several countries, most importantly El Salvador (where the situation could develop into a Nicaragua-type civil war).* Armed violence continued in Colombia, where guerrilla warfare has been a way of life for almost three decades. Kidnappings, bombings, ambushes, bank robberies, and raids on military arsenals led the new government of President Turbay Ayala to implement severe security measures.** The by now almost routine terrorism of both left and right increased in Guatemala; an estimated 2,000 persons were killed, including a former foreign minister (*WP*, 6 December). Low-level guerrilla activities and terrorism continued in Venezuela, where kidnapped U.S. businessman William Niehous was rescued after nearly four years in captivity. Reports of guerrilla activity in Mexico declined, while isolated acts of terrorism took place in Chile and Argentina, among other countries.

The Communist Party of Cuba remained the sole political movement in that Caribbean country. Due in part to worsening economic conditions, serious problems emerged within the party and government, among them conflicts between several older and younger leaders. Fidel Castro criticized "indiscipline, softness, the buddy system, and tolerance" in the government and party and conceded that these were "the shortcomings of our system, of our socialism." (*Granma*, 15 July). Several months later, his brother Raul promised to "settle accounts" with internal dissidents (ibid., 11 November). The Cuban Revolutionary Armed Forces are estimated to number 180,000 men, by far the most powerful military force in Latin America. The government's commitment abroad was maintained, with an estimated 50,000 troops in Africa and the Middle East. Of these, some 20,000 troops serve in Angola and 15,000 in Ethiopia (*NYT*, 21 October). Some speculate that the presence of a Soviet combat brigade in Cuba, which caused tension during the year between Havana and Washington, may be intended to guarantee internal security if Castro decides to deploy Cuban troops in the Americas (see letter to editor, *CSM*, 19 December, p. 23). Soviet support for the Cuban economy was believed to have totaled around $3 billion in 1979 or approximately $8 million per day.

Previous conferences of the nonaligned countries, notably the 1976 one at Colombo, had taken stands that were in essence pro-Soviet. However, at the one in Havana from 3 to 9 September, Castro, as leader of the host state, pleaded in his opening speech for close association with the Soviet Union. Tito of Yugoslavia, the only surviving founder of the movement, urged delegates to avoid alliance with power blocs. Although this advice was followed in form, much of what appeared in the final document could have been written in Moscow (e.g., condemnation of "imperialist nations" by name, including in this category Australia, Canada, and Israel). The majority of delegates from the 94 countries represented for the most part remained silent (*Economist*, 15 September).

The conference divided on two concrete issues, leading to compromises. While supporting Castro in condemning U.S. support for peace negotiations in the Middle East, delegates rejected his recommendation that Egypt be expelled or suspended from the nonaligned group. This question was referred to a coordination bureau of 36 heads of state or government for study and decision. The conference also divided over who should represent Kampuchea—the Pol Pot or Heng Samrin regime. It compromised by leaving the Kampuchean seat vacant until a future conference makes a decision.

---

* The main groups involved were the Popular Liberation Forces, the People's Revolutionary Army, and the Armed Forces of National Resistance. Radio Moscow (10 December) broadcast an interview made in El Salvador with communist party leader Jorge Shafik Handal.

** The four major groups involved were the pro-Soviet Revolutionary Armed Forces of Colombia, the Maoist People's Liberation Army, the Castroite National Liberation Army, and the independent M-19. A fifth group, the Movement for Workers' Self-defense, appeared in September 1978 and claimed credit for the assassination of a former government minister.

Communist parties maintained varying degrees of significant influence in several other countries. In Guyana the People's Progressive Party of Cheddi Jagan, the major opposition to the ruling People's National Congress, called for the resignation of Prime Minister Forbes Burnham. It warned that unless conditions change, a civil war is inevitable (Gwynne Dyer article, *San Francisco Examiner & Chronicle*, 23 December). In neighboring Venezuela, three outspoken communist parties occasionally exercised crucial influence in parliament and constituted the most important communist legislative force found in any American country except Guyana. Communists secured or maintained representation in a number of the region's other democratic or quasi-democratic countries where national elections took place: Costa Rica, Peru, Colombia, Guadeloupe, Martinique, and Mexico, the last one of particular note since it culminated a long campaign for legality (see *Pravda*, 24 November, for 60th anniversary message). Communists also participated in the electoral process in some form in other countries, among them the United States, Canada, Puerto Rico, Bolivia, Ecuador, Jamaica, Grenada, Dominica, St. Lucia, and the Dominican Republic.

Some governments continued to suppress all communist activities (particularly those in Chile, Paraguay, Uruguay, and Haiti), although organizations from these and other countries operated underground at home and openly abroad. The Marxist parties banned from Chile were particularly active in European and Latin American exile, most of them cooperating in the Popular Unity Movement, while several groups continued to advocate armed resistance against the Chilean government.

Pro-Soviet organizations influenced labor developments in Guyana through the Agricultural and General Workers' Union, in Peru through the General Confederation of Workers, in Ecuador through the Confederation of Ecuadorian Workers, and also in Venezuela, Bolivia, and Colombia. Pro-Chinese groups continued to attract support among workers in Colombia, peasants in Peru, and students in several of the Andean countries. Communists led or participated in disruptive strikes in Guyana, Honduras, Peru, and other countries.

In the United States, the communist movement sought leftist unity outside of the two main political parties. At a congress in Detroit during 22–26 August, delegates nominated Gus Hall and Angela Davis as candidates for president and vice-president in the November 1980 national elections. Canadian communists attempted to gain broad support, but secured election to only a few municipal positions. Their party congress, originally scheduled for November 1979, was postponed to 5–7 January 1980.

Communists in Africa and the Middle East. Leaders in the Soviet Union look to a series of national-democratic revolutions as stepping stones on the path to socialism in the Third World. Their strategy emphasizes the importance of forming alliances that will embrace "progressive sections" of the middle class and the petite bourgeoisie, as well as peasants and workers, in the common struggle against Western "imperialism" and "racism" (see Africanus, "The Imperialist Counteroffensive in Africa," *African Communist*, London, no. 76, pp. 44–53). Soviet propaganda places special stress on the real and imaginary evils of the South African government, which supposedly plays a key role in the alleged global network of monopoly capitalism.

Tactics to assure Soviet objectives vary widely. They entail cooperation with incumbent governments and ruling parties that are not necessarily socialist or communist. Moscow, of course, always backs orthodox communist parties. However, because these are weak in sub-Saharan Africa, it collaborates with other forces, especially with "national liberation movements" trained to carry on guerrilla warfare. Bodies such as the FRELIMO or the MPLA consistently had described themselves as nationalist before they seized power. Once installed as the only political party, the leaders declared themselves to be Marxist-Leninist and set about transforming the fronts into orthodox working-class movements. This process has been assisted by the dispatch of USSR, East European, Cuban, and even Chinese communist technicians. Even more important has been the deployment of military advisers, who total 41,680 in sub-Saharan Africa alone, from these countries (U.S. Department of State, *Communism in Africa*, 18 October, p. 2). The same source gives the number of technicians as 37,225.

The extent of communist success, however, has varied. Orthodox movements, such as the Parti africain de l'indépéndance in Senegal, are of negligible importance. The South African Communist Party (SACP) and the African National Congress (ANC) are linked through ties of doctrine and leadership, but remain exile organizations. Moreover, the SACP is composed essentially of intellectuals. It has been unable to succeed in its avowed objective of becoming a mass organization based on the urban proletariat in alliance with the rural population. The ANC's attempts to provoke urban resistance have failed to make progress (Alfred Nzu, "ANC calls for Unity," *Sechaba*, London, October, pp. 16–20). Nevertheless, in the course of the year, South African revolutionaries have intensified their activity. On 6 December Radio Peace and Progress reported a meeting between Boris Ponomarev and ANC President Oliver Tambo held in Moscow (also see *Pravda*, 7 December). In Namibia, the South West African People's Organization (SWAPO) attempts to carry out a guerrilla struggle by using sanctuaries in Angola. Drawing support from the Ovambe ethnic group, it has not made any impact on the South African military establishment stationed in Namibia and continues to suffer from numerous political and organizational weaknesses.

The Soviet Union and its allies also support the Zimbabwe African People's Union (ZAPU), another guerrilla organization. Although following an essentially pro-Moscow line, ZAPU is uneasily linked to the Zimbabwe African National Union, a rival Marxist group, in an alliance that strives for power (see "Statement of the Political Position of the Patriotic Front," in Zimbabwe Information Group's *Bulletin*, London, No. 12, November-December, pp. 3–4). This alliance, known as the Patriotic Front, is militarily much more powerful than SWAPO. But ZAPU, like SWAPO, is limited to restricted support. The former derives the majority of its supporters from the Ndebele ethnic group. The ZAPU's guerrilla effort remains limited, and much of its energy has been devoted to building a semiregular force on Zambian territory for future intervention. They may indeed participate after the February 1980 elections in the new government of what had been Rhodesia.

For policymakers in the Kremlin, the pursuit of revolution in Africa and the Middle East requires the transformation of liberation movements into progressive organizations and of front groups into disciplined cadre parties. This process commenced first in Angola and Mozambique. It is now under way in South Yemen and Ethiopia. The new parties are expected to accept Marxism-Leninism, perhaps gradually, as the Mongolians and Cubans had done earlier. At the same time, these parties are supposed to cement their solidarity with the Soviet bloc.

The new mass parties originated from guerrilla movements or from the military. The rulers of Ethiopia, themselves army officers, have combined the ostensible establishment of a Marxist-Leninist regime with the use of Cuban troops and Soviet advisers to solidify control over non-Ethiopian areas (for example, Amhara and Eritrea). A meeting of military commissars and cadres agreed to convert the Union of Ethiopian Marxist-Leninist Organizations into a working-class party. The new movement faithfully follows the Soviet party line in foreign policy and looks to "victories for the peoples of Angola, Mozambique, Ethiopia, Democratic (South) Yemen, Vietnam, [and] Kampuchea" as a way of further undermining Western imperialism (Radio Moscow, 5 September). As in Soviet bloc states, the new ruling party is to be sustained by a variety of mass organizations. How successful this will be in a country where the urban proletariat is weak, farmers are difficult to organize, ethnic strife continues, and discipline is lax can be decided only in the future.

The FRELIMO in Mozambique previously had transformed itself from a liberation front into a "vanguard party" dedicated to proletarian internationalism, scientific socialism, and democratic centralism of the Marxist-Leninist variety. Although farmers, who make up the bulk of Mozambique's population, are heavily represented among party cadres, they constitute only one-fourth of the representatives in local assemblies. At the same time, about 45 percent of these deputies are drawn from the armed forces, security services, the bureaucracy, and the revolutionary intelligentsia (*WMR*, August, p. 64).

Although similar in orientation to the FRELIMO, the MPLA in Angola (unlike the FRELIMO) depends on Cuban troops to hold major parts of the country nominally under its control. Moreover, the Gulf Oil Corporation supplies Angola with the bulk of its foreign exchange. In addition, the MPLA also depends on the "mesticos," Angolans of Afro-European origin, a major handicap for a ruling party that claims to be founded on the principle of class rather than ethnicity.

In the Maghreb, although allowed to function legally, the Moroccan Communist Party has done poorly in elections. It held its Second Congress at Casablanca during 23–26 February. Algeria and Tunisia both proscribe communist activities, and the movements operate clandestinely.

Similarly, in the Middle East orthodox communist movements are weak. A conference representing nine parties and the Bahrein Liberation Movement was held, apparently in Damascus (*IB*, no. 4). The best organized party is the Iraqi, which derives much support from discontented Shi'ite Muslims, intellectuals, and Kurds. It sought to establish cells within the ranks of the armed forces, but with little success. Arrests and executions have been reported (*Le Monde*, 6 April). Most other parties are proscribed or forced to operate within a framework of semilegality. The Lebanese movement, for example, held a secret congress sometime in May at an undisclosed location. News of this meeting came out only two months later. Communists appeal to Arab national sentiments; all condemn the "defeatist" peace treaty between Egypt and Israel (*IB*, no. 10). In the latter country, communists may organize legally, but they derive most of their support from the Arab minority, which lacks its own nationalist party (see greetings on its 60th anniversary in *Pravda*, 17 November). Many communists were arrested in Egypt because they allegedly had been involved in a plot to overthrow President Sadat.

The pro-Moscow movement (Tudeh) in Iran is now legal. It must compete with several other Marxist-Leninist organizations, to say nothing of Islamic revolutionaries who are bitterly anticommunist (*WP*, 3 December). The Tudeh Party enjoys friendly relations with the Palestine Liberation Organization, which has been welcomed even by Khomeini himself. For the time being, however, the Tudeh appeal is confined mainly to some intellectuals, part of the industrial workers (especially in the oil industry), and some of the ethnic minorities (on 31 December, some 10,000 demonstrators burned the Soviet flag at the USSR embassy in Teheran to protest the invasion of Afghanistan).

From the Soviet point of view, the Middle East picture looks brightest in the People's Democratic Republic of (South) Yemen, which occupies a vital strategic position along with Ethiopia. South Yemen provides naval and air facilities to the USSR. Soviet, Cuban, and East German advisers have played a major role in strengthening South Yemen's armed forces. At the end of 1978, the Yemeni Socialist Party (YSP) held its first congress. It looks toward unification of all national democratic bodies into a single political movement based on "scientific socialism" and emphasizes "cooperation on the principle of proletarian solidarity with socialist community countries headed by the Soviet Union" (*WMR*, no. 12, 1978, p. 23). Because of the closeness of party links between the YSP and the CPSU, South Yemen can be described as a Soviet base on the Indian Ocean. Moreover, it is linked to Ethiopia, where a large USSR arms depot exists. Reportedly, the training of a multinational revolutionary paratroop brigade is proceeding in Aden, which would provide a quick reaction force of Muslims under Soviet command.

International Communist Front Organizations. Throughout 1979 and into 1980, these movements continued to support the interests and foreign policies of the Soviet Union. Interwoven with their basic effort to expand membership and influence by attracting the collaboration of nonpolitical associations through the use of slogans (détente, peace, and disarmament) were general denunciations of South Africa, Chile, Israel, and the United States. The Chinese communists also came under attack for not participating in disarmament efforts and thereby providing de facto aid and comfort to the "Western imperialists." There was praise for the Palestine Liberation Organization, the Sandinistas in Nicaragua, and the Soviet satellite regime in Afghanistan. Moreover, front organizations at various meetings also expressed support for Vietnamese efforts to oust the Pol Pot regime from Kampuchea while criticizing Beijing for its border conflict with Vietnam. At the same time, leaders of certain fronts appeared to be embarrassed by the internecine wars of communist-ruled governments.

The World Peace Council organized an international conference in Kabul, attended by delegates from nearly sixty countries, to express solidarity with Afghanistan. Several documents were issued at the conclusion of the conference, mainly expressing support for the Kabul regime and condemning the imperialist "campaign of lies and slander" against the Democratic Republic of Afghanistan. This condemnation included the People's Republic of China.

Staff members and several of the associate editors were responsible for some of the writing and research and most of the data-collecting effort that produced this *Yearbook*. Profiles were contributed by 65 outside scholars, many of whom prepared more than one. Names and affiliations appear at the end of individual essays. Mrs. Ica Juilland and Mrs. Lynn Ratliff assisted in the processing and filing of research materials as well as in the assembling of some of the data. Much of the final typing was done by Mrs. Margit Grigory, who also handled most of the correspondence with contributors. Special appreciation is due the curators and the staff as well as the members of the readers' services department at the Hoover Institution for their response to emergency requests and for the bibliography.

The following abbreviations are used for frequently quoted publications:

CSM   *Christian Science Monitor*
FBIS   *Foreign Broadcast Information Service*
IB   *Information Bulletin* (of the *WMR*)
NYT   *New York Times*
WMR *World Marxist Review*
WP   *Washington Post*
YICA *Yearbook on International Communist Affairs*

January 1980   Richard F. Staar

EASTERN EUROPE AND THE SOVIET UNION

Albania

The Albanian Communist Party was established on 8 November 1941. At its First Congress, November 1948, the name was changed to the Albanian Party of Labor (Partia e Punës e Shqipërisë; APL). According to the 1976 Constitution of the People's Socialist Republic of Albania (Article 3), the APL is the only legal political party in the country. Party members hold all key posts in the government and in mass organizations. All 250 seats in the People's Assembly, the national legislature, are held by members of the Democratic Front (DF), the party-controlled mass organization to which all Albanian voters belong.

At the Seventh APL Congress (1–7 November 1976), it was announced there were 101,500 party members. Of these 88,000 were full members and 13,500 candidate members. In 1976, 37.5 percent of APL members were reportedly laborers, 29.0 percent peasants, and 33.5 percent white-collar workers (*Zëri i popullit*, 2 November 1976). Women in 1979 comprised about 27 percent of the party's membership (ibid., 8 March). Approximatley 4 percent of the Albanian people are party members, the lowest ratio of party members to the general population among the communist-ruled states of Eastern Europe.

According to a nationwide census conducted between 7 and 16 January, Albania's population at the beginning of 1979 was 2,626,000. It was also revealed that the average annual rate of increase of the Albanian population for the period 1970–1979 was 23.2 per 1000, the highest of the East European party states (ibid., 1 May). According to 1975 census data, peasants comprise 49.4 percent of the population, laborers 36.2 percent, and white-collar workers 14.4 percent. In 1975 about 42 percent of the population was under the age of fifteen (ibid., 28 May, 8 June 1975).

Leadership and Organization. In August APL Politburo member and Central Committee Secretary, Hysni Kapo entered a Paris hospital for medical treatment (*Le Monde*, 10 August). On 25 September it was announced that the 64-year-old Kapo, the third-ranking member of the APL hierarchy, had died of cancer (*Zëri i popullit*, 25 September). Kapo was a charter member of the Albanian Communist Party. He had been elected to the Central Committee in 1943 and had served on the Politburo since 1946. During the late 1940s and early 1950s, he had held a number of important state posts including those of ambassador to Yugoslavia, minister of agriculture, and first deputy prime minister. In 1956 Hoxha selected him to serve as one of the secretaries of the Central Committee. In this capacity he devoted most of his attention to organizational matters and played a major role in transforming the APL into an organization that was thoroughly loyal to First Secretary Enver Hoxha. Since the mid-1960s, Kapo had been mainly responsible for the day-to-day operations of the party. He most likely worked closely with Hoxha in the rebuilding of the party leadership following the high-level purges of the mid-1970s. (See *YICA,* 1975, pp. 3–4; *YICA,* 1976, pp. 1–4; *YICA,* 1977, pp. 1–3.) Owing to his close ties with, and unquestioned loyalty to Hoxha, Kapo had been expected to play a key role in Albanian politics during the post-Hoxha era. Prime Minister Mehmet Shehu, the second-ranking member of the ruling elite, best summarized Kapo's relationship to the APL first secretary when he characterized Kapo as a "loyal pupil and close comrade-in-arms of . . . Enver Hoxha" (*Zëri i popullit,* 28 September). To commemorate Kapo's numerous contributions to the party, the APL Central Committee decreed that several public buildings and institutions in his native Vlorë district be named in his honor. It also authorized the publication of several volumes of his speeches and articles (ibid., 18 November). Kapo's death was undoubtedly both a personal and political loss to Hoxha, who turned 71 in October. Since both Hoxha and his 66-year-old second-in-command, Shehu, have suffered from health problems in the recent past (see *YICA,* 1973; *YICA,* 1976, p. 1), they had apparently counted on Kapo to serve as a stabilizing force in the party leadership after their passing.

Simon Stefani, a candidate Politburo member and first secretary of the Tiranë district party organization since 1976, was added to the Central Committee secretariat in April (*Zëri i popullit,* 1, 8 May). It is still not clear whether Stefani has assumed Kapo's position as secretary for organizational matters or whether there has been a reshuffling of responsibilities within the Central Committee secretariat following the death of Kapo. Stefani apparently came to the attention of the APL leadership while he was serving as first secretary of the Permet district party organization between 1972 and 1976. His latest promotion marks him as one of the most potentially important of the second echelon party officials catapulted into top-level leadership positions following the party purges of the mid–1970s. Stefani was also elected to the largely honorific office of president of the People's Assembly in December 1978 (ibid., 28 December 1978). Gaqo Nesho, first secretary of the Vlorë district party organization since 1973 and a member of the APL Central Auditing Commission since 1971, was appointed to succeed Stefani as party leader for the Tiranë district (ibid., 1, 8 May). Stefani and Nesho are typical of the new leadership that is emerging within the APL. Both are relatively young (in their mid- to late-40s) and have had extensive experience in the party organization outside Tiranë. They seem to be competent administrators and are apparently loyal to Hoxha and committed to the continuation of his policies. Sulejman Baholli, chairman of the Executive Committee of the People's Council of the Durrës district, replaced Nesho as party first secretary for the Vlorë district (ibid., 3 June). Baholli was a member of the Central Committee between 1956 and 1976 when he was demoted to candidate membership. In 1974 he had lost his post as minister-without-portfolio owing to his lack-luster performance in this capacity. His appointments to the important Durrës and Vlorë positions indicate he has regained the confidence of the APL leadership.

With the death of Kapo, the APL Politburo at year's end consisted of eleven full members: Enver Hoxha, Ramiz Alia, Adil Carcani, Kadri Hasbiu, Hekuran Isai, Spiro Koleka, Rita Marko, Pali Miska, Manush Myftiu, Mehmet Shehu, and Haki Toska; and five candidates: Lenka Cuko, Llambi Gegprifti, Qirjako Mihali, Pilo Peristeri, and Simon Stefani. In addition to Hoxha, the secretaries of the Central Committee are: Ramiz Alia, Hekuran Isai, Prokop Murra, and Simon Stefani (ibid., 29, 30 November).

Enver Hoxha made a number of public appearances both in Tiranë and outside the capital city. He attended the Congress of the Democratic Front held in Vlorë (ibid., 5–7 June) and toured the earthquake-devastated areas of northern Albania (ibid., 18–23 October). The APL leader also participated in many of the events held to commemorate the 35th anniversary of the liberation of Albania from Nazi occupation and the establishment of the communist regime (ibid., 25 October; 29–30 November).

Auxiliary and Mass Organizations. The Fifth Congress of the Democratic Front met in Vlorë on 4–6 June. Enver Hoxha was re-elected DF chairman, a position he has held since 1945. Xhorxhi Robo was re-elected secretary (ibid., 7 June). On the eve of the congress, the DF newspaper *Bashkimi* (3 June) published a lengthy article written by Hoxha. He appealed to the patriotism of the Albanian people by reminding them that, prior to the establishment of the current regime, it was widely believed both within and outside Albania that the country could not survive without foreign assistance. The Albanian leader claimed, however, that since 1945 the nation had repeatedly demonstrated it could survive by relying on its own resources and efforts. The key to Albania's success in this regard, he asserted, was the unity and self-confidence of the people, which resulted from the efforts of the DF working under the leadership of the party. In an obvious appeal for national unity at this critical juncture in Albania's history, he urged the members of the DF to continue to support the party and its programs. DF Vice-Chairman Ramiz Alia delivered the main report to the congress. After his recital of what he termed the domestic and external "successes" of the Hoxha regime, Alia indicated there would be no changes in Tiranë's current policies in both these areas. He also noted that the DF would continue to play a significant role in Albanian life as the country's most important agency for the "revolutionary education" of the masses (*Zëri i popullit*, 5 June).

The Central Committee of the Union of Albanian Labor Youth (UALY) met twice during 1979. Its 23–24 February session was devoted to a discussion of the responsibilities of the organization in the fulfillment of the 1979 economic plan. The plenum acknowledged that many young laborers did not take their work duties sufficiently seriously and were not making an honest effort to upgrade their job qualifications (*Zëri i rinisë*, 28 February). At its 27–28 July meeting the UALY Central Committee focused its attention on the need to increase the supply of skilled laborers and professional personnel as the country's economy was becoming more sophisticated. The organization agreed to encourage workers with an eighth grade education to complete a secondary school program. It also pledged to impress upon students currently attending school that they must be willing to be trained in those areas where there are shortages of qualified personnel and to serve in those parts of the country where their talents are most needed (ibid., 28 July). In August the UALY celebrated the 35th anniversary of the first congress of its predecessor, the Union of Albanian Anti-Fascist Youth. On this occasion APL spokesmen stressed the valuable service the organization has rendered in strengthening the loyalty of the nation's youth to the party (*Zëri i popullit*, 8, 9 August).

The plenum of the Albanian League of Writers and Artists (ALWA), which met in Tiranë on 16–17 April, was devoted to a discussion of recent developments in the field of music. It declared that the most important purposes of music and musical productions included "inspiring workers to perform their tasks in a self-sacrificing manner," "strengthening the national character of the people," "fostering party mindedness," and "supporting the teachings of the party and comrade Enver Hoxha." The plenum concluded that Albanian music and choreography have for some time been following the correct party line (*Nentori*, June). This session provided further evidence of the extent to which the party has asserted its control over Albanian intellectuals since the 1973 party cultural crackdown and purge.

Party Internal Affairs. The Sixth APL Central Committee Plenum (29–30) January) focused on the problems plaguing the economy (see below). Hysni Kapo presented the main report, which reviewed the performance of the economy during the first three years (1976–1978) of the current five-year plan (*Zëri i popullit*, 29–30 January). A lengthy commentary on this session in the party newspaper (ibid., 1 February) left no doubt that the APL leadership was clearly distressed by the failure of many sectors of the economy to meet their assigned targets in 1976, 1977, and 1978. The Central Committee apparently decided to attempt to make up the 1976–1978 shortfall during 1979. It was emphasized that the major factor in erasing the accumulated deficits and in meeting the 1979 economic goals would be increased worker productivity. The APL leadership further indicated it was becoming increasingly impatient with those administrators and workers who habitually blamed the weather or forces beyond their control for their personal failures. In addition to implied reprisals against those unwilling or unable to meet their obligations to the state, the Central Committee also appealed to the patriotism and pride of the masses. It noted that, given the hostility Albania faced in the international arena, it was essential for the nation to realize its economic objectives. To fail to do so would leave the country vulnerable to criticism and ridicule from its enemies and would also disappoint its many friends who regard Albania as the last bastion of socialism in the world.

On 24 March the APL Central Committee announced its decision to commemorate the 100th anniversary of Joseph Stalin's birth with an elaborate year-long program of lectures, radio and television presentations, photo exhibitions, and scholarly conferences (ibid., 24 March). Albania was apparently the only communist-ruled state to honor the memory of the late Soviet dictator in this manner. Tiranë used this occasion to reiterate that it considers the Stalin issue to be one of those fundamental ideological questions that serves to differentiate "true Marxist-Leninists" from "revisionists, opportunists, and counterrevolutionaries" (ibid., 27 March). So far as the Albanians are concerned "all true Marxist-Leninists are loyal to the teachings of Stalin" (*Bashkimi*, 27 April). They also proudly observed that Stalin's life and deeds had been and continued to be an inspiration in the building and defense of socialism in Albania (*Zëri i popullit*, 27 March). The attitude of the APL leadership on the Stalin question reflects its determination not to retreat from its long-standing positions on the issues that have led to its estrangement from the greater part of the communist camp. The unwillingness of the Albanians to compromise on these matters was underscored by the tone and content of the major papers presented at the National Conference on the Problems of Socialist Construction held in Tiranë on 22–23 November. Without exception, these presentations stressed the "correctness" of the Hoxha line in every aspect of the building of socialism in Albania (23, 24 November).

Domestic Affairs. *Political Developments.* The first session of the People's Assembly elected on 12 November 1978 (see *YICA*, 1979, p. 4) met on 25–26 December 1978. Of the 250 deputies, 35 percent were serving their first term, 32.4 percent were women, 72.8 percent were graduates of universities or higher professional institutes, and 55.2 percent were under the age of 40 (*Zëri i popullit*, 27 December 1978). The composition of the Council of Ministers elected by the assembly was: Mehmet Shehu, prime minister and defense minister; Adil Carcani, first deputy prime minister; Manush Myftiu, deputy prime minister; Pali Miska, deputy prime minister; Qirjako Mihali, deputy prime minister; Petro Dode, chairman of the state planning commission; Kadri Hazbiu, minister of the interior; Nesti Nase, minister of foreign affairs; Xhafer Spahiu, minister of heavy industry and mines; Kristaq Dollaku, minister of light and food industry; Themi Thomai, minister of agriculture; Rahman Hanku, minister of construction; Tefta Cami, minister of education; Haki Toska, minister of finance; Luan Babamento, minister of communications; Nedin Hoxha, minister of foreign trade; Viktor Nushi, minister of domestic trade; and Llambi Zicishti, minister of health (ibid., 28 December 1978). Aranit Cela was re-elected president of the Supreme Court. All the sitting members of the cabinet at the time of the 1978 election were reappointed to their posts. This development seemed to indicate that the extensive purge of the cabinet between 1972 and 1977, which had resulted in 21 changes in that body, had run its course.

It was announced in March that the year 1979 would be dedicated to the celebration of the 35th anniversary of the "liberation of Albania from Nazi occupation" and "the triumph of the people's revolution" (ibid., 21 March). Two other anniversaries especially significant for the current regime were observed during the year; 24 May was the 35th anniversary of the First Anti-Fascist National Liberation Congress held at Permet (ibid., 24, 25 May). At this meeting the communist-dominated Anti-Fascist National Liberation Council was proclaimed the "repository of Albanian sovereignty." This congress forbade the return of King Zog to Albania, appointed Hoxha supreme commander of the Albanian Army of National Liberation, and took other initiatives to "ensure that the National Liberation Front (predecessor to the DF) would be able to play a major role in determining the future political status of Albania" (*Rruga e partisë*, May). In October appropriate ceremonies commemorated the

35th anniversary of the Congress of Berat (*Zëri i popullit*, 21, 23 October). This congress voted to transform the Anti-Fascist National Liberation Council into the provisional government of Albania, the event which marked the advent to power of the present Albanian regime.

Natural Disasters. On 15 April northern Albania was hit by the most devastating earthquake to strike the country in the twentieth century. The quake caused 35 deaths, 382 injuries, and left 100,000 persons homeless. It also damaged or destroyed 17,122 buildings. (Ibid., 17 April, 1 October.) The government immediately launched a relief program to aid the victims of this disaster and decreed that the damage caused by the earthquake be repaired by 1 October. On 3 October it was announced that "the effects of the earthquake had been completely eradicated" (ibid., 3 October). Between April and October, 2,441 new houses and apartment buildings as well as 165 new public buildings had been constructed, and an additional 14,522 buildings had been repaired. APL leaders hailed this accomplishment as proof of the superiority of the socialist system. In speeches to the inhabitants of the area (ibid., 18, 20 October), Hoxha and Shehu reminded them that the rehabilitation program had been completed without any outside assistance. They contrasted the efficiency with which the communist regime had carried out this operation with the bungling and corruption that had characterized similar efforts in the time of King Zog. The Albanian leaders emphasized that the earthquake relief program had been completed without disrupting other sectors of the economy. Hoxha observed that the mobilization of resources along with the discipline and dedication displayed during the rehabilitation campaign had demonstrated "the great possibilities that exist for the further development of our national economy if we always remain as resolute as we were at this time." He also stressed in his remarks in this region, where there is still considerable sympathy for Catholicism on the part of older Albanians, that the damaged homes and buildings were not rebuilt by the "Pope, the Holy Spirit, or the Immaculate Mother," but rather by "the strong shoulders and sharp minds of Albanian workers." Albanian authorities reported a number of minor earthquakes during the year, but none of these resulted in any loss of life or significant property damage. (Ibid., 14 May, 22 September, 4 December.)

Between 16 and 18 November the entire Albanian coastal plain from Shkodër to Sarandë was buffeted by unusually heavy rains (ibid., 20 November). In addition to homes, factories, warehouses, and other public buildings, some 40,000 hectares of prime farm land—including 23,000 under cultivation—were inundated. Although there were apparently some crop losses, the government claimed the flood damage had been repaired by the end of November (ibid., 28 November).

The Economy. The Albanian economy continued to be plagued with a variety of problems. In addition to the loss of Chinese assistance, the nation's economic performance has been adversely affected by such factors as unfavorable weather, worker apathy, lack of skilled labor, and a shortage of well-trained managerial personnel (*Rruga e partisë*, July; *Probleme ekonomike*, April–June). The APL leadership, which has done little to conceal its unhappiness with this situation, made a concerted effort during the year to revitalize the economy (ibid.). It appears to have been moderately successful in this undertaking. In his annual report to the People's Assembly, Petro Dode, chairman of the state planning commission, revealed that industrial production in 1978 rose by 6 percent, somewhat below the planned target of 8.5 percent (*Zëri i popullit*, 21 February). It appears that in 1979 industrial production will grow by 9 percent, only slightly less than the 10.1 percent rise envisaged in this year's plan (ibid., 29 November). There was a similar improvement in the agricultural sector, where 1979 output will rise by 12 percent (ibid.). Although this result is considerably below the projected 30 percent increase, it does represent the best performance of Albanian agriculture during the current five-year plan. The overall performance of the Albanian economy during the year is even more impressive when one takes into account the natural disasters the country experienced as well as the loss of Chinese aid.

On the occasion of the 35th anniversary of Albania's liberation, the regime sought to publicize the economic advances the nation had made since the end of World War II (ibid., 5 June, 2 September, 29

November). Albania asserts it is the only country in the world today that is free of inflation. It claims to have eliminated its balance of trade deficits and to have become primarily an exporter of processed and finished goods. The nation is now reportedly self-sufficient in the production of bread grains and energy. It maintains that it produces 95 percent of its spare parts needs and 85 percent of its consumer goods requirements. Foreign visitors to Albania report that stocks of consumer goods and food seem to be ample and that living conditions in the country now probably are better than ever (*CSM*, 2 February). When compared to the other East European party states in respect to its per capita gross national product and other measures of economic progress, Albania, however, is still the least developed of this group of nations.

Albanian leaders continue to be concerned about the persistence of capitalist and revisionist influences in the economy. Accordingly, the regime intensified the drive initiated in 1976 to merge private livestock holdings with those of the collective farms. Tiranë was apparently disappointed that this process had thus far been completed in only 5 of the nation's 26 districts (ibid., 24 July). There is also considerable uneasiness about the growing influence of the workers' councils in the administration of some factories and farms. The APL has reiterated its position that the councils are exclusively consultative bodies established solely to ensure that party and state economic directives are implemented at the plant or farm level. Party spokesmen have warned that attempts to transform these bodies into "management organs" would lead to the emergence of a system of "revisionist self-management" akin to that found in Yugoslavia (*Rruga e partisë*, February, July).

Social and Cultural Developments. In an effort to blur the distinctions between physical and intellectual work as well as industrial and farm labor, the People's Assembly in February passed a new law further reducing wage differentials in the country. According to this legislation, "the ratio between the average wage of the workers in all sectors of the economy and the highest wages of functionaries shall not be greater than 1:2" (*Gazeta zyrtare*, March). In this manner the Albanians hope to prevent the rise of a "new class" such as that which has arisen in the Soviet Union and other "revisionist countries" (*Zëri i popullit*, 18 October).

Although Albanian officials have sought to play down the gravity of what appears to be a growing indifference toward the regime on the part of the country's youth, the preoccupation of the press with this theme suggests the leadership does not view this development lightly (*Rruga e partisë*, January, February; *Zëri i rinisë*, 28 February; *Zëri i popullit*, 18 March; *Bashkimi*, 6 April). The problems relating to younger generation Albanians seem to be most acute in the Tiranë district where the "liberal ideas" associated with the youth elites deposed in 1973 (*YICA*, 1974, pp. 3–5) have apparently not yet been extirpated (*Zëri i popullit*, 18 March). In this connection, there was a recognition of the fact that much "scientific research" needs to be done on the social problems confronting the country and that party policy should be based on these studies. Among the areas suggested for investigation were the programs of moral and political education in the schools, the uses of free time by school children, and the youth programs of the mass organizations. (Ibid.)

The Albanian leadership has been exceedingly displeased by the softer line toward religion that has become evident in such revisionist countries as the Soviet Union and China, and among the so-called communist parties of Western Europe. Tiranë clings to the "traditional" Marxist view that religion is a "counterrevolutionary" and "anti-scientific" force that must be continually combatted (*Rruga e partisë*, February). Hoxha and his associates understand that merely closing and destroying churches has not eliminated the practice of religion in Albania. They agree that all influences and traces of religion can only be eliminated gradually by political action, ideological work, and meeting the material needs of the people so that they will not feel constrained to seek the help of God in their daily lives and activities. (Ibid., July.)

Since assuming power, the regime has extensively publicized the many advances in the social and cultural life of the nation. As a consequence of the improvement in health services, there is currently one physician for every 687 inhabitants of the country, the death rate is 37 percent below the average for Europe, and life expectancy has risen to 69 years (*Zëri i popullit*, 29 November). Approximately 70 percent of the Albanian people live in housing constructed since 1945 (ibid.). There were approximately 700,000 students enrolled in the school system during the 1979-1980 academic year. Since 1951 the nation's secondary-level vocational schools and higher pedagogical institutes have produced 143,790 graduates. In 1978 there were 38,900 university graduates in the country in contrast to the 380 in 1938 (*Zëri i rinisë*, 15 September).

Foreign Affairs. The People's Socialist Republic of Albania (PSRA) during 1979 established diplomatic relations with Nicaragua (*Zëri i popullit*, 16 November), the Democratic Republic of Sao Tome and Principe (ibid., 20 November), and Colombia (ibid., 5 December), and had diplomatic relations with 85 countries at the year's end.

There were no significant changes in Albania's foreign policy during 1979. Both Hoxha and Shehu in major foreign policy statements (ibid., 20 October, 29 November) reiterated the PSRA's stand on major international issues. They reaffirmed Albania's desire to maintain normal diplomatic relations with all countries except the United States and the Soviet Union, "or states such as South Africa which are under fascist or racist rule." Tiranë repeated its willingness to resume diplomatic ties with the Federal Republic of Germany and Great Britain once these countries "had fulfilled their well-known material obligations toward Albania." In the case of West Germany, the Albanians are demanding the payment of reparations for the human and material losses the country suffered while under Nazi occupation. The main obstacle to the normalization of British-Albanian relations is Tiranë's insistence that Great Britain return approximately $17 million in Albanian gold held in London since the end of World War II. The British, however, desire to withhold approximately $2 million of this gold to satisfy the award given Great Britain by an international tribunal following the 1946 Corfu Channel incident. Thus far, the Albanians have been unwilling to accept this arrangement. The PSRA has continued its cautious economic and cultural opening to the West and in September was reportedly preparing to send students to study in France, Austria, Sweden, and Italy (*The Economist*, London, 29 September).

PSRA spokesmen again stressed that the country was not pursuing an isolationist foreign policy and pointed to the steady expansion—especially during the 1960s and 1970s—of Albania's diplomatic, economic, and cultural ties with a broad spectrum of nations (*Zëri i popullit*, 5 June, 29 November). In his address marking the 35th anniversary of Albania's liberation (ibid., 29 November), Prime Minister Shehu observed that the country's foreign economic policy has been designed to establish and ensure the PSRA's economic independence. This objective, he claimed, had been realized during 1979 and constituted Albania's "second liberation." In this connection he reported that the nation's imports and exports were in balance and that henceforth Albania would never have a trade deficit. Shehu asserted that the PSRA was not pursuing a policy of autarchy, but one intended to enable the country to develop and modernize by means of its domestic resources and only those imports that could be financed on a pay-as-you-go basis from the nation's production. Thus, those who expected the Albanians to seek handouts from either the United States or the Soviet Union again have been proved wrong. He contrasted Albania's policy in this respect to that of the COMECON countries and China, which have opted for modernization and "economic enslavement" by borrowing heavily from "capitalist states and multi-national corporations."

With few exceptions, Albanian foreign policy commentaries during 1979 were heavily ideological in tone and overly optimistic—indeed unrealistic—in their appraisal of the world situation (ibid., 28 January, 5 June, 4 October, 29 November). According to Tiranë's view of the world, the pro-Albanian Marxist-Leninist movement is doing well, gaining in strength, and making headway in its struggle with the forces of imperialism, social imperialism, and revisionism. The Albanians purport to be much encouraged by the economic, social, and political crises that are allegedly undermining the present regimes in the capitalist and revisionist countries and that are further preparing the way for the popular revolutions that will result in the eventual triumph of Marxism-Leninism. At the same time, however, they claim to be dismayed and angered that the Soviet Union and China, along with their followers and friends in the communist camp, have abandoned the revolutionary cause in order to pursue their respective national interests.

The PSRA reaffirmed its support of "genuine" national liberation movements and wars. So far as the Albanians are concerned, it is only by means of the latter that the "oppressed peoples of the world" will obtain "freedom, national independence, democratic rights, and social justice." (Ibid., 4 October.) Albania thus strongly backed the anti-Somoza movement in Nicaragua. It hailed the overthrow of Somoza as "another case" where a people "determined to fight to the end for their rights" could "topple even the most ferocious regimes supported by imperialism." Tiranë viewed this event as a "signal to the people of Latin America to rise up against regimes that allow their peoples to be exploited by the United States and American monopolies." (Ibid.) The Albanians also closely followed the events in Iran. They applauded the downfall of the shah, but sought to minimize the religious influences in the Iranian revolutionary movement by asserting that the end of the monarchial regime stemmed mainly from "the democratic aspirations" of the people rather than from their religous convictions (ibid., 18 February). Albania was one of the few countries to endorse the Iranian student occupation of the U.S. Embassy in Teheran (ibid., 10 November). Tiranë subsequently called on the United States to return the deposed shah to the Iranian people along with his "plundered wealth." The Albanians also held the United States responsible for the seizure of the Great Mosque in Mecca by "Muslim fanatics." (Ibid., 24 November.)

Albanian-Chinese Relations. China and Albania resumed diplomatic relations at the ambassadorial level in 1979. The countries had reduced their representation to the chargé d'affaires level following the termination of Beijing's economic and military aid programs in Albania during the summer of 1978. China dispatched its new ambassador to Tiranë in April (ibid., 29 April) and in October, Jonus Mersini, a former counselor of the Albanian Foreign Ministry, was named ambassador to Beijing (ibid., 3 October). Although China and Albania have decided to maintain diplomatic ties, their relationship remains cool. It appears that the Albanians have decided to return some unused equipment furnished by the Chinese. Hoxha also has publicly declared that Albania has no foreign debts (*Bashkimi*, 3 June). It would seem from this statement that the PSRA has repudiated its debts to China.

In July and October, respectively, the Albanians published and made available in translation two volumes of Hoxha's *Reflections on China*, a compilation of the APL leader's notes and observations on the Sino-Albanian relationship between 1962 and 1977. These books, which had originally been published for distribution to party members in 1978, were clearly intended to justify Albania's break with China. Hoxha maintains that the fundamental problem in the Sino-Albanian relationship was Beijing's persistence in pursuing an "opportunistic line aimed at furthering its own national interests" rather than a "principled revolutionary line" such as that followed by Tiranë. According to Hoxha's account, the specific areas of disagreement between China and Albania included: China's efforts to effect a reconciliation with the USSR in the early 1960s; China's promotion of the cult of Mao while allegedly downgrading the importance of Stalin; China's unwillingness to assume leadership over the anti-Moscow Marxist-Leninist movement and to transform it into a viable force within the world communist movement; China's launching of the Great Proletarian Cultural Revolution, which resulted in domestic chaos and Beijing's withdrawal from the international arena; China's unwillingness to consult with Albania on matters of concern or interest to both countries; and China's rapprochement with the United States and other capitalist and revisionist states in conjunction with Beijing's decision to become a "superpower." Hoxha observes that by the time of Mao Zedong's death in 1976 China was in a state of ideological and political confusion. These "degenerative trends," according to Hoxha, became more pronounced after Mao's death and led to China's abandonment of Marxism-Leninism and its slide into revisionism and social-imperialism. The publication of Hoxha's *Reflections on China* clearly demonstrated that Tiranë did not intend to halt or mute its ideological polemics with Beijing in the foreseeable future.

Throughout the year, the Albanians were harshly critical of both Beijing's domestic and foreign policies. Tiranë charged that China's establishment of diplomatic relations with the United States demonstrated how deeply Beijing had sunk into the heresy of revisionism (Tiranë radio, 4 January). China's attack on Vietnam was likened to the 1968 Soviet invasion of Czechoslovakia and held to be proof that Beijing has become an "aggressive superpower seeking a sphere of influence" (*Zëri i popullit*, 21 February). The Albanians branded Hua Guofeng's autumn swing through Europe a failure, because he was not able to realize his alleged goal of "provoking" the Western European nations to adopt a more aggressive stance toward the USSR (ibid., 29 November). Tiranë predicted that China's decision to permit the establishment of "joint companies" in partnership with Western firms would result in the further infiltration of "capitalist influences and practices" and lead to the exploitation of Chinese workers (*Zëri i rinisë*, 11 July).

Albanian-Soviet Relations. During the latter part of 1978 and in early 1979, the USSR reaffirmed its willingness through Bulgaria and Yugoslavia to resume commercial relations with the PSRA. Moscow apparently hoped that the Albanians might be inclined to alter their position on this matter following China's decision to end its Albanian aid programs (*WP*, 28 January; *CSM*, 2 February, 6 March). The Albanians, however, ignored these overtures. They similarly did not respond to a Soviet invitation to rejoin the Warsaw Pact (Moscow radio, 15 May). Tiranë reacted to these Soviet initiatives by escalating its polemics with Moscow. APL spokesmen emphasized that Soviet revisionism was probably the most dangerous variant of revisionism because it was the oldest and most prominent and had served as the model for other revisionist heresies, such as the Chinese (*Zëri i popullit*, 8 January). The Albanian leaders' decision to commemorate the 100th anniversary of Stalin's birth coupled with Tiranë's claim that Stalin was the last Soviet leader to rule in accordance with the teachings of Marxism-Leninism (*Bashkimi*, 31 March) underscored the fact that the Albanians were in no mood to give any ground in their struggle with Moscow. Additionally, Tiranë stepped up its criticism of Soviet foreign and domestic policies. The PSRA, for example, took the Soviets to task for having transformed CMEA into an agency to exploit its East European satellites (*Zëri i popullit*, 27 February, 23 July). An Albanian commentary on the Carter-Brezhnev summit meeting in Vienna characterized the SALT II agreement as merely a ploy to enable the two superpowers to preserve their monopoly on strategic nuclear weapons (*Zëri i rinisë*, 23 June). Finally, Tiranë continued to publicize alleged problems—such as inflation, crime, the breakup of the family, and unemployment—that had arisen in the USSR (ibid., 16 June, *Zëri i popullit*, 18 October) as a consequence of Moscow's having embraced "revisionism."

Relations with Eastern Europe. Tiranë's ties with the East European communist party states continue to focus on commercial relations. The Albanians maintain that these states have been reduced to economic appendages of Moscow owing to the Soviet policies of the "socialist division of labor" and "economic integration" (*Zëri i popullit*, 5 September). Further undermining the independence of these nations is the presence of Soviet troops in the region (ibid., 21 August). The Albanians see little prospect for improving relations with these countries as long as current conditions prevail (ibid., 4, 5 June).

Albania's relations with Yugoslavia continued to flourish, especially in respect to trade and cultural exchanges. Yugoslavia is currently the PSRA's leading trading partner. The trade volume between the two countries has steadily risen during the 1970s and is expected to amount to about $80 million in 1980, more than twice the 1978 figure of $34 million (*Wall Street Journal*, 3 May; *NYT*, 21

October). In April Tiranë and Belgrade concluded an agreement which provides for the linking of the rail systems of the two countries (Tiranë radio, 6 April). Cultural exchanges between the two countries have grown steadily in recent years. These exchanges for the most part involve the ethnic Albanians of the Autonomous Province of Kosovo-Metohija, and they are highly prized by both sides. Relations between the two states continue to be complicated by their ideological differences as well as the condition of the Albanian majority in Kosovo. This latter issue surfaced briefly in April, when the Albanian monthly illustrated magazine *Ylli* published an article critical of the tempo of modernization in Kosovo. Although offended by both the tone and content of the article, the Yugoslavs left no doubt of their desire to improve their ties with the PSRA (*Borba*, 25 June; *Rilindja*, 3 July).

Both Albania and Greece appeared satisfied with the pace at which their relations are progressing (*Bashkimi*, 25 March). The Albanians have indicated that they are ready to expand their economic and cultural ties with Greece "on the basis of the common interests of the two states" and noted that only the "common enemies" of the two countries could be opposed to the further strengthening of their relationship (*Zëri i popullit*, 25 March).

Relations with Western Europe and the United States. There were expectations of a rapid rise in Albania's trade with Western Europe at the beginning of the year (*CSM*, 10 January; *WP*, 12 January), but these hopes did not seem to have been fully realized by the end of the year. Among the problems confronting Western European businessmen in opening new markets in Albania are the relatively difficult access to the country, the nation's cumbersome bureaucratic procedures, and the regime's insistence that there be no deficit in its balance of payments (*CSM*, 10 January; *NYT*, 21 October). These difficulties notwithstanding, it was estimated that Albanian trade with Western Europe would grow by 20–30 percent per year for the foreseeable future (*NYT*, 21 October). For the most part, the PSRA's cultural programs in Western Europe are focused on the activities of the Albanian friendship societies found in these countries.

Albanian party and government spokesmen left no doubt that Tiranë is unwilling at present to enter into any type of relationship with the United States (*Zëri i popullit*, 5 June, 29 November).

International Party Contacts. During 1979 Albania maintained contacts with pro-Tiranë Marxist-Leninist parties and groups as well as with various revolutionary groups, primarily from Third World countries. Throughout the year, representatives of these organizations were much in evidence in Albania. (Ibid., 6 April, 11 July, 17 September.)

The APL's current position within the world communist movement was reflected by the foreign party representation at the celebration commemorating Albania's World War II liberation. A total of fourteen Marxist-Leninist parties sent delegations, and an additional fifteen dispatched greetings or messages of support. There were no delegations present from ruling parties, and messages were received from only three ruling parties—Vietnam, North Korea, and Laos (ibid., 1–6 December). The 1974 celebration, on the other hand, was attended by delegations from 4 ruling parties and 27 Marxist-Leninist parties, and received messages of solidarity from 6 additional Marxist-Leninist parties (*YICA*, 1975, p. 11). The 1979 celebration was attended by delegates from the following Marxist-Leninist parties: West Germany, Spain, Peru, Denmark, Colombia, Portugal (Reorganized), Italy, Japan (Left), Greece, Canada, France (Communist Party of French Workers), Mexico, Ecuador, and Iran (Workers and Peasants) (*Zëri i popullit*, 30 November). Messages were received from the Marxist-Leninist parties of Brazil, Indonesia, Dahomey, New Zealand, Turkey, Upper Volta, San Marino, Venezuela, Ethiopia, Tunisia, Sweden, Chile, Great Britain, Angola, and the Dominican Republic (ibid., 1–9 December).

Only two ruling parties, those of Vietnam and Romania, sent condolences to the APL on the occasion of Hysni Kapo's death (ibid., 29 September).

Publications. The APL daily newspaper (with a claimed circulation of 108,000) is *Zëri i popullit*. The party's monthly theoretical journal is *Rruga e partisë*. Another major publication is *Bashkimi*, the daily organ of the DF (claimed average circulation of 45,000). The newspapers of the Union of Albania Labor Youth, *Zëri i rinisë*, and the Albanian Trade Unions, *Puna*, are published twice weekly. The official news agency is the Albanian Telegraphic Agency (ATA).

Western Illinois University   Nicholas C. Pano

Bulgaria

The Bulgarian Communist Party (Bulgarska komunisticheska partiya; BCP) dates it separate existence from 1903 when the Bulgarian Social Democratic Party, founded in 1891, split into "broad" and "narrow" factions. The latter took the name "Bulgarian Communist Party" and became a charter member of the Comintern in 1919. Outlawed in 1924, the party re-emerged in 1927 as the "Workers' Party" and changed its name again in 1934 to "Bulgarian Workers' Party (Communist)." The BCP designation was restored in 1948 after the party was firmly in power. Its best-known leader was Georgi Dimitrov, secretary general of the Comintern from 1935 to 1943 and premier of Bulgaria from 1946 to his death in 1949.

Although the BCP commanded the support of nearly one-fifth of the Bulgarian electorate in the early 1920s, a combination of inept leadership and government repression reduced its membership to about 15,000 by World War II. The party's resistance efforts during the war were not extensive, nor were they significant in bringing it to power. On 5 September 1944 the Soviet Union declared war on Bulgaria, and three days later the Red Army entered the country unopposed. During the night of 8–9 September the communist-inspired "Fatherland Front" coalition seized power from the week-old, pro-Western government of Constantine Muraviev. Following the coup d'etat, the BCP employed tactics that included force and violence to consolidate its hold on the country. The trial and execution of opposition leader Nikola Petkov in 1948 marked the end of organized internal resistance to communization. Stalinist purges, including the trial and execution of the party's general secretary, Traycho Kostov, for "Titoism" in 1949, turned the party into an obedient Soviet tool. Todor Zhivkov, the most durable of the Soviet bloc leaders, became the party's first secretary in 1954 and increased his authority during the period of "destalinization." Since 1962 he has combined state and party leadership, maintaining a firm hold on power with obvious Soviet backing. Domestically Zhivkov's regime has been one of the least liberal in Eastern Europe, and its foreign policy has been marked by unswerving loyalty to the Soviet Union.

Party membership as of 1 January was estimated at about 817,000, and the population at about 8.9 million.

Leadership and Organization. The structure of the BCP is modeled on that of the Communist Party of the Soviet Union (CPSU). Zhivkov, who has encouraged the development of a "personality cult," has consistently been able to eliminate potential or actual rivals, and this year's changes in party leadership reflect his undiminished influence. On 17 July a Central Committee plenum added three new members to the Politburo: Peko Takev, a deputy chairman of the State Council and Chairman of the Bulgarian Tourist Union; Todor Bozhinov, a deputy prime minister and an apparent architect of recent economic reforms; and Lyudmila Zhivkova, chairman of the Committee on Culture. Zhivkova is the daughter of Todor Zhivkov and has increasingly played the role of Bulgaria's "first lady" since her mother's death in 1971. Since no demotions or retirements were announced, these changes increase the size of the Politburo from its customary eleven to fourteen. (The other members are Zhivkov, Ognyan Doynov, Tsola Dragoycheva, Dobri Dzhurov, Grisha Filipov, Pencho Kubadinski, Alexander Lilov, Ivan Mikhaylov, Petur Mladenov, Stanko Todorov, and Tano Tsolov.) Takev's promotion reduced the number of candidate members to three, but the plenum added two new ones: Andrey Lukanov, a deputy prime minister and Bulgaria's representative to the Council for Mutual Economic Assistance (CMEA); and Georgi Yordanov, a deputy prime minister and former head of the Sofia municipal party committee.

The plenum also named two new Central Committee secretaries: Milko Balev, head of Zhivkov's office; and Misho Mishev, chairman of the Central Council of Trade Unions. Bozhinov was relieved of his duties as a Central Committee secretary in connection with his move to the Politburo.

Zhivkov is 68, and these new appointments seem to reflect his tendency in recent years to look for able younger leaders. Takev is 70, but Bozhinov, whose rise has been extremely rapid, is 49 and Zhivkova only 37. All the new appointees are Zhivkov loyalists. Bozhinov and Lukanov (age 41) are expected to play major roles in economic affairs. Lyudmila Zhivkova, although reportedly not without charm, is reputed to be extremely ambitious, and her rapid advance may be considered premature and provoke resentment. (*Radio Free Europe Research [RFE], Situation Report*, 30 July, item 1.)

Auxiliary and Mass Organizations. Bulgaria possesses a number of organizations whose functions are to relay the decisions of the BCP to major social groups and to maintain contact with their foreign counterparts, either directly or through international organizations. Among the more important are the Central Council of Trade Unions (2.5 million members), the Communist Youth (1.4 million), and the Civil Defense organization, which provides mass training in paramilitary tactics and disaster relief. A Committee of Bulgarian Women has had a tenuous existence since 1944. In May its national leaders admonished local committees for being too assertive and too eager to point out shortcomings. They were reminded that the organization "has no field of activity of its own, that its only task is to help other public organizations in fulfilling some of their duties." (Ibid., 13 June, item 2.)

A special place is occupied by the 120,000-member Bulgarian Agrarian National Union (BANU), which in theory shares power with the BCP. Although the BANU recognizes the unquestioned leadership of the BCP, it remains a separate organization. Three ministries and a number of provincial administrations, including that of Plovdiv, are held by Agrarians. Until his death in 1974, BANU leader Georgi Traykov was prominent in the state leadership and very visible in the press. His successor, Petur Tanchev, although not so well known, is first vice-president of the State Council and has accompanied Zhivkov on several of his diplomatic travels. On 6–7 June the government organized an international celebration of the centenary of Alexander Stamboliski, the BANU's greatest leader. Delegates from approximately 25 countries attended. (*Zemedelsko zname*, 8 June.)

Most mass organizations are collective members of the party's Fatherland Front (over 4 million members), whose main function is to stimulate patriotism and enthusiasm for party goals.

Party Internal Affairs. Two Central Committee plenums were held during the year. The first, 2–3 March, was devoted to problems of agriculture, and demonstrated the growing importance of

Bozhinov, who delivered the major speech. A number of individuals in the old Ministry of Agriculture and Food Industry were singled out for criticism and apparently demoted. The second plenum, 16–17 July, although ostensibly devoted to discussion of the educational system, also approved the Politburo and Central Committee changes described above. The exchange of party cards, begun in September 1978 and scheduled to be completed next year, has apparently not brought about any major purges or significant changes in party membership.

When Traycho Kostov was fully rehabilitated in 1962, it was recommended that a volume of his most important works be published. After a delay of sixteen years, the book finally appeared at the end of 1978, but it reportedly says literally nothing about Kostov's trial and even omits to mention the date of his death. When Central Committee member Petko Kunin died in December 1978, his obituary similarly failed to mention that he had been imprisoned as a "Kostovite" from 1951 to 1956. The party is apparently still unwilling to face up to this era of its past. (*RFE, Situation Report*, 26 January, item 2.)

Domestic Affairs. *Elections.* Elections for members of the People's Councils and for town and village mayors, originally scheduled for November 1978, were delayed until 25 March while an administrative reform was implemented. Bulgaria's former 1,399 municipalities were merged and reorganized into 283 units. The number of towns and villages electing mayors for the first time was 3,977. Although the final list of nominees contained only one name for each constituency, public meetings to choose nominees were given the opportunity of selecting from two or more candidates. According to the published results, 99.95 percent of the eligible voters cast ballots, and 99.98 percent of those voted for the official list. Only one candidate failed to win. When compared with the last elections in 1976, the results show slight declines in the proportion of BANU members, unaligned persons, women, and youths. (*Rabotnichesko delo* [*RD*], 27 March; *RFE, Situation Report*, 2 April, item 2.)

Culture, Education, and Youth. At the end of December 1978, the Politburo issued a statement entitled "The Development and Self-fulfillment of Youth Are an All-Party and All-Nation Affair." Although it praises the younger generation for its "correct political positions" and maintains that a "serene political atmosphere" prevails in the country, a number of "shortcomings" were described. These included a lack of coordination among party, government, and Komsomol organs, the failure of critics to castigate ideological and artistic shortcomings effectively and consistently, and "gaps" in the Marxist-Leninist upbringing of youth. To correct these problems, the Politburo recommended the regular holding of conferences, courses, and seminars devoted to the "profound study of Marxist-Leninist classics and party documents," the post-1944 period of Bulgarian history, and the "centuries-long Bulgarian-Soviet friendship." Established artists and writers were encouraged to involve themselves in these programs in order to point out to young people that the only correct road is the one "linked inseparably with the party's policies." The Committee on Culture is to coordinate these activities. (*RD*, 27 December 1978.) The Politburo's statement was probably in response to a growing undercurrent of dissent that began to surface for the first time last year (see *YICA*, 1979, p. 12).

On 16–17 July the Central Committee held a plenum on the development of the educational system. The draft theses, published on 22 May for nationwide consideration, emphasized the unsatisfactory educational level of "workers and employees in material production," three-quarters of whom were said to have at most only an elementary education. The most important of the plenum's proposed reforms involve children starting school at age six rather than seven and the expansion of compulsory secondary education. In the future, schooling will extend over three "degrees": the first, lasting ten years, will emphasize general education; the second and third, which together will take two years, will emphasize the mastering of an area of specialization "under conditions of real production." The entire twelve-year program will be compulsory. Implementation of the plenum's decisions will begin with the 1981–82 schoolyear and is scheduled to be completed by the end of 1985. In an address to the plenum, Zhivkov pointed out that most of the proposed changes had been recommended ten years ago at the last plenum on education in 1969 but had for various reasons not been acted on. He pledged that such "deviations" from plenum decisions would not be allowed to recur. (*RD*, 22 May; *FBIS*, 18 July.)

The Sixth Komsomol Central Committee plenum was held on 23 March and was attended by Zhivkov. Komsomol First Secretary Boycho Shteryanov, who had held this post for three years, was replaced by Georgi Tanev. Shteryanov was appointed a deputy minister of transport. Although little of substance was reported about this plenum, Shteryanov's transfer was apparently a demotion. (*RFE, Situation Report*, 2 April, item 1.) An article in the May issue of *Armeyski komunist* was highly critical of the performance of the Komsomol in the military, describing the life of its units as "boring, apathetic, and insufficiently attractive." Komsomol committees were urged to make their meetings and discussions more relevant to real life, and troop commanders were encouraged to take greater interest in Komsomol affairs.

The humiliation of the Bulgarian soccer team at the hands of England in the European championship prompted the Central Committee Secretariat to order a major shake-up in athletic administration in order to eliminate reportedly widespread corruption, incompetence, and partiality.

Economy. The Central Committee's report on fulfillment of the 1978 plan indicated that economic growth fell well short of the targets set at the beginning of the Seventh Five-Year Plan in 1975 and also failed to meet the lower revised goals published in December 1977. The percentage increases for 1978, together with the targets published in 1977 in parentheses, are national income, 6 percent (6.8 percent); industrial production, 7 percent (7.7 percent); agricultural production, "about 5 percent" (5.0 percent); labor productivity, "about 6 percent" (6.7 percent); and real income, "about 3.1 percent" (3.6 percent). The increases targeted for 1979 are national income, 7 percent; industrial production, 7.8 percent; agricultural production, 7 percent; labor productivity, 6.7 percent; and real income, 3.2 percent. Foreign trade, however, was reported to have increased by 11.1 percent over 1977. Moreover, Bulgaria was said to have achieved a positive balance of trade with the nonsocialist countries. This apparently resulted from a stagnation in imports, due to the large Bulgarian debt and to an expansion of exports to Asia, Africa, and Latin America. (*FBIS*, 26 December 1978; *RD*, 28 April; *RFE*, Situation Report, 15 February and 22 May.)

Decrees from the State Council in January, the Central Committee plenum of 2–3 March, and the 26–27 April session of the National Assembly brought substantial changes in the system of agricultural organization and management. The Ministry of Agriculture and Food Industry, which was criticized by Zhivkov for "excessive centralism, bureaucracy, and apathy" (*RD*, 30 March), was abolished. Its place was taken by the newly organized National Agro-Industrial Union, led by Vasil Tsanov. Further reforms reduced the role of central planning in favor of the "new economic mechanism," i.e., quasi-market relationships to encourage productivity. Agricultural enterprises, in setting up their plans, must first arrange contracts for marketing all production above the compulsory minimum. Procurement organizations are obliged to buy only products for which there is a demand on the home or foreign market. They may also encourage output of high-demand products by offering bonuses above the state procurement prices. Agricultural enterprises will no longer be taxed according to their income, but according to the amount and quality of their land. Thus, the more productive enterprises will have a higher surplus for wages and investment. According to Bozhinov, architect of the new plan, within two years subsidies to less productive organizations will be phased out. This was expected to lead to higher domestic prices for agricultural products, and substantial price increases were in fact announced in November (*WP*, 13 November). At the BCP plenum, Bozhinov and Politburo member Lilov referred to opposition to the new system from bureaucratic conservatives. Lilov warned that administrators "either must comply with what is being done, or they will be confronted, in a way rather unpleasant for them, with the objective needs of agriculture and with resolute countermeasures by the party and the state" (Bulgarska telegrafna agentsiya [BTA], 5 March; *FBIS*, 15 March). The status of private plots was not affected by these reforms. A conference devoted to the role of private farm holdings in January praised their contribution to the economy and called for increased efforts to make small-size farming equipment, improved seeds, and fertilizer available to them (BTA, 18 January; FBIS, 19 January).

In May and June the Council of Ministers issued decrees aimed at reducing fuel and power consumption. Some major industrial enterprises will be converted to burn coal rather than oil, and coal production, which has been declining since 1970, is to be stepped up through around-the-clock work in the mines. Among the measures affecting the general public are a doubling of gasoline prices, the setting of thermostats at 64.4°F in the winter, and a sharp rise in the price of all electricity consumed over a fixed base amount. Gasoline for official cars will be colored to increase the difficulty of diverting it to the black market. (RFE, Situation Report, 11 July, items 2 and 3.)

Reports from the Plovdiv International Trade Fair, held on 3–10 September, suggested that as of 1 January 1980 Bulgaria would make substantial changes in its regulations governing foreign investment. Deputy Trade Minister Atanas Ginev was quoted in the British press as saying that Bulgaria, in its desire to produce goods for sale on the world market, would even permit 100-percent foreign management (Financial Times, 8 September).

Foreign Affairs. The Bulgarian government continued to emphasize its adherence to Soviet positions on all major international questions. In an April address to the National Assembly, Zhivkov stated: "It is a well-known fact that the Bulgarian Communist Party is firmly conducting a policy of all-round cooperation and closeness between the People's Republic of Bulgaria and the Soviet Union. In July N. P. Tolubeev, a full member of the Central Committee of the CPSU, was appointed ambassador to Bulgaria. His predecessor, V. N. Bazovsky, who completed a tour of duty begun in 1972, frequently attended meetings of the Bulgarian Politburo and accompanied Zhivkov on his travels around the country. Further, on the occasion of the 35th anniversary of the Ministry of Internal Affairs, Interior Minister Dimitur Stoyanov referred to the close cooperation between the Bulgarian and Soviet security organizations (RD, 14 September).

In January Leonid Brezhnev spent five days in Bulgaria, his first visit since 1973. Although his stay was described as a "vacation" and little of substance was reported, Brezhnev met three times with Zhivkov and his advisers. Presumably they discussed the state of Bulgaria's relations with Yugoslavia, since during the visit Brezhnev sent a letter to Marshal Tito. Its contents, however, were not revealed either by the Soviets or the Yugoslavs. (RFE, Situation Report, 26 January, item 1.) In late February the Reuters news agency reported a rumor that Soviet ground and air forces were being transferred to Bulgaria over the Varna-Ilichevsk ferry link. This report was promptly denied by Bulgaria (BTA, 26 February; FBIS, 26 February) and received no further confirmation.

Zhivkov paid his annual visit to the Crimea in August. While little specific information was given, Rabotnichesko delo (9 August) indicated that the theme of economic cooperation between the two countries received particular attention. Zhivkov, in an interview taped for Soviet television at the Plovdiv International Fair on 3 September, reiterated his desire for close economic ties with the USSR (Sofia Domestic Service, 3 September; FBIS, 4 September). Two weeks later a Soviet delegation came to Bulgaria to sign an agreement dealing with economic specializtion and production sharing for the period up to 1990 (Sofia Domestic Service, 15 September; FBIS, 17 September). As Bulgaria's principal trading partner, the USSR usually accounts for between 50 and 60 percent of Bulgaria's imports and exports. In November 1978, the world's longest ferryboat link, between Varna and Ilichevsk, began service. It is intended to facilitate Bulgarian-Soviet trade by reducing the importance of the long overland route through Romania (WP, 9 August).

The Bulgarian State Council marked the 75th birthday of Soviet Premier Kosygin by awarding him the Order of Georgi Dimitrov for his contributions to Bulgarian-Soviet relations (Pravda, 22 February). Brezhnev was given this award last year. Tremendous attention was given to the spaceflight of Maj. Georgi Ivanov, who accompanied a Soviet cosmonaut in an attempt to link up with space station Salyut 6 in April. Although the mission failed, it was seen as an important symbol of Soviet-Bulgarian scientific cooperation.

Other East European and Balkan Countries. In a review of Bulgaria's foreign relations, Zhivkov emphasized that Bulgaria "is a socialist country, a member state of the Warsaw Treaty Organization and the Council for Mutual Economic Assistance. The constant consolidation of the fraternal alliance of the countries of the socialist community is the key, the main line, in the foreign policy of our party and state." Relations with the other CMEA and Warsaw Pact states remained generally good, and several head-of-state visits occurred. Edward Gierek visited Bulgaria in January. He was followed by Nicolae Ceausescu in February and János Kádár in June. Zhivkov paid official visits to Czechoslovakia in September and to the German Democratic Republic in October. Reportedly, Zhivkov has used these occasions to urge firmer support for Soviet foreign policy, particularly with regard to the Soviet-backed Vietnamese invasion of Kampuchea (Cambodia), and stressed economic issues, especially those relating to energy shortages, and planning for the 1980s (*RFE, Situation Report*, 26 February, item 1, and 11 July, item 4; *RD*, 28 April and 26 June.) Despite Romania's independent stance on many issues, Ceausescu and Zhivkov have usually preferred to emphasize their points of agreement and their desire for economic cooperation. The Romanian decision of 1 August, however, to require payment in hard currency for gasoline stranded many Bulgarian travelers, which brought an official protest, as well as the imposition of the same requirement on Romanians in Bulgaria (Sofia Domestic Service, 2 August; *FBIS*, 3 August).

Relations with Albania have improved noticeably. A trade protocol providing for a 7-percent trade increase was signed in October (BTA, 4 October; *FBIS*, 5 October). Zhivkov has also called for the unconditional normalization of relations between the two countries (*RD*, 28 April).

In the last few years, Bulgaria has developed excellent relations with her southern neighbors, Greece and Turkey. Zhivkov met with Greek Prime Minister Constantine Caramanlis on Corfu in April; the two signed an economic agreement providing for several cooperative industrial projects and for a doubling of trade over the next five years. At this meeting Zhivkov also partially abandoned his opposition to multilateral Balkan negotiations and expressed Bulgaria's willingness to take part in regional conferences devoted to limited, specific issues such as transport telecommunications, and the health of livestock. (*RFE, Situation Report*, 22 May, item 3.) Zhivkov confirmed this change of policy during a meeting from 9 to 11 July with Prime Minister Bulent Ecevit in Turkey. Afterwards it was announced that the first such meeting, dealing with communications, will be held in Ankara (*RD*, 12 July). Later in the year it was reported that the ten-year agreement covering the emigration of ethnic Turks from Bulgaria had been allowed to expire. (Over 50,000 Turks have migrated to Turkey from Bulgaria since 1968.) The failure to renew or extend the agreement probably results from the Turkish government's unwillingness to receive new immigrants during a period of economic difficulties and seems to indicate no deterioration in Bulgarian-Turkish relations.

Yugoslavia. Controversy over the Macedonian issue continued to dominate Bulgaria's relations with Belgrade. Celebration of the centenary of Bulgaria's liberation from Turkey (when Bulgaria's frontiers briefly included nearly all Macedonia) and the approaching 1300th anniversary of the formation of the first Bulgarian state provided many opportunities to stress Bulgaria's historic and cultural ties to Macedonia. Yugoslavia, for its part, has during the last two years increasingly accused Bulgaria of having designs on the territory of Yugoslav Macedonia and of "the denial of the rights of the Macedonian national minority in Bulgaria" in violation of the U.N. charter and the Helsinki accords (*YICA*, 1979, p. 16). Yugoslav charges have continued to escalate; in a speech celebrating the Yugoslav party's 60th anniversary, Tito himself stated that by refusing to acknowledge the existence of a Macedonian nationality in Bulgaria, the Bulgarians were attempting "to deny the legitimacy of one of our sovereign republics" (Tanjug, 19 April).

Having failed to defuse the issue, the Bulgarian government and press began to reply more energetically to the Yugoslav charges. During the year, the Bulgarian Academy of Sciences published a massive volume of documents dealing with the history of Macedonia before World War II that stressed the Bulgarian character of the region and Yugoslav persecutions. More significantly, in January, *Septemvri*, the journal of the Bulgarian Writers' Union, published extensive excerpts from the forthcoming third volume of the memoirs of Tsola Dragoycheva. These excerpts, which deal exclusively with the Macedonian issue, were also serialized in the newspaper *Otechestven front*, broadcast on Bulgarian radio, and published in a separate pamphlet for broad distribution and for discussion in the schools and the army.

Born in 1898, Dragoycheva is one of Bulgaria's "oldest living revolutionaries." During the Second World War she was a Central Committee secretary and in charge of the party's relations with Tito's partisans. Her current status as a member of the Politburo of course gives her statements special authority. In her memoirs, Dragoycheva made three basic points. First, the BCP, unlike Bulgaria's bourgeois governments, never supported Bulgaria's annexation of Macedonia but favored Macedonian self-determination, including the possible creation of an independent Macedonian state. Second, during World War II Yugoslavia's partisan leaders became increasingly anti-Bulgarian, and at the second session of the Anti-Fascist Council of the National Liberation of Yugoslavia, held in Jajce on 29 November 1943, "unilaterally" and "secretly" decided to unite Macedonia and include it within the borders of Yugoslavia. Third, after the war Yugoslavia treated the Bulgarian communist government as a defeated ally of the Nazis and sought to impose its "hegemony" on the Balkans. Since the end of the war, Dragoycheva continued, Yugoslavia has sought by "permissible and impermissible means" to create an artificial Macedonian nationalism on an anti-Bulgarian foundation. This is bad enough in Yugoslav Macedonia, which "from time immemorial has been flesh of the flesh and blood of the blood of the Bulgarian land and the Bulgarian people," but when applied to Bulgarian Macedonia it amounts to "a crude intervention in Bulgaria's internal affairs." (Tsola Dragoycheva, *Iz moite spomeni*, Sofia, 1979.)

The Yugoslav response to Dragoycheva was vitriolic. In an article entitled "I Have No Proof, But I Assert . . . ," the president of the Macedonian Academy of Sciences, Mihailo Apostolski, suggested that the memoirs may have been the result of Dragoycheva's "illness" or that they were entirely forged. He added that the Bulgarian people were genetically "disposed toward evil." (*NIN*, 4 March.) Dragoycheva replied to the Yugoslav criticisms in two interviews in March and April. In the second, given on Bulgarian television, she told interviewer Ivan Slavkov, Zhivkov's son-in-law, that "obviously the anti-Bulgarian feelings that have possessed certain circles in Belgrade and Skopje border on the hysterical . . . Everybody there, both the ordinary scribblers and the authoritative academicians, regard all means, all sorts of falsehoods and allegations as moral and permissible, as long as they serve their impure aims." (*Otechestven front*, 6 April.)

On 27 April Zhivkov took the unusual step of delivering a state-of-the-nation address to the National Assembly, a task usually performed by Prime Minister Todorov. He devoted the bulk of his substantive comments to relations with Yugoslavia, repeating that Bulgaria had no claim on Yugoslav territory and would not consider ceding any territory of its own. He stated that it was in Bulgaria's interest to improve relations with Yugoslavia and invited Tito to come to Bulgaria for negotiations "without any preconditions." He added that he would be willing to meet with Tito "at any time and at any other place that is suitable and acceptable to the Yugoslav side." (*RD*, 28 April.) In reporting this speech, the Yugoslav press emphasized that Zhivkov had refused to admit the existence of a "Macedonian minority" in Bulgaria and ignored the invitation to Tito. The Yugoslav government did not respond. (*RFE, Situation Report*, 22 May, item 2.)

The Macedonian issue flared up again in August, when Bulgarians learned that Yugoslav Macedonia would celebrate (on 7 December) the 70th anniversary of the birth of the poet Nikola Vaptsarov as a Macedonian holiday. Vaptsarov, who was born in a village in Bulgarian Macedonia and wrote in the Bulgarian literary language, is regarded as a major literary figure. His widow and other relatives asked the Bulgarian press to make public their "profound indignation," and the Bulgarian Writers' Union issued a sharply worded denunciation of those attempting to lay their "unclean hands" on one of the jewels of Bulgarian culture (*RD*, 3 August).

Asia, the Middle East, Africa, and Latin America. Bulgaria continued to echo Soviet criticism of China but maintained diplomatic and trade relations with the PRC. Bulgaria strongly endorsed the Vietnamese invasion of Kampuchea, recognizing the Heng Samrin government in January and organizing medical assistance after a Kampuchean delegation visited Sofia in April. At the opening of the U.N. General Assembly's 34th session, Zhivkov's daughter called for the expulsion of the representatives of the "genocidal" Pol Pot regime (ibid., 29 September). Zhivkov himself paid official visits to Vietnam, Laos, and Kampuchea in October, probably at the urging of the Soviet Union, which wishes to demonstrate socialist bloc support for its Asian policies.

The visit of Abu Mayzar, an official spokesman of the Palestine Liberation Organization (PLO), to Sofia in August provided the Bulgarian government with the opportunity to express its solidarity with the PLO and to denounce "Zionist imperialism," the Israeli-Egyptian negotiations, and America's Middle Eastern polices (Voice of Palestine, 6 August; *FBIS*, 15 August). Diplomatic relations with Egypt, broken off in December 1978 after a disturbance at the Bulgarian embassy in Cairo, were not renewed. Although Bulgaria had developed good relations with Iran—the shah visited Sofia in May 1978—the Bulgarian government hailed the victory of the "anti-imperialist" revolution (BTA, 4 April; *FBIS*, 5 April).

Bulgaria has continued to expand its ties to African nations. *Rabotnichesko delo* (18 April) reported that between 1970 and 1977 the value of trade with Africa rose from U.S. $90 million to $473 million and that "Bulgaria has exported over 300 complete enterprises, installations, and items of technical equipment to African countries alone, as well as having given highly qualified assistance and having trained hundreds of local cadres for those countries." During the year an economic cooperation agreement was signed with Mozambique (BTA, 23 July; *FBIS*, 24 July) and a military cooperation agreement with Zambia (Sofia Domestic Service, 18 July; *FBIS*, 19 July). Tanzanian President Julius Nyerere met with Zhivkov in Sofia on 15 September to discuss expanded economic cooperation (*RD*, 17 September).

An emerging theme in Bulgarian diplomacy has been the expansion of contacts with Latin America. Zhivkov reported that in the last five years "42 agreements and contracts in the fields of economy, science, technology, and culture were signed, not counting those signed with Cuba" (ibid., 28 April). Zhivkov spent five days, 3–7 April, in Mexico, where he was warmly welcomed by President José López Portillo. Their discussions emphasized expanded trade and economic cooperation. After Mexico Zhivkov visited Cuba from 7 to 12 April. About 750 Bulgarian specialists are engaged on various Cuban projects, and the large-scale mechanical engineering complex at Holguin is presumed to be the biggest project built by Bulgaria abroad. (*RFE*, Situation Report, 27 April, item 2.)

Western Europe and the United States. Bulgaria has generally cordial relations with Western Europe, but enormous Bulgarian deficits continue to hinder the expansion of trade. On the negative side, the murder of Bulgarian defector Georgi Markov in London last year continued to receive wide publicity and to focus attention on Bulgarian agents abroad. Helmut Schmidt, chancellor of the Federal Republic of Germany, Bulgaria's largest nonsocialist trade partner, visited Bulgaria from 2 to 4 May. The two issued a long joint declaration calling in general terms for increased economic cooperation, including joint industrial construction and expanded cultural and athletic exchanges (*RD*, 5 May). Relations with the Vatican continued to improve; two new bishops were appointed, and the status of the Plovdiv vicariate upgraded. There is now a full complement of three bishops for Bulgaria's 70,000 Roman Catholics (*RFE, Situation Report*, 22 May, item 4).

Although Bulgarian leaders endorse Soviet criticisms of the United States, direct Bulgarian-American relations have been stable and businesslike. Cultural and scholarly exchanges have continued, and the volume of trade rose significantly in 1979. In September an agreement was signed with Pepsi Cola providing for the marketing of the soft drink in Bulgaria and for the opening of a chain of Pizza Huts at major border crossings and in the larger cities (*CSM*, 13 September).

International Party Contacts. During the year the BCP played host to the leaders of or high-level delegations from the communist parties of Greece, Cyprus, Chile, Paraguay, Peru, and Cuba and from the Southwest African Peoples' Organization and sent delegations to observe congresses or participate in the celebrations of the communist parties of India, Libya, Ethiopia, Belgium, France, Italy, and the United States. Reports of these meetings consisted of statements in support of peace, cooperation, and solidarity. Yusef Dadoo, chairman of the South African Communist Party was awarded the order of Georgi Dimitrov on the occasion of his 70th birthday (BTA, 3 September; *FBIS*, 4 September).

Publications. The official daily of the BCP is *Rabotnichesko delo* (Workers' Cause), its monthly is *Partien zhivot* (Party Life), and its theoretical journal is *Novo vreme* (New Times). Government legislation and decrees are published in *Durzhaven vestnik* (State Newspaper). The mass Fatherland Front organization publishes the newspaper *Otechestven front*, and the Agrarian Union *Zemedelsko zname* (Agrarian Banner). Economic events are surveyed in *Ikonomicheski zhivot* (Economic Life) and cultural ones in the weekly *Literaturen front* (Literary Front) and in *Septemvri* (September), the monthly journal of the Bulgarian Writers' Union. The Sofia Press Agency publishes an English-language weekly, *Sofia News*. The official news agency is Bulgarska telegrafna agentsiya (BTA).

University of Maryland, Baltimore County   John D. Bell

Czechoslovakia

The Communist Party of Czechoslovakia (Komunistická strana Ceskoslovenska; KSC) is a latecomer among the European communist parties. It was constituted at the Merger Congress in Prague (November 1921) of the left wing of the Czechoslovak Social Democratic Workers' Party and a host of leftist splinter groups. Its formal admission to the Communist International followed soon afterwards. In a coup d'etat in February 1948, the KSC seized absolute power in Czechoslovakia, which until then had been a parliamentary democracy. It rules through the mechanism of the National Front of Working People, a formalized coalition in which the KSC holds two-thirds of the seats. The three top political officials—President of the Republic Gustav Husák, Federal Prime Minister Lubomír Strougal, and Federal Assembly Chairman Alois Indra—are all members of the KSC.

A constitutional reform carried out in October 1968 made Czechoslovakia a federal state comprising two units: the Czech Socialist Republic and the Slovak Socialist Republic. The federal structure is the only significant remnant of an ambitious liberalization program launched in January 1968 by the KSC leadership headed by Alexander Dubcek. Reforms in other vital areas of Czechoslovak political and economic life were stopped or reversed after a Soviet-led military intervention of the Warsaw Pact nations in August 1968. The intervention also arrested the development of the KSC into a federalized party. Although a regional party for Slovakia exists under the name Komunistická strana Slovenska (KSS), there is no counterpart to the KSS in the Czech provinces.

The KSC is among the largest communist parties of the world in terms of per capita membership. According to the latest membership statistics, released in 1978, the party had about 1.5 million members and candidates; 62 percent reportedly are of worker origin (*WMR*, June 1978). The total population of Czechoslovakia in June 1979 has reached 15.2 million (Radio Prague, 9 August).

Leadership and Organization. The two supreme organs of the party executive are the Central Committee and the Presidium. Its present composition dates from the Fifteenth Congress (April 1976). This congress should actually have been the sixteenth, but the Soviet-imposed leadership of Gustav Husák does not recognize the validity of the Extraordinary Congress called by the reformists in August 1968 during the Soviet-led military occupation of Czechoslovakia. The next congress is scheduled for 1981.

There are 121 full and 52 candidate members on the Central Committee and 11 full and 2 candidate members on the Presidium. The working organ of the Central Committee is the Central Committee Secretariat, led by the secretary general, with eight secretaries and two Secretariat members. The organizational structure of the KSS replicates that of the KSC, with the sole difference being the title of the top secretary, who in the KSS bears the title of "first secretary." Gustav Husák is the secretary general of the KSC; the first secretary of the KSS is Jozef Lenárt.

Party Internal Affairs. The year 1979 was the tenth anniversary of the replacement of Dubcek by Husák and his group. This anniversary gave party spokesmen and the media an opportunity to denounce the liberalization course of 1968 anew and to extol the takeover by Husák as a "return to Marxism-Leninism," while asserting that the goal of the reformists had been "to change the party into a social-democratic free association of ideologically diverse people—a mere debating society founded on the principles of the so-called right of the minority" (*Rudé právo*, 5 April). Jan Fojtík, a prominent party ideologist, claimed that the ten years of Husák's rule "unequivocally bore out our firm conviction that the road that we took then and that has led our party and society out of the crisis was and remains the right one" (*Hospodárské noviny*, no. 15, 13 March). Another positive assessment of Husák's policies was drawn by speakers at the thirteenth session of the Central Committee, held in Prague 21–22 March. However, one of the principal arguments in favor of the Husák leadership, its economic performance, had become considerably weakened by serious problems connected with the production, supply, and quality of goods and services, as well as the energy crisis and shortages in agriculture. A substantial part of the Central Committee's agenda, therefore, focused on economic questions (Radio Bratislava, 27 March).

Another important party concern in 1979 was the "membership cards exchange," a process to be completed in 1980 (*Rudé právo*, 4 January). In the past, such operations have led to a purge in party ranks. This time, however, informed observers believe that the number of people who are likely to lose their membership will not compare with the mass expulsions of 1970, following the Soviet military intervention (Radio Free Europe–Radio Liberty, *Situation Report*, no. 3, 24 January).

During 1979 the party lost two of its foremost theoreticians and ideological supervisors, both well-known before 1968. On 16 May Jirí Hendrych, former member of the Presidium and chairman of the

Ideological Commission, died in Prague. On 1 July Vladimír Koucký, ambassador to Italy and Malta, former editor-in-chief of the party daily *Rudé právo*, and Central Committee secretary, died in Rome. Both were considered conservative followers of First Secretary Antonín Novotný before his ouster in January 1968. Koucký was regarded as more of a hard-liner than Hendrych. The fall of Novotný ended both men's party careers. Their close affiliation with him made both unacceptable in the eyes of Husák, whose feud with Novotný was irreconcilable. The third prominent person to die in 1979 was ailing ex-President Ludvík Svoboda, former defense minister and Presidium member. Svoboda played an important role in party history on two different occasions: in 1948 he made possible the communist takeover by refusing to support President Eduard Benes, and in 1968, as president of the Republic, he persuaded Soviet leaders to return the reformist Dubcek group, whom they had deposed and interned in Moscow, to power temporarily. Neither of these exploits was recalled in the official obituaries (Radio Hvezda, 20 September).

Domestic Affairs. The year also saw the commemoration of the 35th anniversary of the Slovak national uprising of August 1944. President Husák's speech in Banská Bystrica and other official comments stressed the unity of the Czechs and the Slovaks and the "fraternal help" from the Soviet Union as the most important lessons of the uprising (CETEKA [the official news agency], 25 August). No reference was made to the fact that the Red Army did not significantly help the Slovak rebels, who eventually succumbed to the Nazi troops. Despite the constitutional reforms of 1968, trends in party policy during the last ten years seem to point in the direction of gradual erosion of Slovak autonomy; the self-contained ethnic personality of the Czechs is not even recognized in the party's centralist structure. The goal of the ultimate "merger" of the two ethnic elements, however, may be difficult to achieve.

Indicative perhaps of the mood prevailing in the country is a new decline in demographic growth. Only two years ago, media and economic experts asserted that the declining birthrate had finally been reversed in Czechoslovakia (*Statistická rocenka*, 1978). Recently published figures, however, suggest that the change might have been only temporary (*Demografie*, no. 2).

The Charter Movement in 1979. The opposition, which for some time has taken on more organized forms in Czechoslovakia than in most other communist countries, to the course actually adopted by the party continued to be very articulate in 1979. The so-called Charter Group, constituted in 1977 and comprising prominent persons as well as simple citizens from all walks of life, remained active despite systematic repression by the regime. Charter '77, so-called because of the respect for human and civil rights in the U.N. Charter and the Helsinki agreements of 1975, pointed to a number of violations of these rights by the Czechoslovak government. The harsh treatment of the Chartists by the Czechoslovak authorities has become a new source of disagreement within the international communist movement.

On the eve of the new year, Charter spokesmen Václav Havel and Ladislav Hejdánek reaffirmed the determination of the group to pursue its activities despite increasing persecution (Reuters, 30 December 1978). In January a prominent Charter leader, Jaroslav Sabata, a university lecturer and communist party member of long standing, was tried by the district court in Trutnov, in northeastern Bohemia, and sentenced to nine months of strict confinement. This was Sabata's second condemnation for protest activities (Agence France Presse [AFP], 11 January). His attorney, Josef Daniš, declared at the trial that the court was biased and its methods resembled the infamous political trials of the "personality cult" era. This criticism led to the expulsion of Danis from the Czechoslovak Lawyers' Association (United Press International [UPI], 22 March). Following the condemnation of Sabata, the group designated new leaders, radio journalist Jiří Dienstbier, mathematician and philosopher Václav Benda, and Mrs. Zdena Tomínová, writer and interpreter (Reuters, 8 February). In March the Charter activists established a fund for the support of the victims of persecution and their families, using donations from home and abroad (AFP, 6 March). Early in the year, the Chartists urged Austrian Federal Chancellor Bruno Kreisky to take up the case of the dissidents with party and government officials during his scheduled visit in Prague (Reuters, 18 January). The human rights activists also appealed to the Fifteenth Congress of the Communist Party of Italy (ibid., 1 April). In May three members of the French Communist Party transmitted a letter from the Charter group to Secretary General Georges Marchais; in this letter, Charter leaders complained about systematic intimidation and harassment from the police (*Guardian*, 11 May).

During the first half of 1979, the group continued to disseminate critical analyses of various aspects of Czechoslovak political and social life, which official information sources failed to mention. The publication of these facts by the Chartists probably prompted the authorities to take systematic repressive measures against the group. At the end of May, a number of arrests were made, including among others new Charter spokesmen Dienstbier and Benda (Radio Hvezda, 4 June). Although two other activists, Jirí Hájek and Ladislav Hejdánek, immediately took over their responsibilities (Reuters, 5 June), the Charter movement was nevertheless seriously restricted in its impact. For some time it was uncertain if and when the arrested leaders would be tried. Some informed circles believed that the regime would be wary of the reaction of world opinion and that Soviet politicians would counsel moderation (*Observer*, London, 29 July). In early October the case of the playwright Pavel Kohout, another prominent dissident who was denied return to the country after a temporary stay in Austria, seemed to indicate that the Czechoslovak government might consider other ways in which the opposition could be neutralized. Kohout was forcibly expatriated because of the publication of an allegorical book entitled *The Woman Executioner* and because of his contacts with a previously exiled former Central Committee secretary, Zdenek Mlynár (AFP, 8 October).

Nevertheless, the trial of the Charter activists finally took place in late October. The Prague City Court condemned six defendants (Václav Benda, Václav Havel, Jirí Dienstbier, Petr Uhl, Ota Bednárová, and Dana Nemcová) to jail sentences of between two and five years. The formal accusation centered on the creation of the Committee for the Defense of Unjustly Persecuted Persons, which the public prosecutor said constituted an activity "against the state, aimed at causing harm to the Czechoslovak socialist system, in collusion with hostile forces from abroad" (Czechoslovak Television, 23 October). Many Charter publications had been made accessible to Western media, and this was the basis for the charge. It was also considered an act of conspiracy that the dissidents had held talks with a similar group in Poland. The repression of dissent in Czechoslovakia brought protests in many European countries. The communist party of France condemned the verdicts as unjust and called for the release of the prisoners (*L'Humanité*, 25 October). French Foreign Minister Jean Francois Poncet postponed his planned visit to Czechoslovakia after the French cabinet stated that the measures taken against the activists were contrary to the Helsinki agreements (AFP, 25 October). A spokesman of the Communist Party of Italy declared the verdicts to be "grave and inadmissible" (*L'Unità*, 25 October). A group of prominent American personalities, among them novelists Arthur Miller and Kurt Vonnegut, marched in protest in front of the Czechoslovak mission to the United Nations in New York. The U.S. State Department denounced the imprisonment of the civil rights workers in a statement made by Hodding Carter in Washington (*NYT*, 25 October). Amnesty International in New York announced that it had adopted the sentenced human rights activists as "prisoners of conscience" and would endeavor to obtain their liberation (Amnesty International press release, 28 October). Moreover, 350 Czechoslovak citizens sent a letter protesting the persecution of the Chartists to Pope John Paul II (ibid., 1 November).

Culture and Religion. Close supervision of cultural activities, which had been gradually re-established in Czechoslovakia after the Soviet intervention in 1968, became even more evident in 1979. Although Czech Minister of Culture Milan Klusák abstained from the traditional New Year's review of the cultural scene, programmatic statements in party press and media left no doubt that political criteria would continue to dominate the assessment of cultural products (*Tvorba*, 3 January; Radio Hvezda, 30 December 1978). The 1979 Month of the Book (March) was dedicated to the International Children's Year. Children's books on display showed that many independently minded authors had "escaped into fairy tales" in order to avoid the pressure felt in the area of current fiction. On the other hand, the clandestine publication series "Edice-Petlice" (Padlock Editions) continued to bring out works that the official publishing houses refused to accept. The underground media were joined by a new political and cultural periodical, *Ctverec* (The Square), commenting on current events from a dissident point of view (*Le Monde*, 22 March).

Relations between the state and the Roman Catholic church remained burdened by a number of unresolved issues, among them the regime's unwillingness to lift the restrictions on the training of priests in seminaries. Although the communist media commented positively on the election of a Polish cardinal to the papacy, the basically antireligious attitude of the party became manifest in various statements and analyses (*Tvorba*, 3 January). Many individual priests and church workers suffered persecution and harassment (*NYT*, 24 February). Relations between communist Czechoslovakia and the Vatican were clouded by these circumstances, but it was reported that the party was anxious to come to an agreement with the Holy See, especially in the matter of the appointment of dignitaries to vacant dioceses (*Die Presse*, Vienna, 5 February).

The mistrustful attitude of party leaders toward the Roman Catholic church came to the fore on the occasion of the trip of Prague Archbishop Frantisek Tomásek to Salzburg. The Austrian president had invited Tomásek to participate in ceremonies commemorating the 250th anniversary of the canonization of St. John Nepomuk. Czechoslovak leaders put various administrative obstacles in the way of his trip, apparently to capitalize on the somewhat ambivalent reputation of this saint in the Czech historical tradition. The canonized martyr was perceived in the eighteenth century by the forcibly re-Catholicized Czech population as the Counter-Reformation substitute for John Huss. However, the interference of the authorities with Tomásek's travel plans was strongly resented in Austria (Austrian Television, 9 May), and eventually Tomásek was allowed to go to Salzburg, while the regime's media denied any intention to restrict the cardinal's freedom of movement (*Rudé právo*, 14 May). The Husák leadership has wanted to reap political benefits from the activities of Catholic groups willing to support the system but not enjoying recognition among the mass of believers. In 1979 the pro-regime association of the Catholic clergy, Pacem in Terris, organized an international conference in the Tatra mountain resort Dolný Smokovec in which 60 high church officials from fourteen countries took part. The endorsement of the "peace initiatives of the Czechoslovak and Soviet governments" was the main point on the agenda (*Katolické noviny*, 9 September). Pacem in Terris subsequently held its second Czech national congress in Hradec Králové in Eastern Bohemia, 8–9 October. The congress was visited by an important delegation of party officials (*Lidová demokracie*, 9 October). The situation of other Christian churches was not much different. The present party leaders appeared to have adopted a policy of persecution against all true believers and to encourage those prepared to put religion at the service of political indoctrination (*Der Spiegel*, 29 January).

Auxiliary and Mass Organizations. The national organization of collective farmers, the Union of Agricultural Cooperatives (UAC), held its ninth congress in Prague, 9–11 April. The date of the congress, which had been due for several years, had been deliberately postponed so as to coincide with the 30th anniversary of the Ninth Party Congress, which formulated the guidelines that resulted in the collectivization of 95.2 percent of arable land. Since the last UAC congress, the average size of collective farms has tripled, reducing their number by about two-thirds. This concentration, however, has not been matched by a corresponding increase in productivity. Media commentaries pointed out that for many UAC officials the goal was successful amalgamation, regardless of consequences in the area of efficiency (*Ekonomika pol'nohospodárstva*, no. 10, 1978). Federal Prime Minister Lubomír

Strougal, in his opening speech at the congress on 9 April, pointed out that overall gross production in agriculture had more than doubled since the communist takeover in 1948, but that severe shortcomings in the field of staple products, such as sugar beets and potatoes, persisted. Vegetables, fruits, and fodder also constituted a serious bottleneck, and Czechoslovakia had lost its primacy in the world export of barley (*Rudé právo*, 10 April). The closing resolution exhorted all collective farmers to work toward the improvement of this situation but at the same time pointedly stressed the need for Czechoslovak industry to supply the countryside with quality modern implements. It also praised the Husák leadership for the results achieved during the preceding ten years (*Zemedelské noviny*, 12 April).

The year under review saw a statewide congress of the Czechoslovak Association of Women, held in Prague 14–15 May. The meeting was attended by a thousand delegates representing a million members organized in about 12,000 units. Maria Kabrhelová, who has headed the association since its inception in 1976, was re-elected (*Rudé právo*, 16 May). In this capacity, she participated at the World Conference for the Peaceful and Happy Future of Children in Moscow, 7–11 September (CETEKA, 6 September). The media news and analyses prior to the congress stressed the duties of Czechoslovak women in the process of "building socialism" rather than the grievances and demands of women during the period of the Prague Spring in 1968. Nevertheless, it was admitted, for example, that the needs of working women were still neglected in Czechoslovakia (*Hospodárské noviny*, 16 February).

As for the activities of other mass organizations, representatives of the Central Trade Union Council, led by Chairman Karel Hoffmann, met with their Polish counterparts in the High Tatra region in August. In this working session, "further broadening and deepening of mutual cooperation in all spheres of union life" were discussed (Radio Prague, 29 August). A national meeting of the Pioneer organizations, a component of the Czechoslovak youth movement, was held in June in the Julius Fučík Park of Culture and Recreation in Prague. The Pioneers prepare elementary-school children for later activities in the Czechoslovak Socialist Youth Union. A Central Committee delegation led by Lubomír Strougal opened the meeting, and Strougal delivered a festive address (ibid., 2 June).

The Economy. Nineteen seventy-nine was a difficult year for the Czechoslovak economy. In addition to such problems as low productivity and unsatisfactory quality of goods and services, it had to face adverse external factors over which it had little control, among them the world shortage of oil. A report on the fulfillment of planned targets in 1978, published in early 1979, indicated that performance during the previous year had left a great deal to be desired, especially in the areas of capital investment, export to countries with hard currencies, and energy (*Rudé právo*, 29 January). The continuing unfavorable foreign-payments balance threatened to deteriorate further when it became known that Soviet oil and natural gas deliveries to Czechoslovakia would not be increased above their present levels (Radio Prague, 8 September). This meant that any additional oil would have to be purchased in non-CMEA countries. Substantial price increases for Soviet oil, which in 1979 sold at approximately 60 percent of OPEC prices (*Vecerník*, Bratislava, 2 July), resulted in an overall increase in the cost of living. In July the federal government made public new prices for commodities and services (clothing, gas, electricity, postal fees, etc.), which on the average were 50 to 250 percent higher than the old ones (Radio Hvezda, 20 July). Fixed incomes, such as old-age and widows' pensions or children's allowances, were raised by only about 33 percent (*Rudé právo*, 16 May), which brought hardship to many households. Considering that the Husák leadership had used the improvement in the standard of living as its main justification, this deterioration dealt a serious blow to the legitimacy of the regime. Poor plan fulfillment in the first half of 1979, energy shortages, and a bad harvest added to the general economic plight (Czechoslovak Television, 19 June; Radio Prague, 12 July) and stimulated panic purchasing and hoarding (*Rudé právo*, 18 August; *Pravda*, 31 August). The crisis imperiled the efforts to improve efficiency and the quality of industrial production started in 1978 and known as the Complex Economic Experiment. The experiment was launched in 150 enterprises in twelve key sectors, to which another three sectors were added in 1979 (*Práca*, 31 January; *Hospodárské noviny*, 4 May). It was supposed to last three years, but the anticipated failure of plan fulfillment for 1980 has cast doubts on the success of the operation.

In 1979 special measures designed to improve the quality of products were introduced in Czechoslovakia, including penalties for plants turning out rejects (*Práca*, 4 January). Previous experience with similar actions does not justify great optimism. Energy conservation has been receiving priority among economic goals, hardly surprising in a nation whose per capita energy consumption is among the highest in Europe. However, little has thus far been undertaken toward real savings except for extensive discussion of the problem among experts and in the media (*Plánované hospodárství*, no. 3, March). The development of alternative energy sources has made slow progress. Although the first nuclear power unit began trial operations in December 1978 (one year behind schedule), it will achieve full capacity only in 1985 (*Pravda*, Bratislava, 23 May).

Foreign Affairs. As in the past, party leaders followed faithfully and without reservation the foreign policy line laid down by the Soviet Union. This was reflected in acts and statements of Czechoslovak representatives on diplomatic missions and in international organizations. The coverage of important world events by Czechoslovak media confirmed the unqualified dependence on the Soviet example. Thus, when the shah was deposed in Iran, the Czechoslovak press, radio, and television declared him "a key figure in the anti-Soviet policies in the Middle East sponsored by the United States." The authors of these stern lines seemingly forgot that a little more than a year earlier, the shah and his wife had been received with great pomp by President Husák and the whole federal cabinet and the highest honors bestowed on the imperial couple, such as the Order of the White Lion with Chain and an honorary doctoral degree in philosophy and jurisprudence from Charles University (Radio Prague, 27 August 1977). The radical change of tune in official comments on Iran was, of course, in agreement with the needs of Soviet global policies. So was the somewhat embarrassed position of Czechoslovakia on the seizure in Teheran of the U.S. embassy and hostages. The Czechoslovak delegate at the United Nations condemned the act (UPI, 1 December), but the media kept blaming the Carter administration because of its alleged designs to return the shah to power. On the whole, the position of the party and the government on Iran betrayed the hope, shared with the Soviets, that the upheaval would pave the road for a change of regime favorable to Soviet interests.

The identity of views between Moscow and the Moscow-sponsored leadership in Prague became even more evident during the Vietnamese intervention in Kampuchea (Cambodia) and the conflict between Vietnam and the People's Republic of China. On both occasions, party officials echoed the Soviet stand, sometimes even verbatim. On 18 February the federal government and the Central Committee issued a joint statement in which "the Chinese armed aggression" was "condemned with great indignation." In the same statement, Vietnam was assured of the "full solidarity and support of the Czechoslovak people" (*Rudé právo*, 19 February). The previous Vietnamese invasion of Kampuchea, on the other hand, was presented as an "internal affair of a country" (ibid., 24 February). An unreserved pro-Vietnam declaration was also jointly made by Czechoslovak Foreign Minister Bohuslav Chnoupek and his Soviet colleague Andrei Gromyko during Chnoupek's visit to Moscow (CETEKA, 22 February).

Communist Czechoslovakia followed the same policy line as the Soviet Union concerning the Middle East peace treaty. It rejected the agreement between Egypt and Israel as a step serving the "Eisenhower doctrine," i.e., "the search for U.S. superiority in the world" (Radio Prague, 27 March). The official press agency, CETEKA, released declarations by the World Federation of Trade Unions and the International Organization of Journalists, both based in Prague, stating that Egypt "had abandoned the national liberation struggle of the Arabs." A just and comprehensive peace in the Middle East could be achieved only if Israel pulls out of all occupied territories and all rights of the Palestinian people are vindicated. (CETEKA, 28 March.)

Nor did the coverage of the recent phases of the SALT II negotiations between the United States and the USSR differ in any notable way from that presented by the Soviet media (Radio Hvezda, 28 May). Not unlike their Soviet counterparts, Czechoslovak analysts appeared apprehensive about the reception of the treaty in the U.S. Congress, especially the Senate (*Rudé právo*, 20 June). The Czechoslovak ambassador to the United Nations, Ilja Hulínský, transmitted to U.N. Secretary General Kurt Waldheim a letter from Czechoslovak Foreign Minister Chnoupek in which, among other things, the significance of SALT was underscored (Radio Prague, 24 June).

As for relations between communist Czechoslovakia and its Western neighbors, contacts with Austria appeared to be the most frequent although not always the most friendly. On 25 January Austrian Chancellor Kreisky visited the international industrial fair in Brno (Radio Prague, 26 January). He and Czechoslovak Premier Strougal briefly discussed matters of common interest, especially those concerning trade between the two countries. Even more significant in form and rank was the subsequent four-day state visit of Austrian President Rudolf Kirchschläger, Foreign Minister Willibald Pahr, and Trade and Industry Minister Josef Steinbacher. The Austrians met with President Husák and other members of the federal government. Kirchschläger also visited Archbishop Tomášek.

Important on the agenda of the talks between Kirchschläger and Husák were "humanitarian issues, in harmony with the Helsinki Final Act" (CETEKA, 14 March). These concerned, among others, the reunion of families of exiles, but the Austrian head of state also used the opportunity for raising the question of human rights activists and dissidents within Czechoslovakia. Austrian interest in the fate of opponents of the regime has been a delicate element in relations between the two nations. After Kirchschläger's return from Prague, he reported in a radio interview that Husák had assured him that "in his own opinion no one should be imprisoned for political reasons, if possible." The Austrian president expressed the hope that the Czechoslovak government would "at least reflect on the matter of dissidents" (Austrian Radio Network, 22 March). This hope dimmed considerably when later in the year Czechoslovak authorities denied Pavel Kohout and his wife the right to return home from Vienna (see above). The action against Kohout had repercussions in official Austrian-Czechoslovak relations. When prominent Austrian personalities and groups condemned the forcible expatriation of Kohout, the Czechoslovak embassy in Vienna released a statement minimizing the impact of the condemnation, on the grounds that "Austria needs and will need Czechoslovakia more than vice versa, for political, economic, and strategic reasons" (Associated Press, 8 October). This statement was retracted by the Czechoslovak Ministry of Foreign Affairs the following day, after Chancellor Kreisky called it "a concoction of naiveté and arrogance" (*Die Presse*, 10 October).

The harsh treatment of political opponents also elicited indignation in the neighboring Federal German Republic, where former Chancellor Willy Brandt deplored the persecution of Chartists. The relatively cool relations between West Germany and Czechoslovakia did not warm appreciably during 1979. In March, notes on the cultural agreement signed in 1978 and subsequently ratified were exchanged in Prague (Radio Prague, 16 March). In August Deputy Federal Premier andPrime Minister of the Czech Republic Joseph Korcák visited West Germany and held talks with economic and business personalities in Bonn on the further development of economic cooperation (ibid., 28 August).

Another Western politician to visit Czechoslovakia in 1979 was Greek Premier Constantine Caramanlis. Czechoslovak spokesmen called his visit "an example of realism in cooperation between states with different social systems" (ibid., 8 October). On the other hand, Czechoslovak Foreign Minister Chňoupek visited Spain from 6 to 9 March, where he was received by Prime Minister Adolfo Suárez and King Juan Carlos. World political problems, such as questions of disarmament and peace, were on the agenda of their talks (Radio Hvezda, 6 March).

The foreign minister also undertook an official tour of Ethiopia, Mozambique, and Zambia during April and May (ibid., 30 April). The object of his trip was to manifest the solidarity of the party and the government with the radical regimes of these nations, but economic questions were also discussed (CETEKA, 5 May). Czechoslovak representatives also visited North Africa and the Middle East. Prime Minister Strougal and three members of the federal cabinet paid a three-day official visit to Libya. Economic cooperation was the main topic of talks with Libya's leader, Colonel Qadhafi, but the communiqués also stressed agreement on political questions regarding the Middle East region (Czechoslovak Television, 5 February). Foreign Minister Chnoupek signed two Czechoslovak-Tunisian treaties on legal procedures in the city of Tunis in April (Radio Prague, 12 April). President Gustav Husák, accompanied by the foreign minister and two other members of the federal government, spent four days in Syria on an official "friendship visit." They discussed cooperation in the political and economic spheres with the Syrian president and other politicians and signed several documents on these subjects. In the closing communiqué, the further development of political relations was emphasized, and the Israeli-Egyptian treaty was denounced as being "contrary to U.N. resolutions and to Arab interests" (CETEKA, 24 May).

As for contacts with communist nations on the governmental level, the most important event of 1979 was the meeting of Husák with Leonid Brezhnev in the Crimea in July. The results of these talks were hailed by the Czechoslovak party Presidium as "a new important impulse for further strengthening of cooperation" (Radio Prague, 17 August). The Soviet Union was also visited by Foreign Minister Chnoupek in February. He spent six days in the USSR and had talks with his opposite number, Andrei Gromyko, "on bilateral relations and international issues" (CETEKA, 22 February). Bulgarian First Secretary and President of the State Council Todor Zhivkov headed a top-level delegation that came to Prague for a three-day state visit in September. The most important part of the agenda was economic cooperation between Czechoslovakia and Bulgaria in the "eighties and nineties." The ground for these talks was prepared by the earlier visit of Bulgarian Prime Minister Stanko Todorov to Prague (Radio Prague, 10 June).

Foreign Trade. The unfavorable foreign-payment balance of Czechoslovakia, recently aggravated by the worldwide oil crisis, influenced the development of foreign trade in 1979. As a consequence of a poor harvest, Czechoslovakia will have to import, among other things, 2 million tons of fodder in 1979–1980 (*Rudé právo*, 18 October), which will put additional stress on the country's meager currency reserves. The uncertain future of Iran made dubious an early realization of an ambitious but vital pipeline project across the Soviet Union to and through Czechoslovakia, by means of which Czechoslovakia is supposed to receive almost a third of its oil and natural gas needs. A substantial part of the cost of these deliveries is to be covered by transit fees to be paid to Czechoslovakia by West Germany, at the westernmost end of the pipeline (*Czechoslovak Life*, no. 4, April). Considering the recent restriction of Soviet oil deliveries, Czechoslovakia may face very difficult choices if the pipeline project is canceled. Another serious foreign trade problem has been the quality of exported products. Complaints from customers about Czechoslovak goods have been heard for some time, not only in the West, but also in other communist countries, including the USSR (*Nové slovo*, Bratislava, 22 March). The reportedly deteriorating quality of export items has posed a new threat to the foreign-payments balance. Czechoslovak economic decision makers may in this situation look for additional sources of foreign currency. One such potential reserve appears to be tourism. Tourist traffic in 1978, for example, reached the record figure of 20 million visitors, either for temporary stays or in transit (Presidium press release, 17 March). However, tourist traffic with the West, which is most interesting from the point of view of hard currency, still suffered from a number of administrative restrictions, especially the cumbersome and lengthy visa-granting process.

In an attempt to alleviate the energy crisis without significant outlays in Western currencies, the government decided to participate in a Soviet nuclear energy project in Khmelnitski in the Ukraine. Czechoslovakia will provide equipment worth 240 million rubles (U.S. $360 million) for this enterprise and will receive in exchange 3.6 billion kilowatt hours of electricity per year between 1984 and 2003

(*Rudé právo*, 29 May). Various trade and economic agreements were signed with other communist nations in 1979, including a mining agreement with Mongolia (Radio Prague, 4 September), a general trade agreement with Bulgaria (CETEKA, 14 September), an economic cooperation treaty with Hungary (Radio Prague, 28 August), a general agreement with Yugoslavia (Radio Hvĕzda, 14 June), and a trade and payments protocol with Albania (Radio Tirana, 20 October). Czechoslovak politicians visiting African and Middle East countries either initiated or agreed to economic exchanges and cooperation.

Trade relations with Austria are important for both partners but have encountered a number of problems, among them the small volume of Austrian purchases in Czechoslovakia, due chiefly to the low quality of Czechoslovak commodities (*Die Presse*, 16 March). Certain initiatives of the Czechoslovak government during 1979 indicated that Western help and cooperation in industrial production might be welcome to the regime. The Skoda Automobile Works in Mladá Boleslav, for example, approached the West German Volkswagenwerk in August for the purchase of a license to manufacture Rabbits (*Der Spiegel*, 6 August). A similar step had been undertaken during the brief liberalization period in 1968 but was abandoned after the Soviet military intervention.

International Party Contacts. Czechoslovak party leaders, anxious not to displease their Soviet mentors, had to exercise circumspection in the area of contacts with other components of the world communist movement. Recent exacerbation of the Sino-Soviet dispute because of the events in Indochina made caution twice as indispensable in 1979. The major West European communist parties, especially the Italian and the Spanish, drifted further away from what the Soviet party considered the only correct course, making contacts with these parties complicated and risky. On the whole, relations between the KSC and Western parties have been rather delicate for more than a decade. None of the latter has yet assimilated the shock of the Soviet military action in Czechoslovakia in August 1968. Relations have worsened further as a consequence of the regime's handling of the dissidents. Under these circumstances, adherence to the Soviet line signified disagreement with a large number of the communist parties in the world.

Chinese military operations in Vietnam provided an occasion for Czechoslovak leaders to display unconditional loyalty to their sponsors. Official statements and media commentaries blended into a concerted anti-Chinese campaign. It was asserted that "aggression is a permanent and characteristic feature of Maoist policy" (Radio Hvezda, 18 February). The action in Indochina was denounced as "a reactionary, antisocialist and antipeople policy of great power chauvinism and hegemonism, directed against peace in the world, international security, and the vital interests of mankind" (*Rudé právo*, 19 February). Secretary General Husák, in his opening speech at the meeting of the Interparliamentary Union in Prague, criticized the Chinese position as "a serious threat, which all Czechoslovaks vehemently oppose, to peace in the world" (Radio Prague, 17 April). In a similar vein, the participants at the meeting of nonaligned nations in Havana were accused of not giving "a clear answer to Beijing" and thus "trying to set the nonaligned movement against world socialism" (ibid., 29 August). The KSS organized a seminar on "the battle against the great-power and hegemonist policies of Chinese Communist Party leaders" in Kosice in May (*Pravda*, Bratislava, 14 May).

Skirmishes with other communist parties not obedient to Moscow continued in 1979. Despite renewed contacts with Yugoslavia on the governmental level, the ideological disagreement between the parties of the two nations did not abate. The Yugoslav party press charged that Czechoslovak radio and television commentators "gave a falsified picture of Yugoslavia by spreading untruths and half-truths (*Borba*, 13 April). The Communist Party of Spain became a target of concentrated attacks in the Czechoslovak media for its adherence to the idea of Eurocommunism. In the opinion of Czechoslovak critics, Eurocommunism was "the revisionism of the seventies," i.e., "views and ideas that benefit only and solely international anticommunism in its struggle against progress, peace, and socialism"

(*Tribuna*, no. 19, 19 May). The Spanish, Italian, and French parties also reaped the wrath of their Czechoslovak comrades when they protested against the trial of the Chartists in October (*Rudé právo*, 26 October).

Among the most important interparty contacts of the year were the visit by Alexei Kosygin to Prague in May (Radio Prague, 22 May) and the meeting between Gustav Husák and Leonid Brezhnev in the Crimea in the summer (Tass, 22 August). In the course of the year, KSC officials met with representatives of several other parties in various regions of the world. On the occasion of his state visit to Damascus, Husák had a talk with the Syrian party leader Khalid Bakdash (Radio Prague, 24 May). At about the same time, KSC functionaries exchanged views with the Danish Communist Party in Copenhagen (ibid., 21 May), and a KSC delegation attended the Ninth Congress of the Communist Party of Portugal in Lisbon (ibid., 30 May). Tomás Trávnícek, a member of the KSC Central Committee, attended the congress of the Communist Party, U.S.A. in Detroit as an official delegate (ibid., 25 August). The Central Committee of the KSC also sent a congratulatory telegram to the American communist party on the 60th anniversary of its founding (*Rudé právo*, 1 September). The interest of the KSC in this tiny party is perhaps more understandable if we recall that the U.S. party was the only Western communist party that unreservedly approved the Soviet-led military intervention in 1968.

Publications. The party's central daily, *Rudé právo*, has the longest history of any communist paper, dating from the period before the formal constitution of the KSC. The official organ of the KSS is *Pravda*, published in Bratislava. General policy problems of the party are treated in the Czech weekly *Tribuna* and its Slovak counterpart *Predvoj*. Questions of party life and organization are dealt with in the fortnightly *Zivot strany*, for which there is no equivalent Slovak version. The long-standing weekly *Tvorba*, which had been discontinued for several years, is now devoted to topics of international politics. The trade union movement owns two dailies, *Práce* in Prague and *Práca* in Bratislava. *Mladá fronta* is the organ of the Czechoslovak Socialist Youth Union; its opposite number in Slovakia is *Smena*. The name of the official press agency is Ceskoslovenská tisková kancelár, abbreviated as CTK or CETEKA.

University of Pittsburgh   Zdenek Suda

Germany:
German Democratic Republic

The Communist Party of Germany (Kommunistische Partei Deutschlands), banned under the Third Reich, was reactivated in June 1945. Soviet authorities forced the merger of the larger Social Democratic Party of Germany (Sozialdemokratische Partei Deutschlands) with the KPD the following spring. The resulting Socialist Unity Party of Germany (Sozialistische Einheitspartei Deutschlands;

SED), under control of its deputy chairman and Moscow's trusted agent, Walter Ulbricht, has served ever since as an instrument of the Communist Party of the Soviet Union (CPSU). The first East German constitution was modeled in several aspects after the Weimar constitution, but in 1968 was replaced by a "socialist" one. In 1974, it was amended with references to the "German nation" and "German reunification" eliminated.

The SED succeeded in creating the political, social, and economic structure of a "people's democracy" by utilizing terror and various means of intimidation, including erection of the Berlin wall and massive border fortifications. Moreover, Moscow exercises control by various means, among them an ever increasing economic and military integration with the Soviet Union and the other communist-ruled states. The GDR is the largest single trading partner of the USSR and provides the most forward Western location for Soviet military forces. In September 1950, the GDR joined the Council for Mutual Economic Assistance (CMEA) and in May 1955 became a full member of the Warsaw Treaty Organization.

The SED has some 2.1 million members and candidates, comprising every sixth GDR citizen over eighteen years of age. By percentage, the party includes workers (56.7), collectivized farmers (4.8), intelligentsia (21.5), white-collar employees (11.5), and others (5.5). Women account for 32.5 percent; some 28 percent of all members and candidates are graduates of post-secondary or vocational schools. The social origin of the large majority is claimed to be working class. (*Deutsche Lehrerzeitung*, East Berlin, 13 March.)

Leadership and Organization. During 1979, no major alteration occurred in the Politburo, Secretariat, or Central Committee (for their composition, see *YICA*, 1979, p. 26), except the one caused by the death in December of the oldest Politburo member, Friedrich Ebert. Within the government, however, several changes did take place. The longtime head of the main political administration of the National People's Army (NVA), Adm. Waldemar Verner, resigned—allegedly for health reasons—and was succeeded by a deputy defense minister, Col. Gen. Heinz Kessler, a close confidant of SED Secretary General Erich Honecker. This change reportedly increased Honecker's influence within the military. (Deutsche Presse Agentur [DPA], Hamburg, 9 January; *FBIS*, 10 January.) In June, the minister of coal and power, Klaus Siebold, was replaced by Wolfgang Mitzinger. This dismissal was related to the severe winter (1978–79) energy crisis (DPA, 28 June). Klaus Gysi, minister of culture from 1966 to 1973, replaced Hans Seigewasser as state secretary for church affairs after the latter's death. Dr. Guenther Mittag, Politburo member and secretary in charge of economic affairs, and Werner Seifert were appointed to the State Council (ibid.).

At its 5 March session, the National Front (an SED-controlled alliance of parties and groups) elected four new vice-presidents: Manfred Grund and Günter Jähne of the Liberal Party, as well as Prof. Dieter Ebert and Dr. Lothar Nöring of the Democratic Peasant Party. Two members of the SED Politburo, Joachim Herrmann and Erich Mückenberger, as well as Hermann Kant (president of the Writers' Association) were elected to the National Front Presidium. (Bundesminister für innerdeutsche Beziehungen, *Informationen*, no. 6, p. 19.)

Auxiliary and Mass Organizations. One of the most important auxiliaries is the youth organization, Freie Deutsche Jugend (FDJ), which claims a membership of over 2.3 million and supervises the children's organization (Ernst Thählmann Pioneers), with a claimed membership of 1.7 million (GDR, Ministry of Foreign Affairs, Press Department, *Foreign Affairs Bulletin* [hereafter cited as *Bulletin*], 21 June, p. 147; *Pädagogik*, 12 December 1978, pp. 972–81). First secretary is Egon Krenz, candidate SED Politburo member. Hans-Joachim Willerding replaced Christel Zillmann as secretary of the FDJ. (*Informationen*, no. 2, p. 4.)

The Free German Trade Union Federation (FDGB), headed by Politburo member Harry Tisch, has a membership of over 8.3 million. Like the FDJ, it contributes to the realization of SED internal and foreign objectives. Domestic tasks include political indoctrination and premilitary training of members. Externally, the FDGB provides ideological and material support to foreign revolutionary organizations and movements.

The Society for German-Soviet Friendship, another mass organization, has over 5.5 million members. (For other mass organiations, see *YICA*, 1976, p. 26.)

Party Internal Affairs. At the tenth SED Central Committee meeting (26–27 April), candidate Politburo member Werner Jarowinsky reported on the party elections held between 1 November 1978 and 18 February 1979, which involved 456,359 officials in basic party organizations in countries and districts. Among the 262 first secretaries of county organizations, 238 were re-elected and 24 were newcomers. At the district level, 91 secretaries were re-elected and only 5 replaced (*Informationen*, no. 5, pp. 7–10). The re-election of such a large number of party secretaries was interpreted as proof of trust in local officials by rank-and-file members. Since the Ninth SED Congress (1976), a total of 177,743 candidate members have been accepted into the party. Of these, 74.5 percent are workers; 76 percent are under 25, and 39 percent are women. (Allgemeiner Deutscher Nachrichtendienst [ADN], 6 April; *FBIS*, 27 April.)

Domestic Affairs. Local elections took place on 20 May. More than 261,000 candidates had been nominated by the National Front (*Neues Deutschland* [*ND*], 28–29 April) and were approved by 99.97 percent (12.1 million) of those casting valid ballots. Only 0.17 percent (20,990) voted against the candidates. A total of 27,168 deputies and 8,103 replacements were elected to serve at the various levels of local government. (Ibid., 23 May.)

Reforms enacted during the year included an amendment to the national electoral law providing for East Berlin to have its own delegates to the People's Chamber under the same voting procedures as the rest of East Germany. This legislation violates several agreements, including the Four Power Agreement of 1971 (*NYT*, 29 June). The foreign ministers of the three Western powers and of the Federal Republic of Germany (FRG) protested this violation, but the Soviet Union maintained that the change was an internal affair of East Germany (*Frankfurter Allgemeine Zeitung* [*FAZ*], 2 July). This move, intended to undermine the Four Power status of the city further, had been preceded by the gradual remilitarization of East Berlin and by the establishment of a new city district (Berlin-Marzahn) located outside the original Soviet sector boundaries (ibid., 2 April).

Changes in the GDR penal code were approved on 28 June. They substantially increase jail terms for antigovernment demonstrations and membership in underground organizations, legalize internal exile for persons who have completed prison sentences, and provide up to five-year terms for persons passing to the West published materials or manuscripts considered damaging to East German interests. The last regulation is designed to prevent works from being published outside the Bloc. Three-year jail terms are provided for those who distribute published materials belittling or disturbing the socialist way of life, a rule intended to hinder contacts with Western journalists. This represents a violation of the 8 November 1972 intra-German agreement concerning journalists, as well as the 1 August 1975 Final Act of the Conference on Security and Cooperation in Europe. Also new is the threat of twelve years imprisonment for any citizen who gives even unclassified information to a foreign power or its representatives, any secret service, or foreign organization. Theoretically the law could even cover criticism expressed by East Germans in letters to relatives living in the West. (*ND*, 29 June; *WP*, 27 July; *NYT*, 29 July.) These changes and additions to the penal law seem to have at least two objectives: to reduce contacts of citizens with the West substantially and to provide a legal basis for state action in case of civil unrest or outspoken criticism following expected price increases. The GDR penal laws also apply to crimes committed on ships or airplanes outside the country, as well as to criminal activities perpetrated by citizens abroad (*FAZ*, 2 July).

The year witnessed the 25th anniversary of youth consecration (*Jugendweihe*); 272,500 fourteen-year-old students solemnly dedicated their lives to "socialist society." Political indoctrination and pre-military training of youth received increased attention by Honecker in his address to the FDJ National Youth Festival in East Berlin (1–4 June), which was attended by "hundreds of thousands" (*Informationen*, no. 9, p. 9). He paid tribute to the 31,000 youth brigades for their efforts to increase GDR economic efficiency. The honorary title of "outstanding youth collective" was awarded to 200 units for strengthening and protecting the GDR (ADN, 1 June; *FBIS*, 2 June).

Millions of children and youngsters participated in the military-political and military-sport activities whose objective is to strengthen GDR defense capability. Organizers were the FDJ and the Society for Sport and Technology (*FAZ*, 22 February; *ND*, 3 May). The NVA also provided support. Heinz Hoffman, Politburo member and defense minister, was the overall patron (*Volksarmee*, East Berlin, no. 7). Hoffmann called upon the FDJ to intensify political indoctrination work within the NVA (*IWE-Tagesdienst*, Bonn, 25 April).

Compulsory military education for ninth and tenth graders, commenced in 1978, encountered continuing opposition from the churches. Protestant Bishop Hans Joachim Frankel warned that this policy entailed the danger that children at an early age can form a premature picture of friend and foe that may lead toward hatred (*WP*, 27 April).

Because West German television penetrates about 80 percent of the GDR, the latter wants to prevent children from being exposed to its "manipulation." Parents are requested to help by preventing them from watching this alien TV and by exposing them to GDR educational TV (*FAZ*, 5 July).

Perhaps the outstanding event of the year was the celebration of the GDR's 30th anniversary. Preparations began in 1978, and numerous "socialist competitions" were initiated and dedicated to carrying out socialist goals. The anniversary was highlighted by the presence of Leonid I. Brezhnev, secretary general of the CPSU, and other leaders from the Bloc. A broad amnesty freed 20,000 to 25,000 criminals sentenced before 7 October. A number of political prisoners also were released, not including those held in fulfillment of international agreements and obligations or sentenced for military espionage or Nazi war criminals and murderers (*Calgary Herald*, 11 October).

The churches continued to find themselves under great pressure despite their acceptance of "socialism." Protestant Bishop Albrecht Schönherr stated that since the end of World War II, the number of Christians in the GDR decresed from 16 to about 8 million. He claimed that this drop had been caused primarily by atheist propaganda (*FAZ*, 24 April). Representatives of eight Protestant church organizations met in January and proposed to establish a united Protestant church in the fall of 1981 because of financial constraints and government pressure (*WP*, 2 February; *FAZ*, 24 September).

The Catholic Church, with some 1.3 million followers, was also attempting to find a modus vivendi with the GDR regime. After a meeting on 13 February between the chairman of the Berlin Conference of Bishops, Alfred Cardinal Bengsch, and the state secretary for church affairs, Hans Siegewasser, a press release included the assurance "that the church wants to serve the cause of peace" (*Begegnung*, April).

Military Affairs. The GDR continued to increase its military capability, allegedly because of the aggressive intentions of the military-industrial complexes in the United States, the FRG, and the other "imperialist countries," by stressing political indoctrination and training, as well as by adding up-to-date Soviet weapons systems. Defense Minister Hoffman asserted that NATO's intention is to achieve military superiority and to use its armed forces increasingly as an instrument of imperialist power politics (*FAZ*, 3 February). In a lecture at the Karl Marx Higher Party School, he declared that the intensity of the international class struggle has increased, necessitating greater GDR defense (*ND*, 13 June).

The new head of the armed forces' main political administration, General Kessler, announced an ideological campaign and told party officials in the military that ideological persuasion work was becoming even more important for an understanding of the party's military policy (DPA, 16 May; *FBIS*, 17 May).

Despite economic and financial difficulties, defense expenditures for fiscal 1978 were increased by 4.5 percent, or 11.7 billion marks. Volunteer groups competed in the civil defense initiative "GDR 30" and reportedly demonstrated their ability to protect population, production, and essential institutions. The Institute for Civil Defense received college status the following month. (*ND*, 28 May, 25 and 29 June.)

Party influence over the military establishment has increased as a result of an amendment to the October 1978 national defense law that provides that the National Defense Council, headed by SED chief Honecker, will take "all necessary measures for defense of the country and for protection of the socialist order," even if these measures conflict with other existing laws and regulations (DPA, 9 January; *FBIS*, 10 January). Changes among key military personnel also increased Honecker's influence. For example, his close confidant, Lt. Gen. Fritz Streletz, became armed forces chief-of-staff. Almost all officers, about 70 percent of NCOs, and about half the enlisted men are active SED members, which helps to assure party control over the military (*Die Zeit*, 15 June).

Dissent and Repressive Measures. Opposition to GDR cultural policy surfaced when eight authors signed a letter of concern to Honecker, protesting the criminal proceedings against well-known East Berlin writer Stefan Heym, a former American citizen, and objecting to the increasing defamation of dissident authors. Moreover, other GDR writers sent individual letters to East German leaders criticizing cultural policies (DPA, 22 May; *FBIS*, 23 May).

This expressed dissatisfaction followed the crackdown on political dissidence in April. As a way of silencing writers, the GDR government tied copyright laws to foreign-exchange regulations so that any author who publishes without permission in the West commits a serious offense and can spend up to ten years in jail (*Calgary Herald*, 28 April). Two of the regime's leading critics were prosecuted on this basis. In May Stefan Heym, who had returned to East Germany, was fined $4,500. The previous month, he had been refused permission to give lectures in West Germany. Philosophy Professor Robert Havemann, whose 30-month house arrest was unexpectedly terminated on 9 May and just as suddenly reinstated on 15 October, was fined over $5,000 (*FAZ*, 10 May and 15 October). The Presidium of the Writers' Association took the next step to silence critical writers and expelled Stefan Heym and eight others, thus virtually depriving them of any opportunity to publish or earn a living. They were accused of "having fought from abroad in a slanderous manner against our socialist state, the German Democratic Republic, against our socialist jurisdiction and against the policy pursued by our party and our government" (*NYT*, 9 June). Professor Havemann was not silenced. In an open letter to the authorities, he called for freedom of speech, the release of political prisoners, and the abolition of the laws proscribing "antistate agitation" (*CSM*, 22 June). The new penal laws point to an even more vigorous suppression of dissident activity.

Two amendments to the 1973 regulations concerning foreign correspondents that greatly restrict activities of Western newsmen were issued on 11 April. Formerly they had to inform the authorities only on leaving East Berlin. One of the new regulations requires that the Foreign Affairs Ministry be given notice providing exact information on destination and purpose not less than 24 hours before beginning any journey. A second change requires that permission for interviews involving any social institution (formerly only government authorities) must be obtained (*Die Zeit*, 20 April). At least three West German journalists were expelled for alleged violations of these new regulations (DPA, 14 May; *FBIS*, 15 May).

During the year, the GDR continued to guard against potential escapees. West German Interior Minister Gerhard Baum revealed that an estimated 1 million land mines, some 34,800 automatic firing devices of the SM-70 type, almost 1,000 bunkers, about 675 watchtowers, and nearly 1,000 watchdogs are located along the border (*Los Angeles Times*, 22 March). Nevertheless, in the first half of the year, a total of 1,568 persons managed to escape (*Calgary Herald*, 16 August). The dramatic voyage by two families in a homemade hot air balloon precipitated strict controls along the twelve- to eighteen-mile border strip and closure of several small airfields (*FAZ*, 21 September).

Erich Mielke, the GDR's state security minister and a Politburo member, called for more work by his ministry. "During a period of increasing subversive attacks by the opponent, it is necessary to intensify the struggle against imperialist intelligence services, centers of ideological sabotage, and other hostile organizations, institutions, and forces." Mielke paid tribute to the "selfless work of [espionage] agents on the invisible front." (*ND*, 18 February.)

The official press reported that the population is contributing to public order and security. Its support was demonstrated by the claim that 135,000 citizen-volunteers assist the German People's Police. "More than 80,000 collectives in industry and agriculture . . . have made it their target in the current socialist competition to win recognition as areas of 'exemplary order and security.' " (Ibid., 30 June–1 July.)

The Central Registry, an office in West Germany charged with compiling cases of East German human rights violations, reported 1,360 identified acts of violence and despotism during 1978. In 1,148 cases, prison sentences resulted for political reasons. Along the borders, 60 instances of the use of fire-arms and automatic firing devices or the explosion of mines were heard (*Informationen*, no. 1, p. 12).

There are at least 6,000 political prisoners in the GDR, about one-sixth of them women, the largest number being held for attempting to escape or for opposing the regime. They include about 400 West German and West Berlin citizens; most of them were jailed for assisting escapees (*Die Welt*, 2 June). The amnesty granted to "criminals" (see above) included some political prisoners. Niko Huebner, jailed for refusing military service on political grounds, and the dissident economist Rudolf Bahro were released and permitted to leave for the FRG (*FAZ*, 13 and 18 October). The practice of "selling" political prisoners for fees of U.S. $25,000 and more to West Germany continued. No total figures are available, although one group of 22 former political prisoners arrived in the FRG on 9 October (ibid., 13 October). In December it was announced that a total of 21,928 prisoners were re-leased and an additional 1,272 persons already sentenced to prison terms were freed. In contrast to the amnesty of 1972, when about 25,000 prisoners were released and about 2,100 were extradited to the West, this time only 3 or 4 were permitted to leave the GDR. (*FAZ*, 18 December.)

Economy. East German leaders used the severe winter of 1978–79 as an explanation for various bottlenecks in the country's economy. The report of the Central Administration for Statistics claimed great achievements in fulfillment of the economic plan, though the targeted 5.2-percent increase in GNP was actually closer to 4 percent in 1978 (*Informationen*, no. 3, pp. 7–8). The greatest shortfalls were in foreign trade, and therefore only percentage figures were released. Export to the Bloc went up by 10.3 percent, to the developing countries by 32 percent, and to the Western industrialized states by only 6 percent (*ND*, 19 January). About half of GDR imports, especially of raw materials, come from the Soviet Union. The repeated price increases in these raw materials necessitated larger exports to the USSR and a greater indebtedness to Moscow, apart from the debt to the West. The GDR owed be-tween $3.5 and $5 billion to Western financial institutions (*WP*, 7 January). Another indication of the poor state of the economy was a 20-percent decrease from 1977 in government investments, a reduc-tion from 7.1 to 5.7 billion marks (*ND*, 29 June).

The economic plan for 1979 projected a 4.3-percent growth in GNP (ibid., 16–17 December 1978). The official statistical report on the economic situation for the first six months of 1979 indicated that even this projected increase was not being reached. Total exports were reportedly increasing by 7 percent (to the Soviet Union and socialist countries by 9 percent). No percentages were given for ex-ports to capitalist states. (*FAZ*, 16 July.)

The net income of the population also showed a lower percentage increase, 3 percent compared with 5.6 in 1977. During the first half of 1979, government subsidies for food, gas, and rents rose by 7.5 percent, i.e., by more than $5 billion a year. Housing construction required an additional 12.3 percent in investments (ibid., 19 July; *NYT*, 8 August). Higher prices for many industrial products are expected as of January 1980 (*FAZ*, 29 September).

Two main reasons for GDR economic stagnation are the manpower shortage and dependence on foreign sources of energy and raw materials. The former is responsible for the slow implementation of the 40-hour workweek and for the high percentage, 87.6 percent, of women in the labor force (ibid., 2 January and 2 October). Low old-age income (about 300 marks per month) induced 0.6 of the 3.1 million pensioners to continue working (*Informationen*, no. 9, p. 12).

The GDR's imports have been costly. In 1978, for example, the country imported 11.9 million tons of oil, 2 million tons of iron ore, some 70,000 tons of asbestos, over 25,000 tons of titanium oxide, and 85,000 tons of cotton. These represent the total needs of the East German economy for those materials (*WP*, 7 January). About 80 percent of petroleum requirements are supplied by the Soviet Union. The remaining oil must be obtained from OPEC sources and paid for with hard currency (*NYT*, 16 April). Lignite coal, which normally accounts for two-thirds of all energy requirements, was difficult to strip-mine because of the severe winter, which necessitated importing about 120,000 tons of coal from West Germany (ibid.). With coalfields being depleted and prices for imported oil, gas, and hard coal steadily increasing, the GDR considers nuclear energy the only alternative. At present, only 10 percent of all electricity is produced in nuclear power plants (*FAZ*, 15 September), but by the year 2000 this is expected to rise to 50 percent (*NYT*, 16 April).

On 5 October the GDR and the Soviet Union signed a "program of specialization and cooperation of production" to extend until 1990. Moscow guarantees delivery of raw materials, oil, gas, and equipment for nuclear power plants in exchange for ships, machine tools, and equipment for the chemical, textile, and photocopying industries (*Calgary Herald*, 6 October).

Over $250 million in hard currency, badly needed by the regime, is earned from about 150 "intershops," where prices are quoted in West German marks. Since 1974, GDR citizens had been allowed to hold foreign currencies, which they could obtain as gifts from friends and relatives in the West. The West German mark gradually became a second currency for a new privileged class. In the service industry sector, it was virtually the first currency. On 15 April the GDR introduced a voucher system; gifts of money from the West must be deposited with state banks in exchange for coupons to make purchases at intershops. Restriction on the circulation of foreign currency is primarily designed to combat widespread black market activities. It also enables the government to ascertain who receives money from abroad. The vouchers, made out in the name of the holder, are not transferable and cannot be converted into foreign currency. (*Frankfurter Rundschau*, 6 April; *U.S. News and World Report*, 20 August.)

Foreign Affairs. *Relations with the Federal Republic of Germany.* Although officials have underscored East German willingness to normalize relations with the FRG, they remain stagnant and cool. At the beginning of October, party chief Honecker offered to negotiate a number of issues, including the situation in West Berlin and a reduction in travel fees to that city. He also expressed the view that the two German states could cooperate on disarmament. Honecker's "olive branch" and Brezhnev's warning to all European NATO allies against installing newer missiles on their territory came at the same time. (*Calgary Herald*, 17 October.) One of the major causes for cool relations was the apparent increase in GDR military, industrial, and political intelligence operations in West Germany (*Die Zeit*, 23 February). A former member of the GDR State Security Ministry asserted that in 1977 alone, industrial espionage saved about $160 million in research and development costs (*FAZ*, 23 May). A large number of East German agents, some in sensitive positions, were arrested during the year.

The restrictions placed on West German journalists were another reason for strained relations. Harassment of travelers along transit roads and the GDR's refusal to react to official complaints further aggravated the situation. At least 214 West Germans were in prison for alleged violation of the intra-German transit agreement (ibid., 8 March).

Bonn also accused East Berlin of serious human rights violations and referred specifically to suppression of free speech and assembly. At the same time, the West German government made it possible for about 26,000 persons to leave the GDR under the "family reunion program." In addition, the release of about 13,000 prisoners was purchased (ibid., 22 September).

On the other hand, East Berlin resents the FRG's refusal to recognize GDR citizenship (*Bulletin*, 11 May, p. 117), election of representatives from West Berlin to the European parliament (*ND*, 6 April), and alleged interference in East German internal affairs, e.g., West German criticism of the new penal code (*FAZ*, 4 August).

The GDR continued to receive substantial financial benefits from the West German government and private citizens in the form of transit and visa charges (about $280 million per year), contributions toward construction of an expressway between Hamburg and Berlin ($660 million), mandatory exchange of currency by visitors, and various services rendered to the GDR (*U.S. News and World Report*, 20 August). At the end of 1978, the estimated income from the FRG and West Berlin governments, the federal postal service, federal railroad, and private individuals totaled $3.2 billion (*FAZ*, 1 December 1978). At the end of October, the FRG and GDR signed an agreement that will enable West German citizens to drive their cars into and through East Germany after 1 January 1980 without paying tolls. In return, the FRG will pay the GDR some $28 million (50 million marks) a year over the next ten years (*Süddeutsche Zeitung*, 31 October).

Intra-German trade for the first six months of 1979 showed, for the first time since 1965, more exports to the FGR than imports. West German exports decreased by 7.2 percent, while imports from the GDR increased by 4.8 percent, resulting in a slight reduction in East Berlin's debt to $1.98 billion, or about 3.6 billion DM (*FAZ*, 24 August).

Relations with the Soviet Bloc. A Politburo report to the SED Central Committee (13–14 December 1978) summarized East Germany's policy toward the Soviet bloc: "The SED of Germany unswervingly adheres to its course of firm integration into the community of socialist states, and it will always make its contribution to the cohesion, political effectiveness, and defense capability of our historic alliance" (*Bulletin*, 8 January, p. 5).

Implementation of the policy of specialization, international division of labor, and cooperation with other socialist countries (especially the USSR) made further progress during the year. The 24th session of the Intra-governmental Commission for Economic and Scientific-Technological Cooperation convened at Moscow during 19 to 21 March and produced new agreements, covering the period until 1990 (ibid., 11 May, p. 120). The GDR will specialize in manufacturing small- and medium-size electrical motors, leaving production of larger ones to the Soviet Union (*FAZ*, 24 March). On 16 August Honecker received a group of Soviet scientists whose purpose was to further scientific-technological cooperation (*Bulletin*, 29 August, p. 185).

The 1980 annual protocol on establishing industrial enterprises in the GDR and on delivery of equipment from the Soviet Union was signed on 19 April in East Berlin (ibid., 23 May, p. 127). Cooperation also includes agriculture. At the beginning of 1979, there were 25 comprehensive projects jointly managed by the GDR Academy of Agricultural Science and the USSR All-Union Academy of Agricultural Science (*ND*, 11 January).

The SED regime continued to give full support to Soviet foreign policies. Close liaison was maintained between the political leaders of both countries. Honecker, while vacationing in the USSR during July, met with Brezhnev in the Crimea (*Informationen*, no. 11, p. 9). The latter's participation in the 30th anniversary celebration at East Berlin was intended as a demonstration of the close relations between the countries (*FAZ*, 10 October). On that occasion, Honecker presented Brezhnev with the

Karl Marx Order and awarded him the title "Hero of the German Democratic Republic" (ADN, 4 October; *FBIS*, 5 October).

On his 75th birthday, Prime Minister Aleksei Kosygin also received the Karl Marx Order (*Informationen*, no. 5, p. 2); while on his 65th birthday, his counterpart in the GDR, Willi Stoph, was made a "Hero of Labor" and received the Order of the October Revolution from the Supreme Soviet (ibid., no. 11, p. 6). Kurt Hagen, a SED Politburo member, was honored with the Karl Marx Gold Medal by the USSR Academy of Science for contributions to social science, especially his struggle against ideological enemies of communism (*FAZ*, 7 May).

The annual GDR-USSR trade exchange protocol was signed in Moscow on 28 December 1978 (*Bulletin*, 22 January, p. 18). The estimated commercial turnover for 1979 was expected to be $17 billion (*NYT*, 7 October).

Contacts were maintained by SED leaders with their colleagues in other bloc countries of Eastern Europe, Cuba, and Vietnam. Party leaders and delegations visited each of the "fraternal" states, and East Berlin played host to numerous government and party officials from those countries. Special agreements were signed with Cuba (ADN, 5 April; *FBIS*, 6 April) and Vietnam (*Informationen*, no. 1, p. 3, and no. 11, p. 9).

The GDR, as a member of CMEA, participated in the 88th (January) and 89th (March) sessions of the CMEA Executive Committee. Both meetings dealt with international specialization and cooperation in production (*Bulletin*, 21 February, p. 48, and 4 May, p. 110). Foreign Minister Oskar Fischer participated in a conference in Budapest during mid-May on the foreign affairs of Warsaw Pact states (ibid., 1 June, pp. 129–31). A social science conference devoted to "Thirty Years of the GDR: A Victory of Marxism-Leninism" was held in East Germany and attended by representatives from other socialist countries (ADN, 21 June; *FBIS*, 28 June). East Berlin hosted (3–5 July) a "consultation of secretaries of the central committees from communist and workers' parties" in charge of international and ideological problems from eleven socialist countries (*Informationen*, no. 11, p. 5).

Relations with Industrialized Capitalist Countries. East Berlin continued to improve its political and economic relations with these states. The official publication of the Foreign Affairs Ministry reported that "since Helsinki, the GDR had signed some 90 agreements and arrangements with Western participants in the European Security Conference" (*Bulletin*, 8 January, p. 6). Among the most important were consular agreements with Austria (*Informationen*, no. 6, p. 2) and the United States (*FAZ*, 15 September). Cultural agreements were signed in January with Denmark (*Informationen*, no. 2, p. 5) and in the fall with Belgium (*FAZ*, 15 September).

Foreign Minister Fischer visited his French counterpart in Paris (*Informationen*, no. 6, p. 5) and received in East Berlin the foreign ministers of Norway (March), Ireland (May), France (July), the Netherlands, and Belgium (both in September). Negotiations for trade, preferably barter, arrangements were conducted with France, Italy, Canada, and the United States (ibid., no. 7, p. 10, and no. 9, p. 4). The GDR hosted a group of American senators (*Bulletin*, 16 April, p. 56) and parliamentarians from Denmark, France, the Netherlands, and Portugal (*Informationen*, no. 7, p. 10).

These diplomatic successes did not modify the GDR's propaganda efforts against NATO countries, especially the United States and West Germany. The report of the Politburo to the ninth Central Committee plenum (13–14 December 1978) asserted that "influential circles in the imperialist states, notably in the USA and the FRG, are increasing their activities designed to revert to 'cold war' policies." The report also accused NATO powers of attempting to shift "the current approximate military equilibrium" to their favor in order to use "military force as a political instrument of threat and blackmail." (*Bulletin*, 8 January, p. 5.) General Kessler claimed that the real purpose of NATO, "an alliance against peace and progress," was to implement the political and economic interests of the monopolies (*ND*, 14–15 April). Honecker, in an address to units of the air force, also used the alleged NATO arms race as reason for achieving a high degree of combat readiness by the East German military. The armed forces "must meet the requirements of the class struggle of our time . . . and of a possible war forced upon us" (*FAZ*, 31 August).

Relations with Africa, Asia, and Latin America. The Politburo report to the tenth Central Committee plenum, delivered by Werner Jarowinsky, referred to the tasks set by the Ninth SED Congress regarding assistance to "liberated countries" and those struggling for liberation and economic independence. The visit of a GDR party-state delegation led by Honecker to India (8–12 January), Libya (15–17 January), Angola (17–20 February), Zambia (20–22 February), Mozambique (22–24 February), South Yemen, and Ethiopia (in November), as well as meetings Honecker had with leaders of the Southwest African People's Organization (Sam Nujoma), the Patriotic Front (Joshua Nkomo) and the African National Congress (Oliver Tambo) during his stay in Luanda, demonstrated the extent of East German support. A military delegation, headed by Defense Minister Hoffmann, visited Zambia, Mozambique, and Ethiopia in May and pursued the same objectives. Hoffmann declared his support for increased political, economic, and military aid "to sovereign states in crisis areas that are threatened by imperialist powers or their surrogates" (*Informationen*, no. 4, p. 5).

There were numerous other consultations by East German officials with representatives from developing countries. Foreign Minister Fischer declared: "The GDR views development of relations with nationally liberated countries as its international duty" (*Bulletin*, 22 January, p. 24). East Berlin maintains relations, under intergovernmental agreements, with 52 developing countries; they cover trade, economy, science, and technology. More than 900 specialists worked in the developing countries (ibid., 24 September, pp. 215-16). This figure probably includes FDJ "friendship brigades" in eight different countries, including Mozambique, Angola, Guinea-Bissau, and Mali (ibid., 5 September, p. 200).

The GDR also provided technical training for developing countries. Since 1961 over one thousand specialists from Africa, Latin America, and the Palestine Liberation Organization were graduated from agricultural colleges (*ND*, 28 February). Approximately 250 experts from 54 African, Asian, and Latin American countries have so far been trained at the Institute of Tropical Agriculture of Karl Marx University at Leipzig (*Bulletin*, 15 October, p.240). This activity includes courses for journalists, such as the one for 30 citizens of the Congo (ibid., 4 October, p. 220). By now almost 450 reporters from 38 Asian and African countries have attended the College of Solidarity in East Berlin. About 900 others took part in courses organized by the GDR Journalists' Union in twelve Asian and African countries (ibid., 12 February, pp. 19 and 40). Much of the coordinating work was performed by solidarity committees, friendship societies, and intergovernmental commissions (which become more numerous every year). Deputy Foreign Minister Willerding confirmed that the African fighting liberation movements have been supported by the solidarity committees in many ways (ibid., 15 October, p. 238).

Friendship treaties with Angola (19 February) and Mozambique (24 February) closely tied these countries to the GDR, which continues to provide them with military aid (ibid., 1 March, pp. 51–52, and 12 March, pp. 65–67). Diplomatic contacts with the revolutionary regime of Nicaragua were established at the earliest possible moment (*FAZ*, 3 August). Relations with Zaïre, which had been broken off in May 1977, were re-established on 20 January (*Informationen*, no. 2, p. 5). Military support provided to a number of developing countries came mostly in the form of GDR instructors. In the cases of Mozambique, Angola, and Ethiopia, they numbered in the hundreds. About 2,500 "advisers" were reportedly stationed in Angola (*FAZ*, 5 September). The liberation fighters from South Africa are about the only group that still receives military training in East Germany. Guerrillas from other African countries are trained by the GDR in the so-called front-line states. The regime's preferred area of "assistance" is the organization of internal security forces, such as the secret police. East German experts also assist in the fields of communication, news media, prisons, and penal camps (ibid., 14 August).

Middle East. In this region, the East German regime utilized mixed committees for economic, technological, and cultural cooperation to increase trade and to strengthen political relations. The common denominator remained the anti-Israeli and anti-American policies of the "rejectionist" Middle East states and the GDR. Honecker met with Yassir Arafat, and they agreed that the Israeli-Egyptian treaty represented a serious obstacle to the establishment of a just peace. According to East Berlin, this treaty is a "conspiracy against the Arab peoples and world peace" (ADN, 29 March; *FBIS*, 4 April). This, however, did not prevent the GDR from continuing to trade with Egypt, based on the protocol concerning the exchange of goods concluded in January (*Informationen*, no. 1, p. 13).

Yugoslavia, China, and Albania. Andrei Marinc, deputy chairman of the Federal Executive Council and chairman of the Social Planning Commission in Yugoslavia, visited East Berlin during March in order to negotiate an agreement on long-range economic and scientific-technological cooperation (ibid., no. 6, pp. 5–6).

On 20 January an agreement on exchange of goods for 1979 was concluded in Beijing by the GDR (ibid., no. 2, p. 5). However, China's "punitive action" against Vietnam, which began on 17 February, was strongly condemned by East Berlin. Beijing was accused of cruel aggression against the "fraternal country of Vietnam" and of having concluded an "unholy alliance" with the United States. The rapprochement with the United States and termination of the 30-year treaty with the Soviet Union were two sides of the same coin (*Bulletin*, 11 May, p. 116). Beijing was also accused of having engineered Kampuchea's (Cambodia's) raids into Vietnam and of misusing Vietnamese citizens of Chinese origin as a fifth column to cause tension inside that country (ibid., 8 January, p. 7).

The GDR also signed a protocol on exchange of goods with Albania (*FAZ*, 2 October). An important indication of improvement in these relations was the official visit of high SED official Paul Verner, and not a government representative, to the Albanian embassy for the purpose of expressing his party's sympathy on the death of a high-ranking Albanian party official. This was the first contact on the party level since 1961 (ibid., 1 October).

Collaboration with International Organizations. During the year, the GDR continued to exploit all opportunities for participation in activities of the United Nations and its specialized agencies. Since its admission, East Germany has signed 75 conventions and submitted over one hundred resolutions to the General Assembly. The GDR belongs to sixteen U.N. organs, and an East German international lawyer is a member of the Human Rights Commission (ibid., 21 September).

East Berlin played host to a number of U.N. officials. The official visit by Secretary General Kurt Waldheim was utilized by the SED regime to support its interpretation of that city's status. Waldheim attended a military ceremony in "demilitarized" East Berlin, apparently without any comment. Also, he was photographed with Maj. Gen. Karl Heinz Drews, "city commandant of the capital of the GDR, Berlin." The three Western allies had repeatedly protested this type of violation of the Four Power Agreement concerning all sectors of Greater Berlin (ibid., 7 April).

The report on talks Waldheim held with GDR Foreign Minister Fischer indicates that the U.N. secretary general had accepted the communist interpretation of the Four Power Agreement. Emphasizing the development of détente in Europe after the Helsinki conference, the report stated: "In this context, an important role was to be attributed to the set of European treaties and to the Quadripartite Agreement on West Berlin, the central provision of which is that West Berlin continues not to be a constituent part of the FRG and not to be governed by it" (*Bulletin*, 16 April, p. 90). Waldheim also paid tribute to East Germany's active and constructive cooperation with the United Nations (ibid.).

East Germany will become one of the nonpermanent members of the U.N. Security Council during 1980 and 1981 (*FAZ*, 21 September).

International Party Contacts. As in previous years, the SED maintained contacts with most communist movements throughout the world. Delegations led by Politburo members participated in several congresses of fraternal parties, including those of Italy, Belgium, Portugal, and France. Party officials received numerous delegations and high functionaries of communist or workers' parties from Chile, Italy, Guatemala, Brazil, Vietnam, Belgium, the FRG, West Berlin, Israel, Greece, Great Britain, and Finland. Representatives of mass organizations, such as the FDJ and FDGB, actively participated in nurturing contacts abroad by visiting corresponding organizations. A delegation of the FDJ visited the Socialist Student League in the FRG; in May another one attended the Sixth Congress of the West German communist youth organization, the Socialist German Workers' Youth (*Junge Welt*, 27–28 January: *Informationen*, no. 8, p. 3).

The meeting of the World Peace Council in East Berlin during early February, attended by representatives from almost one hundred countries, also provided opportunities for contacts with fraternal parties and "mass organizations" loyal to Moscow. In addition to top-level party contacts, the Politburo encouraged district party organizations to intensify existing contacts with communist parties in East and West (*Informationen*, no. 5, p. 6).

Publications. The GDR attempted during 1979 to strengthen party control not only over individual authors, but also over the already highly centralized state-owned publishing enterprises (*FAZ*, 2 July). Book production in East Germany is high; almost 6,000 titles (about 140 million copies) were published during 1978. Between 1949 and 1978, more than 150,000 titles (2.9 billion copies) were published. The largest number consisted of works by Karl Marx, Friedrich Engels, and V. I. Lenin (*Informationen*, no. 7, p. 17). (For information concerning the central SED organ, *Neues Deutschland*, and other newspapers and periodicals, see *YICA*, 1977, pp. 43–44, and 1979, pp. 40–41.)

University of Calgary   Eric Waldman

Hungary

Hungarian communists formed a party in November 1918 and were the dominant force in the Hungarian Soviet Republic that lasted from March to August 1919. Thereafter the party functioned as a minute and faction-ridden movement in domestic illegality and in exile. With the Soviet occupation at the end of World War II, the Hungarian Communist Party emerged as a partner in the coalition government, exercised an influence disproportionate to its modest electoral support, and gained effective control of the country in 1947. In 1948 it absorbed left-wing social democrats into the newly named Hungarian Workers' Party. On 1 November 1956 during the popular revolt that momentarily restored a multiparty government, the name was changed to Hungarian Socialist Workers' Party (Magyar Szocialista Munkáspárt; HSWP).

The HSWP rules unchallenged as the sole political party, firmly aligned with the Soviet Union. Its exclusive status is confirmed in the revised state constitution of 1972: "The Marxist-Leninist party of the working class is the leading force in society." Current party membership is 797,000 out of a population of 10.7 million. At the time of the HSWP's Eleventh Congress (March 1975), physical workers constituted 45.5 percent of the membership; "immediate supervisors of production," 6.1 percent; intellectual workers, 40.0 percent; and dependents and others, 8.4 percent. In the 1971–1975 parliament, 71 percent of deputies were party members. About 47 percent of municipal and local council members belong to the HSWP as do about 90 percent of officers in the police forces.

Leadership and Organization. Ultimate political power in the HSWP and therefore in Hungary remains in the hands of the first secretary, János Kádár. The 67-year-old Kádár has been party leader since November 1956. He holds no state office. Current Politburo members are Kádár, György Aczél, Antal Apró, Valéria Benke, Béla Biszku, Jenö Fock, Sándor Gáspár, István Huszár, György Lázár, Pál Losonczi, László Maróthy, Dezsö Nemes, Károly Németh, Miklós Óvári, and István Sarlós. In addition to Kádár, the Central Committee Secretariat includes Sándor Borbély, András Gyenes, Imre Györi, Ferenc Havasi, Mihály Korom, Németh, and Óvári. János Brutyó is chairman of the Central Control Committee, Óvári of the Agitprop Committee, Havasi of the Economic Policy Committee, and Arpád Pullai of the Youth Committee. Minister of Agriculture Pál Romány is chairman of the Central Committee's Cooperative Policy Team, Óvári of the Cultural Policy Team, Németh of the Economic Team, and Béla Biszku of the Party Building Team (see *YICA*, 1978, p. 37, for a discussion of party committees). Németh, Kádár's de facto deputy, has special responsibility for the party apparat; Havasi and Borbély are both responsible for economic policy; and Korom is charged with party and organization as well as defense and security matters. Sándor Jakab, who had served as head of the Central Committee's Party and Mass Organizations Department, was replaced in March by his deputy, Tibor Baranyai, and shifted to the National Council of Trade Unions (NCTU).

Losonczi is chairman of the Presidential Council and therefore nominal head of state. Lázár is prime minister, and Aczél and Huszár are among the five deputy premiers. Apró is chairman of the National Assembly. Gáspár is secretary general of the NCTU, Maróthy of the Communist Youth League, and Sarlós of the Patriotic People's Front. Recent changes in state posts include the appointment of Péter Veress, former ambassador to France, as minister of foreign trade, replacing József Biró; and the replacement of József Bálint as director of the National Statistical Office by his deputy, Mrs. Ferenc Nyitrai. Both new appointees possess sound professional qualifications.

Auxiliary and Mass Organizations. On 30 March the NCTU elected Sándor Jakab second deputy secretary general; the other is László Gál. Jakab has no trade union experience. He has worked his way up through the party apparatus and from 1966 to 1968 served as first deputy minister of the interior. The NCTU also endorsed the economic tasks set by the HSWP's Central Committee on 19 March, including the painful process of improving enterprise efficiency by cutting and reallocating manpower.

Apart from its domestic mobilizing tasks, the NCTU serves external functions. Its secretary general, Sándor Gáspár, was elected president of the World Federation of Trade Unions (WFTU) at the Prague congress in April 1978. In March Gáspár led a delegation to Moscow and signed an agreement on trade union cooperation with his Soviet counterpart; in April he attended the meetings of the WFTU Bureau and General Council in Sofia; and in September he led an NCTU delegation to Romania and was received by Ceauşescu.

Over 500 delegates attended the national conference of the Communist Youth League, 19–20 May. Secretary General Maróthy reviewed the "creative youth" competition program, noted that nearly half of working league members participate in the socialist brigade movement, and praised student contributions to the economy through summer work camps. The league has 840,000 members.

The seventh national conference of Pioneer Leaders was held in Kecskemét, 9–11 April. The Pioneer movement (including the Drummer Boy organization for younger children) has almost 1.1 million members in the eight to fourteen age group. Its functions are the organization of political education, volunteer social work, and normal cultural and sports activities. Surveys show that members regard the movement's self-government and political programs (including staged demonstrations to protest imperialist outrages) as its most boring activities (*Magyar Nemzet*, 8 April). The conference resolved that the movement's activities should be better attuned to children's natural sense of playfulness.

Party Internal Affairs. The party's activity throughout the year was increasingly concentrated on preparations for the Twelfth Congress, which is scheduled for March 1980. It is anticipated that the congress will serve to confirm the current policy of full implementation of the original New Economic Mechanism as a remedy for Hungary's economic troubles.

Kádár, in a speech to a mass meeting of party officials and activists at Csepel on 25 September that was broadcast over radio and television, reiterated his policy of a "two-front battle" against revisionism and dogmatism. Explaining and defending the ongoing price reform and austerity measures, he stressed the need for a more rational distribution of manpower, for work discipline, and for the linking of pay to productivity.

In a report to the March Central Committee meeting, Németh, who is responsible for party matters, called for a commitment to party democracy and personal responsibliity. He denounced the "incorrect view" that difficult economic circumstances make party democracy (i.e., the free expression of opinion) untimely. Party work needs to be more efficient, he said, so as to eliminate superfluous conferences and resolutions and to allow more party activity to be conducted outside normal working hours. He reported that the Politburo had decided not to increase the size of the full-time party apparat. Noting that 30,000 new members had been admitted to the party in 1978, Németh deplored the decrease in the number of workers admitted. He also lamented the abuse of power or, at the other extreme, the inactivity of some party members (*Pártélet*, May.) Later in the year, the party publicized an exemplary disciplinary action by the Central Control Committee, which had expelled the deputy director of the National Association of Cooperatives for gross corruption and recommended that criminal charges be brought against him (ibid., September).

Domestic Affairs. *Culture, Ideology, and Society.* The regime's perennial quest for popular legitimacy was manifested in a conference at Eger, 19–20 October 1978, sponsored by the Ministry of Defense and the Writers' Association. The theme was the historic role of the working class and the "workers' movement" in fostering patriotism as distinct from nationalism, the stress being on the identification of "progressive national traditions." The related phenomena of patriotism and nationalism are politically more sensitive when they concern the fate of Hungarian minorities in neighboring countries. Hungary's greatest writer, Gyula Illyés, continues to test the regime's tolerance in his campaign on behalf of the cultural rights of Hungarians in Romania and Slovakia. An anthology of his writings on the subject has been printed, but the book has not been released (*NYT*, 26 August).

The state's direction of culture and science remains in force but is subject to strains. The status of the Hungarian Academy of Sciences has been altered by decree to give it greater responsibility for directing research in pursuit of national tasks identified by the government (*Magyar Közlöny*, 14 April). The Young Writers' Circle, founded in 1973, was criticized in *Kritika* (April) for lacking in internal democracy, a reflection of the overall "rigid hegemony of centralized bureaucracy." The author regretted that cultural liberalism, which gave rise to such initiatives as the Young Writers' Circle, lost its momentum and failed to engender a genuine socialist democracy in which there would be no restrictions on free expression, so necessary to resolve basic contradictions. Official concern has been expressed over declining attendance at film and legitimate theaters, in the latter case despite the organized distribution of tickets at places of work. The elusive limits of cultural tolerance were suggested by media criticism of avant-garde plays by István Orkény and Gyula Hernádi.

The crackdown on Charter 77 dissidents in Czechoslovakia prompted several letters of sympathy and protest from Hungary in early November. Some 254 writers and scholars, including the journalist János Kenedi and the philosopher János Kis, participated in the protest, which affirmed that "your cause is also our cause." (For earlier manifestations of dissent, see *YICA*, 1978, pp. 48–49, and 1979, pp. 44–45.)

A reported survey among young communist leaders indicated widespread political ignorance of the functions of the Patriotic People's Front (the broad umbrella organization for political mobilization) and of such historical figures as Stalin, Khrushchev, and the Hungarian Stalinist leader Mátyás Rákosi (*Ifju Kommunista*, July). Another survey, conducted by the Central Committee's Institute of Social Sciences, found that perceptions of social stratification and status were influenced by the respondent's social background and education; perceptions of social injustice were most prevalent among semiskilled and unskilled workers (*Valóság*, no. 12, 1978).

A new penal code, the first major reform since 1961, came into force on 1 July. In part, the new code reflects a revision of the old view that crime would disappear with the creation of socialist man. Some offenses, such as libel and minor "economic crimes," are decriminalized, i.e., transferred to the civil code or other spheres of justice. The new code differentiates between grades of severity for each crime and favors fines over imprisonment.

The National Demographic Registration Center is establishing a new central, computerized data bank; each citizen is being assigned an identification number that will also appear on the mandatory identity cards.

The official party policy on religion is one of tolerance, although in its application severe constraints and discrimination remain. In December 1978 Pope John Paul II sent a message of encouragement to the Hungarian church and its flock. At the same time, he dispatched a Vatican diplomat to conduct negotiations with the regime; the outcome was the appointment of four new bishops in April. Moreover, the State Office of Church Affairs approved three-year extension courses for lay Catholics at the Budapest Theological Seminary; demand in the program's first year, 1978–79, exceeded the number of places. Other manifestations of religious tolerance are the greater freedom of Catholic bishops to travel abroad and the establishment of a nursing home for elderly Catholics and of a spiritual retreat center for laymen. The head of the State Office, Imre Miklós, also observed that the government had renounced its right to confirm the appointment of parish priests, but in reality the party closely monitors and influences such appointments. Cardinal Lékai was present on the occasion of the pope's visit to Poland in June, and in October he made an official visit to Moscow at the invitation of the Russian Orthodox church.

Economy. At the National Assembly's summer session, 14–15 June (the usual spring session was simply omitted), Finance Minister Lajos Faluvégi concluded that "the picture of economic management in 1978 was unsatisfactory." There were severe internal and external imbalances. Domestic consumption exceeded the 4-percent rise in national income, while consumer prices rose an average of 4.6 percent and real wages by 3.1 percent. Excessive raises were given in 250 enterprises; consequently no profit shares were paid. Some enterprises produced more than could be absorbed by the domestic and export markets, and inventories rose to record levels. Energy consumption increased by 8 percent, although the plan had called for a 6-percent rise. The balance of trade continued to deteriorate.

These dismal results were attributed to unfavorable changes in the terms of trade and to the inadequate response of the state and enterprise bureaucracies. Government officials admitted that enterprises had been treated too leniently and were sheltered from the impact of world market changes. Exceptions to the application of economic regulators had become widespread. Profitability and efficiency, the original objectives of the New Economic Mechanism, had to be vigorously pursued. A measure of the country's economic weakness is that industrial productivity is only 35 to 40 percent of that in the leading West European countries. Wage differentiation rather than egalitarianism will henceforth be the guiding principle. "Wage increases cannot be demanded without adequate performance," declared Labor Minister Ferenc Trethon (*Magyar Hirlap*, 22 December 1978). Not all social groups could be guaranteed an increase in the standard of living.

The emphasis on labor discipline and productivity was accompanied by a series of austerity measures. At the National Assembly's summer session it debated a draft bill on the management of state finances; one clause reserves to parliament the authority to levy new taxes. The government subsequently indicated that public expenditures for state offices and agencies would be drastically cut. Austerity was anticipated in the guidelines for the 1979 economic plan and state budget approved by the Central Committee on 6 December 1978. National income was slated to grow by 3 to 4 percent (lower than in the preceding two years); industrial production by 4 percent; agricultural production by 3.0 to 3.5 percent; real wages by 1 percent; and consumer prices by 4.7 to 4.9 pecent. Investment was to increase by only 1 percent, and no new major projects were to be launched.

The first round of austerity measures took effect in January. The general profit tax for enterprises was raised from 36 to 40 percent, and the contribution to the compulsory reserve fund was raised from 15 to 25 percent of after-tax profits. For most enterprises automatic wage increases unrelated to enterprise performance have been prohibited and are to be linked to an "efficiency index." Increases over 6 percent are subject to a progressive wage development tax, whose rate, however, was reduced. Reductions were planned in subsidies and tax exemptions, and export credits are to be allocated on the basis of the profitability of proposed exports and of the enterprise as a whole. Staff retrenchments are another aspect of the drive for efficiency. For instance, at the Györ Wagon and Machine Works, 246 employees were dismissed, and the enterprise's 1979 target was a 2 to 3 percent reduction in its 25,000-strong labor force. These staff cutbacks have created much confusion over the problem of reallocating dismissed workers. Since officially unemployment cannot exist in Hungary, there are no unemployment benefits to ease the burden of layoffs.

Initial price increases in January included gasoline (20 percent), rice (50 percent), tobacco (30 percent), beer (20 percent), and printed matter (40 percent). At the same time, the smaller pensions, as well as social allowances, were increased. In June the price of gasoline was raised another 25 percent. The regime took pains to prepare the public for the rapid increase in the cost of living. Warnings were issued in the National Assembly, at the eighteenth congress of economists in Szekszárd, 21–23 June, and in the Central Committee resolutions of 29 June, but there were no specific forecasts. The shock finally came on 21 July with the announcement of a comprehensive set of major price increases, most of them to become effective two days later. The price of foodstuffs rose by 20 percent, of fuels by 34 percent (including a 51-percent hike in electricity rates), of building materials by 12 to 40 percent, of cars by 20 percent, and of cultural services by 30 percent. To offset the impact of these measures partially, compensatory increases were granted to most of the working population (and to pensioners), the exceptions being the liberal professions, artisans, and private tradesmen and farmers. In another concession, the ceiling on building loans was raised.

The magnitude of the price increases caused widespread dismay, and in the industrial stronghold of Csepel overt protests, including the dressing of Lenin's statue in rags, occurred. Party and government leaders fanned out to still the unrest by explaining that austerity and reforms were necessary to maintain the standard of living in the difficult times head. They stressed the careful planning that had preceded the price increases, indicated that without the increases state subsidies would have risen to 75 billion forints out of a state budget of 400 billion, and announced that upward adjustments in producer prices were scheduled for 1980. Sándor Gáspár also defended the measures, admitting that they had provoked differences of opinion (*Népszava*, 9 August). By official estimates the price increases represent a 9-percent aggregate increase in the cost of living (*Népszabadság*, 24 July), but unofficial calculations suggest that for the average consumer the added burden may amount to twice that figure.

A key factor in Hungary's economic distress was the rapid deterioration in the balance of trade. In the ruble sector, trade in 1978 failed to meet either import or export targets, and the terms of trade deteriorated by some 2 percent. In the nonruble sector, imports rose by 23.2 percent rather than by the planned 3 percent, and exports by 8.9 percent instead of 10 to 12 percent, generating a U.S. $2.2 billion deficit, double that of 1977. This imbalance was due in part to an insufficiency of agricultural products for export and to excessive imports in the machine, chemical, and light industries (*Világgazdaság*, 3 March).

Hungary is a net importer of energy, and the Soviet Union is the principal supplier. The latter has been relatively responsive to Hungary's energy needs, but prices have risen steadily. In 1978 Hungary had a large trade deficit with the Soviet Union, which accounts for 30 to 32 percent of all Hungarian trade. Energy, raw materials, and semifinished products account for 70 to 75 percent of Hungary's imports from the Soviet Union. There have been substantial increases in Soviet deliveries of natural gas (over the Orenburg pipeline) and of electrical power. Hungary's annual oil consumption amounts to approximately 10 million tons; in 1978 the Soviet Union supplied 8.5 million tons, 1 million of which was in excess of the plan and paid for in hard currency. Hungary's exports to the Soviet Union consist of machinery and equipment, notably buses (35 percent); semifinished products, particularly alumina (20 percent); and foodstuffs and other consumer goods (45 percent).

Accounts are normally settled on a bilateral basis, but Hungarian economists continue to favor development of the transferable ruble to facilitate multilateral clearing within the Council for Mutual Economic Assistance (CMEA). Some 15 to 20 percent of Hungarian trade within CMEA is cleared in dollars, mostly for over-plan transactions; all trade with Yugoslavia is cleared in hard currency. Foreign credits of over $500 million were negotiated by the Hungarian National Bank in 1978, and Hungary's indebtedness in the West stands at some $2.5 billion. The emergency measures related above are beginning to take hold, for in the first half of 1979 the balance of trade deficit was significantly lower than in the corresponding period of 1978.

At the 89th CMEA Executive Committee session in Moscow in March, an agreement was signed by Hungary, Czechoslovakia, Poland, and the Soviet Union for the joint financing of a nuclear power plant at Khmelnitski in the Ukraine. The proposed plant is part of a major CMEA electric generation and distribution project; a 750-kilovolt line from the Ukraine to Hungary was completed in 1978. The new plant is scheduled to become operational in 1984, with the East European investors being repaid in electric power by 2003. The communiqué of the 33rd CMEA Council session in Moscow, 26–28 June, outlined a target program in transportation that includes a new rail-freight transfer facility on the Soviet-Hungarian border.

In the agricultural sector, at the end of 1978 there were 1,369 cooperatives and 125 state farms. Concentration through mergers and improvements in the quality of management have enhanced the agricultural cooperatives' capacity for independent activity. This in turn has led to tensions between the cooperatives and the many layers of administration over them. The government therefore enacted a reorganization of the control system, reducing its extent and complexity (*Magyar Közlöny*, 6 April). Small-scale farming, with the active involvement of some 1.5 million families, continues to receive official endorsement and promises of material support, particularly for suitably scaled equipment and transport. Household plots and other small-scale farms are the principal producers of milk, meat, and vegetables for domestic consumption.

Inefficiencies continue to bedevil the construction and building materials industries. In a report to the Central Committee on 12 October 1978, Borbély identified shortcomings in completion rates, the preparation of investment projects, and labor organization. He recommended improved planning and management from the ministry down, the expansion of industrial methods and mechanization, more efficient use of manpower, improvements in the living conditions of the over 600,000 construction workers, and incentives for quality. At the same meeting, Havasi presented a plan for 1.2 million new homes, of which 70 percent are to be privately funded and 30 percent publicly funded.

Private car ownership has grown rapidly in recent years to some 800,000, with a current waiting list of over 500,000. In addition to raising gasoline prices, the government has also raised the minimum down payment on new car orders from 20 to 50 percent of the purchase price. Another new rule, designed to cut down on speculative purchases, prescribes that cars up to three years old can be resold only through state agencies, at no more than the original purchase price. Most Hungarians are still paid and make purchases in cash rather than by checks or bank transfers. Planning is under way to modernize cash turnover for the public by extending transfer-deposit accounts and introducing checking accounts at the National Savings Bank.

Foreign Affairs. *Main Trends.* The Kádár regime continues to echo the main lines of Soviet foreign policy faithfully. In East-West relations this currently means promotion of détente and arms control, specifically SALT II. Communist China is regularly denounced for its anti-Soviet stand and its flirtation with the imperialists; a notable example was Kádár's September speech at Csepel. Hungarian media sharply condemned the Chinese incursion into Vietnam and alleged American complicity. On the other hand, the Vietnamese-sponsored Heng Samrin regime in Kampuchea (Cambodia) was promptly endorsed by the Hungarian government. The regime also criticized the Islamic revolution in Iran once it became apparent that the left-wing forces would derive no immediate benefit. The government sent greetings to Castro on the occasion of the nonaligned conference in Havana, while the media hailed the failure of China and the West to split the conference. The Warsaw Pact's Council of Foreign Ministers met in Budapest on 15 May and issued proposals for expanding détente and disarmament. The following day the pact began its "Shield 79" maneuvers in Hungary.

Relations with Capitalist Countries. On the occasion of Finance Minister Faluvégi's visit to the United States in February, an agreement was signed on the elimination of dual taxation in order to facilitate commercial relations and the operation of joint companies. Deputy Premier Huszár led a delegation to the United States in July to promote the expansion of trade under Hungary's recently acquired most-favored-nation tariff status. In 1978 Hungary's exports to the United States increased by 40 percent.

Helmut Schmidt's official visit to Budapest (4–6 September) was the first visit by a West German chancellor. He was returning Kádár's visit to Bonn in July 1977. Schmidt met with Kádár three times, as well as with Losonczi and Lázár. The two sides agreed to intensify high-level contacts and cultural relations and to facilitate economic cooperation. West Germany is Hungary's most important Western trading partner and will establish a trade office in Budapest.

The election of Pope John Paul II was promptly and accurately reported by Hungarian media, and a state delegation attended the investiture. Other notable visits included those of Losonczi to Austria and Foreign Minister Frigyes Puja to Thailand and Indonesia (May), of Portuguese President Antonio Eanes to Budapest (March), and of U.N. Secretary General Kurt Waldheim to Budapest (July).

The new passport regulations for Hungarians retain the limitation on the frequency of trips to nonsocialist countries—one trip every two years for sponsored visitors, every three years for tourists. Interior Minister András Benkei has indicated that in 1977 only 4 percent of applications were denied (*Népszabadság*, 29 October 1978). The new grounds for refusal are similar to the old: national security, intention to visit a hostile person or agency, and no guarantee of adequate funding for the stay abroad. The rules have been relaxed to allow older Hungarian emigrants to retain their new citizenship and return for visits. The shortage of hard currency is the official reason for the restrictions on the frequency of trips abroad.

Relations with the Third World. The intensification of Soviet bloc interest in the Third World in recent years, particularly Black Africa, has been reflected to a moderate extent in Hungary's relations with the area. Hungarian policy has been selective, however, focusing on socialist or pro-socialist African states (where the objective is to win political advantage over the West) and more generally on states that promise fruitful commercial relations.

"Interparty cooperation agreements" have been concluded with the ruling political groups in Angola, Congo, and Mozambique, giving rise to reciprocal party visits. Party contacts were also established in 1978 with Benin and Ethiopia; with Marxist parties in Guinea and Cape Verde, Madagascar, Tanzania, and Mali; and with the Zimbabwe revolutionary groups. The NCTU has fostered contacts with and given financial aid to a number of African trade unions.

By 1978 Hungary's commercial relations with 86 developing countries accounted for 9 percent of its foreign trade; 45 percent of this trade was with Asian, 31 percent with Latin American, and 24 percent with African countries. The developing countries are increasingly regarded as a promising market and source of commodities. African trade is mostly with Arab states. Black Africa's share of total Hungarian trade doubled from 0.4 percent in 1960 to a still modest 0.8 percent in 1977; much of it consists of aid and cooperation projects, apparently with little coordination by CMEA. The biggest partners are Angola, Nigeria, Guinea, Sudan, and Mozambique.

Technical and scientific cooperation is a prominent feature of Hungary's relations with Africa. In 1977–78 some 453 African students were attending Hungarian post-secondary institutions at Hungarian expense (giving rise incidentally to some domestic resentment). Development aid cannot be reliably estimated. The Soviet bloc's military aid to the area is better coordinated than are economic relations, and in 1978 Hungary played its part by concluding a military agreement with Mozambique covering military assistance and training at Hungarian military academies.

Prime Minister Lázár visited Kuwait in March and signed an airline agreement, as well as agreements on cultural affairs and on exchange of health care information. Hungary's large trade surplus with Kuwait may lead to eventual oil deliveries through the Adria pipeline. Defense Minister Lajos Czinege visited Syria, the People's Democratic Republic of Yemen, and Ethiopia in March. Deputy Premier Gyula Szekér visited Nigeria in April. István Sarlós visited the Palestine Liberation Organization's Executive Committee from 30 January to 2 February and met with Yassir Arafat; the joint communiqué denounced Israeli occupation and resettlement policies and asserted the rights of the Palestinian people.

International Party Contacts. Kádár visited Brezhnev, 5–6 March. Although bilateral economic relations and prospects were discussed, the joint communiqué highlighted international issues, including condemnation of China and reiteration of the Warsaw Pact's proposals for the expansion of détente. Kádár was followed by Lázár, who held talks with Soviet Premier Kosygin. Brezhnev paid a visit to Hungary from 30 May to 1 June. His previous visits were in November 1972 and in March 1975, on the occasion of the HSWP congress. He praised the progress of socialism in Hungary and the healthy state of Hungarian-Soviet cooperation, acknowledging in passing the need to consider the unique features of the two countries. Both he and Kádár referred to difficult economic problems. The final communiqué anticipated more joint economic planning, production cooperation and specialization, joint scientific activities, and an improvement in CMEA's activities. Kádár made an official visit to Bulgaria, 18–20 June, and held talks with Todor Zhivkov, mainly on economic matters.

The latest in a series of ideological conferences under the auspices of the Prague-based *Problems of Peace and Socialism* was held at Tihany, Hungary, 25–27 April. Thirty-nine communist and workers' parties were represented; the Hungarian participants included János Berecz, head of the Central Committee's Foreign Affairs Department, and Sándor Lakos, director of the Central Committee's Institute of Social Sciences. The main topic was "revolution and democracy." Berecz reported that the relatively low-level conference did not produce agreement on the question of pluralism; the HSWP's view was that the working class should gain power with or without pluralism, but this was apparently too restrictive or too liberal for some participants. The HSWP was represented at a conference of party secretaries for ideological matters held in East Berlin, 3–5 July.

Hungarian-Romanian relations did not improve noticeably in 1979. An HSWP delegation of Secretaries Gyenes, Havasi, and Óvári visited Bucharest on 9 November 1978 to discuss delays in the implementation of the 1977 Kádár-Ceauşescu agreements on consular facilities and other improvements involving the cultural life of the Hungarian minority in Romania. In a television interview on 16 December 1978, Foreign Minister Puja referred to insufficient progress in normalizing economic, cultural, and tourist contacts between the two countries. Puja's "official friendship visit" to Romania did not produce visible improvement. Romanian Prime Minister Ilie Verdet conducted talks in Budapest with Lázár and Kádár, 16–17 July, "in a cordial and sincere atmosphere," a formula usually indicating differences. It was coincidentally announced that the proposed consulates in Debrecen and Cluj-Napoca would be opened "in the near future." Difficulties of a different order arose when on 1 August Romania imposed restrictions on the purchase of gasoline by tourists. This affected a large number of Hungarian and other East European visitors, and Budapest issued an official protest. Hungary resorted to emergency aid for the stranded tourists, as well as to certain countermeasures. The dispatch of a delegation to Romania to discuss the problem proved largely fruitless, and on 13 August Romania canceled two bus services to Hungary.

Prime Minister Lázár met in Prague with his counterpart Lubomír Štrougal and Czechoslovak party leader Gustav Husák, 27–28 August. The talks focused on bilateral economic relations, including completion of the Adria pipeline and a joint hydroelectric project on the Danube. Biszku led a delegation to Cuba in January for the twentieth anniversary celebrations of the revolution, and in March Deputy Premier Huszár also traveled to Cuba for talks on economic cooperation. The HSWP was represented at the congresses of the French, Italian, Belgian, and Portuguese communist parties. Károly Németh paid a "friendship visit" to Poland in April.

Foreign party visitors to Hungary included delegations from the Tanzanian Revolutionary Party (April) and the East German (April), West German (April), Costa Rican (April), Finnish (June), Cuban (June), North Korean (June), Vietnamese (August), and Venezuelan (August) communist parties. Portuguese party leader Alvaro Cunhal came to Hungary for a rest and met Kádár in August.

Publications. The HSWP's principal daily newspaper is *Népszabadság* (People's Freedom), edited by Dezsö Nemes, with a circulation of 750,000. The theoretical monthly *Társadalmo Szemle* (Social Review) has a circulation of 40,700. The monthly organizational journal *Pártelet* (Party Life) has a circulation of 130,000. Other major newspapers are *Magyar Hirlap*, the "government" daily; *Magyar Nemzet*, published under the auspices of the Patriotic People's Front; and *Népszava*, the organ of the trade unions. The official news agency is Magyar Távirati Iroda (Hungarian Telegraphic Agency).

University of Toronto   Bennett Kovrig

Poland

The history of the communist movement in Poland goes back to the formation in December 1918 of the Communist Workers' Party of Poland; the name changed in 1925 to Communist Party of Poland. The party operated underground until its dissolution in 1938 by the Comintern.

In January 1942 the Comintern revived the movement under the name Polish Workers' Party. This party seized power after the war and consolidated control by gradually eliminating its potential competitors. In December 1948 the communists forced a merger with the Polish Socialist Party and established the Polish United Workers' Party (PUWP). The PUWP has since maintained a dominant position in political and economic life. Two other existing political organizations, the Democratic Party (DP) and the United Peasant Party (UPP), have been restricted to essentially supportive functions. The PUWP's leading role was legally formalized in 1976 through a constitutional amendment.

The PUWP has always maintained operational control over elective state organs and public institutions. The main instrument for coordination of electoral activity is the Front of National Unity, a formal coalition of all social and political groups, which has been chaired since February 1976 by PUWP Politburo member Henryk Jabłonski. No organized group capable of competing with the candidates proposed by the Front of National Unity has been allowed to exist. Since the last parliamentary election in March 1976, the communist party has held 262 out of the 460 seats in the Sejm (parliament); 112 are held by the UPP and 37 by the DP. The remaining 49 seats are filled by nonparty deputies, including thirteen from various Catholic groups (five PAX, five Znak, two Christian Social Association, one Caritas). The next parliamentary election is to be held in 1980.

The most important government functions are in the hands of PUWP leaders. By the end of 1979, Politburo members occupied four of the seventeen positions on the Council of State (Henryk Jabłonski as chairman or titular head of state, Edward Babiuch and Władysław Kruczek as deputy chairmen, and Edward Gierek). Members of the Politburo also held the offices of prime minister (Piotr Jaroszewicz) and three of the eight deputy prime minsters. Four other Politburo members held ministerial posts (Jozef Kepa, administration, local economy, and the protection of the environment; Stanisław Kowalczyk, internal affairs; Wojciech Jaruzelski, national defense; and Jozef Tejchma, instruction and upbringing). Tadeusz Wrzaszczyk, a deputy prime minister and deputy member of the Politburo, is chairman of the Planning Commission.

The PUWP is the largest political organization in the country, with about 3.1 million members (*Trybuna ludu*, 8–9 September). Of these, about 45.6 percent are workers, 33.5 percent are white-collar employees, less than 10 percent are peasants, while the rest are retirees, artisans, and others. About 26 percent of party members are women. The UPP has about 446,000 (*Wies wspolczesna*, September) and the DP approximately 100,000 members (*Nowe drogi*, April, p. 32). The population of Poland is 35.4 million.

Leadership and Organization. The PUWP leadership was stable throughout the year. Edward Gierek continued as leader of the party, and the composition of both the Politburo and the Secretariat of the Central Committee remained unchanged, as in the previous two years (for the list of incumbents, see *YICA*, 1978, p. 50).

The PUWP organization consists of over 75,000 primary units (including about 3,500 in military formations), 2,000 communal and town committees, and 49 provincial committees. The distribution of power is based on the principle of democratic centralism: each organizational unit elects its executive organs, which conduct party work in their respective spheres of competence and are accountable to their membership, while decisions taken by higher organs are binding on lower ones.

According to party rules, the highest authority within the organization is the Congress, which is convened at least every five years (the last one met in December 1975, the next Congress is to meet at the beginning of February 1980). It elects the Central Committee and Central Control Commission. The Central Committee, presently composed of 141 full and 110 deputy members, directs and controls all party activities between congresses. To effectively perform its tasks, it elects from among its members the Politburo and the Secretariat. The Politburo acts as the main policymaking body between Central Committee plenary meetings (plenums). The Secretariat is the executive organ of the Central Committee and is charged with supervision of party work. The Party Control Commission watches over internal discipline and also serves as an appellate office for decisions made by lower units. Corresponding structures are maintained at lower organizational levels.

Auxiliary and Mass Organizations. The PUWP's relation with society revolves around the principle of a centrally directed coordination of all organized political and social activities. Foremost among the mass public organizations are the 23 trade unions, with a total membership of over 12.5 million. Their activities are coordinated by the Central Council of Trade Unions. Under the leadership of Politburo member Władysław Kruczek, this body serves as a policy organ for the entire trade union movement. The Central Council plays an advisory role in the formulation of government economic plans and policies on wages for employees. Its most important task, however, is to secure cooperation between workers and management to achieve economic targets. The legally defined scope of the unions' work ranges from supervision of work safety standards to administration of social programs, such as health services and recreational facilities. Local unions also act to prevent production slowdowns or work stoppages and function as arbitrators in disciplinary conflicts between workers and management. The effective role of the unions and the 5,814 conferences of workers' self-management, however, is restricted to cooperation with appropriate government bodies in preparing and implementing existing labor legislation.

The party also maintains close links with the three youth organizations: Union of Polish Socialist Youth (about 2.7 million members); Socialist Union of Polish Students (300,000); and Union of Polish Scouts (3 million). All three are united in the Federation of Socialist Unions of Polish Youth, chaired by Krzysztof Trebaczkiewicz, a PUWP Central Committee member. The organized youth movement constitutes the main base for recruitment into party ranks.

Among other mass organizations are the Union of Fighters for Freedom and Democracy, a veterans' group (640,000 members); the League of Women, active in propagating a proper model of socialist family life (450,000); the Volunteer Citizens' Military Reserve, a parapolice force frequently used in quelling social dissent and disturbances (350,000); and the League for Defense of the Country, a civil defense organization (1.9 million). All are headed by members of the party's Central Committee.

Party Internal Affairs. The PUWP Central Committee met three times during the year, with economic issues clearly dominating agendas. The Fourteenth Plenum, held on 11 April, debated the problems of small-scale industry and ways to expand its productivity. No firm decisions were taken, however, and the discussion ended with Gierek's call for a new conceptualization of the role of small-scale industry "in our economic policy, in annual plans, and in the future five-year plan. It should also be accorded a place in the theses for the [forthcoming] congress of our party" (*Trybuna ludu*, 12 April).

The Fifteenth Plenum, which took place on 12 June, was devoted to a discussion of Poland's current agricultural difficulties. In the keynote address, Gierek attributed these difficulties to bad weather conditions in 1978, the severe winter that followed, the spring floods, and the summer drought. To compensate for losses, Gierek explained, Poland would have to import about 7.5 million tons of grain and 400,000 tons of soy beans in 1979. At the same time, the country would have to reduce its agricultural exports, producing a trade deficit in agricultural products of some U.S. $700 million (ibid., 13 June). In other matters, the plenum agreed that the next PUWP Congress would take place in February 1980, and a 195-member committee was elected to prepare the country and the party for that occasion.

The Sixteenth Plenum, which met on 19 October, was devoted to discussion of the centrally formulated guidelines for the forthcoming party congress, scheduled to convene on 11 February 1980. As outlined by Gierek in a keynote speech to the plenum, the guidelines centered on two basic themes: the need to continue the essential features of existing economic policies in order to preserve and consolidate the accomplishments of the past and an appeal for public unity behind the leadership, coupled with a call for greater popular involvement in the centrally directed efforts to fulfill the tasks at hand. These themes provided the main issues for a centrally developed mobilization campaign of preparation for the forthcoming congress. Through numerous organizational meetings and public gatherings held in offices and plants throughout the country, the people were made aware that the goal was support for the party and its leaders and acceptance of current policies.

Such insistence on political and operational continuity appeared rather incongruous given Poland's steadily deteriorating economy and a growing dissatisfaction within the party with its leaders' policies. In December 1978, during the thirteenth session of the Central Committee, a provincial party secretary, Tadeusz Grabski, attacked the party's economic programs by openly decrying "unrealistically prepared economic plans that lead to shortages of resources, materials, and energy, as well as inefficient market supply" and put the responsibility for that situation on "the state, the authorities, and, above all, our party." Needless to say, Grabski's speech was not printed in the official reports on the session but was subsequently published in an underground dissident journal (*Głos*, February-March).

Later, a comprehensive assessment of Poland's economic and political conditions prepared by a semiofficially organized and soon dissolved group of intellectuals called Experience and Future—most of whom were party members—described the situation in Poland as characteristic of "a severe, deep, and multifaceted crisis . . . inherent in the way of conducting policy and exercising power" (*Report on the State of the Republic and the Methods of Its Reform*, prepared in May but published by a dissident publishing house in October).

It is impossible to say how widely shared are such views, but they did not seem to affect the direction of policymaking. The great majority of the party rank and file seemed to support the leaders. To what extent this unity might represent a party-wide consensus on the need to continue current economic and social policies, or simply indicated a prevailing concern for system maintenance, is difficult to judge. In any case, the broad pattern of organizational discipline provided a strong argument for assuming Gierek's continuing ability to preserve internal party cohesion and political conformity.

On the other hand, economic and political problems cannot be glossed over by internal party unity. As Mieczysław F. Rakowski, a Central Committee member and well-known political journalist, pointed out: "It is simply impossible to ride out or outlast the current difficulties or to assume that they somehow will go away . . . to reminisce about our great achievements of the past decade or to complain about all those things that make our life miserable . . . is not good enough. The main task of the day should be an effective elimination of all those practices that pull us back. This concerns everyone, both the creators of material and spiritual values as well as those who occupy positions of leadership" (*Polityka*, 17 November). Despite these clear warnings and admonitions, there was no indication that Rakowski's appeals would be taken into consideration by the authorities. The general impression at the end of 1979 was that the prevailing political and economic inertia would continue.

Domestic Affairs. The main domestic efforts of the party concentrated on finding ways to deal with the mounting economic difficulties. The main sources of these difficulties were essentially twofold: particularly adverse weather conditions during the first half of the year and the continuing deterioration of international economic conditions. The harsh winter was followed by massive spring floods and a prolonged early summer drought. The inclement weather also affected implementation of production plans in several other important areas of the economy, such as transport, power, construction, and raw materials. Commenting on the weather conditions, Gierek affirmed at the end of June that disturbances that affected "the functioning of the economy at the beginning of the year were so far-reaching that it has become impossible to make up lost production in several major sectors and to overcome the difficulties" (Radio Warsaw, 25 June). In addition, rapidly rising prices for imports, especially for fuels and raw materials, created an important and growing burden for Poland's economy.

Some observers were convinced that the downward economic trend was due even more to the persistent failure of the country's leaders to adjust policies and streamline management of both agricultural and industrial enterprises. One of the most important reasons for agricultural problems continued to be the official insistence on socialization of land, as well as the discrimination against private farmers in the allocation of fertilizers, equipment, and other needs (see *YICA*, 1979, p. 54). Similarly, no improvement was made in the long-established patterns of industrial management, which remained under strict administrative control of centralized bureaucratic institutions despite growing criticism from the country's economic experts. A leading economic official, Jozef Pajestka, even resigned in March from his position as vice-chairman of the Council of Ministers' Planning Commission in protest against the stultifying centralization of economic decision making. To improve the existing situation in economic management, one Polish expert advised "a clear division of rights and responsibilities among various levels of administrative management . . . for a new phase in the process of streamlining the existing system of economic leadership in the 1980s" (B. Glinski, *Ekonomista*, January). There was no indication, however, that this call for change would find an echo in the party's leading organs.

The practical effects on the country's economy of these exogenous and endogenous factors were serious. Reporting on the estimated plan fulfillment for 1979, Deputy Premier Tadeusz Wrzaszczyk revealed at the end of November that total agricultural production was expected to be over 2 percent lower than in 1978. In comparison with the previous year, grain production fell by some 4.2 milion tons to 17.3 million tons, about 5 million tons less than that planned for the year. Industrial production was said to have grown by only 2.6 percent, instead of the planned 5 percent. The only plan likely to be fulfilled was coal extraction—it is to reach about 200 million tons—while the production of rolled steel, copper, plastics, fertilizers, paper, cement, and electric power would fall below targets. (*Tribuna ludu*, 3 December.)

The draft outline of the forthcoming plan for 1980 called for continuing austerity and tightening of economic activity. Food supplies were to increase by about 4 percent, less than half the growth rate of 10.2 percent planned for 1979. Poland will need to continue massive imports of grain—in 1978 about 8.4 million tons were imported, mostly from the United States and Canada—but even that did not guarantee improvement in the supply of food, particularly of meat. "We will have to deal with essential structural problems, especially in the supply of meat," admitted Wrzaszczyk (ibid.). Supplies of consumer goods were to rise by 6 percent, compared with the 8 percent planned for 1979. Growth in industrial production for 1980 was scaled down to 3 percent. In 1979 it was to have reached about 4.9 percent, but the final figure was a mere 2.6 percent, the lowest officially admitted increase in over thirty years. No indication of the growth of national income during 1979 was provided, but authorities admitted that it "would be significantly below" the planned rate of 2.8 percent (ibid.). The planned growth in national income for 1980 was set at only 1.4 to 1.8 percent, the lowest target ever. Real wages were to rise in 1980 by about 1 percent, implying a clear possibility of an effective lowering of the standard of living for the entire population.

Throughout the year major efforts were made to reduce adverse balance of payments in trade exchanges with Western countries. After the first six months, imports increased by only 3.7 percent over the comparable period of 1978, and exports grew by 10.3 percent (*Biuletyn Statystyczny*, no. 7). Yet Poland's indebtedness to noncommunist, primarily Western, countries further increased. It is estimated to have reached $708 million during the current year. This constituted a 20-percent drop in comparison with 1978 but exceeded the planned deficit by some $108 million. There was no firm information on the overall deficit in the balance of payments with Western countries, but Poland's foreign debt with the West was estimated at $15 billion at the end of 1978, with servicing charges amounting to $4.1 billion during 1979 (*Financial Times*, 23 November).

During the year, the government introduced several measures aimed at energy savings. Prices of petroleum products were raised twice—in January and in July—and speed limits were lowered to reduce fuel consumption. Furthermore, periodic daily cuts of electric power were introduced. These measures were designed to avoid a repetition of the major energy breakdowns that occurred at the end of 1978 and during the early months of 1979 and seriously damaged the production capability of the entire industrial sector. Nonetheless, it is estimated that power shortages during 1979 would exceed those of 1978—2,500 compared with 1,800 megawatts (Radio Warsaw, 24 September). To improve the situation, Poland decided to expand work on nuclear power stations. The first station was to be constructed on Zarnow Lake in the Gdansk (north-central) region and was scheduled to begin operating in 1986 (Polska Agencja Prasowa [PAP], 18 November).

Among other political developments, on 22 July Poland celebrated the 35th anniversary of the formation of the socialist state. On 1 September there was a massive commemoration of the 40th anniversary of the German invasion of Poland.

There were numerous changes in government personnel during the year, primarily at lower levels. One major change, involving two Politburo members, took place at the beginning of February. Jozef Kepa and Jozef Tejchma, both members of the Politburo, and Franciszek Kaim lost their jobs as deputy prime ministers. Kepa was given the post of minister of administration, local economy, and the protection of the environment, while Tejchma took over the Ministry of Instruction and Upbringing. On 8 February nonparty journalist and writer Edmund Osmanczyk was elected by the Sejm to the Council of State, filling the vacancy created by the death of Bolesław Piasecki, leader of the pro-government Catholic organization PAX.

Political Dissent. Throughout the year there were numerous indications that the semiorganized and open movement of opposition against party policies remained active. The political and social dynamics of this movement could not be fully established because it remained divided into several permanent organizations as well as various ad hoc groupings defending specific interests. Although the goals and methods of operation of these groups have differed and even contradicted one another at times, they appeared to share a common denominator—the rejection of state control over areas of their concern.

All available sources agree that even if the number of openly active dissidents remained relatively small—the estimated combined membership of all opposition groups could hardly exceed a thousand persons—they were remarkably successful in developing effective patterns of activity. There is every reason to believe that since the emergence of the first opposition organization three years ago (see

YICA, 1978, pp. 53–55, and 1979, pp. 55–57), all social strata have been affected directly or indirectly by the dissidents' operations.

The dissidents' work is carried on mainly through the dissemination of written materials. By the end of 1979, there were about twenty "underground" publications appearing regularly in different cities throughout the country. In addition, during the year separate groups issued numerous appeals, proclamations, and statements. The dominant emphasis in these publishing efforts was on breaking the state's monopoly over communications. The dissidents' activity acquired a character of a broad and wide-ranging campaign against all aspects of state censorship. It included the unrestricted publication of full-length novels by well-known Polish and foreign writers, the dissemination of confidential regulations from the censor's or party offices, and a constant flow of information on official abuses of power in all areas of public life.

Another form of dissident activity was participation in mass public demonstrations organized to commemorate significant events in Poland's presocialist history. Three such demonstrations took place in different cities during 1979. One in Warsaw on 31 July marked the 35th anniversary of the popular uprising there against the Germans. Another was a series of public gatherings throughout the country on 1 September to commemorate the 40th anniversary of the German invasion and the outbreak of World War II. The third involved several meetings called to celebrate the 61st anniversary of Poland's independence on 11 November. All three events were organized by the Movement for the Defense of Human and Civil Rights (ROPCO) as solemn manifestations of patriotic remembrance of past instances of national heroism. But they also served to underline the differences still existing between official interpretations of national history, which glorified the achievements of the socialist regime and the communist party, and dissident evaluations of the past, which emphasized national independence, territorial integrity, and patriotic remembrance rather than socialist experience. As if to underscore these differences even further, several dissident organizations—including the Committee for Social Self-defense (KOR), ROPCO, and several others—issued special proclamations commemorating the 40th anniversary of the Soviet invasion of Poland on 17 September 1939. Needless to say, that anniversary was completely ignored by the authorities.

The dissident organizations maintained their strongly internationalist outlook. Some of the groups held regular contacts with the dissident organizations in other East European countries, particularly with Czechoslovakia's Charter 77, and all strongly supported further expansion of dissenting trends throughout the area. In addition, the flow of contacts between the Polish dissidents and the West, either through publication of the opposition's articles and statements in the Western press or through visits by Western intellectuals and journalists to Poland, was constant and broad.

On 1 September a group of dissidents announced the formation of a new organization, the Confederation of Independent Poland (KPN). The organizers of the KPN were quoted by Western correspondents as viewing the group as "a political party" with a secret membership and without formal authorization from the state, whose goal was to promote full "freedom and independence" for Poland (Associated Press, 1 September).

In part, the establishment of KPN confirmed that the dissident movement remained sharply divided politically and was polarized among various groups and tendencies. The existence of such divisions has been known for a long time. During 1977 and 1978 two major centers of influence within the movement developed around KOR and ROPCO, with numerous other organizations and groups oscillating between the two. Differences between KOR and ROPCO were mainly political; the former was concerned more with social problems and the latter's orientation was primarily nationalistic. Since the end of 1978, these differences have grown because of personal animosities between activists and leaders of both groups. Eventually ROPCO split, and its more nationalistic activists established the KPN.

Another important factor contributing to the proliferation of dissident groups was a dramatic increase in the activist mood of the public at large following the visit by Pope John Paul II to Poland in June. If anything, this development seemed to establish in the public mind the impression that the existing balance of political influence had shifted away from PUWP leaders. This impression, although grounded more in perception than in political realities, became even stronger as a result of the apparent inability of party leaders to solve Poland's persistent economic problems and difficulties.

Yet, while the Pope's visit had an undeniable impact on the public, it was clear that the church's position in social and national life should not be identified with the dissident movement. Although openly sympathetic to dissident activity, the church remained determined to preserve its own specific orientation and organizational separateness. This became explicit when on 3 October a group of dissidents went on a one-week hunger strike in a Warsaw church to protest "the detention of human and civil rights activists in Czechoslovakia and Poland" (Reuters, 3 October). This action prompted a rebuke from the secretary of the Episcopate, Bishop Bronisław Dabrowski, who pointedly remarked after a talk with the strikers that "a church serves specific religious and cult purposes, so the use of a church for political ends interferes with this purpose." Bishop Dabrowski affirmed that the church would fulfill its traditional role as defender of those "who fight for human rights" but also remarked that the choice of both the place and the form of political demonstrations are "not always" recognized or approved by church authorities. (Ibid., 4 October.)

The official response to political dissent was ambiguous, mostly antagonistic, but also relatively tolerant. In order to contain the spread and the intensity of opposition, the authorities continually used restrictive measures ranging from press and institutional harassment to police intimidation, physical abuse, and the arrest of individual dissenters. There was no attempt, however, to suppress the operations of the movement. One reason for such relative toleration might be the party leaders' determination to preserve the increasingly fragile structure of civil peace in the country. In addition, it could be argued that from the point of view of the authorities, the continuing activism of the opposition groups, particularly since they cannot seriously challenge the party in power, performs a basically constructive function in the operation of the political system by providing a built-in instrument for mitigating and releasing social tension.

Relations with the Catholic Church. The most important political development in 1979, a development that deeply affected social relations and may have a long-lasting impact on the future evolution of power relations in the country, was the visit of Pope John Paul II (2–10 June). The visit became inevitable following the election in 1978 of Krakow's cardinal as leader of the Roman Catholic church. The visit was preceded by a long period of intense negotiations between church officials and the political authorities over problems of timing, duration, and the program of the pope's trip. The actual process of these negotiations remained secret, although some indications of inevitable pressures and counterpressures were made public in the form of occasional interviews given by government officials to foreign newspapers (e.g., *Corriere della Sera*, 29 January and 2 February), as well as religious activities at home (public prayers for the pope's visit, etc.).

On 24 January Edward Gierek and Poland's primate, Stefan Cardinal Wyszynski, met to "exchange views on the most important questions facing the nation and the church" (PAP, 24 January). On 2 March, following a series of intense bargaining sessions, punctuated by occasional trips by Polish bishops to the Vatican, an official announcement set the date and the duration of the visit.

To prepare for the visit itself, the Vatican's secretary of the Council for Public Affairs of the Church, Archbishop Agostino Casaroli, came to Poland 22–26 March. He took part in a session of the Episcopate, conferred with Cardinal Wyszynski, and had extensive talks with several Polish officials, including Council of State Chairman Henryk Jabłonski and Foreign Minister Emil Wojtaszek. Subsequently the scope of cooperation between church and state agencies charged with the preparation of the visit increased considerably, with an expanding proliferation of preparatory committees, a growing flow of mutual communication links, and a broadening of joint efforts to streamline work on all details related to the papal trip. On a more specifically operational plane, a comprehensive effort was mounted by Catholic bishops to recruit voluntary organizers and church marshals to supervise the preparations for the visit and ensure public order at the religious ceremonies. By the end of May, the number of such voluntary helpers was said to exceed 40,000 (United Press International, 25 May).

On 29 May Giereck and Cardinal Wyszynski met again. At the conclusion of their talks, both leaders affirmed that "the visit of Pope John Paul II will provide new impulses for cooperation between church and state. It will serve to develop further relations between Poland and the Holy See. The visit will contribute toward the unity of the Poles in the implementation of national goals for the prosperity of their fatherland—the Polish People's Republic" (Radio Warsaw, 29 May).

Pope John Paul II arrived in Warsaw on 2 June. During the following eight days, he traveled across central and southern Poland, saw and was seen by millions, and delivered some thirty public addresses and sermons. The pope's visit became a continuous public celebration, a feast of faith and religion, a solemn occasion for a massive uplifting of humanitarian spirits and ideas, and also a joyous happening for the nation at large, which suddenly found itself united through a common euphoria of pride and satisfaction.

The purpose of the pope's visit was religious, although he met and discussed world problems with Edward Gierek and other state officials. However, to the extent that the dominant accent in the pope's pronouncements was on the continuing importance of religous beliefs and on the need to strengthen and consolidate the institutional church, his visit also acquired strong political connotations. This was particularly apparent in Pope John Paul II's insistence on the inalienable rights of man, including the right to religious liberty, as the foundation of all human activities. Clearly implicit in this call, repeated in all the pope's sermons and addresses, was a criticism of the collectivist ethos that has always dominated both the thinking and the actions of the communist government. If one added to that the strong assertion, frequently voiced by the pope, of a historical identification of the church and religion with Polish national existence itself, the inherently political message of the papal statements became unmistakable.

At the same time, the pope stopped short of any explicit condemnation of the communist system of government and instead called for some form of mutually acceptable accommodation between the church and socialist state aimed at reconciliation rather than conflict. But he also made clear that it was not to be a reconciliation at all costs and it would have to lead to an "authentic dialogue [between church and state] respectful of the convictions of believers, so it would ensure all the rights of citizens and also normal conditions for the activity of the church as a religious community to which the vast majority of Poles belong. We are aware," the pope affirmed, "that this dialogue cannot be easy, because it takes place between two world views that are diametrically opposed; but it must be possible and effective, for the good of individuals and the nation demands it." (Address to the 169th episcopal conference of Polish bishops, 6 June.)

As for the more practical aspects of the process of eventual accommodation between the church and the state, Pope John Paul II pointed out that in the future "there must be clarity in rules of procedure, which have been developed within the church community in accordance with the [requirements] of the current situation. Those rules, both with regard to the activity of the clergy and that of the laity, and their correspondence with practice are the sources of moral authority." (Ibid.) This could mean that the flow of contacts, negotiations, and decisions between church and state would in the future be more tightly coordinated within the church and watched more closely by the Vatican. Local church officials would likely see their functions more clearly defined by the Holy See in order to assure that their actions fully conformed to the broader strategies of the Vatican. As for the government, it will likely encounter a substantially different and more cohesive group of adversaries in future negotiations.

There was little discernible movement in the area of church-state relations in the months following the pope's visit. No official statement on this subject was made by political leaders, while the activity of the church was characterized by caution and restraint. On 5–6 September the 170th plenary conference of the Polish Episcopate met in Warsaw to review the most important problems facing the church. The bishops pointedly asserted that "in many spheres the church is not operating under normal conditions for carrying out its mission," especially in view of continuing difficulties in constructing needed church buildings and broadening access to the mass media, and blamed the negligent and restrictive attitude of the government for those problems (Radio Vatican, 11 September). They also declared themselves ready, however, "for further talks on the subject of the normalization of relations between the church and the state . . . which would make possible broader cooperation . . . in many spheres of social life — the strengthening of the family, the social system, respect for life, sobriety, respect for social property, healthy customs, and in the shaping of attitudes about the moral value of work. All this," the bishops declared, "is for the good of the nation, the church, and the state." (Ibid.) There was no response from the government, although during the second part of the year official permits for the construction of fourteen new churches in Warsaw's suburbs were issued.

During the year, the Polish government became more sensitive to the needs of the Jewish community within Poland and became involved in a dialogue with Jews outside the country. In September a government-sponsored committee was established to honor Janusz Korczak, a Jewish educator killed by the Nazis during the war. More attention was devoted to keeping alive Warsaw's Yiddish theater, and in July the members of an American commission on the holocaust were able to tour former sites of concentration camps throughout the country.

Another development, with possibly lasting, long-range implications for political and religious relations in Poland, was the death on 1 January of Bolesław Piasecki, founder and principal leader of the procommunist Catholic PAX Association. His departure greatly weakened PAX's internal cohesiveness and political role as a party tool for infiltrating the Catholic community. Piasecki was replaced on 14 January by Ryszard Reiff.

Party International Affairs. During the year, PUWP representatives took part in several multinational communist meetings. In April Polish delegates participated in an ideological conference in Hungary. Another ideological conference, at the level of Central Committee secretaries in charge of ideological problems, was held in East Berlin, 3–5 July. It "confirmed the resolve of [all participants] to strengthen, on the basis of the principles of Marxism-Leninism and proletarian internationalism, solidarity with all peoples fighting against imperialism and reaction and expressed the conviction that the achievements of real socialism promote new successes for the cause of peace, democracy, national freedom, and social progress." (Tass, 6 July.) Although there was no mention of the papal visit to Poland in the official communiqué, there is little doubt that this event must have played a role in the deliberations.

As for bilateral relations with other communist parties, the PUWP received several ranking representatives of West European parties, including the French, Italian, and West German parties.

Foreign Affairs. In the area of foreign relations, the most important developments were extensive contacts with Soviet party and state officials. Numerous exchanges between the two countries took place at ministerial and party levels throughout the year. Gierek himself visited the USSR twice. On 12–14 March, he went to Moscow to exchange views on the current international situation and to discuss Polish-Soviet relations with the head of the Communist Party of the Soviet Union (CPSU), Leonid Brezhnev. Eventually both leaders expressed "satisfaction with the development of all-round cooperation between the Soviet Union and Poland . . . [and] emphasized the striving of the CPSU and the

PUWP to further deepen ties along party, state, and public lines, to expand cultural exchanges and contacts, to strengthen friendship between the Soviet and the Polish people" (ibid., 13 March).

Between 25 July and 7 August, Gierek spent a working holiday in the USSR, meeting with Brezhnev in the Crimea on 4 August. According to the communiqué, the two leaders "informed each other about problems on whose solution the communists and all the working people of the Soviet Union and Poland are now busy and about plans for the period immediately ahead" (*Trybuna ludu*, 6 August). The meeting was also attended by CPSU Politburo member and Central Committee Secretary Konstantin Chernenko. As if to put the Polish-Soviet conversations in a broader international perspective, Polish media commented subsequently on the "cooperation carried out by the PUWP and CPSU, which . . . forms the cornerstone of cooperation between Poland and the Soviet Union" (PAP, 7 August).

Rapidly increasing economic cooperation between Poland and the USSR continued throughout the year. After the first six months, total trade turnover between the two countries reached 3.7 billion rubles, making a 14.9-percent growth in comparison with the similar period in 1978. Imports from the USSR increased by 18.8 percent during that time, while exports from Poland were up by 10.9 percent. Those figures put Poland in second place among members of the Council for Mutual Economic Assistance in their trade with the USSR (*Zycie Warszawy*, 15–16 September). Most of Poland's imports were in oil and petroleum products (about 74 percent of all Polish imports in this area), natural gas, cotton, iron ore, and other raw materials. Poland exported seagoing vessels, shipbuilding equipment, chemical products, textiles, clothing, and coal.

Among the bilateral contacts with other East European states, the most important were Gierek's visit to Bulgaria (31 January–1 February) and Czechoslovak leader Gustav Husák's visit to Poland (19–20 February). In both cases, exchanges of views on the international situation and on the development of mutual relations were mentioned as the most important themes for discussion. On 17–18 May, Gierek traveled to East Berlin to meet Erich Honecker for talks on organizational matters, as well as on economic relations with the German Democratic Republic.

As for contacts with other communist countries, Premier Piotr Jaroszewicz paid an official state visit to Cuba, 25–31 March. While there, he assured the Cubans of continuing Polish support for Cuban socialist development.

. In relations with Western countries, Poland continued strong efforts to expand economic cooperation and contacts. The Federal Republic of Germany (FRG), Poland's most important trading partner, continued as a primary area for diplomatic activity. Throughout the year numerous official exchanges were held between the two countries. They included working visits by FRG Chancellor Helmut Schmidt (17–18 August) and German Justice Minister Hans-Jochen Vogel (April) and a trip by the parliamentary leader of the FRG ruling Social Democratic Party, Herbert Wehner (April). In addition, numerous lesser personalities from Germany's political, economic, and cultural establishments visited Poland during the year. These visits were reciprocated by an equally large number of Polish officials. The number of individual Polish tourists going to West Germany exceeded 200,000 for the first time.

Poland's trade relations with the FRG improved somewhat during the year. At the end of 1978, Poland had a deficit of $154.8 million, but the estimated deficit by the end of 1979 was expected to drop to about $90 million.

Polish-American relations were also maintained at a cooperative level, with economic issues predominating. In May a session of the Polish-U.S. Economic Council was held in Poland at the same time as the Polish-U.S. Working Group on Agriculture met there. Those meetings underscored the continuing importance of American economic aid and support for Poland's economic stability. On 5 November the U.S. Department of Agriculture announced that Poland had been granted credits and guarantees of $500 million for the 1979-1980 fiscal year to purchase U.S. agricultural products. Inevitably this will adversely affect Poland's already serious balance of payments position with the United States, especially in view of the declining trade volume in the first eight months of 1979: a nearly 14-percent drop in total trade, with exports down almost 15 percent and imports declining by some 13 percent (*Biuletyn Statystyczny*, no. 9). The highlight of official Polish-American relations was the visit by Emil Wojtaszek, Poland's foreign minister, to the United States in July. During the year, several U.S. congressional delegations visited Poland, and numerous American bishops took part in religious celebrations during Pope John Paul II's visit to Poland.

Among other Western contacts, particularly noteworthy were the visit by Edward Gierek to France in September, an official visit by Dutch Prime Minister Andreas A. M. van Agt to Poland (September), and a visit by Austrian Chancellor Bruno Kreisky to Poland in November. In all these events, economic questions and problems of trade relations were clearly at the center of discussions.

Poland was also active in maintaining cooperative relations with numerous Asian, African, and Latin American countries. Polish Foreign Minister Wojtaszek visited several states in the Middle East, presumably to discuss the possibility of oil purchases by Poland. Poland's head of state, Henryk Jabłonski, paid an official visit to Mexico in October. There is no doubt that his trip was also closely related to possible purchases of Mexican oil (*Zolnierz Wolnosci*, 27 October).

Publications. The official organ of the PUWP is the daily *Trybuna ludu*; the party also has daily newspapers in all 49 provinces. Its monthly theoretical journal is *Nowe Drogi*. The monthly *Zycie partii* and the biweekly *Zagadnienia i materialy* are for party activists. Another biweekly, *Chlopska droga*, is for rural readers; the monthly *Ideologia i polityka* is for the general public. The most important popular weekly, *Polityka*, is closely linked to the party without, however, any official political identification.

Radio Free Europe   Jan B. de Weydenthal
Munich, Germany

Romania

The Communist Party of Romania (Partidul Comunist Român; CPR) was founded on 8 May 1921. Throughout most of the interwar period the CPR was outlawed. Factionalized and controlled by the Soviet-dominated Communist International, the party had little popular support. The Soviet occupation of Romania in 1944 ensured the emergence of a people's republic headed by the party, which was renamed the Romanian Workers' Party (Partidul Muncitoresc Romîn) in 1948. Under the leadership of Gheorghe Gheorghiu-Dej, the party gradually initiated in the 1960s a more nationalistic internal course and a more autonomous foreign policy. This orientation has been continued by Nicolae

Ceauşescu, who succeeded Dej after the latter's death in 1965. In that same year the Ninth Congress of the CPR proclaimed Romania a socialist republic, and the party reverted to its original name. Since 1948 the CPR has been the only party in Romania.

As of November, according to the report that Ceauşescu presented to the CPR's Twelfth Congress (*Scînteia*, 20 November), party membership totaled 2.93 million, of which "nearly" 54 percent were workers, "nearly" 18 percent were peasants, and 29 percent were intellectuals and white-collar personnel. Women constitute 28 percent of the membership. Ceauşescu also indicated that the party was 90 percent Romanian, 8 percent Hungarian, and 2 percent German and other nationalities—approximately the ethnic composition of the total population. Total population as of 5 January 1977 was about 21.6 million; it is currently estimated at over 22 million.

Organization and Leadership. The CPR is organized into committees and basic units at various local work places and into organizations at the communal, town, municipal, county, and national levels. Ceauşescu reported to the Twelfth Congress that there were 7,000 party organizations with committee structures and 60,400 basic party units (ibid., 20 November). Every five years the 39 county organizations and the Bucharest party organization elect deputies to the national congress which, according to party statutes, is the supreme authority of the CPR. In practice, though, congresses have merely ratified decisions made by other party bodies: the Central Committee, the Secretariat, the Political Executive Committee, and the Permanent Bureau. The CPR's Twelfth Congress was held 19–23 November. Supplementing the work of these ongoing bodies is the National Conference of the CPR, which meets between congresses to review the implementation of party decisions. The last conference met 7–9 December 1977.

Despite the plethora of party leadership bodies and other party organizations, meetings, and conferences, political power has been highly centralized in the hands of the CPR secretary general, Nicolae Ceauşescu, and increasingly his wife, Elena. The latter, in addition to being a member of all leading party bodies, is chairman of the party's Central Committee Commission of Party and State Cadres—a position from which she reputedly exercises considerable control over personnel assignments. She is generally considered the second most influential political figure in Romania (*NYT*, 27 November). In 1979 she was appointed president of the National Council of Science and Technology and of the Commission for Economic Standardization (*Scînteia*, 8 June; *Buletinul Oficial*, 1 September); the functions of the latter body are not yet clear.

Unlike most other communist parties, the CPR does not have a politburo. Decision making is centered in two bodies: the 45-member Political Executive Committee and the fifteen-member Permanent Bureau. The nine-member Secretariat is also a key power center. However, with the increasing personalization of power by the Ceauşescus and their almost unceasing leadership reshuffles ("cadre rotation"), formal lines of authority have become somewhat blurred and the power of party bodies reduced.

In 1979 Ceauşescu organized several "waves" of leadership changes. The first was announced through presidential decrees and a Central Committee plenum (*Scînteia*, 31 January and 1 February). Of the eight officials shifted, two were in the Secretariat, Emil Bobu (cadres) and Vasile Musat (foreign affairs). Bobu, downgraded to minister of labor, had been viewed as working with Elena Ceauşescu in cadre appointments; his loss of this position appeared to reinforce Mme. Ceauşescu's power (Reuters, Bucharest, 17 September). Also included in the reshuffle were several economics ministers and the mayor of Bucharest, a position given to Gheorghe Pana, who had held the Labor Ministry portfolio.

Another leadership realignment was announced after a 29 March Central Committee plenum (ibid., 30–31 March). Ilie Verdeţ, a long-time Ceauşescu confidant, replaced Manea Manescu as prime minister. Verdeţ's previous position as president of state planning was assigned to a party economic technocrat, Nicolae Constantin, who also became a candidate member of the Political Executive Committee and a deputy prime minister. The Secretariat, reduced in number by earlier reshuffles, was replenished by the appointments of Ilie Radulescu, who appears to have the culture portfolio, and Dumitru Popa, whose responsibilities are not clear—he may be handling security matters. Radulescu took over the duties of party secretary Virgil Cazacu, who appears to be handling the foreign affairs slot in the Secretariat. Foreign Minister Stefan Andrei, however, remains the most influential member of Ceaușescu's foreign policy team.

A shake-up of the cultural-educational apparat (ibid., 29 August) saw Miu Dobrescu removed as president of the Council for Socialist Culture and Education, with Sazana Gadea replacing him and turning over her position as minister of education to Aneta Spornic, deputy minister of labor. The latter appointment suggests an intensification of Ceaușescu's efforts to tie education more closely to the needs of economic production at the expense of the liberal arts.

The CPR's Twelfth Congress formally elected members to the leading party bodies, and once again there were substantial membership changes. In general, the congress, following Ceaușescu's repeated calls for more women and more representation of local party people, considerably expanded the number of female and county party members on the Central Committee and Political Executive Committee (ibid., 24 November). The Political Executive Committee, increased from 41 to 45 members (full and candidate), experienced a sweeping shake-up. Four full members were removed— Gheorge Cioara, Emil Draganescu, Manea Manescu, and Iosif Uglar—while another (Gen. Ion Ionita) was dropped to candidate status. Six new full members were appointed: Minister of Defense Ion Coman, State Planning Chief Nicolae Constantin, Minister of Forestry Ludovic Fazekas, Vice-President of Trade Unions Cornelia Filipas, Minister of Education Aneta Spornic, and Bacau County First Secretary Alexandrina Gainuse. The first three had previously served as candidate members. Those dropped from candidate status were Teodor Coman, Mihai Dalea, Ion Iliescu, Vasile Patilinet, and Mihai Telescu. Nearly all these people had been brought to the top by Ceaușescu but in recent years had apparently fallen out of favor. The eleven new candidate members were drawn heavily from the ranks of the county party first secretaries, many of whom are political unknowns. While the Secretariat had only one change—Ludovic Fazekas replaced Iosif Uglar as the nominal Hungarian representative—the Central Committee was increased from 518 to 571 full and candidate members. Among the new appointees were an increased number of women. Ceaușescu's son Nicu was given candidate status.

Probably as a result of Elena Ceaușescu's influence, women have emerged for the first time in significant numbers in the party and state leadership. The previous Political Executive Committee, for example, had only two women, while it now has nine. The year also saw the first assignment of women at the level of county party first secretary. The leading state educational and research ministerial posts are now held by women.

The only leading party body where women did not increase their representation was the Permanent Bureau. It was expanded from eleven to fifteen members by adding Emil Bobu, Virgil Cazacu, Nicolae Constantin, Constantin Dascalescu, and Dumitru Popescu and dropping Manea Manescu.

Mass and Auxiliary Organizations. The CPR sponsors a large number of mass organizations, conferences, and meetings covering nearly all major groups and activities in the society in order to integrate them with the policies of the party. The CPR's conception of democracy revolves around building up the membership of the mass organizations, which usually meet in plenary session at least once every few years. Most sessions have a keynote speech by Ceaușescu in which he outlines the problems and prospects for the group's activities. Ceaușescu recently has been emphasizing the importance of the mass organizations as centers for "debating" party policies, but thus far none of them appear to be involved significantly in decision making.

The Socialist Unity Front received particular consideration in 1979. Ceauşescu announced (*Scînteia*, 31 October) that this mass umbrella political organization would be restructured to create numerous local units that would receive noncommunists as members and provide them with a means of addressing party leaders with their views on domestic and foreign policy. It was also pointed out, however, that the new units would operate under "the guidance of party organizations."

Other mass organizations of note are the Union of Communist Youth and the General Union of Trade Unions. In response to sporadic worker unrest in the past few years, Ceauşescu has also been giving more attention to the workers' control councils, charged with monitoring ways of improving economic performance at the enterprise level. The councils of working people of Hungarian and German nationality have also been receiving more media attention.

Internal Party Affairs. Ceauşescu, often referred to as the "most beloved son" of Romania, continued to dominate the CPR. His personality cult remained unabated in 1979 and was extended to include his wife, Elena. She is now described in terms only slightly less effusive than those applied to her husband. The National Council of Women, for example, proclaimed that because of her high qualities as "a person, wife, and mother, she is a perfect model for millions of Romanian women" (ibid., 25 October). Her role in the early days of the CPR is now given increasing attention (e.g., *Magazin Istoric*, October). The Ceauşescus' personal power is unparalleled in contemporary Eastern European communist parties.

Confronted with growing economic problems, Ceauşescu voiced a variety of criticisms of the ability of the CPR to rectify the situation. In a major speech to leading party cadres on 7 September (*Scînteia*, 9 September), he came down hard on "deficiencies in the activity of party bodies and organizations, working people's councils, and other party-state bodies." County party bodies were particularly criticized for "serious shortcomings" and were told that they would be held responsible and accountable for meeting economic plan targets, especially in agriculture. At the same time, he was critical of the lax procedures connected with admitting and monitoring CPR members and called on the party to be "stricter" and "more demanding." In this respect he stressed that next year's exchange of party membership cards (the first since 1948) "should not be limited to replacing an old card by a new one but should constitute an act of great political significance, an opportunity for discussing with each communist his tasks, how he fulfills them, and how he meets the requirements inherent in membership in the CPR." The implication was that some members would be weeded out, although it is unlikely that the exchange will turn into a major purge.

In the same speech, Ceauşescu reasserted the need for the CPR to perfect its ideological and propagandistic activity in the face of efforts by Romania's "enemies," both internal and external, to "denigrate" it. He renewed his opposition to emigration from Romania (except in cases of "family reunification"); called on the party to combat "foreign circles" that deliberately distort Romania's nationality situation; condemned people who "for money will serve any master" for degrading the country; urged that the "confusion created by certain circles in connection with human rights" be eliminated; and warned against international efforts by "certain religious denominations and certain religious elements" to intervene in the state's internal affairs.

The Twelfth Party Congress. The major party event of the year was the CPR's Twelfth Congress, 19–23 November. Except for one incident, the congress was a generally pro forma affair that reelected Ceauşescu to a five-year term as secretary general, carried out more party leadership changes, and adopted several previously drafted programs. The most important programs were the 1981–1985 economic plan, the program for scientific research and technological development in 1981-1990, and the energy program for 1981–1990.

Ceauşescu's marathon speech to the congress emphasized economic and political issues over foreign policy ones. The Romanian leader, however, broke little new ground and, setting aside his wide-ranging criticisms of two months earlier, tried to put a relatively positive accent on Romania's road in the 1980s. The only real domestic news in his speech was the announcement that Romania had discovered oil in the Black Sea, but Ceauşescu gave no indication of the size or accessibility of these deposits.

The congress confirmed Ceauşescu's pre-eminent position in Romanian political life, which may have provoked the most dramatic incident of the meeting. On the last day of the conclave, an 84-year-old delegate and onetime CPR leader, Constantin Pirvulescu, was granted permission to speak. He launched into an attack on Ceauşescu's arbitrary exercise of power at the expense of party bodies. Because the event unfolded in front of foreign delegations and could not be suppressed, Agerpres, the Romanian news agency, was compelled to issue a statement(23 November) in which it described Ceauşescu's retort to Pirvulescu and expressed the "deep indignation" of the delegates, who voted to strip him of his congressional seat. Ceauşescu called Pirvulescu an "instigator" who was "alien to the country" and hinted that he was doing Moscow's bidding since he is "probably longing for the time when the fate of the party and of the people was not decided here but elsewhere." This unprecedented defiance of Ceauşescu suggests that some elements of the CPR may be getting restless over his heavy-handed ways of governing.

Domestic Affairs. The key domestic goal of the CPR — rapid multilateral socioeconomic development — absorbed continuing attention and elicited growing concern. The decrease in domestic resources, especially oil and gas, and the international energy crisis combined to lower Romania's industrial growth rate, which had been among the highest in the world. As indicated by data on 1978 economic plan performance (*Scînteia*, 2 February), many of Romania's key economic sectors did not fulfill their targets. Industrial production declined from a 12.5-percent growth rate in 1977 to 9 percent in 1978 (as opposed to the planned 10.6 percent); agriculture grew by only 2.4 percent (as opposed to the planned 6.9 percent); industrial investments were seriously down; foreign trade grew by 10 percent (failing to meet a 19-percent growth target), with a trade imbalance well over $600 million; and national income grew at 7.6 percent (versus a planned 11 percent).

The 1981–1985 economic plan reflects Ceauşescu's determination to push ahead with industrialization, leaving agriculture and the standard of living shortchanged in the process (ibid., 5–7 and 12 July). At the same time, Romania is being forced to scale down its rate of growth. Industrial production, for example, is set at an average annual growth rate of only 8 to 9 percent. But even this moderated plan is premised in part on a new energy package that seeks to decrease Romania's reliance on oil and gas by shifting first to coal and later to nuclear energy. As Ceauşescu said to a mass meeting of coal miners:

> It will be impossible to buy oil in coming years. That is why we must see to restructuring the activity of our national economy in the years ahead. We must place greater stress on developing those sectors that consume less energy and oil . . . The need for energy will increase and it is therefore necessary to seek new resources . . . We will also try to seek new resources which must hold an increasingly greater share in the future . . . what is essential in the coming period is coal production. (Ibid., 11 August.)

Since coal production has failed to meet recent targets and coal miners have been sporadically restive, Ceauşescu's positing of domestic coal production as the short-term solution to the goal of energy self-sufficiency by 1990 seems somewhat optimistic, if not unrealistic. In the meantime, the already pressed Romanian consumer is bearing the brunt of new conservation efforts — price hikes in gasoline, alternate weekends for private driving, rationing of electricity, and increased prices for domestic use of energy.

The low standard of living and poor working conditions fueled a short-lived dissident group, the Free Trade Union of Romanian Workers. Formed in February by twenty Romanians and initially headed by a Bucharest physician, Dr. Ionel Cana, the group claimed support in a number of working centers throughout the country. The group's charter (for the text, see *Free Trade Union News*, May) specified that the members would "fight for the respect of the rights of Romanian citizens," especially in the field of labor. It complained of de facto unemployment, forced retirements, excessive work norms, poor wages, and involuntary political activity.

The Ceauşescu regime moved quickly against the leaders of the dissident group. Reports reaching the West, especially France where a group of intellectuals had taken up the dissidents' cause, indicated that the leaders had been harassed, detained, or imprisoned. Although the movement appeared to dissipate within Romania, its imprisoned leaders generated continuing interest in the West and this, in turn, seemed to provoke sporadic Romanian blasts against reactionary "foreign circles." Ceauşescu's 7 September speech seemed to allude to this Western-backed human rights agitation in Romania:

> We must resolutely fight attempts by certain foreign circles to denigrate our country, to misinform public opinion about the true situation in Romania . . . We should not content ourselves with saying: enemies can say what they will, we know that we are right. It is not enough to know that we are right, we must also explain our viewpoint and make others grasp it too, including people abroad.

International Affairs. Romania's foreign policy in 1979 remained assertively independent, balancing the country's membership in Soviet-dominated organizations—the Warsaw Pact and Council for Mutual Economic Assistance (CMEA)—with active ties to China, the West, and the Third World. At the same time, Ceauşescu seemed particularly disturbed by international trends. In his speech to the Twelfth Congress, he pinpointed continuing conflicts between communist states, increasing underdevelopment, lack of progress in disarmament, and the energy crisis. He also reiterated one of his favorite foreign policy themes: the tendency to divide the world into spheres of influence and domination, which he specifically linked to the quest for hegemony.

China and Asia. The year was heralded by two crises in Southeast Asia: the invasion of Kampuchea (Cambodia) by Vietnam in January and the invasion of Vietnam by China in February. Romania, because of its close relations with China, condemned Vietnamese actions but expressed only concern over Chinese behavior. On the Kampuchean invasion, Romania asserted that it "greatly disapproves of the support granted to some elements that rose against the government of their own country, acting by means of military force, [this being] a heavy blow for the prestige of socialism" (*Scînteia*, 10 January). Although never so stated, Romania probably saw Soviet backing of Vietnam against Kampuchea as an ominous precedent for international communist relations that one day might manifest itself in the Balkans. Romania subsequently refused to recognize the Heng Samrin regime and continued to maintain contact with officials of the ousted Pol Pot government.

Bucharest's response to the Chinese invasion of Vietnam was more restrained. Agerpres (19 February) issued a statement saying that "public opinion in our country took notice of the declaration of the People's Republic of China as to starting wide-scale military actions, as also of the declaration of the Socialist Republic of Vietnam regarding the amplification of the armed confrontations at the Sino-Vietnamese frontier." Saying that "nothing can justify resorting to military actions," Romania called on both sides to negotiate (*Scînteia*, 20 February). Moscow complained that the Romanian statement "does not contain any condemnation of the Chinese aggression against Vietnam" (Moscow Domestic Service, 20 February).

As a result of Romania's stance on the Indochina crises, its relations with China remained on a steady, positive course. The major Chinese visitor was Foreign Minister Huang Hua, who stopped in Bucharest to brief Ceauşescu, following Chairman Hua's tour of Western Europe. Both sides pledged to combat "any form of domination and dictation" (ibid., 13 November). There was, in addition, an unceasing flow of Chinese delegations to Romania, including exchanges of military officers.

The Middle East. In keeping with its earlier approval of the Camp David accords, Romania gave low-key backing to the Egyptian-Israeli peace treaty. *Lumea*, the Romanian foreign affairs journal, called the treaty "a noteworthy event in the context of actions aimed at politically resolving the conflict in the Middle East" but went on to assert that a lasting peace had to be "global" in nature and thus needed the participation of "all interested parties, including the Palestinians represented by the Palestine Liberation Organization [PLO]" (22 March). Romania recommended the convening of a "Geneva-type" peace conference.

Toward this end, Ceaușescu contacted the major Middle East actors and offered them his services as a channel of communication. Thus, he visited Libya's Qadhafi (8–9 April), Egypt's Sadat (25 April), hosted former Israeli Prime Minister Rabin (7 August), visited Syria's Assad and PLO leader Arafat (13–17 August), and then received Arafat in Bucharest (25–26 August). Following Ceaușescu's second meeting with Arafat in nine days, both sides issued a communiqué that expressed "their complete satisfaction with the close ties of friendship and solidarity," called for the "total, unconditional, and immediate Israeli withdrawal" from occupied Arab territory, and "denounced" Israeli military action against Lebanon, as well as Israeli attempts to "annex" occupied territories (*Romania Libera*, 27 August).

Following these meetings, Ceaușescu sent his personal envoys to brief the major interested parties. Vasile Pungan delivered messages to Israeli Prime Minister Begin (31 August) and Egyptian President Sadat (11 September). Foreign Minister Andrei, en route to the nonaligned summit in Havana, stopped in Washington for a discussion with Secretary of State Cyrus Vance (31 August). And Deputy Foreign Minister Cornel Pacoste met his Soviet counterpart (4–5 September).

Supplementing Ceaușescu's renewed intermediary efforts in the Middle East crisis was an intense Romanian quest for new sources of Middle East oil to compensate for lagging domestic oil output and the temporary suspension of Iranian oil deliveries during the Iranian revolution. Iran had supplied a considerable part of Romania's oil imports. The need for new supplies may have contributed to the urgency with which Ceaușescu seemed to touch base with the Middle East states and the PLO. If Romania obtained additional crude oil supplies, it was not announced.

Other Third World Activity. Romania, which defines itself as a "European, socialist, developing" state, continued its association with the nonaligned movement as a "guest." Foreign Minister Andrei attended the 3–9 September nonaligned summit in Havana. Although a peripheral participant, Bucharest sided with Yugoslavia's efforts to prevent the success of Castro's move to have the non-aligned movement side with the pro-Soviet communist world as a "natural ally." The Romanian press declared that the major problem facing the movement was "the preservation of the initial orientation of nonalignment policy as an independent factor in international relations, above exterior influences and rivalries, above military blocs" (ibid., 29 August).

Ceaușescu, with his penchant for state visits, undertook a marathon tour of Africa (8–25 April), visiting Libya, Gabon, Angola, Zambia, Mozambique, Burundi, Sudan, and Egypt. He also met with the leaders of the major African black liberation movements. Seeking to boost Romania's ties to the continent, Ceaușescu signed friendship and cooperation treaties with six states and over thirty assorted economic cooperation agreements (*Scînteia*, 9–26 April). The treaties constituted general statements endorsing political independence and sovereignty and pledging more consultations and cooperation.

Western Europe and the United States. Interactions with the West continued in a generally positive vein, despite the pique caused by Western human rights critiques of the Romanian regime. The major European visitors to Bucharest were French President Valéry Giscard d'Estaing (8–10 March), Greek Prime Minister Constantine Caramanlis (18–20 March), and West German Foreign Minister Hans-Dietrich Genscher (11–12 October). Giscard endorsed Romania's independent foreign policy, and Ceauşescu agreed in principle to the French proposal for a conference on disarmament in Europe; Ceauşescu and Caramanlis discussed prospects for Balkan collaboration; and Genscher signed a document on reciprocal governmental guarantees for capital investments in the respective countries. Ceauşescu's major European foray was to Spain (21–24 May), where he became the first communist head of state to be received by King Carlos, an event that received great publicity in the Romanian media (*Lumea*, 24 and 31 May) but was negatively treated by the Spanish press, which found the Ceauşescus' personal demeanor objectionable.

Romania continued its negotiations with the European Economic Community (EEC) over the establishment of a mixed trade commission outside the purview of any EEC-CMEA understanding. Bucharest has also been active in promoting consultations before the 1980 Madrid conference on European security follow-up sessions, a forum Romania hopes can be used to achieve European security arrangements that would limit both NATO and Warsaw Pact activities, thereby constraining the Pact's ability to pressure Romania.

Relations with the United States remained rather active. Foreign Minister Andrei met twice in the United States with Secretary of State Vance; the latter, however, had to postpone his December trips to Romania and Yugoslavia because of the Iranian crisis. Secretary of Commerce Juanita Kreps led the U.S. delegation to the U.S.-Romanian Economic Commission's meeting in Bucharest in April. Numerous lower-level meetings also took place.

Soviet Union and Eastern Europe. Romanian-Soviet relations, which deteriorated markedly in 1978, appeared cool but more correct in 1979. Although Ceauşescu did not greet Soviet leader Brezhnev on 12 January during the latter's train stop in Romania en route to Bulgaria, both sides subsequently manifested a readiness to project a businesslike public attitude toward each other. At the same time, Romania did not retreat from its considerable foreign policy differences with Moscow.

The two major Romanian-Soviet political meetings—Foreign Minister Andrei's visit to the USSR, 29 January–2 February, and Ceauşescu's meeting with Brezhnev in the Crimea, 1 August—seemed geared to avoid a further widening of disagreements. Andrei's talks with Gromyko were described as "useful" and taking place in a "friendly, working atmosphere" (*Scînteia*, 4 February), while Ceauşescu's brief visit with Brezhnev was described as "frank and comradely" (ibid., 2 August). At the latter meeting, Brezhnev presented Ceauşescu with the Order of Lenin to commemorate the Romanian's 60th birthday, which had occurred in January 1978. The delay was no doubt caused by the tense state of bilateral relations in that year.

Except for certain aspects of European security issues, Romania continued to resist a host of Soviet foreign policy directives. This was particularly manifest at the 3–5 July meeting in East Berlin of communist party secretaries in charge of ideology and foreign policy from the Warsaw Pact states, Mongolia, Cuba, Vietnam, and Laos. The meeting issued a bland concluding "announcement" signed by all participants. A second document, signed by all but Romania, endorsed the various Soviet foreign policy priorities.

Romania did not send troops to the Warsaw Pact military maneuvers in Hungary, 12-19 May, and Ceauşescu was the only Warsaw Pact leader who did not join Brezhnev in East Berlin for the 6 October festivities marking East Germany's 30th anniversary. Romania did, however, endorse Brezhnev's announcement that Moscow would withdraw some Soviet troops and tanks from East Germany as part of the Soviet campaign to forestall NATO's medium-range nuclear force modernization plans (ibid., 9 October). But even here Bucharest felt compelled to put its own accent on the matter, claiming that Brezhnev's unilateralism confirmed the wisdom of Ceauşescu's repeated calls for unilateral European security initiatives, like Romania's stance against increased defense spending.

If for the most part Romania avoided widening its conflict with Moscow, such was not the case with its relations vis-à-vis Eastern Europe, which took a sudden negative turn. On 26 July Romania promulgated a decree, effective 1 August, stating that individual tourists motoring in Romania must purchase gasoline with hard currency or, if they were from Eastern states, with tickets issued under governmental agreements that such purchases would be covered "in free currency, in fuel or other goods, mutually agreed on" (Agerpres, 27 July). None of the CMEA states rushed to negotiate, with the result that after 1 August thousands of East European motorists found themselves barred from entry into Romania, while those already in the country were unable to leave since only hard currency could be used to purchase gasoline (*NYT*, 2 August; 5 August).

The East European states issued heated formal and informal protests. Said, for example, a Hungarian spokesman: "These measures came quite unexpectedly. They are unilateral measures which . . . are contrary to the highest level Hungarian-Romanian agreements and, beyond these, to bilateral agreements concerned with tourism between the two countries" (Budapest Domestic Service, 4 August).

Romania subsequently relented a bit by postponing implementation of the decree to 10 August and worked out some ad hoc arrangements with several of the East European states. But Romania steadfastly argued that since it had to pay for its oil imports in hard currency (not being a recipient of Soviet oil), the measures were justified in light of the international energy crisis.

Although the final resolution of the issue remained unclear at year's end, Romania's provocative move against its formal allies illustrated that it continued to place national interests above any wider grouping. Whether it could continue to act as boldly in the 1980s, given likely economic constraints at home and abroad, is a key question for Ceaușescu and the CPR.

Publications. *Scînteia* is the daily newspaper of the CPR, and *Era Socialista* is its theoretical journal. *Romania Libera* is the other major daily paper. *Lumea* is the weekly foreign affairs journal. *Revista Economica* is the major periodical devoted to economic policy. The two most important historical journals are *Anale de Istorie* and *Magazin Istoric.* Agerpres is the Romanian news agency.

Washington, D.C.   Robert L. Farlow

Union of Soviet Socialist Republics

The Communist Party of the Soviet Union (Kommunisticheskaia Partiia Sovetskogo Soiuza; CPSU) traces its origins to the founding of the Russian Social Democratic Labor Party in 1898. The party split into Bolshevik (claiming "majority") and Menshevik (alleged by the Bolsheviks to be the "minority") factions at the Second Congress held at Brussels and London in 1903. The Bolshevik faction led by Vladimir I. Lenin was actually a minority of the party membership after 1904. Unable to regain the policymaking dominance attained at the Second Congress, the Bolsheviks broke away from the Mensheviks in 1912 at the Prague Conference to form a separate party. In March 1919, after the seizure of power, this party was renamed the "All-Russian Communist Party (Bolsheviks)." When

"Union of Soviet Socialist Republics" was adopted as the name of the country in 1924, the party's designation was changed to "All-Union Communist Party (Bolsheviks)." The present name was adopted in 1952. The CPSU is the only legal political party in the USSR.

As of 1 May 1979, party membership approximated 16.5 million (*Rude pravo*, 1 May). The party has sought to stabilize membership growth under the present leadership, in contrast to the rapid growth that characterized the Khrushchev era. The 23rd Congress in 1966 adopted stricter rules concerning membership, and the goal of stabilization was furthered by an exchange of party cards carried out between 1973 and 1975. The 25th Congress in 1976 established even more stringent standards for individual admission and verification of progress among candidates. In the exchange of party cards, about 347,000 members were excluded, and between 1971 and 1976, more than 100,000 candidates were denied full membership cards. As a result of these measures, the trend in membership has been steadily downward. Between 1961 and 1966, the average annual increase in CPSU membership was 6.0 percent; between 1973 and 1976, only 1.96 percent. In 1976 and 1977, the average annual increase declined to 1.85 percent and in 1978 the increase was under 1.25 percent. Present party membership is about 9.2 percent of the adult population and approximately 6.3 percent of the total USSR population of 262 million (Tass, 21 April).

Some 70 percent of new candidate members are drawn from the ranks of the Komsomol. Over 4 million communists are women, representing slightly less than one-fourth of total membership. Only about 14 percent of the members are collective farmers, compared with the worker component of approximately 42 percent. The remainder of the membership is composed of professional people, white-collar employees, and military personnel. The most recent data on educational levels show that 24.3 percent of party members have higher and 41 percent have incomplete higher or secondary educations. Great Russians continue to be disproportionately represented in party ranks, accounting for about 60 percent of the members. Ukrainians constitute approximately 16 percent, Belorussians more than 3.5 percent, and other nationalities about 20 percent of party membership.

Organization and Leadership. The CPSU's structure parallels the administrative organization of the Soviet state. There are approximately 390,000 primary party organizations. Above this lowest level are 2,857 rural *raion* committees, 815 city committees, 10 *okrug* ("area") committees, 149 *oblast'* ("district") committees, 6 *krai* ("territorial") committees, and 14 union-republic committees. There is no separate organization for the Russian republic (RSFSR), the largest constituent unit of the country. At the top, the All-Union Congress is, according to party rules, the supreme policymaking body. The Congress elects the Central Committee and the Central Auditing Commission. The 24th Congress, in 1971, set the maximum interval between congresses at five years. In the interim, the highest representative organ is the Central Committee. Actually power is concentrated in the Politburo, the Secretariat, and the 22 departments of the Central Committee, including the newly created Correspondence Department.

Two plenums of the Central Committee were held in 1979. The first, in April, devoted special attention to matters of party work and ideological training (see below). Two organizational changes were announced. Yakov P. Ryabov was relieved of duties as Central Committee secretary for the defense industry following appointment as first deputy chairman of the USSR State Planning Commission (Gosplan). Leonid Borodin, first secretary of the Astrakhan *oblast'* party committee, was promoted from alternate to full member of the Central Committee (ibid., 17 April). Borodin's election brings to 270 the number of active full members of the Central Committee. A total of 26 of the 287 full members elected at the 25th Congress have died or retired, and Borodin is the ninth new member elected since 1976 (Radio Liberty, 23 March; *Pravda*, 18 April).

The second plenum of the year was held in late November. It was devoted mainly to economic questions. Two major organizational changes were announced. Nikolai S. Tikhonov, 74, first deputy prime minister, was promoted from candidate to full member of the Politburo. Mikhail S. Gorbachev,

48, Central Committee secretary for agriculture, was named a candidate member of the Politburo. (*Pravda*, 28 November.)

Elections for the Supreme Soviet, the first under the new constitution, were held on 4 March. Election procedures and results, controlled by the CPSU, were essentially the same as under the old constitution. Approximately three-fourths of the 1,500 members of the two houses of the Supreme Soviet are members of the CPSU, and all deputies are officially designated by the party. Attempts were made to nominate nonofficial candidates in two districts, in Moscow (Roy A. Medvedev was the proposed candidate) and in the Lithuanian capital of Vilnius (*CSM*, 2 March). In both cases, authorities ruled that the endorsing groups lacked the required status of "public organizations." Composition of the new Supreme Soviet is similar to that of the previous one. One-third of the deputies are workers, one-fifth collective farmers, and the remainder "intelligentsia." One-third are women, one-fifth under 30 years of age, and half are new members. (*Pravda*, 2 March.) The new Supreme Soviet held its first session in Moscow, 18–20 April. Principal officers of the Supreme Soviet were reconfirmed in their posts and the USSR Council of Ministers re-elected, with no changes in personnel (Tass, 19 April).

The current Politburo is as follows:

Members:	Other Positions:
Brezhnev, Leonid I.	General Secretary, CPSU Central Committee; Chairman, Presidium of the USSR Supreme Soviet
Kosygin, Aleksei N.	Chairman, USSR Council of Ministers
Suslov, Mikhail A.	Secretary, CPSU Central Committee
Kirilenko, Andrei P.	Secretary, CPSU Central Committee
Pelshe, Arvid I.	Chairman, Party Control Commission
Chernenko, Konstantin U.	Secretary, CPSU Central Committee
Grishin, Viktor V.	First Secretary, Moscow City Party Committee
Kunaev, Dinmukhamed A.	First Secretary, Kazakh Central Committee
Shcherbitsky, Vladimir V.	First Secretary, Ukrainian Central Committee
Andropov, Yuri V.	Chairman, Committee of State Security (KGB)
Gromyko, Andrei A.	Minister of Foreign Affairs
Romanov, Grigori V.	First Secretary, Leningrad *Oblast'* Party Committee
Ustinov, Dimitri F.	Minister of Defense
Tikhonov, Nikolai S.	First Deputy Chairman, USSR Council of Ministers

Candidate Members:

Demichev, Piotr N.	Minister of Culture
Rashidov, Sharaf R.	First Secretary, Uzbek Central Committee
Masherov, Piotr M.	First Secretary, Belorussian Central Committee
Solomentsev, Mikhail S.	Chairman, RSFSR Council of Ministers
Ponomarev, Boris N.	Secretary, CPSU Central Committee
Aliev, Geidar A.	First Secretary, Azerbaidjan Central Committee
Kuznetsov, Vasily V.	First Deputy Chairman, Presidium of the USSR Supreme Soviet
Shevardnadze, Eduard A.	First Secretary, Georgian Central Committee
Gorbachev, Mikhail S.	Secretary, CPSU Central Committee

The present Central Committee Secretariat is composed of ten men. Their names and reported functions are: Brezhnev (general secretary), Kirilenko (organizational affairs), Suslov (ideology), Chernenko (Politburo staff work), Ponomarev (nonruling communist parties), Vladimir I. Dolgikh (heavy industry), Mikhail S. Gorbachev (agriculture), Ivan V. Kapitonov (cadres), Konstantin V. Rusakov (ruling communist parties), and Mikhail V. Zimianin (culture).

The ethnic composition of the Politburo and Secretariat reflects the domination of the CPSU by Great Russians, which apparently has intensified in recent years. Ten of the fourteen full members and two of the nine candidate members of the Politburo are listed in Soviet sources as ethnic Russians. Nine of the ten members of the Secretariat are listed as ethnic Russians. Zimianin is Belorussian. Chernenko, who hails from Siberia, is listed as Russian but has a Ukrainian name.

Republic first secretaries are Karen S. Demichyan (Armenia), Geidar A. Aliev (Azerbaijan), Piotr M. Masherov (Belorussia), Karl Vaino (Estonia), Eduard A. Shevardnadze (Georgia), Dinmukhamed A. Kunaev (Kazakhstan), Turdakun V. Usbaliev (Kirgizia), August E. Voss (Latvia), Piatras P. Griskiavicus (Lithuania), Ivan I. Bodiul (Moldavia), Dzhabar R. Rasulov (Tadzhikistan), Mukhamednazar G. Gapurov (Turkmenia), Vladimir V. Shcherbitsky (Ukraine), and Sharaf R. Rashidov (Uzbekistan).

Auxiliary and Mass Organizations. The most important of the many "voluntary" organizations allied with the CPSU is the Communist Youth League (Kommunisticheskii Soyuz Molodezhi; Komsomol), headed by 46-year-old First Secretary Boris N. Pastukhov. The Komsomol has over 38 million members.

Other large mass organizations include the All-Union Central Council of Trade Unions, headed by Aleksei I. Shabaev, with more than 107 million members; the Voluntary Society for Promotion of the Army, Air Force, and Navy, whose members seek to "instill patriotism and pride" in the armed forces; the Union of Soviet Societies for Friendship and Cultural Relations with Foreign Countries; and the Soviet Committee of Women.

Party Internal Affairs. The aging of the leadership continued to pose a problem for the image and organizational effectiveness of the CPSU, particularly the gradually declining but changeable physical condition of Brezhnev. Although the issue of Brezhnev's health was downplayed by Soviet spokesmen, efforts were made to relieve him of less important duties. The leadership continued to apply stopgap remedies to meet the obvious practical difficulties involved in directing the Soviet system with top officials hampered by age and infirmity. Although Brezhnev had established an unprecedented ascendancy at the Central Committee plenum of November 1978, there were indications during 1979 of intense infighting among key political figures as the succession to Brezhnev approached more closely. Meanwhile the party sought to upgrade cadre selection and performance and launched another campaign to improve ideological indoctrination. In the wake of this campaign, several union-republic secretaries for ideology were dismissed. Trouble spots continued to plague the party, and party and government positions at various levels, particularly in Georgia, which has been a chronic problem area for the party throughout the 1970s, were reshuffled.

The Leadership. Brezhnev's physical condition produced serious doubts about his ability to remain long in office and appeared to create some problems for the efficient dispatch of party and government business. He is reportedly suffering from cerebral arteriosclerosis and other diseases; in early 1979, there were indications of limited attention span, speech difficulty, and senility. In early spring, Brezhnev became seriously ill with a lung inflammation. Reports circulated in Moscow that a contingency plan had been drawn up in case the illness proved fatal or totally disabling, with Andropov slated for party leader, Ustinov for prime minister, and Kosygin for president (*Newsweek*, 25 June). Brezhnev recovered, but his general condition continued to pose political problems for the leadership.

While recovering from the lung infection, Brezhnev appeared enfeebled and disoriented at a Kremlin banquet in honor of French President Valéry Giscard d'Estaing. In April Brezhnev missed a meeting with a visiting group of U.S. congressmen and important sessions of the new Supreme Soviet. As titular president (chairman), Brezhnev should have presided over the opening session of the Supreme Soviet Presidium and the joint meeting of the Councils of Elders from the two chambers; Deputy Chairman Kuznetsov substituted as presiding officer at both conclaves. The Soviet leader also absented himself from the opening session of the Council of the Union on 18 April and the Lenin anniversary ceremonies two days later. (*Pravda*, 18, 19, and 21 April.) However, he reportedly attended a match of the world ice hockey championship (*NYT*, 23 April).

Brezhnev played a rather vigorous role as host to Yugoslavia's President Tito in May, and in mid-June he was able to meet the physical demands of the Vienna summit conference. There were indications, however, that he was relying increasingly on subordinates to perform many of his party and government duties. Suslov apparently took over as chief spokesman at the Central Committee and Supreme Soviet sessions during April (Radio Liberty, 2 May). At Vienna, Brezhnev leaned heavily on Gromyko, Chernenko, and Ustinov. Unwilling to confront the uncertainties of succession, the top Soviet leaders were seemingly mapping out an aloof leadership role for Brezhnev similar to that of Mao in his later years, with other officials carrying out the ordinary duties. Whether Brezhnev would be able to maintain even such a limited role was doubtful. After early summer, Brezhnev was not seen in public for two months (*NYT*, 24 August).

Amid mounting uncertainty about Brezhnev's tenure, there were indications of possible discord among his potential successors. A photograph of the principal CPSU leaders reviewing the May Day Parade in Red Square appeared in a Moscow evening newspaper, with Kirilenko missing (*Vechernyaya Moskva*, 1 May). The obviously doctored photograph was replaced the following morning with an accurate one showing Kirilenko next to Suslov (*Pravda*, 2 May). The evening newspaper involved in the incident is under the jurisdiction of Moscow party chief Grishin, but it seemed unlikely that he could have safely challenged Kirilenko without support from other members of the hierarchy. The Moscow first secretary has not appeared particularly secure in his position; in press reporting of Supreme Soviet campaign speeches, Grishin was accorded less coverage than any other Politburo member. Kirilenko, who had been given equal press attention with Suslov in the 1974 campaign, clearly ranked behind Suslov in 1979, while newcomer Chernenko was remarkably accorded a position right behind Kirilenko, outranking seven more senior Politburo members. (Radio Liberty, 12 March.)

A protégé of Kirilenko was involved in an important change of position in early 1979. Yakov P. Ryabov, Central Committee secretary for the defense industry since 1976, was appointed first deputy chairman of the State Planning Commission (Gosplan), succeeding Viktor D. Lebedev, who had died on 3 December 1978. The official decree on the appointment stressed that it was "in connection with the necessity of further strengthening the USSR Gosplan" (*Sobranie Postanovlenii Pravitel'stva SSSR*, no. 7, 1979). The decree listed Ryabov as a party secretary, but the subsequent session of the Central Committee relieved him of that post (*Pravda*, 18 April). The change in position amounted to a formal demotion, but there were indications that his transfer actually reflected a rise in status. Given the severe criticism aimed at Gosplan by Brezhnev at the Central Committee plenums during 1978, it was obvious that the party leader had given highest priority to upgrading the work of Gosplan and strengthening party influence in the planning agency. A close associate of Ryabov, N. L. Ryshkov, was also appointed a first deputy chairman of Gosplan (*CSM*, 17 April).

Organizational Matters. Regular *krai* and *oblast'* party conferences in December 1978 and January 1979 produced no major changes in personnel. However, a number of important appointments occurred before these conferences, and some governmental posts were reshuffled at the union-republic level during the first quarter of 1979. Some of the appointees simply filled existing vacancies; in other cases, the appointments coincided with expressions of dissatisfaction concerning the work of previous holders of the positions. In general, the tendency toward appointment of somewhat younger cadres was marked (Radio Liberty, 5 March). When these changes are considered in conjunction with the personnel reshuffle at the November 1978 Central Committee plenum, it is obvious that the party has finally been forced to confront in some measure the problem of generational turnover.

Vsevolod S. Murakhovsky, 52, former head of the Karachaevo-Cherkess party organization, was named first secretary of the Stavropol *krai* party committee, replacing Mikhail S. Gorbachev following the latter's promotion to Central Committee secretary for agriculture. Murakhovsky's former post was filled by Aleksei A. Izhievsky, previously first secretary of Stavropol *gorkom*. New first secretaries were appointed in Kalinin (Pavel A. Lenonov, 60), Novosibirsk (Aleksandr P. Filatov, 56), and Kalmyk *oblast's* (V. L. Nikulin, 50). All three replaced retirees. In Magadan, Sergei A. Shaidurov was dismissed as first secretary "for unsatisfactory work in the management of the *oblast*'s party organization" and replaced by Nikolai I. Mal'kov. (*Pravda*, 5, 17, 20, 24, and 27 December 1978.)

Vladimir I. Brovikov, 47, deputy chief of the CPSU Central Committee's Organizational Party Work Department since 1973, became second secretary of the Belorussian Central Committee, succeeding Aleksandr N. Aksenov, 54 (*Sovetskaya Belorussia*, 28 December 1978). Aksenov had been appointed Belorussia's prime minister, replacing Tikhon Y. Kiselev, 61, shifted to Moscow as a deputy chairman of the USSR Council of Ministers.

In Kirgizia, the secretary for industry, Absamat G. Masaliev, was transferred to the post of first secretary of the Issyk-Kul' *oblast'* (*Sovetskaya Kirgiziya*, 13 January).

A significant change in the Ukraine involved the dismissal of Andrei S. Sushchenko as chairman of the party's Auditing Commission and as second secretary of the Kiev *oblast'* party committee (*Pravda Ukrainy*, 13 and 23 December 1978). Party chief Shcherbitsky has been sharply critical of organizational work in Kiev during recent years; this criticism, directed against the Kiev *gorkom* and its first secretary, Aleksandr P. Botvin, continued in 1979 (ibid., 19 May). Nevertheless, Botvin retained his membership in the Ukrainian Politburo and the CPSU Central Committee, and occasional favorable references to the Kiev *gorkom* organization appeared in the national party press. There are some indications that Shcherbitsky is not as secure either in Kiev or in Moscow as Western observers assume; notably, he ranked next to last among full Politburo members in the extent and precedence of press coverage during the Supreme Soviet election campaign (Radio Liberty, 12 March). A further development that may affect Shcherbitsky came in April when Valentin E. Malanchuk, Ukrainian party secretary for ideology since 1972, was dismissed from his post (*Radyans'ka Ukraina*, 27 April). The Ukraine was one of three union-republics that replaced party secretaries for ideology, as the CPSU launched a new campaign for improvement of ideological work.

Georgia experienced an extensive reshuffle in government posts during January. Earlier, Viktoriya M. Siradze had been dismissed as secretary for ideology and replaced by Guram N. Enukidze, former chairman of the Georgian SSR State Committee for Television and Radio Broadcasting (*Zarya vostoka*, 20 and 22 December 1978). Siradze became deputy head of the Georgian SSR Supreme Soviet Presidium.

The ideological secretary in Tadzhikistan was also demoted. Ibodat R. Rakhimova, 56, who had held the position since 1966, was shifted to secretary of the Tadzhik SSR Supreme Soviet Presidium and also lost her seat on the Tadzhik party's governing Buro. She was replaced by Guldzhikhon B. Bobosadykova, 41, formerly party first secretary in Dushanbe. The latter position was filled by Yuldash A. Shakirimov. (*Kommunist Tadzhikistana*, 14, 15, and 22 December 1978.)

The selection, placement, and education of cadres received major attention at party conferences preceding the Supreme Soviet elections. They were also the subject of a major *Pravda* editorial on 30 January: "Cadre policy is a powerful lever by which our party actively influences the course of social development." The editorial singled out Kokchetavskaya *oblast'* for "poorly trained people with no initiative" and for many cases of "breaches of party and state discipline and abuse of office" and praised the Moscow and Kiev city committees and the Leningrad, Sverdlovsk, and Gorkovskaya *oblast'* organizations for "particularly valuable work."

Ideology and Propaganda. Another major theme of the pre-election party conferences, which was stressed in campaign speeches by full and alternate Politburo members holding field commands, was the need to improve the party's ideological work. Following the elections, a Central Committee resolution signaled the opening of another broad offensive on the ideology/propaganda front. Both Western and Soviet observers have noted indifference toward ideological questions among the masses in recent years; the resolution's frank and direct confrontation of the problem represented a new departure. The Central Committee attacked "trite" and "formalistic" propaganda work and presented a detailed program for improvement in ideological education, stressing the roles of the media and party lecturers. The resolution noted two major deficiencies in ideological education work: the failure to take sufficient account of "the increased educational and cultural standards and requirements of Soviet people" and the "dynamic nature of socioeconomic processes and the spiritual life of contemporary Soviet society"; and the lack of consideration for the "nature of the sharply aggravated ideological struggle in the international arena." (*Pravda*, 6 May.)

At the outset of the campaign, correction of the first of these deficiencies was accorded priority. But the unrestrained rhetoric of the media and party leaders soon made it clear that "ideological struggle" was paramount and that the offensive was a manifestation of an intensified hard-line approach to "alien ideologies." An editorial called for "raising the attacking spirit of propaganda" and spoke of "the organic link" between propaganda and "the living practice of communist construction in the USSR and the development of the world revolutionary process" (ibid., 14 May). An editorial in the principal army newspaper viewed the strengthening of ideological work as essential for raising the "combat readiness" of USSR armed forces (*Krasnaya zvezda*, 13 May).

Moscow party chief Grishin, in a speech to the Moscow Writers' Organization, charged that some members had failed to expose "bourgeois and revisionist ideology" and "manifestations of views and morals alien to us." Grishin called for "the further strengthening of the patriotic and international education of Muscovites" and warned Moscow residents against succumbing to ideological contamination from the thousands of foreign visitors expected during the 1980 Olympics. (*Moskovskaya pravda*, 8 May.)

At the close of the academic year, another editorial on the ideological campaign called for educational work that would avoid "formalism" and a "superficial approach." Ideological training should emphasize "proletarian internationalism," "love for the socialist fatherland," and opposition to "manifestations of alien ideology." (*Pravda*, 28 May.)

Ukrainian First Secretary Shcherbitsky delivered several major speeches on the themes of the campaign, stressing the struggle against "alien ideologies." At Dnepropetrovsk he warned against "anticommunist propaganda" purveyed by a "network of state establishments and various anti-Soviet centers, including nationalist and Zionist ones." Shcherbitsky charged that "organizers of ideological subversion are stepping up their efforts to implant in the consciousness of students political indifference, individualism, petty proprietary and consumer psychology, and various technocratic views, in a word, to disarm the younger generation ideologically." At the celebration of the 325th anniversary of the Ukraine's reunification with Russia, Shcherbitsky acknowledged "shortcomings" and the need for reform in ideological work. He called for efforts to "increase the political vigilance of our people and to rebuff bourgeois ideology and the intrigues of imperialist propaganda, particularly of nationalist and Zionist centers abroad." (*Pravda Ukrainy*, 17 and 19 May.)

Reflecting the party's concern with the persistence of religous belief and practice, Shcherbitsky called for intensification of atheist propaganda in a speech in Kiev to party activists. He charged that legislation concerning cults has sometimes been violated and urged that more attention be given to Soviet secular ceremonies. (Ibid., 8 June.) The importance of atheist propaganda was also emphasized in an editorial of the Georgian party's principal newspaper, which stressed the usefulness of sociological research in determining the "state of the population's religiosity" and the effectiveness of atheist propaganda (*Zarya vostoka*, 17 April).

The continuing need to seal off Soviet borders and protect the country against external influences was emphasized by Maj. Gen. Ivan P. Polezhayev, first deputy chief of political administration of Border Guard Troops, who charged that "foreign centers of psychological warfare" were "using the expansion of economic and cultural links with our country" and "the development of international tourism" to smuggle anticommunist and anti-Soviet literature into the USSR (Moscow Domestic Service, 26 May; *FBIS*, 29 May).

Domestic Affairs. The most important concern during 1979 was the economy. The party was confronted with serious shortcomings in the mechanism of plan fulfillment and the first manifestations of an approaching energy shortage. Despite a highly successful 1978 on the farm, the underlying problems in agriculture remained as intractable as ever. Sluggish performance in production inspired no initiatives for fundamental reform of the economy, however. Policy remained essentially unchanged in another major area of concern, that of dissent. The general policy of repression continued, but there was a striking upsurge in Jewish emigration.

Economy. Complete figures on 1978 production, released in January, showed somewhat less favorable results in both industry and agriculture than had been indicated by the November preliminary report. The earlier report of a record grain harvest of 235 million tons in 1978 was confirmed, i.e., 53.4 million tons more than the 1971–1975 annual average. However, the meat and dairy industries fell 3 percent short of targets.

Overall industrial production rose by 4.8 percent, about 0.2 percent less than the November estimate but still in excess of the planned 4.5 percent. Productivity increases were disappointing and barely surpassed the percentage increase in the number of workers and employees. The construction industry continued to be a major problem area, and productivity rose only 2.2 percent (*Pravda* and *Izvestiia*, 20 January).

The chronic shortcomings in construction were underscored by a joint resolution of the CPSU Central Committee and the USSR Council of Ministers, "On Measures to Further Improve Training of

Skilled Cadres and Establish Them in Construction." The resolution instructed party and government agencies to give highest priority to improving the quality of construction and to set goals for improving vocational training for construction workers and stimulating productivity by emphasizing "progressive forms of remuneration" (*Pravda*, 13 February).

Continuing the drive to upgrade performance in the service sector of the economy, the government announced a wage increase for 18 million workers in the "nonproductive branches" (Tass, 12 January; *FBIS*, 16 January).

Growing concern with energy matters was reflected in a number of official pronouncements during the year. A joint party-government resolution set goals for electric power consumption of 170 to 180 billion kilowatt-hours in 1985. The government plans to increase electricity available for agricultural production by 160 to 180 percent and rural per capita consumption for utilities and consumer needs by 180 to 200 percent between 1981 and 1985 (*Pravda*, 16 February). Another party-government decree established plans for construction of a new fuel-energy complex at Kansk-Achinsk in Siberia (Moscow Domestic Service, 5 April; *FBIS*, 7 April). According to another report, by 1980 atomic power stations will account for approximately one-tenth of all electricity generated in the European part of the USSR (Tass, 10 April).

Although long-range Soviet projections on energy availability are generally optimistic, spokesmen have expressed concern about the possibility of energy shortages in the 1980s and an awareness of the difficulties in meeting short-run production targets. A report by geologist I. Khvedchuk pointed to inadequate progress in Soviet offshore oil and gas extraction (*Pravda*, 3 April). In a later broadcast, Viktor A. Ryabov, head of the All-Union Petroleum Industry Association, explained the difficulties involved in attaining an additional 3.2 million tons of fuel oil between July and December 1979. He also revealed that goals for energy conservation were not being met in all sectors of the economy. (Moscow Domestic Service, 17 June; *FBIS*, 18 June.)

Improvements in any economic sector were scant during the first half of 1979. In the first quarter, average wages rose 2.3 percent compared with the same period of 1978 (Tass, 24 April), but industrial production grew only 3 percent against the planned 5.6 percent (Moscow Domestic Service, 17 May; *FBIS*, 21 May). Marketing output for the quarter was only 99.7 percent of the planned figure (Moscow Domestic Service, 24 April; *FBIS*, 27 April). Continuing slow growth in the construction industry also was reported (Moscow Domestic Service, 7 May; *FBIS*, 8 May). Shortfalls for the first five months of the year were reported in several industries, including ferrous metallurgy, chemicals, and timber procurement and wood processing. Overall production output increased by only 3.6 percent in May, still far short of planned goals (*Pravda*, 12 June). In November, Gosplan chief Nikolai K. Baibakov acknowledged shortfalls in production plans for coal, oil, and steel and announced lower growth rates in 1980 for consumer goods, heavy industry, and food supplies (*NYT*, 28 November).

Failure to meet production targets has often been covered by downward revision of annual plans. a practice banned by a Central Committee decree. From 1980 onward, the five-year plan is to be the basic tool of economic policy, rather than the yearly plan. According to the decree, factory performance is to be gauged by specific items produced and not by total value of output; supposedly this will increase production of scarce consumer goods. Further, the problem of construction delays is to be met by rewarding construction enterprises for completed projects, rather than merely for projects started (*Pravda* and *Ivestiia*, 28 July). The new approach points toward greater centralization of the economy, with increased sanctions available to Gosplan (*NYT*, 16 August). Following Brezhnev's sharp criticism of Gosplan at the November 1978 Central Committee plenum and appointment in April of Yakov P. Ryabov as deputy head of Gosplan, the July decree provided further evidence of party leaders' determination to secure greater control over and to revitalize economic administration. But the action involved no fundamental reform and decreased flexibility in the consumer sector. The goal of sharply accelerated productivity seemed likely to remain elusive.

Prospects in the agricultural sector were no brighter. The USSR appeared certain to fall far short of its record 1978 grain harvest, necessitating substantial increases in imports from the United States. Bad weather was identified as the major reason for the reversal. An official report in May lamented that "the late spring has created unprecedented difficulties for farm workers" (Moscow Domestic Service, 6 May; *FBIS*, 8 May). Shortcomings in the supply of spare parts for tractors were noted as a special problem for the 1979 harvest (*Izvestiia*, 29 May). In November Brezhnev reported to the Central Committee a harvest of 179 metric tons, the lowest since the crop of 140 million tons in 1975 (*NYT*, 28 November).

Agricultural development of the non–black earth zone, a pet project of Brezhnev, has been a top priority goal of the Ninth Five-Year Plan. Nevertheless, serious problems have appeared in construction, road building, land improvement, and establishment of livestock farms (*Stroitel'naya gazeta*, 18 May). Most importantly, unsatisfactory living and working conditions have made it difficult to recruit and retain workers for the new farm projects (Radio Liberty, 7 June). A joint party-government decree laid out measures to correct this problem. The decree guaranteed year-round employment for workers, raised wages to the levels of virgin lands state farms, and established wage supplements for senior workers and strict standards for housing and other construction (Tass, 6 June).

Dissent. Jewish emigration from the USSR reched record levels in 1979. It was expected that the number of emigrants for the year might total more than 50,000 (*NYT*, 5 May). Some observers attributed the upsurge to Soviet efforts to win most-favored-nation trade status with the United States and to promote a favorable climate for adoption of SALT II. Dissidents attributed the rise to an increase in applications, triggered by a rash of official publications and speeches denouncing Zionism and growing discrimination against Jews in universities.

The upsurge in Jewish emigration certainly foreshadowed no general liberalization in Soviet policies toward dissent. Prominent dissidents, whatever their religion or nationality, continued to be denied exit visas, and various forms of harassment were still employed against civil-rights activists (ibid., 30 April). The desire to emigrate has spread to other minorities, and although emigration of Jews may serve regime purposes both at home and abroad, the authorities have made it clear that general freedom of emigration will not be permitted, regardless of the 1975 Helsinki agreement.

Five dissidents were released in exchange for two Soviet officials at the United Nations, Valdek Enger and Rudolf Chernyayev, who had been convicted of espionage in the United States (ibid., 28 April). Most prominent among those freed was Aleksandr Ginzburg, who had administered a fund for persecuted dissidents set up by Aleksandr Solzhenitsyn. The others were Valentine Moroz, longtime activist in the Ukrainian nationalist movement; Georgi Vins, leader of a reform Baptist group; and two participants in the 1970 Leningrad airplane-hijacking escape attempt, Eduard Kuznetsov and Mark Dymshits. At the same time, five other participants in the thwarted highjacking attempt by Jewish activists were released. Ginzburg, Vins, and Moroz were greeted in New York by a parade of 100,000 people on Fifth Avenue, led by Sen. Daniel Patrick Moynihan (ibid., 30 April). All of those freed (except Ginzburg) had served most of their sentences; so the USSR's concession was negligible.

Andrei Sakharov, leader of the human rights movement, seized the opportunity afforded by the exchange to renew his call for an amnesty for all Soviet political prisoners. A statement released by Sakharov and his wife, Elena Bonner, identified fifteen other imprisoned human rights activists, including Yuri Orlov and Anatoly Shcharansky, as victims whose freedom was demanded (*WP*, 29 April).

The latest Sakharov appeal had no more effect upon USSR authorities than his previous efforts. A letter received by Shcharansky's wife from one of his fellow prisoners reported her husband to be seriously ill in Chistobol prison (ibid., 11 May). The underground press reported that the property of Shcharansky's parents had been confiscated and that his father, who also is in poor health, had been denied an opportunity to see his son (*Arkhiv samizdata*, no. 3,366, 10 May). After a visit to the prison, Shcharansky's mother confirmed that he was in bad condition and charged that he was not being given adequate medical care (*NYT*, 9 August). The wife of Georgi Vins told a Western reporter that she and her family were being kept under virtual house arrest in Kiev, although the U.S.-Soviet exchange agreement had specified that the families of freed prisoners would be allowed to emigrate to the United States (*WP*, 3 May).

Meanwhile, the regime continued to apply repressive measures against dissidents but with less publicity than in previous years. Having imprisoned or exiled most of the leading dissident figures, particularly activists in the democratic movement, the police apparatus concentrated during 1979 on less well known dissidents, especially those active with religion, nationalities, labor, and literature.

Sakharov reported that a 50-year-old Orthodox nun, Valeria Makiyeva, had been sentenced indefinitely to a psychiatric hospital for making and selling belts embroidered with words from the 90th Psalm (*NYT*, 14 April). The *samizdat* press revealed that members of dissident priest Dimitri Dudko's congregation in the village of Grebnevo had been detained and beaten and that the priest himself had been the victim of an "armed attack by people dressed in police uniforms" (*Russkaya mysl*, 8 March). In Tashkent five members of the Seventh-Day Adventists were sentenced to prison for anti-Soviet activity. Prosecution of the Adventists was defended in a lengthy article (*Izvestiia*, 13 May).

Ukrainian human rights activist Vasyl Ovsiyenko was sentenced to three years in a strict-regime camp for "resisting police" (*WP*, 12 February). Andrei Sakharov claimed that he had evidence that Ovsiyenko had not resisted the police but was being persecuted for his ties with the Helsinki group and political prisoners (Radio Liberty, 13 March). The KGB searched fourteen homes of people in the Ukraine, Leningrad, and Moscow linked to the Helsinki monitoring group. The searches in the Ukraine were reportedly aimed at prosecution of Oles Berdnik, a founder of that group. One of the search victims in Kiev, historian Mikhail Melnik, reportedly committed suicide following the KGB raid (Reuters, 12 March).

Mustafa Dzhemilev, a former labor camp prisoner and a leader of the campaign to allow Crimean Tatars exiled to Central Asia after World War II to return to their homes, renounced his Soviet citizenship and applied for permission to emigrate to the United States (*NYT*, 8 February).

Officers of the KGB filmed American correspondents who were leaving a news conference held by Jewish dissidents. Most of those present at the meeting in a Moscow apartment had been denied permission to emigrate. Soviet authorities reportedly had prevented other dissidents from coming to the gathering from Leningrad, Vilnius, Kiev, and Kharkov (ibid., 11 March).

Persecution of workers active in attempts to organize an independent labor movement continued during 1979. Responding to complaints filed with the International Labor Organization, a Soviet official reported that Vladimir A. Klebanov, founder of the dissident labor union, had required psychiatric treatment due to head injuries suffered while working in a mine. According to the statement, this union was a "foreign-inspired group of malcontents being used for political purposes." (Ibid., 1 March.) Dissident sources in Moscow revealed that Vladimir Skvirsky, a founder of the "Free Interprofessional Association of Workers" organized in October 1978, had been sentenced to five years of internal exile on the charge of stealing library books (Associated Press, 17 May). Leo Volokhonsky, one of the founders of the Klebanov group, received a two year labor camp sentence from a Leningrad court (*L'Unità*, 13 June).

Attempts to establish independent literary outlets were defeated by Soviet authorities during the year. Several prominent literary personalities organized a new, unofficial, and largely apolitical magazine called *Metropol*. The most prominent of the magazine's five editors was Vassily Aksyonov; the 23 contributors to the first issue included Andrei Voznesensky and Bella Akhmadulina (*WP*, 24 January). The Writers' Union refused to approve publication, but several copies were circulated, both in the Soviet Union and abroad. Following the union's rejection, the authors appealed to Brezhnev to prevent reprisals (*NYT*, 28 January). The Writers' Union called in and reprimanded the editors and subsequently expelled two of the authors, Yevgeny Popov and Viktor Yerofeyev (*Le Monde*, 27 June).

Five issues of the unauthorized journal *Searches* were published before authorities could suppress publication. It included articles defending the Russian Orthodox Church, private property, and Eurocommunism. Two of the editors, Raissa Borisovna Lert and Pyotr M. Yegides, identified themselves as Eurocommunists. Police searched the apartment of one of the editors and initiated a criminal investigation (*NYT*, 28 February).

In a Supreme Soviet election campaign speech, Yuri V. Andropov, head of the KGB, reaffirmed the hard-line stand against dissidents. He asserted that prosecution of dissidents was democratic and had the full approval of the Soviet people. Andropov noted that dissidents were depicted in the West as defending human rights. "But," said the KGB chief, "Soviet police have never given and will never give anyone the right to act to the detriment of socialism, for whose triumph they gave up so many lives and put in so much work." (Tass, 22 February.)

Despite wide-ranging police repression, dissident activity continued. Activists in the Moscow group monitoring observance of the Helsinki accords issued a public statement defending their persecuted colleagues in Czechoslovakia (*NYT*, 31 July).

Dissidents won a moral victory when Andrei Sakharov was able to participate in an unprecedented rebuff to a high party leader well known for his support of repressive policies. As a member of the Academy of Sciences, Sakharov took part in the debate and vote on the proposed admission of Sergei P. Trapezhnikov. The academy is the only Soviet institution that has retained the secret ballot which made possible the defeat of Trapezhnikov's nomination by a vote of 212 to 137 (*CSM*, 27 March). Trapezhnikov has been a full member of the Central Committee since 1965, chairman of the Science Commission of the Supreme Soviet since 1966, and head of the Central Committee's Department of Science and Educational Institutions throughout the Brezhnev era. A close associate of the latter since the general secretary led the party in Moldavia, Trapezhnikov is generally considered the most outspokenly pro-Stalinist and reactionary figure in the Soviet hierarchy.

Ecology. Environmental concerns are usually given low priority in the USSR, and official spokesmen rather consistently and enthusiastically support the development of atomic power. A major article in the party's theoretical journal by two energy specialists may signal a more cautious approach to such problems. Nikolai A. Dollezhal, chief of the Energy Production Department of the Academy of Sciences, and economist Yuri Koryakin warned that unless the atomic energy program is radically altered, the more densely populated areas of European Russia may soon reach the limits of their "ecological capacity" to cope with new nuclear power stations. The authors emphasized three special problems in the program: technical reliability and safety; increased danger of accidents in transporting nuclear fuel; and the strain on land resources and the overall environment (*Kommunist*, no. 15, October).

Foreign Affairs. The most dramatic Soviet foreign policy activity during 1979 concerned the SALT II agreement. Following nearly seven years of negotiations on a second round of strategic arms limitations, the treaty was signed at Vienna in mid-June by Brezhnev and Carter. Before and after the summit meeting, the Soviet media praised and encouraged SALT II advocates in the West and denounced those who questioned the strategic balance, especially critics in the United States. Although generally disdaining any linkage between the treaty and behavior in other matters, Soviet leaders did permit a spectacular upsurge in Jewish emigration during the months preceding the Vienna summit. On the matter of revisions proposed by some members of the U.S. Senate, the USSR maintained an adamant "all-or-nothing" position, but there were indications in late summer that the latter would accept qualifications and reservations, provided these were not incorporated in the text of the treaty.

The belated discovery of a Soviet combat brigade in Cuba during August threatened ratification of the arms pact since several key senators indicated that approval of the treaty was contingent on removal of the troops. Amid USSR denials of any combat capability in Cuba and uncertain signals from the United States, the two sides entered into negotiations on the issue. Confronted by an unyielding stance, President Carter announced in October a policy of surveillance and containment of Soviet-Cuban military forces in the Caribbean. This response appeared to effect no real change in the status quo, which Secretary of State Cyrus Vance had declared unacceptable. Perhaps more important, the subdued American reaction left untouched what many analysts regarded as the core of the problem, the utilization of Cuban troops as Soviet proxies both inside and outside the Western hemisphere.

The apparent fizzling of this issue seemed to confirm the official USSR view of an increasingly favorable "correlation of forces" in the world, as did other significant events during the year. Confident of the USSR's military power, Soviet leaders seemed inclined to pursue the role of the world's number one superpower, aided in no small measure by the relative American passivity in global politics since the Vietnam war. *Pravda* (29 November) summarized the favorable foreign policy trends in a front-page editorial: "The events of this year have shown once again that the mighty alliance of the three main revolutionary forces of the present—world socialism, the international working class, and the national liberation movement—is being strengthened, scoring new victories over the forces of imperialism and reaction."

In Southeast Asia, an important change in the balance of power favorable to Soviet interests was effected at minimal cost to the USSR. After an escalation of tensions extending over three years, Vietnam invaded Kampuchea (Cambodia) in December 1978/January 1979 and overthrew the Chinese-backed Khmer Rouge regime. China responded two months later with a limited incursion into North Vietnam to "punish the aggressor." With threats emanating from Moscow, Chinese forces withdrew, leaving the Soviets more firmly ensconced in Southeast Asia's affairs than ever before. As a result, China's strategic position in the Sino-Soviet negotiations, which resumed following the "proxy war" and the aborted Chinese intervention, has become less favorable. Meanwhile, the USSR increased pressure against Japan, which in 1978 had signed a friendship treaty with China containing an "anti-hegemony" clause, evidently aimed at the Soviet Union.

The "arc of instability" stretching from North Africa to Afghanistan became even more unstable in 1979, with somewhat mixed results for the USSR. The overthrow of the shah in Iran represented a major blow to anticommunist elements in the Middle East and to the United States. On the other hand, Moscow sustained a loss when key communist party leaders in Iraq were forced to flee Baghdad in March. The 1978 Soviet gains in Afghanistan were threatened by a civil war, requiring increased aid for its client regime. The Soviet position in Kabul was rendered more uncertain by the ouster and subsequent death of the Moscow-backed leader, Nur M. Taraki. In the Near East, the improved diplomatic position of the PLO seemed to tilt the correlation of forces in Moscow's favor. However, in this area, Moscow's room for maneuver was severely limited due to its inflexible support for Arab "rejectionist" forces.

One area of particular concern in any Soviet assessment of the correlation of forces has been Western Europe, where NATO has undergone substantial reorganization in recent years. Apparently aiming to counteract the renewed cohesion and retooling of NATO, Brezhnev proposed in 1979–1980 Soviet troop and tank reductions in East Germany contingent on restraint in the West European arms buildup (*Facts on File*, 12 October, p. 761).

Despite some setbacks and the uncertain future of SALT II, Soviet leaders should be satisfied with their overall record in foreign affairs during 1979. Looking ahead, they presumably could anticipate further gains under cover of the USSR's steadily expanding military might, particularly in view of the anticipated Western inferiority in strategic arms during the first half of the 1980s. There are, however, certain negative aspects to the correlation of forces that might inhibit Soviet exploitation of its advantages: the tendency toward ever closer collaboration among the United States, West European countries, China, and Japan; the potential USSR vulnerability due to its heavy reliance on communist allies and "national liberation" forces not fully controlled by Moscow; the expected leadership change in Moscow; and Soviet internal problems, especially in the economy and among restless non-Russian nationalities.

Soviet-American Relations. At the beginning of the year, the USSR faced two major tasks in relations with the United States: completing the SALT II package and coping with the consequences of the American diplomatic recognition in December 1978 of China. The progress of the Sino-American rapprochement seemed to evoke genuine alarm in the Kremlin. China continued to be depicted by Moscow as subservient to imperialist interests; closer relations between Washington and Beijing posed the threat of "imperialist encirclement" of the USSR. The initial Soviet reaction to President Carter's surprise recognition of China consisted of warnings about adverse consequences for détente and truculence during the final stages of the SALT II negotiations. However, the treaty could not be used as leverage against the new Sino-American relationship because Soviet leaders clearly regarded the agreement in the interests of the USSR. The official position on détente, or *razriadka*, had been that it reflected success in the "diplomatic struggle of the two worlds"; SALT II was the culmination of the *razriadka* policy pursued throughout the 1970s. Given the growing skepticism about the treaty among many prominent American political figures, a tactical problem for Moscow was reconciling the correlation of forces rationale with the political exigencies involved in securing U.S. Senate ratification. It met this problem by exerting as much diplomatic pressure as possible on Washington, by playing down the two worlds rhetoric, and by launching a propagandistic peace offensive.

A planned Brezhnev visit to the United States in January had been postponed; a later trip was precluded by his physical condition. Soviet officials acknowledged that the postponement took place because of Deputy Prime Minister Deng Xiaoping's visit to Washington that same month (*NYT*, 12 January). At the same time, a tour of China, Japan, South Korea, and Southeast Asia by a delegation under Sen. Sam Nunn of Georgia apparently aroused USSR fears of a linkage between the "China card" and opposition to Moscow's objectives in SALT II.

The activities of Nunn, perhaps the most articulate American critic of SALT II, and his colleagues drew special attention from the Soviet press, which charged that the purpose of the visit was encouragement of increased military expenditures by countries opposed to the USSR. This view conformed to the continuing propaganda campaign against a wide-ranging anti-Soviet, militaristic collaboration among American "hawks," the Pentagon, and NATO officials (*Pravda*, 4, 5, and 13 January, 5 February; Tass, 24 January). Particular attention was devoted to arms sales by the United States. A Central Committee report charged that the United States had not lived up to its 1977 promise on restraining such sales, which rose from $11.4 billion that year to $15 billion in 1978 (*Pravda*, 2 March). Concern over this matter was presented as a manifestation of USSR support for peace and stability but more likely reflected serious losses in arms sales competition with the United States. The CIA reported a 65 percent decline in Soviet arms sales, from a record $5.2 billion in 1977 to $1.8 billion in 1978. The 1977 figure for American arms sales was $6.9 billion (United Press International, 21 October).

Brezhnev used the occasion of a visit by six U.S. senators, led by Howard Baker of Tennessee, to urge speedy completion of SALT II and to denounce "certain circles" opposed to Soviet disarmament goals. The senators met with Brezhnev, Foreign Secretary Gromyko, and A. M. Aleksandrov-Agentov, Brezhnev's chief foreign policy aide (*Pravda*, 12 January). Baker attributed Brezhnev's urgency about SALT II to Soviet anxiety concerning U.S. diplomatic recognition of the PRC in the previous month (*NYT*, 11 January). Uncommitted at the time on the matter of ratification, the influential Republican senator subsequently turned against SALT II and unsuccessfully introduced a "crippling" amendment concerning large missiles (ibid., 23 October).

Evidently aiming for a wider American audience, Brezhnev granted an interview to three repre-sentatives of *Time* magazine (*Pravda*, 10 January). Speaking mainly about China, Brezhnev indicated that the USSR would not allow itself to be provoked into abrogating its 1950 treaty with the PRC but warned that the United States, in its moves toward Beijing, was "playing with fire." Subsequently the Soviet press reported favorable reception of the interview in the United States, indicating widespread awareness of the "Soviet desire for peace" (Tass, 18 January).

The tensions that had characterized U.S.-USSR relations since American recognition of the PRC were exacerbated in February due to circumstances surrounding the death of the American ambassa-dor to Afghanistan, Adolph Dubs. The United States charged that after Dubs had been abducted by Afghan rebels, Soviet advisers ignored American requests to proceed with caution and instead directed the police to attack the Kabul hotel room in which Dubs was being held. In the crossfire, the envoy was killed (*NYT*, 15 February). Moscow denied the American allegations. A government state-ment admitted that Soviet representatives had been at the scene but asserted that they had "nothing to do with the decision of the Afghan authorities as regards the character of actions directed at saving the life of the American ambassador" (Tass, 17 February).

At the same time, a flurry of charges and countercharges regarding the outbreak of revolution in Iran appeared. The United States formally accused the Soviet Union of efforts to help foment anti-American actions in Iran (ibid., 15 February). The Soviet media suggested that a 14 February attack on the American embassy in Teheran had been inspired by the CIA to provide a pretext for American military intervention in Iran (Tass, 15 February). Soviet officials also complained that the United States did not rebut many of the anti-Soviet remarks of PRC Deputy Prime Minister Deng during his January visit (*NYT*, 15 February).

Amid the rising tide of hostility, both Moscow and Washington pulled back and sought to promote an improved climate for SALT II. In a late February press conference, President Carter spoke favor-ably of the increase in "out-migration" of Jews during the previous six months to more than 40,000 and "guessed" that the Soviet Union would qualify for most-favored-nation trade status within a few months (United Press International, 27 February).

An article signed by "I. Aleksandrov" in *Pravda* (28 February) scored the United States as an accomplice of "the Chinese aggression against Vietnam." Brezhnev's Supreme Soviet electoral speech two days later offered a striking contrast in its moderate tone vis-à-vis the United States and the absence of any specific criticism of the American government. He did issue a mild warning about "encouragement of the Chinese policy of 'great-power hegemony,'" without naming the United States. The Soviet leader expressed the hope that the SALT II treaty would soon be completed and that he would meet with President Carter to sign it "in the near future" (*Pravda*, 3 March).

An incident reminiscent of Soviet actions against Americans that had heightened tensions during the previous year occurred in April. The U.S. embassy in Moscow delivered a strong protest against the alleged drugging of Robin Knight, Moscow correspondent of *U.S. News and World Report*, in Tashkent and abuse of both Knight and his wife by Soviet police (*NYT*, 23 and 24 April). Knight had been a frequent target of the USSR press for his reporting on dissident activities. This incident was quickly overshadowed by the U.S.-Soviet prisoner exchange (see above). A "senior" administration official said in Washington that the exchange had improved "the atmosphere" between the United States and USSR for the solving of other issues, including SALT II (ibid., 28 April).

A Soviet grain purchase brought the total of grain and soybeans ordered from the United States in 1979 to 10.3 million tons. The secretary of agriculture stated that completion of SALT II could lead to greater Soviet-American agricultural trade (Reuters, 9 May). Subsequently, U.S. grain exports to the USSR were considerably increased, due not to SALT II but to the worst Soviet harvest in five years.

As SALT II negotiations neared completion, the USSR press stepped up both its attacks on "anti-Soviet" figures in the United States and its laudatory comments about American proponents of détente.

National security affairs adviser Zbigniew Brzezinski was attacked in an article entitled "Doctrine of Dangerous Ventures" (*Sovetskaya rossia*, 25 March). Particularly emphasized was the Twelfth Dartmouth Conference at Williamsburg, Virginia, which brought together Supreme Soviet deputies, members of the U.S. Congress, and academicians and scientists from both countries. The conference considered questions of economic cooperation, SALT II, and other matters. An official Soviet statement reported that the delegates "held a comprehensive discussion on a broad range of problems of Soviet-U.S. relations and searched for ways of insuring international security" (*Pravda*, 14 May).

The United States announced that it had reached a basic agreement on SALT II with the USSR (*NYT*, 10 May). Both sides revealed that formal signing of the treaty would take place at Vienna in June. The Soviet press hailed these events as signifying "a victory for reason and for the two powers' recognition of the cardinal fact of our time, that there really is no sensible alternative to détente" (*Izvestiia*, 13 May).

Confronted with rising domestic questioning of the strategic implications of SALT II, President Carter approved development of the mobile MX ballistic missile (Associated Press, 8 June). The prospect of major American efforts to correct any strategic imbalances did not assuage the apprehensions of the more vocal critics as verification moved to the forefront as a critical issue. The United States had lost the two missile-tracking stations in northern Iran (*NYT*, 24 April), leaving only the one distant base at Sinop, Turkey. It proposed to recover this capability by use of U-2 flights near the Turkish-Soviet border (ibid., 4 April). Turkey made these flights contingent on Soviet approval, which was not forthcoming. Before the revelation of these proposals, Carter had already claimed that the United States possessed adequate means for verifying Soviet treaty compliance (ibid., 1 April). American military chiefs generally supported this view in public testimony, but independent military analysts expressed grave doubts about the American capacity for verification (*WP*, 16 June).

Brezhnev and Carter met in Vienna during 16–18 June. A number of issues were discussed, but other than SALT II, only a pact banning radiological weapons was agreed on. At formal dinners, Brezhnev and Carter exchanged charges about responsibility for world trouble spots (*Pravda*, 17 and 18 June), but the atmosphere was generally cordial, even convivial; at the signing ceremony, Carter surprised onlookers by embracing Brezhnev with a Russian-style hug and kiss (*NYT*, 19 June).

The treaty placed an immediate aggregate ceiling of 2,400 strategic delivery vehicles on both parties and pledged reduction of the ceiling to 2,250 by 31 December 1981. Article V of the treaty sets a subceiling of 1,320 on all ICBMs, SLBMs, ASBMs with MIRVs, and bombers with cruise missiles whose range exceeds 600 kilometers. Under Article V, no more than 1,200 ICBMs, SLBMs, and ASBMs may be equipped with MIRVs; of these, no more than 820 may be placed on ICBMs. Article IV limits the substitution of technologically advanced missiles for less advanced ones and precludes increases in silo volume by more than 32 percent. However, it also permits each side to "deploy one new type of light ICBM."

At Vienna, Brezhnev warned that the Soviet Union "will not accept any backpedaling, any attempt to undermine the treaty, any attempt to rock this elaborate structure, to substitute any of its elements" (ibid., 18 June). Following conclusion of the summit, a lead article in *Pravda* (20 June) warned that no changes would be permitted. The Soviet hard-line approach to treaty changes invited new opposition in the United States; some proponents of the pact saw the USSR posture as needlessly provocative. Confronted with an increasingly probable rejection of the treaty by the U.S. Senate, the Soviets gave an indication of greater flexibility.

A U.S. senate delegation led by Joseph Biden of Delaware met with Prime Minister Kosygin, First Deputy Foreign Minister Georgi M. Kornienko, and Georgi A. Arbatov, director of the Institute on the USA and Canada (Tass, 29 August). Kosygin assured the senators that the Soviet Union would not seek to upgrade the capability of the Backfire bomber. Biden told Kosygin that the Senate was likely to attach three "clarifications" to the treaty: the protocol restricting deployment of cruise missiles in

Europe would not be extended beyond 31 December 1981; the treaty would not inhibit existing U.S. collaboration with its West European allies; and related documents would have the same force as the treaty itself. According to Biden, the Soviets appeared ready to accept these clarifications (*NYT*, 31 August).

Two incidents in early August demonstrated that the Vienna summit had not dispelled continuing tensions in U.S.-Soviet relations. In the Black Sea, USSR planes including Backfire bombers, made over thirty mock missile attacks against the U.S. destroyers *Caron* and *Farragut*. Near Guam, a Soviet espionage ship snared a Mark 37 training torpedo launched by a U.S. submarine during exercises and after first refusing, returned it only after negotiations at a higher level (Reuters, 10 August).

These incidents at sea evoked no major response from Washington but an issue that surfaced in late August proved impossible to overlook; charges concerning the alleged presence of a Soviet combat brigade in Cuba threatened the entire structure of SALT II. After U.S. intelligence definitely confirmed the presence of 2,000 to 3,000 troops in August, Sen. Frank Church of Idaho made a public disclosure. Subsequently, Church led the Senate campaign for withdrawal of these Soviet troops. Several senators indicated the strategic arms treaty would not be ratified until the issue had been resolved; Church termed the issue a "test" directly linked to SALT II ratification (*NYT*, 10 September). The USSR officially denied that the unit was a combat brigade; a Soviet government statement claimed that it had been in Cuba since 1962 on a training mission (*Pravda*, 11 September).

The response of the U.S. administration to the troops issue appeared rather erratic as it sought to cope with both domestic pressures and Soviet intransigence. At the outset, Secretary of State Cyrus Vance declared that he would not accept the status quo. As negotiations proceeded, American spokesmen tended to downgrade the issue. Negotiations extended over a period of more than two weeks, limited initially to Vance and Ambassador Anatoli Dobrynin and in the later stages involving talks between Vance and Foreign Minister Gromyko. The Soviets denied a combat role for the brigade and refused to make any adjustments. In a speech to the U.N. General Assembly on 25 September, Gromyko lashed out at the United States, charging that "all sorts of falsehoods are being piled up concerning the policies of Cuba and the Soviet Union." Further, Gromyko said that "it is high time that you honestly admit that this whole matter is artificial and proclaim it to be closed." (*NYT*, 26 September.) On the same day, in a "town meeting" at Queens College, President Carter called Cuba a Soviet "puppet" and reaffirmed that the Soviet brigade "is a combat unit." He told his audience that if the status quo did not change, he would take "appropriate action." (Associated Press, 26 September.) The Soviet government responded to the latter statement with charges that Carter's tone was "ultimatum-like" and "threatening" (Tass, 27 September).

Vance and Gromyko held their final meeting on the issue, a three-hour session, in New York on 27 September. Afterwards, Gromyko described the discussion as "serious" and Vance concurred. Neither diplomat would discuss specifics, but it was obvious that no breakthrough had occurred. (*NYT*, 28 September.) On the same day, Vance reported on the talks to the National Security Council in Washington.

The U.S. administration evidently concluded the diplomatic episode when President Carter gave a television report to the American people. Noting Soviet assurances that the brigade would not be used outside Cuba, Carter indicated that the unit posed no strategic threat. However, he promised that American military strength in the Caribbean would be augmented and that surveillance over Cuba would be increased. (Ibid., 2 October.) Senate reaction to Carter's performance was mixed, and ratification of the strategic arms treaty remained in doubt. Whatever the effect on SALT II, it was obvious that there had been no change in the status quo as demanded and that the United States had sustained a diplomatic setback.

Two days after Carter's address, the United States announced a decision by the Agriculture Department to give the USSR permission to buy a record 25 million metric tons of American corn and wheat over the coming year (ibid., 4 October). State Department spokesman Hodding Carter defended this by saying that agricultural trade benefits both countries (Associated Press, 5 October).

In September and October, the Kremlin displayed concern about growing linkage among the United States, West Europe, and China and the possible upgrading of military capabilities by its potential opponents in both East and West. An article entitled "Research Provocateurs" in *Pravda* cited a report on a U.S. Defense Department staff study that favored steps to bolster China's military potential against the USSR (*Pravda*, 5 October). It voiced skepticism concerning Secretary Vance's assurance that the United States had no plans to sell arms to China, a move recommended for consideration by the study.

Reflecting Soviet concern about the projected installation of Pershing-2 intermediate-range missiles in Western Europe, East German leader Erich Honecker delivered a threatening speech in which he compared West German and NATO leaders to Hitler and Goebbels. Honecker said that the East Germans and Russians were "strengthening the defense capabilities of our countries" to check the "aggressiveness of West German imperialism" (*Neues Deutschland*, 21 September). Soviet endorsement of Honecker's hard line was indicated by the presence in the audience of Gen. Yevgeny F. Ivanovsky, commander of Soviet forces in East Germany, and Soviet Ambassador Piotr A. Abrasimov (*NYT*, 21 September).

After Honecker's speech, Brezhnev tried a more conciliatory approach. In a speech in Berlin on 6 October marking the 30th anniversary of the German Democratic Republic, the Soviet leader announced that the USSR would withdraw 20,000 troops and 1,000 tanks from East Germany during 1980. Brezhnev also said that the USSR was prepared to reduce the number of medium-range nuclear missiles deployed in the western areas of the Soviet Union "in the event that no additional medium-range nuclear systems are deployed in Western Europe" (Tass, 6 October), an apparent condition for both moves.

Initial reaction to Brezhnev's initiative was mostly negative. West German Chancellor Helmut Schmidt welcomed the troop pullback but cautioned that obsolete Soviet missiles were being replaced by modern, more mobile rockets, carrying three warheads instead of one. A U.S. State Department spokesman said that the withdrawal would be basically symbolic since the USSR has 400,000 soldiers in Central Europe, some 100,000 more than the United States. National security adviser Brzezinski said that "we have to recognize the Soviet Union has an interest in forestalling Western efforts to upgrade our conventional and theater nuclear forces in order to achieve equality." Brzezinski also warned that failure to go ahead with plans for new intermediate-range missile systems in Europe could lead to political intimidation from the Soviet Union "at best, and even war at worst." On 12 October, the Atlantic Treaty Association, representing the fifteen Western allies, endorsed the NATO plan for deployment of new medium-range nuclear-tipped missiles in Western Europe. (*NYT*, 7, 8, 11, and 13 October.)

Marshall D. Shulman, principal adviser on Soviet affairs to the secretary of state, gave a gloomy assessment of U.S.–Soviet relations on 16 October in testimony before a congressional committee. Shulman reported that the United States and USSR were at loggerheads on virtually every issue except the SALT II treaty and that these differences "are unlikely to be reconciled in the future." Further, he said that "the potential for escalation of violence in southern Africa remains the most serious potential problem on the horizon in U.S.–Soviet relations." (Ibid., 17 October.)

Other than agreement on radiological matters, no progress was made in disarmament talks. The most notable event at the 1979 session of the 39-nation Disarmament Conference in Geneva was the submission in July of a joint U.S.–Soviet draft agreement to ban weapons that spread radioactivity by means other than nuclear explosions (ibid., 11 July). However, there was little discussion of the proposal, and the conference disbanded in August with no accord to report to the U.N. General Assembly (ibid., 15 August).

Soviet-Chinese Relations. Relations between the USSR and the PRC during the year were dominated by the successful Vietnamese invasion of Kampuchea and its aftermath. Visibly upset by American recognition of the PRC in December 1978, Soviet leaders grasped the opportunity to inflict a proxy blow to Chinese prestige by strongly supporting the Vietnamese invasion at the end of December and into January. The Vietnamese army overwhelmed the forces of the Beijing-backed Pol Pot regime and quickly occupied most of Kampuchea. China responded by attacking Vietnam across its northern frontier in February (ibid., 18 February).

Confronted by a barrage of Soviet denunciations and threats and aware of its perilous position on China's northern frontier, PRC leadership limited the incursion into Vietnam, although some 20,000 Chinese troops were reportedly killed during the campaign. The PRC announced complete withdrawal of all its forces from Vietnam (ibid., 17 March). The following month, the PRC and Vietnam began peace talks in Hanoi on the disputed frontier area between the two countries (ibid., 19 April).

The outcome was a fundamental change in the Asian power balance unfavorable to Beijing; accordingly, the USSR was able to adopt a patient, cautious attitude. The PRC, on the other hand, was faced with a fait accompli that it was unable to reverse; for Chinese leaders, further negotiations with the Soviets seemed the most likely option, but China's bargaining position had been considerably eroded. However, for a time, the two sides continued on a collision course, at least at rhetorical levels.

At the beginning of March, the United States opened its embassy in Beijing, resuming diplomatic relations with mainland China after 30 years of nonrecognition (ibid., 2 March). Mutual recriminations continued to flow from Soviet and Chinese media. In late March, Moscow emphasized both the continuing border disputes and the ideological differences between the USSR and the PRC by means of a conference on the "struggle against Maoist falsifications in history." Sponsored by the Academy of Sciences and the Academy of Social Sciences, it was held in Moscow 27–29 March; principal speaker was CPSU Central Committee secretary for liaison with ruling communist parties, Konstantin V. Rusakov. The Soviet press reported that the aim of the conference was "to lay bare the Maoist falsifications of history aimed at asserting great-Han chauvinism and attempting to justify the hegemonic desires and the expansionist policy of the present Chinese leaders" (Tass, 27 March; *FBIS*, 29 March).

On 3 April, the National People's Congress of the PRC decided not to extend the Treaty of Friendship, Alliance, and Mutual Assistance between the USSR and the PRC beyond its expiration in 1980 (*Pravda*, 4 April). Termination of the treaty was in accord with the PRC's closer alignment with Japan (Radio Liberty, 4 April) but also clearly reflected the intensified hostility between the two communist powers. Predictably, Moscow's initial reaction was a denunciation of the move, a characterization of the action as a "logical extension of Beijing's anti-Soviet, antisocialist policy, a policy for collusion with rank reactionaries and imperialists" (Radio Moscow, 3 April; *FBIS*, 4 April). An "I. Aleksandrov" article four days after the treaty termination was much more restrained. The writer admitted that "it is possible that certain articles in the treaty do in fact require clarification" but concluded that "the truth is that it is not the treaty that is outdated but that China's policy has degenerated" (*Pravda*, 7 April).

Chinese Foreign Minister Huang Hua presented a memorandum to the Soviet ambassador in early May calling for a resumption of negotiations and containing no reference to territorial disputes. In late May, the Soviet foreign ministry was reported to be preparing a favorable reply to the Chinese proposal (Kyodo, Tokyo, 26 May; *FBIS*, 29 May). The USSR next formally proposed a meeting to be held in Moscow in August (*Pravda*, 5 June). Reacting to Western comments about the forthcoming meeting, Soviet spokesmen angrily denied that the USSR was "playing the China card" in order to "make the United States nervous" (ibid., 10 June).

The PRC responded favorably to the Soviet proposal, and the Soviet government announced that talks would begin at Moscow (*Izvestiia*, 26 July). A border incident in July failed to slow the momentum toward an easing of tensions. Moscow admitted that a Chinese soldier had been killed by Soviet border guards on the East Kazakhstan–China frontier (*NYT*, 25 July).

Chinese negotiators arrived in Moscow on 23 September. Three weeks later, it was reported that both sides had agreed to move ahead to full-scale discussions aimed at normalizing relations between their countries, although negotiators had failed to agree on an agenda. Reportedly the only significant item of agreement had been a decision to alternate discussions between the two capitals (Reuters, 12 October).

Despite the apparent seriousness of the negotiations, each side continued its political maneuvers against the other. The Chinese maintained their efforts to obtain Western arms and PRC Premier Hua Guofeng made a much-publicized visit to France, West Germany, and Britain in October. And the Soviet Union stepped up pressure against the PRC's new treaty partner, Japan.

Japan. Soviet-Japanese relations have been strained during the late 1970s due mainly to Japan's persistent demands for the return of territory lost at the end of World War II; Japanese reluctance to undertake risky investments in Siberia; and, most important, Japan's steady rapprochement with China, which culminated in the signing of a friendship treaty in 1978. During 1979, the USSR increased pressure on Japan through a relatively quiet flexing of its military muscle in the Far East. In January, Japanese authorities reported that the USSR had increased troop strength and was building bases on the southernmost of the Kurile Islands, opposite Hokkaido (*NYT*, 31 January). Other sources revealed an intensification of this activity during the year, and in the fall the Japanese government announced that Soviet troops had fortified an additional island (*Chicago Sun-Times*, 17 October).

While lightly brandishing its military "stick," Moscow did not neglect the economic "carrot" in its relations with Japan. Controversy over fishing rights has long been a source of Soviet-Japanese tensions. In Moscow, Soviet and Japanese representatives initialed an accord providing for the establishment of a joint commission on fishing to promote cooperation and settle disputes (Radio Moscow, 31 March; *FBIS*, 3 April). This agreement followed the outlines of a provisional understanding announced the preceding April and paved the way for a fishing accord providing for the joint fishing of Tanner crab in Olyutorsk waters in the western Bering Sea (Kyodo, Tokyo, 26 April; *FBIS*, 27 April). An article describing prospects for Soviet-Japanese trade and economic cooperation in highly optimistic terms appeared in Moscow (*Izvestiia*, 8 April).

Pravda editor Viktor G. Afanasyev headed a delegation of journalists that visited Japan and was received by Prime Minister Ohira (Tass, 29 May). A month later, two articles by Afanasyev heavily underscored the deepening hostility between the two countries. He denounced Japan for its treaty with China and the continuing claim for return of the Kuriles (*Pravda*, 28 and 29 June).

Southeast Asia. Soviet activities during the year were devoted mainly to consolidation of its expanded foothold in the area. It augmented its military presence in Vietnam and pursued diplomatic initiatives designed to confirm the changed regional power balance.

After the overthrow of the Pol Pot regime, Moscow immediately recognized the new government installed by the Vietnamese army and pledged its support for the "construction of peaceful, independent, democratic, nonaligned Cambodia advancing toward socialism" (*Izvestiia* and Tass, 9 January). The USSR vetoed a U.N. Security Council resolution calling for withdrawal of Vietnamese forces from Kampuchea (*WP*, 16 January) but was unable to prevent U.N. General Assembly seating of the Pol Pot representative (*NYT*, 22 September). Heng Samrin, head of the new regime in Kampuchea dispatched an effusive message of thanks for Soviet support to Brezhnev and Kosygin (Moscow Domestic Service, 11 May; *FBIS*, 14 May). Moscow announced appointment of Oleg Bostorin as Soviet ambassador to the People's Republic of Kampuchea (Tass, 12 May). Bostorin, 48, is a career diplomat with previous experience in Thailand, Singapore, and the Philippines.

Moscow also moved to reassure Thailand, which was uneasy over the invasion of neighboring Kampuchea and subsequent clashes along its frontiers. Soviet leaders were presumably concerned that Thailand might move more closely into the American orbit, following President Carter's pledge of increased military aid to Bangkok (Associated Press, 22 January). Thailand's Prime Minister Kriang-sak Chamanan was received in Moscow on his first visit to the Soviet Union with an unusually warm public greeting by Brezhnev. Talks with the latter and Kosygin yielded no agreement or substantive pronouncements on policy (*Pravda*, 21, 22, 23, and 28 March). The only positive sequel to the meeting was a seminar on Soviet-Thai trade held in Bangkok (ibid., 27 May).

Soviet fears about a Sino-Japanese alliance and the possible outflanking of its sphere of influence in Southeast Asia were reflected in a strong denunciation of the new trade agreement between Japan and the Philippines (ibid., 21 May).

Europe. The primary USSR concerns vis-à-vis Western Europe during the year were the revitalization of NATO and the projected stationing of American intermediate-range missiles on the continent. Soviet efforts to dissuade the West Europeans from accepting the missiles reached a climax with a strident press campaign in which Defense Minister Ustinov participated (ibid., 25 October), underlining Moscow's sense of urgency. Earlier, an editorial had warned Norway against increasing its role in NATO (ibid., 6 October). West European leaders publicly held firm on the issue, but there was some private wavering in both West Germany and Britain. When Chinese leader Hua Guofeng visited Bonn, he was asked to tone down his anti-Soviet statements. A spokesman for Chancellor Helmut Schmidt said that the West German government "would not find it particularly auspicious" for Hua to repeat statements that he had made in Paris urging the West Europeans to increase their capability to resist possible Soviet aggression (United Press International, 21 October).

The following month, there were indications of a possible favorable response to Brezhnev's overtures. Leonid M. Zamyatin, head of the CPSU Central Committee's Foreign Information Department, said that Warsaw Pact countermeasures would become "inevitable" if NATO stationed U.S. missiles in Western Europe (Tass, 3 November). On the following day, West German Foreign Minister Hans-Dietrich Genscher said that NATO was ready to negotiate deployment of middle-range nuclear missiles with the Warsaw Pact (United Press International, 4 November). However, as of the year's end, most West European governments had agreed to accept the missiles.

Despite a minor furor over Hua's remarks in Paris, Soviet relations with France were generally good. Foreign Minister Jean François Poncet visited Moscow (*Pravda*, 13 and 14 February). Later the USSR signed a contract with French companies for a computer similar to the one denied the Soviets by executive order of President Carter in 1978 (Tass, 27 March). Following a postponement due to Brezhnev's ill health, President Valéry Giscard d'Estaing arrived in Moscow. The visit produced several agreements, including accords on expanded economic cooperation and computer and electronics sales (*Pravda*, 29 April).

Foreign Minister Gromyko visited Rome in January for talks with Foreign Minister Arnaldo Forlani. The conversations produced only a joint communiqué supporting détente and disarmament, with no specified matters of agreement released (ibid., 27 January).

The USSR made progress in one area where its influence previously had been minimal. It negotiated agreements with Greece on the Soviet supply of natural gas and electricity, as well as on the construction of an aluminum plant. Agreement was also reached on the general outlines of economic cooperation and a political declaration of principles to be signed during a later visit to Moscow by Prime Minister Constantine Caramanlis. However, the budding Moscow-Athens rapprochement was dampened by mutual criticisms appearing in Soviet and Greek newspapers (*NYT*, 14 August).

Middle East. Soviet policy in this area remained generally unchanged. The USSR sharply criticized the new Israeli-Egyptian accord, maintained support for Arab "rejectionist" forces, and attempted to strengthen its diplomatic and military position in the area. However, Moscow was forced to respond to events over which it had little control, with some unfavorable consequences.

The Arabian peninsula continued to be a point of friction between East and West. It was reported that a Soviet missile-carrying nuclear submarine had entered Aden, the South Yemen port close to Middle East tanker routes (United Press International, 5 August). South Yemen and the USSR subsequently established closer links through a twenty-year treaty of friendship. This and other documents of cooperation were signed in Moscow by Brezhnev and President Abdel Fattah Ismail (ibid., 26 October). Saudi Arabia's anger over the Israeli-Egyptian treaty and Soviet desire for additional oil supplies combined to produce hints of a possible new relationship between Moscow and Riyadh, including diplomatic relations (Tass, 15 May; *Literaturnaya gazeta*, 5 June).

The USSR made some attempts to improve its frequently delicate relations with Syria; prospects were rendered more favorable by the latter's reaction to the Israeli-Egyptian treaty. Foreign Minister Gromyko journeyed to Damascus for talks with Syrian leader Hafiz al-Asad (Tass, 26 March; *FBIS*, 27 March). Soviet sources described the visit as "friendly" (*Pravda*, 26 March). The following month, Brezhnev and Kosygin sent warm greetings to Asad on the 33rd anniversary of the withdrawal of foreign troops from Syria (ibid., 17 April), and Asad visited Moscow in October for conversations with the Soviet leaders.

Moscow's commitment to the Arab rejectionist front was tested by continuing persecution of Iraqi communists. The leaders of the party, headed by Secretary General 'Aziz Muhammad and including one cabinet minister, were forced to flee Iraq and reportedly went into exile at Moscow (Radio Free Europe, 30 April).

The USSR welcomed the overthrow of the shah and attempted to come to grips with the situation posed by installation of an Islamic theocratic regime in Teheran. It was the second government (after Pakistan) to recognize the new regime dominated by the Ayatollah Khomeini (Tass, 12 February). During the following weeks, charges and countercharges concerning alleged interference in the internal affairs of Iran were exchanged between Moscow and Washington. The USSR played down the basic anticommunism of the Khomeini regime and the wave of terror and emphasized the anti-American thrust of the Iranian revolution (*Pravda*, 10 April, 22 May). Clearly worried about the potential spillover of Islamic revivalism into their own Central Asian areas, the Soviets proclaimed a fundamental harmony between goals of Muslims and communists (Radio Moscow 24 May; *FBIS*, 29 May). However, the Khomeini movement clearly had a negative influence upon USSR interests in neighboring Afghanistan.

Afghanistan. The newly won Soviet sphere of influence in Afghanistan was threatened by a revolt against the pro-Moscow regime of Nur M. Taraki, which erupted at the beginning of the year and gradually gained momentum. At the outset, Radio Moscow repeated Afghan government denials of trouble in various parts of the country (Tass, 15 January). However, when rebels abducted the American ambassador in Kabul, the Taraki government's fragile position became obvious. The ambassador's death produced severe strains in Soviet-American relations (see above). By the end of March, exiled rebel leader Silghatallah Mojaddidi claimed that his forces occupied large areas of the country and that Turkoman tribesmen were fighting government troops near the Soviet border. Taraki's control was threatened both by Muslim traditionalist opposition to the modernizing regime and by ethnic resistance to centralized authority.

Moscow increased its military aid to Taraki, reportedly delivering twelve rocket-armed helicopter gunships (*NYT*, 4 March). Two months later, the Supreme Soviet ratified the 1978 treaty with Afghanistan (*Pravda*, 21 May). The USSR reportedly asked Prime Minister Morarji Desai of India to persuade Pakistan to refrain from assisting Muslim rebels in Afghanistan (*NYT*, 15 June).

The USSR escalated its assistance to Taraki, but the extent of its direct involvement remained uncertain. Moscow apparently became wary of involvement in a "Vietnam" type adventure in which it could not rely exclusively upon proxies. Prime Minister Hafizullah Amin stated that there were no more than 1,600 Soviet "advisers" in Afghanistan (United Press International, 20 August). Meanwhile,

Ambassador Vasili Safronchuk was reportedly making an urgent attempt to induce the Taraki government to broaden its political base beyond the ruling Khalq party.

Taraki visited Moscow on his way back from the Havana conference of "nonaligned" countries (Tass, 12 September). Shortly after his return to Afghanistan, Radio Kabul reported that he had resigned. There were unconfirmed reports that he had been wounded during a coup. Prime Minister Amin emerged as the new leader (ibid., 17 September), and there were indications that although pro-Soviet, he might be less amenable to Moscow's lead than was Taraki. American officials reported that USSR paratroopers had been put on alert across the border (*NYT*, 25 September) and that 400 Soviet soldiers had taken over an airfield near Kabul. On 9 October, Radio Kabul reported the death of Taraki without specifying the cause. In the final months of 1979, the Soviet foothold in Afghanistan appeared increasingly precarious.

India. Kosygin visited India during 9–15 March. He and Prime Minister Desai signed a ten-to fifteen-year agreement on trade and scientific-technical cooperation and another agreement on cooperation in medical and public health matters. However, Kosygin apparently failed to nudge India toward an overt anti-Beijing stance (ibid., 16 March). Desai returned the visit and was welcomed by Brezhnev. Their talks yielded a communiqué opposing foreign intervention in Southeast Asia and Afghanistan (*Pravda*, 15 June), but Desai was clearly unwilling to modify India's meticulous stance of nonalignment on key Middle Eastern and Far Eastern issues.

Africa. The USSR consolidated friendly relations with its client regime in Addis Ababa. The Soviet-Ethiopian treaty signed in November 1978 was ratified by both countries (ibid., 20 February). Brezhnev and Kosygin cabled greetings to Ethiopian leader Mengistu Haile Mariam on the occasion of Ethiopia's "Victory Day" (ibid., 6 April). Kosygin later visited Addis Ababa for talks with Mengistu (Tass, 10 and 11 September; *FBIS*, 11 September).

Deputy Foreign Minister Leonid F. Ilichev visited Angola for talks with President Agostinho Neto (Tass, 10 February). Subsequently, a CPSU delegation led by Central Committee candidate member Aleksandr Vlasov traveled to Angola for discussions on cooperation between the two countries' ruling parties (Luanda Domestic Service, 20 March; *FBIS*, 21 March). The following month, an agreement on cooperation in fishing between the Soviet Union and Angola for the years 1979 to 1981 was signed at Luanda (Radio Moscow, 10 April; *FBIS*, 11 April).

Nigeria, evidently opting for American trade and aid, ordered the USSR to reduce the number of its "advisers" from 40 to 5 (*NYT*, 22 August).

A front-page editorial described Africa as "marching confidently toward total liberation" and accused China of attempting to undermine African unity in the struggle for independence and "supporting Western-inspired counterrevolutionary movements." It charged that "the imperialist powers are trying to drag the African continent into the orbit of their aggressive policy" and that "this is a serious threat to the cause of peace." (*Izvestiia*, 10 April.)

The Americas. The Soviet alliance with Cuba was strengthened further during the year. A protocol for a trade exchange of more than 4 billion rubles in 1979 was signed (*Pravda*, 2 February). Deputy Prime Minister Ivan V. Arkhipov led a Soviet delegation to the ninth session of the Soviet-Cuban Commission for Economic and Scientific-Technical Cooperation in Havana (Tass, 9 March). Raul Castro conferred with USSR Defense Minister Ustinov in Moscow, and the Cuban received the Order of Lenin from Brezhnev (*Pravda*, 16 and 22 February). The conference of "nonaligned" countries in Havana was hosted by Fidel Castro. The USSR press viewed it as demonstrating that the nonaligned countries would no longer "sing to the tune called by imperialism" (Tass, 9 September) and accused the United States of raising the Soviet combat brigade issue to divert attention from the Havana meeting.

Moscow gave strong verbal support to the anti-Somoza revolutionary forces in Nicaragua (ibid., 29 March) and, after a period of silence on the subject, came out with its strongest denunciation yet of the military regime in Uruguay (ibid., 3 April).

Prospects for expansion of Soviet-Cuban influence in the Caribbean appeared to be enhanced by the visit to Moscow of Prime Minister Michael Manley from Jamaica. Following conversations with a Soviet group headed by Kosygin, agreement was announced on exchange of Jamaican aluminum and Soviet commodities, as well as on cooperation in fishing. The two governments agreed to hold talks on cultural and scientific exchanges later. (Ibid., 13 April; *FBIS*, 19 April.)

International Party Contacts. Boris N. Ponomarev, Central Committee secretary for liaison with nonruling communist parties, continued to face the difficult task of maintaining or establishing friendly relations with movements outside the bloc against a backdrop of CPSU insistence upon "proletarian internationalism" and opposition to Eurocommunism and other manifestations of independence by individual parties.

Ponomarev was the main speaker at a conference in Moscow commemorating the 60th anniversary of the Third (Communist) International. He praised "proletarian solidarity" as the "guarantee of universal peace" and attacked the Chinese communists for betraying their Marxist-Leninist heritage (Tass, 17 March). Ponomarev was main speaker again in May at an international theoretical conference also in Moscow on "The Scientific-Technological Revolution and the Deepening of the Economic and Social Conditions of Capitalism at the Contemporary Stage." Delegations from Bulgaria, Hungary, Vietnam, East Germany, Mongolia, Poland, Romania, and Czechoslovakia attended and there were several representatives from nonruling communist parties. Ponomarev's speech was devoted to the "scientific-technological revolution" and "the struggle of the two systems" and contained no direct references to Eurocommunism or to China (Moscow Domestic Service, 21 May; *FBIS*, 22 May).

In late December 1978, Ponomarev played the "China card" when he received a delegation from the pro-Soviet Communist Party of Bolivia (PCB). Mindful of its domestic competition with the pro-Chinese Communist Party of Bolivia Marxist-Leninist, the PCB delegation issued a statement condemning China for its policy of "siding with the imperialists" and Chinese "acts of aggression against Vietnam" (Moscow World Service, 20 December 1978; *FBIS*, 21 December 1978).

A much more important movement with an anti-Chinese orientation, the Japanese Communist Party, sent a delegation to Moscow in May for talks with Ponomarev and other CPSU officials. The PRC-Japan treaty of 1978 and the U.S. diplomatic recognition of the PRC provided some common ground for the Soviet and Japanese parties in attempts to improve their long-strained relations; however, the latter's staunchly nationalistic position on the Kurile Islands issue remained a stumbling block. Ponomarev held conversations with the deputy chairmen, Tomio Nishizawa and Hiroshi Murakami, and the deputy chief of the JCP Central Committee's International Department, Koito Masuda (Tass, 7 May). Before their departure for Tokyo, Nishizawa and Presidium member Hiroshi Tachiki met with CPSU secretary and Politburo member Mikhail Suslov. No agreement was reached on the holding of a summit meeting between the respective party heads (Kyodo, Tokyo, 15 May; *FBIS*, 16 May).

Ponomarev welcomed a delegation from another small pro-Soviet party, that of Switzerland, led by Secretary General Armand Magnin. On the Soviet side, Ponomarev was assisted by the Central Committee cadres secretary, Ivan V. Kapitonov, and the deputy head of the International Department, Vadim V. Zagladin. At the conclusion of the visit, representatives of the two parties issued a noncontroversial communiqué supporting "détente and the strengthening of international peace" (*Pravda*, 7 May).

Ponomarev led the CPSU delegation to the 23rd Congress of the French Communist Party. The major speech by First Secretary Georges Marchais was generally supportive of the USSR, although mildly critical of the "underestimation of general democratic demands." A mass meeting in conjunction with the congress was held to honor the CPSU delegation; Ponomarev gave a speech denouncing the policies of NATO and the PRC (ibid., 11, 12, and 14 May).

The CPSU Central Committee sent greetings to its Italian counterpart on the eve of the Fifteenth Congress and denounced capitalism, imperialism, and the PRC (ibid., 30 March). The CPSU delegation to the congress was headed by Politburo member Arvid Y. Pelshe (Moscow Domestic Service, 5 April; *FBIS*, 6 April). The congress maintained the Italian Eurocommunist stance, but party leader Enrico Berlinguer's major speech was not critical of the USSR (*Pravda*, 31 March). Pelshe delivered a speech at a rally in Bologna warning against Eurocommunism and denouncing the policies of the PRC (Tass, 31 March).

CPSU relations with the dominant faction of the Spanish party, led by Secretary General Santiago Carrillo, continued to be strained due to the issue of Eurocommunism. Moscow gave strong verbal support to the pro-Soviet faction of the party; CPSU officials welcomed the veteran leader of that group, Dolores Ibarruri, to Moscow for an extended visit (*Pravda*, 4 February).

Relations with the Portuguese movement were much more satisfactory from Moscow's standpoint. Candidate Politburo member Eduard A. Shevardnadze led the CPSU delegation at the Ninth Congress, held in Lisbon. In his speech, Shevardnadze praised "the glorious traditions of internationalism of Portuguese communists" (ibid., 3 June). Communist leader Alvaro Cunhal, in his major address, reaffirmed his party's loyalty to "proletarian internationalism" (Tass, 1 June).

While at Vienna for the SALT II summit, Brezhnev met with the Austrian party chairman, Franz Muhri. The meeting constituted a break with the practice of avoiding contacts with local party leaders while on formal visits to the West and emphasized the pro-Soviet orientation of the Austrian movement. Muhri lauded USSR foreign policy, and Brezhnev praised the Austrian party for its adherence to "proletarian internationalism" (*Pravda*, 19 June).

A delegation from Finland, led by party Chairman Aarne Saarinen, held discussions with Suslov and other CPSU officials in Moscow (ibid., 3 February).

The CPSU Central Committee sent greetings to the Third Congress of the Congolese Labor Party. The message emphasized the "common interests" of the two parties in "the struggle against imperialism, neocolonialism, racism, and Chinese hegemonism" (Moscow Domestic Service, 25 March; *FBIS*, 26 March). A national school for cadres of the Congolese Labor Party, built with Soviet help, was opened at Brazzaville (*Pravda*, 3 February).

A delegation from the Communist Party of Lebanon also visited Moscow. The joint communiqué called for creation of a Palestinian state (ibid., 7 June).

CPSU relations with ruling movements were highlighted by three visits made by General Secretary Brezhnev to East European countries, despite his uncertain health. Accompanied by Politburo member Konstantin U. Chernenko, he journeyed to Sofia for several days of talks with Bulgarian leader Todor Zhivkov (Tass, 15 January). On the way to Bulgaria, Brezhnev was met by several Romanian party and government officials at Jassy (Agerpres, Bucharest, 12 January; *FBIS*, 15 January). When Brezhnev's train stopped in Bucharest, Romanian leader Nicolae Ceauşescu pointedly avoided a meeting.

Hungarian leader János Kádár met with Brezhnev at Moscow (*Pravda*, 7 March), and the Soviet leader returned the visit later. Brezhnev spoke on Hungarian television, emphasizing the cooperation between the Soviet and Hungarian parties and peoples (Tass, 1 June). According to the official USSR statement on the June meeting, matters discussed included the implementation of the "decisions of the 25th CPSU Congress and the 11th Hungarian Congress" (Moscow Domestic Service, 30 May; *FBIS*, 31 May).

Brezhnev participated in the celebration of the 30th anniversary of East Germany and held conversations with East German chief Erich Honecker (*Pravda*, 7 October). While in East Berlin, Brezhnev delivered a major speech directed against the upgrading of NATO missile capabilities in Western Europe (see above).

In the wake of Ceauşescu's diplomatic slight to Brezhnev in January, relations between the CPSU and the Romanians continued to be strained. Ceauşescu did confer with Brezhnev in the Crimea during the summer (*NYT*, 2 August), but the only positive result was the removal of the requirement that East European vacationers in Romania pay for oil and gas with Western currency (ibid., 4 August).

First Secretary Edward Gierek of Poland visited Moscow for talks with Brezhnev (*Pravda*, 14 March).

Yugoslav leader Josip Broz Tito also led a delegation to Moscow. Radio Moscow expressed the hope that the visit "will lead to further consolidation of the all-round cooperation between the two countries" (Radio Moscow in Serbo-Croat to Yugoslavia, 16 May; *FBIS*, 17 May); however, both sides apparently were unusually frank in expressing differences. At a Kremlin dinner, Tito declared that better relations require "a full acknowledgement of certain differences in our views and policies" (*NYT*, 18 May).

Kosygin visited Czechoslovakia for meetings with General Secretary Gustav Husák and Premier Lubomír Strougal (*Izvestiia*, 27 May).

A delegation of Mongolians led by N. Jagbaral, member of the Politburo and secretary of the Mongolian Central Committee, visited the USSR. Mikhail S. Gorbachev, Central Committee secretary for agriculture, and Vladimir A. Karlov, head of the Central Committee Agricultural Department, held talks with this delegation (*Pravda*, 14 April).

Publications. The main CPSU organs are the daily newspaper *Pravda* (circulation more than 11 million), the theoretical and ideological journal *Kommunist* (appearing seventeen times a year, with a circulation over 1 million), and the semimonthly *Partiinaia zhizn*, a journal of internal party affairs and organizational matters (circulation more than 1.16 million). *Kommunist Vooruzhennikh sil* is the party theoretical journal for the armed forces, and *Agitator* is the same for party propagandists; both appear twice a month. The Komsomol has a newspaper, *Komsomolskaia pravda* (six days a week); a monthly theoretical journal, *Molodoi kommunist*; and a monthly literary journal, *Molodaia gvardia*. Each USSR republic prints similar party newspapers in local languages and usually also in Russian. Specialized publications issued under supervision of the CPSU Central Committee include the newspapers *Sovetskaia rossiia*, *Selskaia zhizn*, *Sotzialisticheskaia industria*, *Sovetskaia kultura*, and *Ekonomicheskaia gazeta* and the journal *Politicheskoye samoobrazovaniie*.

University of New Orleans   R. Judson Mitchell

Yugoslavia

Yugoslav communists date the origin of their party to April 1919, when a "unification congress" in Belgrade set up the Socialist Workers' Party of Yugoslavia, including both noncommunist and communist components. In June 1920 this party was dissolved and the Communist Party of Yugoslavia was founded. At the Sixth Congress, in November 1952, the CPY changed its name to the League of Communists of Yugoslavia (Savez komunista Jugoslavije; LCY). The LCY alone of the political parties in the Socialist Federative Republic of Yugoslavia (SFRY) exercises control over the country by playing the leading role in the Socialist Alliance of the Working People of Yugoslavia (Socijalisticki savez radnog naroda Jugoslavije; SAWPY). The SAWPY is a front organization that includes all the mass political organizations; it also includes individuals representing diverse social groups.

At the beginning of 1979, Yugoslavia had 22,074,000 inhabitants (Tanjug, 27 December 1978). On 30 June, membership of the LCY numbered 1,855,638 (*Borba*, 19 October 1979), broken down by nationality as follows: Serbs 903,325 (or 48.68 percent); Croats 279,088 (15.04 percent); Moslems 120,802 (6.51 percent); Macedonians 116,163 (6.26 percent); Slovenes 109,112 (5.88 percent); Montenegrins 108,369 (5.84 percent); "Yugoslavs" 103,730 (5.59 percent); Albanians 68,102 (3.67 percent); Hungarians 24,309 (1.31 percent); others 22,638 (1.22 percent).

The only available official data concerning the social composition of the LCY dating back to 1977 (*Borba*, 7 January), when the party numbered 1,623,735 (*Komunist*, 1 September 1978), follows.

Social Group	Number of Party Members	Percentage
Blue-collar workers	470,883	29
White-collar workers	113,661	7
Peasants	81,187	5
Humanist intelligentsia	227,323	14
Administrative officials	194,849	12
Managers and functionaries	113,661	7
Army and police forces	97,424	6
Unemployed	48,712	3
Pensioners, students, etc.	276,035	17
Total	1,623,735	100

In early 1979, 599,000, or 33.75 percent of the LCY's membership, which was then 1,774,624 (*Vjesnik*, 13 September), were blue-collar workers. In his report to the eighth plenary session of the LCY Central Committee, Branko Mikulić said that, of the 1,885,638 party members at the end of June 1979, 630,904 (34 percent) were "highly qualified, qualified, semiqualified, and nonqualified workers, plus peasants" (*Politika*, 19 October). He also said that "more than 650,000 party members" (35 percent) were 27 years of age or younger. There were also 451,000 female members (24 percent). He did not disclose how many white-collar workers there were, saying only that, if one took engineers, technicians, economists, jurists, and other persons "who directly participate in the production process, as well as young people attending schools which prepare them for productive jobs, then a workers' majority in the party has been achieved" (ibid.).

Leadership and Organization. The supreme forums of the LCY are the 116-member Central Committee and its 24-member Presidium (23 plus Tito, LCY president for life). At the sixth plenary session of the LCY Central Committee in June, several changes in the composition of the Presidium were introduced (see below).

Auxiliary and Mass Organizations. The SAWPY has 113 million members (*Borba*, 28 June). Its supreme body is the Federal Conference (FC), the president of which is the 60-year-old Serb Todo Kurtović, who has said that "in the SAWPY, all well-meaning people have the same rights, regardless of their ideological affiliation" (*Komunist*, 15 June). Following the 15 November session of the FC (*Borba*, 16 November), the term of the FC president was reduced to one year, in accordance with President Tito's idea of collective leadership. The main SAWPY publication is the daily *Borba*.

The Confederation of Trade Unions of Yugoslavia (Savez sindikata Jugoslavije; CTUY) has 6 million members. It was the first mass organization in Yugoslavia to implement President Tito's idea of collective leadership. At the 20 April plenary session, the title of the president was changed to chairman and the term of office cut to one year. The 63-year-old Croat Mika Spiljak, elected president for a four-year term in November 1978, became the first one-year chairman. A new 30-member Presidium was elected (4 members from each of the six republics and three from each of the two autonomous provinces). The chairman of the CTUY is simultaneously chairman of the CTUY Presidium (ibid., 21 April). The daily *Rad* is the CTUY's official publication.

In December 1978 the League of Socialist Youth of Yugoslavia (Savez socijalisticke omladine Jugoslavije; LSYY) had 3,610,000 members organized into 35,500 basic organizations; this was 65.6 percent of the 5.5 million young people living in Yugoslavia (*Komunist*, 22 December 1978). On 29 June a conference of the LSYY in Belgrade decided to introduce the system of collective leadership and reduce the size of the Presidium from 41 to 27 (3 from each of the six republics, 2 from each of the two autonomous provinces, 3 representing various social organizations, 1 from the army, and the editor of the LSYY official weekly *Mladost* as an ex officio member). The 28-year-old Slovene Lev Kreft, who was elected president of the LSYY at its Tenth Congress in December 1978, was replaced by his deputy, Vasil Tupurkovski, also 28, a Macedonian professor from Skoplje, but only for a one-year term. The Secretariat of the LSYY was abolished and a secretary of the Presidium was elected: Darko Mrvos of Croatia. He is to remain in office for a one-year term (*Komunist*, 6 July; *Politika*, 30 June).

Party Internal Affairs. The death of Edvard Kardelj on 10 February caused a number of changes to be made in the LCY, most of them designed to implement Tito's idea of collective leadership. Kardelj's death left two important seats vacant: one in the Presidency of the SFRY (popularly called the State Presidency), the nine-member top state collective leadership, and one in the Presidium of the LCY Central Committee, the 23-member supreme party forum. With the exception of Tito, who has been occupying all three supreme posts in country and party (president of the republic and the Central Committee Presidium, and supreme commander of the armed forces), only eight persons have simultaneously held office in the State Presidency and in the Presidium: the late Slovene Edvard Kardelj, the Croat Vladimir Bakarić; the Serbs Petar Stambolić, Cvijetin Mijatović, and Steven Doronjski; the Montenegrin Vidoje Zarković; the Macedonian Lazar Kolisevski, and the Albanian Fadil Hodza.

On 28 June, the sixth plenary session of the LCY Central Committee decided to relieve three members of the Central Committee Presidium of their posts (citing Kardelj's death as the main reason) and elected four new members to replace them (the fourth for Kardelj). In the State Presidency, Kardelj was replaced by his 65-year-old Slovene countryman Sergej Kraigher; another Slovene, 49-year-old Andrej Marinc, was elected to the Presidium. Mijatović of Bosnia-Herzegovina, Kolisevski of Macedonia, and Zarković of Montenegro were relieved of their duties in the Presidium (they remained members of the State Presidency) and were replaced by 56-year-old Hamdija Pozderac, a Moslem from Bosnia-Herzegovina, Lazar Mojsov, 59, of Macedonia, and Dobroslav Ćulafić, 53, of Montenegro (*Politika*, 29 June).

After the 28 June changes, the new composition of the Presidium is as follows: President Tito; for the Slovenian League of Communists (LC), Stane Dolanc, Andrej Marinc, and Franc Popit; for the Croatian LC, Vladimir Bakarić, Dusan Dragosavac, and Milka Planinc; for the Serbian LC, Petar Stampolić, Milos Minić, and Tihomir Vlaskalić; for the Bosnian-Herzegovinan LC, Branko Mikulić, Hamdija Pozderac, and Nikola Stojanović; for the Macedonian LC, Aleksandar Grlickov, Lazar Mojsov, and Angel Cemerski; for the Montenegrin LC, Veselin Djuranović, Dobroslav Ćulafić, and Vojo Srzentić; for the Vojvodina LC, Stevan Doronjski and Dusan Alimpić; for the Kosovo LC, Fadil Hodza and Mahmut Bakalli; for the People's Army, Gen. Nikola Ljubičić.

The ethnic composition of the Presidum is as follows: eight Serbs (Alimpić, Doronjski, Dragosavac, Ljubičić, Minić, Stambolić, Stojanović, and Vlaskalić); four Croats (Tito, Bakarić, Mikulić, and Planinc); three Slovenes (Dolanc, Marinc, and Popit); three Montenegrins (Ćulafić, Djuranović, and Srzentić); three Macedonians (Cemerski, Grlickov, and Mojsov); two Albanians (Bakalli and Hodza); and one Moslem (Pozderac). By electing Pozderac a member of the Presidium, the problem of Moslem representation in the top party forum was, at least temporarily, resolved.

At the 15 May session of the Presidium, Stane Dolanc, hitherto the secretary, resigned and was replaced by a Serb from Croatia, Dusan Dragosavac (*Politika*, 17 May). The announcement of Dolanc's resignation on the eve of Tito's trip to Moscow provoked speculation about whether Dolanc had been demoted. No doubt, after Kardelj's death, his position had been notably weakened. Dragosavac is known as a "tough man," not very popular with the Croats but extremely loyal to Tito. In contrast to the chairman of the Presidium (until October 1979 the Croat Branko Mikulić and since then, until October 1980, the Serb Stevan Doronjski), who is rotated every year, the secretary retains his position for two years (*Komunist*, 18 May), which makes him, theoretically, a little stronger. In fact, the standing rules of the Presidium provide that neither the chairman nor the secretary, nor any other member of the Presidium, can take any important measures without consulting the president of the LCY (Tito) or all other members of the Presidium.

The death of Edvard Kardelj left a big gap in the Yugoslav leadership. There is no one today in Yugoslavia who could replace him as the second man in the state and in the LCY. On the other hand, his death relieved some party members of their fear that his idea of the "pluralism of self-management interests" might really have become the guiding rule, not only in the state, but also in the party. Interestingly, after Kardelj's death, party members, organizations, and forums were continually warned that they must act according to the principle of "democratic centralism" provided for in the party program and statutes, rather than on the basis of the pluralism of self-management interests (*Vjesnik*, 8 November).

At the eighth plenary session of the LCY Central Committee on 18 October, it was reported that between June 1978 and 25 September 1979 the Presidium met 33 times, during which "more than 90 current ideological-political questions were discussed" (*Borba*, 18 October). From June 1978 to October 1979, the LCY Central Committee held eight plenary sessions. In his major report to the committee plenum, Mikulić complained that "there is still very little initiative and direct decision-making on the part of workers" and attacked the "technobureaucrats," whom he accused of being mainly responsible for workers' lack of influence in enterprises and for the ever-increasing inflation (*Komunist*, 19 October). In connection with the proposed one-year term for various leading party posts, Mikulić said that the same principle would apply to the communal level and would be set forth in a special decision next year. The secretaries of local committees would be elected for two-year terms and executive secretaries would serve for four years (ibid.).

At the 34th session of the Presidium, held in Karadjordjevo on 23 October under Tito's chairmanship, the latter approved Mikulić's report. He hailed the work of the committee and the Presidium, urged the removal of "serious problems" in the country's economic development, mentioned the nonaligned summit in Havana, and praised "the successful work" of the collective leadership (*Komunist*, 23 October).

At the 35th session on 13 November, the Presidium discussed "current ideological-political problems concerning implementation of the policy of equality" of Yugoslavia's nationalities and national minorities. The introductory report was submitted by Dusan Dragosavac. The session also discussed the information media, the sciences, culture, and education, "especially in the sphere of historiography and publishing" (*Borba*, 15 November). However, on 7 and 20 November two joint sessions of the Presidium and the State Presidency took place in Belgrade at which Yugoslavia's economic difficulties were discussed. A long resolution was published in which it was said that inflation had "reached a very high point," causing the country's economic situation to deteriorate seriously. All state and party bureaus and communists in general were invited to do their utmost to resolve existing problems (*Vjesnik*, 24 November).

On 19 April a formal session of the LCY Central Committee commemorated the 60th anniversary of the Communist Party of Yugoslavia. President Tito delivered a major speech, stressing that although it is "a small country, Yugoslavia is prepared to resist any possible attack against its achievements" (*Borba*, 20 April). The commemoration could not but be imbued with memories of the conflict against Stalin and Moscow. Tito's speech gave an extensive explanation of what has happened during the past sixty years, emphasizing his own role (since 1937) in bringing about the consolidation of the party, which led to the communists' rise to power in 1945.

LCY's Ideological Problems. An international symposium was held in the Adriatic town of Cavtat, near Dubrovnik, from 1 to 5 October. Some 113 Marxists from 57 countries took part in a discussion of "The Subjective Forces of Socialism," i.e., the problems of communist parties. The Soviet and Yugoslav Marxists engaged in heated polemics about whether the "Leninist type of communist party" was still valid more than fifty years after Lenin's death. The Yugoslav and Polish delegates clashed over the problem of self-management. Delegates from China attended for the first time, but their names were not published nor is it known if they took part in the discussions (*Vjesnik* and *Borba*, 6 October). Most participants in the symposium agreed that capitalism had survived despite all prophecies of its imminent death; no one, however, was ready to make any new prophecies about its death. Regarding the situation within the world communist movement, Veljko Cvijeticanin of Zagreb said that "it is an exaggeration to say that everybody has his own Marx, but, without any doubt, there have existed various tendencies and different interpretations within Marxism" (ibid.). In his major report, read at the symposium, Aleksandar Grlickov denied the existence of any "leading center" of the international communist movement, insisting only that "various roads to socialism are the strongest elements in the construction of socialism as a world process" (*Socijalizam*, no. 10, October).

Domestic Affairs. *The Problem of the Succession: "Collective Leadership."* Kardelj's death and the fact that President Tito celebrated his 87th birthday on 25 May have intensified the problem of Tito's succession. On the state level the idea of collective leadership was born in 1970, when Tito announced the creation of a collective state forum, which was set up in June 1971 and was composed of 23 members. The constitution of 1974 provided for a 9-member State Presidency; its members were confirmed for a second term in February 1979, only a week before Kardelj's death (*Borba*, 3 February). Since then the composition of the State Presidency has been as follows: Tito (president for life); Sergej Kraigher (Slovenia); Vladimir Bakarić (Croatia); Petar Stambolić (Serbia); Cvijetin Mijatović (Bosnia-Herzegovina); Lazar Kolisevski (Macedonia); Vidoje Zarkovic (Montenegro); Stevan Doronjski (Vojvodina); and Fadil Hodza (Kosovo). From May 1979 to May 1980 the vice-president has been Lazar Kolisevski, deputizing for President Tito.

New Constitutional Changes. At its 4 October session the State Presidency decided to submit a proposal to the Assembly of the SFRY to change the constitution adopted in February 1974. On 31 October the Federal Chamber of the Assembly discussed Tito's idea of collective leadership, which they felt should be reflected in a change of Article 151 of the constitution (which provides for a four-year term of office for various leading officials in the national assemblies and governments). In October 1978 President Tito had suggested that a one-year term for most elected and appointed bodies should become the rule. In the State Presidency a one-year term for the vice-president had been the practice even before the new constitution was adopted in February 1974. Article 327 of the constitution provides for the election of both the president and the vice-president "for a one-year term," anticipating the period after Tito, when there will be no president for life. In its proposal to the SFRY Assembly, signed by Tito, the State Presidency justified the proposed constitutional change as being a "more consistent implementation of the principle of collective work, decision-making, and responsibility in assemblies and other collective arms of authority and social self-management" (*NIN*, 28 October).

Since 1946 the Yugoslavs have changed their constitution four times: in 1946, 1953, 1963, and 1974. The real reason behind these repeated changes has been the leaders' attempts to preserve party control over the state apparatus. The changes are also intended to ensure that, after Tito, no single individual can usurp power and proclaim himself a "new Tito."

The Struggle Against Pan-Islamic Nationalism. In the March 1971 census, more than 1.7 million people were permitted to register themselves as Moslems by nationality, distinct from Moslems by faith (*Yugoslav Survey*, no. 1, February 1973). More than 88 percent of these Slavic Moslems live in Bosnia-Herzegovina, where in the past they have had to declare themselves as Serbs, Croats, or "Yugoslavs." Presumably, in 1971 they were recognized as a separate ethnic group in order to discourage a struggle between the Serbs and Croats to claim them as "pure Serbs" or "pure Croats."

Although the regime insisted that to be a "Moslem by nationality" had nothing to do with Islam as a religion, Yugoslavia's communist leaders used the country's Moslems as a bridge between themselves and the Arab countries—to which dozens of young Yugoslav Moslems were sent to study. When in 1973 Libyan Col. Mu'ammar al-Qadhafi paid an official visit to Yugoslavia, he was taken to Sarajevo, the capital of Bosnia-Herzegovina, where the communist leaders took him from one mosque to another. In the meantime, however, most of Yugoslavia's Moslems have begun to feel themselves closely linked with the Pan-Islamic movement, i.e., they have begun considering themselves Moslems by faith. Along with the Albanians and Turks, the Moslems by faith are today believed to number "between 3.5 and 4 million persons" (*Frankfurter Allgemeine Zeitung* [*FAZ*], 22 May).

Even though all Slav Moslems in Bosnia-Herzegovina are Sunnites, their admiration for the Pan-Islamic revolution, mainly carried out by the Shiites in Iran, has been great. The head of Yugoslavia's Moslems, the ulama Ahmed Smajlović, considered the country's Moslem spiritual leader, has criticized Iran's Ayatollah Ruhollah Khomeini for his anti-Western orientation and "backward" attitude toward women; but he did not hide his joy concerning "the victory of Islam" in Iran and elsewhere. Smajlović also hailed Islam's "rejection of Marxism-Leninism, which cannot be ideologically accepted" (ibid., 7 June). Sarajevo's Muhamed Filipović indicated that there has been "a clear revival of the revolutionary role of Islam," for which he was sharply criticized (*Komunist*, 26 October).

This may explain the organized anti-pan-Islamic campaign that began in the second half of 1979; in its course almost daily criticisms have been directed against the leaders of the Moslem religious community. The mufti of Belgrade, Hamdija Jusufspahić, and the imam of Bugojno, Husein Djoza, a counselor to the ulama Smajlović, were sharply denounced for having addressed as "dear Moslem brothers" a mass meeting at the opening of a new mosque in a Bosnian village (*Politika*, 29 October). Jusufspahić had claimed that "anyone who eats pork will acquire the characteristics of the animal he eats" (*Borba*, 28 October). The imam Djoza, editor-in-chief of the Moslem religious paper *Preporod*, was also attacked because his periodical began a polemic by discussing an anti-Moslem book called *Parergon* by Dervis Susić, that deals with the pro-fascist leanings of some Moslem individuals and groups prior to and during World War II (ibid., 26 September).

The strongest general attack against pan-Islamic ideas and activities in Yugoslavia has come from Hamdija Pozderac, the only Moslem representative in the LCY Central Committee Presidium. During a symposium in the Bosnian town of Banja Luka, Pozderac said there had been attempts to persuade the Moslems in Bosnia-Herzegovina to identify their Islamic religion with the idea of nation, using the slogan of "religious brotherhood." He resolutely rejected the idea of a "pan-Islamic, universal link based on faith," which may have created a type of "pan-Islamic nationalism" that is in opposition to the nationality policy of the LCY and therefore is a "misuse of faith for political purposes." Pozderac insisted that "pan-Islamic nationalism" had to be rejected because "it has been misusing, not only democratic freedoms within Yugoslavia, but also our openness toward the situation in the world . . . [and] the principles of socialist self-management" (*Komunist*, 23 November).

Dissident Forces and Amnesty. During 1979, the Yugoslav authorities strengthened their efforts to curb the increased activities of dissidents. "Open anti-Communism and bloc exclusiveness" are said to have formed the ideological basis for a group of oppositionalists who began attacking the regime "under cover of 'the struggle for human rights' " (*Borba*, 5 January). The Yugoslav information media published only a few names of people who were tried for "hostile anti-state activities." In January, the 53-year-old Dubrovnik baker Zvonimir Kisić was arrested for "the criminal deed of engaging in dissemination of hostile propaganda" and sentenced to ten years' imprisonment (ibid., 8 March). In Serbia, people who celebrated the Serb Orthodox new year's eve (January 14) were proclaimed "enemies" (*Stuttgarter Zeitung*, 12 January). In February, a 26-year-old Serb was sentenced to two years' imprisonment in Novi Sad for "enemy activity" (Tanjug, 10 February). In Sremska Mitrovica, the 31-year-old Nedeljko Martinović was sentenced to ten years' imprisonment for having joined, while working in West Germany, "an extremist Croat exile organization" (*Politika ekspres*, 28 February). The Macedonian exiled politician Dragan Bogdanovski, who, it is claimed, was kidnapped and brought back to Yugoslavia, was sentenced in Skoplje to thirteen years in jail for "anti-Yugoslav activities in the West" (*Politika*, 17 February).

In April, Milovan Djilas, Yugoslavia's most prominent dissident, was summoned by the secret police and warned to cease his "criminal activities" (*NYT*, 8 April). Government spokesman Mirko Kalezić stated that Yugoslavia "is not a multiparty system of the Western type," nor does it have "a shadow opposition which is waiting to take over the government tomorrow." After saying this, he refused to comment further on the warning to Djilas (Associated Press, 8 April). In August, a county court in the Serbian town of Sabac sentenced an unidentified "group of persons" accused of "subversive activities" to prison terms ranging from eighteen months to six years. No names of the convicted persons were given, but it was said that they belonged to an illegal organization called "The Realistic Unification of Europe—Yugoslav Movement of Europeans," whose leader was described as "a certain Bogdan Stefanović," living abroad (Tanjug, 8 August).

Eight Belgrade university professors and lecturers (Mihajlo Marković, Svetozar Stojanović, Ljubomir Tadić, Zagorka Pesić-Golubović, Milan Zivotić, Nebojsa Popov, and Triva Indzić—all contributors to the banned Zagreb philosophical bimonthly *Praxis*, who were suspended in 1975 but continued to receive a reduced monthly salary, would lose even that should a new law be passed in Serbia (*NIN*, 14 October). In a letter addressed to a West German daily, the eight professors complained about "political discrimination" and about having been put on a "blacklist" (*Die Welt*, 27 October).

In September, Milovan Djilas and his two friends Dragoljub Ignjatović and Momcilo Selić put out a mimeographed literary magazine called *Casovnik*. About 800 copies were printed of the 200-page periodical, which contains only short stories and poems, including an essay on Dostoevsky by Mihajlo Mihajlov, who toured the United States during 1979. Djilas, Ignjatović (nominal editor of the periodical), and Selić were summoned to court on October 15 (*NYT*, 16 October). Djilas was fined 10,000 dinar (about $530) for his "spiritual fatherhood" of the periodical and Ignjatović was sentenced to 30 days' imprisonment; Selić was only reprimanded (*Vecernje novosti*, 16 October). On the same day, the Belgrade daily *Politika* published an anti-Djilas article, "Provocation in 'Literary' Disguise," with the subtitle "Milovan Djilas, Together with His Followers, Has Continued to Pursue Anti-Yugoslav Activities." Djilas is accused of having found "one of his main platforms in the pages of certain West European and American newspapers" and of maintaining contacts "with the extremist Chetnik terrorists in America." Stressing that Djilas "has been warned several times about his anti-Yugoslav activities," the article ends: "For this reason, one must rightly ask the question: How long does Djilas, with this kind of behavior, intend to go on defying the democratic patience of our public?" (*Politika*, 16 October.)

At its 23 November session, the State Presidency amnestied 51 prisoners on the occasion of the 29 November national holiday: 19 were set free and 32 had their prison terms reduced. There were no details about how many were political prisoners (*Borba*, 24 November).

Economy. In the first nine months of the year, Yugoslavia's exports totaled 83.3 billion dinars (about U.S. $4.3 billion; $1 = 19 dinars), which is 14 percent more than in the same period of 1978. However, imports reached 171.1 billion dinars (about $9 billion) in value, which is 31 percent more than in 1978. Only 49 percent of the imports could be covered by exports. More than 70 percent of the trade deficit was with Western countries, to which goods costing 35.6 billion dinars (about $1.87 billion) were exported, but from which goods valued at more than 100 billion dinars (about $5.26 billion) were imported. Only 35 percent of the imports from Western countries could be covered by exports to them. In the first nine months, the country's general foreign trade deficit jumped from 57.4 billion dinars (about $3.02 billion) to 87.8 billion dinars (about $4.62 billion). Yugoslavia exported to the developing countries goods totaling 14.6 billion dinars (about $768 million) i.e., 2 percent less than in 1978; it imported from them goods valued at 26.7 billion dinars (about $1.40 billion), 33 percent more than in 1978. The "most harmonized" trade was achieved with the East European countries, to which exports costing 3.63 billion dinars (about $191 million) were made, and from which imports worth 5.86 billion dinars (about $308 million) were brought in, which means that 75 percent of the imports from socialist countries was covered by exports to them (*Ekonomska politika*, 15 October). It was estimated that by the end of 1979 Yugoslavia's exports would reach the sum of $7 billion, its imports $12 billion (ibid., 1 October).

On 7 and 20 November, the Presidium of the LCY Central Committee and the State Presidency, plus "several top state officials of the federation, as well as the presidents of the six socialist republics and two socialist autonomous provinces," held joint sessions at which the serious economic situation of the country was discussed. A resolution was published on 24 November dealing with two essential problems: a) the causes of Yugoslavia's economic difficulties and b) the measures that should be taken to eliminate, or at least alleviate, them. Along with "significant results" achieved in the economic sphere, the resolution said, "numerous disproportions in the economic structure and shortcomings in economic operations are becoming greater and, under the circumstances of a deteriorating international economic situation, have led to serious economic difficulties" (*Komunist*, 30 November). In the view of the Presidium, the difficulties can be attributed to the following factors: a) improper implementation of existing laws and regulations; (b) disruption in the relationships between existing goods and money: "An excessively high boom on the domestic market has accelerated price rises and produced a deficit in the balance of payments"; c) the fact that inflation has reached "a very high level and is tending to increase to such an extent as to upset all economic processes" — in the first nine months, inflation reached 30 percent (*Dnevnik*, Ljubljana, 15 October), but it was estimated that by the end of the year it would reach only 22–23 percent (*Ekonomska politika*, 22 October); d) the fact that the trade and balance of payments deficit has become the country's key problem — Yugoslavia's indebtedness abroad has reached a level that "must not be exceeded" (ibid.). The serious earthquakes in Montenegro (April and May) and "other natural disasters" were also given as causes of the difficulties.

This year, Yugoslavia's foreign debts totaled about $13 billion (*FAZ*, 25 September); it is estimated that the debt service over the next three or four years will run from $1.8 billion to $2.9 billion annually (*Journal of Commerce*, 25 September). It is also estimated that about 22 percent of Yugoslavia's foreign currency earnings will have to be used for the payment of interest on debts (*FAZ*, 25 September).

In the first nine months, about $1 billion was earned from foreign tourism (*Borba*, 21 September) and roughly $2.8 billion by Yugoslav workers abroad (*Vjesnik*, 13 August). In September there were 1,185,000 Yugoslavs in Western Europe (*Vecernji list*, 12 October). Of these, 695,000 were employed and 490,000 were dependents (including 250,000 school-age children). Yugoslav statistical data are not reliable concerning the absolute figures of citizens working abroad. For instance, in August it was reported that "about 900,000 Yugoslavs" were working in West European countries, "with more than 2,000,000 family members both in the old [Europe] and new [United States and Canada] world" (*Ekonomska politika*, 20 August). According to other statistics, there were 360,000 Yugoslav citizens in Australia, 130,000 in Canada, and "more than 1,000,000" in the United States (*Vjesnik*, 4 August).

In September there were 5,280,000 employed persons in the so-called socialist sector and "about 735,000 unemployed" (*Borba*, 27 September). In November there were 750,000 unemployed (*NIN*, 2 December). The rate of unemployment in Slovenia was 1.5 percent, in Kosovo 27.1 percent. It was claimed that, among the unemployed, "only 400,000 are socially and economically truly unemployed, while the others are students, peasants waiting for employment," etc. (ibid., 26 September). In 1978 there were 472,863 persons "seeking a first job"; 52 percent were women, 72 percent young people, and 40.3 percent "experts" (ibid.). There were 380,000 persons engaged in the "private sector" of the Yugoslav economy (about 280,000 private shop or workshop owners and about 100,000 workers employed by them); about 3 million "active citizens" tilled their own land in the countryside (*Ekonomska politika*, 10 September).

Full statistical data on personal incomes in Yugoslavia were given only for 1978; for 1979 it was reported that the average monthly salary was 5,740 dinars, or about $302 (Tanjug, 4 December). The average monthly salary of a Yugoslav worker in 1978 was 5,075 dinars (about $267); in the economic branches it was 4,914 dinars (about $259) and in the noneconomic branches 5,923 dinars (about $312). Bank officials had the highest personal income (6,815 dinars, or $359 a month), followed by administrative officials (6,388 dinars, or $336 a month). It was also revealed that 40 percent of all employed persons earned 5,000–6,000 dinars a month (about $263–316) and that only 5.7 percent of the employed, most of them in the state and party apparatuses, received 9,000 dinars a month, or about $474 (*Vjesnik*, 19 June). More than one-fifth of all employed Yugoslavs "earn about 4,000 dinars [about $211] monthly," with workers employed in industry and mining occupying thirteenth place on the list of wage earners (*Politika*, 2 August). About 400,000 workers in Yugoslavia were receiving 2,500–3,000 dinars (about $132–158) monthly (*Vjesnik*, 1 July).

Foreign Policy. *The Soviet Union.* The culminating point in Yugoslav-Soviet relations in 1979 was President Tito's official visit to Moscow from 16 to 21 May, of which only two days were devoted to official meetings with Prime Minister Leonid Brezhnev. Summarizing these official talks as briefly as possible, one might say that the Yugoslav and Soviet leaders again agreed to continue to disagree. To be sure, this is nothing new in relations between the two countries and parties, but President Tito's advancing age put the old formula into a somewhat different perspective. It is not so much a problem of what Moscow's approach to Yugoslavia has been up until now, but rather what the Russians might do after Tito's disappearance from the Yugoslav scene. On this point, Brezhnev did his best to persuade Tito that he has nothing to fear, saying in his toast on 17 May that all rumors of possible Soviet interference in post-Tito Yugoslavia are "absurd fantasies" (*Politika*, 19 May).

The joint communiqué (officially called "the press release about the Yugoslav-Soviet meeting") repeated some well-known generalities (ibid.). President Tito in his toast mentioned the June 1955 and June 1956 Belgrade and Moscow declarations (ibid.) in which various roads to socialism had been recognized by Nikita Khrushchev and reconfirmed by Brezhnev. Upon his return home, Tito said that he and Brezhnev had "tried, as much as possible, to understand one another's point of view, on which differences existed, but which are, I should say, logical" (*Borba*, 22 May). The Soviet information media called these differences "natural—which must not be an obstacle to our all-round cooperation" (*Pravda*, 20 May).

One of the main differences between Belgrade and Moscow has been in views on nonalignment. Tito made a long reference to nonalignment in his 17 May toast, but Brezhnev did not once mention the subject. The most controversial topic in relations between Moscow and Belgrade was not mentioned at all: the Vietnamese invasion of Kampuchea (and the Chinese invasion of Vietnam). This was the question in 1979 over which the Yugoslav and Soviet media constantly exchanged volleys (see below). In his 14 June press conference, Stane Dolanc confirmed that there were "quite definitely" differences between Yugoslavia and the Soviet Union, especially in their respective views about the nonaligned movement (*Politika*, 16 June).

Nevertheless, throughout the year, the two countries and parties exchanged visits of delegations at all levels, both from individual republics and from the two federations. Although similar visits have been recorded in the past, Moscow's interest in the individual Yugoslav republics and nationalities deserves special attention. Between 22 and 30 October, a delegation of the Yugoslav National Assembly, headed by Chairman Dragoslav Marković, visited the Soviet Union; Marković said on his return from Moscow that, "regardless of differences, those points that are mutual to us have been much more significant" (ibid., 1 November).

Trade. In 1979 the "planned volume" of Soviet-Yugoslav deliveries was $3.3 billion (*Zurnaleksport*, August). In the first months of 1979, however, 92 percent of Yugoslav exports to and 93 percent of Yugoslav imports from the Soviet Union had already taken place. This meant $1.28 billion for Yugoslav exports and $1.474 billion for Soviet exports to Yugoslavia (*Economic Review*, April-May). By September, 98 percent of the contracted arrangements had been carried out (Tanjug, 21 September).

At the end of September, a Soviet delegation headed by Vice-Prime Minister Ivan Arkhipov arrived in Belgrade for the seventeenth session of the Yugoslav-Soviet Committee for Economic and Scientific-Technical Cooperation. Arkhipov and Yugoslavia's Vice-Prime Minister Gojko Ubiparip signed a trade protocol covering the 1981–1985 period that provides for an expansion of the volume of trade to the level of $2–2.1 billion. The committee announced that, in the first eight months of 1979, Yugoslav and Soviet enterprises contracted for $1.6 billion worth of imports from the Soviet Union and $1.4 billion worth of exports from Yugoslavia. Up to that time, the Yugoslavs had exported $800 million worth of goods to the USSR and imported $900 million worth from it (*Borba*, 27 September).

Between 30 October and 5 November, another Soviet vice-prime minister, Vladimir Novikov, conferred in Belgrade with Ubiparip and other Yugoslav economic leaders. They mainly discussed cooperation between the two countries' machine-building industries (Tanjug, 5 November). Ten days later, it was reported that trade between the Soviet Union and Yugoslavia in 1980 was projected at about $4 billion, of which Yugoslav exports should amount to $1.8 billion and imports from the Soviet Union $2.1 billion (ibid., 16 November).

The Conflict Over Vietnam's Invasion of Kampuchea. The January invasion of Kampuchea (Cambodia) by Vietnamese troops aroused great concern in Yugoslavia. Kampuchea and Vietnam are communist-ruled countries and members of the nonalignment movement. The fact that Vietnam has been supported by Moscow and Cambodia by Beijing has led to conflict between two mutually hostile ideological trends. The Yugoslavs have worried that there might be a revival of the Brezhnev Doctrine, proclaimed in 1968 after the Soviet invasion of Czechoslovakia in justification of subjugating a communist country that opposes Moscow-type "real socialism." The official Yugoslav stand has been that the Vietnamese invasion should be condemned, not only because no invasion of a foreign territory or overthrow of the government of an independent and sovereign country can be accepted "in contemporary international politics . . . but rather as a precedent which might endanger the security of other countries" (*Vecernji list*, 6/7 January). In a talk with several Yugoslav journalists, Dusan Dragosavac said that no invasion "can be justified by any kind of theory of limited sovereignty" (*Borba*, 29 January).

Criticism of Yugoslavia's "unobjective reporting" of the conflict in Indochina (mostly by the Soviet Union and Czechoslovakia) was resolutely rejected in Yugoslavia. The Yugoslav information media wrote that the Vietnamese invasion "opened a Pandora's Box," making possible some "unpredictable surprises." They asked: "Who is next? (*NIN*, 25 February). The general tenor in the Yugoslav media has been that: a) the conflict between China and Vietnam will continue (*Vecernji list*, 24/25 February); b) it can be resolved only if the Vietnamese withdraw from Kampuchea; c) the Kampuchean events "have dramatically displayed all the weaknesses of a power which tried to impose its solution on others by force"; and d) the Vietnamese action "has also shown that armed confrontations between nonaligned and socialist countries reflect negatively on both the strength and the prestige of the non-aligned movement" and that the invasion has "obviously harmed the causes of socialism in the world" (*Borba*, 21 February).

These four points prevailed in Yugoslav commentaries about the affair throughout the year. The commentaries mainly deplored wars between communist countries (ibid., 27 February) and concentrated their responses on the attacks coming from the East European countries, particularly from the Soviet Union (*Sovyetskaya Rossiya*, 16 March). Even though the Yugoslavs insisted that they were impartial in their appraisal of the Vietnamese invasion of Kampuchea and the Chinese invasion of Vietnam, they did not conceal their sympathy with the Chinese (*Vjesnik*, 9 April). They strongly attacked the Czechoslovak information media for "falsifying the image of Yugoslavia in presenting untruths or half-truths" concerning the alleged Yugoslav approach to the war in Indochina (*Borba*, 11 April). In their counterattacks against Vietnamese reporting, the Yugoslavs claimed that the Vietnamese anti-Yugoslav campaign recalled the Cominform's anti-Yugoslav attacks in 1948 (ibid., 18 April).

Two Yugoslav army generals, Dzemil Sarac and Rahmia Kadenić, both Moslems, warned all would-be aggressors that any attack on Yugoslavia similar to that on Cambodia would not pay, because the Yugoslavs are ready to defend their country and their independent communist system at any price (*Vjesnik*, 21 April; *Borba*, 12 April). Similar attacks and warnings were voiced in the Yugoslav press throughout the year (*Vjesnik*, 28 September; *Borba*, 29 September). In November, the Yugoslav-Soviet polemics over Cambodia sharpened after Tass (20 November) rebuked *Borba* for an article (18 October) in which it allegedly joined the United States and China in rejoicing over Vietnam's second defeat in the United Nations. Tass reminded the Yugoslavs that the Vietnamese "fraternal help" to Cambodia was identical with the Red Army's help to the Yugoslav partisans in 1944. It was this comparison that disturbed the Yugoslavs most. "We do not accept such an analogy, not even conditionally," a Yugoslav commentator said (*Borba*, 22 November). A radio commentator asserted that the comparison was "very insolent and a huge lie." Although "no one in Yugoslavia has been ready" to belittle the Red Army's contribution in World War II, no one is prepared to tolerate the assertion that freedom was gained for Yugoslavia's nationalities by anyone other than themselves (Radio Zagreb, 22 November).

The Sixth Nonaligned Summit in Havana. The sixth nonaligned summit was held in Havana from 3 to 9 September. It was attended by representatives of 116 countries: 96 full members, 12 observers, and 8 guests (*Vjesnik*, 28 September). Before, during, and after the summit, sharp polemics were exchanged concerning the role to be played by the nonaligned movement. Castro's Cuba and Tito's Yugoslavia played the main roles in the struggle over leadership of the movement: Tito succeeded in attracting a large number of the nonaligned countries in defense of the "original idea" of nonalignment; Castro propagated the idea that the communist countries, headed by the Soviet Union, were the "natural allies" of the nonaligned countries.

In January (17–20), Cuban Foreign Minister Isidoro Malmierca paid an official visit to Belgrade, where he and Yugoslavia's Foreign Minister Josip Vrhovec clashed over the Vietnamese invasion of Kampuchea. In his 17 January toast, Vrhovec warned his Cuban colleague that "conflicts between individual nonaligned countries, especially when they assume the form of armed clashes and interventions, always provide an opportunity for foreign interference, bloc competition, and the infiltration of foreign interests" (Tanjug, 17 January). In his toast, Malmierca interpreted the nonaligned movement as a group of countries fighting "imperialism and oppression." He added that the nonaligned movement would succeed "on the basis of the struggle against imperialism, colonialism, neocolonialism, racism (including Zionism), and apartheid" (ibid.). Contrary to normal practice, neither Malmierca's nor Vrhovec's toast was published in any major Yugoslav paper; they were released only by Tanjug in English.

In his efforts to gain the support of as many nonaligned countries as possible, President Tito started a four-state tour of the Middle East in 1979: Kuwait (1–4 February), Iraq (4–8 February), Syria (8–11 February), and Jordan (11–12 February). Commenting on his tour, a Belgrade weekly said that "a relatively small, but aggressive group of nonaligned movement members seeks (and wherever it can, tries to force) the transformation of the nonaligned countries into a strategic reserve, into 'a natural ally' and, in fact, a follower of a military-political coalition" (*NIN*, 11 February). The Yugoslavs complained that Iraqi leaders were stressing "exclusively the anti-imperialist and anti-Zionist aims of the nonalignment movement" but not displaying "a like stand on the equally important direction of our struggle against hegemony and all forms of political and economic domination which are not classic imperialism" (Radio Belgrade, 6 February).

From 6 to 10 March, North Korean Foreign Minister Ho Tam paid an official visit to Yugoslavia; he came closer to the Yugoslav than to the Cuban approach to nonalignment (*Politika*, 8 March). President Tito, in his major (15 May) speech before the National Assembly, warned against "the danger of isolation and particularly the danger of division within the movement" (*Borba*, 16 May). On 28 May, Tito left for Algeria, where he remained until 31 May; from 31 May to 3 June he visited Libya, and afterward Malta. Neither in Algeria nor in Libya did he succeed in mobilizing the leaders' support for the line to be followed by the nonalignment movement. In Libya, al-Qadhafi spoke of "certain difficulties which accompany Libyan-Yugoslav bilateral co-operation" (Tanjug, 2 June).

The foreign ministers of 91 nonaligned countries held a preliminary conference from 6 to 10 June in Colombo, Sri Lanka, where they prepared the agenda for the sixth nonaligned summit in Havana. The problem of Kampuchean representation was not resolved and was to be discussed in Havana (*Politika*, 11 June). The Yugoslav information media described the heated behind-the-scenes struggle during the Colombo conference, especially several "traps" which some "forces, striving to reorient the nonaligned movement," tried to set with the aim of dividing the movement (*NIN*, 17 June). In the meantime, the Yugoslav information media accused the Warsaw Pact countries, particularly Czecho-slovakia, of trying to split the nonaligned movement (*Borba*, 28 July; Radio Belgrade, 28 July).

In Havana, the struggle over the interpretation of nonaligned goals continued. Tito's 4 September speech at the summit was considered moderate. After months of attacks and counterattacks in defense of the "basic orientation" of the nonaligned movement, one might have expected the Yugoslav leader to deliver a more inflammatory speech. He deplored differences between nonaligned countries, but in principle recognized them as "quite natural"—a development that will probably continue in the future. "The only thing which we must not tolerate is any unprincipled attitude, because this contradicts the essence of the movement and causes it great harm" (*Vjesnik*, 5 September). Despite the optimistic tone of the Yugoslav media during and after the Havana summit, the Yugoslavs did not conceal their misgivings about "undemocratic activity" within the nonaligned movement. They were especially angered by Cuba's Foreign Minister Malmierca, who "employed undemocratic means, hammering on the chairman's table while chairing one of the sessions . . . to impose his own concept on nonaligned policy and its implementation" (ibid., 10 September).

In Belgrade, Stane Dolanc said in an interview that the behavior of Cuba during the conference "was strange, to put it very mildly," and indirectly criticized Moscow for trying to impose its will upon some of the nonaligned countries (Radio Ljubljana, 6 September). Upon his return home President Tito claimed victory, with the Yugoslav newspapers announcing that "the nonaligned countries are following Tito's line" (*Vjesnik*, 8 September). This sentence became a slogan in Yugoslavia. In his speech in Belgrade, Tito made it clear how satisfied he was with the results of the summit, although the other side (Cuba and its protector, the Soviet Union) also claimed satisfaction. Yet neither Tito nor Dolanc, nor any of the Yugoslav commentators, dared to point out the strange fact that a totally aligned country such as Cuba had become the nominal leader of the nonaligned world for the next three years.

In his 23 September speech in the Serbian town of Titovo Uzice, the Yugoslav president said that "there are still some people who cannot conceive that the nonaligned movement is no one's mouth-piece" (*Borba*, 24 September). In a belated accusation of Cuba's Prensa Latina news agency, the Yugoslavs revealed how fierce had been the Yugoslav-Cuban struggle over nonalignment, especially over the Vietnamese invasion of Kampuchea (*Politika*, 24 September). The Yugoslavs visibly waited to see how the U.N. General Assembly's vote (21 September) on Kampuchean representation would turn out, and once the majority had decided in favor of the anti-Vietnamese and anti-Soviet Pol Pot regime, Belgrade gave Tanjug the go-ahead for a counterattack on Prensa Latina.

The United States. Yugoslav officials did not conceal their satisfaction over Washington's apparent understanding of Belgrade's nonaligned stance. On 15 March, the Yugoslav information media reported a message President Carter had sent to President Tito "as a part of the usual exchange of opinions between the two presidents on current questions of international relations" (*Borba*, 16 March). Ten days earlier Tito had sent a message to Carter in connection with the Middle East crisis, the current events in Southeast Asia, "and other current international questions" (ibid., 4 March). In late January/early February, a delegation headed by Serbia's Prime Minister Ivan Stambolić paid an official visit to Washington and discussed economic cooperation between Yugoslavia and the United States (*Politika*, 8 February). According to Ilija Vakić, chairman of the Yugoslav Federal Economic Chamber, Yugoslavia's imports from the United States in the first eight months of 1979 were worth $671 million; exports to the United States totaled $246 million (*Borba*, 20 October).

It was this huge deficit ($425 million) that, according to Vakić, restricted any expansion of Yugoslav-American trade (ibid.). Vakić made his statement during the Yugoslav-American economic meetings in Belgrade (19-22 October), when representatives of eighteen U.S. companies conferred in Yugoslavia about their interest in joint ventures and long-term cooperation between the two countries (Tanjug, 22 October). The president of the U.S. Overseas Private Investment Corporation, J. Bruce

Llewellyn, observed that the meetings and contacts of U.S. economic experts with Yugoslav business-men and economists had convinced them of the "great possibilities the Yugoslav economy can offer for wider and more meaningful cooperation" (ibid.).

In April, a U.S. State Department team headed by Under Secretary of State for Political Affairs David D. Newsom met in Belgrade with Yugoslav officials to discuss "questions about bilateral rela-tions and the most immediate international political and economic issues" (Tanjug, 24 April). Newsom talked with Yugoslavia's Foreign Minister Vrhovec and Deputy Foreign Minister Budimir Loncar and Serbia's Prime Minister Ivan Stambolić (*Politika*, 26 April).

Some difficulties in Yugoslav-American relations emerged in connection with what Belgrade called "exile terrorists" in the United States. A court decision easing the life sentence imposed upon a group of "anti-Yugoslav émigrés" who had hijacked a passenger plane in 1976 was received in Yugo-slavia "with indignation" (*Borba*, 15 April). On the other hand, the heavy sentences given Nikola Kavaja, the Serbian Orthodox priest Stojiljko Kajević, Rados Stevlić, and Nikola Zivović were received in Yugoslavia with satisfaction (Tanjug, 23 June).

In May, Gen. Bernard W. Rogers, then U.S. Army chief of staff, arrived in Belgrade, where he met with Yugoslav army leaders; he visited Yugoslavia from 6 to 11 May (Tanjug, 11 May). On 25 May, a Yugoslav government spokesman said no date had been set for a proposed visit by President Carter to Yugoslavia (ibid., 25 May). Mrs. Joan Mondale, wife of the U.S. vice-president, spent six days in Yugo-slavia, where she opened the U. S. art exhibition "America Now" (ibid., 16 June). Representatives of 90 U.S. enterprises and 140 Yugoslav enterprises held their fifth annual meeting in Dubrovnik, 3–6 June (*Ekonomska politika*, 11 June). An LCY delegation headed by Tihomir Vlaskalić, president of the LCY of Serbia, paid an official visit to Washington from 26 June to 9 July. The delegation had been invited by the chairman of the Republican and Democratic National Committees and by the American Council of Young Political Leaders. The delegation visited California, Chicago, New York City, and Niagara Falls. The Yugoslav information media reported that the party delegation's visit was "a great success" (Tanjug, 10 July).

Chairman of the U.S. Export-Import Bank John Moore visited Belgrade in July to discuss credits and financial cooperation with Yugoslav Finance Minister Petar Kostić. The two discussed conditions for a $90-million credit granted by the American bank for the reconstruction of Yugoslav regions hit by a severe earthquake in April (ibid., 27 July). In October, U.S. Treasury Secretary William Miller met Kostić in Belgrade to discuss Yugoslavia's serious trade deficit with the United States, Yugoslavia's fourth largest economic partner (ibid., 3 October). Also in October, President Tito had "a lengthy con-versation" with Henry Kissinger in Belgrade (*Borba*, 15 October).

On 20 November, Yugoslavia's new ambassador to Washington, Budimir Loncar, presented his credentials to Deputy Secretary of State Warren Christopher (*Politika*, 21 November). A visit to Yugo-slavia, Romania, and West Berlin in the first half of December by U.S. Secretary of State Cyrus Vance was officially postponed because of the Iranian situation (Tanjug, 5 December).

Relations with China. Throughout the year, Yugoslavia's information media were full of reports about China, especially in view of the Vietnamese invasion of Kampuchea and Beijing's reaction to it. China's "opening to the world" was greeted enthusiastically (*Ekonomska politika*, 15 January). Several Yugoslav delegations visited China, and Chinese delegations toured Yugoslavia. Some of the Yugoslav delegations (for instance, the Vojvodina delegation, headed by Prime Minister Nikola Kmezić) were received by Hua Guofeng (Tanjug, 21 February). In March, Hua also received Yugo-slavia's Deputy Prime Minister Branislav Ikonić and members of the Yugoslav economic delegation who took part in a session of the Yugoslav-Chinese Committee for Economic, Scientific and Technical Cooperation (*Borba*, 3 March). A series of economic agreements were signed in Beijing doubling the 1978 trade between the two countries from $200 million to $420 million in 1979 (Tanjug, 5 March). Re-garding China's internal developments, the Yugoslav papers wrote about "de-Maoization" as something new (*NIN*, 18 March). A large Yugoslav industrial fair opened in Beijing in April (*Politika*, 9 April), with displays of some 200 Yugoslav enterprises. Again, Chairman Hua received the Yugoslav trade delegation, headed by Ilija Vakić (ibid., 15 April). In May, China's Deputy Foreign Trade Minister Zhou Huamin visited Yugoslavia officially (*Borba*, 16 May), and several days later a delegation of the Chinese trade union federation, headed by Vice-Chairman Huang Minwei, arrived in Belgrade (ibid., 22 May).

In June, a Chinese agricultural delegation headed by Deputy Minister for Agriculture Zhao Fan arrived in Yugoslavia, where an agreement on cooperation was signed (Tanjug, 13 June). Also in June, a Yugoslav party study delegation headed by Svetozar Durutović, executive secretary in the Central Committee Presidium, went to China (Tanjug, 22 June). They were received by Chairman Hua in Beijing (*Borba*, 3 July). Yang Yong, deputy chief of the Chinese General Staff, stopped briefly "while flying through Yugoslavia's airspace" in Belgrade, where he was welcomed by top Yugoslav army leaders (ibid., 27 June). In July, a Chinese party study delegation, headed by Central Committee member Song Renqiong, arrived in Belgrade (Tanjug, 4 July); they were received by Branko Mikulić, then chairman of the Presidium. Ikonić and Chinese Vice-Premier Wang Zhen conferred about Yugoslav-Chinese economic cooperation in September (*Vjesnik*, 14 September). A Chinese military delegation led by Deputy Chief of Staff Wang Shangrong, traveling "from Belgium en route to Romania," arrived in Belgrade, where they were met by Yugoslav military leaders (Tanjug, 19 September). Also that month, President Tito received Deputy Prime Minister Wang Zhen (ibid., 21 September). In October, China's Minister of Culture Huang Zhen arrived in Belgrade for an official visit (*Borba*, 16 October).

Trade difficulties between China and Yugoslavia were announced at the end of October; it was said that only $75 million had been realized in both directions in the first nine months of the year, although it had been planned that total trade in 1979 would be $420 million (*Politika*, 26 October). The culminating point in Yugoslav-Chinese relations in 1979 was the official visit of China's Foreign Minister Huang Hua to Yugoslavia between 6 and 9 November, after he had toured Western Europe with Chairman Hua. Huang was received by Tito and, in an interview, praised Tito's "positive and constructive role in international politics" (Tanjug, 9 November). A member of the Presidium, Milka Planinc, spent seven days in Beijing as the head of a Yugoslav party delegation (*Borba*, 21 November).

Publications. The main publications of the LCY are *Komunist* (weekly) and *Socijalizam* (monthly). The most important weeklies are *NIN* (*Nedeljne informativne novine*; Belgrade) and *Ekonomska politika* (Belgrade). The most important daily newspapers are *Borba* (with Belgrade and Zagreb editions), *Vjesnik* (Zagreb), *Oslobodjenje* (Sarajevo), *Politika* (Belgrade), *Nova Makedonija* (Skoplje), and *Delo* (Ljubljana). Tanjug is the official news agency.

Radio Free Europe   Slobodan Stanković
Munich, Germany

Council for
Mutual Economic Assistance

The Council for Mutual Economic Assistance (abbreviated as CMEA, CEMA, or Comecon) was established in January 1949 in response to the Marshall Plan and consisted originally of the Soviet Union and its then European allies. Today it has ten members: the Soviet Union, Bulgaria, Czechoslovakia, East Germany, Hungary, Poland, Romania, and the non-European communist states of Cuba, Mongolia, and Vietnam. Yugoslavia has associate member and Angola, Ethiopia, Laos, Korea, and Yemen (the last since 1979) have observer status.

Although the original goal was the economic integration of the member states, the CMEA remained dormant during Stalin's lifetime. Instead, Moscow opted for direct domination and exploitation of its European satellites, despite the organization's lofty principles of "sovereign equality" and independence of each member state and the unanimous-vote provision incorporated in its charter. Only since the mid-fifties and especially during the seventies has the CMEA shown signs of vitality, reacting to such problems as the Hungarian revolution, the Sino-Soviet split, and recent economic upheavals, including the energy crisis. Because the wholesale adoption of Soviet economic priorities in each communist country had led to gross duplications and inefficiencies, the CMEA first attempted to coordinate economic plans (1956–60) and then tried to establish specialization and cooperation in production, expressed in bilateral agreements for the 1961-1965 planning period. It was not until 1971, however, that the so-called "comprehensive program" for economic integration was enacted, establishing committees on coordination, planning, and technical and scientific cooperation. This was followed in 1975 by the adoption of a "coordinated plan" for multilateral integration, beginning with 1976-1980, and the establishment of joint committees on energy and raw materials, supplemented in 1978 by "target" (long-term) programs for cooperation in fuel, energy, and raw materials; in agriculture and food industries; and in machine-building; and by similar programs in manufactured consumer goods, and in transportation.

In 1979 the CMEA celebrated its 30th anniversary at its 33rd regular session in Moscow (26–28 June). Attending were the heads of government of the member states, a Yugoslav delegation, representatives of the observer states, delegates from Afghanistan, Finland, Mexico, and Mozambique (states with which the CMEA has cooperation agreements), and envoys from the U.N. Economic Commission for Europe and the U.N. Industrial Development Organization. The solemn session heard Soviet Premier Kosygin's opening address, adopted a statement, and issued a communiqué, all of which reviewed the past and outlined future goals. During the session, fourteen agreements to implement previous decisions were signed. (*FBIS*, 27 June–5 July.)

The session extolled the achievements of the CMEA since its inception and presented numerous statistical data showing the CMEA's share of the world economy (territory, 18.7 percent; population, 10.7 percent; national income, 25 percent; industrial production, 34 percent; electric power, 21.6 percent; natural gas, 27.8 percent; steel, 29.4 percent; mineral fertilizers, 36.8 percent; and cement, 27 percent). Foreign trade turnover within the CMEA in 1978 increased by 12 percent over 1977, with intra-CMEA trade accounting for over 60 percent of the member countries' total trade. The central theme revolved around the energy problem, a growing concern of communist as well as of Western countries.

In the opening address, Premier Kosygin stressed the need for joint efforts in the energy field and promised that Soviet supplies of fuel and other energy materials during the 1980–1985 period would be increased by about 20 percent over the expected base of the current five-year plan (including 1980) of about 370 million tons of crude oil, 46 million tons of petroleum products, 88 billion cubic meters of natural gas, and 64 billion kilowatt hours of electricity. It is estimated that the USSR presently meets over 80 percent of its European partners' (other than Romania) needs for oil and 25 percent of their total energy needs. However, the USSR has had difficulties in meeting its own goals, which together with the widely anticipated peaking of Soviet production in the eighties (when only about 60–70 percent of the CMEA's oil needs will be met by Soviet supplies), have brought shortages, price adjustments, and the development of alternate sources.

Thus, the Soviets imposed a change in the CMEA pricing system. In future years, the price of crude oil is to be determined on the basis of the preceding five-year average of adjusted world prices, rather than by making changes every five years as in the past. This formula led to considerable price increases (about triple the 1974 level), even though Soviet oil sales to its allies are well below world (OPEC) prices (perhaps one-fourth less) and wide fluctuations are minimized by the five-year spread. Another new feature is the setting of maximum limits for Soviet exports and the charging of higher prices in convertible currencies for extra quantities, if available, as the Hungarian case seems to indicate (Radio Free Europe–Radio Liberty, no. 148, 3 July).

Individual CMEA countries continued domestic price increases and conservation measures. Thus, during 1979 gasoline prices jumped nearly 100 percent in Bulgaria and 50 percent in Czechoslovakia, various restrictions on automobile transport were decreed, and in July Romania—a major oil-producing country—requested foreigners to pay for Romanian oil in coupons obtained with hard currency at U.S. $2.65 per gallon, a measure that generated strong reactions from other CMEA countries.

A longer-term goal, which had been announced and gradually implemented but is to be stepped up, is the development of nuclear power for electricity generation. Nuclear power is to account for over one-third of the electric power produced in Cuba and the European part of the CMEA by 1990 and for about one-half by the year 2000. The plans foresee a total yield of 37,000 megawatts (*Economist*, 26 May), in addition to two plants in the USSR proper. One-half of the power generated will be used by the Eastern European countries in proportion to each state's share in its development. In March, Hungary, Poland, Czechoslovakia, and the USSR signed an agreement for the construction by 1984 of the 400-megawatt Khmelnitski station and a 750-kilovolt power transmission line connecting the USSR and Poland. These plans call for the generation of electricity equivalent to about 75 million tons of "ideal fuel" annually (*Ekonomicheskaya gazeta*, 4 June). Many, often jointly constructed, high-tension power lines, such as the 750-kilovolt Vinnitsa-Albertirsa line, are to be integrated in order to supplement the "Peace" grid and to connect with Yugoslavian and Western European networks.

The Soviet Union can supply its allies with 15.5 billion cubic meters of natural gas per year over the *Soyuz* (Alliance) pipeline between Orenburg and the USSR's western frontier, which was completed in 1978. Other agreements were signed on modernizing the Moscow-Berlin and Moscow-Sofia highways and on constructing wide-gauge railroad tracks from the Soviet Union to Czechoslovakia, Romania, and Poland.

The year under review also saw the continuation of joint investments for the development of natural resources, primarily in the Soviet Union, with reciprocal deliveries covering the CMEA member states' needs almost completely for coal and natural gas, 70 to 75 percent for oil, and 75 to 80 percent for iron ore (ibid.). Thus far, the major projects have been the Orenburg pipeline, the Ust Ilimsk cellulose plant, the Kuyembaev asbestos mining and enriching combine, the Kursk iron ore project, the Norilsk copper and nickel development, and the Vinnitsa-Albertirsa power line, as well as the nickel ore project in Cuba. The long-term plans (1981–1990) provide for a fourfold increase in direct joint investment over 1976–1980. During this period, 28 such projects are scheduled. These and the joint scientific-technical research projects planned for the current five-year span amount to 9.6 billion transferable rubles (about $14.5 billion), of which the East European countries are responsible for nearly one-half. For the period until 1990, additional investments of over $100 billion will be required. (Radio Free Europe–Radio Liberty, *Background Report*, no. 59, 13 March, and no. 77, 2 April.) Much of the needed credits and hard currency for Western equipment will be financed by the CMEA's International Investment Bank (IIB), established in 1971, which supplemented the earlier International Bank for Economic Cooperation. The IIB was reportedly negotiating the first Eurocurrency loan for noninvestment purposes, mainly for oil purchases in Western markets, which indicates the difficulties faced by East European countries in earning foreign exchange and the reluctance of the USSR to assist its allies beyond certain limits (*Financial Times*, 13 March).

The CMEA allies face a growing burden vis-à-vis the Soviet Union as a result of these joint investment schemes on Soviet territory. The Soviets are granted a hidden interest subsidy since the difference between CMEA and Euromarket interest rates is large (well over 10 percent at the present time). Moreover, repayment in kind will not begin before the expiration of the gestation period. (Radio Free Europe–Radio Liberty, *Background Report*, no. 59, 13 March.) In addition, the terms of trade have generally been unfavorable to the smaller states. Finally, inflation will also favor the Soviets.

Inroads into Third World countries have continued, but their markets are not too attractive, and their resources are more in demand in the industrialized West.

The position of the CMEA vis-à-vis the West is also troublesome due to serious trade imbalances, especially of the smaller member states. The trade deficit of the European CMEA countries, including the USSR, amounted to nearly $60 billion by 1979, with little relief in sight. Aside from Soviet oil and other raw materials, few other CMEA products are competitive in the West.

If projections of slackening Soviet oil production in the eighties are borne out and declining growth rates in the CMEA countries in general continue, the future will be more problematic. In 1979, the 30th anniversary of the CMEA, it seemed that various successes and a greater degree of cooperation and integration had been achieved. However, obstacles and deficiencies—some endemic to centrally planned economies of the communist type and others arising because of nationalistically minded populations—will no doubt continue to plague the CMEA and to dramatize the contrast between the assertive giant, the Soviet Union, and the less than equal partners.

The University of Vermont   L. A. D. Dellin

Warsaw Treaty Organization

Established as a multilateral military alliance on 14 May 1955, the Warsaw Treaty Organization (WTO) came into being one day before the state treaty in Vienna that restored sovereignty to Austria and obligated the USSR to evacuate its armed forces from Hungary and Romania. The WTO provided a legal basis for Soviet troops stationed in Poland and East Germany.

Status-of-forces agreements with Poland (1956), East Germany, Romania, Hungary (all 1957), and Czechoslovakia (1968) remain in effect except for Romania, which lapsed in 1958 upon withdrawal of USSR troops from that country. Albania de facto left the WTO in 1961, although it did not announce its withdrawal until 13 September 1968. Yugoslavia never became a pact member. There were reports that during November 1976 Brezhnev's attempts in Belgrade to affiliate that country with the WTO had been rejected by Tito (see *YICA*, 1977, p. 105).

During the year under review, joint Soviet-Czech maneuvers, code-named "Friendship 79" and involving some 26,000 troops, were held from 2 through 7 February in the western regions of Czechoslovakia that border on the Federal Republic of Germany. They reportedly included live infantry, artillery, and tank fire, while the "enemy" [NATO] employed simulated weapons of mass destruction. Chemical warfare units from the Central Group of Soviet Forces decontaminated their own and Czechoslovak troops (*Rude pravo*, 6 February). The following month, the Northern Group of the Soviet Army with Gen. Afanasiy Shcheglov of the USSR (representing the supreme WTO commander) in attendance, conducted war games with Polish troops in the Pomeranian military district (*FBIS*, 27 March).

More extensive maneuvers, code-named "Shield 79," took place in Hungary under WTO commanding officer Marshal Viktor G. Kulikov of the Soviet Union. Contrary to early reports (*CSM*, 15 May), Romanian troops did not participate, although Romanian staff officers were present. At the end of the exercises, Kulikov addressed a rally of military units from Bulgaria, Czechoslovakia, Poland, and the USSR. He praised the troops' professional and political training as well as their military fitness. Moreover, he stressed the possibility of peaceful coexistence but warned that the successes of détente were not yet firm. Finally, he asserted that the hegemonistic aspirations of Beijing's leaders represented a threat to peace. (*Népszabadság*, 20 May; *FBIS*, 23 May.)

Simultaneously with "Shield 79," meetings of WTO defense and foreign ministers took place in Budapest. The highlight of the foreign ministers' communiqué appeared to be a proposal that an all-European conference (including the United States and Canada) be held later in the year "to begin discussing and implementing practical measures to facilitate the building of trust . . . and easing military confrontations" (*Pravda*, 16 May). The ministers spoke in favor of a reduction in military spending and a readiness to disband both WTO and NATO simultaneously.

In a similar vein on the eve of the annual military parade in East Berlin, Brezhnev announced on 6 October that the USSR would withdraw as many as 20,000 troops and 1,000 tanks from East Germany over the next twelve months. Moreover, he said that Moscow was prepared to reduce the number of medium-range ballistic missiles from the western areas of the Soviet Union on the condition that NATO not install any new weapons systems that could reach the USSR from Western Europe (*Facts on File*, 12 October, p. 761). Nicolae Ceauşescu of Romania was the only WTO chief of state not to attend these East German 30th anniversary celebrations.

The WTO Military Council, presided over by Marshal Kulikov, met during 23–26 April in Warsaw and again on 29–31 October in Bucharest. Aside from the statements that the sessions had passed "in an atmosphere of friendship and close cooperation," little else was reported. At the second meeting, the Council was said to have drawn up "a balance sheet of operational readiness and preparedness for 1979 and analyzed tasks for 1980" (*FBIS*, 1 November).

Parliamentary representatives of WTO countries held a consultative meeting in Prague during mid-October and concluded that "the strengthening of peace and détente remained of utmost importance" (Radio Prague; *FBIS*, 23 October). Earlier, WTO representatives at the mutual and balanced force reduction talks in Vienna had urged the West to accept the "initiative of the socialist countries" and to respond (*Pravda*, Bratislava, 5 July).

Among other developments during the year, Marshal Kulikov made visits to WTO capitals. Colonel General Dmitrii T. Yazov assumed command over Soviet troops comprising the Central Group of Forces, stationed in Czechoslovakia, replacing Lt. Gen. Dmitrii S. Sukhorukov (Radio Prague, 15 and 24 January).

Hoover Institution   Alex N. Dragnich

Document: Eastern Europe

FOR INTERNATIONAL SOLIDARITY

(Central committee secretaries for international and ideological questions from Bulgaria, Hungary, Vietnam, East Germany, Cuba, Laos, Mongolia, Poland, the Soviet Union, and Czechoslovakia meeting in East Berlin from 3 to 5 July issued the following statement:)

The delegations emphasized once again the resolve of their parties to strengthen, on the basis of the principles of Marxism-Leninism and proletarian internationalism, the solidarity with all peoples fighting against imperialism and reaction and expressed the conviction that achievements of real socialism promote new successes of the cause of peace, democracy, national freedom, and social progress.

. . . they expressed complete support for the Vietnamese people, who gave a firm rebuff to Chinese aggression, and for Vietnam's struggle for peace, national independence, sovereignty, territorial integrity, and socialism . . .

They expressed solidarity with the Lao People's Democratic Republic, which is fighting against the maneuvers and subversive provocations of imperialism and reaction and making efforts to implement profound political and social transformations and socialist construction. They welcome new Kampuchea [Cambodia], whose people, led by the sole lawful government, the People's Revolutionary Council of Kampuchea, having overthrown the tyrannical regime of Pol Pot, set the course toward revival of its country on a truly democratic basis.

It was stressed that Beijing's great power hegemonistic aims, which are being used by imperialism in its struggle against socialism, constitute a threat to the security of all peoples, above all in Southeast Asia, and go against the interest of the Chinese people itself.

The fraternal parties condemn resolutely imperialist and colonialist provocations against Asian and African countries that have chosen a socialist orientation and solidarize with their struggle.

They expressed solidarity with the struggle of the Nicaraguan people against the dictatorial regime and for freedom and independence of their motherland and declared against imperialist attempts to implement military intervention in that country, which would be a gross violation of the principles of peaceful coexistence and would contradict the interests of détente.

The delegation confirmed the invariable support for Arab peoples, particularly the Palestinian Arab people, and noted protests of the majority of Arab countries against the Egyptian-Israeli separate deal, which was concluded under Washington's auspices. They expressed solidarity with the peoples of Namibia, Zimbabwe, and South Africa in their struggle against imperialism and for attaining and defending national rights, peace, and social progress.

Source: *Pravda*, 7 July 1979.

Note: Romania refused to sign the statement, in part because of the condemnation of China and Israel.

WESTERN EUROPE

Austria

The Communist Party of Austria (Kommunistische Partei Österreichs; KPÖ), founded 3 November 1918, has been a legal party throughout the democratic history of the Austrian republic. Between the wars, the KPÖ's insignificance was due largely to the leftist orientation of the Social Democratic Party (Austromarxismus). The free elections in all zones of occupation in Austria in 1945 were a great disappointment to the KPÖ, which, as one of three contestants in that election, received only 5 percent of the vote. The party was kept in this weak position by the impact of the Soviet occupation of northeastern Austria. The military intervention in Hungary brought its vote share down to 3 percent, and that in Czechoslovakia down to roughly 1 percent in the seventies.

The party's membership is now estimated at 25,000 in a country of 7.5 million people. Although the party stressed national concerns after further electoral defeats in 1979, it has continued its rigid adherence to a pro-Moscow position.

A plethora of elections in Austria during 1979 gave the KPÖ ample opportunity to display its unpopularity with Austrian voters. Foremost among these was the national election of 6 May 1979, which gave the party its all-time postwar low, with the exception of 1966, of 0.96 percent of the national vote. In 1966, the KPÖ decided to run a list in one district only and to support the Socialist Party (SPÖ) elsewhere. In that election, the KPÖ exerted its only significant influence on Austrian politics; its support defeated the Socialists and gave an absolute majority to the conservative People's Party. The following table shows the KPÖ vote, by province, in the last fully contested election before the invasion of Czechoslovakia and compares it with the four elections won by Bruno Kreisky's SPÖ in 1970, 1971, 1975, and 1979:

	1962	1970	1971	1975	1979
Vienna	5.04	1.48	2.13	1.99	1.48
Styria	3.43	1.22	1.64	1.21	1.11
Carinthia	3.22	1.19	1.58	1.44	1.10
Lower Austria	2.61	0.90	1.24	1.00	0.74
Upper Austria	1.82	0.58	0.83	0.83	0.72
Salzburg	1.76	0.59	0.77	0.73	0.61
Vorarlberg	1.26	0.49	0.66	0.78	0.92
Burgenland	1.04	0.44	0.47	0.44	0.38
Tyrol	0.98	0.42	0.56	0.65	0.55
Nationwide	3.04	0.98	1.36	1.19	0.96

The ranking of the provinces has remained amazingly constant, and the Czechoslovak crisis cost the KPÖ two-thirds of its already meager vote almost everywhere. After 1970, there was a slight upsurge, but the 1979 vote shows a decline from 1975 in all provinces except Vorarlberg. Vorarlberg has a fair amount of small-scale industry, especially textiles, but a very conservative electorate. In fact, with the exception of Vienna, the ideological preferences of the general population are unrelated to the vote for the KPÖ; Burgenland, now with the lowest KPÖ vote, has an SPÖ-led provincial government.

There were many other elections during 1979. Six of the provinces chose members of their legislatures. Provincial elections began on 25 March with Lower Austria and Salzburg. The KPÖ vote in Lower Austria dropped from 8,869 to 7,007 and in Salzburg from 1,466 to 1,108 (*Die Press*, 26 March). The other provincial elections took place in the fall. No KPÖ list was entered in the Tyrolian election of 30 September. Upper Austria and Carinthia voted on 7 October. The KPÖ vote in Upper Austria dropped from 6,301 to 4,311 (*Oberösterreichisches Tagblatt*, 8 October). In Carinthia, where 2 percent of the vote had gone to the KPÖ in 1975, the party's vote was cut in half, dropping from 6,013 to 3,112 (*Salzburger Nachrichten*, 8 October). In the final election, in Vorarlberg on 21 October, the KPÖ managed to increase its vote from 1,317 to 1,611 (*Arbeiter-Zeitung*, 22 October; *Wiener Zeitung*, 29 October).

In the two communal elections held in 1979, the KPÖ vote was nearly cut in half. On 25 March in Klagenfurt, the capital of Carinthia, the party's vote dropped from 1,407 to 755 (*Die Presse*, 26 March). The KPÖ vote in communal elections on 14 October in the province of Salzburg declined from 992 to 558 (*Wiener Zeitung*, 16 October).

Student elections were held throughout Austria in May, soon after the general election. Voter turnout was low, having declined to 33 percent from 39 percent in 1977. The vote share of the Communist Student Union (KSV) rose from 2.97 to 3.51 percent and that of the Trotskyist Revolutionary Marxist Group (GRM) from 3.29 to 3.5 percent. At the University of Vienna, the KSV increased its representation from one to two seats and the GRM from zero to two seats. The KSV made substantial gains at the University of Vienna, Salzburg, and Klagenfurt, and at the Mining College in Leoben; the GRM achieved substantial gains at the University of Salzburg and the Academy of Fine Arts in Vienna. The KSV sustained substantial losses at the Economic University in Vienna and the Technical University in Graz; the GRM, at the University of Graz and the Agricultural University in Vienna. (Ibid., 19 May.)

Elections to the Chamber of Labor were held on 10 and 11 June. The Trade Union Left Bloc, the communist group, lost 6 of its 10 seats (out of a total of 810), keeping 2 seats in Vienna and 1 each in Lower Austria and Styria (ibid., 13 June).

According to a report in *Die Presse* (28 March), the KPÖ was alarmed by the results of the provincial elections of 25 March in which the party lost one-third of its vote. Hans Kalt, editor-in-chief of the *Volkstimme*, "admitted that many anti-Kreisky workers considered the KP[Ö] 'too weak' to secure jobs more effectively. The KP[Ö] no longer counts seriously on a return to Parliament." Just before the general election, however, KPÖ Chairman Franz Muhri felt that a seat could be won in Vienna (*Wiener Zeitung*, 4 May). After the election, Muhri referred to the "particularly disappointing showing of the KPÖ" and called for discussion of the results at county and provincial levels, culminating in a discussion by the Central Committee in late June (ibid., 12 May).

Leadership and Organization. Franz Muhri remained at the helm of the KPÖ throughout 1979. Since party leaders now submit to occasional press conferences, questions about the leadership are no longer completely taboo. This is shown by the report of the *Wiener Zeitung* (30 June) of the press conference of 29 June: "KP[Ö]-chief Muhri was then asked about a possible change at the top of the party leadership. He answered that this problem would not be discussed until early fall. Should the party congress express confidence in him, he would accept the election to the chairmanship."

The KPÖ's poor showing in the general election of 6 May led to interesting self-criticism in the daily *Volksstimme* (reported in *Die Presse*, 14 July):

> During the campaign, the KPÖ was identified with a completely negative picture of conditions in the Eastern states, in response to which "wide circles of our party" assumed "a defensive, evasive position," which was also the fault of the party leadership, which had done too little to counteract generalized notions that people in communist countries are worse off than in Austria. The resolution of the Politburo, to assume a public position toward this difficult question [literally, "hot potato"], had not been implemented. "Not a few leadership groups [in the KPÖ] refuse in principle to hold public discussions of fundamental questions because they consider them too risky."

Domestic Attitudes and Activities. In October 1978 the Central Committee of the KPÖ discussed domestic policy. It demanded an immediate reform of Austria's tax system, with an increase of taxes on domestic and foreign corporations (*IB*, no. 20, 1978).

On the occasion of the KPÖ's 60th anniversary, Muhri contributed an article, "Sixty Years of Struggle," to *Pravda* (3 November 1978). Its domestic aspects contained the usual claims of compatibility of communism with socialism and democracy. Muhri warned against Austria's penetration by multinational corporations, especially from countries in the European Economic Community (EEC). In discussing communist relations with socialists, Muhri made this remarkable statement: "The communists and socialists acted together during the impressive October 1950 strike." Readers of Austria's recent history will know that the incident was the KPÖ's Soviet-supported effort to gain control of Austria's labor movement, and possibly of the government, through a general strike, which was put down without blood being shed by the socialist trade unions.

The national conference of the KPÖ to nominate candidates for the 6 May election received Muhri's report, "For the Expansion of Democracy, the Right to Work, for Social Progress, and Peace," in which he stated: "The CPA [KPÖ] is the only party in the country that points a way out of the crisis situation and fights for the maintenance of existing jobs and the creation of new ones. It always encourages development of all-round ties with the socialist countries, thanks to which more than 150,000 Austrians are ensured jobs." (*IB*, no. 7.)

The May 1979 issue of *World Marxist Review* (pp. 16–22) contained Muhri's annual contribution to the international movement. The focus was on the desirability of working with the SPÖ and on deploring the SPÖ leaders' collaboration with state monopoly capitalism, especially through Austria's "social partnership." Unfortunately a careless or subversive printer twice printed CPA [KPÖ] instead of SPA [SPÖ]:

> A considerable body in the CPA leadership, with their incomes running into millions, belong to the privileged segment of society. [T]hey hold key positions in the state apparatus, the administration of provinces and municipalities, the management of nationalized industry, banking, insurance companies and consumers' cooperatives. In short, the CPA leaders have made common cause with the system of state-monopoly capitalism.

Muhri then turned to the current economic crisis and pointed out that blue- and white-collar workers and tenants, especially the younger ones, are beginning to resist "capitalist rationalization." He felt that the KPÖ should be able to make use of the widening gulf between left-wing socialists and the SPÖ leaders.

In a press conference of 29 June, the KPÖ brought up a number of domestic questions. Muhri emphasized that the KPÖ should not concede to the SPÖ a monopoly of the "Austrian way" but should emphasize its national character. The party, Muhri said, was working on a concept of democracy, including referenda, the electoral system, and the mass media. A KPÖ Central Committee secretary, Erwin Scharf, warned against SPÖ efforts to change the electoral system (*Wiener Zeitung*, 30 June). The national orientation of the KPÖ received further emphasis in the *Volksstimme* (*Die Presse*, 14 July).

In a press conference of 21 September, Muhri emphasized the usual policy lines: more work places, control of multinational corporations, higher taxes for corporations instead of workers, and no increases in pension premiums and rents. Hans Kalt warned against further violence in dealing with Carinthia's Slovene minority. Muhri stated that the Central Committee had not yet decided whether to nominate a candidate in Austria's presidential election of 1980 (*Wiener Zeitung*, 22 September).

International Views and Positions. In Muhri's 60th anniversary article in *Pravda*, he bemoaned Austria's one-sided pro-EEC and pro-NATO positions, praised the KPÖ's stand for peace, and acknowledged the USSR's merit in liberating Austria in 1945.

On 20 February *Volksstimme* printed the Central Committee's resolution "Hands Off Vietnam," in which the KPÖ strongly assailed the Maoist attack on the unyielding people of Vietnam.

International Activities and Party Contacts. From 12 to 15 December 1978, Muhri attended the International Conference on Socialism in Sofia (*Volksstimme*, 30 December). From 11 to 13 February, Muhri, Hans Kalt, and KPÖ Secretariat member Hans Steiner visited Prague. The culmination of the visit was a conference with Czech President Gustav Husák (*FBIS*, 13 February). The visit resulted in a long joint communiqué of the Czech party and the KPÖ (ibid., 22 February). Muhri, accompanied by Politburo member Hans Karger and Otto Treml, visited Poland from 14 to 16 May. The visit climaxed in a meeting between Polish leader Edward Gierek and Muhri (*Volksstimme*, 18 May).

The peak of the KPÖ's international travel season was the visit of Leonid Brezhnev, who came to Vienna to meet with President Carter. On 18 June Muhri and Steiner met with Brezhnev. Brezhnev stated that "Soviet communists . . . value highly the Austrian Communist Party's faithfulness to the great principles of Marxism-Leninism and proletarian internationalism" (*FBIS*, 19 June). Muhri told a press conference: "All Austrian communists . . . are deeply grateful to Comrade Brezhnev for expressing fraternal solidarity with the KPÖ's activity" (ibid., 7 July).

On 18 July Muhri, on holiday in Bulgaria, visited Todor Zhivkov in Varna (ibid., 9 July). Four days earlier, Steiner visited the Hungarian party in Budapest (ibid., 16 July). In late September, Muhri, Politburo member Anton Hofer, Steiner, and Filzwieser held talks in Moscow, mostly on international matters, with Soviet party officials Mikhail A. Suslov, Boris N. Ponomarev, and Vadim V. Zagladin (ibid., 28 September).

Publications. Publication of *Volksstimme*, the daily newspaper, and *Weg und Ziel*, the KPÖ's theoretical monthly, continued.

Other Marxist Groups. Austria's Trotskyists, the GRM, publish the monthly *Rotfront*. After 50.5 percent of Austrian voters in a plebiscite on 5 November 1978 had voted against a nuclear power plant, *Rotfront* published a special issue hailing the outcome as a "victory" of "the mass movement." The GRM claimed credit for having started the Austrian antinuclear movement:

> The antinuclear movement . . . after a fairly rapid upswing . . . in June 1977, had entered a phase of decline. At that time, the GRM put forward the slogan of a referendum. We argued that this would make it possible to . . . broaden out the movement . . .
>
> Today we can see that in the last few months, opposition to nuclear power has become a broad mass movement.

A class-struggle orientation for the antinuclear movement can . . . help to build a socialist alternative to the SP[Ö].

The GRM considers it its task to promote discussion of this central question among nuclear activists. (*International Press*, 27 November 1978.)

The Maoist League of Austria used the 11 September 1978 issue of their daily newspaper, *Klassenkampf*, to publish a joint statement with the Workers' and Peasants' Party of Turkey, saying that Vietnamese leaders were attacking Kampuchea (Cambodia) at the instigation of the social-imperialists (*Peking Review*, 1 December 1978). On 5 January the Communist League staged demonstrations against Soviet social-imperialism in Graz, Linz, Salzburg, Innsbruck, and Klagenfurt and held a mass rally in Vienna followed by a protest march to the Soviet embassy (*FBIS*, 10 January).

University of Alberta   Frederick C. Engelmann

Belgium

The Communist Party of Belgium (Parti communiste de Belgique/Kommunistische Partij van België; PCB/KPB), founded in 1921, has an estimated 10,000 members in a population of 9.8 million. Its political influence has been weak, except during the period when it participated in the immediate postwar coalition governments (1945–1947). At the end of the 1920s, it suffered the loss of its "left opposition" members (Trotskyists). In the December 1978 legislative elections, the PCB/KPB received 180,000 votes (3.2 percent), compared with 151,000 (2.7 percent) in the 1977 elections. In the House of Representatives (212 seats), the party rose from 2 to 4 seats; in the Senate (181 seats, of which only 106 are elective), it now has 2 seats compared with 1 previously. Six months later, at the 10 June elections for the European parliament, the PCB/KPB obtained 145,800 votes (2.6 percent), a decline of 0.6 percent. None of its candidates was elected to the parliament at Strasbourg.

The party has always been stronger in the Walloons—in the old industrial centers—than in Flanders. In December 1978, 5.1 percent of the French speakers but only 1.9 percent of the Flemish speakers voted for the PCB. The PCB/KPB does not have its own trade union organization. It exercises a minor influence within the Walloon-dominated Belgian General Confederation of Workers (FGTB/ABVV), which is linked to the French-speaking Socialist Party and the Flemish Belgian Socialist Party. PCB/KPB Senator Robert Dussart is also the principal trade union delegate at Ateliers de construction electrique de Charleroi, one of Belgium's largest firms. On the other hand, the party's presence is practically nonexistent within the Flemish-dominated Confederation of Christian Trade Unions (CSC/ACV), whose links with the Social-Christian parties are becoming less and less intimate. At the last congress of the PCB/KPB, 33 of the participants were trade union delegates of the FGTB/ABVV while only 1 came from the CSC/ACV (*Le Drapeau rouge*, 2 April).

Leadership and Organization. The new Central Committee (72 members) resulting from the 23rd Congress of the PCB/KPB (30 March–1 April) re-elected Louis Van Geyt chairman and Claude Renard and Jef Turf vice-chairmen. The number of members of the Political Bureau was increased from thirteen to fifteen and that of the National Secretariat from four to five. Other members of the Political Bureau are Pierre Beauvois, Jean Blume, Urbain Coussement, Marcel Couteau, Jan Debrouwere, Albert De Coninck, Augustin Duchâteau, Robert Dusart, Georges Glineur, Rosine Lewin, Jaak Withages, and Ludo Loose. In addition to the chairman and the two vice-chairmen, the Secretariat includes Marcel Couteau and Albert De Coninck. Rosine Lewin remains political editor of *Le Drapeau rouge* and Jef Turf of *Rode Vaan*. Jacques Moins is director of the party's publishing house, and Susa Nudelhole is coordinator of committees for the Central Committee. (Ibid., 3 April.)

In contrast with the Socialists, the Social-Christians, and the Liberals, who are split into Flemish- and French-speaking parties, the PCB/KPB has remained unified, while comprising three regional councils: one Flemish (Dutch-speaking), one Walloon (French-speaking), and one for Brussels (bilingual).

Three organizations are directly linked to the PCB/KPB: the Communist Youth of Belgium (dynamic despite its small number of activists), the National Union of Communist Students (its influence in the universities is insignificant), and the children's Union of Belgian Pioneers. The expression of pro-Soviet communist views occurs as well through front organizations, such as the Belgian Union for the Defense of Peace (BUDP). Canon Goor, winner of the Lenin Peace Prize, is the driving force behind the International Committee for Security and European Cooperation, which organized the European Forum for Disarmament at Ostend from 26 to 28 October in which Vadim Zagladin, the director of the International Section of the Communist Party of the Soviet Union (CPSU), participated (ibid., 30 October). The foreign policy of the USSR is often backed by the National Action Committee for Peace and Development, to which some Christian, socialist, pacifist, and Third World aid organizations belong.

Since the PCB/KPB's condemnation of the military invasion of Czechoslovakia in August 1968, certain Walloon federations, particularly that of Liège, have constantly criticized the orientation of party leaders as insufficiently deferential toward the USSR. The most remarkable element of the 23rd Congress was the disappearance of the fear of a split, which has haunted the party's leaders (ibid., 3 March). In fact, the texts on Eurocommunism, human rights, and the "socialist camp" adopted at the beginning of 1978 (see *YICA*, 1979, p. 119) were modified to tone down criticism of the USSR. In the end they met no opposition, and the leaders of the Liège federation (excluded from the Central Committee at the 22nd Congress in 1976) were re-elected. After preparations for the 23rd Congress began, the party's daily, *Le Drapeau rouge*, avoided reference to repression in Eastern Europe.

Domestic Attitudes and Activities. "Our preceding congress in 1976," said Louis Van Geyt at the 23rd Congress,

> made it possible to specify our concept of the beginning of an antimonopolist stage toward a socialism that is consonant with Belgian conditions and to propose a program and some means for a democratic and progressive solution to the crisis. At that time, however, that idea was somewhat abstract. But during the three years that have passed since then, there has been an enormous acceleration and deepening of the crisis, making it possible for our party to work successfully in an increasing number of cases and to give a political extension to struggles, especially with regard to employment, through the constitution of timely pluralistic fronts, including at the parliamentary level. (*Le Drapeau rouge*, 31 March–1 April.)

On the eve of the Congress, 50,000 people assembled in Namur in response to the call of the Walloon common trade union front (FGTB/CSC) to demand a 36-hour work week coupled with the creation of new jobs (unemployment stands at 300,000 people—10 percent of the wage earners) and real power for the regions. For the PCB/KPB, the agreement reached on 3 April by the Socialists, the Social-Christians, and the Democratic Front of Brussels French-Speakers to permit the formation of a government led by Wilfried Martens did not answer the demands expressed at Namur. The reduction of the work week was not made obligatory. The regions still have no directly elected assemblies, and their executives are not independent of the central government (being made up of members of that government).

The PCB/KPB considers that the Martens government is playing into the hands of the right and organizing social regression by blocking wage levels, making social security more expensive for workers, and raising the price of public transport (ibid., 31 October–1 November). The PCB/KPB remains faithful to its policy of supporting the defense of urban life, anti–nuclear movements, and demonstrations in favor of the de-penalization of abortion.

International Views and Positions. In an introductory report to the 23rd Congress, Van Geyt specified the limits of his adherence to the concept of Eurocommunism:

> Our approach to things leads us to express some differences about the repression of opponents and the restriction of freedom of expression and creativity that exists in certain socialist countries or in countries that are trying to build socialism. But this position does not imply for us the slightest question of our internationalist solidarity with all anti-imperialist forces and, in particular, with the socialist countries. In this area we were wrong to hesitate for so long to grasp in a positive way the concept of Eurocommunism, leaving our opponents to interpret this concept negatively.   (Ibid., 31 March–1 April.)

Nevertheless—and this is surprising—the return of the leaders of the Liège federation to the Central Committee (see above) has not led the PCB/KPB to be even more discreet in its disapproval of repression in Eastern Europe and in its declarations of Eurocommunist faith. Shortly before the conviction of Jaroslav Sabata, the spokesman for Charter 77, in Prague at the beginning of May, the PCB/KPB interceded with Czech leaders "to demand that they stop the prosecutions for crimes of opinion" (ibid., 11 May). After his conviction, the party announced its "disagreement with such repressive practices" (ibid., 9 June). On the anniversary of the Warsaw Pact invasion of Czechoslovakia, Rosine Lewin wrote: "For us 21 August remains a painful date . . . Let us repeat it: as far as we are concerned, socialism is inseparable from the exercise of human rights—economic, social, and political." At the end of October, the day after the conviction in Prague of six members of the Czech Committee for the Defense of Unjustly Prosecuted Persons, Van Geyt, questioned on the Belgian radio, termed the trial "scandalous." However, the Political Bureau of the PCB/KPB had not "the slightest intention of encouraging any opposition whatsoever to Czech leaders." (Ibid., 20–21 October.)

After Enrico Berlinguer and Santiago Carrillo announced in Madrid on 10 October an initiative of the Eurocommunist parties to combat the economic crisis, the director of the Belgian communist press, Jacques Moins, wrote in an article entitled "Eurocommunism Is in Good Health": "Eurocommunism is becoming a precise reality and is playing its role in the overall workers' movement; it is participating in the wide debate that is shaking the movement up at this time of crisis, [a crisis] that could lead to authoritarian solutions if the left does not find a strategy of assembling the progressive forces that will permit [us] to respond to the crisis and to impose change on society." (Ibid., 15 October.) But the PCB/KPB daily echoed neither the speech, which was violently hostile to Eurocommunism, made at the same time by Boris Ponomarev (the Soviet leader responsible for relations with foreign communist parties), nor the reply, published in *L'Unità*, that Enrico Berlinguer made to Ponomarev's attack.

The manifesto of the PCB/KPB for the European elections of 10 June stated: "Today the European Economic Community [EEC] is a permanent reality, one of the expressions of contemporary Europe . . . The active participation of workers is one of the essential conditions for democratization of European institutions." Contrary to the French Communist Party, the PCB/KPB does not oppose the participation of Greece, Portugal, and Spain in the EEC, and in agreement with the Italian and Spanish communists, it demands that political and trade union rights identical to those accorded to the workers of host countries be granted to immigrant workers (ibid., 3–4 March).

On the whole, the PCB/KPB remains true to its tradition of supporting Soviet diplomacy. It reproached Belgian Foreign Minister Henri Simonet for having advocated during his trip to Washington in October linking ratification of the SALT II agreements to the acceptance—notably by Belgium—of new strategic arms. For the Belgian communists, this is unacceptable since the USSR, through Leonid Brezhnev's speech in East Berlin on 6 October, has taken "an important initiative aimed at limiting conventional arms" and has formulated "propositions, as well, for limiting nuclear armaments." (Ibid., 11 October.) The PCB/KPB daily accorded an important place to the conferences held in Belgium, at the initiative of the National Action Committee for Peace and Development, under Italian Gen. Nino Pasti, former deputy for nuclear affairs to the Supreme Command of NATO. General Pasti, now a senator elected on the list of the Italian Communist Party, claims that the Soviet military threat is an invention of NATO aimed at justifying an increase in its budget (ibid., 31 March–1 April).

In January the PCB/KPB approved the formation of the pro-Vietnamese Popular Republic of Kampuchea (Cambodia) in Phnom Penh, and at the time of the Sino-Vietnamese war in February, it did not hesitate to take a position entirely favorable to Hanoi. *Le Drapeau rouge* violently reproached the Belgian government for supporting continued recognition of Pol Pot as the holder of Kampuchea's seat at the United Nations (ibid., 24 September).

International Activities and Party Contacts. A delegation of the PCB/KPB led by Vice-Chairman Renard visited Moscow in January at the invitation of the CPSU. That same month Albert De Coninck headed a delegation that held meetings in Prague with leaders of the Czech party. After this visit the PCB/KPB refused to confirm or deny that its delegates had asked their hosts for explanations of the fate of Jaroslav Sabata, the spokesman of Charter 77 (see above). On 4 May Van Geyt met in Berlin with Erich Honecker, general secretary of the Socialist Unity Party of the German Democratic Republic. The joint communiqué published at the end of the visit included several attacks on Chinese leaders. On 31 May Van Geyt and other leaders of the PCB/KPB held an exchange of views in Brussels with two members of the Executive Committee of the Communist Party of Spain (CPS). (For over ten years CPS General Secretary Santiago Carrillo has not had a summit meeting with the PCB/KPB despite three stays in Belgium—the last in 1975).

During the summer, Jean Du Bosch, a member of the Central Committee and leader of the BUDP, traveled to Afghanistan before the overthrow of President Taraki (*Le Monde et la paix*, September). At the end of September, Van Geyt had talks in Belgrade with Branko Mikulić, the present chairman of the League of Yugoslav Communists. On this occasion the PCB/KPB announced its disagreement with Yugoslavia on the question of Kampuchea (Belgrade continued to recognize Pol Pot's regime). With an eye on the European elections, the PCB/KPB met in Brussels with the French Communist Party in April and with the Italian Communist Party in May. A further meeting between Belgian and French communists took place in Paris on 1 October.

Publications. Like all Belgian dailies, *Le Drapeau rouge*, the French-language daily of the PCB/KPB, receives a government subsidy. Its circulation is no more than 10,000, of which an estimated 2,000 copies are sent to subscribers registered in countries of the "socialist camp." The Flemish communists publish a weekly, *De Rode Vaan*. The French-language ideological review of the party, *Les Cahiers marxistes*, is a monthly, while its Flemish counterpart, *Vlaams Marxistisch Tijdschrift*, appears quarterly. The French-language version is published by the Jacquemotte Foundation and the Flemish version by the Masereel Foundation. In 1979 the Jacquemotte Foundation also published the latest work of the Marxist Economic Group (MEG), *Contre-projet Europe*. The prime mover of MEG is Jacques Nagels, a member of the Central Committee and a professor at the Free University of Brussels.

Other Communist Groups. In November the most important organization of the extreme left, All Power to the Workers (Alle Macht aan de Arbeiders/Tout le pouvoir aux ouvriers; AMADA/TPO) became the Party of Labor of Belgium (Parti du travail de Belgique/Partij van de Arbeid van België; PTB/PVDAB). Founded by former Flemish students of the Catholic University of Louvain, this party is well established in Antwerp, especially among dockworkers. In the December 1978 legislative elections, AMADA/TPO, which is Maoist in orientation, obtained 43,500 votes (0.7 percent). In the June European elections, it advanced to 0.8 percent with 45,400 votes. The PTB/PVDAB is not officially recognized by the Chinese Communist Party, but several of its leaders visited China in 1979. It publishes two weeklies, *Alle Macht aan de Arbeiders* in Flemish and *Tout le pouvoir aux ouvriers* in French.

The Marxist-Leninist Communist Party of Belgium (Parti communiste marxiste-léniniste de Belgique), which is officially recognized by Beijing, merged in December 1978 with another small group, Communist Struggle (Lutte communiste-marxiste-léniniste). The new formation, which has retained the name Marxist-Leninist Communist Party of Belgium, has only a few dozen members. It publishes a weekly, *Voix communiste*.

The Workers' Revolutionary League (Ligue révolutionnaire des travailleurs/Revolutionaire Arbeiders Liga; LRT/RAL) is the Belgian section of the Trotskyist Fourth International. In the December 1978 elections, it received 9,000 votes (0.1 percent), and in the June European elections, it obtained 17,000 votes (0.3 percent). The LRT/RAL, which at most has 1,000 members, publishes two weeklies, *La Gauche* in French and *Rood* in Flemish.

The combined votes of the AMADA/TPO and the LRT/RAL in the 10 June elections were equivalent to 43 percent of those cast for the PCB/KPB.

Brussels   Willy Estersohn

Cyprus

The original Communist Party of Cyprus (Kommonistikon Komma Kiprou) was secretly founded in 1922 by Greek Cypriot cadres trained in mainland Greece. Four years later, the party openly held its first congress after the island became a British crown colony. Finally outlawed in 1933, it survived underground until April 1941 when its direct successor appeared under the name of the Progressive Party of the Working People (Anorthotikon Komma Ergazomenou Laou; AKEL). The party was again proscribed by the British in 1955, as were all political organizations during the EOKA insurgency. The AKEL took no part in that four-year anti-imperialist campaign and has suffered criticism to this day from many sources for its "attitude to the EOKA struggle during which the communists prevented masssive labor participation" (*Cyprus Mail*, 7 June). Since the establishment of the Republic of Cyprus in 1960, the AKEL has had legal status.

As the oldest and best-organized political party in Cyprus, the AKEL commands a following far larger than its estimated 12,000 members (ibid., 26 May 1978). Virtually all its overt support comes from the Greek Cypriot majority in the island, who constitute about 80 percent of the estimated 640,000 population. The proportion of party members to national adult population probably ranks AKEL second only to its Italian counterpart among nonruling communist parties. Despite its overall potential, the AKEL has played down its strength in past parliamentary and presidential elections, and no member has ever held any cabinet post.

Since the Turkish invasion and subsequent occupation of about 36 percent of the northern part of the island in July 1974, the sociopolitical setting in Cyprus has been one of fragile calm. Pending a final resolution of constitutional problems in the government, the Turkish Cypriots formed a Turkish Federated State of Cyprus (TFSC) in 1975 and have held separate elections within their own community for the past fifteen years. Within the Greek Cypriot community, AKEL leaders claim their party is "well-organized, close-knit and capable of coping with difficulties" (*WMR*, July). In the parliamentary elections of September 1976, the three cooperating parties—AKEL, the Democratic Front led by Spyros Kyprianou, and the United Democratic Union of the Center (EDEK)—won about 75 percent of the vote (ibid., February 1978). The AKEL contested only its nine previously held seats and received a minimum of 30 percent of the coalition vote. (For the election results, see *YICA*, 1977, pp. 127–28.) In the February 1978 presidential election, the AKEL preserved the parliamentary coalition and backed the incumbent, Spyros Kyprianou, who won by acclamation. While intentionally never seeking the presidency in the past, AKEL leaders boasted that they could have "put forward an able presidential candidate" (*IB*, 15 March 1978).

The AKEL's reluctance to show its true strength in the elections in Cyprus may change in the future. One right-wing newspaper stated "that AKEL—which has grown very brazen—is promoting the current education minister, Mr. Sofianos, as its own candidate for president at the next election in 1983" (*To Tharros*, 17 September). To be successful with this tactic, the AKEL must overcome two historic realities: the 1959 Zurich and London agreements—which gave Cyprus its original and subsequently unworkable form of government—include a legal rationale for the three guarantor powers (the United Kingdom, Greece, and Turkey) to intervene against an illegal subversion of the republic; and the probability that a legal push for power by the AKEL would surely unite nationalists and rightists against the left-wing parties. Thus, the main reason that AKEL did not enter a candidate in the last presidential election was "the assumption that his victory in the election could create a situation bordering on civil war," which the communists "wish to avoid" (*WMR*, February 1978).

Party leaders believe that Cyprus has not reached the stage that would enable the party to achieve its "more distant goal—the socialist transformation of society" (*IB*, 15 March 1978). Nevertheless, the AKEL asserts that it is a "Marxist-Leninist party, a party of the working class and of the other working people, whose goal is socialism and communism" (*WMR*, June 1978). Cypriot communists consider their "vanguard role" effective since it has evolved "on the basis of scientific analysis of the specific situation in our country and its international position" (ibid.). Party General Secretary Ezekias Papaioannou reaffirmed this position during 1979 in the Soviet Union when he promised to "devote all his energies to the struggle for the freedom of Cypriots, for the ideals of communism, for peace, progress, and socialism" (Tass, 24 January).

The most consistent policy that the AKEL has espoused in recent years has been the open endorsement of "the line and tactics of the struggle for the solution of the Cyprus problem as defined by the national and ministerial councils in March 1977 under the chairmanship of the late President Makarios" (Nicosia Domestic Service, 21 August). Party leaders feel that "the government most suited to the people would take the form of a politically representative government based on a common minimum program" (ibid.). The communists believe that for the time being "not only general democratic, but also socialist goals" can be reached by "democratic means" and "parliamentary activity" (*WMR*, June 1978). Therefore, the "participation by AKEL deputies in the work of all the parliamentary committees and the party's very presence in parliament have an effect on the adoption of important decisions and laws" (ibid.). In 1974 AKEL first put forward its demand for a "coalition government of anti-imperialist parties and a seat in the Cabinet of Ministers" (ibid.). Unable to achieve the latter goal, the AKEL now supports "the inalienable right of parties and organizations to judge and criticize the work of the president, including the choice of ministers" (*Cyprus Mail*, 28 September).

The AKEL continued to downplay its differences with the Greek Orthodox Church of Cyprus, particularly over the redistribution of church-owned land to tenant farmers. Instead, AKEL economists tend to include this issue tacitly in the more comprehensive call for "the more just distribution and redistribution of the national income" (*Kharavyi*, 10 December 1978). The AKEL has learned from bitter experience that the church in Cyprus is still influential in secular politics—even after the passing of Archbishop Makarios—hence the communists do not try to appeal to the Greek Cypriots by attacking their Orthodox faith.

Although the AKEL is the only professed Marxist-Leninist party in Cyprus, there is a much smaller socialist party, the EDEK. This political grouping is tightly controlled by a 58-year-old physician, Dr. Vassos Lyssarides, who at one time was personal medical adviser to President Makarios. The socialists were part of the coalition with the communists and the Kyprianou forces in the last parliamentary and presidential elections and consequently now hold four seats in the House of Representatives. Leaders of both parties normally refer to one another as "the progressive forces in Cyprus" and try to avoid open feuding. However, a crisis did develop when Dr. Lyssarides allegedly told "the Supreme Soviet leadership" during a visit to Moscow of the "many extravagances that have recently been taking place inside AKEL" (*To Tharros*, 22 January). In June an open "dispute started with the debate in the House about British bases" and soon widened to reveal "a divergence of views between AKEL and EDEK over the approach to a Cyprus settlement" (*Cyprus Mail*, 6 June). Dr. Lyssarides accused AKEL of actions ranging from "concessions that would aid Turkish aims" to "allying with the right wing." In reply, AKEL leaders countered that Dr. Lyssarides had in reality been "trying for the last two decades to cause the disruption of AKEL." The AKEL then reportedly "served notice that it is ending its election collaboration" and "will not give any AKEL votes" to EDEK in the 1981 parliamentary elections (ibid., 7 June). Dr. Lyssarides accepted the challenge "for an election contest and hoped they would be held under the proportional representation 'when the people will dispel many a myth'—meaning apparently claims for exaggerated vote strength" (ibid.). These bitter exchanges undoubtedly served to open up old wounds and may have caused a permanent rupture in relations between the two left-wing parties.

Leadership and Organization. The leading personalities in the AKEL are General Secretary Ezekias Papaioannou, who has held the office since 1949, and Deputy General Secretary Andreas Fantis. Both were re-elected at the party's Fourteenth Congress, held 25–28 May 1978. The Congress is the supreme authority and meets every four years. It elects the Central Committee, Political Bureau, and Secretariat. (For the names of key AKEL officials, see *YICA*, 1979, p. 123.)

After the Turkish invasion in 1974 and the subsequent movement of refugees to the south, "more than 250 Party organizations disintegrated, [which] created extremely difficult problems for Communist activity" (*WMR*, July). To replace the cadres who were killed during the invasion, "many capable functionaries have emerged, especially among the young people." Recruitment remains an acute problem since "the progressive movement has been steadily growing, producing a constant need for cadres on whom the demands tend simultaneously to increase as well." (Ibid.)

At the Fourteenth Congress, the AKEL was able to report to the delegates that its "goal of winning hundreds of new members, especially young men and women," resulted in membership surpassing that reported at the previous congress (ibid). Regarding the composition of the party, the report stated: "The bulk of the Party members—67 percent—are industrial workers and employees, 20 percent come from the peasanty and the middle sections; 24 percent of the total membership are women, 30 percent of the new Communists are under the age of 30. In the recent period, there has been a marked increase among AKEL members of young scientists, whose number has nearly doubled since the 13th Congress." (Ibid.)

The party leadership is notable for its stability and comparatively advanced age; many are over 60. General Secretary Papaioannou, at January ceremonies in Moscow, was presented the Order of the October Revolution "for his revolutionary activity over half a century and in connection with his 70th birthday" (Tass, 23 January).

Party Internal Affairs. There have been occasional reports of friction between the "hard-core" leaders and some younger cadres over such issues as Eurocommunism, the "Brezhnev Doctrine," and the correct line for the Cyprus solution. The attacks by Lyssarides also struck at some vulnerable areas in the AKEL. In fact, the AKEL "temporarily suspended" its countercharges to EDEK's last list of accusations, which covered "six pages" (*Cyprus Mail*, 9 June). It chose instead to call a special meeting of the Political Bureau to formulate "a detailed analytical decision on the Cyprus problem" (ibid.).

Each September, the AKEL holds a "fund-raising drive to provide money for the resumption of the party's normal activity" and to demonstrate "a symbolic expression of mass support for the Party" (*WMR*, July). Even in 1974, "the year of the putsch," the AKEL raised 18,000 Cypriot pounds, "but in 1977 the figure was already 80,200 pounds, or 30,000 more than in 1973" (ibid.). Additional operating capital is generated from at least two industrial enterprises: the Popular Distiller's Company of Limassol, which produces wines and brandies, and the People's Coffee Grinding Company in Nicosia.

Auxiliary and Mass Organizations. The total membership of all elements within the AKEL apparatus, including various front groups and allowing for overlaps, is estimated to exceed 60,000, or five times its card-carrying party membership. The most influential front is the island's largest labor union, the Pan-Cypriot Workers' Confederation (PEO), to which about 45 percent of the 100,000 organized Greek Cypriot workers belong. It is an affiliate of the World Federation of Trade Unions (WFTU). Andreas Ziartidhes, a labor leader for over 35 years, was re-elected PEO general secretary in April 1975. Pavlos Dinglis is his deputy. Both are active in AKEL affairs, and Ziartidhes is a member of the House of Representatives from Nicosia. The PEO maintains relations with the Turkish Cypriot left-wing union, Dev-Is, which is also a member of the WFTU. In February the PEO was denied entrance into the Turkish side to meet with its counterpart, but a formal meeting between the two unions' leaders was held on neutral ground in July (*Kharavyi*, 12 July).

The AKEL-sponsored United Democratic Youth Organization (EDON) claims to have over 10,000 members in Cyprus and a branch in London, where more than 125,000 Cypriots live. Secretary General D. Khristofias of the Central Council of EDON, Executive Office member and secretary of the Nicosia EDON P. Lapithiotis, and Central Council member L. Sinderzis paid a five-day visit to Athens where they briefed counterparts in the Greek communist youth organization "on the growth of the youth movement in Cyprus" (ibid., 9 December 1978). The EDON holds a seat on the World Federation of Democratic Youth and through a secondary school organization called PEOM, it extends its influence to over three times its stated membership.

The Pan-Cyprian Federation of Students and Young Professionals (POFNE) is composed of students and graduates of universities in Eastern Europe, who comprise about 8 percent of Cypriots studying abroad. A communist front, the International Union of Students (IUS), organized a conference in Nicosia in December 1978 stressing its "solidarity with the students and people of Cyprus" (*Cyprus Today*, September-December 1978). The conference was hosted by POFNE members and was attended by 118 delegates, representing 65 international, national, and district student organizations. At the conference, an official meeting took place between the Secretariat of POFNE and the Turkish Cypriot representatives of the Revolutionary Youth Organization and the Federation of Turkish Cypriot Students and Youth. Following the meeting, representatives of the IUS and POFNE visited the "occupied areas of Cyprus as guests of their Turkish Cypriot colleagues" (ibid.).

Other communist-dominated front groups in Cyprus include a farmers' union; the Confederation of Women's Organizations; the Pan-Cyprian Peace Council, a member of the World Peace Council; and a number of friendship clubs sponsored by Eastern European countries. The "London branch of AKEL," the Union of Greek Cypriots in England, has about 1,200 members (*Kharavyi*, 24 July).

Domestic Attitudes and Activities. The AKEL's line on domestic issues has been consistent in recent years. For example, it continually exploits anticolonial sentiments by attacking the 1959 Zurich-London agreements that created the Cyprian dyarchy. The presence of British sovereign base areas (SBA) and troops on the island, under terms of these agreements, provides a ripe and ready target for communist propaganda. In New York, Papaioannou reasserted that "U.S. imperialism seeks to turn Cyprus into 'an unsinkable aircraft carrier' of NATO in the eastern Mediterranean" (Tass, 15 November 1978). After the dismantling of the U.S. bases in Iran, the AKEL claimed that the SBAs had been placed at the "disposal of the U.S. Pentagon—in violation of the [Zurich-London] treaties" (*Kharavyi*, 16 March). After the British government denied this charge, AKEL challenged it and recommended that the government of Cyprus prevent non-British forces from using the SBAs and ultimately abolish them (ibid., 25 April).

In May both AKEL and EDEK deputies placed the SBA issue on the agenda of the House of Representatives by means of a resolution that expressed "opposition to the existence of the British military bases and the U.S. spy stations in Cyprus" (Nicosia Domestic Television, 31 May). The resolution was debated but was tabled after the government declared that it did "not have any pertinent information" that the bases were being used "for purposes other than those stipulated in the agreements" (ibid.). The communists did manage to mount a "peace march" against the bases on 3 June. Finally, on 21 June the House of Representatives passed a resolution on the British bases, but it was far less critical than either the communists or the socialists would have preferred.

The United States and Great Britain came in for more criticism from the leftists during an initiative in November 1978 to the Cypriot people about a "framework for a Cyprus solution." Concurrently, the Cyprus issue was debated in the U.N. Security Council. The result was that Secretary General Waldheim was asked to submit a report by May 1979 with recommendations "on efforts made concerning the intercommunal talks and on the progress toward the implementation of the Security Council's decisions" (*IB*, 3 March). But the AKEL viewed this "framework" as the work of countries that have "stood against Cyprus' recourses to the United Nations" and that "continue to oppose the proposals of the Soviet Union and Cyprus to convene an international conference, within the framework of the U.N., for discussing the international aspects of the Cyprus problem" (ibid.). Regarding the internal aspects of the problem, the AKEL maintains that these are "exclusively matters which must be solved by the Cypriots themselves" (ibid.).

Secretary General Waldheim did visit Cyprus in May to meet with Cypriot President Kyprianou and TFSC President Rauf Denktash. Through his efforts, the much postponed intercommunal talks were rescheduled for 15 June, but they lasted only one week. The AKEL was clearly disappointed by this breakdown, and Papaioannou emphasized "that the Cyprus question would be solved through a mass, peaceful struggle and he supported the creation of a defense shield and the need for a representative government of politicians" (Nicosia Domestic Service, 11 September).

Papaioannou continued his attack on the "coupists" still in the government: "it is inadmissible that four and a half years after the treacherous coup d'etat, the purge and cleansing of the state machinery has not been accomplished" (*Kharavyi*, 9 November 1978). A resolution of the AKEL Political Bureau in March added that in order "to speed up the purge," it is necessary "to confiscate all illegally held weapons, to dissolve all underground teams, and to democratize the country's political and social life" (Nicosia Domestic Service, 10 March). In September Papaioannou spoke of the re-emergence of the EOKA-B terrorists and of "a dangerous new situation" due to the "government's reluctance to punish the coupists, carry out the purge and disarm illegal groups" (*Cyprus Mail*, 28 September).

On 8 July village elections were held for the first time in over fifty years, and the communists were pleased with this obvious development in "true representative government" at the grass roots. On 15 July the House passed a new electoral law, which will base future elections on a "re-enforced" proportional representation instead of party slates determined in advance. It was supported by the AKEL, but opposed by EDEK.

In January the AKEL issued its "third emergency economic development plan." Its goal is "the highest possible rate of economic development in order to substantively and steadily improve the standard of living of the working people and the people in general" (Nicosia Domestic Service, 20 January). The basic target "must be the fair distribution and redistribution of the national income and the fair allocation of economic and tax burdens." The implementation of this "requires improving the balance of trade and the balance of payments, settling the problems that result from the shortage of manpower, combating inflation, and in general a sound fiscal policy" (ibid.). Despite the geographic division of the island, Greek Cyprus has experienced astonishing economic growth, while Turkish Cyprus has not fared as well.

International Views and Positions. At the Fourteenth Congress in 1978, the AKEL set four objectives:

1. To facilitate in every way the common struggle of the peoples for the ultimate victory of the policy of peaceful coexistence on the principles of the Helsinki Final Act, for the consolidation of détente and its extension to the military sphere;

2. To facilitate in every way the common struggle against the arms race, against the production of the neutron bomb and for general and complete disarmament;

3. Vigorously to support and display our solidarity in every way with the common struggle of the peoples for freedom, national independence, democracy, economic and social progress;

4. To further promote ties between Cyprus and the nonaligned and other friendly countries which are in solidarity with and extend valuable support to our struggle (*Kharavyi*, 8 June 1978).

The AKEL has "always been unshakably loyal to the immortal principles of Marxism-Leninism. Thus, the party sees anti-Sovietism in any form as "tantamount to anticommunism and determinedly resists it." (*WMR*, December 1978.) On the Iranian situation, the AKEL sent a congratulatory cable to Ayatollah Khomeini on the occasion of his "great victory against the forces of fascism and imperialism" (*Kharavyi*, 13 February). As a result of the U.S. loss of bases in Iran, Deputy General Secretary Fantis stated in a speech that "NATO has already decided to grant increased military aid to Turkey, arm it to the teeth, and convert Turkey into its main fortress in the Mediterranean and the Near and Middle East" (*O Filelevtheros*, 18 February).

In a review of international developments since the Fourteenth Congress, the AKEL Central Committee noted that the most important event is the

> treaty between the Soviet Union and the United States for the control and limitation of strategic nuclear arms—SALT II—that will be signed in a few days during a summit meeting between Comrade Brezhnev, president of the Presidium of the Supreme Soviet and secretary general of the Central Committee, and U.S. President Carter.

> This treaty, which is the result and continuation of the Helsinki Final Act on European Security and Cooperation, constitutes an important step toward international détente and security, promotes disarmament and the consolidation of peace, and opens the road for new talks in order to conclude a SALT III treaty. (*Kharavyi*, 17 June.)

Seeing the possibility for further détente in the military field, AKEL General Secretary Papaioannou had these further thoughts:

> The SALT II agreement could and should be followed by an agreement to reduce armament in Europe for the sake of an all-European military détente as proposed by the foreign ministers of the Warsaw Pact member states on 8 June 1978.

> European and world peace and security require the limitation of all military forces and military détente as a step toward general and complete disarmament, which is the ideal to which mankind aspires. The peoples of Europe, just like the peoples of all the world, will struggle for a reduction in armed forces, for military détente, as an inseparable part of the struggle for a multifaceted consolidation of détente, peaceful cooperation, and lasting peace. (Ibid., 18 June.)

International Activities and Party Contacts. The AKEL maintains extensive and frequent contacts with both ruling and nonruling communist parties, as well as with all the various international front groups. Perhaps one of the more unusual contacts was the tripartite meeting at an undisclosed time and place between the AKEL and representatives of the communist parties of Greece and Turkey, which was reported by the Athens newspaper *Rizospastis*, on 4 February. A joint communiqué was issued, signed by Papaioannou for the AKEL, General Secretary Kharilaos Florakis for the Greek party, and General Secretary I. Bilen for the Turkish party. In part, the communiqué noted that the "three parties call on the Turkish, Greek and Cypriot working class, the village toilers, and the intellectuals to increase and harmonize their efforts exerted to strengthen peace, friendship and cooperation among the three peoples and their struggle waged to purge the eastern Mediterranean region from imperialist war bases and to transform it into a region of peace, security and cooperation . . . [and] favor the legalization" of the Turkish party (*IB*, 15 April).

Following the January visit of EDEK leader Lyssarides to Moscow where he charged the AKEL with "extravagances," the Central Committee of the Communist Party of the Soviet Union invited an AKEL delegation for talks. On the surface, the meeting was reportedly "held in an atmosphere of fraternal friendship and complete mutual understanding" (Tass, 23 January). According to another report, however, General Secretary Papaioannou was scolded by Supreme Soviet leaders "for what is going on in the party, for . . . not following the correct line" on the resumption of the intercommunal talks in Cyprus (*To Tharros*, 22 January). The "recent controversy between AKEL and EDEK through their press organs, *Kharavyi* and *Ta Nea*," was seen as confirming this (ibid.). On returning to Cyprus, Papaioannou strongly criticized "the intrigues of the USA and NATO, which seek to solve the Cyprus problem within the narrow circle of allies of this aggressive bloc." He insisted that the Cyprus problem "should be settled by means of intercommunal talks under the aegis of the U.N. secretary general and without interference from outside." (Tass, 29 January.)

In March an AKEL delegation went to Beirut where talks were held with leaders of the Palestine Liberation Organization (PLO) and representatives of the communist parties of Lebanon, Iraq, and Jordan (Nicosia Domestic Service, 12 March). Papaioannou was not at the meeting but later sent a cable to PLO Chairman Yassir Arafat condemning the "treacherous U.S.-inspired Carter-Begin-Sadat treaty, which is a threat to world peace" (*Kharavyi*, 27 March). In the same month, the Cypriot leader visited Libya and Greece, where he addressed "a gathering organized by Cypriot students in Athens" (Nicosia Domestic Service, 26 March).

An AKEL delegation visited Sofia in March to "have talks on topics of mutual interest, particularly the Cyprus problem" (ibid., 19 March). In August Papaioannou was invited by Bulgarian First Secretary Todor Zhivkov to receive the Georgi Dimitrov Order. This was "festively presented" to the AKEL general secretary "on the occasion of his 70th birthday for his services in the development of the fraternal ties between the Bulgarian Communist Party and the AKEL" (Sofia Domestic Service, 11 August).

Publications. According to Central Committee member Dinos Konstantinou, the AKEL has "always given special attention to the ideological front: education, agitation and propaganda." Hence, the communists have "re-opened Party schools . . . [are] organizing seminars and lectures on current affairs, and [are increasing] the circulation of the Party press." After the Turkish military action in 1974, the circulation of the party's two papers, *Kharavyi* and *Demokratia*, "fell to nearly 2,000 copies." However, the party "sorted out the situation in due time and took all the necessary measures to increase the size of the printings." As a result, "by the end of 1977, the Party papers had printings close to the average reached before the putsch and the invasion."

The AKEL has long had an influential press in Cyprus. Its central organ is the large-circulation daily, *Kharavyi* (Dawn), but there are sympathetic writers and editors on most of the island's other periodicals. The AKEL also publishes a weekly newspaper, *Demokratia* (Democracy), and a magazine, *Neoi Kairoi* (New Times). Its scholarly journal is an occasional publication entitled *Theoritikos Demokratis* (Theoretical Democrat). The PEO labor union publishes a weekly named *Ergatiko Vima* (Worker's Stride), and the EDON youth organization has a weekly called *Neolaia* (Youth). Cypriot communists in London have published a weekly called *Ta Vima* (The Stride) for the past 38 years.

Puebla, Mexico   T. W. Adams

Denmark

The Communist Party of Denmark (Danmarks Kommunistiske Parti; DKP) sprang from the left-wing faction of the Social Democratic Party (Socialdemokratiet; SD) in the turbulent aftermath of World War I. The DKP was organized on 9 November 1919, and except for the German occupation during World War II, it has always been a legal party.

The DKP has traditionally drawn most of its support from among urban industrial workers, together with some leftist intellectuals in Copenhagen and other urban centers. Membership edged upward during the mid-1970s after a decade of stagnation. Before the internal party turmoil of autumn 1979, party membership was estimated at between 7,500 and 8,500. The population of Denmark is about 5.1 million.

The DKP celebrates its 60th anniversary under the most trying conditions in more than a decade. In recent months the party has lost all seven of its parliamentary seats and has been forced to expel one of its most influential figures. The sudden reverses were quite unexpected; during 1979 the party's support of the anti-European Economic Community (EEC) movement was crowned with success in the first direct elections to the EEC parliament, and DKP standings in the frequent public opinion polls were stable. Such instant reverses of political fortunes have characterized the political spectrum since the first protest election of 4 December 1973 and have been repeated in the three subsequent elections. The surprise parliamentary election on 23 October once again saw twelve parties vying for representation, and ten finally gained entrance to the new parliament. Despite five elections in eight years, the government returned to a Social Democratic minority cabinet, which replaced the unlikely Social Democratic-Liberal minority government that had lasted only a little over a year. With only 69 (a gain of 4) of the Folketing's (parliament) 179 seats, the new government will have to seek a majority on an issue-by-issue basis—a well-established if frustrating procedure in postwar Danish politics.

For the DKP the October elections were a disaster. Receiving only 1.9 percent of the votes (a loss of 1.8 percent since February 1977), the party fell below the 2-percent barrier normally necessary for a party to participate in the proportional representation division. All seven DKP members lost their seats. In the March 1978 municipal and county elections, the DKP had made some gains. Between 1973 and 1979, the party had stabilized its electoral strength at around 4 percent; this was an improvement upon the period 1953–1973, when it typically polled only 1 percent. In the first two postwar elections (1945 and 1947), DKP strength was considerably greater, owing in large part to the prominent role of communists in the wartime resistance movement.

The DKP was only one of four socialist parties to the left of the reformist Social Democrats to contest the 1979 elections. The Left Socialists (Venstresocialisterne; VS), who had fallen below the 2-percent minimum in the 1971 and 1973 elections, returned to parliament in 1975 and added a seat in 1977 and another this October for a total of six mandates (3.6 percent of the votes). The Socialist People's Party (Socialistisk Folkeparti; SF) won ten seats in October (5.9 percent of the vote), a gain of three. The internal party strife within the SF that reached a peak in 1976, with a large turnover of elected representatives and gains for the party's more radical wing, seems to have abated in 1979.

Finally, the Communist Workers' Party of Denmark (Kommunist-Arbejder Parti; KAP), formerly the Communist League of Marxist-Leninists, appeared on the ballot for the first time in 1979. It received only 0.4 percent of the vote, far short of winning any representation.

Leadership and Organization. The supreme party authority is the DKP's triennial Congress, which held its 25th meeting in September 1976. It received the report of the Central Committee, adopted the party program and rules, and elected the leading party bodies—the Central Committee (41 members, 11 alternates), a 5-member Control Commission, and 2 party auditors. The Central Committee elects the party chairman, the Executive Committee (15 members), and the Secretariat (5).

Jørgen Jensen was elected party chairman by the Central Committee on 10 December 1977 following the death of Knud Jespersen, DKP chairman since 1958. Jensen, 60, is a veteran of many years of DKP activity and has been a member of the Central Committee since 1952. He is active in trade union affairs and is a member of the Danish Metalworkers' Union (Dansk Metalarbejderforbund) Executive Committee, even though the union is controlled by Social Democrats. He has also been chairman of a union local in Lyngby (a Copenhagen suburb). Ib Nørlund, who was acting DKP chairman briefly during Jespersen's illness, was until October the party's parliamentary leader; he remains its chief theoretician. Paul Emanuel is party secretary.

Until 1979 the DKP seemed unique among the several Marxist parties in Denmark in that personality conflicts and policy differences, if any, had not been discussed in public since the last party split in 1958. In late 1977, however, the party criticized Central Committee member Preben Møller Hansen for his autocratic behavior as chairman of the communist-dominated Seamen's Union (Dansk Sømaendenesforbund) (*Berlingske Tidende*, 28 November 1977). In 1979 this argument erupted with bitter public exchanges between Hansen and DKP leaders, both before and after the electoral disaster. In late September Hansen and two of his close supporters simultaneously resigned from and were excluded by the DKP Central Committee. Hansen then published a letter sharply critical of the DKP leadership. A month later, the fiery union leader was expelled from the DKP. He threatened to start a new communist party and recommended to the 2,700 members of the DKP's maritime division that they resign from the party (*Aktuelt*, 30 October; *Berlingske Weekendavisen*, 2 November). Earlier in September the party faced a local organizational split in the city of Helsingør (*Aktuelt*, 6 September). It is likely that these internal struggles contributed significantly to the party's poor electoral showing, especially in the Copenhagen region. Others have felt that Chairman Jensen, though tried and true, lacks his predecessor's personal popularity and political skills.

Not much is known about party finances other than that they seem to be adequate and that there are frequent collection campaigns for the party's daily newspaper, *Land og Folk*. Until it lost its parliamentary representation, the DKP, like all parties represented in the Folketing, had received a monthly subvention from the public treasury amounting to some 355,000 Danish kroner (about U.S. $66,230) per year.

The party's two main auxiliary organizations are the Communist Youth of Denmark (Danmarks Kommunistiske Ungdom; DKU), led by Gerda Kristensen, and the Communist Students of Denmark (Danmarks Kommunistiske Studenter; KS), chaired by Frank Aaen. Founded in 1974, KS held its Fourth Congress in Copenhagen in November 1978. In April, KS activist Bent Thaarup won the chairmanship of the leftist-dominated National Union of Danish Students (Danske Studenters Faellesraad; DSF). In recent years the DSF has promoted student activism along a wide front in order to gain increased state grants for students (*Berlingske Tidende*, 30 April). Communists have also won a substantial number of seats on university councils, on which students are entitled to representation.

The autonomous Faroese Communist Party (FKP), active on the Faroe Islands, was formed in 1975 and is headed by Egon Thomsen. The FKP did not participate in either the 1977 or 1979 parliamentary elections, and it failed to gather even the few hundred signatures necessary to appear on the ballot during the November 1978 local elections. The DKP is not directly active in Greenland, which received home rule in 1979. The leftist Siumut (Forward) Party, which won control of the Greenland legislature, has been loosely allied with SF. Preben Lange is the party's new representative to the Danish parliament.

Domestic Activities and Attitudes. Although the Danish economy appeared to be making some progress in early 1979, with unemployment declining to below 6 percent, the soaring price of petroleum undermined the recovery. For years Denmark has suffered from high unemployment, particularly among young and female unskilled workers, large deficits in trade and in the state budget, and modest economic growth. These issues dominated internal Danish politics and were the cause of the collapse of the Social Democratic-Liberal coalition in September. The formation of the two-party coalition, which did not command a parliamentary majority, in August 1978 sparked strong protests not only among the three left-socialist and Marxist parties but also in the trade union movement and among some left-wing Social Democrats. The alliance between the Social Democrats and the main opposition party confirmed the swing to the right of the Social Democratic leadership under premier Anker Jørgensen. The Social Democratic chairman of the Trade Union Confederation (Landsorganisationen; LO), Thomas Nielsen, called the coalition a break with all principles of the workers' movement (*Nordisk Kontakt*, no. 12, 1978).

Not surprisingly, the coalition was the target of DKP domestic political activity during 1979. Just after its formation, DKP Chairman Jensen denounced the new government and vowed total opposition to thousands of trade unionists demonstrating outside the parliament building (ibid., no. 13, 1978). This stance was reiterated at the DKP party conference in late November 1978 and again in the 1 May speeches by communist leaders. In addition, the DKP program stresses sizable wage increases for industrial and unskilled workers, a 35-hour workweek, and 35 days' paid vacation per year. The current economic crisis has been hard on heavy industry (especially the shipyards), the areas of DKP union strength.

The failure of employers and unions to reach a general collective bargaining agreement resulted in parliamentary action in March to prolong the current agreements for two years. Some improvements in wages and vacation benefits were included, but both parties expressed dissatisfaction. In the wake of governmental intervention, which has become the rule in recent years, there was a series of wildcat strikes.

Dissatisfaction among trade unionists could provide an opportunity for increased DKP activity because the party has long been stronger in the trade union movement than in electoral politics. Although the LO is firmly controlled by unionists previously loyal to the SD, some communist and other Marxist activists are prominent in union locals. Mention has already been made of communist strength in the seamen's and metalworkers' unions, although this may be undermined by the DKP internal uproar. The DKP along with the other leftist parties have opposed SD proposals to introduce "economic democracy"—various forms of collective investment funds based on business profits. Since the scheme is also opposed by most nonsocialist parties (at least in its compulsory forms), various SD and LO efforts to introduce the proposals have thus far been frustrated. The leftist opposition has denounced the scheme as a substitute for nationalization and worker control of industry.

Another instrument of DKP labor activity has been the Shop Stewards' Initiative Group (Formands-initiativet), in which unionists sympathetic to the DKP compete with SF, VS, and other activists for control. The Initiative Group has lost much of its original visibility, and there are signs that it is moribund (*Politiken*, 23 June). Its failure was one of the sources of contention between Preben Møller Hansen and DKP leaders.

As in many other Western countries, nuclear power has been a matter of increasing political sensitivity in Denmark. The nation, currently without nuclear generators, remains nearly totally dependent on imported energy, although North Sea oil and gas have become more promising in recent years. Ironically, the Copenhagen metropolitan region (of 1.3 million people) is located only fifteen miles from two large Swedish nuclear reactors. Until 1979, the DKP had been staunchly pronuclear; but two weeks after the Harrisburg, Pennsylvania, nuclear incident, it joined the antinuclear forces (*Information*, 10 April). In August the Danish government announced that a popular referendum would be held (presumably in the spring of 1981) before the introduction of nuclear power to Denmark.

International Views and Positions. The 25th DKP Congress (1976) and more recent statements have reaffirmed the party's established international views, which include support for the foreign (and domestic) policies of the Soviet Union and the regimes of Eastern Europe, support for anti-Western movements in the Third World, and vigorous opposition to Danish membership in NATO and the EEC. Communist support and activity have been prominent in the Popular Movement Against the EEC (Folkebevaegelsen imod EF), formed in the early 1970s as a nonpartisan alliance to keep Denmark out of the EEC. As the June election to the EEC parliament approached, the Popular Movement's efforts intensified; it ran its only list of fifteen candidates, including the communist editor of its weekly newspaper, *Det ny Notat*, (The New Notice), Jens Peter Bonde. The SF anti-EEC forces, critical of communist dominance in the Popular Movement, ran their own slate. In the June elections, which were characterized by much lower voter participation than usual, the Popular Movement received 20.7 percent of the vote and elected four candidates including Bonde and Else Hammerich, who has previously been associated with communist-front organizations (*Berlingske Søndag*, 28 January; *Information*, 15 January). The SF list received 4.8 percent of the vote and elected a single representative. The VS received 3.5 percent but no EEC seats, although, as with the SF, this list participated in a technical ballot coalition with the Popular Movement—which accounted for the fourth Popular Movement mandate. Finally, the single mandate from Greenland was won by an anti-EEC Siumut candidate. Throughout the campaign, the DKP and other anti-EEC groups denounced the EEC for its nature (a conspiracy of rich capitalist states) and for its intentions (political union) (*Berlingske Tidende*, 23 April).

Like other leftist groups, the DKP devotes considerable effort to anti-NATO policies and attacks on Danish defense expenditures (already among the lowest in NATO). Denmark's commitment to purchase the F-16 fighter and American consideration of the neutron bomb have been recent targets (*WMR*, no. 3); to these, the DKP and other anti-NATO forces have added American plans for modernization of NATO missiles, debated late in 1979. It was Social Democratic and nonsocialist concern about the missile modernization program that motivated the Danish government's unenthusiastic caution at the December Brussels meeting of NATO.

International Activities and Party Contacts. Like their non-Marxist countrymen, Danish communists like to travel; so again in 1979 the DKP maintained close contacts with other European communist parties. The DKP has been present at and supported all of the Soviet-sponsored functions: the 1976 meeting of European communist parties in Berlin, the 60th anniversary of the Bolshevik revolution in Moscow in 1977, and others. Loyalty to the Soviet party remains the sine qua non of DKP international activity, as indicated by its wholehearted support for Vietnam's adventures in Kampuchea (Cambodia) and the resistance to Chinese retaliation (*Politiken*, 28 January).

In May the DKP leadership received Herbert Mies, from the East German Socialist Unity Party, and in July there were talks between Danish communists and their Bulgarian comrades (Allgemeiner Deutscher Nachrichtendienst, 28 May). In June, a DKP Central Committee secretary, Jørn Christensen, visited with party officials in Romania; DKP Chairman Jensen visited Prague briefly in July. Finally, another DKP delegation visited Moscow and Azerbaijan in July (Tass, 29 July).

Publications. *Land og Folk* (Nation and People), a daily newspaper, is the DKP's central organ. Its circulation of some 10,000 increases on weekends to 12–14,000. *Tiden-Verden Rund* (Times Around the World) is the party's theoretical monthly journal. The DKU publication is *Fremad* (Forward).

Other Marxist Groups. Mention has already been made of the two principal competitors with the DKP for left-socialist support. In domestic politics, both the VS and the SF try to maintain independent profiles, but their differences in practice are in nuance only. Both parties, like the DKP, were sharply critical of the Social Democratic-Liberal coalition, the compulsory collective bargaining settlement, and the SD plans for "economic democracy." Since 1959, when the SF was formed by the purged DKP Chairman Aksel Larsen, it has been the most pragmatic of the various leftist groups. In 1966–1967 and 1971–1973 it provided parliamentary support for minority SD governments in domestic matters. Its earlier pragmatism caused several splits, in 1967 and 1976–1977, and recently, it has presented a more radical profile. Ten of the purged former SF moderates, known as Larsenists, issued a statement supporting the Social Democrats prior to the October elections (*Berlingske Tidende*, 16 October). As noted above, the SF gained significantly in the October parliamentary elections, apparently at the cost of the DKP, and in June an SF candidate was elected to the European parliament. Gert Petersen, who has been a prominent SF parliamentarian and theorist since 1961, remains party chairman. Although the SF is a purely Danish party, it has had close ties to an analogous party in Norway (Sosialistisk Venstreparti), and it expresses enthusiasm for the leading advocates of Eurocommunism.

The VS is also a native party without institutional ties to foreign movements. It stresses the limitations of parliamentary action in its program and has been vocal in support for student activists and minority elements in the trade union movement. Although not uncritical of events in communist countries, the VS, like the SF, directs most of its foreign policy criticism against the United States, NATO, and the EEC. The VS has been anxious to avoid strongly institutionalized leadership, and it demands continuous activity by its members. One result has been recurrent intraparty policy struggles. It is estimated that the VS has at present 2,500–3,000 active members (ibid., 13 July 1978). As noted, the VS gained a single seat (for a total of six) in October.

In addition to these two small parties, there is a myriad of "parties," cultural groups, and publications reflecting various Marxist viewpoints. The KAP is headed by Copenhagen University lecturer Benito Scocozza; it appeared for the first time on the ballot in October but received meager support. The KAP has remained loyal to its pro-Beijing line on foreign policy, also supporting the positions of North Korea and the beleaguered Pol Pot regime in Kampuchea. It has also been active in student protest movements and in the most radical factions of the trade union movement. Finally, there are the Trotskyists, who in late 1978 adopted the name Socialist Workers' Party (Socialistisk Arbejderparti; SAP) (previously the Revolutionary Socialist Union). They remain critical of all foreign powers and domestic competitors (*Socialistisk Dagblad*, 14–15 October 1978.)

Among the many non-DKP leftist publications are the SF's *Socialistisk Dagblad* (Socialist Daily), formerly *Minavisen*; the KAP's *Arbejderavisen* (Worker's News), formerly *Kommunist*; the SAP's *Klassekampen* (Class Struggle); and the independent and radical socialist *Politisk Revy* (Political Review).

University of Massachusetts
Amherst

Eric S. Einhorn

Finland

Consistently attracting nearly a fifth of the electorate, the Communist Party of Finland (Suomen Kommunistinen Peuole; SKP) remained in 1979 the only European communist party (except for the special case of Iceland) participating in a democratic parliamentary government. Given the internal party strains and the party's 1979 electoral losses, the SKP's distinction was perhaps of mixed value. Nevertheless, the history of the Finnish communist movement has been one of dramatic changes reflecting the country's special history and geographic position. The SKP was established in Moscow on 29 August 1918 by "reds"—dissident Social Democrats—escaping from Finland's bloody civil war. Until 1930, the SKP operated through a variety of front organizations, but during the 1930s it was forced underground by a government ban on its operations. It became legal again in 1944, as stipulated by the Finnish-Soviet armistice. During the years of Soviet-Finnish armed conflict (1939-1940 and 1941-1944), nearly all Finnish communists remained loyal to their country.

The SKP draws most of its members from either the industrialized urban areas of southern Finland or the small farming communities of the northern and eastern districts, where a "northland" radical tradition remains strong. Membership of the SKP is estimated at about 45–48,000, out of a total Finnish population of 4,780,000.

The year 1979 brought considerable political activity centering on the parliamentary elections of 18–19 March. The four parties supporting Social Democrat Kalevi Sorsa's left-center government—including the communist-controlled electoral and parliamentary front organization, the Finnish People's Democratic League (Suomen Kansan Demokraatinen Liitto; SKDL)—all suffered major setbacks, while the opposition parties generally gained support. The SKP had participated in the Sorsa government, and the SKDL saw its share of the votes reduced by 1 percent (from 18.9 percent in 1975 to 17.9 percent in 1979). The SKDL parliamentary group lost 5 seats (from 40 to 35 in the 200-seat Eduskunta). The other coalition parties fared similarly: the Social Democrats lost 2 seats (to 52), the Center Party lost 3 (to 36), and the Liberal People's Party was decimated by its loss of 5 seats (to 4). The principal victor of the election was the National Coalition (Conservative) Party, which gained 12 seats (to a total of 47). President U. K. Kekkonen asked the Conservative leader Harri Holkeri to investigate the possibility of forming a new government in early April; but the Social Democrats refused unconditionally, while the Centrists would not join a coalition without the Social Democrats. The president then asked the Social Democrats to attempt to form a coalition, and after nearly four weeks of negotiations, a new four-party majority government was finally assembled. It resembled the old Sorsa left-center coalition with the substitution of the Swedish People's Party for the badly decimated Liberals. The new premier, Mauno Koivisto, governor of the Bank of Finland, has been a leading Social Democratic politician since the mid-1960s and has served as finance minister (1966-1967, 1972) and as premier (1968–1970). The new government controls 133 out of 200 parliamentary seats, although some of the hard-line communists refused to support the previous Sorsa government on certain issues. As before, the communist-dominated SKDL holds 3 cabinet seats; Kalevi Kivistö, the new chairman of the SKDL, is vice-minister for education, Veikko Saarto remains transport and communications minister, and SKP Secretary-General Arvo Aalto continues as labor minister (*Nordisk Kontakt*, nos. 6–10).

Leadership and Organization. Aarne Saarinen, aged 66, a "liberal" communist and popular former union leader, has been SKP chairman since 1966 and a consistent supporter of SKDL participation in left-center coalitions. The Eighteenth Party Congress in 1978, which re-elected Saarinen, also re-elected the so-called Stalinist (hard-line, particularly on parliamentary and cabinet issues) Taisto Sinisalo, the liberal Olavi Hänninen as vice-chairmen, and the liberal Arvo Aalto as secretary general. The 1978 congress confirmed the relative strength between the two factions, which has remained quite stable throughout the decade. The 50-member Central Committee has 29 majority (liberal) and 21 minority (Stalinist) members, and the ratio in the party's Executive Committee (politburo) is 9 majority to 6 minority. The SKDL Executive Committee maintains similar proportions (with some variation on particular issues), and the new SKDL chairman, Kalevi Kivistö, is a left-socialist (not formally a communist) like his predecessor, Ele Alenius. The Central Committee is the SKP's highest decision-making body between the triennial congresses (ibid., no. 11, 1978; *Helsingin Sanomat*, 4 June).

Party Internal Affairs. It is not easy to define the issues that split the two SKP factions, even though their disagreements over day-to-day political tactics are argued in public. The division can be traced back at least to the ideological turmoil following the 1956 "de-Stalinization" congress of the Soviet communist party. Among the issues widening the split have been different reactions to the Warsaw Pact invasion of Czechoslovakia in 1968, domestic political tactics (especially the continuing political collaboration with the Social Democrats), and interpretations of Moscow's preferences. Personality issues have undoubtedly also played a role. A majority of the SKP activists support continuing participation in the left-center government and political pragmatism despite the electoral setback in March 1979. Both factions suffered in the loss of seats, and Vice-Chairman Sinisalo, leader of the hardliners, lost his parliamentary seat. Finland may rightfully claim to have a "working model" of Eurocommunism, a phrase that Chairman Saarinen does not disown. Some have felt that the continuing public debate between the two factions attracts public attention to the party. While this may be so, the recent electoral losses may raise the question of the consequences of that publicity.

Mutual toleration between the two factions is not easy. The Eighteenth SKP Congress occasioned an energetic struggle for the election of delegates. An attempt at a pre-congress compromise failed, and the liberals won a majority of the delegates (278 to 215). Nevertheless, at the congress itself, the two factions avoided direct confrontation by formulating statements in rather general terms and avoiding votes (by previous agreement). The party program adopted at the congress, "For a Democratic Change," reflects this compromise. Worded in generalities, the document focuses on the continuing economic crisis and the sacrifices borne by the workers of Finland. It warns the Social Democrats of the necessity to institute changes in the economic system. Moreover, it contains the usual references to international solidarity and "proletarian internationalism." The North Atlantic Treaty Organization (NATO), the organization for Economic Cooperation and Development (of which Finland is a member), and the European Economic Community (EEC) are singled out for attack as tools of American and capitalist domination (*WMR*, nos. 16–17).

Relations between the SKP and its political front organization, the SKDL, have received less attention. The Sinisalo faction has been critical of SKDL Chairmen Alenius and has issued warnings to his successor, Kivistö (*Helsingin Sanomat*, 4 June). The Twelfth SKDL Congress in June 1979 reflected the broader focus of the front. Its statements are decidedly less ideological and more pragmatic. The leadership of the SKDL has been enthusiastic about continued participation in the left-center coalition. Relations between the SKP and the SKDL have continued to be disturbed by the critical remarks of some noncommunist front politicians: for example, Ilkka-Christian Björklund, who has been critical of domestic suppression of dissidents in the Soviet Union and East Germany and has drawn analogies to hard-line elements within the SKP. The reaction of both factions of the SKP to such open criticism indicates that Finnish communists clearly draw a line between their own internal debates and criticism directed at neighboring communist regimes. (*Demari*, 2 June.)

Domestic Attitudes and Activities. The electoral setback suffered by all four of the left-center coalition parties and the impressive gains registered by the Conservatives (and two other rightist parties) reflect broad dissatisfaction with the economic difficulties of the past four years. Although the economy improved considerably in 1979, unemployment continued to hover around 6 percent. Both the former Sorsa and the current Koivisto governments have made domestic economic stabilization and the reduction of inflation principal policy priorities. This has involved various forms of wage and price controls. The hard-line faction of the SKP has been especially critical of the former government. The majority wing of the SKP has recognized the necessity of economic stabilization and supported the government's bill reducing the inflationary impact of indexed collective bargaining agreements (*Helsingin Sanomat*, 11 January).

The reconstituted left-center government under Premier Koivisto has kept to the pattern of seeking to stimulate employment while paying close attention to the country's balance of payments and price developments. This was reflected in the new government's first budget, presented in September. Public spending is to increase only modestly, while the target for domestic inflation has been set at 7.5 percent (*Nordisk Kontakt*, no. 12). In conjunction with the government's goals, the central Bank of Finland revalued the Finnish *markka* by 2 percent in September so as to reduce external inflationary pressures. The dramatic improvement in the Finnish balance of payments, following several devaluations in recent years, made possible this step. Although a majority of the SKP has gone along with its coalition partners, the party program still advocates much more radical measures, such as: (1) expansion of the state sector in industry and services, along with better parliamentary control of such activity, (2) nationalization of all banks and major financial institutions, and (3) dismantling of Finnish economic and trade ties with the West and increased economic and technological ties to the Soviet bloc (*WMR*, January 1977). These options have not been pursued by the recent left-center governments.

In contrast to the consensus that dominated the re-election of President Kekkonen in January 1978 (he faced only token opposition, despite his advanced age and his incumbency since 1956), the March 1979 parliamentary elections were vigorously fought. The sharp gains for the Conservatives were anticipated some weeks before the actual elections, and the SKP divided its efforts between electioneering and preventing formation of a Conservative government. All leading SKP figures rejected beforehand the possibility of cooperation with the Conservatives (*Helsingin Sanomat*, 11 February). After the election, the Social Democrats as well made it clear that they could not participate in a government with the Conservatives, and the Centrists refused to join any coalition containing the Conservatives without the Social Democrats. Outside influences may also have been strongly felt, a phenomenon not unprecedented in postwar Finnish politics. When SKP Secretary-General Aalto speculated about the possibility of a Finnish version of "historical compromise," i.e., a broad coalition from the left to the moderate right, including the Conservatives, *Pravda* denounced such a scenario (*Pravda*, 10 March). In light of such attitudes, the post-election effort of the Conservatives to assemble a coalition was merely pro forma.

Another important sphere of communist domestic activity is the powerful domain of the Finnish labor unions. Although the Social Democrats control 23 of the 28 sectoral trade unions within the Finnish Confederation of Trade Unions, communists currently control several important unions including the construction workers, food distributors, rubber and leather workers, and building maintenance workers. The Social Democrats enjoy only a slight majority among the metal workers and paper workers. Nevertheless, despite competition for influence, the unions have reflected the collaboration between the SKP and the Social Democrats. As noted above, the unions have accepted, with some dissent, the government's economic policies limiting wage indexing. During the long search for a viable government following the March elections, the unions agitated for continuation of the left-center coalition. The Center party's discussion with the Conservatives brought strong attacks from several unions, particularly those under communist control. Finally — as reflected in the conference of the communists' largest union, the construction workers, in May — the Social Democrats, who account for about a quarter of the delegates, have been given increased influence, while the "Stalinist" communists have seen theirs reduced (*WMR*, no. 5; *Helsingin Sanomat*, 12 May).

In 1979 the pattern of SKP/SKDL influence in domestic politics was strengthened through close collaboration with the Social Democrats and cooler ties to the Centrists. The Conservative electoral gains are likely to strengthen the already preponderant role of Saarinen's "liberals" within the SKP, since the result of division among the parties and factions of the left could be continued growth for the moderate right.

International Views and Positions. Both SKP factions support similar foreign policy goals, and given the country's geography and history, foreign policy issues do not tend to be used in partisan maneuvers. The Helsinki Accords of 1975 remain the keystone of SKP foreign policy views, along with the party's traditional opposition to NATO, the EEC, and other ties with the Western community. Finland's special relationship with the Soviet Union is symbolized by the 1948 Treaty of Friendship, Cooperation, and Mutual Assistance. On the occasion of the 30th anniversary of the treaty in 1978, the SKP reaffirmed its foreign policy views. The SKP position is that the treaty guarantees the independence and security of Finland. President Kekkonen's special foreign policy responsibilities were evident in his re-election campaign in 1978. One widely displayed campaign poster pictured the president and his signed initials, with the statement, "Confidence beyond our borders."

Statements by the SKP reflect the party's position that Finnish neutrality cannot be compromised by words and actions sympathetic to Soviet foreign policy goals. Closer ties to Western Europe immediately raise suspicions. Chairman Saarinen attacked China for its failure to accept Soviet moves toward reconciliation, and on the same occasion he specifically attacked the Chinese embassy in Helsinki for publishing and spreading anti-Soviet propaganda (*Nordisk Kontakt*, no. 7, 1978). The 1978 SKP program focuses mainly upon domestic issues, but it includes the usual references to the principles of "proletarian internationalism" and the "mutual solidarity of the workers of all countries" (*WMR*, nos. 16–17, 1978).

Foreign policy issues frequently are tied to domestic politics. The SKP minority Sinisalo wing differs from the majority in its especially passionate denunciation of Finland's economic and political ties to the West. Sinisalo has observed that the true political color of every communist is unstinting loyalty to the foreign policy goals of the Soviet Union (*Pravda*, 4 September 1978). Such remarks are unusual among contemporary Western European communist leaders. The Stalinists created a major foreign policy episode for Finland when their daily newspaper *Tiedonantaja* several times called for joint maneuvers between Soviet and Finnish military units. Coming after the visit of Soviet Defense Minister Dimitri Ustinov in the summer of 1978, the articles created serious concern inside and outside of Finland. Finnish political leaders including President Kekkonen have been quite critical in recent years of Norway's role in NATO, including plans for participation of West German units in NATO maneuvers in Norway. On 10 October 1978 Centrist Defense Minister Tänkämaa (in the Sorsa government) responded to questions in the Finnish parliament and denied that the Soviet defense minister or government had demanded joint maneuvers. *Tiedonantaja* editor Urho Jokinen claimed that his paper's editorials had been misinterpreted, and that only social contacts between the two countries' armed forces had been intended (*Nordisk Kontakt*, no. 13, 1978; *NYT*, 15 November 1978).

Nothing more was heard of such proposals in 1979; but as noted above, Soviet commentators made it clear that they were opposed to conservative participation in any new government coalition. Moreover, Finnish and Soviet commentators emphasized the importance of Finnish-Soviet economic ties. Typically, the USSR takes 20 percent of Finnish exports and provides 18 percent of imports (*Yearbook of Nordic Statistics*, 1978). The fifteen-year plan for Finnish-Soviet economic cooperation, concluded in November 1977, called for significant expansion of trade, energy supplies, and joint projects, including nuclear power plants (*Nordisk Kontakt*, no. 15, 1977).

International Party Contacts. The SKP maintains intensive and close relations with the communist parties of both Western and Eastern Europe. Party leaders Saarinen, Sinisalo, and Aalto led a delegation to East Germany and to the Soviet Union in January, while another SKP delegation visited Romania. In Moscow the Finnish delegation met with top Soviet leaders, including Soviet Politburo members Mikhail Suslov and Arvid Pelshe. The upcoming Finnish elections and the SKP program were discussed (*Helsingin Sanomat*, 1 February). Such high-level attention is rarely accorded other Nordic communists; it reflects the pattern that brought Soviet Premier Aleksei Kosygin to Helsinki in December 1977 on the occasion of the 60th anniversary of Finnish independence, as well as a substantial Soviet delegation to the SKP Congress in June 1978.

In June another Finnish communist delegation visited Hungary, while in July a group of communist women headed by SKP Politburo member Anna Liisa Hyvonen visited Romania (*Magyar Tavirati Iroda*, Budapest, 5 June; *Agerpres*, Bucharest, 13 July). Finally, SKP Chairman Saarinen gave a lengthy interview to a reporter from the Italian communist daily *L'Unità* on the practical problems of communist participation in a left-center coalition (*L'Unità*, 27 March). Saarinen noted the problems of frustration in promising more than could be delivered in light of political and economic realities.

Other Marxist Parties. Given the range of Marxists found within the two SKP factions and the associated SKDL front, Finland is unique among the Nordic countries in not having significant independent leftist groups. The only noteworthy Marxist-Leninist group outside the SKP/SKDL family is the pro-Chinese "Marxist-Leninist Group of Finland," whose activities are regularly reported in the Chinese press. The group remains without political significance in spite of visits to Peking and occasional demonstrations against Soviet "social imperialism." It did not figure in the March elections. Nevertheless, the SKP has been quite critical of the propaganda activities of the Chinese embassy in Helsinki and its Finnish contacts.

Publications. The SKP/SKDL *Kansan Uutiset*, published daily in Helsinki, is the main organ of the liberal majority of the SKP (circulation 55,600). *Kommunisti* is the monthly theoretical journal. *Tiedonantaja* and *Hämeen Yhteistyö* speak for the SKP hard-line minority faction. The weekly *Folktidningen* is the communist newspaper for Finland's small Swedish-speaking minority. The Finnish "Maoists" circulate several publications including *Lakakuu* and *Aamulehti*, perhaps the only violently anti-Soviet publications in the country.

University of Massachusetts   Eric S. Einhorn
Amherst

France

The French Communist Party (Parti communiste français; PCF) was founded in December 1920, as a result of the division of the Socialist Party (Parti socialiste; PS). Since the early 1960s, the PCF has followed a policy of electoral alliances with the PS, left-center forces, and in some cases left-Gaullist movements. The PCF, the PS, and the Movement of Left Radicals (Mouvement des radicaux de gauche; MRG) signed the "Common Program of Government" in 1972. This was repudiated on 21 September 1977, marking the conclusive failure of the three parties to agree on the extent of nationalization to be sought. Nevertheless, an electoral alliance, the Union of the Left, has remained in effect. While contributing to large parliamentary and municipal gains for the left as a whole, the alliance has benefited the PS far more than the PCF. In the March 1978 parliamentary elections and the June 1979 elections for the European Assembly, the PCF was unable to re-establish its traditional dominance of the French left, which it lost to the PS between 1973 and 1976. Nevertheless, the PCF's membership is the largest and most militant of all French parties.

The PCF continues its post-1958 stagnation, with about one-fifth of the total vote, despite the Union of the Left alliance. The success of this alliance in the 1976 departmental elections and the 1977 municipal elections was not followed by victory in the 12–19 March 1978 legislative elections. Of the 491 deputies to be elected, the Union of the Left won 201, compared with its previous total of 184, with 45.3 percent of the vote. The majority, composed of the Union for French Democracy (Union pour la démocratie française; UDF) of Prime Minister Raymond Barre and the Rally for the Republic (Rassemblement pour la république; RPR) headed by Jacques Chirac, the Gaullist leader, polled 46.5 percent of the vote. Communist candidates received 5.8 million votes, or 20.6 percent, compared with 21.41 percent in 1973, 20 percent in 1968, and 22.5 percent in 1967. Eighty-six PCF deputies were elected. The figure for 1973 was 74, including one deputy from the Guadeloupe Communist Party. The PS received 22.6 percent of the votes, compared with 19.2 percent received in 1973, and the MRG got 2.1 percent. The PS's position as the largest party of the left was reaffirmed. All political observers concurred that the electoral defeat of the Union of the Left resulted from the split on implementation of the "Common Program." Allocating the blame for this rupture and the ensuing defeat at the polls has become the principal subject of controversy between the PCF and the PS, as well as within the PCF, since March 1978.

Departmental elections on 18–25 March to fill half the seats on the general councils of the French departments enabled the PCF and the PS to register some gains and to show that the Union of the Left has vitality on the electoral front. In general the principle of second-round withdrawal was respected by the two parties. The PS received 27 percent of the votes(26.5 percent in 1976), and the PCF received 22.5 percent (22.8 percent in 1976). The Union of the Left increased its hold on presidencies of general councils from 37 to 43, of which only 5 are headed by PCF members. (The majority heads 52). The gap between the PCF and the PS is considerable, but this type of election is not the best terrain for the PCF.

There was only one round of voting in the 10 June elections for seats in the European Assembly, the first elections of this kind in the European Economic Community (EEC). The results confirmed the contrast between the PCF's electoral stagnation and the progress of the PS. Comparing these results with those of March 1978 is difficult because the PS and the MRG formed a common list of candidates, which received 23.7 percent of the votes. The PCF received 20.6 percent, or 4.1 million votes. (The difference in the number of votes received compared with March 1978 results from the high level of abstention, 38.8 percent.) In the PCF's judgment, these results showed progress for itself and a weakening for the PS. The two parties took strongly opposed positions for these elections, with the PCF taking a "national" stance while the PS assumed a more "European" posture. The PCF won 19 of the 81 French seats. Georges Marchais headed the PCF list. Others who won election included E. Maffre-Baugé, a noncommunist agricultural leader; R. Chambeiron, a progressive; and Paul Vergés, the secretary general of the Réunion Communist Party. The Martinique Communist Party called on its members to vote for the PCF list, while the Guadeloupe Communist Party asked its members to abstain. The electorate of both parties more or less respected these wishes. On 11 June the Political Bureau of the PCF stated that the "dreams" of "pushing the PCF to the sidelines, of diminishing its role to that of mere support, an instrument of social-democratic policy" were reduced to nothingness by the European elections, which had produced a "positive" result for the PCF.

The growth in PCF membership contrasts sharply with its electoral frustration. After stagnating at around 300,000 to 350,000 members in the 1960s, the total number of members reached 543,000 in 1976, 632,000 in 1977, and 702,864 by the end of 1978 (Paul Laurent, *L'Humanité*, 28 April). Each September, the *Humanité* festival is the occasion for an intense recruitment campaign; 10,000 new members joined in 1979. This figure is, however, somewhat ambiguous since many who sign membership forms never receive party cards or buy only a few of the monthly dues stamps. In November the party's Organizing Committee launched a campaign for all members to get their party cards, because "thousands of communists have been waiting, some for several months, to obtain their card" (*Humanité*, 16 November). The party stated that the number of members would "slightly, but clearly" exceed the 1978 figure (*France nouvelle*, 17 November). But the goal of a million members, reiterated at the 23rd Congress, remains distant. This year's slackening of membership growth clearly results from the new line of denouncing the PS and from the problem of integrating and retaining members who have joined in recent years.

In April Paul Laurent of the Political Bureau announced the results of the first study of the PCF's social composition since 1967 (*L'Humanité*, 28 April). He emphasized the increase in female members (from 25.5 percent in 1966 to 35.7 percent). The percentage of party members under 25 years of age increased from 9.4 to 11.8. Sixteen percent of the membership is over sixty years of age. Laurent pointed out that 51 percent are from the working class, but his definition of the working class includes "certain categories of production management and salaried employees." Employees not ranked in the working class constitute 28 percent of party membership; technicians 4.4 percent; and intellectuals 13.5 percent, of whom 35,606 persons—50 percent of the "intellectuals" category— are teachers. Unemployed persons make up 3.2 percent of the membership, and retired persons account for 12.8 percent. Only 10 percent of the party's voters are members. (J. Burles, *France nouvelle*, 9 June.) The party's constituency does not correspond exactly to the social composition of its membership. To judge from the March 1978 and June 1979 elections, the party has not made significant inroads in the middle class.

A return to the policy of reciprocal withdrawals of candidacy in second-round elections is presently the only form of cooperation between the PCF and the PS. The bipolarization that was so characteristic of French politics in recent years has given way to a condition of permanent confrontation, at times open, at times hidden, between the two majority parties (the UDF and the RPR) and between the PCF and the PS in the opposition. None of these parties in this two- and four-way game wants to break with its partner. The PCF's tactic of "union from the ground up" vis-à-vis the PS may well lead to serious consequences for the PCF's electorate and its members if the many factions within the PS come into conflict and break apart.

Leadership and Organization. The national leadership of the PCF was elected at the party's 23rd Congress, held on 9–13 May. The Central Committee has 145 members. The distinction between full and candidate members on both the Central Committee and the Political Bureau has been abolished. Sixteen of the Political Bureau's 21 members were re-elected: Gustave Ansart, Mireille Bertrand, Jean Colpin, Charles Fiterman, Maxime Gremetz, Guy Hermier, Henri Krasucki, André Lajoinie, Paul Laurent, Roland Leroy, Georges Marchais, René Piquet, Gaston Plissonier, Claude Poperen, Georges Séguy, and Madeleine Vincent. The five new members are: Philippe Herzog, Pierre Juquin, Francette Lazard, René Leguen, and Giséle Moreau. Colpin, Fiterman, Laurent, Plissonier, Gremetz, and Moreau make up the Secretariat of the Central Committee. Georges Marchais remains secretary general. (*L'Humanité*, 14 May.)

Four members of the preceding Political Bureau left "at their request": Etienne Fajon (who had been a member since 1945), André Vieuguet, Guy Besse, and Jacques Chambaz. A fifth, Jean Kanapa, died in September 1978. Two members, Roland Leroy and René Piquet, left the Central Committee's Secretariat. The departure of Leroy, who is the director of *L'Humanité*, was the major surprise of the 23rd Congress, according to many observers. Although the number of members in the party's leadership organizations has never been so great (18th Congress, 1967: 96; 19th Congress, 1970: 107; 20th Congress, 1972: 118; 22nd Congress, 1976: 121; 23rd Congress, 1979: 145), membership in these groups has become increasingly unified in support of Georges Marchais.

At the end of 1978, the PCF had "28,000 cells, of which more than 10,000 were work-site cells" (Georges Marchais, report to 23rd Congress). The PCF gave even greater emphasis in 1979 than in the preceding two years to the necessity of increasing the number and percentage of work-site cells in order to foster membership recruitment and to reinforce the party's position vis-à-vis the Socialists, in conformity with the new party line of "union from the ground up." Marchais asked the 23rd Congress to increase the number of work-site cells from 10,000 to 12,000, although he did not establish a target date for meeting this goal. There were 9,550 work-site cells in 1977, 40 percent of the total number of cells, while at the end of 1978 this category represented only 35 percent of all cells.

Party Internal Affairs. As a result of the PCF's outwardly "democratic" image, the PCF leadership has in recent years been faced with demands for a certain liberalization in the party's internal affairs as well. But since September 1977, the disavowal of the "Common Program" with the Socialists, the electoral failure of the left in March 1978, and the party's mobilization against the PS and the return to a harder line (union from the ground up as opposed to union at the top) have provoked debate and dissension within the PCF.

Disputes within the PCF began in 1977, marked at first by stands taken by militants from the ranks of the party's intellectuals, who were troubled by the party's severe anti-Socialist attitude. The current of discord continued in 1978, growing in magnitude after the March 1978 elections. The principal spokesmen for the position critical of the party line were Gérard Molina (the former secretary general of the Union of Communist Students) and Yves Vargas, both of whom wrote *Dialogue à l'intérieur du P.C.* (Conversations Inside the Communist Party) in February 1978, reprinted in April 1978, as well as Jean Rony, a well-known communist journalist, whose article "The PCF Has Not Been Heard by the Masses" appeared in *Le Monde* on 24 March 1978. In addition, many party members from southern France have opposed the party's leadership. On 3 April 1978, Marchais stated that the party leadership had received only "31 letters" expressing dissent and that "the period of excluding members of the party is completely over for us." In the next several days, criticism of the party leadership swelled. On 5 April *Le Monde* published a collective letter from five party intellectuals (Althusser, Balibar, Labica, Bois, and Moissonier), followed on 13–15 April by three articles by Jean Elleinstein, a historian and assistant director of the party's Center for Marxist Research and Study (Centre d'études et de recherches marxistes). Then Jean Rony's book *Trente ans de parti: Un Communiste s'interroge* (Thirty Years in the Party: A Communist Questions Himself) appeared, and in the daily newspaper *Libération* Kehayan and Panzani, two party members from Marseilles, stated that Jean Elleinstein had been "too prudent" (19 April 1978). Louis Althusser, a communist philosopher, then published a series of critical articles in *Le Monde* (25–27 April 1978). And finally the dissidents issued the first petitions signed by protesters.

At the end of April 1978, party leaders began to react. René Andrieu, editor-in-chief of *L'Humanité*, wrote an editorial entitled "Fruitless Speculations" about the commentaries on the party's internal situation. On 11 May 1978, the Political Bureau issued a release that mentioned "the political response that would be necessary" against "those activities that threaten the policies and the basic principles of the party," and an Andrieu article attacked communist journalist Frémontier for revealing certain practices of PCF leaders. On 13 May 1978, Paul Laurent rebuked Althusser for statements that he had made to the Italian daily *Paese Sera.* Nevertheless, the protests continued.

On 17 May 1978 *Le Monde* published a declaration signed by 100 party militants calling for an extraordinary party congress. Then Jean Elleinstein openly criticized the Soviet weekly *New Times*, and a new petition, circulated by militants in Aix-en-Provence, was signed by 300 persons. These events caused party leaders to react because the protests were threatening a portion of the communist press, especially *Nouvelle critique* (New Criticism) and *France nouvelle* (New France). During the first two weeks of June 1978 the entire party mobilized against the protesters. *L'Humanité* published many statements from cells, committees, and federations that attacked the "unacceptable behavior" of "certain communists" who were taking part in "an activity directed from without against the party" (*L'Humanité*, 5 June 1978). The protests quickly waned; and the signers of the petitions no longer dared to publish them. By the summer, PCF leaders had the situation under control once again. Jean Elleinstein publicly shook hands with Georges Marchais at the *Humanité* festival in September. The dissenters were really too divided among themselves to threaten serious danger; and the movement was made up essentially only of intellectuals. In June 1978, while reporting to the Central Committee, Marchais spoke of "5 sections out of 2,724, 65 cells out of 27,000, 1,000 members out of 630,000" who had openly protested some aspect of party policy.

In the fall of 1978 the problem of protest within the communist press surfaced again with the condemnation by the Political Bureau on 11 October of an issue of *Nouvelle critique*, the periodical of the intellectuals. This problem grew worse in 1979 when several editors of *France nouvelle*, the principal weekly of the PCF, resigned in February. Although Marchais had noted that the time when members would be excluded had passed, a Paris cell of the party refused to give a 1979 card to Guy Konopnicki, a former president of the French National Student Union (Union nationale des étudiants de France; UNEF) and former leader of communist students, who had published a humorous pamphlet titled *Vive le centenaire du PCF* (Long Live the Centennial of the PCF), which was critical of party leadership. On 24 February a hundred dissidents held a general assembly in Paris as preparatory work for the 23rd Congress got under way. Nevertheless, party leaders were able to maintain complete control over the preparation and operation of the congress.

The Fizbin affair was the only case of protest within the ranks of party leaders against other leaders. In January Henri Fizbin left his position as first secretary of the Paris federation of the party "because of bad health." It became clear in November that he had resigned for political reasons. Marchais offered a new post to Fizbin in September, which he refused. On 29 October the leaders of the Paris federation openly supported Fizbin in a private meeting; this support at once became publicly known. On 8 November Paul Laurent brought the Fizbin affair before the Central Committee in a roundabout way. By mid-November, party leaders assumed control of the Paris federation but failed to impose unanimity on its leaders. On 19 November Fizbin resigned the presidency of the communist group of Paris municipal councillors, and two days later he gave up his post in the Central Committee. Several Paris leaders of the PCF have expressed solidarity with him. The principal differences between Fizbin and the Political Bureau related to the social makeup of the Paris federation.

The protest movement is concentrated among intellectuals, female party members, and environmentalists (who consider that the party does not go far enough on their issues) in the Paris federation. These groups publish several periodicals: *Positions* (Bordeaux), *Luttes et débats* (Struggle and Debate; Paris), and *Dialectiques* (Dialectics), an intellectual review.

Auxiliary and Mass Organizations. The Communist Youth Movement (Mouvement de la jeunesse communiste de France; MJCF), which had grown significantly in membership and activities by the end of 1977, made little progress in 1978. At the 23rd Congress in May, Jean-Michel Catala, its secretary general, stated that the MJCF had "more than 100,000 members" and that the PCF had 83,000 members under 25 years of age, or 11.8 percent of its total membership. He admitted that the MJCF had "too often" confused "independence and autonomy" in its relations with the PCF. Despite the youth festivals held in June 1978 at Ivry, which had a reported attendance of 150,000, and at Argenteuil, where there were "tens of thousands" of persons, the MJCF suspended publication of its weekly in May. Catala was replaced as secretary general of the MJCF in October by Pierre Zarka, a communist deputy from Saint-Denis.

The Union of Communist Students (Union des étudiants communistes de France; UECF), part of the umbrella organization of the MJCF, is the PCF's organization among university students. F. Combes, its secretary general, has had to deal with disturbances among its members beginning in spring 1978 in Paris and especially in Bordeaux, where groups critical of the UECF's leaders have sprung up. The UECF's monthly magazine has been suspended since that time. The UECF is the dominant group within the UNEF, whose influence has diminished in the French universities because of challenges from Trotskyist and Socialist student groups. The party's organization among high school and preparatory students is the National Union of High School Action Committees (Union nationale des comités d'action lycéens).

The PCF dominates two of the large teachers unions, the National Union of Higher Education federal Bureau at the 40th Congress held at Grenoble from 26 November to 1 December 1978. Eight and assistants, and the National Union of Secondary Teachers (Syndicat national du second degré), whose members are high school teachers. The PCF does not control the most powerful teachers' union — that of the lower-level teachers — which is close to the PS. Consequently it has been unable to take control of the National Education Federation (Fédération de l'education nationale; FEN), which encompasses all the teachers' unions, including the SNES and the SNESup, and has a completely noncommunist leadership. Communist elements within the FEN nevertheless comprise the second strongest of the five main tendencies within the federation.

The General Confederation of Labor (Confédération génerale du travail; CGT) remains the major mass organization within the communist sphere of influence and therefore continues to occupy a crucial position in the PCF's efforts to mobilize working-class support for its policies. Still the largest union organization in France by far, the CGT claims to have 2.3 million members (40th Congress, Grenoble, 1978). According to the results of professional elections and in terms of its ability to mobilize militant activity, the CGT is the dominant union in all sectors of the French economy — private, nationalized, and public, although, as noted above, it does not dominate the education federation.

The CGT's general secretary, Georges Séguy, as well as its second-ranked figure, Henri Krasucki, are both members of the PCF Political Bureau. They were re-elected to the CGT's Confederal Bureau at the 40th Congress held at Grenoble from 26 November to 1 December 1978. Eight of the sixteen members of the bureau are communists; the eight noncommunists are considered "fellow travelers." The Executive Committee of the CGT has 93 members, 63 of whom are known communists of orthodox leanings. The seven socialists on the Executive Committee represent several tendencies. All of the CGT's professional federations are run by communist secretary generals, and its 97 departmental unions also have communist directors. The confederation's leaders were able to control a number of minor opposition challenges at the Grenoble congress. There was some dissidence from socialist elements and protest from hard-line communists against liberalization within the CGT. (G. Frischmann, a former member of the Political Bureau of the PCF, represented this latter view. He was not re-elected to the Executive Committee.)

A number of other mass organizations had varying impact on French political and social life. In rural areas, a communist-dominated group, the Movement for the Coordination and Defense of Agricultural Enterprises (Mouvement de coordination et defense des exploitations agricoles) campaigned actively against the extension of the European Economic Community to Spain and protested the importation of British agricultural products. In foreign affairs, the French Association of Friendship and Solidarity with African Peoples (Association française d'amitié et de solidarité avec les peuples d'Afrique) and the French Association of Friendship and Solidarity with the People of Iran (Association française d'amitié et solidarité avec le peuple d'Iran), whose leaders are communists, organized or participated in many demonstrations against French policy in Africa (especially in Zaire and the Central African Empire), the shah's government in Iran, and the United States. The Peace Movement (Mouvement de la paix) strongly supported Vietnam in its conflict with China (February-March) and backed the Brezhnev disarmament proposals. It was particularly active among Catholic elements. The Movement Against Racism and For Friendship Among Peoples (Mouvement contre le racisme et pour l'amitié entre les peuples; MRAP) is active in struggling against racism and seeks to extend its influence among African workers living in France. Its influence has been compromised by the failure of its leaders (its secretary general is communist) to respond to the measures taken by PCF municipalities that oppose further settlement of immigrant laborers in their areas. The MRAP did, however, demonstrate in Paris against the Shcharansky trial in the Soviet Union in June 1978, as did the PCF, and criticized episodes of Soviet anti-Semitism. The People's First Aid Association of France (Secours populaire français) is led by J. Lauprêtre, a member of the PCF Central Committee. It claims a membership of 369,350 (1977) and solicits funds for relief of poor persons in France and throughout the world. Known particularly for its "green Santa Clauses," this group directed a campaign in 1979 for solidarity with Kampuchea (Cambodia), in conjunction with the pro-Vietnamese government. In 1978 it came to the aid of people in the Sahara, working with the Polisario Front.

In keeping with the relative feminization of PCF membership in recent years, the Union of French Women (Union des femmes françaises; UFF) increased its membership from 100,000 in 1976 to 130,000 in 1979 (ibid., 30 January). The UFF is headed by J. Gelly, who is a member of the PCF Central Committee. It has encountered serious difficulties because other feminist movements have attacked the UFF for its reticent positions and its relative conservatism on feminist issues.

Domestic Views and Activities. The general line of the PCF was presented at the 23rd Congress in May 1979 (see *Cahiers du communisme*, June-July). The present goal of the party is "the democratic advance of socialism" by means of "union" and "struggle." The means of union consist of forging and developing a popular mass movement that would constitute a majority, which implies an electoral alliance with the PS. The party must accord "absolute priority" to this union "from the ground up" in order to "put the left back into balance the correct way," in other words, to advance the PCF ahead of the PS. Marchais criticized a number of illusions about the union idea and drew upon the experience of the "Common Program": "By signing the 'Common Program,' the PS saw itself identified as a revolutionary party, which was false both as to its veritable nature and as to the strategy of its leaders." Marchais asked that union should be "placed permanently under the control of the workers." He repeated the statement made by the PCF on 20 March 1978: "The PS has led the left to an electoral defeat for which it bears full responsibility." Nevertheless, he maintained that the PCF's decision to sign the "Common Program" in 1972 was "the only fitting and realistic decision." By means of struggle, the PCF refers to "a process of mass struggle" that will lead to "modification, little by little, of the balance of social and political forces to the benefit of the masses." The means of struggle to be used are mass actions and universal suffrage.

This return to a harder line, at least until the next major electoral event, the presidential elections in 1981, was accompanied by a number of other policy statements articulated at the congress. The party repudiates layoffs, unemployment, the austerity program, and the attempt to create a consensus — the government's request to the population to face up to the energy crisis. For the PCF, the basic cause of the economic crisis is the operation of multinational enterprises and European integration. To fight against these trends is to fight "against the decline of France," "against the loss of its independence and sovereignty." The PCF wants to protect all social classes and strike down "the domination of capital," and it accuses the PS of rejecting its approach. According to Marchais, the superiority of the PCF over the PS lies in the PCF's theory of "scientific socialism," which is materialistic and dialectic. Marchais reminded his audience of "the historical necessity of the leadership role of the working class," of which the PCF is the "vanguard."

The PCF modified its statutes during the 23rd Congress. Articles 18 and 19 now speak of the necessity for members to belong to a work-site cell. Party activities should be organized by priorities in and around the place of work. This change was the most discussed question among party officials (Paul Laurent, report to the 23rd Congress). The distinction between full and candidate membership on the Central Committee and the Political Bureau was abolished. The term "scientific socialism" replaced "Marxism-Leninism," and the national character of the PCF was emphasized in the preamble. Article 8 condemns currents of opposition within the party and states that the PCF remains under "democratic centralism." These were the most important changes.

The 23rd Congress took place at Ile Saint-Denis, north of Paris, from 9 to 13 May. There were 1,992 delegates present. Before the congress there was discussion at all levels of the party. *L'Humanité* and *France nouvelle* had opened their pages to opinions of members and had published 230 contributions, the vast majority of which were favorable to party leaders. At the congress of the Paris federation, for instance, the vote on the resolution for the congress presented by the leaders obtained 600 votes, with 1 vote opposed and 4 abstentions (*L'Humanité*, 2 May).

The attitude of the PCF toward the PS was characterized by repeated attacks upon François Mitterrand, first secretary of the PS. At a meeting of the Italian Communist Party in Turin on 21 May, Marchais stated, "François Mitterrand represents permanent failure" (ibid., 23 May). Mitterrand and Marchais came into direct conflict over whether they had in fact met on 5 May 1974 at the time of the presidential elections, one denying what the other affirmed. In June and November the two leaders referred publicly to controversial aspects of each other's personal life. Gaston Defferre, the deputy and Socialist mayor of Marseilles, is also a favorite target of the PCF, which criticized him for the subway strike in Marseilles in November. The anti-Socialist attacks of the PCF also extended to J. P. Chevènement, the leader of the Center for Socialist Studies, Research, and Education (Centre d'études, de recherches et d'éducation socialistes), the most left-wing faction of the PS. This faction had given its support to Mitterrand after the Metz Congress of the PS.

In April, the Directors' Committee of the PS renewed its appeal to the PCF for a "nonagression pact" between the two parties and called on the PCF to choose "between the union strategy that it continues to affirm and its persistent desire to appear as the sole party of the working class." At

Anglet on 20 August Mitterrand proposed to the PCF a program of "unified action at the founda-tions" and suggested a meeting without pre-established agenda. The meeting took place on 20 September at PCF hadquarters, with Charles Fiterman leading the PCF delegation and Chevènement, Poperen, Beregovoy, and J. P. Cot representing the PS. It was virtually a complete failure. On 23 September Marchais stated that the "nonagression pact" was just a "little political tactic" of Mitterrand's. Then, in October and November, there were a number of conflicts between the PS and the PCF in cities that they govern jointly in the Union of the Left. At Angers, Valence, and Marseilles there were transit strikes supported by the PCF and the CGT against Socialist mayors. Other conflicts between the parties took place at Lille, Castres, Albi, Rennes, and Pessas, as well as in other cities. Most recently, the PCF denounced as a political maneuver a brief meeting between Jacques Chirac, the Gaullist mayor of Paris, and Mitterrand at the Paris City Hall in November.

The PCF participated in all the major labor disturbances that broke out in several regions of France because of business shutdowns or slowdowns. Operating either directly, through its local officials or its sections in the affected businesses, or indirectly, through its influence in the CGT, the PCF played a role in the steel industry disturbances at Denain in the Nord department and at Longwy in Lorraine from the fall of 1978 to the spring of 1979. One of the most spectacular events of these strikes was a march on Paris held on 23 March,organized by the CGT with PCF support. The PCF gave a decidedly anti-European and anti–West German slant to these strikes and factory occupations by adopting the slogan "Produce French, Buy French." "Longwy and Denain have become symbols . . . of the struggle against Giscard d'Estaing's policy of national abandonment." (Jean Colpin, in a speech to the 23rd Congress.) the PCF gave the CGT its support in the labor union's disputes over union strategy with the French Democratic Labor Confederation (Confédération française démo-cratique du travail; CFDT). In March, Edmond Maire, the secretary general of the CFDT, had criti-cized the PCF for its "desire for hegemony." When the oceanliner *France*, which had been pur-chased by a foreign company, was scheduled to leave Le Havre in August, the PCF backed the CGT's efforts to prevent the ship from leaving. The ship was to be refitted in a German shipyard, and the controversy took on anti–German coloration. And the Manufrance affair gave the party an op-portunity to step in directly during an important labor conflict. Manufrance, a large manufacturing concern in Saint-Etienne, had laid off a number of employees. The city of Saint-Etienne, a major shareholder in the company, was headed by J. Sanguedolce, a member of the PCF's Central Com-mittee. The municipal government threw its weight behind worker grievances, and the compromise reached in negotiations enabled the city to maintain that the extra financial support came as a result of its activities.

On 29 March the PCF published a document entitled *The PCF and the Labor Movement*, which emphasized the importance of the labor movement in social conflict. The document pointed out that unionized communists reject the "social-democratic" concept of syndicalism. The PCF affirmed that it would respect the independence of all unions, but recognized a "special nature" in its relations with the CGT. While it judged positively the agreements for joint action reached by the CGT and the CFDT, it warned the CFDT against its "centrist" tendency (its retreat from political activism) and against dis-crimination toward communist militants within its ranks. The PCF took note of its differences with the other unions and expressed the desire to have "fruitful cooperation with all unions," the princi-pal obstacle being "anticommunism." In September Georges Marchais treated the labor issue again, attacking Edmond Maire and the CFDT as well as the leaders of the FEN and the General Confed-eration of Managers (Confédération générale des cadres). He described the "constructive ties be-tween the CGT and the PCF" (ibid., 14 September). Above all, he called on communists within the CGT to increase their activity, and he affirmed that consolidation of the party at the work-site is linked with the development of the union movement. The PCF is the best-placed political organiza-tion at the work-site. Compared with the 10,000 work-site cells of the PCF, the PS claims 1,400 work-site groups and sections, and the RPR claims 950 worker and professional associations. With the exception of the extreme left, the other parties have no such institutions (*Le Figaro*, 8 October).

The PCF and the CGT, as well as other organizations, campaigned against administrative provisions concerning the entry and stay of immigrant workers in France. The party has intensified its recruitment efforts among these workers. However, municipalities controlled by the PCF that have a high proportion of immigrant workers have been accused of discrimination against them and of not desiring their stay. At Levallois, a western suburb of Paris, the communist city government held a referendum in September to prevent the location there of a group of immigrant workers. The PCF has treated problems of regionalism, particularly in Brittany and Corsica, with qualified support for regionalist proponents. In June, when there were clashes in Ajaccio between young Corsicans and the police, the Corsican federation of the PCF called for the departure of the police from the island and recognition of "a Corsican presence within national unity." The PCF press has supported the defendants in several Corsican and Breton autonomist trials without, however, going so far as to espouse these causes fully.

The leaders of the PCF accord great importance to the problems of the intellectuals and have held several meetings to deal with these issues. Since late 1977, dissidence in the ranks of the PCF has been largely the work of the intellectuals. In December 1978 at Vitry, a communist stronghold in the Paris suburbs, Marchais held discussions with 400 intellectuals and dealt with a number of criticisms. This meeting ended favorably for PCF leaders. Although the intellectual faction remains under control, there are still many problems brewing beneath the surface, the most notable being the attitude of Jean Elleinstein, whose relations with Marchais have had their ups and downs. The Center for Marxist Research and Study merged with the Maurice Thorez Institute in October, and the new body has taken the name Institute of Marxist Studies. Francette Lazard, a member of the Political Bureau, is the director of this organ, which studies historical and theoretical problems of the PCF and enjoys significant influence in university circles.

International Views and Policies. At the 23rd Congress in May Marchais articulated the proposal put forward throughout the party: "The overall evaluation of socialist countries is positive." He made clear that the defense of socialist countries is "an essential battleground of the class struggle." Marchais also stressed the importance for French communists of "a shift in the balance of world forces" in favor of socialism. He condemned the socialism of the social democrats, recalling that the Soviet Union's communist party had already done so at its Twentieth Congress. He also rejected all foreign models for French socialism and pronounced himself in favor of Eurocommunism, which he defined as being "neither a new center, nor a new model, nor based on any particular party." The 23rd Congress, declared closed by Marchais to shouts of "Long live international solidarity," marked the return of the PCF to a more restrained attitude toward the Soviet Union. In June 1978 the PCF had taken part in street demonstrations in Paris against the Shcharansky trial in the Soviet Union. It had earlier protested the sentencing of Orlov to seven years in a labor camp (*L'Humanité*, 19 May 1978). In the summer of 1978, the PCF strongly publicized the book *The Soviet Union and Us*, published by its own house, Editions Sociales, and written by five communist intellectuals. This book described the Soviet Union in balanced terms, approving the regime while expressing reservations about certain of its practices.

This book was received unfavorably both by pro-Soviet elements and by party liberals, and in December 1978 the Soviet communist party journal *Kommunist* attacked it. The PCF did not respond to this attack. Meanwhile, the Kehayan affair had taken place. Jean and Nina Kehayan had been sent by the PCF to Moscow for several years. They had returned to France disenchanted and wrote *The Street of the Red Proletariat*, which was well received by readers. Guy Hermier, a member of the Political Bureau, responded for the PCF in *L'Humanité* (22 November) by sharply attacking the

Kehayans for "gross distortion of Soviet reality and the policies of their party." Since that time, the intermittent polemical exchanges between the PCF and the Soviet communist party have almost completely ceased. Jeanette Thorez-Vermeersch, former member of the Political Bureau and widow of Maurice Thorez, renewed her attacks against the present leaders of the PCF in a book that appeared in November and accused the PCF of anti-Soviet policies. But her position has become somewhat isolated since the PCF has refrained from criticizing Moscow. *L'Humanité* ran a spate of articles in the fall presenting internal Soviet developments in a favorable light, and the PCF gave its complete support to Brezhnev's disarmament proposals. Maxime Gremetz, a member of the Political Bureau and the successor to the late Jean Kanapa as head of the foreign policy section of the PCF, issued a statement criticizing the "dangerous projects" of the United States and NATO in Europe and has welcomed the "concrete proposals for reduction of forces in Europe" put forward by Brezhnev, accusing the French government of "doing nothing" (*France nouvelle*, 17 November). As of late 1979, there were no foreign policy differences between the Soviet Union and the PCF.

The elections for the European Assembly on 10 June provided an opportunity to verify the PCF's Eurocommunism. The PCF's policy in this campaign opposed that of the Spanish Communist Party, which favored the entry of Spain into the EEC. The PCF opposed Spain's entry and organized demonstrations in southwestern France to mobilize French farmers. The PCF also had differences with the Italian Communist Party (PCI) on the issue of entry into the EEC of Spain, Greece, and Portugal. Despite these differences, the PCF and the PCI campaigned together. Berlinguer and Marchais appeared on the same podium at Marseilles on 19 May and at Turin on 21 May. With non-Eurocommunist parties such as those of Portugal, the German Federal Republic, Luxembourg, and Belgium, on the other hand, the PCF had no policy differences. The basic issues in the PCF's European election campaign were defense of national independence "against a Europe of the multi-nationals" (Marchais, 28 May) and "Europe is not peace" (Marchais, *L'Humanité*, 31 May). The party emphasized the struggle against "[West] German Europe" even more than that against "German-American Europe."

The PCF firmly supported Vietnam in its conflict with China, especially during the "frontier war" of February and March. At a solidarity meeting in Paris on 1 March, Marchais stated that the Pol Pot dictatorship in Kampuchea had nothing in common with socialism, and he demanded the withdrawal of Chinese troops. He proclaimed that "socialism carries peace within itself" and that China suffers from a "dramatic lack" of socialism (ibid., 2 March). On 29 June and 21 July, the Political Bureau expressed its total support for Vietnam on the refugee question, speaking of the refugees as "emigrants." The PCF sent a delegation supportive of Vietnam to the Geneva conference on the refugee question.

In response to the Iranian crisis, the PCF organized demonstrations at the end of 1978 in support of the forces opposing the shah. The Political Bureau attacked the United States in a press release on 2 January, demanding the withdrawal of American military personnel from Iran. After saluting the "victory of the revolution" in February, the party was restrained with regard to the Ayatollah Khomeini for several months, but when the American embassy was taken over in November, the PCF took a favorable stance toward Iran and Khomeini. The party regarded Iran as engaged "in a struggle against imperialism and financial oligarchy, trying to liberate Iran from its dependency upon the United States, to attain popular democracy, and to change the fundamental conditions of economic and social life of the oppressed masses. What Iran requires is what Khomeini expresses." (D. Bari, *L'Humanité-dimanche*, 28 November.)

On the international scene, the PCF judged that the Tokyo summit, the meeting of chiefs-of-state from seven countries, was directed "against the people." The PCF has led intense campaigns in support of "national liberation" struggles, most notably in favor of the Polisario Front, through co-operation with the Algerian government. There was a meeting with front representatives in Paris in

February. The Palestine Liberation Organization (PLO) has also enjoyed strong PCF support; PLO spokesmen met with the PCF representatives in October and November. Following communications between the PCF and the Lebanese Communist Party, arrangements were made for an Arafat-Marchais meeting to be held at an unspecified date in Lebanon. After a first meeting between Marchais and Arafat in Algiers on 31 October, the PCF and the PLO issued a joint communiqué in which the PCF endorsed the demands of the PLO and called on the French government to invite Arafat to Paris and to recognize the PLO. The PCF maintains excellent relations with the Algerian government. In the Americas, the PCF has declared its solidarity with the Sandinistas in Nicaragua and is following the situation in Brazil closely.

The PCF's nationalism does not prevent the party from playing a full role in the international communist movement directed by Moscow.

International Activities and Contacts. Relations between the PCF and the Soviet communist party this year reached a level unheard of in quite some time. Boris Ponomarev, a member of the Soviet Politburo, represented the Soviet party at the 23rd Congress of the PCF in May. Maxime Gremetz, head of the foreign affairs section of the PCF and a member of the Political Bureau, met with Ponomarev at Moscow in July. The two met again in Moscow during the month of October, this time in the company of Charles Fiterman of the PCF's Political Bureau. Vadim Zagladin, the assistant chief of the international politics section of the Soviet party, came to Paris for meetings from 19 to 24 November. Although the official statements subsequent to these meetings have been brief, PCF criticism of Soviet violations of human rights ceased in 1979. There was, nevertheless, some minor discord between Gremetz and Ponomarev over the subject of defining Eurocommunism (*L'Humanité*, 20 October).

Relations with the Czech Communist Party remain rather bad. The PCF's Political Bureau released a statement criticizing the Vaclav Havel trial in Prague (21 October), but the party did not go so far as to take part in street demonstrations occasioned by this event; further, the PCF reproached the French minister of foreign affairs for postponing a visit to Prague because of this trial. At the 23rd Congress of the PCF, J. Haman, a secretary of the Czech Central Committee, represented the Czech party; Czechoslovakia had a display area at the *Humanité* festival in September. The PCF maintained good relations and had frequent contacts with other socialist countries in the Soviet bloc, and with Romania and Yugoslavia. Erich Honecker, the secretary general of the East German communist party, was host to Marchais at the end of December 1978. Todor Zhivkov, the Bulgarian chief-of-state, received Gremetz in August. Marchais spent his 1978 vacation in Romania, as the guest of Nicolae Ceauşescu, secretary general of the Romanian Communist Party. Gremetz made a visit to Poland in January. Marchais had a personal victory in being seen by President Tito in Yugoslavia on 2 July. There had been several contacts before this meeting, which further enhanced the prestige of the French party's secretary general. Relations with China have been marked by the position of the PCF with regard to Vietnam and the pro-Vietnamese government in Kampuchea. The contacts begun in 1978 have not been followed up, although a representative of the Chinese press agency did attend the PCF's congress. And no contacts have been made with Albania, in spite of the wishes of the PCF.

Dealings with the communist parties of Western Europe have been influenced by the question of allowing certain countries to enter the EEC. The consequent differences between the PCF and the other parties have dealt a serious blow to Eurocommunism. The meeting between the French and the Spanish communist parties in Madrid on 18 and 19 January was a failure. Despite many contacts and meetings between Marchais and Berlinguer, differences between the French and Italian parties still exist, although both parties attempt to paper them over. The only "Eurocommunist" meeting of the year was held in Paris between the French, Spanish, and Italian communist parties in November to muster support for the Polisario Front. This meeting followed one at Madrid on 20 September at which the three parties adopted a position in favor of the Polisario Front. The secretary generals of the three parties have not met since March 1977. The PCF has maintained active and cordial relations with the communist parties of Greece, Portugal, Belgium, and West Germany, all of which are non-Eurocommunist parties. In the summer of 1978 Marchais went to Mexico, where he held discussions with the local communist party, which had hitherto been considered as belonging to the Eurocommunist sphere of influence.

Eighty-eight delegations of communist parties and "national liberation" movements attended the 23rd Congress of the PCF. The PCF makes an effort, not always successful, to maintain good relations with all communist parties. It freely admits to being in agreement with the Soviet communist party's international strategy—although it has not mentioned the Eritrean problem for more than a year, since it did not share the Kremlin's views on that issue—but not all problems between the PCF and the Soviet communist party have been resolved, although there has been clear progress in their relations.

The Far Left. It is possible to evaluate the activities of the extreme left during the past year under two rubrics: structure and antigovernmental labor activities. Both aspects of extreme-left activities can be subsumed in the larger framework of what the militants themselves describe as the "crisis of leftism": defections by militants are becoming more numerous, and the influence of these factions has been decreasing steadily. The problems encountered by the press of the extreme left provide ample illustration. *Rouge*, the daily of the Revolutionary Communist League (Ligue communiste révolutionnaire; LCR), a Trotskyist group, became a weekly in February; and *Tribune Socialiste*, the weekly of the Unified Socialist Party (Parti socialiste unifié; PSU), has become a monthly. *Maintenant* (Now), which first appeared on 12 March, had aimed at a readership at the junction point of the extreme left and the dissidents within the PCF. It closed down in August. And the weekly of the Workers' Communist Organization (Organisation communiste des travailleurs; OCT), *Etincelle* (The Spark), has become a monthly.

The strikes and demonstrations in the Lorraine steel industry from December 1978 to May 1979 led the extreme left to think in terms of a movement that might overcome the electoral failure of March 1978. The goal of this movement was the general strike. Had this movement been successful, it would have placed the extreme left in the more comfortable terrain of effecting change through nonparliamentary means, and these factions would have been accorded a "second wind." But in spite of the violent aspects of the movement, it did not grow sufficiently. Moreover, the PCF managed to keep it under control, either directly or, through the CGT, indirectly. The mass demonstration of steelworkers in Paris on 23 March demonstrated that the extreme left's penetration of mass movements was shallow, or at most circumstantial.

Since then, the extreme left has fallen into a pattern of occasional bursts of activity tied to specific issues: solidarity with the Sandinistas in Nicaragua and a campaign against the repression of revolutionaries in Iran. More significant, its mobilization to protest the expulsion of Italian revolutionary militants was only lukewarm. This reticence—almost stagnation—is observable at the structural level: the year was marked by an unprecedented number of congresses and a great proliferation of factions in each group.

The PSU held its congress at Saint-Etienne on 12–14 January. The most lively faction within the party proposed special contacts with Michel Rocard's wing of the PS to keep the PSU in the mainstream, but the congress decided nothing beyond a continuation of what had become the usual PSU issues: industrial self-management; support for the antinuclear movement; decentralization; and support for autonomy movements. The PSU decided to associate itself with the weekly *Maintenant*. And at its National Council meeting on 18 November it named Huguette Bouchardeau as its candidate in the 1981 presidential elections. Her eventual withdrawal in favor of a leftist candidate who does better in the first round will be decided in the context of an explicit political agreement.

The Trotskyist current went through a number of ups and downs. The LCR held its first congress 25 to 28 January at Saint-Gratien; several factions fought to a standstill for dominance. The right wing emphasized the need for aligning with a rival organization, the Internationalist Communist Organization (Organisation communiste internationaliste; OCI) and won 18 percent of the vote; the left wing wanted to move toward the OCT and received 38 percent of the vote. Consequently, LCR leaders found themselves in the minority, and a compromise was necessary—the leadership stayed in power but a Central Committee was elected by proportional representation. As *Libération* summed up on 29 January: "The congress has opened up an extended crisis ... Each side holds to its own position." The preparatory meetings for the world congress of the Fourth International provided the setting for resolving the crisis. At a 1–4 November meeting held at L'Haye-aux-Roses, the pro-OCI faction used the pretext of debates over the nature of the new Nicaraguan state and the support to be given the Sandinistas to withdraw from the LCR. The pro-OCI faction called on its followers and on the other factions to participate in a forthcoming international meeting of the Committee for the Reunification of the Fourth International (Comité pour la réunification de la quatriéme internationale), a rival group. The LCR lost about a fourth of its supporters, who seem to want to form a new organization, the International Communist League (Ligue communiste internationale).

The Internationalist Communist Organization–Alliance of Youths for Socialism (Organisation communiste internationaliste–Alliance des jeunes pour le socialism; OCI-AJS) was also troubled by internal crises. Charles Berg, the secretary general of the AJS, was expelled from the OCI in February for fraudulent practices, including falsification of statements and embezzlement of funds for his personal use. In fact, his expulsion seems to result from his hostility to rapprochement with the LCR. The closed and sectarian nature of the organization prevents outsiders from learning the real reasons behind its announced decisions. The movement held a special congress on 24–27 May at which it threw its continued support behind P. Lambert and confirmed its policy orientations: a workers' front; demonstrations against the National Assembly; and a government composed of the PS and the PCF.

By reason of the OCT's intermediary position between the Trotskyists and the Marxist-Leninist movements, it plays a special role on the French extreme left. Because it has never been able to overcome the difficulties inherent in this position, however, it has moved toward the LCR, with which it formed a common candidate list in the March 1978 elections. The Marxist-Leninists have lost their credibility. The OCT, which lost 40 percent of its militants in December 1977, appears to be in a state of permanent crisis. At the time of its Third Congress on 21 and 24 April, half of its members voted to merge with the LCR. This faction pulled out of the OCT at the beginning of July and began discussions with the LCR. If successful, a merger of these elements would be tantamount to a return of members that had pulled out of the LCR in 1971, when it was called the Communist Revolution Organization (Organisation communiste révolution).

The Marxist-Leninists are fragmented into many parties, groups, and organizations. One of the major events of the year for these factions was the joint announcement by the Communist Revolutionary Party–Marxist-Leninist Faction (Parti communiste révolutionnaire–marxiste-léniniste; PCR [m.l.]) and the Marxist-Leninist Communist Party (Parti communiste marxiste-léniniste; PCML) in their respective newspapers (*Humanité rouge* and *Quotidien du peuple*, 25 October) of a prospective agenda for merger. The essential points of accord are coordination of activities; merger of press organs (their dailies were expected to merge on 1 January 1980); and preparation of a unification congress to elect a common leadership body in which each group will have a proportional share of power. This development culminates a trend that has been at work over the past two years. The PCR (m.l.) and the PCML had presented joint candidacies for the 1978 legislative elections. But other groups of this prevailing political drift have stayed apart from this centralizing trend: the French Communist Union–Marxist-Leninist Faction (Union communiste de France–marxiste-léniniste), which has been very active among immigrant workers, and the French Communist Workers' Party (Parti communiste ouvrier de France; PCOF), which publishes the newspaper *La Forge* (The Forge). The PCOF, a new party, is pro-Albanian and was formed after a split in the PCML in the Strasbourg region.

To bring this summary of the extreme left back into perspective, it should be noted that the candidate list presented jointly by the Workers' Struggle (Lutte ouvrière; LO) and the LCR received 3.1 percent of the votes nationally in the June elections for the European Assembly. Consequently, even though the organizations and the ideologies of the extreme left seem to be on the wane, this force in French politics remains electorally important.

(Sources for this section include *Libération, Le Matin, Rouge, Informations ouvrières, Humanité rouge, Quotidien du peuple,* and *Lutte ouvrière.*)

Publications. There has been a downturn in the expansion of the PCF press since the 1978 elections. A number of recently created publications have stopped publication. *Le Point du jour*, a regional daily started on 29 November 1977 to service the Lyon–Grenoble–Saint-Etienne area, shut down at the end of April 1978. *Paris-hebdo*, the weekly started by the Paris federation of the PCF in October 1976, also stopped publication at the end of April 1978. In both cases financial problems were blamed for the closings, although *Paris-hebdo* was shut down because it allowed publication of certain opinions that were not in conformity with the party line. The publication of the MJCF, a weekly, shut down in May 1979, and *Nouveau clarté*, an occasional monthly of the UECF, has not appeared since May.

It was announced on 16 October that the principal weekly of the PCF, *France nouvelle*, which has been published since 1945, would merge with the intellectual monthly of the party, *La Nouvelle critique*, in early 1980. The new publication will take the title *Révolution*, and its director will be Guy Hermier, a member of the Political Bureau. Its editorial committee includes Jean Elleinstein (but not Louis Althusser, the dissident communist philosopher). The estimated circulation of *Révolution* is 100,000. The changes in layout and content that were made in *L'Humanité*, the party's principal daily newspaper, in 1977 and in October 1978 have not produced the hoped-for expansion of the paper. At the 23rd Congress, Roland Leroy, director of the paper, set the goal of selling 500,000 copies of *L'Humanité-dimanche*, the special Sunday edition of the paper. Leroy criticized communists who had complained that "*L'Humanité* is hard to read." *L'Humanité-dimanche* had a circulation of about 400,000 copies in 1977 and 1978. The daily press run of *L'Humanité* in 1977 averaged 219,232 copies, of which 153,097 were sold. In 1978 sales decreased by 2 percent, and the loss on each issue was 44 centimes (*L'Humanité*, 27 April). On 12 September the Central Committee decided that each cell should constitute a sales committee and should focus attention on sales at the work-site.

The regular party press also includes the monthly theoretical journal *Cahiers du communisme*; a rural weekly, *La Terre*; a literary monthly, *Europe*; a philosophical bimonthly, *La Pensée*; a monthly economic journal, *Economie et politique*; a historical bimonthly, *Cahiers de l'Institut de recherches marxistes*; and a monthly review for teachers, *L'Ecole et la nation*. For intraparty communication the Central Committee publishes *La Vie du parti. Police et nation* and *Armée et nation* are circulated exclusively among the police and the army. It is difficult to estimate the number of publications disseminated by the cells, but it is several thousand, at least. These publications appear irregularly and assume a variety of forms. The party's provincial dailies are *La Liberté* (in the north), *L'Echo du centre*, and *La Marseillaise*.

Editions Sociales, the party's principal publishing house, and its distribution network, the Centre de diffusion du livre et de la presse (Book and Newspaper Distribution Center), went through a serious crisis in 1978–1979. Nearly one hundred employees were laid off because of "reorganization." The Livre Club Diderot, which sells artistic and historical works on the PCF, also laid off a number of employes. Two former directors expressed criticism of the policies of PCF leaders in this domain in *L'Entreprise des patrons rouges* (The Business of the Red Bosses), a book that appeared in September.

Institut d'histoire sociale   Nicholas Tandler
Paris   with Jean Louis Panné

Germany: Federal Republic of Germany

The Communist Party of Germany (Kommunistische Partei Deutschlands; KPD) was founded on 31 December 1918. During the Weimar Republic, the KPD was one of the major political parties. In 1933, after Hitler came to power, the party was outlawed but continued to operate underground. After the end of the war, the KPD was reconstituted. In the first elections following the founding of the Federal Republic of Germany (FRG), the party received 5.7 percent of the vote, giving the communists 15 seats in the Bundestag. In the next elections in 1953, the KPD fell to 2.2 percent, i.e., below the 5 percent required to qualify for representation in the legislature. In August 1956 the Federal Constitutional Court found the KPD's objectives and methods in violation of the FRG's Basic Law and outlawed the party (it continued to operate as an ineffective underground organization). In September 1968 the present German Communist Party (Deutsche Kommunistische Partei; DKP) was founded. At that time the underground KPD had about 7,000 members. Most of the leaders of the DKP were KPD members. In 1971, the Federal Security Service (Bundesverfassungsschutz; BVS) proved that the DKP was a successor of the KPD and could be outlawed by a decree of the federal minister of the interior (see *YICA*, 1975, p. 174). On the occasion of the 60th anniversary of the founding of the KPD (1978), DKP Chairman Herbert Mies declared that his party was the sole legitimate legatee of such former communist politicians as Rosa Luxemburg, Karl Liebknecht, and Ernst Thählmann. (*Frankfurter Allgemeine Zeitung* [*FAZ*], 9 January.)

The DKP is pro-Moscow in orientation. Membership figures reported in the past appear to have been exaggerated. At the end of 1978, the party was supposed to have had 42,000 members, an increase of about 2,000. In North Rhine-Westphalia, the highly industrialized and most populous *Land* in the FRG, DKP membership remains stagnant at about 15,000. (Ibid., 5 June.) The population of the FRG is 61.2 million. The following tabulation is based on the annual report of the BVS and provides an overview of left-extremist organizations in the FRG at the end of 1978.

Type of Organization	Number of Organizations	Membership	
Orthodox communist:			
Basic organizations	2	49,900	
Affiliated organizations	11	29,100	
Organizations influenced by communists	50		50,400[a]
Dogmatic new left (Maoist):			
Basic organizations	11	5,500	
Affiliated organizations	27	6,800	
Organizations influenced by the new left	15		2,780[a]
Trotskyist	11	880	
Undogmatic organizations of the new left, including anarchists	81	4,750	
TOTAL	208	96,930	53,180[a]
Deduction for membership in more than one organization	24,930	13,280	
	72,000	39,900	
TOTAL MEMBERSHIP		111,900	

Source: Bundesminister des Innern, *Verfassungsschutz, 1978*, Bonn, September 1979, p. 66.
Note: The membership of 111,900 for 1978 is 5,700 less than the membership given for 1977.
[a] Including noncommunists

Leadership and Organization. No changes in DKP leaders have been reported since the Fifth Party Congress (Mannheim, 20–22 October 1978). The Socialist Unity Party (SED) of the German Democratic Republic (GDR) remains the major financial contributor to the DKP. The SED also continued to provide direct supervision of DKP activities, including the political schooling of the party's functionaries. The DKP is organized in about 1,400 primary party organizations (factory, residential, and university groups). Above them are 187 county (*Kreis*) organizations, which are led by twelve district (*Bezirk*) organizations. (Ibid., p. 77.)

The most important affiliated organizations of the DKP are the Socialist German Workers' Youth (SDAJ), Marxist Student Union–Spartakus (MSB-Spartakus), and Young Pioneers. The SDAJ, which has about 15,000 members, held its Sixth Federal Congress in Hamburg (5–6 May). It was attended by 728 delegates. Werner Stürmann was elected the new chairman and Vera Achenbach deputy chairman. (*Unsere Zeit [UZ]*, 11 May; *Deutscher Informationsdienst [DI]*, vol. 30, no. 1,503–4, May-June, p. 25; for additional information concerning these organizations, see *YICA*, 1978, p. 143, and 1979, p. 148.) One of the several communist-led organizations that supported the DKP in its promotion of "unity of action" among communists, socialists, Protestant churches, and public figures is the Association of Victims of Nazi Regime–League of Anti-Fascists (VVN-BdA), which held its annual federal congress in Dortmund (25–27 May). It was attended by over 350 elected delegates and representatives from the GDR, the Soviet Union, Yugoslavia, and Israel, as well as from numerous committees of former resistance fighters and victims of Nazi persecution. Organizations with which the VVN-BdA has collaborated in various actions were represented, including the Nature Friend Youth (a Social

Democratic youth organization), Socialist Student League, Association of Democratic Jurists, Anti-Imperialist Solidarity Committee, German Peace Union, DKP, Young Democrats (the youth organizations of the Free Democratic Party), SDAJ, Young Socialists (the official youth organization of the Social Democratic Party [SPD]), and MSB-Spartakus. (*DI*, vol. 3, no. 1,505-6, June-July, pp. 2–7; for other organizations of this kind, see *YICA*, 1978, p. 142–44, and 1979, p. 148–49.)

Party Internal Affairs. At the beginning of 1979, the DKP changed all membership books (*CDU-Documentation*, Bonn, 22 February, p. 7), a standard procedure in communist parties. The purpose was to eliminate passive members who did not participate actively in the realization of DKP policies. The second session of the DKP Directorate in Düsseldorf (3–4 February) discussed preparations for the conference of delegates held on 17 February in Saarbrücken to nominate DKP candidates for the elections to the European parliament (10 June). A list of 78 candidates was elected by the approximately 200 delegates in attendance. (*DI*, vol. 30, no. 1,497, 13 February, p. 3, and no. 1,498, 27 February, p. 8.)

As in previous years, the ideological schooling of party members received a high priority among party activities. The Fifth DKP Congress had made it a duty of party members to study Marxism-Leninism because of its "indispensable" value as "intellectual armament." The DKP Presidium selected the topics for the "education year 1979–80." All of them relate to Marxism-Leninism and current issues, e.g., "Thirty years of the GDR: contemporary problems of the development of socialism," "the value of elections for the struggle of the workers' movement," and "communist and nonpartisan trade unions." (Ibid., vol. 30, no. 1,510, 11 October, p. 2.) The bimonthly "educational evenings" form the basis for the ideological education of members. Party leaders strongly urged members to participate in the regular courses and seminars offered by the party's Marxist Workers' Education (Marxistische Arbeiterbildung; MAB), which maintains throughout the FRG about one hundred Marxist Evening Schools. The MAB was established in March 1969, shortly after the founding of the DKP. The district party organizations were instructed by DKP leaders to organize Marxist Factory Workers' Schools. A number of these "schools" operated in 1979 in most of the industrial cities of the FRG. (Ibid., vol. 30, no. 1,496, 29 January, p. 7, and no. 1,500, 29 March, pp. 18–24.)

The central research and teaching institute of the DKP is the Institute for Marxist Studies and Research, located in Frankfurt. It was founded in December 1969. The institute advises DKP leaders on ideological issues and publishes ideological education materials. In its ten years of activity, it has produced close to 200 titles. About a thousand DKP members attended the party's Karl Liebknecht School at Leverkusen or took courses lasting up to one year at the Franz Mehring School in East Berlin (1978, about 300 participants), the Institute for Social Science of the Central Committee of the Communist Party of the Soviet Union (CPSU), and at the Leninist Komsomol School in Moscow (1978, about 40 participants). (*Verfassungsschutz*, 1978, pp. 89–90.)

The Sixth Federal Congress of the SDAJ in Hamburg (5–6 May) witnessed considerable changes in SDAJ leaders, which is quite usual in youth organizations. Only 33 of the 67 members elected to the Federal Directorate were incumbents. Almost half of the delegates and guest delegates had joined the SDAJ after 1976. The congress adopted the "Action Program for the Five Basic Rights of Youths." (*Arbeitskreis für Landesverteidigung, Radikal Info*, Bonn, no. 3, May-June, pp. 1–6.)

Domestic Attitudes and Activities. Efforts to achieve "unity of action" in order to gain influence among the masses continued to be the focus of DKP domestic activities in 1979. The party was supported in this endeavor, aimed at overcoming its isolation, by DKP-affiliated and -influenced organizations. The fight against the so-called *Berufsverbot* (denial of the right to practice one's own occupation) continued to be used to obtain support from Social Democrats, trade unionists, and Christian groups. For example, about 26,000 persons demonstrated in Bonn on 31 March against the security checks of civil service applicants. (*FAZ*, 2 April.) At the end of 1978, there were 2,309 left-extremists in public service (1,432 belonged to orthodox communist organizations and 877 to the new left). By far the greatest percentage was employed in education (56.7 percent teachers, 13.3 percent faculty of post-secondary institutions, and 8.3 percent support staff). (*Verfassungsschutz, 1978*, pp. 67–68.) Unity of action propaganda also utilized "anti-imperialist, antiwar, antifascist sentiments." For example, a Committee against Fascism and War was formed from the following organizations: League of German Catholic Youth, Young Socialists, VVN-BdA, Citizen Initiative Against *Berufsverbot*, DKP, the Protestant churches, and others. (*Sozialistische Korrespondenz*, Hamburg, vol. 2, no. 13–14, July, p. 21.) Numerous committees, most of them under covert communist leadership, organized protests and demonstrations. The DKP also supported various "citizen initiatives," such as the anti–nuclear power plant movement, in order to gain influence among the people (*FAZ*, 29 May). The International Antiwar Day (1 September), which was commemorated with a demonstration in Bonn, was termed a successful unity of action. It was organized by the communist controlled Committee for Peace, Disarmament, and Cooperation and was supported by the Association of German Students, the MSB-Spartakus, Nature Friend Youth, German Peace Union, Young Democrats, Socialist Youth Organization-Die Falken, SDAJ, VVN-BdA, and local organizations of the Young Socialists, SPD, Free Democrats, and Catholic and Protestant churches. (*UZ*, 27 July and 17 August.)

The selection of Franz-Josef Strauss, the leader of the Christian Social Union, the Bavarian sister party of the Christian Democratic Union, as candidate for chancellor provided the DKP with a new topic, "stop Strauss" for unity of action (ibid., 24 August). The DKP called for unity of action of communists, Social Democrats, Christian workers, and those who do not belong to any party to "stop Strauss' in order to defend social and democratic rights and to assure the continuation of the policy of détente. (*DKP-Pressedienst*, Düsseldorf, 3 September.) The official organ of the DKP, *Unsere Zeit* (24 September), explained that the essence of the "anti-Strauss movement" was the common interest of Social Democrats and communists.

The DKP continued to lose in most *Land* and local elections held during 1979, as the following table illustrates:

Land Elections	1979 Votes	Percentage	1975 Percentage
Rhineland-Palatinate (18 March)	9,012	0.40	0.40
Schleswig-Holstein (29 April)	3,115	0.20	0.40
Bremen (7 October)	3,331	0.82	2.15

The results of local elections were similar. In Rhineland-Palatinate (10 June) the DKP obtained 0.3 percent and in Saarland (10 June) 0.9 percent (down from the local elections in 1975 when the communists reached 2.6 percent). The DKP vote in the local elections in North Rhine-Westphalia (30 September) was 0.7 percent. In the elections held in four communities in *Land* Hesse (8 October), the DKP improved its vote slightly but at most received only 0.8 percent. At the end of 1979, there were about seventy DKP members in local governments throughout the FRG. The communists did poorly in the first direct elections for the European parliament, receiving a total of 112,197 votes, or 0.4 percent.

Members of the DKP and its affiliated organizations were urged to be active trade union members in order to increase the influence of the party among trade unionists. About 85 percent of DKP members belong to trade unions. The percentage of trade union officials who are members of the DKP is minuscule; however, in the youth organization of the trade unions, the communists have achieved considerable influence. (*Rheinischer Merkur*, 16 March; *FAZ*, 13 June.) On the other hand, the DKP emphasizes the trade union affiliation of its candidates standing for elections. For example, 30 of the 78 DKP candidates for the European parliament were trade union officials (*Rheinischer Merkur*, 16 March).

International Views and Party Contacts. The international views of the DKP follow those expressed by Moscow and East Berlin. For example, DKP chairman Herbert Mies accused NATO of escalating the arms race (*WMR*, March, p. 3). The SALT II agreement was referred to as an "important step toward containing the arms race" (Allgemeiner Deutscher Nachrichtendienst [ADN], 16 June; *FBIS*, 19 June). The DKP Presidium demanded that the West German government condemn the Chinese aggression against the Vietnamese people (ADN, 23 February; *FBIS*, 27 February). Chairman Mies also publicly declared his party's opposition to Eurocommunism (*FAZ*, 19 February). The DKP strongly opposed the FRG's "hate campaign" against the GDR and rejected the reports about "alleged dissenters," forced adoption of children of escapees and political prisoners, and intershops (*UZ*, 20 April).

The DKP intensified its contacts with West European fraternal parties because of the elections to the European parliament. Party officials met with leaders of several West European communist parties. A DKP delegation attended the party congress of the Communist Party of Ireland (*DI*, vol. 30, no. 1,499, 15 March, p. 7). Good relations with the communist parties of the Soviet Union and Eastern Europe were maintained. DKP chairman Herbert Mies received the Karl Marx Order, the highest GDR order, on the occasion of his 50th birthday (*UZ*, 23 February). Kurt Bachmann, member of the DKP Presidium, was honored with the International Lenin Peace Prize (*Sozialistische Korrespondenz*, vol. 22, no. 13–14, July, p. 31).

Dr. Yusef Dadoo, chairman of the Communist Party of South Africa, visited the DKP Directorate. In a statement to the press, the support of the "African racist regime by multinational corporations" was condemned and the "Botha-regime" accused of threatening the peace of Africa and of the world (*DI*, vol. 30, no. 1,500, 29 March, pp. 4–5).

Publications. There have been no substantial changes in the field of DKP or communist-influenced publications. The official party organ, *Unsere Zeit*, still has a daily circulation of about 30,000 and a Friday edition of 60,000 to 70,000 copies. The party Directorate continued to publish the *DKP-Pressedienst*, the *DKP-Land Review*, and the monthly *Informationsdienst* for the approximately 730 factory, residential, and university papers produced by local party organizations. The *Land* Hesse has alone about 43 factory, 18 residential, and 5 university newspapers (*FAZ*, 7 July). The major DKP publishing house, *Verlag Marxistische Blätter*, marked its tenth anniversary (*DI*, vol. 30, no. 1,502, 17 May, p. 11). The youth magazine *Elan*, organ of the SDAJ, reportedly has an edition of 70,000 copies (ibid., vol. 30, no. 1,503–4, May-June, p. 3; for other DKP and leftist publications, see *YICA*, 1978, pp. 147–48).

Other Leftist Groups: Rival Communist Organizations. The "new left" is the collective term used for all left-extremists opposed to the pro-Moscow "orthodox" communist organizations and includes numerous organizations and groups espousing various Maoist interpretations or antidogmatist and anarchist views. Membership in and influence of most of these organizations declined during 1979 due to the high demands they make on their members and their continued lack of success.

The strongest of the "Maoist parties" is the Communist League of West Germany (Kommunistischer Bund Westdeutschlands; KBW) which, as a result of membership losses, appears to have assumed again the character of a cadre group. The KBW also suffered further setbacks in the *Land* elections. In Rhineland-Palatinate (18 March) the KBW obtained 0.1 percent of the vote. In Schleswig-Holstein

(April 29) the KBW vote decreased from 0.1 to 0.05 percent and in Bremen (7 October) from 0.4 to 0.13 percent. Substantial membership losses in its auxiliary organizations forced the KBW to combine them in a new mass organization: the "Association of Revolutionary People's Education–Soldiers and Reservists," comprising the former Soldiers' and Reservists' committees, the Society for the Support of the People's Struggle, and the Committees against Paragraph 218 (anti-abortion law).

The Communist Party of Germany (Kommunistische Partei Deutschlands; KPD), a Maoist party, also lost members. Its official organ, *Die Rote Fahne* (edition of 9,000 copies), experienced severe financial difficulties (*FAZ*, 21 June). The KPD issued a statement supporting the "Chinese counter-attack against Vietnamese aggression" (New China News Agency, 27 February, *FBIS*, 1 May). The federal elections scheduled for 1980 provided the party with a new domestic issue. The KPD called for protest actions at election rallies of Franz-Josef Strauss and of Helmut Schmidt because a one-sided "stop Strauss" campaign would prevent the "alternative election alliances" from developing into an independent political force divorced from the interests of the SPD and DKP (*FAZ*, 21 September). The Communist Youth League of Germany (KJVD) held its second "conference of delegates" in Osnabrück (16–18 March). The Central Committee of the KJVD elected Berndt Ziesemer as its chairman. (*Radikal Info*, no. 2, p. 2.)

The Communist Party of Germany/Marxist-Leninist also lost members and experienced organizational difficulties. The Communist League (KB), despite organizational and financial problems, attempted to expand its influence beyond its strongholds in Hamburg and Lower Saxony. Its two main propaganda topics were antifascism and anti–nuclear power. The KB succeeded in establishing unity of action in the anti–nuclear power movement by infiltrating a number of citizen-initiative groups. The KB remained very active at the universities. (*DI*, vol. 30, no. 1,507, 2 July, pp. 8-10.) Groups of the undogmatic left, such as the Revolutionary Cells, gave the anti–nuclear power movement its militant character (*FAZ*, 12 April).

A new left-radical daily newspaper, *Tageszeitung* (TAZ), began publication on 17 April with an edition of 73,000 copies. Its editorial policy is left of the DKP and addresses itself to citizen initiatives, the women's rights movement, trade unions, the "alternative," and ecological and undogmatic left groups. (*DI*, vol. 30, no. 1,501, 25 April, p. 8; for additional information about radical left-extremist parties and organizations, see *YICA*, 1978, pp. 148–50, and 1979, pp. 152–55.)

WEST BERLIN

West Berlin is still under the "occupation status" established after World War II, and the United States, Britain, and France maintain troops in their respective sectors. The 1971 Four Power Agreement concerning Berlin affirms that Berlin is not part of the FRG and has a "special status" based on Allied agreements concluded in 1944 and 1945. The GDR, supported by the Soviet Union, has incorporated the Soviet Sector and made "Berlin" its capital. The Western Allies encourage the FRG to maintain close ties with West Berlin which, without West German support, would not survive economically. Since 1959 the population of West Berlin has declined from 2.3 to 1.9 million.

The SEW. The special status of Berlin allowed the SED to organize a West Berlin subsidiary. The name of the party, founded by East German communists, was changed from Social Unity Party of Germany–West Berlin to Socialist Unity Party of West Berlin (Sozialistische Einheitspartei Westberlins; SEW) to give the illusion that the SEW is an indigenous party.

Leadership, Organization, and Domestic Activities. In 1979 no changes in SEW leaders and organization were observed. Membership probably remained about 7,500. The party continued in its efforts to establish unity of action and unite Social Democrats, Christian workers, and those without party affiliation in the "antimonopoly struggle." Results were negative. Common policies and actions were achieved at the universities with the left-extremist student organizations that control the student parliaments. Another major activity of the SEW was the campaign for the 18 March election for West Berlin's House of Representatives. The SEW vote continued to decline. The communist candidates received 13,723 votes, or 1.1 percent (1975: 1.8 percent; 1971: 2.3 percent). (*FAZ*, 20 March.)

Horst Schmitt, chairman of the SEW, praised his party's "untiring efforts in the defense of the social and democratic interests of the working people to counteract anti-communism, anti-Sovietism, and the continuous slander directed against the GDR" (*WMR*, March, p. 61). A number of "mass organizations" affiliated with the SEW assisted the party's efforts to establish contact with the masses.

International Views and Party Contacts. The SEW's policy on the future of West Berlin mirrors that of the Soviet Union and the GDR. SEW Chairman Horst Schmitt declared that West Berlin, located within the GDR, should be recognized under international law as an independent and special political entity that should establish normal and neighborly relations with the GDR instead of continuing the present "confrontation policy" (*FAZ*, 12 January). The achievement of independent political status for West Berlin would bring it closer to complete integration with the GDR, the final objective of Moscow and East Berlin. The SEW's other foreign policy positions are identical with those held by Moscow and East Berlin. Horst Schmitt stated: "As socialism and communism grow stronger as a result of the policy of peaceful co-existence of states with different social systems and as further successes are scored on the road of détente, the bourgeoisie is finding it increasingly more difficult to cope with the inner contradictions of the capitalist system" (*WMR*, March, p. 62).

The SEW maintained close relations with fraternal communist parties, especially with the SED and the CPSU. In May a SEW delegation visited the USSR (Tass, 19 May; *FBIS*, 21 May). Horst Schmitt conferred with SED party chief Erich Honecker in East Berlin (*Neues Deutschland*, 25 May).

Publications. *Die Wahrheit*, the official organ of the SEW, continued to appear six times weekly. No changes have been reported concerning the size of its edition, which in 1978 was about 16,000 copies. (For publications of the "mass organizations" controlled by the SEW, see *YICA*, 1975, p. 191.)

Other Leftist Groups: Rival Communists. West Berlin's student population provided most members of the various left-extremist groups, which also operate in the FRG. Their influence is neglible. At the elections for the West Berlin legislature, the KBW obtained 1,367 votes, or 0.1 percent (*FAZ*, 5 April). The "Alternative List" (AL) participated for the first time in West Berlin's elections and received 47,534 votes (3.7 percent). A number of AL candidates were known as left-extremists. In four of the twelve district boroughs, the AL was able to elect ten candidates, including at least four members of the Maoist KPD. (Ibid., 21 March.) In elections at the Free University of Berlin, leftist groups obtained a majority among the 33 percent of students who voted (ibid., 6 June; for further details, see *YICA*, 1977, p. 169).

University of Calgary   Eric Waldman

Great Britain

The Communist Party of Great Britain (CPGB) was founded in 1920. It remains Britain's most significant Marxist political party due to its influence in the trade union movement. The CPGB is a recognized political party and contests both local and national elections but did not participate in the June elections for the European parliament. The party does not function in Northern Ireland, which it regards as the domain of the Communist Party of Ireland. The CPGB has had no members in the House of Commons since 1950, when it had two. The party has one member in the House of Lords, Lord Milford, and eight council members at various levels of local government. On 18 May 1979 Annie Powell became the first communist mayor in Great Britain when she became mayor of Rhondda in south Wales. Current membership of the CPGB is given as 20,599, but dues-paying membership is probably considerably less. The population of Great Britain is just under 56 million.

Leadership and Organization. The CPGB is divided into four levels: the National Congress, the Executive Committee and its attendant departments, the districts, and the various local and factory branches. Constitutionally the National Congress is the supreme authority in the party. It meets biennially; the last meeting was held in November. It elects the 42-member Executive Committee, considers documents on future policies and activities, and listens to reports on the party's activities since the previous Congress. Delegates to the Congress are from the party's districts and branches. However, the power of the Congress is more apparent than real; it endorses the decisions of the Political Committee as a matter of course, although it has made amendments on occasion.

Responsibility for party activity on specific issues is ostensibly in the hands of the Executive Committee, which meets once every two months and chooses the members of special committees, the full-time heads of departments, and the sixteen-member Political Committee. The Political Committee is the real controlling body in the party and meets every week or as the occasion requires.

During 1979 leading officers and heads of departments were Gordon McLennan (general secretary), Reuben Falber (assistant secretary), Mick Costello (industrial organizer), Jack Woddis (international department), Dave Cook (organization), George Matthews (press and publicity), Jean Styles (women), Betty Matthews (education), Malcolm Cowle (election agent), Dennis Ellwand (treasurer), and Martin Jacques (editor of *Marxism Today*).

The CPGB's youth organization, the Young Communist League (YCL), is in a state of severe decline, with membership now about one thousand. In April 1979 it held its 36th National Congress, which gave more attention to the problem of falling membership. It is generally felt within the YCL that the group has suffered from being exploited to do party chores. Accordingly, more emphasis is being given to the social side of the movement. The YCL publishes *Challenge*. The new general secretary is Nina Temple. The YCL continues to be active in youth groups, such as the Anti-Nazi League (ANL), which was established to counter the neo-fascist National Front, and the Campaign Against Youth Unemployment. Compared with the activities of other ultra-left forces, however, it tends to play a minor role.

The real significance of the CPGB is in the trade unions, where it enjoys a degree of influence grossly disproportionate to its electoral strength. Most British union executive councils have at least one communist member. The 38-member General Council of the Trades Union Congress (TUC) has two communist members, George Guy of the National Union of Sheet Metal Workers and Ken Gill of the Technical and Supervisory section of the Amalgamated Union of Engineering Workers. Minor union successes scored by the CPGB in 1979 included the election of John Gelait as London regional organizer of the National Graphical Association, Jack Collins as general secretary of the Kent area of the National Union of Mineworkers, and John McFadden to the national executive of the National and Local Government Officers' Association. The National Graphical Association, a key printing union, elected its first communist national officer in November.

The communists continue to sponsor the Liaison Committee for the Defence of Trade Unions (LCDTU), founded in 1966 as the party's chosen instrument for spreading communist propaganda in industry. It has not enjoyed any notable success since it was the principal organizer of a strike in 1970 by some 600,000 people against the Industrial Relations Bill. However, it hopes that the performance of the new Conservative government will give it the opportunity once again to mobilize mass support. The LCDTU lobbied the TUC's annual conference in Blackpool on 5 September in a bid to make it adopt more communist-inclined policies.

The party is paying particular attention to building up more factory branches; it currently has about 200. To this end the CPGB held four regional work-place conferences in the autumn. There were signs that the party's policy was having some success. In November a communist shop steward, Derek Robinson, was sacked by the ailing British Leyland company for his continual agitation. The dismissal led to a major strike and lessened hopes for the company's survival.

But it is not simply directly through the trade unions that communist power can be brought to bear. Some 80 percent of Labour Party funds are based on trade union contributions, and 88 percent of the votes at the annual Labour Party conference are controlled by trade unions. At the 1979 conference, Roy Grantham, general secretary of the clerical workers' union, Apex, described the process as a "grotesque picture" with "members of other parties" directing votes that may change the Labour Party.

Party Internal Affairs. Internal party debate focused primarily on the vexing question of membership. Once a party of over 40,000, the CPGB is now down to 20,599, a drop of nearly 5,000 from the 1978 figures. Moreover, it is likely that this low figure masks a much smaller dues-paying membership. This was suggested by an interesting survey that the party conducted in June 1978 of twenty London branches. It demonstrated that so many "members" were behind on their dues that the party had only 20 percent of its nominal membership. (*Comment*, 3 February.) The party could indeed take no comfort from this, especially since London is usually thought to have one of the best dues-paying records in Britain.

The subject received renewed attention at the party's 36th National Congress in London in November. Gordon McLennan, general secretary of the CPGB, blamed the losses on differences within the international communist movement, armed conflicts between socialist states, and limitations on democracy in communist countries. The four-day congress was dominated by discussion of the party's future role and concern for its loss of support. Indeed the fall in membership was the worst the party had sustained since the Soviet invasion of Hungary in 1956. A resolution put forward by hardline Stalinists criticized party leaders for not doing enough "to publicize the achievements of the socialist countries." The resolution was defeated 163 to 114, a narrow majority when it is remembered that nearly a thousand pro-Soviet dogmatists left the party in 1977 to found the New Communist Party. This pro-Soviet resurgence underlines the difficulty the party is having in establishing a clear role for itself. Even its own program, *The British Road to Socialism* (see *YICA*, 1978, pp. 153–54), does not allocate a very distinctive role for the party to play. At a time when the left is making great advances within the Labour Party itself, it is becoming more difficult for party leaders to explain the need for a communist party to left wingers. The resurgence of pro-Soviet feeling is probably an attempt to re-establish a clear-cut identity for the party, albeit one of simple pro-Sovietism. This feeling of a weakening of purpose was also demonstrated by many delegates who expressed concern that the party fielded only 38 candidates in the 3 May elections and none in the European elections.

The conflict between traditional Soviet-oriented communists and those seeking new traditions also found expression in the party's debate on "inner-party democracy." In fact, although new proposals on intra-party democracy were accepted by the congress, they represent no fundamental change of direction from traditional communist practices. Outgoing executive committees will still recommend candidates, but in the future there is to be more discussion before balloting. "Democratic centralism" is not really affected. The alternative proposals, which mustered about a third of the congress's votes, would have represented a victory for a more democratic approach. Elections to the new Executive Committee produced fifteen new names.

Most resolutions were of a predictable nature. The principal one was a basic statement of current party policies and was passed unanimously. In addition, the congress pledged the communist party to total resistance to the new Conservative government's proposals to encourage secret balloting in trade union elections and to restrict secondary picketing. A resolution on British Leyland called for a "vigorous campaign" against the management's proposals to rationalize the ailing company. The congress further decided to hold a national conference on industrial strategy and reasserted its opposition to the Abortion Amendment Bill by stressing that abortion on demand was a woman's right. More interesting was the defeat by a 20-percent majority of a motion to oppose the further development of nuclear plants. The antinuclear cause is one that has been wholeheartedly supported by most far-left groups, and it was of note that the CPGB has decided to disassociate itself from it. The conference was attended by "fraternal delegates" from the Palestine Liberation Organization, Chile, Vietnam, South Africa, Cyprus, Ireland, and Iraq.

Communist party income is difficult to estimate. Although the party is in many respects declining and possesses an aging membership, it retains a wide range of business interests and front organizations, indicating a more substantial income than first impressions might suggest. These interests include Central Books Ltd.; Lawrence and Wishart, publishers; Farleigh Press and London Caledonian, printers; Rodell Properties Ltd.; the Labour Research Department; and the Marx Memorial Library. Annual income from dues and donations is probably in the neighborhood of £250,000. In addition, the daily communist newspaper, *Morning Star*, which is financially independent of the party, is kept afloat by substantial orders from Eastern Europe. Including these sales, the daily circulation of *Morning Star* is 34,000. The National Finance Conference held in Birmingham on 30 September gave particular attention to the 1980 "national appeal" due to be held from 18 February to 22 March. It was announced that in the five years of its operation, the national appeal had raised £263,762 for the party.

Domestic Attitudes and Activities. During the first quarter of 1979, communist domestic strategy focused on the disruption of the Labour government's incomes policy. A series of strikes during the winter certainly played a role in souring public opinion against the government, which finally fell to a vote of no confidence on 28 March; but the communist role was marginal. Of particular note, however, was that businesses often claimed that communist agitators had played a big role in causing a major strike by 100,000 lorry drivers of the Transport and General Workers' Union in January.

When general elections were finally declared, the communist party launched its campaign under the slogan: "Defeat the Tories and Strengthen the Left." The party fought in 38 constituencies — more than in the October 1974 elections but below the 50 required to win radio and televison time.

The communist platform called for a ban on nuclear and chemical weapons, an immediate reduction of £1 billion in defense spending, and withdrawal from Northern Ireland. It also called for various measures to reduce inflation, including a refusal to comply with price increases of the European Economic Community (EEC), a complete price freeze for at least six months, taxation of corporate profits, the abolition of the value-added tax, and a reduction of interest rates. It also advocated establishing national assemblies for Scotland and Wales.

In the general elections of 3 May 1979, the CPGB returned its worst result in postwar politics. The full figures were as follows:

Party	Votes	Percentage	Seats won
Conservatives	13,697,753	43.9	339
Labour	11,509,524	36.9	268
Liberal	4,313,931	13.8	11
Ulster Union	289,835	1.0	10
Scottish National	504,259	1.6	2
National Front	191,267	0.6	0
Plaid Cymru	132,544	0.4	2
Communist	15,958	0.05	0
Others	565,692	1.75	2

Even though the communists contested only 38 seats, their average vote fell to a mere 420 per constituency—in the party's best and most carefully chosen areas. With such poor results, it came as no surprise when the party announced that it would not field candidates for the European parliamentary elections shortly afterwards.

Following the change of government, communist activities were concerned with two objectives: opposition to the new Conservative government's policies and attempts to get the official Labour opposition to adopt a more communist-inclined strategy. In the first case, the CPGB was especially concerned to mobilize mass public campaigns against the government's proposed trade union reforms and public spending cuts. The party attributed the Labour Party's defeat to the "right-wing" policies pursued by Labour leaders. The party, working according to its program, *The British Road to Socialism*, advocated the adoption of what it called an alternative economic strategy (AES). The AES claims that Britain's economic ills are attributable to "state monopoly capitalism" and that wholesale nationalization, import controls, and export planning are essential to national recovery. This extreme left-wing strategy is to be achieved by pushing the Labour Party to the left by pressure from a broad democratic alliance, which includes the CPGB. By increasing investment, overcoming inflation, and reducing unemployment, the AES will, it is claimed, unite disparate groups of people, not necessarily socialists, around a platform of shared interests. The Labour Party did indeed move much further to the left later in the year, but it is most unlikely that the CPGB played a significant role in this process.

A campaign in favor of devolved assemblies for Scotland and Wales was also rejected at the polls on 1 March. The Labour government had proposed creation of local assemblies under the Scotland and Wales Acts of 31 July 1978, which provided for referenda the following year. The Communists campaigned for the assemblies, but in Scotland only 32.85 percent of those entitled to vote approved while in Wales the proposal was decisively rejected.

International Views and Party Contacts. The international views of the CPGB echo those of the Soviet Union, with the exception of the party's attitude on Czechoslovakia. Having condemned the Soviet invasion of August 1968, the party still occasionally feels constrained to issue criticisms of Soviet policy in Czechoslovakia. In October the Political Committee denounced the heavy jail sentences imposed on five supporters of Charter 77. The official statement called for their release and commented: "Continued attempts by the authorities in Czechoslovakia to respond to political criticism, arguments and actions by resort to the police, courts and prisons run directly counter to fundamental principles of Socialist democracy" (*Morning Star*, 25 October).

As is often the case with communist parties, the CPGB has had to change its attitude on international events as the posture of the Soviet Union has changed. In April 1975 the victory of the Khmer Rouge was heralded as a victory for peace and progress; by 1979 the party was consistently castigating the Khmer Rouge and lauding the Vietnamese puppet Kampuchean (Cambodian) government of Heng Samrin. Similarly, the party had in the past praised the progressive role of the Iraqi government; in 1979 the same regime was consistently denounced for its harsh treatment of Iraqi communists. The shah's government, always a favorite butt of communist propaganda, finally fell in February, but the CPGB was suspicious of the clerical complexion of the new government.

South Africa and Chile remained key targets of communist propaganda. The party supports the anti-apartheid movement and is affiliated with the Chile Solidarity Campaign. It continued to criticize the EEC and was opposed to Britain's joining the related European Monetary System (which Britain did not join in any case). It accused Lord Carrington, the British foreign secretary, of attempting to organize a "sellout" in the discussions over the future of Zimbabwe-Rhodesia and consistently supported the Patriotic Front. It condemned China's February invasion of Vietnam. The party continued to denounce Britain's nuclear force, which is now undergoing a modernization review, and called for the country's unilateral nuclear disarmament. Predictably, it was totally opposed to the deployment of medium-range U.S. nuclear missiles in Europe and welcomed President Brezhnev's proposals to reduce Soviet force levels in Eastern Europe.

Various international contacts were made in 1979. These included a visit to Cuba by Michael McGahey, party chairman, in January. Jack Woddis, head of the International Department, was received on 17 July by Hermann Axen, Politburo member and secretary of the East German party's Central Committee. On 20 September Nicolae Ceauşescu, secretary general of the Romanian Communist Party, received Reuben Falber. They exchanged views on international affairs and expressed the desire to develop closer cooperation between their two parties. The most important conference was held on 25 September in Moscow. Boris Ponomarev, the head of the CPSU's International Department, and his deputy Anatoli Chernyayev met Woddis and the chief of the CPGB's Scottish Committee, Jack Ashton. The Soviet delegation was powerful; the International Department is regarded as Moscow's key arm in controlling foreign communist parties and is in some respects a more significant body than the Soviet Foreign Ministry. McGahey also visited Bulgaria in August in his capacity as vice-president of the National Union of Mineworkers. Bert Ramelson, former CPGB industrial organizer, participated in the International Conference of Historians of the Second World War in Moscow in October.

Publications. The Communist organ is the daily *Morning Star*. Another leading paper is the fortnightly *Comment*, which contains all major Executive Committee statements and regular reports on party activities. *Marxism Today* is a theoretical monthly that contains articles of original research. *Link*, a woman's quarterly that had been in trouble with the Executive Committee for its independent stance, circulated again in 1979. *Challenge* is the YCL's monthly. In addition, the Communists publish several journals of specialized interest. *Economic Bulletin* appears twice yearly and contains articles of a largely theoretical character. *Education Today and Tomorrow* appears five times a year. *Science*

Bulletin is a quarterly covering a wide range of issues, particularly the relation between science and socialism. *Euro-Red* is a quarterly journal of comments on political developments in Western Europe. *Our History Journal* appears four times a year and is devoted to the history of the CPGB. Irregular journals include *Red Letters*, which is concerned with cultural affairs, *Socialist Europe*, on East European affairs; and *Music and Life*, which contains Marxist views of music. *Medicine in Society* is a discussion forum for communist health workers.

Other Marxist Groups. Britain's largest Trotskyist group is the Socialist Workers' Party (SWP), formed in December 1976. Membership is nearly 5,000. The SWP has a weak industrial base but claims groups of militants in the auto industry, the docks, the railways, the National Union of Mineworkers, the National Union of Teachers, and the National and Local Government Officers' Association. It tries to build up support in the working class through its rank-and-file organization. It is also active in sponsoring protests for the unemployed. The ANL has been a successful source of new recruits for the party in the past, but in 1979 the ANL was in relative decline since neo-fascist activity in the country was insubstantial. There is an SWP section called *Chingari* (Spark), which produces papers in Bengali, Punjabi, and Gujarati. The SWP is also associated with Women's Voice, a socialist feminist organization, and Flame, a black group.

Despite its smallness, the SWP eschews cooperation with most other ultra-left forces and in particular denounces the CPGB-sponsored "broad democratic alliance" as both utopian and leading to reformist politics. Rejecting the parliamentary road to socialism, the SWP believes in the necessity of an armed revolutionary struggle in which representative bodies capable of governing the country will be spontaneously created.

The SWP has a full-time Central Committee of ten members, paid from party funds. The party is centrally organized and has about 70 districts and branches. Its claimed main support is in Glasgow and the north of England. The SWP's chairman is Duncan Hallas; but its best-known personalities are its theoretician Tony Cliff (pseudonym of Ygael Gluckstein) and the polemical journalist Paul Foot.

The various party sections often produce their own papers for trade union circulation. The party's principal organ remains the weekly *Socialist Worker*, with a claimed circulation of over 20,000. The SWP also has a publishing press, the Pluto Press, closely associated with it. Unemployment, anti-racism, opposition to the police, and single-issue solidarity campaigns were the leading propaganda issues for the party.

The International Marxist Group (IMG) is the British section of the Trotskyist United Secretariat of the Fourth International; it has about 1,500 members. The IMG's national secretary is Bob Pennington, but Tariq Ali is probably a better-known spokesman. Robin Blackburn and Norman Gervas are its chief theorists. The IMG has been closely involved with single-issue campaigns, such as support for the revolutions in Iran and Nicaragua. It campaigned for the devolution referenda in Scotland and Wales. Like the SWP, anti-police propaganda was a key issue for the IMG. The party's paper, *Socialist Challenge*, implicitly supported the terrorism of the Provisional Irish Republican Army by characterizing the British as the source of the violence and tacitly approving the murder of Lord Mountbatten in August. *Socialist Challenge* has paid sales of about 6,000. Continuing the work of former years, the IMG cooperates with the International Socialist Alliance to construct a common program. Under the name Socialist Unity Party, they fielded some candidates in the May general elections; all were heavily defeated.

The third significant Trotskyist group is the Workers' Revolutionary Party (WRP), an affiliate of the Fourth International (International Secretariat). It publishes a daily newspaper, *Newsline*, with claimed sales of 3,000, and an irregular journal, *Fourth International*. It has a large youth section, the Young Socialists, which has a sizable black component. The WRP operates in a highly clandestine manner, and comparatively little is known about its activities; it is known, however, to have small groups in the docks and in engineering, mining, the theater, and the auto industry. It has a small trade union organization, the All Trade Union Alliance, to promote its industrial campaigns. Membership is around 1,000, although it claims 5,000. Party general secretary is Mike Banda, but its former head and veteran revolutionary is Gerry Healey. Its best-known personalities are from the world of stage and cinema, including Ken Loach, Tony Garnett, and Corin and Vanessa Redgrave. The WRP fielded 60 candidates in the May general elections, largely as a means of securing greater publicity. Although it took the elections seriously, it regards Parliament merely as a "facade to hide the conspiracies taking place outside." Its candidates all scored poor results. The party has a tradition of taking a tough sectarian approach to revolutionary politics and has had several splits. The most recent was the Workers' Party established in Manchester in August under the leadership of Royston Bull and Steve Johns, both former *Newsline* reporters. It is holding talks with the Workers' Socialist League of Alan Thornett, itself an earlier breakaway from the WRP. The WRP itself is believed to receive substantial aid from Libya.

In addition, there are various small Trotskyist groups, including the International Communist League, the Revolutionary Communist Group, Workers' Action, and the Spartacist League. Probably the most important Trotskyist group is not a party at all. The Militant Tendency of the Labour Party is about 1,500 strong and holds *all* seats on the executive council of the Labour Party's Young Socialists. Its influence on the future development of the Labour Party itself should not be discounted.

The small New Communist Party has made little impression on political life. Membership is about 800, and its rigid pro-Soviet attitudes make it unlikely that it will gather support from the young. It continues to produce the weekly *New Worker*, and its banners are often seen in demonstrations. The party suffered a serious setback in February when its head, Syd French, died from a heart attack.

There are two small Maoist organizations of note: the Revolutionary Communist League of Britain, which admires the Pol Pot regime in Kampuchea, and the Communist Party of Britain (Marxist-Leninist), which is pro-Albanian.

London   Richard Sim

Greece

The Communist Party of Greece (Kommunistikon Komma Ellados; KKE) evolved from the Socialist Workers' Party of Greece founded in November 1918 by a small group of leftist intellectuals. After several years of internal feuds and a period of forced "illegality" under the Metaxas dictatorship in the late 1930s, the KKE emerged as a major political force during the country's occupation by the Axis. Its attempts to use the resistance movement as a route to power failed. A guerrilla campaign (1946–1949) also failed, and the party remained outlawed from 1947 to 1974.

During the military dictatorship of 1967-1974, the party split into two factions, which became known as the KKE (Interior) and the KKE (Exterior). With the collapse of the military regime in July 1974, both factions were legalized, but the split remained.

Today, the Marxist left is represented by four political parties: the United Democratic Left (EDA), which was initially created in 1951 to act as a stand-in for the outlawed KKE and continues to exist primarily because of the personality of its leader, Elias Iliou; the KKE (Interior), which follows a moderate course patterned after the Eurocommunist parties in Western Europe; the KKE (Exterior), which regards itself as the genuine KKE and vehemently rejects the adjective "exterior" and is clearly pro-Moscow and orthodox in its ideological positions; and the Pan-Hellenic Socialist Movement (PASOK), founded by Andreas Papandreou in 1974. Papandreou is the son of former Greek Premier George Papandreou, long associated with the liberal democratic center in Greece. The PASOK espouses a Marxist-nationalist line that in its socioeconomic doctrines reflects a mixture of Marxism-Leninism, Chinese communalism, and Yugoslav self-management and in its political pronouncements is vehemently anti-American and anti-NATO with some overtones of nonalignment. In the Soviet-Chinese dispute, the PASOK tends to side with Moscow.

The relative strength and significance of these four parties may be estimated by the results of the last parliamentary election in November 1977. The EDA, in an electoral coalition with the KKE (Interior), received a total of 2.72 percent of the popular vote. The KKE (Exterior) received 9.29 percent of the vote. The PASOK received 25.33 percent and emerged as the major opposition party, with 92 seats in the 300-seat legislature. In contrast, the KKE (Exterior) has 11 seats in the legislature. The KKE (Interior) has none, while the EDA is represented by its veteran leader, Elias Iliou.

The municipal elections of October 1978 indicated a growing influence for PASOK. The professed goals of PASOK (total withdrawal from NATO, rejection of Greece's membership in the European Economic Community [EEC], total elimination of American or NATO military installations in Greece, and a socialist transformation of the economy) and its occasional denunciations of Western liberal democracy or West European social democracy reveal PASOK as a party of the Marxist left— in fact, PASOK appears to espouse more radical positions than the EDA or the KKE (Interior). During the closing months of 1979, PASOK leader Papandreou began to tone down some of his more extreme rhetoric in an apparent effort to expand the party's influence in the area of the traditional center, which is now virtually leaderless.

Despite the unwillingness of the parties of the Marxist left to join forces in a single electoral coalition, they can still play a decisive role during the next parliamentary election, which is to take place no later than November 1981. Together they command the support of approximately 37 to 40 percent of the electorate.

During 1979 the influence of the Marxist left, spearheaded by PASOK, showed no sign of diminishing. Although the Caramanlis government remains stable and basically pro-Western in its policies, a large number of Greeks, even among those who support the liberal democratic center or the governing Party of the New Democracy, harbor a deep resentment toward the United States for its alleged pro-Turkish policies in the disputes over Cyprus and the Aegean. This anti-Americanism inevitably benefits the Marxist left, primarily the consistently anti-American, anti-NATO, and anti-EEC parties—PASOK and the KKE (Exterior). The KKE (Interior) has publicly accused the rival KKE of hoping to aid a PASOK electoral victory and then playing the role of the true power behind the throne. This may happen if PASOK fails to win a majority in the legislature in the next parliamentary election and has no alternative but to form a government with the support of KKE (Exterior) votes in the legislature. The domination of PASOK by its founder and leader poses a serious question regarding chances of surviving as an independent political force without him. Most likely, the party itself will slide into obscurity, but a large segment of its radicalized followers may shift their allegiance to the KKE (Exterior). It is worth noting that in the municipal elections of 15 and 22 October 1978, the KKE

(Exterior) realized significant gains that proportionately surpassed the gains in mayoral seats registered by PASOK. Perhaps when voters were not thinking in terms of parliamentary seats, they tended to vote for those candidates for mayor or city council seats who most closely reflected their ideological preferences.

In anticipation of the forthcoming parliamentary elections in 1980 or spring 1981, Mikis Theodorakis, the internationally known composer, has organized the United Left Movement—not as a new political party but as a grass-roots movement designed to press the KKE (Exterior), the KKE (Interior), and the EDA to join forces in an electoral coalition. Theodorakis contends that such a coalition will win a sufficient number of seats to prevent either the Caramanlis or the Papandreou party from forming a government. In such a case, Theodorakis expects PASOK to seek some form of cooperation with the communist left in order to form a government.

Leadership and Organization. The KKE (Exterior) is governed by a Politburo elected by its Central Committee. The present Politburo consists of Kharilaos Florakis (the party's secretary general), Nikos Kaloudhis, Andonios Ambatielos, Grigoris Farakos, Mina Giannou, Roula Koukoulou, Kostas Loules, Kostas Tsolakis, Loula Logara, Dimitrios Gondikas, and Stratis Tsambis. At a December 1978 plenum, the Central Committee elected a Secretariat composed of Florakis, Kaloudhis, Farakos, Giannou, Logara, Stefanos Papayiannis, and Orestis Kolozov, who is in charge of the party's foreign contacts. The party's youth organization (KNE), at its Second Congress in April, elected Spyros Khalvatzis as its new secretary, replacing Dimitrios Gondikas. The KNE is directed by its Central Council.

The other communist party, the KKE (Interior), has an Executive Office instead of the traditional Politburo, which was abolished at its Second Congress in April 1978. The Executive Office is composed of Babis Drakopoulos (the party's secretary), B. Georgoulas, G. Giannaros, P. Dimitriou, L. Kyrkos, G. Banias, T. Benas, I. Straveris, and K. Filinis. The members of the Executive Office are elected by the party's Central Committee.

The EDA is governed by an eleven-member Executive Committee led by Elias Iliou, the EDA's leading personality since the early 1950s and the party's only deputy in the legislature. The EDA appears to be on the decline and survives primarily because of the presence of Iliou in the Greek legislature. Erstwhile party notables such as Manolis Glezos of resistance fame and Mikis Theodorakis, the composer, are no longer associated with the EDA. Theodorakis has now joined the KKE (Exterior).

The PASOK is directed by an Executive Office dominated by party Chairman Andreas Papandreou. The Executive Office includes Giannis Alevras (a deputy in the legislature), Paraskevas Avgerinos, Giorgos Gennimatas, Kostas Laliotis, Kostas Simitis, Akis Tsokhatzopoulos, Giannis Kharalambopoulos (also a deputy), and Andreas Khristodoulidis. The Executive Office is elected by the 80-member Central Committee. Twenty Central Committee members are deputies in the Greek legislature.

Party Internal Affairs. The KKE (Exterior), stronger financially and with a larger following, appears to be solidifying its position as the genuine communist party in Greece. Most Greek publications, regardless of political leaning, have dropped the adjective "exterior" when referring to this party and simply identify it as the KKE. Even the KKE (Interior) has ceased to use the adjective "exterior" and now refers to its rival merely as "the dogmatic KKE." (All references to the KKE below refer to the "exterior" party.) In March 1979 both the KKE and PASOK vehemently attacked the refusal of the Greek government to allow members of the wartime communist-led resistance units to participate in the parades held on Independence Day (25 March).

Domestic and International Views and Positions. The KKE's views remained constant and predictable during 1979. The party's Central Committee (in its resolutions) and the party's leading theoreticians Grigoris Farakos and Manolis Kaloudhis (in articles published in foreign journals, such as the Soviet periodical *Kommunist*), as well as party Secretary General Florakis (in public statements and interviews), condemned "imperialist" efforts to promote "monopolistic totality" in the EEC through creation of a common monetary system, through the direct election of the European parliament, and through the admission of Greece, Spain, and Portugal into the EEC system. The party also condemned the Egyptian-Israeli Camp David agreement and the official resumption of diplomatic relations between China and the United States.

The KKE continued its strong opposition to Greece's induction into the EEC. However, in view of the signing of the treaty in May, the KKE is now promising to organize "a mass struggle to curb the agreement's adverse impact on the working people" and "to coordinate our working people's struggle with the struggle of the working people in other EEC countries."

The formal signing of the accession treaty in Athens led to renewed attacks on Greece's induction into the EEC by PASOK and the KKE.

The party predictably opposes Greece's return to NATO and advocates an immediate suspension of negotiations and Greece's complete withdrawal from NATO. It also rejected American mediation efforts to resolve the Cyprus problem during the year.

In October the visit of Premier Caramanlis to Moscow was most favorably greeted by all political parties except the National Front, which speaks for the extreme conservative right. Both PASOK and the KKE in particular pointed to the visit as a long overdue "opening to the East" and called on the Greek government to withdraw from NATO completely.

On the domestic scene, the KKE voiced strong opposition to a new law on incentives to attract foreign investment, which in the party's view gives "new privileges to the monopolies." Efforts to undermine the Congress of the Greek General Confederation of Labor, which is dominated by noncommunist labor leaders, failed because "the party's efforts did not embrace the broad masses of workers and employees." In fact, the party's influence remains limited. "The pace of bringing in new members remains slow," to quote a January Central Committee resolution.

The KKE (Interior) favors Greece's entry into the EEC, but for reasons fundamentally different from those of the Greek government. This party sees Greek participation as a way for "the Greek working people to join forces with all those people who are struggling for a different Europe . . . free of the regime of the monopolies . . . a continent of independence, democracy, peace, and socialism." With regard to NATO, this party opposes Greece's return and supports a gradual withdrawal from the alliance. During 1979 the KKE (Interior) launched a campaign for the political cooperation of the leftist parties to promote "a democratic way" to bring about significant changes in the political and socioeconomic system. The party sees this "democratic way" in terms of electoral cooperation and overall coordination of political activities; each participating party, movement, and organization is to retain its own identity. In this regard the KKE (Interior) is opposing the KKE's efforts to bring about a "leftist party of the EAM [the wartime National Liberation Front]," which in its view is merely an effort to bring all leftist forces in Greece under the aegis of the KKE.

The PASOK in many ways expresses views that are in harmony with the basic positions held by the KKE. It advocates complete withdrawal from NATO, an end to all NATO and American bases on Greek soil, an end to American "imperialist domination" of Greece, and increased cooperation with the Soviet bloc. It considers the improvement of American relations with China "a destabilizing factor for world peace." It "hailed the victory of the Iranian people against American imperialism" at the time of the shah's overthrow. It has consistently opposed Greece's entry into the EEC, which Papandreou considers a device for placing Greece even more tightly "under the domination of the monopolies." For a period of time, Papandreou pressed for a popular referendum on the issue of EEC membership. In a speech in October, however, he made no reference to this demand and, instead of his usual strong denunciation of the EEC, merely expressed "misgivings" on the effects the accession will have on Greek farmers and workers. Papandreou, in an obvious effort to gain increased support from more moderate segments of the Greek electorate, has toned down his rhetoric on the "socialization of the economy" and on the merits of a single party system. On the contrary, he has stressed that other parties would be allowed to function under a PASOK government "provided they respect the socialist constitution" PASOK plans to enact.

Papandreou is confident that in the next electoral confrontation PASOK will receive sufficient support to gain a majority in the legislature, form its own government, and then proceed with constitutional changes to fashion its own brand of socialism. He realizes that in order to win a parliamentary majority he needs the support of many voters who may not entirely share his views of a socialist society or agree with his anti-American and anti-NATO rhetoric. One may expect that during 1980, as the time for the parliamentary elections draws nearer, Papandreou will tone down his socialism and focus more and more on his nationalist, anti-American arguments. His main problem will be the possible alienation of some of his radical followers. Keeping them in the fold while expanding into the moderate center will require a very delicate political strategy.

International Party Contacts. During 1979 both the KKE and the KKE (Interior) continued their efforts to improve their status by obtaining the endorsement of foreign parties. The KKE appeared to be somewhat more successful in this effort. In January this party invited delegations from the Italian and the French communist parties. The Italian delegation under Giancarlo Pajetta, a member of the Italian Secretariat, met with KKE Secretary General Florakis on 9 January. Despite the KKE's efforts, the Italians avoided an exclusive endorsement. Asked at a press conference which party he recognized, Pajetta replied: "We recognize reality . . . It is not up to me to recognize or not recognize this or the other party."

The KKE was much more successful with the French. The delegation headed by French Secretary General Georges Marchais arrived in Athens on 18 January for a four-day visit. In an airport statement, Marchais made it clear that his party considers the KKE the only legitimate communist party in Greece, thus dealing a heavy blow to the Eurocommunist pretensions of the KKE (Interior). In March a delegation of the Danish Communist Party under Secretary General Ib Jorgen Nørlund came to Athens at the invitation of the KKE. In a joint communiqué the two parties affirmed their opposition to the EEC, condemned China's "anti-Soviet policies," and declared their determination to expand their "friendship and cooperation on the basis of the principles of Marxism-Leninism."

In addition to these contacts with Western European communist parties, the KKE continued its contacts with governing parties in the Soviet bloc. In early May, Politburo member Ambatielos visited Budapest and held talks with Hungarian party leaders. In June a KKE delegation under Florakis visited East Germany at the invitation of the East German Central Committee. In late July, a delegation under Florakis went to Moscow and had talks with Boris Ponomarev. From Moscow the delegation flew to Bulgaria where they met with Todor Zhivkov on 2 August.

The KKE (Interior) made similar but less extensive efforts to maintain its international contacts. In late February 1979 a party delegation including Babis Drakopoulos, E. Voutsas, and veteran communist Dimitrios Partsalidis visited Yugoslavia at the invitation of the Yugoslav party. Later in the year, on 27 August, Romanian party chief Nikolai Ceauşescu met with Drakopoulos in Bucharest. A month later, the Romanian Central Committee invited EDA leader Iliou for a short, ceremonial visit.

Other Marxist-Leninist Organizations. For the record, one may mention the Revolutionary Communist Movement of Greece (EKKE), which is pro-Chinese; the Organization of Marxist-Leninists of Greece (OMLE); the Greek Revolutionary Liberation Front; and the Greek Communist Party/Marxist-Leninist (KKE/ML). These organizations have very limited followings, and their political significance should not be exaggerated.

Publications. The KKE's official organ is its daily *Rizospastis*, which has existed for over 55 years, although as an underground newspaper for a considerable part of this time. The KKE (Interior) and the EDA voice their views through the daily *AVGI*. The KKE (Interior) youth organization "Rigas Fereos" publishes the monthly *Thourion*. The monthly theoretical review *Kommunistiki Epitheorisi*, which has been in existence since the 1930s, is controlled by the KKE. The OMLE occasionally publishes the tabloid *Laikos Dromos*; the EKKE, *Laikoi Agones*; and the KKE/ML, *Kokkini Simaia*. The PASOK does not publish its own newspaper or periodical. Instead, it relies on large circulation publications such as the dailies *Elevtherotypia* and *Ta Nea*, the weekly *Oikonomikos Takhydromos*, and *Politica Themata* or *Anti* for favorable coverage of the party's activities and pronouncements. Most significant is the continuing anti-Americanism evident in the editorials and the reporting of most Greek newspapers, which further legitimizes the political arguments of the Marxist left.

Howard University   D. G. Kousoulas

Iceland

Iceland's special political culture, with its emphasis on personalities, egalitarianism, and fervent nationalism, has produced various left-socialist movements over the years. Although analogies can be made with other Western European countries, Icelandic political institutions retain certain unique styles and characteristics. For more than a decade the main left-socialist party has been the People's Alliance (Altydubandalagid; AB), which while advocating fairly radical alternatives to current domestic and foreign policies, nevertheless does so without any direct reference to communist pronouncements and slogans from abroad. The AB is thus the latest form of a solidly established native radical tradition, but one that is quite concerned about international and foreign policy questions. Depending on one's definitions, Iceland has either nearly no communists whatever or one of Western Europe's strongest communist parties. The AB is composed of a heterogeneous collection of trade union members, radical teachers and students, extreme nationalists, and disenchanted Social Democrats. Until the 1978 parliamentary elections, the AB was considerably stronger than the reformist Social Democratic Party (Altyduflokkurinn; SDP); Iceland had been the only Nordic country in which the Social Democrats were not the largest party. The AB has an estimated 3,000 members, out of a total population of about 225,000. Its main strength rests in the Reykjavik area (where half the population lives) and in the smaller fishing and processing towns along the eastern and northern coasts.

Communism has had a rather confusing and maverick history in Iceland. Its first organizational form was a successionist left-wing splinter from the SDP in 1930. There has never been any legal prohibition against the communists. In 1938 the communist party withdrew from the Third International (Comintern), reconstituted itself to include more radical Social Democrats, and took the name of

United People's Party–Socialist Party (Sameiningar flokkur altydu–Sosialista flokkurinn; UPP-SP). Even before the realignment, the Icelandic Communist Party (Kommunistaflokkur Islands; ICP) had actively sought a "popular front" with the Social Democrats. The new UPP-SP based its ideology on "scientific socialism—Marxism," and although there were no longer organizational ties to Moscow, the UPP-SP generally echoed Moscow's viewpoint on international affairs. In 1956 an electoral alliance was formed between most of the UPP-SP, the National Preservation Party, and dissident Social Democrats. This People's Alliance of 1956 strengthened the electoral position of the socialist left and paved the way for the UPP-SP's participation in a broad national coalition (1956–1958). Moreover, the merger with the National Preservation Party (formed in 1953 to protest NATO membership and the NATO airbase at Keflavik and to promote a return to neutrality in foreign policy) made the AB the principal opponent of NATO membership. The AB became an avowed "Marxist political party" in November 1958 and so replaced the UPP-SP. Several elements in the National Preservation Party objected and under the leadership of Hannibal Valdimarsson formed the Organization of Liberals and Leftists (Samtök frjalslyndra og vinstri manna; OLL). In domestic policy the OLL was more pragmatically socialist than the AB's leading elements. There is also a pro-Soviet Marxist faction, the Organization of Icelandic Socialists, and the Trotskyist Revolutionary Communist League (Fylking Byltingarsinnadhra Kommunista; FBK). The Icelandic Communist Party–Marxist-Leninist (ICP-ML) was formed in April 1976, and its chairman, Gunnar Andresson, claimed that the new party was the rightful heir of the original ICP. With its warning against modern revisionism and Soviet "social imperialism," the ICP-ML has close ties to the Chinese Communist Party and is mentioned occasionally in the *Beijing Review*.

The main left-socialist/communist group, currently represented by the AB, has consistently polled between 12 and 22 percent of the popular vote in postwar elections. Between 1971 and 1974 the AB participated in a coalition government formed by the Progressive (agrarian centrist) leader, Olafur Johannesson, along with the OLL (Trond Gilberg, "Patterns of Nordic Communism," *Problems of Communism*, Washington, May/June 1975).

The AB gained substantially in the June 1978 elections to the 60-member Althing (parliament). Polling 22.9 percent of the vote (up 4.6 from 1974), the AB won 14 mandates (a gain of 3). Their advance was overshadowed by the dramatic gains of the SDP, which polled 22 percent (a gain of 12.9 percent) and won 14 seats (a gain of 5). The OLL polled only 3.3 percent (a loss of 1.3 percent) and lost both of its parliamentary seats. These leftist gains were largely erased by the sudden parliamentary elections of 2–3 December. The AB received 19.7 percent of the vote (a loss of 2.2 percent) and only 11 seats (down 3), and the SDP polled 17.4 percent (a loss of 4.6) and had their parliamentary holdings reduced to 10 (a loss of 4).

The Progressives won 24.9 percent and 17 seats (a gain of 5), while the opposition Independence (moderate conservative) Party won 35.4 percent and 21 seats (a gain of 1). (Icelandic Embassy, Washington, D.C., 11 December.) Although the Progressives had headed the center-left government, the elections seem to be a repudiation of the previous coalition, whose breakup occasioned the hasty elections.

The 1978 elections were followed by a lengthy period of political negotiations. The SDP's leader, Benedikt Gröndal, was the first to try to form a government; then Independence leader Geir Hallgrimsson tried unsuccessfully. When the leader of the AB, Ludvik Josefsson, was given a chance, Iceland attracted considerable attention from other NATO countries. Would Iceland be the first NATO country to have a Marxist premier, one who had campaigned vigorously against the alliance? Josefsson failed when the SDP refused to accept him as premier, and the AB leader later blamed politicians in Norway, Washington, and Brussels for this decision (*Nordisk Kontakt*, no. 12, 1978). The fourth and successful effort was made by a former Progressive premier, Olafur Johannesson, in August 1978. The new coalition consisted of the Progressives, the Social Democrats, and the People's

Alliance. Social Democrat Gröndal, with his strong pro-NATO stand, became foreign minister, while three AB leaders received cabinet posts: former AB Chairman Ragnar Arnalds became minister of education and communications, Hjörleifur Guttormsson became minister of industry, and Svavar Gestsson became minister of commerce. The new center-left government issued a lengthy declaration. On the sensitive issue of foreign and NATO affairs the declaration noted that the AB maintained its position against NATO membership and the stationing of American forces in Iceland, but that this would not affect the government's policies (ibid.). The compromise reflects a necessary virtue, but the government soon found other obstacles.

Domestic affairs proved to be the coalition's nemesis, and when the Johannesson government resigned in early October, the Social Democrats formed a caretaker government until the December elections. Benedikt Gröndal became premier and continued to serve as foreign minister in the six-man cabinet (*News of Iceland*, November).

Leadership and Organization. The AB limits leadership positions to one term, and so in November 1977 former Fisheries Minister Ludvik Josefsson replaced Ragnar Arnalds as party chairman. The new vice-chairman is Kjartan Olafsson, editor of the party daily, *Thjodhviljinn* (*Nordisk Kontakt*, no. 15, 1977). Josefsson is also leader of the AB parliamentary group. The Management Council is the party's highest authority between meetings of the 32-member Central Committee.

Personalities weigh heavily in Icelandic politics, and over the years the Communists have had their full share of factionalism, splits, and realignments. This has been especially true of the AB, whose parliamentary strength has fluctuated more because of internal strife than because of changing public support. The 1968 formation of the OLL cost the AB several parliamentary seats. In recent years such turmoil has declined, despite the AB's participation in several coalitions.

Domestic Attitudes and Activities. The governmental crisis that led to the collapse of the center-left coalition in October was caused by the continuation of severe domestic inflation. Although the Icelandic economy grew during 1978-1979 and unemployment remained minimal, wage drift, the complex wage-indexing system, and soaring petroleum prices sent the rate of inflation toward the 50-percent mark. The government's 1979 budget sought to counter these tendencies by reducing the growth of state spending and reforming the indexing system, but from the start there were clear disagreements within the coalition. Josefsson proposed several alternatives to the government's economic policies, including reduced cutbacks in public works, larger state subsidies for specific consumer goods, postponement of tariff reductions (between Iceland and her partners in the European Free Trade Association), and greater reductions in nonsocial state expenditures (ibid., no. 14, 1978). Although the Progressives and Social Democrats were able to agree on specific economic measures, including a reduction in the rate of increase through wage indexing, the AB resisted these proposals through early 1979. Instead AB representatives proposed sharpened control of private personal and business financial transactions in order to reduce tax frauds (ibid., no. 16). In early 1979, the AB proposed greater state and municipal subsidies for child-care institutions. Although AB Education Minister Arnalds attacked the government's economic policies, a settlement was reached at the end of March, and there seemed to be hope for a reduction in the rate of inflation to 35–40 percent. The government's measures resulted in a series of strikes, including a prolonged stoppage of the merchant marine that was finally ended by legislation (ibid., nos. 10, 12).

Labor strife has been a frequent phenomenon in highly unionized Iceland. Until the 1968 split in the AB, communist influence in the Iceland Trade Union Federation (Altydusamband Islands) was significant. Direct control has been less during the past decade, but the AB consistently supports the more radical demands of organized labor. Wage demands have been high in both the public and private sectors, and both sectors have experienced strikes. Coupled with the previously generous indexing system, successive governments have been unable to stop spiraling inflation.

The AB has regularly proposed greater state control of all sectors of the economy, including direct price negotiations between farmers and the state, publication of the names of bank loan recipients, and public ownership and control of all economic resources in the seas, on and under Icelandic land, or otherwise part of the country's resources (ibid., no. 6, 1978). None of these proposals were advanced by the center-left coalition. Continuing disagreements over economic policy was the principal cause of the SDP decision in early October to end the coalition and seek new parliamentary elections. Moreover, there seems to have been considerable tension within the AB, specifically between the AB's ministers and the AB parliamentary group (*Morgunbladid*, 15 October).

International Views and Positions. No Icelandic party is more consistently suspicious of things foreign than the AB. This has meant continuing opposition to Icelandic membership in NATO and to retention of the U.S.-Icelandic defense force (the Keflavik base) in any form. There are currently some 3,000 American troops stationed at the base, and their main missions are reconnaissance, anti-submarine warfare, and air interception (*NYT*, 1 December 1978). The AB's long-term objective has been and is an unarmed (except for the Coast Guard) and neutral Iceland.

The AB, when last in the government (1971-1974), forced the United States to reopen negotiations with Iceland over the Keflavik NATO base. The AB advance in the 1974 elections may have been promoted by anti-NATO feeling, but the even larger gains of the Independence Party and the mass "Defend Our Land" petition indicated that most Icelanders favor a more moderate security policy. The NATO base continues, however, to give the Icelandic government considerable leverage in political and economic dealings with other Western states. This occurred during the 1975–76 "Cod War" between Iceland and Great Britain, which ended with an agreement very favorable to the Icelandic position. The use of the British navy to protect British fishing trawlers provided the context for an attack on NATO membership by AB foreign policy spokesman Gils Gudmundsson, who characterized the connection as a "political swindle" (*Nordisk Kontakt*, no. 15, 1976).

During 1979 Iceland began negotiations for demarcation of territorial waters between Iceland and the sparsely populated Norwegian island of Jan Mayen. Iceland's position is that Jan Mayen is not a regularly inhabited island, and thus Iceland's territorial waters should be the 200-mile limit and not a line halfway between the two islands. Although the government's position has been to bargain realistically with Norway, AB spokesman Stefan Jonsson opposed any concessions (ibid., no. 9).

Svava Jakobsdottir, an AB member of parliament, proposed a measure banning nuclear weapons on Icelandic territory and demanded Icelandic inspection of all areas on the Keflavik base to ensure compliance. She noted that the base authorities had not responded to questions about the use of Icelandic territory for such weapons (ibid., no. 15, 1978). There was no action on the proposal.

Nearly 80 percent of Icelandic exports are fish or fish-related products, which explains the broad national consensus that Iceland must have exclusive control of its coastal waters. The threat of depletion of fish stocks has forced the government to impose severe limitations on the size of the catch in recent years. For years Iceland has had substantial trade with the USSR, and the AB has been among the most enthusiastic for increasing trade with non-Western nations. About 10 percent of Iceland's foreign trade is with the USSR, while nearly 30 percent is with the United States. Although Iceland has greatly developed its natural geothermal and hydroelectric resources in recent years, all of the country's petroleum comes from the USSR. Iceland must pay the Rotterdam spot prices for petroleum, and this was a severe burden in 1979. Efforts to renegotiate the basis for petroleum prices with the USSR during 1979 were unsuccessful (ibid., nos. 11 and 12).

International Party Contacts. Icelandic communists connected with the AB have been consistently absent from international communist meetings and have avoided contacts with foreign communist movements. In fact, no other Western European communist party has maintained such an isolationist position (see Gilberg, "Patterns of Nordic Communism," pp. 34–35).

The AB maintains no formal ties with the Communist Party of the Soviet Union, and it condemned the Warsaw Pact invasion of Czechoslovakia in 1968. Accordingly, no AB representatives have been present at periodic gatherings of pro-Soviet parties, such as the 25th Congress of the Soviet party in February 1976 or the meeting of European communist parties in East Berlin in June 1976. In the past the AB has offered moral support for communist parties, most notably those of Romania and Yugoslavia, that are known for their independent or nationalistic views. The AB has also maintained occasional contacts with the Italian Communist Party, including a visit to Rome by then party Chairman Ragnar Arnalds in 1976.

During 1979 Icelandic Foreign Minister Gröndal visited East Germany on an official visit (Allgemeiner Deutscher Nachrichtendienst, 16 May). In addition a Soviet parliamentary delegation visited Iceland in September (Tass, 11 September). Earlier a new friendship and cultural cooperation agreement was concluded between the "friendship societies" of the two countries (ibid., 13 April).

Publications. The AB's central organ is *Thjodhviljinn* (Will of the Nation), a daily newspaper in Reykjavik. It has a national circulation of some 10,000. The party also publishes a biweekly theoretical journal, *Ny Utsyn* (New Views). Outside the capital, there are at least two procommunist weeklies: *Verkamadhurinn* in Akureyri and *Mjolnir* in Siglufjördhur.

Other Marxist Groups. Mention has been made of the OLL, which split from the AB in 1968, as well as two smaller Maoist and Trotskyist groups formed in the mid-1970s. The OLL's parliamentary support steadily declined through the 1974 elections. In October 1976, the OLL Executive Committee decided to cancel the party's National Congress and dissolve itself in favor of the two-man parliamentary group. In some regions of the country OLL activists seemed anxious to support the AB, in others the SDP, and in still others to continue an independent political organization. Although candidates were run in all electoral districts in 1978, the OLL polled only 3.3 percent of the vote and failed to elect any members. With the disintegration of the center-left coalition government in fall 1979, it is possible that the OLL may attract some support from disappointed AB and SDP voters.

The Maoist ICP-ML drew little voter support but continued its active support of Chinese foreign policy goals. Ari T. Gudmundsson, chairman of the ICP, joined with his Danish comrades in the Communist Workers' Party of Denmark to denounce the Vietnamese invasion of Kampuchea (Cambodia) and Soviet foreign policy in general (New China News Agency, 7 December 1978). The ICP's main publication is *Stettabarattan* (Class Struggle).

The Trotskyist FBK ran parliamentary candidates in 24 electoral districts in 1978, but none received any significant number of votes. Although active in most leftist activities, the FBK is critical of the AB and most other competitors for leftist support. Its publication is *Neisti* (The Spark). (Intercontinental Press, 10 April 1978.)

University of Massachusets
Amherst

Eric S. Einhorn

Ireland

The first Irish communist party was founded on 14 October 1921 following a schism in the Socialist Party. It disappeared during the ensuing civil war (1922–1923), although small groups of Marxist-Leninists known collectively as Revolutionary Workers' Groups remained. In June 1933 a conference of these cells led to the formation of the Communist Party of Ireland (CPI). This is the date now adopted by Irish communists for the party's formation.

The Second World War, known as the "emergency" in the south, severely disrupted the party's organizational structure, largely because of the belligerent status of Northern Ireland and the neutrality of the south. In 1941 the southern organization suspended its activities and the present-day general secretary of the party, Michael O'Riordan, was interned. Two separate Irish communist groups then emerged: the CPI and the Irish Workers' League, later renamed the Irish Workers' Party of Northern Ireland, in the North. At a special Unity Congress held in Belfast on 15 March 1970, the two groups reunited to form the CPI.

Today the CPI has a membership of about 600, based mainly in Dublin and Northern Ireland. Members in the north are usually of a Protestant background. In the south there are numerous Marxist groups, and it is more usual for left-wing militants to join either the Socialist Labour Party (SLP) or the Sinn-Fein-Workers' Party (SFWP). The population of the Republic of Ireland is about 3 million and of Northern Ireland about 1.5 million.

Leadership and Organization. The CPI is divided into two area branches, northern and southern, corresponding to the political division of the country. The Congress is the supreme constitutional authority of the party but in practice serves largely as a rubber stamp for the National Executive. The innermost and effective controlling body is the National Political Committee, which includes Andrew Barr (chairman), Michael O'Riordan (general secretary), Tom Redmond (vice-chairman), Johnny Nolan (national treasurer), and James Stewart (assistant general secretary). The other, non-office–holding members are Joseph Bowers, Madge Davison, and Fergal Costello.

The CPI holds no seats in any significant legislative assembly in either north or south and has little prospect of doing so. It has one local councillor in the south. The communists do, however, have some influence in the trade unions and in the Northern Ireland Civil Rights Association. The CPI also controls a small youth organization, the Connolly Youth Movement.

Domestic Attitudes and Activities. The key event of the year was the Seventeenth National Congress, held in Belfast at the end of February. The congress was attended by 117 delegates from party branches in Dublin, Belfast, Cork, Coleraine, Limerick, and other centers. The conference was also attended by visiting delegations from the communist parties of Great Britain, Chile, Cuba, Cyprus, Czechoslovakia, France, East Germany, West Germany, Portugal, the Soviet Union, and the United States, and from the international Marxist journal, *World Marxist Review*. The presence of the Czechoslovak delegation underlined a salient characteristic of the CPI—its total loyalty to the Soviet Union.

The general objectives of the CPI were confirmed in a long composite resolution passed by the congress. The fundamental party aim is to achieve a unified socialist Ireland. This is to be won through the unity of all working people, including small farmers, small businessmen, fishermen, and professional people. The party recognizes that it is still a long way from achieving this goal and attributes this failure to British interference, which it holds divides the working people of Northern Ireland and dominates the economy of the south. The congress adopted other resolutions on industry and organization, the party constitution, women and youth affairs, and international solidarity.

A new National Executive Committee was elected, which in addition to Political Committee members, includes Sean Morrissey, Michael Fox, James Graham, Betty Sinclair, Brian Gormaly, Bill Somerset, Tommy O'Flaherty, Eoin O'Murchu, Edwina Stewart, Mick Wall, Gerry McIntyre, Eddie Glachin, and Michael Mooney.

The party still hopes to create a far-left grouping embracing the CPI, SLP, and SFWP. It suggests its own draft program for a national left program and offers the pages of the party organ, *Irish Socialist*, for an open discussion between interested groups. It attributes the breakdown of the former grouping of far-left groups — the so-called Liaison Group of the Left — to an abandonment by the SFWP of its wholehearted commitment to a left-republican posture.

In local government elections held in the summer, the CPI polled badly. The party contested two areas in Dublin, but both candidates were near the bottom of the poll. Johnny Montgomery polled 199 first preferences in Ballyfermot and Sean Lambe 149 in North Central. The only success was that of Declan Bree, who campaigned as a candidate of the communist-controlled Connolly Youth Movement. Bree was elected to both Sligo Corporation and Sligo County Council.

Although a marginal influence in Irish political life, the CPI retains an element of influence in the trade union movement and has been active in unemployment campaigns. Andrew Barr, the party's national chairman, is also a president of the Irish Congress of Trade Unions and a member of the Executive Committee of the European Confederation of Trade Unions. The party campaigned in support of a wholesale reform of the tax system, a popular cause in Ireland in 1979, and against the use of nuclear energy. While not overtly critical of Pope John Paul II's visit to Ireland of 29 September to 1 October, the CPI attacked the church's positions on contraception and divorce, which the party maintained were major obstacles to Irish unity.

In the north the CPI seeks a phased British withdrawal. First, troops should be withdrawn to barracks, then a bill of rights should be introduced to protect the Catholics, next British financial aid should be given to the province, and finally the troops should be withdrawn. Although the CPI itself eschews violence, it holds the British ultimately responsible for the violence. In the long run, secular education should be introduced.

International Views and Party Contacts. The CPI is totally loyal to Moscow and has never been known to criticize the policies of the Soviet Union. Its papers give much attention to the apparent achievements of the USSR and the Eastern European states. Its foreign policy declarations are therefore predictable — apart perhaps from its advocacy of Irish neutrality and its unremitting hostility to Irish membership in the European Economic Community. At its February congress the party unanimously adopted a resolution hailing what it termed the historic victories of the peoples of Afghanistan, Angola, Ethiopia, Kampuchea (Cambodia), Laos, and Mozambique and strongly condemned the Chinese attack on Vietnam.

James Stewart was received by Dimitur Stanishev, secretary of the Bulgarian Communist Party, on 11 July. They discussed the activities of the two parties and some aspects of international affairs. They emphasized the complete unanimity of their views. In August Stewart and Edwina Stewart had talks with President (formerly Prince) Souphanouvong of Laos. On 30 July Vasil Bilák, member of the Presidium and secretary of the Czechoslovak Communist Party's Central Committee, received CPI

General Secretary O'Riordan. They discussed the work of their two parties and views on the international communist movement. At the invitation of the Soviet Central Committee, O'Riordan visited Lithuania on 8 August where he had a meeting with Piatras Griskiavicus, first secretary of the Lithuanian party.

Publications. The CPI publishes the weekly *Unity* and the *Young Worker* in Belfast and its principal party organ, the monthly *Irish Socialist*, and the theoretical quarterly *Irish Socialist Review* in Dublin.

Other Marxist Groups. There are many small Marxist groups in Ireland. The leading one, which enjoyed some electoral success in the 1979 local elections, is the SFWP, the political wing of the official Irish Republican Army. It is pro-Moscow and publishes the monthly *United Irishman.* Other groups include the Trotskyist Movement for a Socialist Republic, the League for a Workers' Republic, the Irish Republican Socialist Party, and a CPI splinter, the Irish Marxist Society. There is a Maoist organization, the Communist Party of Ireland–Marxist-Leninist, which is pro-Albanian and hostile to current developments in China. In June a delegation from this party visited Albania and had talks with Ramiz Alia, a member of the Albanian party Politburo.

London   Richard Sim

Italy

The Italian Communist Party was founded in January 1921 when a radical faction of the Italian Socialist Party (PSI) led by Amedeo Bordiga, Antonio Gramsci, Palmiro Togliatti, and others seceded from the PSI and formed the Partito Comunista d'Italia, later renamed the Partito Comunista Italiano (PCI). Declared illegal under the fascist regime, the PCI reappeared on the political scene in 1944 and participated in governmental coalitions in the early postwar years. Excluded from office in 1947, it remained in opposition at the national level until the mid-seventies. Since the parliamentary elections of 1976, the PCI has played a significant role in national politics. From summer 1976 until January 1979, the PCI has been part of the governmental majority but without holding cabinet posts. In the parliamentary elections of 3 June, the electoral strength of the PCI decreased from 34.4 to 30.4 percent of the popular vote, and the PCI lost 26 seats in the Lower House and 7 seats in the Senate. Partly as a result of the elections, the PCI moved into the opposition in July but has continued to press for the formation of a broad coalition of national solidarity and communist representation in the cabinet. At the local level, the PCI has been in power in a number of municipalities since the late 1940s, particularly in the regions of Emilia-Romagna, Tuscany, and Umbria. Following the municipal elections of 1975, the PCI gained control of an even larger number of local governments. Since then it has shared power, generally with the PSI, in all major urban centers of the country (Rome, Milan, Turin, Bologna, Florence, Venice, Naples, and others).

Leadership and Organization. The basic unit of party organization is the section. The smaller units that existed in the past (the cells) no longer function. Party members belong to 1 of the 11,000 sections organized in neighborhoods, villages, or places of work. Activities of the sections are coordinated through plant, town, and area committees. Sections are grouped into federations, which usually coincide with the area of the province. In turn, federations are grouped into regional committees. Young communists are organized in the Youth Federation, which has approximately 150,000 members.

The national organization includes a Central Committee (169 members), a Central Control Commission (55 members), a Directorate (32 members), and a Secretariat (7 members). In addition, there are several bureaus staffed by experts in different policy areas. After the July reorganization, the most important departments are International Affairs (Giancarlo Pajetta), Party Problems (Giorgio Napolitano), Propaganda and Information (Adalberto Minucci), Cultural Activities (Aldo Tortorella), Economic and Social Problems (Gerardo Chiaromonte), Women (Adriana Seroni), Regional and Local Governments (Armando Cossutta), Problems of the State (Ugo Pecchioli), and Education (Achille Occhetto) (*L'Unità*, 12 July).

No significant changes in the composition of the leadership occurred as a result of the Fifteenth Congress held at the beginning of April. Party Chairman Luigi Longo and General Secretary Enrico Berlinguer were unanimously reconfirmed in their offices. Other posts were not filled immediately after the Congress to assure continuity in party leadership until the parliamentary elections of 3 June. In early July the Central Committee chose the members of the Directorate and the Secretariat. The latter body was reduced in size from nine to seven members; in addition to Berlinguer, it includes Mario Birardi, Gerardo Chiaromonte, Pio La Torre, Adalberto Minucci, Giorgio Napolitano, and Alessandro Natta (ibid.). Natta was expected to become deputy leader. The most notable change in the composition of the Secretariat was the exclusion of Giancarlo Pajetta and Paolo Bufalini (Agenzia Nazionale Stampa Associata [ANSA], 11 July). Both, however, remained members of the Directorate.

The number of party members claimed at the end of 1978 was nearly 1.8 million. In reporting the membership figures in preparation for the Congress, party leaders pointed out that although the party had grown from 1.6 million members in 1974, there had been difficulties in recruiting members in 1977 and 1978, and in the latter year membership had decreased by 25,000. Among the reasons given were the difficulties "encountered by our cadres and members in trying to understand the innovations that were introduced after 20 June 1976 and in trying to comprehend fully the positions that the party was assuming one after another" (*Rinascita*, 30 March). The social composition of the party membership in 1978 was laborers (40 percent); retirees and housewives (28 percent); white-collar workers, small businessmen, artisans, and professionals (18 percent); farmhands and small farmers (11 per cent); and students (3 percent). Party officers expressed concern "about the persistent underrepresentation of women among party members" and even more about the age composition of the party. In 1977 about 55 percent of party members were over 40, while only 11 percent were under 25. Party leaders stressed the need for "a broad recruitment program among the younger generation." (Ibid.)

The volume of the activities carried out by the party can be gauged in part by the PCI balance sheet. The final budget for 1978 listed a total of 48 billion lire, with a deficit of 482 million. Among the sources of revenue, the most important ones were annual membership fees (36.8 percent), public financing (27.9 percent), and miscellaneous proceeds (32.4 percent), the bulk of which consisted of amounts collected through the Unità Festivals and subscriptions to the communist press. The average annual contribution of card-carrying members was almost 9,000 lire (about U.S. $11). (Ibid.) Almost two-thirds of expenditures were for grants made by the national headquarters to peripheral offices and organizations. The next highest items among expenditures (21 percent) were publishing, information, and propaganda activities. The party daily, *L'Unità*, absorbed approximately 6 billion lire. In making the budget public, the PCI Directorate stressed the toll of inflation "even for a party such as ours that can count on the voluntary work of thousands and thousands of comrades, on its officials working for pay equivalent to that of a worker, and on successful candidates paying a large proportion of their salaries to the party" (*L'Unità*, 21 January).

Domestic Views and Activities. Among the most important domestic developments during 1979 were the Italian cabinet crisis that began in January; the PCI Congress that convened in April; the parliamentary elections of 3 June; the European parliamentary elections of 10 June; and the negotiations for the formation of a new cabinet in July and August.

Although the cabinet crisis officially began in January, there were many signs that the coalition of which the PCI was a part was gradually becoming less politically viable as early as fall 1978. In November the cabinet was reshuffled and a new minister of industry appointed. Party leaders made it clear that they were happy neither with the procedure followed by Premier Giulio Andreotti nor with the person chosen. Furthermore, PCI leaders were unhappy about other issues. Asked whether the PCI would provoke a governmental crisis if its demands were not satisfied, party leader Giorgio Napolitano stated: "Failure to provide a satisfactory solution to any one of these problems would certainly be enough to make the political situation difficult and eventually untenable" (*Corriere della Sera*, 26 November 1978).

Another element of friction was added in mid-December 1978 when the Christian Democrat (DC) cabinet decided that Italy should join the European Monetary System, a move that the PCI had opposed. The PCI announced "its staunch opposition to the move" (*Wall Street Journal*, 13 December 1978). The gradual deterioration of the coalition continued. In mid-January *L'Unità* launched a strong attack against the DC (ANSA, 15 January). The next day, the PCI daily commented on the visit to the United States of DC Secretary Benito Zaccagnini and objected to the fact that he had apparently discussed with the press the issue of communist participation in the government. "Imagine what would happen if the general secretary of the PCI had said that he had discussed in Moscow . . . issues such as the exclusion of the DC or of any other party from the government" (*L'Unità*, 16 January). A few days later, the PCI accused the DC of "undemocratically and unjustifiably refusing to create a government made up of all democratic parties" and announced that its representatives in parliament would vote against the three-year economic plan if it were not modified (ANSA, 18 January).

On 26 January after attending a meeting of the secretaries of the five parties supporting the coalition, Berlinguer openly withdrew PCI support of the cabinet: "After a careful examination of the facts, we have come to the conclusion that our presence in the majority that backs the government has become impossible" (ibid., 26 January). Throughout the ensuing consultations, which lasted two months, the position of the communists remained the same: the PCI would re-enter a parliamentary majority only in exchange for full participation in the new government, including their own cabinet ministers (*NYT*, 4 February). When it became clear that the DC would not accept PCI participation in the cabinet, Berlinguer proposed a government having the parliamentary support of the two major parties but without DC participation in the cabinet (*L'Unità*, 16 February). As the crisis continued, it became clear that some parties were thinking of early elections following an anticipated dissolution of parliament. On 5 March Berlinguer attempted to forestall this possibility by declaring: "Majorities without the communists are possible in this parliament, but it is certainly not up to us to suggest them . . . so, do not tell us that if the communists are not in the majority, there is no solution other than early elections" (ibid., 5 March). By mid-March it had become apparent that new elections were unavoidable. On 19 March the PSI refused to back a DC cabinet that included Social Democrats and Republicans, and elections became a certainty.

The Fifteenth Congress. Scheduled for 20-25 March, the Fifteenth Congress was postponed for a week due to the prolonged government crisis. The congress had been preceded by section meetings and federation congresses in which delegates to the national congress had been selected. These meetings also discussed the "theses" that had been approved by the Central Committee in December.

The congress was attended by approximately 1,500 Italian delegates. Delegations from about one hundred communist and socialist parties and national liberation movements numbering some 8,000 guests convened in the huge Sport Palace in Rome. The Soviet delegation was headed by Arvid I. Pelshe, a member of the Politburo of the Communist Party of the Soviet Union (CPSU). According to some observers, "Moscow's failure to send a more prominent official was interpreted as a snub" (*NYT*, 4 April). The Chinese Communist Party did not send a delegation, but the Chinese ambassador to Rome did attend the proceedings and had a talk with Berlinguer (ibid.).

One of the tasks of the congress was to approve a new set of bylaws. One of the more controversial issues, which had been a focus of debate in the past few years, was Article 5, which states that it is a member's duty "to acquire and to extend an acquaintance with Marxism-Leninism and to apply its teachings in resolving specific problems." The new formulation (now Article 6) states that every party member must "increase his cultural and political knowledge and carry out a thorough study of the history and heritage of ideas of the PCI and of the entire workers' and revolutionary movement." The introduction to the new bylaws also states that "the party identifies with the ideological and cultural traditions whose mold and inspiration lies in the thought of Marx and Engels and which received an impulse of historic significance from Lenin's innovative ideas and his work." (*L'Unità*, 4 April.) As for "democratic centralism," another trait of the PCI that had been under attack by other parties, a special commission in charge of studying the question reported that "a very broad segment of the party had spoken out in favor of retaining democratic centralism—viewed, however, not as an instrument of entrenchment but as a stimulus for progress toward an ever increasing responsibility shared among party members" (ibid.).

Some observers had thought that the congress would provide an opportunity for a confrontation between those favoring a return by the party to the opposition stance of an earlier period and those favoring the pursuit of a broad coalition strategy. Some juxtaposition of points of view occurred. Thus, hard-liner Cossutta stated: "The PCI cannot stop being itself and cannot abandon its internal democratic centralism, its ideological inspirations found in the work of Marx, Engels, and Lenin, its internationalist feelings, and its ties of cooperation and fraternity with the Soviet Union and other socialist countries, with communist workers and parties and with liberation movements . . . Nor can we be expected to become a strong social democratic party, especially in view of the problems and failures of the European social democracies. We are and we will remain ourselves." (Ibid., 1 April.)

On the other hand, Emanuele Macaluso, widely regarded as a proponent of the "softer" Eurocommunist line, argued against a return to the opposition and stated that the PCI was a "governing" force. "To this end," he added, "emphatic proclamations of fraternal relations with the USSR serve no purpose." Moreover, "the fundamental factor from which we must proceed is that for the first time in the history of the European workers' movement, there is a possibility of unity, or at least of convergence, among the communist, socialist and social democratic forces," with the possibility of building "a new society based on political democracy and the guarantee of all freedoms." (Ibid., 2 April.) Pietro Ingrao, a prestigious leader who has served as chairman of the Lower House of parliament since 1976 and is expected to return to party work and possibly challenge the present leadership, took, instead, a balanced position: "It is not out of caution that we speak of a transformation rather than of a revolution. We believe that upheaval in society requires an entire historical stage. This is the rationale for the 'third path' to socialism. And we say 'third path' not in order to establish an impossible and static point of equidistance between East and West, between the Eastern bloc countries and the social democracies, but in order to emphasize the innovation, its significance, and its distinctiveness . . . We have learned from the USSR and [the] October [Revolution]. I can see no harm in our learning from the vicissitudes of social democracy." (Ibid., 3 April.)

On the issue of what stance to take in domestic politics, the congress approved the line proposed by the leaders and summarized by Berlinguer as follows: "It must therefore be stressed that the government needed now is a coalition government composed of the democratic forces, a government including the full participation of the PCI on the basis of equality and with positions consistent with its role and responsibility" (ibid., 31 March).

In his closing remarks, Berlinguer returned to the theme of the party's ties with the Soviet Union and restated a position that he had articulated on earlier occasions: "According to many politicians and journalists, an assessment of our international stance comes down to measuring with a ruler how far away we are from, or how close we are to this or that communist party or this and that socialist state. According to them, our party's autonomy will only be acknowledged when we decide to proclaim that the Soviet Union and the socialist countries are the perfection of evil and that it is therefore necessary to break away from them . . . I have already said and I will now repeat that it is absurd to ask us to cut off our roots, the ties with the October Revolution, with Lenin's work and thoughts." (*FBIS*, 17 April.)

The Parliamentary Elections. Although the election was not held until June, the PCI began on its campaign immediately after the conclusion of the congress. The party's leaders did not look forward to the election. This was partly because of the electoral defeats suffered in many areas by the party in the partial administrative elections of 1978. The leaders also sensed some discontent among party followers. Moreover, while the PCI was forced by the logic of the campaign to attack the DC, the party's strategy still envisioned a broad alliance after the election. Because of these difficulties, there was some pessimism about the electoral outcome, and Berlinguer reportedly believed that the party would do well if it did not drop more than 2 percent at the polls (*CSM*, 5 May). Early estimates from public opinion polls indicated that the PCI was likely to lose about 4 percentage points (*Panorama*, 8 May).

The PCI presented its electoral platform on 4 May. Although several issues surfaced during the campaign (the economy, terrorism, the implementation of health care reforms), the election was seen by many observers as a referendum on the single issue of PCI participation in a governing majority. (*Corriere della Sera*, 2 June.)

The losses suffered by the PCI in the election (4 percent in the election for the House and 2.5 percent in the election for the Senate) were not unexpected. They were significant nevertheless. It was in fact the first time that the overall level of support for the communists had declined in the postwar period. Furthermore, given the general stability of the Italian electorate, a loss of 4 percentage points was likely to be considered a setback of consequence. In general the PCI managed to retain part of the gains made in 1976, but its decline in 1979 was particularly pronounced in those provinces in which gains had been more marked in 1976.

On 10 June Italian voters were called to the polls to elect members of the European parliament, and in this election, the party again did not fare well. Twenty-four PCI candidates were elected to the Strasbourg assembly, but the PCI share of the vote (29.6 percent) declined slightly compared with the national election (30.4 percent). Finally, on 17–18 June regional elections were held in the island of Sardinia. Once again the outcome showed that the electoral strength of the PCI was declining from the high point reached in the mid-seventies.

Party leaders met at the end of June to assess the situation and to determine the causes of the decline. Berlinguer, in his report, could point out that the defeat of the communists had not benefited either the PSI or the DC; this was seen as a positive aspect. The reasons for the decline were attributed to the attacks waged against the party both domestically and internationally: "Overseas there was pressure from the U.S. government and other Western European governments . . . At home the DC sabotaged and delayed the implementation of the most radical parts of the program that had been agreed on" (*L'Unità*, 3 July). In addition, party leaders explained the returns as being due to short-comings of the party, i.e., "defects of direction, orientation, work, and organization" (ANSA, 3 July). Lastly, they referred to events that had occurred earlier in the year in Asia: "We cannot disregard the fact that such tragic situations as those of Kampuchea (Cambodia) and Vietnam and the Chinese-Vietnamese conflict helped to damage the image that socialism has established so far, and this accentuated confusion and doubt in the ideological sphere, especially among the younger generation" (*L'Unità*, 3 July).

When the new round of negotiations among parties opened in early July, the PCI position was the same as at the beginning of the year. After two unsuccessful efforts by Craxi and Pandolfi, DC leader Cossiga formed a cabinet with the support of the Social Democrats and the Liberals and with the vital abstention of the Socialists. The PCI announced its decision to vote against the new coalition. Directorate member Aldo Tortorella explained his party's decision as follows: "After seven months of crisis . . . we are faced with a new minority cabinet marked by a clearly provisional character and by a composition and program entirely unequal to the serious problems of the working masses and of the country . . .[The problems] demanded and still demand authoritative leadership based on consensus, moral strength, operational ability, and commitment . . . Nobody can doubt that our opposition will have the same characteristics of involvement, responsibility, rigor, and steadfastness that our activity has always demonstrated." (Ibid., 12 August.)

International Views and Positions. The most important international events on which the PCI took positions during 1979 were the China-Vietnam conflict, the direct election of the European parliament, and the deployment of a new generation of missiles in Western Europe.

Although the other Italian parties contested the European election as part of one or another transnational federation (Socialist, Liberal, Christian Democratic), there was no corresponding group of communist parties. Five months before the election, Antonio Rubbi of the party's Foreign Section announced: "The PCI will contest the election with its own lists, symbols, and program. It has never been and it is not now the PCI's intention to form a European communist party. This would contrast with the essence of the Eurocommunist line, which rules out the establishment of organizational centers and which is based instead on the autonomy and independence of every party." (Ibid., 28 January.) At a later date, asked if the inability of the European communists to present a common program signified that Eurocommunism was not a viable option, Berlinguer stated in a televised press conference: "Eurocommunism is by no means dead. Of course, matters could be considered otherwise if one regarded Eurocommunism as a kind of single party comprising the communist parties of the various European countries. But we have never considered Eurocommunism this way. Eurocommunism is the meeting point of original formulations by the various national parties, all of which identify with one essential objective: the building of socialism in Western Europe along a road that differs from that pursued by countries in which socialism has been created. And naturally, in a manner different from that pursued by the social democrats." (Ibid., 30 May.)

During the campaign PCI leaders acknowledged the existence of differences in the PCI's position vis-à-vis that of the French Communist Party (PCF). At a joint PCF-PCI rally in Marseilles, Berlinguer stated: "Of course, it is no secret that our two parties still diverge and take different lines on major questions of European policy, such as the expansion of the [European Economic] Community to include Greece, Spain, and Portugal, which we favor, or the question of the powers of the European parliament, which we think should be strengthened" (*L'Humanité*, 2 May). But it was clear that more than these two issues separated the two parties. Although the French had gone so far as to suggest that in the new European parliament they wanted "to be in a separate political group unless administrative concerns oblige us to cohabit with the PCI" (*Le Monde*, 30 January), the Italian communists exhibited a more open posture regarding collaboration with other political groups: "The European left can perform a key function in building Europe if it can lay aside its ancient divisions and at the same time commit itself to collaboration with other democratic forces and particularly with the more advanced segments of the Catholic and Christian movement" (*L'Unità*, 22 April).

The armed conflict between China and Vietnam was a source of concern for PCI leaders. Commenting on the mounting tension in Asia, Giancarlo Pajetta observed in early January: "Differences on various issues, even on significant issues, should not become causes for warfare among communists. There are many points of Chinese policy, especially foreign policy, concerning the well-known concept of the inevitability of war with which we do not agree. However, we do not support a crusade against China, nor do we seek its isolation." (*Rizospastis*, 9 January.) When the conflict broke out, Berlinguer expressed his concern in a speech in Leghorn: "Armed clashes between China and Vietnam . . . are a serious and distressing event that disturbs all men who love peace, but it arouses particular emotions in the hearts of our comrades and workers because two countries that fought and won great revolutionary battles and gave a socialist direction to their development have come to blows" (*Unità*, 19 February).

The controversy over the changes in the balance of military power in Europe became a central issue in Italian politics in the fall. The PCI's posture on this issue became an important consideration in the debate over the formation of a new governmental coalition with communist participation. Shortly after Brezhnev's speech of 6 October in East Berlin, a commentary in *Rinascita* (12 October) stated: "The speech appears to open new perspectives for concrete negotiations on arms control." The party's position was formalized at a meeting of the Directorate on 17 October, which was later summarized by Paolo Bufalini: "We have not said that the equilibrium of military forces is intact and that the United States is in the wrong. We have said that neither Italy nor other nations have sufficient, decisive elements to determine what the situation is . . . and we have asked that the existing armament situation be verified . . . If from this process of verification it is determined that the equilibrium has been altered, we believe — and this is the essence of our proposal — that it should be re-established but at a lower rather than a higher level, i.e., by removing the factors (specifically the missiles) that have caused the disequilibrium." (Ibid., 9 November.)

International Party Contacts. As in previous years, the PCI maintained extensive international contacts in 1979. In January a delegation headed by Giancarlo Pajetta went to Greece at the invitation of the Central Committee of one of the two Greek communist parties (the KKE), but the Italian guests also had contacts with the KKE (Interior) (*Rizospastis*, 6 January). Another delegation led by Guido Fanti visited Vietnam (*L'Unità*, 23 January). In the same period, a PCI group went to Sweden and met with the chairman of the Social Democratic Party, Olof Palme (ibid., 20 January). In February Paolo Bufalini and Antonio Rubbi traveled to the USSR and had talks in Moscow with Boris Ponomarev of the CPSU (Tass, 12 February). Shortly afterwards, Sergio Segre of the PCI Foreign Section had conversations in France with the secretary of the French Socialist Party, François Mitterand, and a PCI delegation traveled to Amsterdam for a meeting with leaders of the Communist Party of the Netherlands (*L'Unità*, 20 and 23 February). In March Ugo Pecchioli and other PCI officials traveled to Spain, where they were received by Spanish party leader Santiago Carrillo, and then went on to Lisbon for talks with Portuguese communist leaders (ibid., 14 March). Later in the month another PCI group traveled to Copenhagen for a meeting with Danish communists (ibid., 24 March).

The PCI Congress provided an opportunity for contact with a large number of foreign parties and political groups. In addition to delegations of communist parties from the five continents, a number of other groups were represented at the congress, including delegations from the socialist parties of Belgium, France, Japan, Sweden, the Netherlands, Switzerland, and the United Kingdom, as well as representatives of "national fronts" from Algeria, Angola, Eritrea, the Western Sahara (the Polisario), Mozambique, and Zimbabwe (*FBIS*, 2 May).

Additional contacts took place after the PCI Congress. In mid-May Directorate member Giovanni Cervetti led a delegation to the 23rd Congress of the PCF (*L'Unità*, 12 May). A week later, Berlinguer participated in a joint PCI-PCF meeting in Marseilles (*L'Humanité*, 2 May), and Giancarlo Pajetta traveled to Brussels, where he had contacts not only with Belgian communists but also with representatives of the Walloon and Flemish Socialist parties (*L'Unità*, 19 May). In August, after vacationing in the USSR, Berlinguer visited Leningrad and met with Leonid Brezhnev (ANSA, 6 September). At the end of September, Berlinguer met with PCF Secretary Georges Marchais in Strasbourg, where the two leaders were attending the European parliamentary session (*L'Unità*, 27 September). And in early October the PCI secretary traveled to Lisbon to meet with Alvaro Cunhal, the Secretary of the Portuguese Communist Party.

Publications. The official PCI newspaper, *L'Unità*, appears daily in both Milan and Rome and is edited by Central Committee member Alfredo Reichlin. The weekly *Rinascita*, edited by economics expert Luciano Barca, is a cultural journal that primarily attracts an audience of intellectuals. The theoretical journal of the party is *Critica Marxista*, edited by Aldo Tortorella. Other specialized journals dealing with history, international affairs, and economics are, respectively, *Studi Storici, La Nuova Rivista Internazionale*, and *Politica ed Economia*.

A popular periodical, *Donne e Politica* is addressed to women. In October another popular periodical catering to an audience of young people, *La Città Futura*, ceased publication after two and a half years (*Rinascita*, 26 October). The Foreign Section of the party publishes a trimonthly bulletin in four languages entitled *The Italian Communists*. The publishing house of the party, Editori Riuniti, annually produces a large number of volumes in a wide variety of fields.

Other Communist Groups. Other communist groups operate to the left of the PCI. Two of them, the Democratic Party of Proletarian Unity for Communism (PDUP) and the United New Left (NSU), presented lists of nationwide candidates in the parliamentary elections of June. The PDUP list received 1.4 percent of the popular vote and the party obtained six seats in the Lower House. The NSU list received 0.8 percent of the vote but failed to obtain parliamentary representation. In the election for the European parliament, the PDUP polled 1.1 percent of the vote, and another leftist group (Proletarian Democracy) received 0.7 percent. They each obtained a seat in the Strasbourg assembly.

A number of self-styled "real" communist groups exist, and many of them have been involved in episodes of political violence. In addition to the Red Brigades—whose original leaders are all in jail—acts of terrorism have been claimed by such groups as Prima Linea, Brigate per il Comunismo, and others.

Ohio State University   Giacomo Sani

Luxembourg

The Communist Party of Luxembourg (PCL) was founded in January 1921. Before World War II it played an insignificant role in Luxembourg politics. Following the war, the party increased its influence to some extent, partly because of the enhanced prestige of the Soviet Union. Since 1945 the PCL has been represented in parliament and in the town councils of Luxembourg City and several industrial centers of the south. From 1945 to 1947 the cabinet included one communist minister. The party's influence decreased after that but increased again following the elections of 1964. It reached a new climax in the elections of 1968 and decreased again in the elections of 1974 and 1979.

In the 10 June parliamentary elections the PCL obtained approximately 5 percent of the votes and 2 out of the 59 seats (compared with 5 in 1974). This result is by far the lowest in the postwar period. On the occasion of the first elections to the European parliament, on 10 June, the PCL won only 5.01 percent of the vote, not enough to win a seat. During the municipal elections of 12 October, the PCL presented a list of candidates in eight of the nineteen municipalities applying the system of proportional representation. In 1969 it had presented nine lists in fifteen municipalities having proportional representation. In these eight municipalities the PCL won sixteen councillor seats (compared with eighteen in 1969). The party now participates in only three majority coalitions with the Luxembourgish Socialist Workers' Party (POSL), in Esch-Alzette, Differdange, and Kayl-Tétange. Compared with former years, the results of the 1975 elections were another sign of the decreasing popularity of the PCL.

Leadership and Organization. The PCL, strongly pro-Soviet, presents the image of a united party. Differences of opinion are usually not made public. During the past few years, however, a few dissenting members were excluded from the party; their departure was extensively discussed in the media. In parliament party members normally vote as a bloc. Since the last elections, the communist presence in the legislative assembly has been almost insignificant. With only two representatives, the PCL cannot form a party-fraction of its own, and no other splinter party is willing to cooperate with it. (A party must have at least five representatives to form a party-fraction. Actually each of the three largest parties forms its own fraction, and the four other parties are unable or unwilling to build a common fraction.)

Party membership is estimated at between 500 and 600. The population of the Grand Duchy is about 357,000 (1978). Only 0.17 percent of the population are members of the PCL.

The decisions of the PCL Congress and of its leading bodies are usually passed unanimously. The Congress meets every three years, most recently on 26 and 27 December 1976 in Luembourg City. At that time the Central Committee was enlarged to 31 full and 4 candidate members (formerly 28 full and no candidate members). Since then four members have died and have not been replaced. The Executive Committee remained at 10 members (actually 9 after the death of Arthur Useldinger). The 3-member Secretariat consists of the new party chairman, René Urbany; his father, the honorary chairman, Dominique Urbany; and in Useldinger's place, the new party treasurer and Central Committee member, Joseph Ruckert (a steelworker who is very dedicated to the Urbany clan).

The leadership of the PCL is strongly centralized. This point is emphasized by the complete absence of regional party organizations, although local party sections do exist. The party heads the League of Luxembourg Women (Union des femmes luxembourgeoises) and has a youth auxiliary organization, whose name, Jeunesse progressiste luxembourgeoise, was changed on 9 July 1977 to Jeunesse communiste luxembourgeoise (JCL). In addition, it dominates a group of former resistance members (Le Réveil de la résistance), the Luxembourg Committee for European Security and Cooperation, and various societies that cultivate friendly relations with East European countries (Association Luxembourg-URSS, Luxembourg-Tchécoslavaquie, Luxembourg-RDA, etc.)

Members of the Urbany family occupy key positions. René Urbany succeeded his father Dominique as party chairman at the first meeting of the Central Committee after the 22nd Party Congress. He remains director of the party press. The post of party secretary is apparently still vacant. The Réveil de la résistance is directed by François Frisch, brother-in-law of René Urbany and member of the Central Committee. He is also active as secretary of the Luxembourg Committee for European Security and Cooperation. René Urbany's sister, Yvonne Frisch-Urbany, leads the Soviet-sponsored "Cultural Center Pushkin"; his father-in-law, Jacques Hoffmann, is a member of the Central Committee and the Executive Committee. He is also a member of the executive board of the communist printing company Coopérative ouvrière de presse et d'édition (COPE).

The board of directors of COPE includes Grandgenet Joseph (president); René Urbany (administrator-director); François Frisch, Jacques Hoffmann, Théo Bastian, and Camille Muller (administrators); and Dominique Urbany (auditor).

Domestic Attitudes and Activities. During the most recent national conference of the PCL (28 October 1979), Chairman René Urbany presented the position of his party, without, however, deviating from the political standpoint adopted by the party at the end of World War II.

In his address, he stated that the elections of June 1979 saw the coming into power of a rightist government, which by its policy would only contribute to the deterioration of the nation's standard of living, above all because it would not fight unemployment and inflation effectively and would thus jeopardize the system of social security. Urbany criticized the arms race and the rearmament of the country by the (planned) establishment of a supply base for U.S. armed forces in Luxembourg. The government, says the chairman, has not succeeded in guaranteeing an adequate representation of the Grand Duchy in the institutions of the European parliament.

The president also violently attacked the "Americanization" of Europe and stressed that the failure of European communist parties is due mainly to the libelous campaigns of their opponents.

He concluded that despite the party's failure in the elections, the activity of the party has not slowed down.

Analyses and discussions, said Urbany, have shown that PCL policy responds to the demands of modern times and that a modification of the program is not to be considered. The PCL will continue to fight for international détente, for disarmament in the Grand Duchy and the world, for the maintenance of national sovereignty, for the establishment of a socialist system in the Grand Duchy, and for mutual understanding of all communist parties under the leadership of the Communist Party of the Soviet Union (CPSU).

The small leftist groups of Trotskyist and Maoist allegiance sprang up spontaneously and not because of disagreement with the party line, said Urbany. They created minor problems for the party, which at one point saw recruitment of young members endangered. But the party succeeded in stopping this evolution by creating structures better adapted to the mentality of young people. These groups have remained minorities and did not succeed in developing roots in the political life of Luxembourg. The disastrous results of the last elections even discouraged some militants, who later joined the PCL.

International Views and Positions. During the national conference, the question arose of the necessity of fighting external dangers from imperialism and internal dangers from so-called dissidents, who are supposedly only agents of imperialism. Eurocommunism was banned, and the attitude of certain parties favoring this tendency was rejected. These parties (the French, Italian, and Spanish), it was said, have been able to grow and expand because they were helped by the same CPSU whose predominance they now contest.

The policy of the People's Republic of China was violently criticized because China is continuously attacking the USSR and is seeking an alliance with capitalism.

Leaders of the PCL often visit the USSR and other East European countries, where they also spend their holidays. Aeroflot, the Soviet national airline, links Luxembourg with Moscow and Havana. The USSR embassy in Luxembourg is better equipped than would be necessary for diplomatic representation in a small country. There are sixteen legal representatives associated with the USSR embassy. Recently Ambassador E. A. Kossarev left Luxembourg after ten years of service and was replaced by K. B. Oudoumian.

Besides the diplomatic representatives, the East–West–United Bank has three permanent and one temporary Russian employees, Aeroflot has three, and the Cultural Center A. S. Pushkin has a teacher of Russian.

During 1979 a Bulgarian embassy with six representatives (four of them diplomats) was established in Luxembourg. Recently Romania established an embassy in Luxembourg. Yugoslavia has one representative at the Yugoslav embassy, and the People's Republic of China established an embassy with sixteen representatives, six of them diplomats.

Publications. The party organ, *Zeitung vum Lëtzeburger Vollek*, has a daily distribution of between 1,000 and 1,500 copies. The party's publishing company, COPE, publishes this paper, as well as the French edition of the *World Marxist Review*, and also distributes foreign communist publications. The PCL distributes its publications periodically to households and also participates in the political programs of Radio Luxembourg.

At the beginning of 1979, the PCL moved into its new party headquarters, doubtlessly constructed with the financial help of the Soviet Union and East Germany. This new building houses the party's printing company and the offices of the party's publications. The technical equipment and production capacity exceed the needs of the PCL by a great margin. Publications from these installations are supplied to other communist parties and organizations beyond the Grand Duchy.

Luxembourg   Leon Zeches

Malta

The Communist Party of Malta (CPM) is currently estimated to have fewer than one hundred members. It was founded during a clandestine congress in November 1968 at Gwardamangia. Currently legal, it generally supports the ruling Labour Party's nonaligned foreign and leftist domestic policies. The most obvious identity of interest has been the successful effort to remove British armed forces from the island, accomplished 31 March–1 April 1979.

Leadership and Organization. The CPM leaders are Chairman Anthony Baldacchino, a General Workers' Union activist, and Secretary General Anthony Vassallo. Both were re-elected at the party's Second Congress, which was held 16–18 February. Others include international affairs secretary Paul Agius (also secretary general of the communist-front Maltese Peace Committee), education and propaganda secretary Mario Vella (also secretary general of the CPM Progressive Youth League [PYL], re-established in November 1975), and documentation secretary (as well as PYL international secretary) Lillian Sciberras. The remaining members of the eleven-person Central Committee are John Agius, Philip Bugeja, Renald Galea, Mario Mifsud, John Muscat, and Paul Muscat (*Proletarjat*, no. 12, February-March, p. 3). Apparently, no politburo exists.

Domestic Activities. The CPM does not endorse all Labour Party positions uncritically. It seeks to support the latter's left wing, while pushing the ruling movement as a whole into a more radical stance. Communist and noncommunist sources attest CPM leverage vis-à-vis the Labour Party and the General Workers' Union, which the Labour Party dominates, suggesting that this is the CPM's chief political importance. The CPM hopes to run candidates in the 1981 national election.

International Views. The CPM follows the Soviet line and supports "proletarian internationalism," according to Article 89 of the "Draft Communist Party Programme" (ibid., no. 11, January, p. 22). The Second Congress condemned China for antagonism toward the USSR and its allies, for its invasion of Vietnam, and for its cooperation with NATO and "fascist" regimes. It also condemned Egypt for allegedly undermining Arab unity. Relations with the Soviet-line communist parties (those of the USSR, Bulgaria, Czechoslovakia, East Germany, and Poland sent delegates to the Second Congress), however, are balanced by relations with the Eurocommunist parties of Italy (PCI) and France (PCF). Another delegate at the Congress represented the Afro-Asian Peoples' Solidarity Organization. However, messages were received from the communist parties of Vietnam, Brazil, Cuba, Jordan, and the United States and the Party of Labor in Angola and the *World Marxist Review* (ibid., no. 13, April, p. 20).

Italian communists sent a delegate to the Second Congress, and Secretary General Vassallo attended the PCI Congress (20–25 March). At least one outside observer has suggested that the desire of the Maltese government to facilitate relations with Italy is a factor (*Sunday Times*, Valletta, 16 February), in addition to the obvious ones of proximity and party strength. Vassallo's attendance at the PCF

Congress (9–13 May) may well be explained by any or all of these three factors. It should be noted that Maltese Prime Minister Dom Mintoff had asked France and Italy, as well as Algeria and Libya, to guarantee Malta's security at the time of the British withdrawal.

Publications. Edited by CPM Secretary General Vassallo, a mimeographed monthly called *Proletarjat* has been appearing since early 1978. A Maltese edition of *World Marxist Review* started in April 1979 and claims a press run of 1,500 copies.

Hoover Institution   Richard F. Staar

Netherlands

The Communist Party of the Netherlands (Communistische Partij van Nederland; CPN) was founded as the Communist Party of Holland in 1918, but the official founding date is that of affiliation with the Comintern, 10 April 1919. The present name dates from December 1935. The party has always been legal (with the exception of the World War II period).

The CPN's policy was based for more than ten years on the "new orientation" proclaimed at its 1964 congress. It gave primary importance to domestic political goals; relations with international communism were subordinated to the goal of creating a united front in which communists and socialists would play the leading role. After 1975, however, increasing involvement in the international communist movement was noticeable and led to the normalization of relations with the Communist Party of the Soviet Union (CPSU), which in fact meant the end of the new orientation policy.

From 1959 (when the party was split) until 1972, the CPN share in elections steadily increased (from 2.4 to 4.5 percent of the vote). Elections for the Lower House of the parliament in May 1977 brought a considerable loss. Compared with 1972, CPN votes declined from 329,973 to 143,420 (from 2.41 to 1.73 percent). The number of CPN seats in the Lower House dropped from 7 to 2 (out of 150).

Provincial and municipal elections in the spring of 1978 confirmed this decline. The number of CPN seats in provincial governing bodies dropped from 19 to 5 and in municipal governing bodies from 129 to 85.

Despite considerable losses in the elections, CPN membership has increased from 10,000 to 15,000 in the past few years. Its followers are scattered over the country, with centers of activity in the provinces of North-Holland and Groningen. It changed from a typical workers' party into a party of broader social composition, including university intellectuals and members of the service sector of society. The population of the Netherlands has passed 14 million.

Leadership and Organization. The CPN's 26th Congress, on 21 January 1978, elected a new Central Committee of 60 members and abolished honorary membership in the Central Committee.

This decision was directed against Paul de Groot, former CPN chairman, and signified the end of his influence in the party.

On 11 February the Central Committee elected a sixteen-member Executive Committee, the principal policymaking body. It includes Henk Hoekstra (chairman), Rinus Haks (organization secretary), Harry Kleuver (general treasurer), Joop IJisberg (propaganda), Marcus Bakker (chairman of the CPN faction in parliament), and Gijs Schreuders (editor-in-chief of *De Waarheid*). The Secretariat, consisting of three members of the Executive Committee and one general member of the Central Committee, is the organizational and administrative center of the party.

The most active of the CPN front organizations is the General Netherlands Youth Organization (Algemeen Nederlands Jeugd Verbond; ANJV). The Netherlands Women's Movement (Nederlandse Vrouwen Beweging; NVB), like the ANJV, works to support CPN demands.

Party Internal Affairs. The main events since the end of 1978 were the celebration of the CPN's 60th anniversary (November 1978), the Festival of *De Waarheid* (May 1979), and a meeting of the Central Committee (June 1979).

The CPN anniversary celebration shed a clear light on the present principles, attitudes, and policies of the party. The CPN is an orthodox communist party, based on the principles of scientific socialism; it is guided by the principles of the class struggle, the dictatorship of the proletariat (although the term "democratic socialism" is used), and proletarian internationalism; and it shows a marked preference for united front tactics and action from "the masses."

The CPN continued its campaign against the Van Agt–Wiegel government, presenting it as a political renewal against the social, economic, defense, and foreign policies of the government.

Domestic Attitudes and Activities. During 1978 the CPN had concentrated on the struggle against the neutron bomb, nuclear weapons, and the arms race; but the struggle against the social and economic policies of the government was taken up again at the end of 1978 under the slogan "Compass 81 must go." A special committee of broad composition (some 800 members) was set up and presented to the general public. This committee, however, was dominated by a group of CPN members. Moreover, both the chairman and the secretary were CPN members. The committee has been active through various meetings and demonstrations on current and controversial social issues. This activity culminated in a meeting under the name "Great Social Forum" on 29 September, which was meant to demonstrate the broad opposition against Compass 81 and to present a common progressive alternative.

The CPN was deeply involved in strikes in Rotterdam that paralyzed the harbor from late June to late September. Although a socioeconomic conflict, it was regarded by its leaders and organizers as a political confrontation with the capitalist system in the Netherlands. The leaders of these strikes belonged either to the CPN or to the so-called Marxist-Leninist groups. Using the discontent of the dockworkers with wages and the shift system, the CPN and the other groups began their activity in the first half of 1979. Despite differences in tactics (the Marxist-Leninist groups did not shrink from violence in an effort to create "revolutionary situations"), they remained united and formed the Common Action Committee of Rotterdam Dockworkers. Because the CPN did not want to become isolated, it accepted the violent action, which it had sought to avoid because of its mediating role between the strikers and those trade unions that opposed the strikes. The strikes continued much longer than had been foreseen. The strikers suffered financially since they were not paid from union strike funds. The number of nonstrikers increased, as did the amount of violent confrontation between strikers and nonstrikers. Better collective labor agreements, promises of higher wages, and strike pay for the trade unions were achieved, and the Common Action Committee decided to end the strike at the end of September.

The CPN's major focus of activity during 1978 was mobilization of Dutch public opinion against the neutron bomb. Together with activities in the socioeconomic field, the campaign against nuclear weapons and the arms race was continued in 1979. Efforts were made to mobilize trade unions and churches for this purpose. In several towns special meetings and demonstrations focusing on such highly emotional issues as deployment of NATO tactical nuclear weapons in the Netherlands were held.

International Views, Positions, and Party Contacts. The CPN's involvement in the international communist movement continued to increase. On many occasions party leaders stressed their solidarity with other communist parties and with Soviet policy.

The CPN campaign against the neutron bomb was developed in concert with representatives of the Soviet Union, other East European countries, and the World Peace Council. In December 1978 an "international symposium" was held against the neutron bomb and in January 1979 a "cultural manifestation." The symposium was attended by some 300 to 400 participants from East and West and was addressed by prominent international speakers who condemned the neutron bomb as well as NATO. Some 6,000 participants from various countries attended the cultural manifestation, in which some 200 artists indicated their opposition to the neutron bomb.

As the CPN broadened its activity against the neutron bomb into a campaign against nuclear weapons, it became increasingly involved in international communist campaigns against nuclear weapons. During the second half of 1979, it took the initiative for an international campaign: Stop the Neutron Bomb, Stop the Arms of Mass Destruction. The campaign was directed primarily against the production and deployment of NATO tactical nuclear weapons on European soil.

The CPN took part in the elections for the European parliament, but did not win a seat. Henk Hoekstra, chairman of the party, rationalized this result as follows:

> Of course it would have been better if the CPN also had been part of the communist representation within the European parliament. That would have accorded with the true political position that our party occupies nationally as well as with its contributions to the international communist movement and the struggle for peace and against capitalism. It would also have accorded with the diversity of communist parties in Western Europe, a diversity that is coupled with agreement on the main issues. But our connections with the French and Italian communist parties, among others, are good and have been strengthened to such an extent that our views will also come up for discussion in the European parliament through the communist representation. (*De Waarheid.* 4 July.)

To prepare itself for the European elections and to coordinate its efforts with those of other West European communist parties, the CPN met on 6 February with the French party in Paris, on 21 February with an Italian delegation in Amsterdam, and with a Belgian delegation in Amsterdam on 9 May.

Publications. The CPN daily, *De Waarheid* (The Truth), has a circulation of about 20,000. The theoretical bimonthly, *Politiek en Cultuur*, is used for training purposes. The ANJV and NVB publish monthly newspapers. The CPN's Instituut voor Politiek en Sociaal Onderzoek issues a quarterly, *Info*, which draws attention to articles published by other communist parties on current problems of communism. The CPN maintains its own publishing house and bookshop, Pegasus, and operates two commercial printing plants, one for *De Waarheid* and one for other printed matter.

Pro-Soviet Groups. The pro-Soviet groups of the years 1964-1975 may, because of the CPN's change in policy toward the Soviet Union, no longer be regarded as dissident groups. Although they sometimes may appear to be front organizations, they are not because of the independence that they developed during the time of the CPN's strained relations with the CPSU, an independence that they do not wish to surrender. The main group is the Nederland-USSR friendship society, which promotes cultural relations between the Netherlands and the Soviet Union. Its monthly paper is *NU* (Netherlands-USSR). The travel agency Vernu BV organizes tourist visits to the Soviet Union.

In 1973 young members of the Nederland-USSR founded a new organization, Jongeren Kontakt voor Internationale Solidariteit en Uitwisseling (Youth Contact for International Solidarity and Exchange; JKU), which issues the paper *Nieuwsbrief* and operates a travel agency (Kontakt BV). The JKU maintains contact with similar organizations in other West European countries and with the co-ordinating Soviet youth organization. The JKU is a member of the World Federation of Democratic Youth.

Pro-Chinese Groups. The emergence of pro-Chinese groups was the result of the autonomous policy of the CPN in the Sino-Soviet dispute. At one time there were eight of these small groups in the Netherlands, all ostensibly governed by Marxist-Leninist principles. Although they often competed, there was a marked tendency—encouraged by the Communist Party of China—for them to act in a more unified fashion. In May 1978 three of these organizations decided to discontinue independent operations and to establish a new organization, the Communist Workers' Organization–Marxist-Leninist.

The new organization tried to include in its coordinating efforts another pro-Chinese group, the Netherlands Communist Unity Movement–Marxist-Leninist. This group consists primarily of students and publishes the paper *Rode Tribune*. The result was combined action in several fields. However, efforts to intensify this cooperation and to absorb other pro-Chinese groups were frustrated by the Chinese policy of cooperating with the Western world against the Soviet Union. This caused confusion in the ranks of the pro-Chinese groups and led to a less pro-Chinese attitude among their followers.

International Documentation and Information Centre　　　　　C. C. van den Heuvel
The Hague

Norway

The Norwegian Communist Party (Norges Kommunistiske Parti; NKP) has remained small and quite isolated since its 1975 decision not to merge with several left-socialist parties and factions. This decision split the party and caused its then chairman, Reidar T. Larsen, and several other leaders to leave the NKP for the new Socialist Left Party (Sosialistisk Venstreparti; SV). The NKP is now the weakest of three Marxist parties to the left of the powerful and ruling Norwegian Labor Party (Det Norske Arbeiderparti;DNA), which is a reformist social-democratic movement. In addition to the SV and the NKP, current Marxist activity in Norway includes the Maoist (and consistently pro-Chinese) Workers' Communist Party (Arbeidernes Kommunistiske Parti; AKP), which has run in the last two parliamentary elections as the Red Electoral Alliance (Rød Valgallianse; RV).

The NKP was organized on 4 November 1923 by a few radical politicians and trade unionists who split from the DNA after the latter ended its brief membership in the Third International. The NKP first demonstrated electoral strength in 1945, when it won 11 of the 150 Storting (parliament) seats, thanks to communist participation during World War II in the Norwegian resistance movement and the Soviet liberation of northern Norway. The Cold War quickly eroded NKP strength, and by 1957 the communists held only a single seat in parliament. In 1961 dissident Laborites started the Socialist People's Party (Sosialistisk Folkeparti; SF), and the NKP lost its last mandate. Not until the formation of the Socialist Electoral Alliance (Sosialistisk Valgforbund—a forerunner of the SV) in 1973 by the SF, the NKP, and dissident left Laborites did communists once again sit in the Storting. Standing alone in the 1977 elections, the postschism NKP received only 0.4 percent of the votes, far short of winning a parliamentary mandate and even down from the party's 1.0 percent showing in 1969. The September 1979 county (*fylke*) and municipal elections confirmed the NKP's electoral weakness. The NKP polled 10,117 votes (0.5 percent) in the county council and 7,397 votes (0.4 percent) in the municipal council elections (*Nordisk Kontakt*, no. 12). No national party did as poorly.

Although exact membership figures for the NKP are not available, there are surely considerably fewer than the 2,000 to 5,000 members estimated before the 1975 schism. The population of Norway is just over 4 million.

Although the SV was initially an electoral alliance of the left under a common platform, the 1975 decision to merge the three factions has not created a stronger left-socialist bloc. Despite the spectacular initial showing in the 1973 parliamentary elections (11.2 percent of the vote, 16 out of 155 seats), the merged party did poorly in the 1975 municipal and county elections, and in the 1977 parliamentary elections the SV drew only 4.2 percent of the vote and won but 2 seats. In the 1979 local elections, the SV averaged about the same as two years earlier but declined relative to the 1975 local elections (ibid.). Norwegian local elections are considered indicators of national political trends despite the obvious influence of local political factors.

The third Marxist party, the AKP, ran in the 1979 local elections under its usual RV banner and drew 16,917 votes (0.8 percent) in the county and 14,035 votes (0.7 percent) in the municipal elections. This was a marginal improvement over 1977 and 1975, and the RV outpaced the NKP.

The surprising strength of the Norwegian left in general and the SV in particular in 1973 resulted from the emotional national campaign against Norwegian membership in the expanded European Economic Community (EEC). Supported by both socialist and nonsocialist political groups, the National Movement Against the EEC was victorious in the September 1972 EEC referendum. Parliamentary elections a year later showed severe losses for those parties (especially the DNA) that had supported EEC membership. By 1975 the issue had faded, however, and surveys showed that the SV was losing strength because of opposition to its anti-NATO line and the internal turmoil connected with the merger efforts. The 1977 parliamentary elections and the 1979 local elections have reduced the Norwegian leftist parties to their pre-EEC fringe position. Nevertheless, the governing DNA is dependent upon the two SV parliamentary votes for a majority in any socialist/nonsocialist confrontation. The government's economic austerity program announced in fall 1978 received the general backing of several nonsocialist parties, but SV support helped the government make several modifications favorable to organized labor (ibid., no. 14, 1978). The rightward drift in Norwegian politics continued in 1979, as evidenced by the local elections and the government's austere policy agenda. The Marxist left ends the decade not only divided into three competing factions, but electorally weak—dividing about 5 percent of the vote among themselves (see Henry Valen, "The Storting Elections of 1977: Realignment or Return to Normalcy?" *Scandinavian Political Studies*, new series, 1, no. 2/3, pp. 83–107). The SV's traditional tactic of pressuring the DNA is likely to be less effective given the continuing strength of the Conservative and other nonsocialist parties.

Leadership and Organization. Personalities are important in a small democracy, and there has been considerable continuity among the three left-socialist parties. Current NKP Chairman Martin Gunnar Knutsen emerged as leader of the rump-NKP after the party's divisive Fifteenth Congress (November 1975), which voted 117 to 30 against merger with the SV. Knutsen was unanimously re-elected chairman at the NKP's harmonious Sixteenth Congress in April 1978, as were Rolf Nettum, organizational vice-chairman; Hans Kleven, political vice-chairman; and Arne Jørgensen, editor of the party's twice-weekly *Friheten* (*Friheten*, 18 April 1978). There were no leadership changes at the party's annual conference in June (*Pravda*, 10 June). The Norwegian Communist Youth League (Kommunistisk Ungdom; KU) is the party's most important affiliate.

The SV can be regarded as a descendant of the SF party that emerged among anti-NATO Laborites in the early 1960s. In a radio interview, SV Chairman and Tromsø University historian Berge Furre was asked whether the SV was not merely the SF all over again. Furre stressed the broader scope of the SV, the merger of several leftist groups in 1975, and the party's commitment to far-reaching social and economic reforms. At the SV's annual convention in March, Furre was re-elected party chairman, while Hilde Bojer, Rune Slagstad, and Torbjørn Dal were elected vice-chairmen, Liss Schanke became party secretary, and Steinar Hansson succeeded to the editorship of the party's newspaper, *Ny Tid* (*Nordisk Kontakt*, no. 5). Furre along with Finn Gustavsen, who had founded the SF in 1961, have been prominent throughout the SV's short history, but Gustavsen retired from active politics in 1977. Both Furre and Gustavsen faced possible Court of Impeachment (Riksrett) proceedings following their disclosure of secret defense information during the 1977 election campaign, but a special parliamentary commission recommended in early 1979 that charges against the two men be dropped (ibid., no. 3).

Less is known about the organization of the AKP, which made marginal gains in the 1979 local elections. An amalgam of various Maoist groups that arose in the late 1960s, mainly as splinter groups from the SF and NKP youth organizations, the AKP was formally organized in late 1972. Paal Steigan remains the party's only chairman. Ideologically, politically, and presumably organizationally and financially, the AKP maintains very close ties to the Chinese Communist Party. Moreover, the AKP has been active in a variety of front organizations, including the party's continuing control of the venerable Norwegian Students' Association (Det Norske Studentersamfunnet). This control continued in 1979, but the association contains only some 1,400 of the roughly 20,000 students at Oslo University (*Aftenposten*, 14 May). Despite the changes in Chinese foreign and domestic policies, the AKP has had no difficulty in continuing its support for Beijing.

Domestic Attitudes and Activities. The past year has seen the fruits of the Labor government's austerity program ripen. Although domestic growth was modest and unemployment climbed slightly (to only 1.2 percent), Norwegian public and international finances improved considerably, and the rate of inflation dropped. The large increases in petroleum prices during 1979, although not of Norway's making, greatly eased the financial problems of the country. Nevertheless, the Labor government's price and wage controls gave the country a sharp cure for its deteriorating international economic balance. Both the SV and the NKP were sharply critical of the wage control aspects of the government's program (*Nordisk Kontakt*, no. 15, 1978). Another symbol of the country's economic difficulties was the bankruptcy of the Tandberg Radio Company, Norway's prestigious consumer electronics firm. The NKP and the SV saw this as another indication of the government's economic mistakes, but both parties were concerned about the hundreds of jobs at stake. Finally, although Norway's petroleum wealth has continued to insulate the country from harsher economic measures, the SV remains critical of the government's decision to start oil prospecting in coastal waters north of 62° latitude (ibid., no. 2).

The NKP's platform, adopted in its current form in 1973 before the party schism, was reiterated at the party's Sixteenth Congress in 1978 and in statements during 1979. Chairman Knutsen stressed that Norway's class struggle could not be waged according to a pattern imported from the Soviet Union or from other socialist countries. Nor could it be waged according to an Italian, French, or Portuguese formula. Even the other Scandinavian countries could not provide a model for political action. At the 1978 congress, NKP leaders defended the 1975 decision not to merge with the SV (*Arbeiderbladet*, 15 April 1978). The NKP remained committed to its 24-point election manifesto issued before the September 1977 Storting elections. The manifesto stressed traditional NKP views: heavier taxes on higher incomes; replacement of the 20-percent value-added tax (on all items) with luxury taxes; improved working conditions through shorter working hours; greater worker participation in enterprise management; better employment security; and specific promises for special groups—more day-care centers, higher minimum old-age pensions, etc. The other Marxist parties also advocated these proposals. Indeed, many are acceptable to the DNA and some nonsocialist parties. Hence, the problem of the NKP in cutting a distinctive profile continues (*Friheten*, 7 October).

These general goals were made somewhat more specific at the NKP's annual conference in June. The 80 delegates at the meeting adopted the theme "Unity and solidarity against right-wing forces—for a new political course." Specifically the party called for increased national economic planning with attention to price controls and regulation of foreign trade. Protection for Norwegian jobs was stressed. The public sector at all levels must take primary responsibility for avoiding and reducing unemployment. Chairman Knutsen stressed the technical electoral alliance with the SV and other socialist lists in the upcoming local elections (*Aftenposten*, 11 June).

The SV's electoral disappointment in 1977, although long predicted by public opinion polls, was seen by the party as stemming from the adverse publicity that the party drew in revealing the location and purpose of certain NATO installations in Norway (particularly Loran-C transmitters, formerly used exclusively by American nuclear submarines but now shared with other maritime services). As noted above, the issue was sufficiently sensitive, especially for the DNA, for the parliamentary commission to recommend dropping the matter in early 1979. During 1979, the SV's domestic line focused on DNA mismanagement of the Norwegian economy and the burdens faced by wage earners under the government's austerity program. Nevertheless, the SV's small parliamentary group supported the government when opposition parties called for sterner income measures.

Although the Maoist AKP has little interest in electoral campaigns except as a forum for propaganda, the party was active in the 1979 local elections and made small gains. As noted above, the AKP has dominated the Oslo Student Association for several years and has gained some important positions in trade union locals, although the larger unions, as well as the Norwegian Trade Union Confederation (Landsorganisasjonen; LO), are firmly controlled by Laborites. Given the continuing importance of special interest and issue organizations in Norwegian politics, the strength and influence of the AKP may be greater than the RV's meager electoral results indicate.

Norwegian communists have traditionally been stronger in the trade union movement than in electoral politics, but neither they nor the other small left-socialist groups have been able to challenge the DNA-LO link. This could change if the government's income policy continues to provoke discontent within the unions. Neither the communists nor the SV are represented in the LO national executive or control any national labor union. At the local level, the NKP is visible in the construction workers' union and to a lesser extent in the metal, wood, and electrochemical fields.

International Views and Positions. The 1975 split in the NKP has not significantly changed the party's views on international issues. This was confirmed in the party manifesto issued at the conclusion of the party's Sixteenth Congress in 1978. The Final Act of the 1975 Conference on Security and Cooperation in Europe (Helsinki accords) was stressed as a prelude to an attack on NATO and

Norway's role in the Western alliance. The United States, NATO, and particularly West Germany were seen as forcing Norway to increase its military activity. The stationing of heavy NATO military equipment in Norway and the participation of West German troops in NATO maneuvers held in Norway were denounced. The neutron bomb and its possible deployment in Europe were attacked as were proposals in 1979 for modernization of NATO's nuclear forces. Various Norwegian-Soviet disagreements, such as the demarcation of territorial limits in the Barents Sea and Soviet violations of Norwegian territorial waters and airspace, were downplayed. The NKP advocated compromise and cooperation. Parallel force reductions and eventual dissolution of NATO and the Warsaw Pact were supported. Outside Europe, the NKP reiterated its support of "national and social liberation movements." Reaffirming its adherence to Soviet international policies, the NKP denounced anti-Soviet propaganda and policies (*WMR*, no. 3).

The manifesto and statements are additional evidence that following the 1975 schism, the NKP has lost its "nonaligned" orientation and has become more strongly supportive of Soviet foreign policy views. As the independent socialist periodical *Kontrast* pointed out in 1978, NKP Vice-Chairman Hans Kleven, writing in his book *Vår Strategi* (Our Strategy), praised the constructive role of Soviet troops in Eastern Europe.

The SV has continued to make its anti-NATO, antimilitary, and anti-EEC position a central plank of its party platform. Public and parliamentary statements devote far more attention to cataloging the evils of American monopoly capitalism and the Central Intelligence Agency than to regretting Soviet civil rights violations or threats toward Norway. In 1979 the SV vehemently attacked the proposed modernization of NATO missiles in Europe while downplaying growing Norwegian-Soviet tensions in the north. In 1977 the SV electoral manifesto called for Norwegian disarmament, and at the 1979 party conference a majority of SV members called for an alternative Norwegian defense based on nonviolence and guerrilla tactics (*Nordisk Kontakt*, no. 5). Commenting at the close of the SV conference, party Chairman Furre stressed the SV's antimilitary stance and noted that as long as Norway belonged to NATO, its defense policy merely reflected American interests (Radio Norway, 5 March).

On civil rights issues, the NKP has taken a low profile. Party officials have refused to regard the trial and imprisonment of dissidents in the Soviet Union as contrary to the Helsinki principles. When asked about the relevance of Soviet policies to a future communist Norway, NKP Chairman Knutsen noted that in accordance with Norwegian traditions, rights of free association and political action would remain as long as opposition parties did not resort to "illegalities" (*Nå* [Now], 4 November 1978).

The AKP remained the exception to the general line of the Norwegian socialist left. Reflecting its ties to China, the AKP denounced the military programs of both the United States and the Soviet Union. Continued attention was directed to Soviet-Norwegian disputes. In addition, the AKP denounced Vietnam's invasion of Kampuchea (Cambodia) and supported the Chinese retaliation against Vietnam in 1979. Despite the changes in Chinese positions since Mao's death in 1976, the AKP has remained loyal.

International Party Contacts. The international position of the NKP is reflected by its close ties to the communist parties of Eastern Europe and the Soviet Union. The NKP's chairman returned from a visit to the Soviet Union in October 1978 with a new Russian wife (ibid.). In April he returned to the Kremlin to receive the Order of People's Friendship from the Communist Party of the Soviet Union (CPSU) (Tass, 12 April). In addition NKP Vice-Chairman Nettum led a delegation to Russia in December 1978 at the invitation of the CPSU Central Committee. These visits concluded with expressions of Norwegian admiration for the USSR (*Pravda*, 13 December 1978). Another NKP delegation visited the Soviet Union in June (ibid., 27 June), while a Soviet delegation visited the NKP in Norway in August (Tass, 18 August).

Representatives of nine foreign communist parties attended the NKP's Sixteenth Congress in April 1978. The low-level Soviet delegation and the relatively small number of international representatives reflects the NKP's limited importance (*Arbeiderbladet*, 15 April 1978).

Official NKP statements on the topic of Eurocommunism have usually been ambivalent. While stressing that different national circumstances dictate varying tactics, the NKP has been critical of the moderate line on specific issues followed by French and especially Italian communists. The dangers of "revisionism" are frequently cited and the importance of "proletarian internationalism" reiterated (*WMR*, no. 11, 1978). Although foreign communist parties are not directly criticized, the example of the Soviet experience is underlined (ibid.)

The SV belongs to no formal network of international contacts but maintains close informal ties with the Socialist People's Party in Denmark, the Left Party—Communists in Sweden, and the People's Alliance in Iceland. On several occasions, the SV has expressed its enthusiasm for Eurocommunism, especially as practiced by the Italian Communist Party.

The AKP looks mainly toward China for international support and inspiration. Chairman Steigan visited Kampuchea shortly before the Vietnamese-led invasion and expressed support for the Pol Pot regime (*Peking Review*, 1 December 1978). In addition, the AKP declared its support for the Albanian and North Korean parties during 1979.

Publications. The main NKP organ is *Friheten* (Freedom), first published as an underground paper during World War II. Dwindling circulation caused its transition from daily to weekly publication in 1967. Fund raising to keep the paper going is a continuous NKP preoccupation and remained so in the party's September 1979 collection drive. During the fall of 1977, *Friheten* increased publication to twice a week. In line with Norwegian policy, the NKP Press Office received 25,000 Norwegian kroner (about U.S. $5,000) in public support in 1978 (*Nordisk Kontakt*, no. 15, 1978). The KU publishes the youth bulletin *Fremad* (Forward). The SV newspaper is *Ny Tid* (New Times), which was intended to absorb the readership of the SF publication *Orientering*. The latter was respected in the 1950s and 1960s by many readers outside SF party circles. In addition to continuous financial and editorial difficulties, the SV weekly was involved in the "espionage" scandal of the 1977 electoral campaign. Nevertheless, given the small size of the SV parliamentary delegation, *Ny Tid* is an important SV mouthpiece. Finally, there is the AKP weekly *Klassekampen* (Class Struggle), which enjoys a small public subvention, and the party's theoretical journal *Rød Fane* (Red Flag).

University of Massachusetts   Eric S. Einhorn
Amherst

Portugal

The left-wing spectrum in Portugal is shaded with many hues, mostly to the far left of the dominant Portuguese Communist Party (Partido Comunista Português; PCP). The latter is the largest, best organized, and most influential of the groups, although it does not retain the impact that it had during the first two years following the 1974 revolution. Elections in December increased the communists' popular vote to nearly 20 percent, but the center-right coalition won majority control in parliament. The PCP claims a membership of 164,000, a growth of 43 percent since 1977 (*Pravda*, 2 June). This makes the PCP the fourth largest communist party in Western Europe but the second largest relative to the size of the population—an estimated 9.9 million in Portugal. Some 5 percent of the PCP members are said to be workers and salaried employees (*FBIS*, 4 June).

The communists effectively control the General Confederation of Portuguese Workers (Confederação Geral de Trabalhadores Portugueses–Intersindical Nacional; CGTP-IN). The latter claims the loyalty of 1.7 million workers in 277 unions out of 2 million workers in a total of 348 unions (*WMR*, April; *Pravda*, 2 June). The communists also dominate the farm worker collectives in the southern wheat belt, although the number of such collectives is gradually being reduced. The PCP asserts that 517 of the 550 collectives organized since 1974 are still in operation on almost 1 million hectares of land (*Pravda*, 2 June).

A potential challenge to the PCP's appeal to the militant left appears to come from the United Workers' Organization (Organização Unida de Trabalhadores), organized in 1978 under the leadership of Maj. Otelo Saraiva de Carvalho. Second-place candidate for president in 1976 and one of the officers implicated in the attempted left-wing putsch of November 1975, the radical-leftist Carvalho is expected to run for president again in the 1981 elections.

Other far-left parties, mostly relatively inactive Maoist and Trotskyist organizations, include the Communist Party of Portugal, Marxist-Leninist (Partido Comunista do Portugal, Marxista-Leninista; PCP-ML), the Portuguese Communist Party, Reconstituted (Partido Comunista Português, Reconstituido;PCP-R), the League for Revolutionary Unity and Action (Liga para a Unidade e Ação Revolucionária), the Communist Party of Portuguese Workers (Partido Comunista de Trabalhadores Portugueses), the Party of the Democratic and Social Center (Partido do Centro Democrático y Social), the Popular Socialist Front (Frente Socialista Popular), the Movement of the Socialist Left (Movimento da Esquerda Socialista), the Portuguese Democratic Movement/Democratic Electoral Commission (Movimento Democrático Português/Comissão Democrática Eleitoral), and the Revolutionary Socialist Party (Partido Socialista Revolucionário). The last is a Trotskyite group organized in 1978 as "a specific alternative to today's social democracy, Eurocommunism, and Maoism." It claims to support unity of the trade union movement within the CGTP-IN. (*Diário de Notícias*, Lisbon, 30 October 1978.)

Leadership and Organization. The Ninth Congress of the PCP met in Lisbon 1–3 June to rededicate the PCP to the defense of the country's "revolutionary gains" and to renovate and rejuvenate the party's central leadership. The latter aim was achieved by enlarging the Central Committee membership from 52 to 72 while retaining all the previously elected members. The number of alternates was increased from 36 to 56. The charismatic Álvaro Cunhal was reconfirmed as secretary general. The Political Committee, as the politburo is known in Portugal, is composed of Álvaro Cunhal, Antonio Dias Lourenço, António Gervásio, Carlos Brito, Carlos Costa, Diniz Miranda, Domingos Abrantes, Blanqui Teixeira, Jaime Serra, Joaquim Gomes, José Vitoriano, Octávio Pato, and Sérgio Vilarigues. Alternate members of the committee are Ângelo Veloso, José Casanova, and Raimundo Cabral. The Secretariat is composed of Álvaro Cunhal, Carlos Costa, Blanqui Teixeira, Joaquim Gomes, Jorge Araújo, Octávio Pato, and Sérgio Vilarigues, with Jaime Félix as alternate member. (*FBIS*, 4 June; *Avante*, 7 June.) Cunhal claimed that the number of primary party cells had increased from 7,000 to 9,000 since the Eighth Congress of 1977 (Tass, 1 June). These units operate in business and educational organizations, on rural estates, and in the armed forces and are organized under eight broad provincial divisions.

The congress reiterated the party's loyalty to the principles of Marxism-Leninism and proletarian internationalism, thereby supporting Cunhal's long-standing position as Europe's staunchest defender of Soviet leadership of the international communist movement. Special guests who addressed the congress at its conclusion were members of the communist parties of the Soviet Union and Vietnam and the national liberation movements of Mozambique and Angola. (Ibid., 4 June.)

On the recommendation of the congress, the 22,900-member Union of Communist Youth merged in November with the 8,600-member Union of Communist Students (*Expresso*, Lisbon, 7 July).

Domestic Attitudes and Activities. With a vote of censure in June, PCP and Socialist deputies precipitated the collapse of the government of Carlos da Mota Pinto, Portugal's tenth since the 1974 revolution. The vote was provoked by the two parties' bitter opposition to the technocratic, nonpolitical cabinet, which they accused of moving steadily to the right. Mota Pinto, an outspoken anticommunist, had been named in November 1978 by President António Ramalho Eanes. The appointment was seen at the time as a temporary solution to the parliamentary stalemate that had prevented previous Socialist attempts at governing. (*CSM*, 8 June.) The PCP denounced Mota Pinto in particular for his forceful, "unconstitutional" policy of "restoring capitalism" and of returning to owners much of the land seized illegally during the first tumultuous years of the revolution (*NYT*, 21 January).

President Eanes dissolved parliament and called for new elections in December as the only democratic solution to the political crisis, even though general elections must according to law be held again in 1980. The Socialists, thwarted in their attempt to organize a coalition government with dissident Social Democrats, charged that the president was yielding to the pressure of a "right-wing minority" that hoped through the elections to end the left-wing parliamentary majority of the Socialists and the PCP. (Ibid., 14 July; *CSM*, 12 September.)

Eanes assuaged his Socialist critics by naming as caretaker prime minister a "moderate leftist Catholic," Maria Lourdes Pintassilgo, who promised to oversee elections impartially (*NYT*, 20 and 29 July). Dubious right-wing politicians charged that her left-wing bias would give their Socialist and PCP rivals an edge at the polls (ibid., 22 July). In spite of this, the right-of-center Social Democrats, Center Democrats, and People's Monarchist Party forged a Democratic Alliance (Aliança Democratica; AD), which they expected to win an "overwhelming majority." Cunhal, who had been urging either a Socialist-PCP coalition or early elections "to prevent a return to right-wing dictatorship," expected the Socialists would continue to be the biggest party. (Ibid., 17 January and 29 July; *Visión*, New York, 25 August.)

The December elections did indeed reconfirm the Socialists as the largest single party, but they were deflated by heavy losses to the PCP and to the AD. A system of proportional representation gave the AD a three-seat absolute majority even though the coalition gained only 45 percent of the popular vote, compared with 51 percent for eight leftist parties (including 27 percent for the Socialists and 20 percent for the PCP). The AD won 128 seats, the Socialists 73 (a loss of 34), and the PCE 47 (a gain of 7). Fortified by PCP gains in every electoral district in the country, Cunhal warned the triumphant Francisco Sá Carneiro, soon named to head the cabinet, against tampering with revolutionary gains. The new prime minister was committed to retrenchment from the socialist policies of previous governments. (*Los Angeles Times*, 4 December; *CSM*, 5 and 13 December.)

Before the elections, interim Prime Minister Pintassilgo presented a moderate program that sidestepped such controversial issues as the implementation of the controversial agrarian reform law. Mota Pinto's implementation of the reforms had provoked some violent clashes between riot police and peasants, although armed resistance by militants reportedly declined. Some 70,000 farm workers in southern Portugal responded to a call by Cunhal in January for a one-day protest strike, and according to the PCP, there were sympathy stoppages in "hundreds" of industrial enterprises. The rural militants were characterized by Mota Pinto as "civil guerrillas," but the PCP leader said his was a "responsible party" that advised against terrorism or any use of arms. (*NYT*, 25 January and 26 February; *CSM*, 15 August; *Economist*, 13 January; *WMR*, April.) The chief means of defending revolutionary gains, he said, was through mass rallies. There were 59 such demonstrations in the first three months of 1979, involving "hundreds of thousands of people." Cunhal asserted that strikes in 1978 had involved 1.8 million people. (*Pravda*, 2 June.)

The PCP voiced alarm over the growing consensus among the major parties, including the Socialists, in favor of revising the constitutional provision for a "transition toward socialism." Such a move was seen by the party as equivalent to a coup d'etat since such matters "are not subject to amendment"; this would lead to a "reactionary or even fascist dictatorship." More specifically, the PCP feared that "every democrat and patriot" (i.e., communist) would be dislodged from his strategic position in the nationalized banks and industries and in the heavily collectivized Alentejo farm belt. (*NYT*, 2 January; *Manchester Guardian*, 4 February; *WMR*, April.)

It was expected that following the 1980 parliamentary elections, a general constitutional reform would be undertaken. President Eanes had urged a revision that would remove the military from its role as an arbiter in the political life of the nation. The PCP continued to refrain from direct attacks on the president but opposed any further weakening of the military's participation in politics. Communists combined with Socialists in May to pass a bill that would grant a general amnesty to all military elements involved during the previous five years in attempted coups. However, much indignation was aroused in the military by this measure, which the president promptly vetoed. He sought thereby to avoid "aggravating tensions" in the armed forces and "to keep them in the barracks." (*CSM*, 31 May.)

International Activities and Party Contacts. The PCP's statements continually reaffirmed the party's rigidly loyal support for Soviet leadership of the international communist movement. Party delegations visiting Moscow and Budapest early in the year joined their hosts in "resolutely" condemning Chinese armed aggression against Vietnam (Tass International Service, Moscow, 29 December 1979; *FBIS*, 2 and 16 January; *Népszabadság*, Budapest, 4 March). The emergence of a "democratic Kampuchea" (Cambodia) following the Vietnamese invasion was hailed by *Avante* as "a failure of Maoism . . . and of the expansionist policy of Beijing's leaders" (Vietnam News Agency, Hanoi, 31 January).

Despite close PCP affiliation with the Soviets, a more conciliatory attitude toward Eurocommunism was displayed. Some significance was seen in the October visit to Lisbon at the invitation of the PCP of Italian Communist Party leader Enrico Berlinguer. The Eurocommunist exponent had been openly critical of the PCP's "antidemocratic" behavior in the left-wing coup attempt of 1975. Observers saw in the visit an effort to lend a more moderate hue to Cunhal's public image in preparation for the upcoming parliamentary elections. Berlinguer, stressing that he wished merely to strengthen ties with the PCP, disclaimed any intention of meddling in the Portuguese elections. (*FBIS*, 3 and 4 October.)

Portuguese communists denounced the failure of the Mota Pinto government to pursue effective reconciliation with the country's former African colonies. Negotiations over Portuguese assets and banking operations in Mozambique could not get under way, according to *Avante* (12 April), because of Portuguese officials' "arrogant" insistence on preconditions that would restrict Mozambique's sovereignty. A PCP delegation visited Luanda in April to strength ties of friendship and cooperation between the Portuguese and Angolan people (Luanda Domestic Radio, 17 April).

In honor of the twentieth anniversary of Fidel Castro's triumph over Batista, the PCP hailed the Cuban Communist Party as "a beloved internationalist bastion of the progressive forces . . . fighting against fascism." Revolutionary Cuba was called the "first free territory in America." (*Avante*, 4 January.) At a Lisbon rally called to express solidarity "with the people of Chile," Cunhal alerted his listeners to the "sinister shadow of the Pinochet-type coup overhanging Portugal," with domestic "fascists and reactionaries" trying to employ the same methods as in Chile (*IB*, no. 9).

Cunhal consulted with communist party officials in Moscow in late 1978 and again in August and with Hungarian officials in March and August. Other PCP delegations also went on "fact-finding" missions to Romania, Bulgaria, Poland, East Germany, and the Soviet Union in June and July. The aim of the Moscow visit was to study Soviet experience in guiding municipal government as an inspiration for Portuguese communist activity (Tass, 19 June). A group of PCP officials also attended the 22nd Congress of the Communist Party, U.S.A. in August. Members of the Communist Party of Venezuela paid a visit to the PCP in Lisbon in July.

Publications. The PCP publishes the weekly *Avante* and *O Militante*, the theoretical bulletin of the Central Committee. A semiofficial PCP daily newspaper is the *Diário de Notícias*.

Rival Far-Left Organizations. A large cache of arms and munitions was uncovered by police near Lisbon in January. Arrested were various unidentified individuals with reputed ties to the "Red Brigades" and the Basque terrorist group, Euzkadi ta Askatasuna. Their plans were said to include the abduction or killing of prominent Portuguese politicians. (*Excelsior*, Mexico City, 7 January.)

The Soviet-Vietnamese treaty of friendship and cooperation, signed in November 1978, and the subsequent Vietnamese invasion of Kampuchea were vigorously denounced by the PCP-ML. In its three publications, *Unidade Popular, O Comunista,* and *Em Luta*, the PCP-ML condemned Vietnam as the "Cuba of Asia"—a "faithful lackey of Russian social-imperialism." It said that the aggressors must be compelled to renounce expansionism and to cease genocide. (New China News Agency, Beijing, 16 and 24 November 1978, 9 January, and 17 July.)

The PCP-R continued its special and cordial relationship with the dissident Albanian Party of Labor, which a PCP-R delegation visited in March. The Albanian party sent a greeting of solidarity to the Third Congress of the PCP-R in June, hailing their common struggle against U.S. imperialism and Soviet and Chinese social-imperialism (Tirana Domestic Radio, 17 March and 16 June).

Elbert Covell College   H. Leslie Robinson
University of the Pacific

Spain

The dominant and most moderate party to the left of the Socialists in Spain is the Communist Party of Spain (Partido Comunista de España; PCE). Throughout most of its history since its founding in 1920, the PCE acted as a hard-line Marxist-Leninist group. In more recent years, especially following its legalization in April 1977, the party quickly evolved into the foremost exponent of Eurocommunism. This movement of European communists professes independence from Moscow and absolute respect for parliamentary democracy. The PCE now officially labels itself "Marxist, revolutionary, and democratic" (see *YICA*, 1979, p. 200). It claims a membership of over 200,000 out of a total population of 37.6 million. The party controls the Workers' Commissions (Comisiones Obreras; "CC OO"), the largest confederation of trade unions in Spain, and has been influential, in cooperation with Socialists, in the chief municipal governments of the country since it drew 13 percent of the vote in the April elections. The 23 communist deputies in the Cortes bask in the glow of the secretary general's charisma.

The most active terrorist organizations of the radical left in Spain are two guerrilla factions of the Basque separatist movement called the Basque Homeland and Liberty (Euzkadi ta Askatusuna; ETA) and the Maoist October First Antifascist Resistance Group (Grupo de Resistencia Antifascista Primero de Octubre; GRAPO). Tightly organized and well armed, the military branch of the ETA (ETA-Militar) has waged guerrilla warfare since 1959 and has intensified its killings since the death of Franco in 1975. The political-military branch (ETA-Político-Militar) has generally eschewed terrorist acts causing deaths. Both factions are Marxist spin-offs from the "bourgeois" Basque Nationalist Party (PNV), which is said to have the support of most Basques.

The remaining radical-left parties in Spain are mainly Maoist, Trotskyist, Marxist-Leninist, and anarchist. The Spanish Workers' Revolutionary Organization (Organización Revolucionaria de los Trabajadores Españoles) merged in July with the Spanish Communist Workers' Party (Partido Comunista de Obreros Españoles). The latter is headed by Enrique Líster, who was expelled from the PCE in 1970. The Communist Organization of Spain, Red Flag (Organización Comunista de España, Bandera Roja) is said to have suffered heavy losses in membership in its Central Committee in June. A new Marxist group, the Feminist Party (Partido Feminista) was formed in June to assert itself in "active solidarity with all female, proletarian, and oppressed peoples of the world . . . fighting against imperialism and for the world feminist revolution" (Madrid Domestic Radio, 2 June).

Organization and Leadership. Basic policy guidelines for the PCE are set at occasional congresses, which also elect the 160-member Central Committee, the 45-member Executive Committee, and the 7-member Secretariat. As secretary general since 1960, 64-year-old Santiago Carrillo continues to govern the party "with discipline." He also holds a seat in the national Cortes as a deputy. Party Chairman Dolores Ibarruri did not run in March for re-election to her parliamentary seat. Pressure from fellow communists in her native Asturias that she retire because of her health and age had been squelched and some complainers expelled from the party. A former editor of *Mundo Obrero* wrote in another publication that this exposed "the survival of a political practice that still makes use of Stalinist methods." (*Opinión*, Madrid, 8–14 December 1978.)

The PCE published its parliamentary campaign expenditures and sources of financing in early March, calling on all other political parties to do the same. Reported were revenues of 137 million pesetas, secured from election-aid bonds and bank loans, and expenditures of 110 million pesetas. (*Mundo Obrero*, 3 March.) The previous month, *El País* had alleged that the Communist Party of the Soviet Union was assisting the PCE financially. *Mundo Obrero* wrote that it was no accident that the authors chose the period of pre-election campaigns to spread this "fabrication." (*Pravda*, 17 February.)

Domestic Attitudes and Activities. Parliamentary and municipal elections in early 1979 marked the end of the "consensus" policy of cooperation between the PCE and the government. Santiago Carrillo nevertheless continued to call for a government of national unity, i.e., of government cooperation with all political parties of the left. (Madrid Domestic Radio, 2 March; *WP*, 3 March; *L Unità*, 28 May.)

In the March elections, Adolfo Suárez's Union of the Democratic Center (Unión del Centro Democrático; UCD) retained its plurality in the important lower house of the Cortes, gaining 3 seats. Its representation of 168 was 8 short of a majority, but it expected the support of a few small parties. Socialist, communist, and several leftist regional deputies then unsuccessfully opposed—149 to 183—the reconfirmation of Suárez as prime minister. The PCE also won 3 additional seats—for a total of 23—in the new Chamber of Deputies, while the Spanish Socialist Workers' Party (Partido Socialista Obrero Español; PSOE) lost 3, for a total of 121. Several left-wing regional parties, including five new ones, won a total representation of 28 deputies, compared with 25 previously. Carrillo, who had opposed holding elections at that time, was convinced that PCE's showing would have been spectacular twelve to eighteen months later since the party was continually improving its public image. Especially detrimental to the left, he said, had been the intervention of Spanish bishops, who had urged Catholics to oppose candidates favoring materialistic ideologies, totalitarian models, abortion, divorce, and lay education. (*Mundo Obrero*, 25 February; *CSM*, 20 February and 2 April; *Keesing's Contemporary Archives*, 15 June.)

The PCE's more pronounced opposition to Suárez related to the increasingly rightward shift of the latter's policies and to his decision to govern alone. Alarmed at the high abstention rate (33 percent) in the December 1978 constitutional referendum (see *YICA*, 1979, p. 201), the prime minister had been pressed to take a more conservative stance in order to attract some disaffected middle-class voters and to calm concerned elements of the armed forces (*WP*, 10 December 1978). The bulk of the army was perceived to be loyal, but an ultra-rightist plot aborted in November 1978 was scarcely reassuring (*CSM*, 8 December 1978). Suárez was also encouraged to move to the right by his slight gains in the March parliamentary elections, in which polls had led to the expectation that the Socialists would be the victors. The UCD's popular vote rose slightly, from 34.7 percent in 1977 to 35 percent (*Keesing's Contemporary Archives*, 15 June).

Government moves denounced by leftists included unpopular wage ceilings of 11 to 14 percent—compared to 16-percent inflation in 1978, the militarization of some striking workers, and decrees that outlawed picketing during strikes and that greatly extended antiterrorist legislation. Then in April Suárez announced the formation of a highly conservative cabinet. Carrillo warned of "political disaster" if the UCD insisted on governing without consensus, for it would be difficult for a government of the right to reach agreement with the unions. He said that communist and socialist unions were planning joint action in the future. (*WP*, 3 March; *Mundo Obrero*, 10 March; *CSM*, 21 March; *NYT*, 25 February and 9 March.)

The PCE was further encouraged to seek a "global accord" with the Socialists by the not unexpected sweeping victories of both parties in the April municipal elections. Although the UCD won the most municipal council seats, the majority of major city councils were dominated by Socialists and Communists, who combined to elect Socialist mayors. The PCE made important gains in Madrid,

Barcelona, and other major cities; in Madrid, the party won as many seats as the UCD. In Córdoba and in some 200 villages, communist mayors were chosen. The PCE drew 13 percent of the popular vote in the April election, compared with 10.7 percent in March. The Socialists held steady both times at 29 percent, while the UCD dropped from 35 to a little over 31 percent. Abstention by 33 percent of the voters in March and by 40 percent in April was thought to favor the left. (*NYT*, 5 and 14 May; *WP*, 5 April; *CSM*, 9 April; *Mundo Obrero*, 19 April.)

The possibility of an even broader electoral alliance between the PCE and the Socialists—along with other "progressive" forces—in future national elections was reportedly viewed by the PCE and by radical members of the PSOE as inevitable and desirable. However, PSOE leader Felipe González stoutly opposed this and insisted on the need for a moderate image for his party that would make it more congenial to middle-class voters. Even though such a centrist policy could lead to the defection of some militant Socialists to the communist party, González was said to feel that this loss would be more than offset by the weaning of progressives from the UCD. As an essential underpinning for a centrist image, González sought to induce the party's 28th Congress in May to abandon its "outdated and meaningless" Marxist definition. A rebuff by 61 percent of the delegates led him to resign as secretary general unexpectedly; however, in a more smoothly controlled extraordinary congress held in September, he recaptured the leadership and won removal of the Marxist label. (*Mundo Obrero*, 25 February and 10 March; *NYT*, 21 May and 8 July; *Economist*, 26 May; *Radio Free Europe Research*, 29 May; *WP*, 28 August; *CSM*, 2 October.) The PCE's leaders were cheered that the PSOE crisis was thus resolved. They had made clear their sympathetic understanding of González's position and their concern that the party feud could have repercussions harmful to Spanish democracy. (*Mundo Obrero*, 24–31 May; *Radio Free Europe Research*, 5 June.)

Relations between the PSOE and the UCD appeared to be more cordial as the government backed a large credit to the PSOE granted by the West German Social Democrats. It also agreed to recompense the socialist-dominated General Workers' Union (Unión General de Trabajadores) for extensive urban properties confiscated under General Franco. This was expected to give the organization an advantage over the communist-dominated "CC OO," to which it had been losing ground. Carrillo announced a massive campaign to increase "CC OO" strength (*CSM*, 2 October). He also accused the PSOE of turning toward social democracy and of being a "foreign party" because of its German ties. There was no need for a socialist party, he said, "if we are going to pursue Willy Brandt's policies . . . the UCD is enough." (*Le Monde*, 22 March.)

International Views and Positions. As Spain prepared for elections early in 1979, PCE leaders continued to draw political capital from violent attacks on a "repressive" Soviet Union. The principal spokesmen for this anti-Soviet campaign were, as in previous years, Santiago Carrillo and Manuel Azcárate, the Central Committee member responsible for relations with other communist parties. Azcárate charged that since socialism is "above all democratic," it could scarcely be said that the Soviet Union was a socialist state. Rather, it retained many of the worst features of the capitalist state in which the laboring masses lacked freedom and were exploited by a blatantly privileged minority. Even today, he said, political freedom in many capitalist countries is greater than in the Soviet Union. (*Mundo Obrero*, 9–15 November 1978; *Radio Free Europe Research*, 14 November 1978; *Avanti*, Rome, 28 February.)

Moscow was also denounced for extending its repressive policies to other communist parties, whose full independence it was unwilling to recognize. All Soviet polemics against Eurocommunist ideas, it was said, were characterized not by critical discussion but by condemnation. Carrillo recognized that the Eurocommunist movement was undergoing a serious crisis. He attributed this to the disunity of the socialist movement in Western Europe and to "Eastcommunist" overreaction to Eurocommunist initiatives. He said the crisis was also a repercussion of the crisis of the "entire system of imperialism." (*Radio Free Europe Research*, 27 December 1978 and 4 January.) Carrillo saw Euro-communism evolving into "Eurosocialism," i.e., a "pluralistic socialism," on both national and regional levels, implemented by broad coalitions of communists, socialists, social democrats, and other "progressives." According to Azcárate, the advantages would be a steady increase in détente and a gradual weakening of NATO as well as of Moscow's control over Eastern Europe. He said there was no question, though, of a "break with the USSR," for that country plays a vital role in the struggle against imperialism. (*Daily Telegraph*, 14 February; *L'Unità*, 29 May; *Radio Free Europe Research*, 4 January and 5 June.)

One example of the disunity of the socialist movement often cited by Carrillo was the failure of the communists and socialists in France to form a government alliance, "a severe setback for Eurocommunism." By implicitly blaming the French Communist Party (PCF) for this situation, Carrillo provided evidence of additional disunity—the growing feud between the PCE and the PCF. The discord derived principally from the PCF's opposition to the incorporation of Spain in the European Economic Community (EEC). The Spanish communists gave assurance that Spain's application for admission to the EEC did not represent a "plot" against the French economy. (*La Vanguardia*, Barcelona, 29 December 1978; *Le Monde*, 8 February.)

A further example of disagreement among the Eurocommunist parties was their contrasting approach to developments in Indochina. Although the Spanish, French, and Italian parties were in accord in condemning the Chinese invasion of Vietnam, only the PCE bitterly denounced the Vietnamese invasion of Kampuchea (Cambodia). Taking a sideswipe at the Soviet Union, the PCE warned that intervention by the big powers through intermediary countries represented a danger to every country's independence. (*Mundo Obrero*, 9 January and 20 February; *Radio Free Europe Research*, 23 January; *El País*, Madrid, 20 February; *BBC Current Affairs Talks*, 6 March.) The PCE saw as a "positive" development the establishment of diplomatic relations between China and the United States (*El País*, Madrid, 19 December 1978).

The PCE continued to oppose Spanish participation in NATO since this would increase Spain's dependence on foreign states, aggravate existing tensions, and require a sharp increase in military spending (Tass, Moscow, 23 May. However, the Spanish communists took offense at "gratuitous" advice offered by Fidel Castro that Spain not join NATO. They instructed the Cuban leader that Spaniards did not need to have their decisions dictated from abroad. (*Mundo Obrero*, 7 September.)

International Activities and Party Contacts. The PCE actively promoted the Algerian-backed Polisario Front as the sole legitimate representative of the people of the disputed territory of the former Spanish Sahara. A joint communiqué of a PCE delegation and the Front concluded in May that the sole guarantee of peace and stability in the region would be provided by the establishment of the Saharan Democratic Arab Republic throughout the zone. Representatives of the Spanish, Italian, and French communist parties met in Madrid in September, promising to intensify their efforts to induce their respective governments to recognize the Polisario Front and to seek U.N. resolutions calling on Morocco to withdraw its forces from the territory. A PCE official indicated a peaceful solution was especially necessary because the turmoil represented a threat to the nearby Spanish-owned Canary Islands. (Algerian Domestic Radio, 8 May; *Mundo Obrero*, 21 September.)

Carrillo visited Yugoslavia twice during the year for talks with Marshal Tito. The "constant expansion" of the circle of countries and movements joining the ranks of the nonaligned was among the principal topics discussed. Carrillo was especially interested to see, as an example for Spain, how nonaligned Yugoslavia organized its defense. The two also talked about the need to develop new forms of struggle for the "new international economic order." (*FBIS*, 17 April; Zagreb Domestic Radio, 10 August; Tanjug, Belgrade, 10 August.) Carrillo followed up the August visit with a stopover in Romania.

A PCE delegation headed by Carrillo visited Iraq in July at the invitation of the Iraqi Ba'th Arab Socialist Party to discuss means "to consolidate cooperation" between the two parties. Carrillo hailed the revolutionary steps being taken in Iraq to repulse "the machinations of imperialism, Zionism, and reaction." (International News Agency, Baghdad, 3 July; Baghdad Voice of the Masses, 6 July.)

Dolores Ibarruri consulted with Soviet officials in February while "on holiday" in Moscow. A delegation of Spanish communist medics spent two weeks in the Soviet Union in July to familiarize themselves with public health activities in that country.

Publications. The PCE's principal publications are the weekly *Mundo Obrero*, the bimonthly *Nuestra Bandera*, a theoretical and political journal, and various small regional newspapers.

Activities of Basque and Rival Communist Organizations. Prospects for bringing peace to guerrilla-torn Spain seemed to improve following a July agreement that conceded limited home role to the Basque provinces for the near future. The pact also provided for the gradual removal of the Spanish paramilitary Civil Guard and riot police. The moderate PNV was able to negotiate this concession despite unrelenting pressure from the militant separatist ETA organization and its affiliated Herri Batasuna (United People) Party, which insisted that only total independence for the Basque region was acceptable. The hope was that the majority of Basques would support the pact and thereby further isolate the terrorist group. (*CSM*, 30 July.)

Hitherto many were said to be protective of the guerrillas out of sympathy for them as instruments of blackmail against the Madrid government (*NYT*, 28 November 1978). Now many Basques more openly articulated their disapproval of violence. Even within the ETA there was a rift. The group's "political-military" branch endorsed the home-rule pact and announced that it was suspending all further violence. Its attitude was ambivalent, however, for it accepted responsibility for the subsequent bombings at Madrid's airport and two railroad stations that killed five people and injured scores of others. The action was called "politically inexplicable" by Juan María Biandrés, a recently elected deputy in parliament with ties to that branch of the ETA. (Ibid., 2 August.) At a clandestine press conference, ETA members apologized for the deaths and injuries, which they blamed on police for not having responded to a warning to evacuate the targeted areas. These were the latest in a series of bombings carried out by that group at tourist resorts to pressure the government into releasing or transferring to the Basque region some one hundred prisoners from a jail in Soria. It was claimed that they were being tortured. (Ibid., 5 and 30 July; *CSM*, 15 August.)

Although the group again announced it would refrain from violence, it resumed its pressure in November with the kidnapping of a prominent UCD member of the Cortes, Javier Rupérez. He was released a month later. Sources close to the ETA speculated that the change of tactics was due to a loss of support for the "soft" approach among squabbling members, who were being attracted to the hard-line "military" branch of the ETA. (*Economist*, 4 August; *CSM*, 13 and 14 November.) The ETA-Militar was unimpressed by Madrid's "too moderate" concessions and by the subsequent October referendum in which 88 percent of Basque voters approved of the home-rule pact. Almost half the electorate refrained from voting, perhaps fearing ETA reprisals. (*CSM*, 30 October.) Approximately the same rate of abstention in that area had characterized the December 1978 referendum in which some 20 percent of voting Basques opposed the new constitution. The high abstention rate at that time had been interpreted as indicating overwhelming disapproval of the document. The PNV had recommended staying away from the polls, and the ETA had urged a negative vote. (Ibid., 30 January; *NYT*, 8 December 1978.) In the March parliamentary elections, Basque nationalist parties won 48 percent of the vote in that region and 12 of the 22 seats. Three of these, plus a Senate seat, went to the Herri Batasuna Party, which decided to boycott Cortes sessions to protest government policy toward the Basques. (*WP*, 3 March.)

Meanwhile, the ETA-Militar guerrillas intensified their campaign of assassinations, robberies, and other violence by which they have harassed Spanish governments since 1959. Over one hundred army officers, policemen, and civilians were killed during 1979 by ETA and GRAPO gunmen. Among the highly placed victims were the military governors of Madrid and Guipúzcoa provinces, a Supreme Court judge, and several mayors. There were 88 killings in 1978, 61 of them by the ETA. (*CSM*, 30 January; *NYT*, 30 May; *Keesing's Contemporary Archives*, 15 June.) To finance their activities, guerrillas continued to rob banks and to extort "revolutionary taxes" from businessmen (*Visión*, New York, 27 January). The avowed objective was total autonomy for a Marxist Basque republic that would embrace a seemingly reluctant Navarre as well. So provocative was the violence that observers presumed that the aim was to ignite a military coup or at least a harsh police repression that would justify the assertion that nothing had changed. Perhaps it was simply felt that continuing intimidation might induce still more concessions.

In response to the stepped-up guerrilla action, the Suárez government coordinated police and civil guard action under a new director of state security, sent massive police reinforcements into the Basque area, and secured an agreement from the French government to deny refugee status to Basque exiles (*CSM*, 15 and 30 January, 6 February). New regulations made it a crime to collaborate in any way with guerrilla organizations or to make public apologies for them. To discourage ransom payments, banks were authorized to refuse to cash especially large checks. (*NYT*, 2 February.) Scores of suspects were detained under the antiterrorist laws, and several top leaders of the ETA and the GRAPO were imprisoned. Police said a series of successful raids had "cut the head off" the GRAPO organization. (Ibid., 28 July, 16 August, 12 September, 15 and 16 October.)

The increased security measures had the support of all the major political parties, including the PCE. Carrillo called the ETA "the number-one support for the extreme right." (*CSM*, 15 January; *Manchester Guardian*, 28 January and 4 June; *L'Unità*, 28 May.) Many right-wing civilians and members of the army continued to fume openly at the government's failure to crack down harder on the terrorists; clandestine groups were able to slay a number of leftist guerrilla leaders on their own (*NYT*, 22 December 1978, 10 and 30 January, 6 August).

Elbert Covell College   H. Leslie Robinson
University of the Pacific

Sweden

The forerunner of Sweden's communist party (Sveriges Kommunistiska Parti; SKP) was founded in May 1917 and joined the Communist International in July 1919. Inner tensions plagued the SKP from the 1920s to the advent of World War II. Following a period of relative insignificance during the 1950s, the party profited from the rise of the "new left" in the 1960s. In 1967 it absorbed new groups from the radical left and changed its name to Left Party–Communists (Vänsterpartiet Kommunisterna; VPK).

A large minority within the party criticized the VPK for being "reformist" and founded the Communist League, Marxist-Leninist (Kommunistiska Förbundet Marxist-Leninisterna; KFML), which is pro-Chinese in orientation. In 1973 the KFML changed its name to SKP.

From 1970 to 1976 the VPK exerted an influence on Swedish politics disproportionate to its number of seats in parliament. In the 1970 elections, Prime Minister Olof Palme and the Social Democratic Party, with 163 seats in the 350-seat parliament, relied on the VPK for the survival of its government. During no other period in Sweden's postwar history has the communist party exerted such influence on parliamentary life. During the 1970–1973 period, it participated in such important parliamentary committees as defense and taxation. Following the 1973 elections, however, Palme frequently compromised with the Liberal Party, thus weakening VPK participation in Swedish parliamentary life. The fall of the Social Democratic government in 1976, however, marked the beginning once more of political insignificance for the VPK, similar to that it had experienced during the 1950s and 1960s.

In October 1978 the non-socialist coalition government (Conservative, Liberal, and Center parties) resigned because it failed to reach agreement on Sweden's nuclear policy, and a minority government was formed by Liberal Party leader Ola Ullsten. At the beginning of 1979, the election polls pointed toward the possibility of the Social Democratic Party returning to power after the September elections and toward a renewed importance for the VPK. The result in September, however, was a slim victory for the nonsocialist parties. The VPK gained three seats in parliament but was later excluded by the nonsocialist parties from all parliamentary committees. Thus, the VPK should continue to play a marginal role in Swedish politics for the next three years.

The latest VPK membership figure is reported to be 17,000. The population of Sweden is about 8.3 million.

Leadership and Organization. The party congress is theoretically the highest organ of the VPK. It elects the 35-member central committee, known since 1964 as the Party Board. The Board in turn selects an eight-member Executive Committee (Verkställande Utskott), which directs party work. There are 28 party districts, corresponding to Sweden's electoral districts, and 395 local organizations. The Communist Youth (Kommunistisk Ungdom) is the party youth organization. Party chairman is Lars Werner (Stockholm), who is generally regarded as less colorful than his predecessor, Carl-Henrik Hermansson.

The feud between the VPK and the Communist Workers' Party (Arbetarpartiet Kommunisterna; APK), which broke away from the VPK in 1977, continued during 1979. The APK was, however, severely weakened by its dismal showing in the 1979 elections: 10,797 votes and no seats in parliament. This result is in contrast to the optimistic views of the organization secretary of the party, Veikko Keteli, in an interview in late 1978: "The APK is continuing to strengthen its position. It is also noted that the party's roots in places of work are becoming more solid. In the Stockholm district, for example, two new work-place organizations were formed just recently . . . the Swedish Communist Youth Organization has begun to take root." (*Norrskensflamman*, 28 December 1978.) Keteli regretted that the APK's invitation to the VPK to join in technical cooperation in the election had been rejected.

Domestic Attitudes and Activities. The most important domestic event for the VPK during 1979 was the campaign for the September elections. The VPK political platform, "Program for the Eighties: Radical Labor Politics—The Way to Socialism," was presented in February. The platform, according to party leader Werner, was formulated so as to attract the support of the entire labor movement. (*Ny Dag*, 9–13 February.)

Concerning tax policy, the VPK urged abolition of the value-added tax on food products and supported a tax reduction of 1,000 kronor on incomes in the 30,000–80,000 kronor bracket to be financed by raising taxes on capital, capital gains, and net profits, as well as increased employer taxes. The VPK supported collective workers' funds but advocated a state fund owned by the state under wage-earner control (the fund was to be used primarily for investments in state-owned firms, be spent in regions with high unemployment, and be financed by higher taxes on capital, gifts, inheritances, and corporate profits). The VPK opposed the Swedish nuclear power program and supported the referendum on nuclear power scheduled for 1980. The party also proposed that all private apartment houses should be transferred to municipal ownership, that the entire building materials industry should be nationalized, and that a rent freeze should be introduced.

In the area of educational policy, the VPK supported elimination of all examination certificates in elementary schools and eventually in high schools.

The VPK election campaign was successful, and the number of VPK seats in parliament increased from seventeen to twenty. The party got 304,689 votes, or 5.63 percent of the ballots cast, compared with 4.8 percent in 1976. One of the reasons for the gain may be the change of generations constituting the Swedish electorate. In the mid-sixties electoral support for the VPK was still dominated by workers. The social base of the VPK changed during the 1970s, and young, educated voters have played an increasingly prominent role.

International Views and Positions. In an interview for the conservative Swedish daily *Svenska Dagbladet* early in the year (5 February), party Chairman Werner commented on Eurocommunism and Indochina. At that time he had recently visited Romania and a VPK delegation was to visit Italy shortly: "We reject all domination by strong communist states, particularly in West Europe. We insist on going our own way and on communist parties being allowed to follow their own countries' traditions within the workers' movement. This includes democratic freedoms and rights, the multiparty system, and the right to strike." The VPK's current major foreign policy problem is Indochina: "We denounce any form of interference in another country's affairs. We denounce the Pol Pot regime's atrocities and its border conflicts with Vietnam. We denounce China's dictatorial demands. We understand that the people of Kampuchea (Cambodia) are rebelling against this regime."

International Activities and Party Contacts. On 2 January a delegation headed by party leader Lars Werner from the VPK visited the Soviet Union and was received by Boris Ponomarev, member of the Politburo and secretary of the Central Committee of the Communist Party of the Soviet Union. The parties "exchanged views on . . . topical issues of the international situation and of the communist and workers' movement . . . They stressed the special importance of intensifying the struggle for a cessation of the arms race" (Tass, Moscow, 6 January). Later in January a VPK delegation headed by Lars Werner, visited Romania. It was received by Nicolae Ceauşescu, the secretary general of the Romanian Communist Party. During the discussions "both sides stressed the need in relations between the communist and workers' parties to ever more forcefully assert the principles of fully equal rights, respect for independence and noninterference in internal affairs, and respect for each party's right to independently formulate its revolutionary strategy and tactics in keeping with the historical, social, and political conditions in its own country" (Bucharest Domestic Service, 16 January). The crowded travel plan in January concluded in East Berlin, where the VPK delegation was received by Politburo member Hermann Axen and Erich Honecker, secretary general of the East German Central Committee. Honecker and Werner "spoke out in favor of consolidating the action unity and cooperation between communists and workers' parties on the basis of the doctrines of Marx, Engels, and Lenin." (Allgemeiner Deutscher Nachrichtendienst, East Berlin, 24 January.) In February a VPK delegation led by Executive Secretary Tore Forsberg visited Poland and met with members of the Polish communist party's Central Committee. In June Executive Committee Secretary Bo Hammar visited Bulgaria and met with Dimitur Stanishev, secretary of the Central Committee of the Bulgarian Communist Party. Another VPK visit was made to Poland in June.

The APK's leader led a delegation to Czechoslovakia in June and met with Central Committee members of the Czechoslovakian Communist Party (KSC). In a joint communiqué on 4 July, both parties expressed their thanks to the peace policies of the Soviet Union, attacked Chinese leaders, and emphasized "their international solidarity with the heroic Vietnamese people." The KSC wished the APK communists "much success in their struggle for democracy and socialism, for peace and progress in the world. At the same time, the two parties stressed the need to restore the unity of Swedish communists on the basis of Marxism-Leninism and proletarian internationalism . . ." (*Pravda*, Bratislava, 4 July.) Carsten Thunborg, member of the APK Politburo, headed an APK delegation to Poland in July. In discussions with Polish leaders, the "unity of all forces of peace and progress, cooperation between communists, social democrats, and other progressive political parties, trade unions, [and] mass social organizations in the struggle for halting the arms race, for détente, against aggression and war" were stressed. (Polska Agencja Prasowa, Warsaw, 13 June.)

Other Leftist Groups: Rival Communist Organizations. There are a large number of extreme-leftist groups in Sweden. The Maoists are represented by two parties. The SKP, as noted earlier, grew out of the KFML and is the party officially recognized by Beijing. Its membership is secret but believed to be around 2,000. The SKP was very active during 1978–1979 in attacking Vietnam for aggression against Kampuchea. In a statement in late 1978 the SKP charged: "Under the cover of a fabricated liberation movement, Vietnam has launched a large-scale offensive against Kampuchea using its bombers to create so-called 'liberated zones.' Since this action is taken with the support of Soviet leaders, the aggression against Kampuchea and the [Soviet] invasion of Czechoslovakia in 1968 are of [the same] sort." (New China News Agency, Beijing, 16 December 1978.) The SKP received only 10,862 votes in the September elections.

The Communist Party of Marxist-Leninist Revolutionaries (Kommunistiska Partiet Marxist-Leninisterna [revolutionärerna]; KPML[r]) grew out of an association of the same name that broke away from the KFML in 1970. Party chairman is Frank Baude. The main center of party strength is in Sweden's second largest city, Göteborg. The party is active in almost 90 localities throughout the country. Membership is believed to be around 1,500. It did not take part in the September elections. The Swedish section of the Fourth International is the Communist Workers' League (Kommunistiska Arbetareförbundet; KAF). It is insignificant but does take part in the elections. The KAF received 1,802 votes in September.

Publications. *Ny Dag* (New Day), the VPK central organ, is published twice weekly. The main organ of the APK is the daily newspaper *Norrskensflamman* (Northern Lights), published in Luleå. The theoretical organ of the VPK is *Socialistisk Debatt* (Socialist Debate). The SKP's central organ is *Gnistan* (Spark). The KPLM(r) publishes *Proletären* (Proletariat) twice weekly. The Trotskyist KAF publishes *Internationalen* (International).

Helsingborg, Sweden   Bertil Häggman

Switzerland

The oldest communist party in Switzerland is the Swiss Labor Party (Partei der Arbeit/Parti du travail/Partito del Lavoro; PdA). It was founded on 5 March 1921 as the Swiss Communist Party, banned in 1940, then re-formed under its present name on 14 October 1944. It is officially pro-Soviet and has been recognized by Moscow as a branch party throughout its existence. Membership is approximately 5,000.

The PdA has been joined in the Lower House of parliament (Nationalrat) by two other left-wing parties. The Progressive Organizations Switzerland (Progressive Organisationen, Schweiz; POCH) calls itself "communist" and is friendly toward the Soviet Union. Founded in 1972 by young critics, primarily radical students, of the coalition government system, it has concentrated from the beginning on domestic issues and criticized the PdA for its elderly leadership. Since the national elections of 1975, when its candidates failed to win a parliamentary seat, it has been careful not to move tactically against the interests of other groups on the left. It presents itself, however, as a more vigorous alternative for the young. Membership is estimated at 900.

The Autonomous Socialist Party (Partito Socialista Autonomo/Parti socialiste autonome/Autonome Sozialistische Partei; PSA) originated in 1969 when young left-wing Social Democrats (Second International) left the Socialist branch of the Ticino canton in protest against the elderly leadership. The PSA and the POCH concluded an agreement to coordinate policy in 1973. Elements of the PSA exist throughout Switzerland and during the year were able to build up a significant following in the French-speaking region of the canton of Berne (after the Catholic north formed the new Jura canton; see *YICA*, 1976, p. 225). Membership is estimated at 680.

Three other communist parties and one nonparty organization also warrant mention. The Marxist Revolutionary League (Ligue marxiste révolutionnaire/Marxistische Revolutionäre Liga; LMR) was created in 1969. At that time some one hundred young leftists, mostly intellectuals and disenchanted members of the PdA from Geneva and Lausanne, demanded a return to an elitist cadre party with strict discipline in order to lay the groundwork for "revolution." The LMR joined the Fourth International (Trotskyist) in 1969. Membership is approximately 500.

Originally a pro-Chinese group, the Communist Party, Switzerland (Kommunistische Partei, Schweiz; KPS) consists of two splinter parties. One party calls itself the Communist Party, Switzerland Marxist/Leninist (KPS/ML) and the other kept the original name. Each accuses the other of having caused the schism. The former follows a pro-Chinese line and advocates expanding the military budget, in line with China's present European policy. The latter is Marxist without being Leninist. Both prefer not to enter elections with candidates of their own. Membership in the KPS/ML and KPS is not known but estimated by sources on the left as 100 to 200 each.

The above list of party groups does not include some fifty, more or less unstructured leftist organizations that represent a broad spectrum of ideologies from anarchy to total central planning.

The population of Switzerland is about 6.3 million.

Leadership and Organization. The PdA is governed by a 50-member Central Committee with representatives from all linguistic areas of Switzerland. The 14-member Politburo has a 5-member Secretariat headed by Armand Magnin (Geneva, age 59); the French-speaking secretary is supported by two German-speaking permanent secretaries of the Central Committee, Hansjörg Hofer and Karl Odermatt. The Eleventh Congress of the PdA was held in 1978 (see *YICA*, 1979, pp. 209–10).

The POCH consists of cantonal sections that send delegates to an irregularly scheduled National Convention, held most recently in May 1978. The last convention, with some 110 delegates present, designated a Party Committee of 53 and, from its members, a Managing Committee of ten, as well as two full-time members of the Central Secretariat, one of them the central secretary, Eduard Hafner. There are POCH sections in only seven cantons: Bern, Basel-Land, Basel-Stadt, Lucerne, Schaffhausen, Solothurn, and Zurich. Cantons with few members — the French- and Italian-speaking cantons among them — have informal organizations.

The LMR is more centrally organized than the POCH. Its cantonal sections convene nationally to elect a Central Committee and a Politburo. The last (fourth) National Congress was held during the summer. The Politburo operates collectively, and LMR sources refuse to divulge names and numbers of members of their committees. The LMR calls itself an activist party, maintains strict discipline, and obligates each member to contribute a substantial part of his income to the party. A leading member is Peter Sigerist, head of the Bern office.

Domestic Affairs. In the October parliamentary elections, the political climate was dominated by an uncertain economic outlook. Although the Swiss franc stayed at a record level (making it the currency that appreciated most strongly against the dollar), exports and the tourist industry generated smaller earnings and their growth rate fell. Unemployment remained low. The record low participation in the elections (48 percent) mirrored the lack of political militancy, and the results showed an increased desire for stability.

Elections for both houses of parliament on 20–21 October brought small but significant gains to the two center parties of the government coalition, and losses both to the Catholic and the Socialist parties. The Christian Popular Party (CVP) demanded social benefits as did the Socialists; but just as the Socialists made moves toward an opening to the left, the CVP moved left to satisfy its blue-collar wing (see *YICA*, 1976, p. 226). The Socialists lost four seats, and the CVP two seats. The Liberal Democrats won four and the Popular Party two seats.

Arithmetically, the loser was the small Independents' Party, not represented in the cabinet. Originally a consumer party, it has become a critic of government in economic matters, trying to be a useful gadfly, and is generally seen as a yardstick for dissatisfaction in the country. In 1979, for the first time, dissatisfaction moved to the left and showed itself in votes given to marginal leftist parties. The Independents declined from eleven to eight parliamentary seats, with the difference of three going to the POCH (two) and the PSA (a second seat).

Before the elections the PdA, POCH, and PSA held a joint press conference on 9 February and announced a common electoral strategy, calling themselves the coalition of the Consistent Left. Following the elections, the representation of the three parties totaled seven seats, despite a loss of one for the old PdA (from four to three). This is the most since the invasion of Hungary in 1956, but it was achieved at the expense of smaller parties. The government coalition retained its 169 seats.

The 200 seats of the Lower House are divided as follows: Liberal Democrats 51, Christian Popular Party 44, Socialists 31, Popular Party 23, Independents 8, Liberal Conservatives 8 (a right-wing group of Liberals not represented in the cabinet but generally voting with the coalition), Protestant Party 23, National Action 2 (the remnants of the anti-foreign movement of the 1973 oil shock and recession fright), others 3, PdA 3, POCH 2, and PSA 1.

While the Independents are accustomed to the vicissitudes of election hazards, the Socialists are expected to undergo a serious crisis in the coming year. The Socialists had gained nine seats in 1975 and their party chairman, Helmut Hubacher, had tried to push the party into an opening to the left in subsequent local elections (see *YICA*, 1977, p. 236). Leftist elements had, moreover, made inroads into party committees. Sensing strong opposition from the rank and file, Hubacher abruptly solicited the support of the more conservative parties two months before the elections; however, the party lost votes in typical blue-collar precincts. Simultaneously, the emergence of new parties to the left showed that the Consistent Left, mostly young people, rejected the Socialist effort. The POCH and the PSA, in addition to the LMR and the KPS, consider the Socialists "bourgeois collaborators."

Other election results of importance during the year were: (1) 3 December 1978: a proposal to create a federal security police to combat terrorism was defeated by an alliance of the left and cantonal rights advocates fearing big government, 920,000 to 724,000, with 43.3 percent of the electorate voting; (2) 18 February: a proposal to reduce the voting age from twenty to eighteen years in federal matters (some cantons have done so for cantonal voting) was defeated narrowly, 965,000 to 934,000, participation being 49.6 percent; on the same date, a proposal for compulsory consultation with adjacent townships prior to building any new nuclear plant was defeated, 966,000 to 920,000; (3) 20 May: a proposed value-added tax was rejected, 940,000 to 497,000, while new, stricter legislation for nuclear plants (which would not have been an issue if the compulsory local consultation process had been passed in February) was accepted, 983,000 to 444,000; participation for both these issues was 37.6 percent.

Domestic Attitudes. For several years the trend toward central planning and leftist militancy has cut across party lines (see *YICA*, 1976, p. 224). The 1979 elections saw a return of ideological boundaries coinciding more precisely with party programs. The new Consistent Left represents opposition parties with little in common with socialist policies and therefore exerts little influence on national affairs. Moreover, the leftist coalition will be put to the test in reciprocal relations among the three parties, with the old PdA's three parliamentarians facing four from the POCH and the PSA. The PdA's efforts to woo back some of the brighter people of the other parties have been visible for some time. But the other two will try to remain on good terms with the PdA, which remains the only standard-bearer of communism officially recognized by Moscow.

The only politically relevant development, apart from the elections, was the designation of PdA member Roger Dafflon as mayor of Geneva. A longtime moderate member of the party, he was in line for the position, which changes hands each year according to seniority and a majority vote by the five city council members. Three other parties, the Christian Democrats, the Liberals, and the Radicals (cantonal parties can have names different form those of their federal alliance), dropped their opposition to the nomination (they had feared that Geneva's reputation as an international meeting ground would suffer) because they felt that Dafflon's administrative reputation made opposition fruitless.

Publications. Circulation figures (in parentheses), where they are given, are uncertified claims of the publishing organizations. The PdA publishes *Voix ouvrière*, Geneva, a daily (7,000), in French; *Vorwärts*, Basel, a weekly (6,000), in German; and *Il Lavoratore*, Lugano, a weekly (3,000), in Italian.

The POCH publishes *POCH-Zeitung*, a weekly (7,000), and *Emanzipation*, a weekly for women's groups, in German; *Tribune ouvriére*, a weekly (3,000), in French; and *Positionen*, a monthly for basic ideological discussion, in German. The Bern section of the POCH, Progressive Organizations Bern, publishes *Venceremos*, a Spanish name inspired by the Che Guevara legend, in German; it is aimed at high-school students and appears six times per year.

The LMR publishes the bimonthly *Bresche* in German and *La bréche* in French. The KPS/ML publishes *Offensiv*, originally antimilitaristic, but now following China's lead in seeking stronger national defense against Soviet hegemonism; *Oktober* and its French and Italian counterparts, *Octobre* and *Ottobre*, monthly. The KPS counters *Octobre* with *Rote Fahne*, a German monthly. The most lively and well-written paper is *Focus*, a monthly (10,000) in German, which merged with *Leserzeitung* in September. It is a poorly edited periodical written by editors of a defunct Socialist paper in Basel, *AZ*, who were joined by leftist editors fired by the biggest Basel daily, *Basler Zeitung*. *Leserzeitung* has not proved successful. The merged product, the first issue of which appeared in October, is *Tell* (after the legendary William Tell); it will be an illustrated monthly and seeks a circulation in excess of 20,000.

Bern, Switzerland   Swiss Eastern Institute

Turkey

In 1979 Turkey experienced a further upswing in political violence; a continuing economic crisis; foreign policy problems involving Cyprus, Greece, the United States, NATO, the Organization for Economic Cooperation and Development (OECD), and Western Europe; and a partial parliamentary election and subsequent change of government. These interrelated developments contributed to a significant increase in social and political tension and consequently provided more fertile ground for extremist agitation and propaganda.

The economic crisis continued unabated through its third year, despite the Republican People's Party (RPP) government's efforts to implement a stabilization plan. In March foreign debts still stood at U.S. $12 billion, while foreign exchange reserves had dwindled to a mere $540 million (*Keesing's Contemporary Archives*, 9 November, p. 29,921). Although the trade deficit in 1978 had been cut by 42.5 percent, this came at a high price since it was due primarily to an import freeze. One consequence of that freeze was a marked slowdown in industry and continuing high unemployment (20 percent). Moreover, the government's stabilization plan was costly to consumers. It included a series of currency devaluations that resulted in sharply increased prices for the few foreign-manufactured goods still available. In addition, government-controlled prices were also steeply increased, including those for such staple items as cooking oil, flour, and sugar. The general rate of inflation reportedly rose from 26 percent in 1977 to 62 percent in 1978 to 99 percent between March and August 1979 (ibid.). Extensive negotiations between the government and the International Monetary Fund, the OECD, and a number of other governments (including oil-producing states, such as Iraq and Libya) did result in extension of foreign credits and refinancing of at least part of the debt. The benefit of these agreements and other anticipated results of the government's plans, however, came too late to prevent a debacle for the RPP in the October parliamentary elections.

The year dawned in a particularly ominous manner. Conflict between leftist and rightist militants in the southeastern provincial capital of Kahramanmaraş of a type that had become endemic during the 1970s exploded into a sectarian massacre. Three days of rioting by the Sunni Muslim majority against Alevi Shi'ites resulted in the loss of over one hundred lives and the destruction of nearly a thousand buildings. The government of Bülent Ecevit was forced against its own democratic commitments to request a parliamentary declaration of martial law in 13 of the country's 67 provinces (including Ankara and Istanbul). The martial law regime was extended to 6 additional provinces in April, all of them in the predominantly Kurdish southeast, in response to expressions of serious concern within the Cabinet itself with what was perceived to be a recrudescence of Kurdish separatism. This concern was obviously fueled by fears of spillover from the conflict across the border between Kurds and the revolutionary government in Iran.

The declaration of martial law (renewed at two-month intervals throughout the year) gave the government an undoubted advantage in dealing with the distressingly high and still escalating level of political violence. One change from the previous year was the apparent shift of the initiative from the extreme right (in particular followers of Alparslan Türkeş's militant National Action Party) to the extreme left. Government crackdowns on two leftist armed groups in June, following attacks on U.S. servicemen in Izmir and Istanbul, failed to stem the tide, however. By August, an estimated 2,000 people had been killed in political incidents since the inauguration of the Ecevit government twenty months earlier. The death rate from political incidents in midsummer averaged twenty per week. During the first eight months of the year, moreover, it was officially claimed that more than $2 million worth of arms, most of Soviet and Czech manufacture, had been confiscated by the government. These arms (and presumably additional quantities that had gone undetected) were allegedly being smuggled into the country from Iraq and Syria for use by leftist terrorist groups (ibid., p. 29,923).

Although the left seemed to become more active than in preceding years, it continued to be plagued by excessive fragmentation. A comprehensive survey of leftist organizations, for example, listed a total of roughly 50 groups, of which 33 were said to be active in 1979 (including the still proscribed Turkish Communist Party [TCP]). Additionally, eight organizations claimed to speak for the Kurds (*Aydinlik*, 5 and 13 March; Joint Publications Research Service [JPRS], tr., "Translations on Western Europe: Factions of the Turkish Left," 14 June, pp. 4–9). Among the most active of these groups were several splinters of the Turkish People's Liberation Party (TPLP), itself a breakaway from Dev Genç (Revolutionary Youth), a leading leftist organization of the 1960s (Landau, *Radical Politics in Contemporary Turkey*, pp. 40ff). Formed and led in 1970 by Mahir Çayan, the TPLP was involved in two spectacular incidents in the early 1970s: the kidnapping and murder of the Israeli consul general in Istanbul, and the kidnapping of NATO technicians near the Black Sea and subsequent shoot-out with security forces in which Çayan himself was killed. Not only has Çayan become a martyr for the extreme left, but he left behind essays written during and after his imprisonment in 1971. In these essays, he argued that the existence of a strong socialist bloc (i.e., the Soviet Union) and the dangers of nuclear weapons have made war unacceptable as an instrument of capitalist imperialism. Consequently, imperialists have tried to infiltrate and modernize formerly colonialized countries by co-opting their national bourgeoisies. The only way to break the hold of these groups on these societies (including, of course, Turkey) is through armed action on the part of first urban and later rural guerrillas (*Aydinlik*, 12 March).

One of the groups that broke away from among Çayan's followers in 1975 called itself Revolutionary Road (or Dev Yol for short). This group disagreed with Çayan's reliance on the support of the socialist bloc, pointing to the Sino-Soviet split. It dismissed both the USSR and China as revisionist rather than revolutionary states and characterized the TCP as a "refugee group." It argued that "the only way to push back fascism [in Turkey] is to refuse to surrender and to go into active struggle." However, since unorganized action was bound to fail, the group favored postponement of armed action until the appropriate organizational groundwork was completed (ibid., 13 March). Impatient with such delays, the Istanbul members of Dev Yol broke away in 1978 to form yet another splinter known as Revolutionary Left, or Dev Sol. This group favored immediate armed action and sought to extend its activities across the country. It was involved in murderous attacks on local officials of the National Action Party (NAP) in Istanbul and launched an effort to organize and control residents of new shantytown districts. It also allegedly played a major role in provoking the December 1978 riots between Sunnis and Alevis in Kahramanmaraş (ibid., 15 March).

Another fragment of the Çayan group was the Marxist-Leninist Armed Propaganda Unit (MLAPU). It surfaced in Paris in 1973 and involved Çayan's widow. Allegedly linked with the international terrorist Carlos, who in turn is said to be backed by Moscow, the MLAPU also allegedly was close to the German Baader-Meinhof gang and the Italian Red Brigades, as well as to the Palestine Liberation Organization, which is alleged to have trained active MLAPU terrorists before their infiltration into Turkey. In May and June, the MLAPU claimed credit for the murder of two U.S. servicemen in Turkey. A crackdown by the government netted thirteen suspects and raised the question of whether the group survived (*San Francisco Chronicle*, 6 June).

Among other notable developments within the fragmented left in Turkey during 1979 was the surfacing of the Kurdish Workers' Party) known colloquially as the Apocular, or Apo-ists). This group announced its existence with an ambush in the southeast, one of whose victims was a Justice Party parliamentary deputy. Declaring support for the Iranian Kurds, the Apo-ists announced their goals as the national liberation of Kurds in opposition to capitalist colonialism and "its local collaborators" (*Hürriyet*, 2 August 1979).

Throughout this turmoil, the still proscribed and exiled TCP carried on frequent commentary and exhortation, particularly over the radio (and increasingly also by means of graffiti, alongside and in competition with Dev Sol and Dev Yol as well as the rightist NAP). Thus, in a report to the party's Central Committee (see *WMR*, October 1978), the TCP characterized the Republican Party as "bourgeois reform" and accused it of having moved toward the reactionaries and the big-business–oriented Justice Party when it took over the government early in 1978. However, the TCP still kept the door open to left-wing Republicans. "Our party is following a policy whose substance is to support every constructive step of the present government . . . while at the same time criticizing its lack of consistency and steps leading back." The TCP responded to the December 1978 riots and imposition of martial law by declaring that Turkey was again on the brink of military dictatorship, noting particularly that several martial law commanders sympathized with the extreme rightist NAP. The TCP called for unity of action between the "TCP, TLP [Turkish Labor Party], TSWP [Turkish Socialist Workers' Party], socialists, social democrats, the left-leaning flank of the RPP, the Turkish democrats, the trade unions, all democratic mass organizations, progressive and revolutionary youth associations, patriotic forces within the army, and everybody who opposes martial law, the suppression of democratic freedoms, the violation of human rights, sectarian provocations, and racist and chauvinist oppression" (Our Radio, 31 December 1978).

Another note that appeared in communist pronouncements during 1979 was support for Kurdish aspirations. According to a report in Beirut, the TCP supported the "just and democratic rights" of the Kurdish people and denounced "Kurdish opportunists and reactionaries who have become a tool of American, Turkish, and Iranian intelligence." The TCP further called for "the closing of ranks of the Kurdish and Turkish nationalists, progressives, and democrats and . . . joint struggle on the road to democracy along with hostility to imperialism, Zionism, and reaction" (*JPRS*, 29 January). More specifically, the TCP supported the Kurdish leader Celal Talabani, who is based in Sulaimaniya, Iraq, and opposed the Barzani group known as the Kurdish Democratic Party (*WP*, 18 April). In view of the extreme sensitivity of Turks generally when it comes to matters involving the Kurds, open communist commentary of this sort is bound to arouse even greater tension.

Additional light on the dynamics of the high level of violence in Turkey was shed by a series of interviews conducted among imprisoned activists of both right and left early in 1979. Published in

Milliyet, the leading independent Istanbul daily, this survey showed that most of the detained activists were under 24 years of age, came from large low-income families whose fathers were relatively uneducated, and had experienced mobility from village to city. Significantly, there were few outstanding differences between those with leftist proclivities and their political opposites (*JPRS*, 25 May). While *Milliyet* was careful to disclaim scientific validity for the survey, it was significant in that it manifested the kinds of strains on individuals generated by the process of rapid socioeconomic development and modernization.

Finally, as a conclusion to the flux of this tense year in Turkish politics, a comment on the partial parliamentary election of 14 October is in order. The magnitude of the defeat suffered by the RPP under the leadership of Bülent Ecevit may be measured by considering the election results in Istanbul, an RPP stronghold in the elections of the preceding decade. The RPP share of the vote fell from 58 percent in 1977 to 38 percent in 1979, while that of the Justice Party rose from 28 to 40 percent. Such is the measure of disillusionment at the inability of the RPP to solve the economic, social, and political problems outlined above. Nor was the extreme left able to capitalize on this disillusionment; none of three parties competing in the election (the TLP, the TSWP, and the Socialist Revolutionary Party) succeeded in polling more than 1.3 percent of the vote, even in Istanbul. Thus, the extreme left remained fragmented but retained its capacity to disturb the Turkish political scene during 1979. Its activities also seemed to help pave the way for a rightist reaction of some magnitude.

University of Illinois, Chicago Circle   Frank Tachau

ASIA AND THE PACIFIC

Afghanistan

Following a coup at the end of April 1978, a leftist, pro-Soviet government was installed in Kabul under the control of the People's Democratic Party of Afghanistan (PDPA). The leaders of the PDPA, or Khalq, which first came into existence in 1965, have consistently argued that the party is not communist. Nevertheless, the use of Marxist jargon is common, and government officials address one another as comrade.

Leadership and Organization. In order to ensure absolute loyalty, extensive purges have been conducted not only of elements of the old regime but within the PDPA itself. Several prominent leaders have been accused of plotting the overthrow of the government. These include Abdul Qadir, leader of the April coup, who was sentenced to death. The sentence was later commuted to fifteen years in prison. The number-two man in the regime and leader of the Parcham faction of the party, Babrak Karmal, was accused of organizing an opposition group (see *YICA*, 1979, p. 215). Karmal and six other top officials were relieved of their government posts and sent abroad as ambassadors. Later they were dismissed altogether and now reside in Soviet bloc countries. Many of the vacancies created in the military, the bureaucracy, and the educational system have been filled by Soviet personnel.

On 16 September a violent confrontation occurred between President Nur Mohammad Taraki and Prime Minister Hafizullah Amin. Taraki apparently intended to remove Amin from power because the latter was gaining too much influence. The plan backfired, however, and Taraki was killed. He was first reported to have resigned due to ill health, but later Bakhtar, the official news agency, said he succumbed to a "grave disease" on 9 October (*FBIS*, 10 October).

Amin had been steadily rising in influence. He was made prime minister in addition to foreign minister on 27 March and given powers to "remodel the government" (*NYT*, 28 March). On 28 July President Taraki assumed direct command of the army, but his orders were issued through Amin. After the elimination of Taraki, Amin took virtually all important posts—president, prime minister, chairman of the Revolutionary Council, chairman of the Council of Ministers, head of the secret police, minister of defense, secretary general of the Central Committee of the party, and chairman of the commission to draft a new constitution.

On 27 December, Amin was overthrown by Babrak Karmal, who seized power with the support of 5,000 Soviet combat troops, which had been airlifted into Kabul during the two days preceding the coup. After the coup, thousands of Soviet troops poured into the country. Karmal proclaimed himself president, prime minister, commander-in-chief, and secretary general of the communist People's Democratic Party. In a radio speech, he called his predecessor a "tool of world imperialism." (*NYT*, 28–31 December; see also Biographies.)

At the time of the 1978 coup, the PDPA claimed a membership of 50,000, but estimates of its real strength are put at no more than 5,000 (*NYT*, 2 August). Government officials report that vigorous recruiting efforts are under way. In April, Taraki said in an interview "every day hundreds and thousands of party membership cards are being distributed" (*FBIS*, 22 May). In September, Amin claimed there may be as many as 100,000 party members (*NYT*, 9 September). Membership in the party requires a trial period of eight months to one year during which the candidate must prove himself.

In addition to expanding the membership of the PDPA, leaders of the regime are attempting to build organizations that touch all aspects of Afghan life, including labor, peasants, women, religious communities, and youth. Membership in the People's Youth Organization alone is put at 300,000 (*FBIS*, 18 September). Because of the declining effectiveness of the regular army, a militia or paramilitary force has been proposed. These forces would have training facilities and equipment equal to or better than those of the regular army. The regular military is conscripted mostly from the illiterate peasantry, who generally are not sympathetic to the political ideology of the regime. The militia would be drawn from the educated and semi-educated youth, mainly from the cities (*Daily Telegraph*, 29 May).

Domestic Policy. The PDPA has undertaken an ambitious program of social and economic change. A major target is education, which the government considers a high priority due to a rate of illiteracy that the Afghans acknowledge may be as high as 95 percent (*FBIS*, 23 May). The government claims that large sums of money are being spent building schools, printing textbooks, and training teachers. Six hundred students and 22 teachers had been sent to Soviet bloc countries for education by the end of 1978 (ibid., 15 November 1978). The government has attempted to change the social status of women. Wearing the veil is discouraged, and the dowry system has been attacked. A maximum of U.S. $10 has been imposed as the sum a family can receive for the marriage of a daughter (*Asian Wall Street Journal*, 17 January). Women have been granted full economic and political rights, including freedom of marriage (*FBIS*, 27 July). These measures have been very unpopular among the traditionally minded Islamic population.

Perhaps the most ambitious program has been land reform. The PDPA claims that before the overthrow of the old regime, 50 percent of the land was owned by 5 percent of the population, which also controlled financing, seeds, implements, and water. Some 36 percent of the population was landless. On 2 January a decree was issued setting limits on the amount of land that one person may own. Anything in excess of 30 jeribs (4 jeribs equals 1 acre) of first-class land was to be confiscated and distributed among the landless. Families were allowed 6 hectares, about 15 acres. By July, the government claimed to have completed land reform by distributing 3 million jeribs to 285,000 families (ibid., 19 July).

The government also undertook to supply farmers with bank credits to obtain necessary supplies and implements. The position of the government is that agricultural cooperatives are the future course for rural Afghanistan (ibid., 5 February).

Within a matter of weeks after the April 1978 coup, opposition, consisting mainly of rural tribal groups, surfaced. Objections were raised about the government's social and economic reforms and the incompatibility between socialist ideology and Islam. Among the more important opposition groups are the Hezb-i-Islami (Islamic Party of Afghanistan) and the Jamiat-i-Islami (Islamic Brotherhood). Although poorly armed in comparison with the army, the rebels have enjoyed considerable success. They claim to be in general control of the countryside, with the government effectively confined to the larger metropolitan areas. Rural inhabitants have suffered heavily, however, since the government has used air strikes against villages suspected of supporting the rebels.

The rebels are operating in part out of bases in Pakistan, although the government of Pakistan denies such bases exist and has taken a neutral position on the fighting. As many as 142,000 Afghan refugees have entered Pakistan (*NYT*, 15 August).

On three occasions elements in the army have mutinied. The first occurred in March in the eastern city of Herat; mutinous troops and tribal rebels held the city for some time. Fighting was intense, and casualties numbered in the hundreds. Many Soviet advisers and their families were killed. On 20 April an army unit mutinied in the city of Jalalabad, near the Pakistan border. The rebel hold on the city was again broken after intense fighting. On 5 August a mutiny occurred in Kabul itself and was put down only after Soviet helicopter gunships were used (*Manchester Guardian*, 27 May; *NYT*, 6 August). In late November, Soviet troops were reported to have gone into action alongside Afghan forces in a major offensive against rebel-held territory (*San Jose Mercury*, 29 November).

International Views and Positions. During the year, Afghanistan has moved even closer to the Soviet Union. Domestic policies and organizational structures are openly patterned after Soviet models, and Afghan foreign policy consistently follows the Soviet line. The number of Soviet personnel in Afghanistan has grown as a result of leadership gaps created by purges and by the government's inability to deal effectively with armed resistance to the regime. Units of Soviet combat troops have been sent into Afghanistan in order to secure the airfields through which Soviet supplies are funneled (*NYT*, 6 September), and after the overthrow of Amin on 27 December, at least 25,000 Soviet combat troops moved into Afghan territory (*NYT*, 28–31 December).

At least thirty agreements have been signed between Afghanistan and the Soviet Union covering economic, technical, cultural, and defense matters. A permanent trade commission has been established, and in February a protocol was signed calling for a 30-percent increase in trade between the two countries (*FBIS*, 22 February). Before the 1978 coup, there were plans to build an east-west railroad linking Afghanistan with Iran. The initial studies and planning for the project, to be funded by Iran, had been completed. Now there are plans to build a north-south transportation system, including a road and railroad bridge across the Amu Darya River, the current border between the Soviet Union and Afghanistan (*Izvestiia*, 7 November 1978). Soviet planning experts have been sent to Kabul to aid in the development of Afghanistan's five-year plan.

The rebellion against the Kabul government has made it increasingly hostile toward its neighbors. China, Pakistan, and Iran are all accused of providing supplies and sanctuary to the rebels. American and Egyptian military advisers are reported in both the Afghan and Soviet press to be providing training (*FBIS*, 20 July). The Kabul government has revived the issue of an independent Pushtunistan for the peoples in the hill areas along the Afghanistan-Pakistan border. Prime Minister Amin referred to this issue as the "freedom movement among Pushtun and Baluch people to achieve the victorious and independent unity with the peoples of their fatherland" (ibid., 1 December 1978).

The role of the United States in Afghanistan has been reduced to a minimum as a result of hostile actions against Americans. On 14 February American Ambassador Adolph Dubs was kidnapped and taken to a Kabul hotel. Within a few hours, the room in which he was being held was attacked by Afghan security forces, and Dubs and his kidnappers were killed. The U.S. government maintains that Soviet advisers were present during this incident and are to some extent responsible for its outcome. The Afghan government denies any Soviet involvement. On 7 September the American air attaché was attacked on a Kabul street by Afghan military personnel. He apparently escaped death only by the timely arrival of other Western diplomats.

Publications. The official organ of the Democratic Republic of Afghanistan is *Sawr Revolution*; the first issue appeared in December 1978. *Khalq* is a weekly newspaper published by the PDPA.

University of Montana   Louis D. Hayes

Australia

The Communist Party of Australia (CPA), founded in October 1920, expanded rapidly in the 1930s and early 1940s but gradually declined both in numbers and influence in the post–World War II era. By 1978 its membership scarcely exceeded 2,000, and party membership has probably fluctuated at that level until the present. The CPA split in 1964 when a pro-Chinese faction of around several hundred broke away to form a separate party. Then in 1971 the Socialist Party of Australia (SPA) was formed and adopted a stance critical of the Soviet Union. Meanwhile, the CPA became more independent in its views and policies, but its overall relations with Moscow still remain warm and sympathetic.

The 26th Party Congress. In June the CPA held its 26th Party Congress, which was attended by communist delegates from the Chilean Socialist Party, the Greek Communist Party, the Japanese Communist Party, the Korean Workers' Party, the Mexican Communist Party, the Front for the Liberation of Mozambique, Maori and Pacific Peoples Revolutionary Front, the Communist Party of Romania, the New American Movement, the League of Communists of Yugoslavia, and the Italian Communist Party. Twenty-six other communist parties sent greetings, among them the parties of Vietnam, Laos, Portugal, Spain, and the USSR. (*Tribune*, 20 June, p. 5.)

The congress elected 35-year-old Judy Mundey to replace party veteran Laurie Carmichael. Mundey, elected unopposed, joined the party in 1963 at the age of 19. She was then a member of the Builders Labourers Union, and her view at that time as now was that the working class must unite and struggle to seize power from the capitalist class (ibid., 27 June, p. 7). Mundey rose in the party's ranks to become the first secretary of the Sydney district party branch and now the party's first woman president.

Other individuals elected to high party office included the two joint national secretaries, Eric Aarons and Bernie Taft; assistant national secretaries Rob Durbridge and Mark Taft; executive members Marvis Robertson, Joe Palmada, Brian Aarons, Richard Walsham, Linda Rubinstein, and Philip Herington; and committee members Hugh Hamilton, Marie Crisp, Murray Broad, Kay Wicks, Darrell Dawson, Vicki Wootten, David McKnight, Aileen Beaver, Denus Freney, Joyce Stevens, Laurie Carmichael, Pete Cockcroft, Merv Nixon, John Alford, Roger Wilson, Dave Davies, Lesley Ebbels, Max Ogden, Pierre Slicer, Tony Evans, Maksina Medigovich, and Vic Slater. The congress praised Charlie Gifford for leading "the party in Queensland for many years," Jack Mundey "for his outstanding work in linking the labour movement with environmental and resources issues," and Laurie Aarons, who "was national secretary during the whole period when the CPA took an independent path and elaborated a new policy." (Ibid.)

President Mundey asserted that in the past few years the CPA had been recruiting more youth, especially women, and the profile of delegates at the 26th Congress bore out her words. The ages of 56 of the delegates (sixteen were women) ranged between 20 and 30, and 25 (eight women) were between 31 and 40. Only 29 (eleven women) were over 50. Moreover, "12 new members were elected to the National Committee, most of them under 30." (Ibid., 20 June, p. 5.)

Not unsurprisingly this new composition of congress delegates coincided with a new party strategy, the first fundamental change in fifteen years. The new party "line," which the CPA adopted after heated debate, can be called a "united front" campaign to give party support to all groups and individuals struggling for greater legal and socioeconomic rights. This is borne out by the congress's pointed statement on "women and social liberation." New committee member Joyce Stevens introduced this new policy in a resolution stressing that "recently a new interest in Marxism has broadened many feminists' analyses of patriarchy under capitalism" . . . and by their attempt to develop a socialist feminism that redefines the practices and understandings of both feminists and socialists" (ibid.). Since the 26th Congress adopted "proportional representation of women on the National Committee (NC) and its executive by a comfortable margin" (25 percent of the NC were women), clearly the CPA intends in the future to mobilize more women into its ranks and champion women's rights throughout Australia.

The congress, however, did not ignore the working classes. Delegates agreed on various resolutions that committed the CPA to struggle on behalf of the working classes for higher wages, shorter working hours, and more programs giving workers a voice in company management. The CPA definitely intends to support the labor union movement and wherever possible to acquire control of these unions. The CPA also condemned the new national budget published by the liberal Fraser government for favoring the wealthy and imposing too great a burden on the poor (see also ibid., 29 August, p. 1).

In the area of foreign affairs, congress delegates spoke out against U.S. military installations in Australia, expressed the CPA's solidarity with Vietnam's struggle against the Pol Pot regime, and called upon the Australian government to grant aid to Vietnam. Finally, it adopted a policy line, very much like that of the southern European communist parties, of deploring the conflict in Southeast Asia between Vietnam and its Soviet ally and China since all parties once had an "outstanding record of struggle for national liberation."

The CPA and Labor. The pattern that emerged in 1979, like that of preceding years, was one in which the CPA seized on every case of work stoppage as an opportunity to show its support for labor and demonstrate its unique right to serve as the champion of workers' rights in Australia. The CPA vigorously expressed its support of the labor union movement and of workers involved in any conflict with management.

In October the CPA tried to mobilize financial support and public sympathy for 50 workers at a Union Carbide firm in Altona, Victoria. These workers had physically occupied the main plant to demand a 35-hour workweek without any decrease in pay. The CPA's *Tribune* published a long account of how the strikers fed themselves and obtained support from the community (ibid., 5 October, p. 1). Then in September the CPA endorsed the Labour Party's appeal to the Fraser government to pass a wealth tax and tighten up penalties for those among the wealthy who practice tax evasion (ibid., 5 September, p. 1).

The CPA also made a public issue of aboriginal workmen laboring in a uranium mine at Narbalik, Queensland. The CPA claimed that many of these workers had already contracted "radiation-induced diseases." The basis for this assertion was a public report that listed the alleged dangers of working in these mines, but the Queensland state government had ignored this report and taken no action (ibid., 1 August, p. 9). In early July the CPA called for all labor unions to unite and oppose the Fraser government. This appeal was made by the party's assistant national secretary, Laurie Carmichael, in a speech calling on all labor unions to set aside their differences and adopt a united front against the Fraser government (ibid., 25 July, p. 1). In the same month the CPA prominently supported a four-day strike of 33,000 rail and tram workers in Victoria, Tasmania, and South Australia (ibid., 4 July, p. 12).

The CPA and Australian Society. The CPA has begun to identify with minorities and so-called "oppressed" groups in Australian society and devotes considerable space in its organ, the *Tribune*, to the plight of such groups. The CPA's rhetoric is passionate, at times vitriolic, and designed to elicit maximum sympathy for these groups instead of promoting clarity of discussion and understanding of their problems. The CPA one-sidedly describes the current difficulties of these groups without any mention of the recent, gradual improvement of their rights, nor does it dwell on any of the profound complexities within Australian society that prevent quicker improvement.

In September, for example, the CPA reported that the Fifth National Homosexual Conference was being held in Melbourne (over 600 lesbians and male homosexuals participated). The CPA's correspondent reporting this event expressed the hope that "next year's Sydney conference will consolidate the theme of fighting back so homosexuals can live, work and love without imposed fear or guilt" (ibid., 19 September, p. 6).

In the same month the CPA took up the cause of Australia's aborigines by describing in glowing terms how aborigines could organize and support their own efforts. The case in point was a group of aborigines who had organized to form the Strelley Community School in Western Australia, found funding for it, and managed the school with success.

The CPA also came out strongly for repealing state abortion laws. An article by Rebecca Albury in the *Tribune* (19 September, p. 16) violently attacked Ed Casey, Queensland Labour Party leader, for petitioning the Queensland parliament to take "strong and definite steps" to prohibit the operation of a Brisbane fertility clinic. Albury's article claimed that this effort was part of a concerted campaign against women seeking to obtain abortion rights throughout Australia. This example of the CPA championing women's rights even when it conflicted with the demands of a labor union is an example of how women's voices are now being heard in the CPA, even when the message severely criticizes organized Australian labor.

The CPA prominently played up the achievements of outstanding women, giving detailed and colorful accounts of their achievements, especially in the labor movement. The *Tribune* (12 September, p. 13) ran a long interview on Barbara Murphy, the first woman to be elected to the powerful New South Wales Labour Council Executive. Murphy was quoted as belonging to no party except the Teachers Federation and involving herself only in interunion activities. Readers were able to learn about her general interests and life style, including her hobbies, such as a love for cooking and preparing a "lovely dinner."

Nor did the CPA miss any opportunity to champion the cause of women who were allegedly the victims of employment discrimination. A 26-year-old woman named Deborah Wardely had applied to become the first woman pilot for Ansett Airlines in Victoria. For reasons not made clear by the CPA, Wardely had been denied the pilot's job and was appealing her case. The CPA made a special effort to document her flying qualifications and raise doubts in the readers' minds why she was the brunt of employment discrimination (ibid., 15 August).

The CPA and International Affairs. The CPA appears to have taken a more flexible position on international affairs, especially where socialist countries are involved. Of course, the CPA continues to criticize the United States and other Western countries as imperialist powers threatening world peace, but the CPA has adopted a rather ambiguous stance toward China.

For example, party veteran Eric Aarons wrote a lead article in the *Tribune* (3 October, p. 13) commemorating the 30th year of China's revolution and warmly praising Maoist doctrine and policies. Yet, Aarons pointed out that after Mao's death and the elimination of the "gang of four" by Hua Guofeng, the new leadership's policies seem to have been supported by "genuine mass enthusiasm for change." Aarons went on to argue that even the Sino-Soviet split in the early 1960s had positive benefits for communist parties around the world. The split accelerated "an irreversible process of the decline of the uncritical imitation of revolutionary 'models' and consequently willingness to accept an external source as the ultimate 'authority.' " This comment strongly suggests that the CPA has taken a flexible position on foreign affairs, even to the extent of criticizing major socialist states.

For example, the CPA made no secret of its contempt for and alarm at China's invasion of Vietnam in early 1979. The party strongly criticized Chinese actions (ibid., 21 February, p. 1) and at the same time expressed the fear that war between China and the Soviet Union might soon follow.

Throughout 1979 the CPA expressed its unswerving support for Vietnam's actions and policies to extend its control over Indochina. It criticized the U.N. resolution declaring the Pol Pot government the legitimate representative of Kampuchea (Cambodia) (ibid., 3 October, p. 2). It solicited funds from its membership to send to Vietnam. The CPA's chief organ always reported events in Vietnam most sympathetically, stressing the correctness and justness of Vietnam's policies and defending its actions to unseat the Pol Pot regime.

Finally, the CPA appears to be making an energetic attempt to establish closer ties with communist parties around the world, irrespective of their ideological disputes or differences with Beijing and Moscow. This activity was certainly indicated by the invitations extended to communist parties to attend the 26th Congress and by their acceptances.

Publications. The CPA publishes a weekly newspaper, the *Tribune*, which in mid-1979 became a sixteen-page paper with color print and one-third more news and comment. The party also publishes the monthly theoretical journal *Australian Left Review* and the occasional internal publication *Praxis*. The SPA has a fortnightly newspaper, the *Socialist*, and a monthly digest, *Survey*. The Communist Party of Australia (Marxist-Leninist) prints a weekly newspaper, *Vanguard*, and the monthly theoretical journal, *Australian Communist*.

Hoover Institution
Stanford University

Ramon H. Myers

Bangladesh

The beginning of 1979 saw the pro-Moscow Bangladesh Communist Party (BCP) legal once again, but declaring its refusal to participate in the national elections scheduled for January. Later the BCP changed its position and joined in the election campaign but performed poorly. The Samyabadi Dal/ Marxist-Leninist (BCP-ML), the pro-Beijing communist party, also performed poorly in the election, although its leader Mohammad Toaha was elected to a seat in the parliament. In the fall the BCP-ML joined with four other parties under the leadership of Toaha to constitute the Democratic Front (DF) in an apparent attempt to increase its political influence. This union provoked strong criticism from the BCP, which interpreted the newly formed group as anti-Soviet, anti-Indian, and anti-BCP. One other Marxist party, the Jatiya Gonomukti Union, also joined the DF. Meanwhile, the pro-Moscow National Awami Party (NAP; not a Marxist or communist party, although sometimes seen as a front for the BCP) split, with one faction retaining close ties with the BCP.

None of the communist, Marxist, or leftist parties had much influence in Bangladesh politics during the year. The three communist parties mentioned above remained small, with membership ranging from 1,000 to 4,000.

Party Leadership. Moni Singh and Mohammad Farhad continued at the helm of the BCP. Mohammad Toaha remained leader of the BCP-ML, although Toaha also became head of the new five-party coalition, DF, in October. Kazi Zafar Ahmed, chairman of the United People's Party, and Enayetullah Khan, vice-chairman of the National Awami Party-Bhashani (NAP-B), whose parties also joined the DF, can also be counted among the DF's leaders. Both are former members of the cabinet and remain influential politicians. Rashed Khan Menon, who is also a member of parliament, is another leader of the DF. These and a number of known and colorful individuals have given the DF considerable attractive power, perhaps indicating why the BCP has been so acutely concerned.

The National Awami Party-Muzaffar (NAP-M), pro-Moscow but technically not Marxist or communist, split during the year. In April the NAP-M leadership expelled its general secretary, Pankaj Bhattacharya, and its organizing secretary, Mrs. Motia Chowdhury. These two formed a new party, which remained steadfastly antigovernment. Pro-Beijing critics contended that the split was engineered by Moscow so that it could maintain close ties with the government through the NAP-M, yet also oppose the Zia leadership at the same time through another party that it controlled.

Anwar Zahid, secretary general of the pro-Beijing NAP-B (technically not a communist party) remained head of his party but was also counted as a leader of the DF. Enayetulla Khan, who runs the influential Sunday newspaper *Holiday*, which is known for its pro-Chinese sympathies, and who has supported the BCP-ML, also joined the NAP-B and appeared to add strength both to that party and to the cause of the DF.

The Jatiya Gonomukti Union, a small Marxist party, and the Gonofront, a leftist though not a Marxist party, also joined the DF, but their leaders did not play a central role in its strategy or activities.

Party Activities. In November 1978 a ban on several parties, including the BCP, was lifted—a result, according to BCP leaders, of a petition with more than 150,000 signatures circulated by the party and submitted to President Mohammed Zia ul Haq. Shortly after President Zia announced that general elections would be held on 27 January, he also issued a decree banning all parties organized with foreign financial help and affiliated with any foreign organization that propagates views detrimental to the sovereignty and security of the nation or that maintained an armed underground organization. At the same time, he required all political parties to keep their accounts in recognized banks in Bangladesh.

Twelve parties, including the BCP but not the BCP-ML, announced in December that they would boycott the elections unless President Zia agreed to "five prerequisites" for free and fair elections: the lifting of martial law, withdrawal of other "repressive" laws, Zia's resignation from the posts of commander-in-chief and chief martial law administrator, the restoration of parliamentary democracy, and freedom of the press.

In the meantime, on 7 December 1978 the BCP held its first Central Committee meeting as a legal party for some time and on 13 December held its first rally since 1975. Pronouncements at the rally called on the people to "struggle for independence and exercise democratic, political, and economic rights." Later in December the government extended the deadline for parties to file nomination papers for the election, and President Zia tried to persuade the boycotting parties to join in the election campaign. At almost the same time, the date of the election was postponed from January to February.

On 27 December the BCP, the pro-Moscow NAP, and several other parties that had proclaimed a boycott of the elections changed their positions and decided to participate by nominating candidates. In fact, the two pro-Moscow parties were the first to break away from the group of boycotting parties. Ironically, one of the reasons given for this switch in policy by the BCP, as well as the NAP, was the repeal of the fourth constitutional amendment, which gave the president dictatorial powers and allowed him to rule with one-party support while banning other parties.

Elections were finally held on 18 February and resulted in a resounding victory for President Zia's Bangladesh Nationalist Party (BNP). The BNP won 203 of 300 elective seats in the parliament. The Awami League-Malek came in second with 40 seats, and the right-wing Muslim League–Islamic Democratic League alliance won 19 seats. In all, 29 parties participated in the election and a number of candidates ran as independents. The BCP fielded 14 candidates and the BCP-ML 19—out of a total of 1,709.

The Marxist or communist parties did very poorly in the elections. Mohammad Farhad, representing the BCP, was badly beaten. Mohammad Toaha, head of the BCP-ML, won the only Marxist or communist seat in the parliament. The election seemed a clear-cut defeat for communist and other leftist parties. On the other hand, a number of leftist politicians had joined the BNP to gain influence from within. The election also seemed a clear defeat for the Soviet-supported parties, although it was rumored at the time of the elections that the Soviet Union had also given some support to several right-wing parties.

In September the DF issued a sixteen-point program, which was described by members of the group as "not a leftist program, but a patriotic, democratic one." Although the DF proclaimed that it did not consider followers of the late Sheikh Mujibur Rahman, including pro-Moscow and pro-Indian groups, its enemies, the BCP weekly newspaper spoke of the DF in terms of the "ominous activities of the Maoists in Bangladesh." Meanwhile, the government did not seem very concerned about the newly formed DF.

International Views and Contacts. Although the BCP retained close ties with Moscow and the BCP-ML continued its contacts with Beijing, neither the Soviet Union nor China relied on their respective supporting parties in their relations with the government of Bangladesh. This is primarily because these parties are too small and do not have much influence with the government.

During the year the BCP supported the Soviet Union's proposals on disarmament and détente with the United States. Party Chairman Moni Singh traveled to Eastern Europe and while there expressed the party's support for disarmament in Europe, as well as for other tenets of Soviet foreign policy. At the same time, however, the BCP claimed to be a nationalist party not controlled by outside forces.

Mohammad Toaha gave his party's support to China, including Beijing's establishing of diplomatic ties with the United States. The BCP-ML also supportd other themes in China's foreign policy during the year, including China's anti-Soviet line.

Publications. See *YICA*, 1978.

Southwestern at Memphis   John F. Copper

Burma

The Burmese Communist Party (BCP), founded on 15 August 1939, was part of the nationalist coalition that led the struggle for Burmese independence. The BCP split with the noncommunist nationalists in March 1948, three months after Burma gained independence, and has since been in insurrection against the government. There are no reliable figures on party membership. Estimates of the size of the BCP's guerrilla force range from 8,000 to 15,000 men operating east of the Salween River in the mountainous area of northern Burma bordering China's Yunnan province. There have been infrequent reports in the Burmese press of BCP terrorist activities in southwestern Burma in the Arakan State, but the relationship between these alleged communists and those in northern Burma is uncertain. They may be remnants of a small radical communist movement that broke away from the BCP in 1947 and has been periodically reported as active in southwestern Burma.

Leadership and Organization. No changes were reported in BCP leadership during 1979. Seventy-year-old Thakin Ba Thein Tin remains party chairman. Long resident in Beijing, he was reported in Burma in 1979 (Voice of the People of Burma Radio [VOPB], 4 September; *FBIS*, 12 September). Party headquarters is in Pang Hseng (also called Wan Long), a Burmese town on the Chinese border, which also serves as the headquarters of the Northeast Command, the BCP's military arm. Zaw Mai, a former Kachin Independence Army (KIA) leader, is believed to command the BCP forces.

Party Internal Affairs. The BCP's 40th anniversary dominated party propaganda during the year. The New Year's statement broadcast on VOPB noted that "despite its attempts to deceive the people, the reactionary military government was in 1978 dragged closer to the brink of death." Commenting on the importance of the integration of "armed struggle with various other forms of struggle," it said that the party will learn from the experiences of 1978 to lay down guidelines for 1979. (VOPB, 2 January; *FBIS*, 9 January.) The anniversary statement, broadcast on 15 August, was less optimistic and tended to stress the difficulties the party has encountered in leading the "people's democratic revolution" over the years. While reaffirming the primacy of armed struggle, the statement repeated the need for integrating it with other forms of struggle. (*FBIS*, 17 August.) Party Chairman Thakin Ba Thein Tin similarly stressed the theme of integrated struggle in his anniversary address. Speaking from a platform reportedly decorated with huge photographs of Marx, Engels, Lenin, Stalin, and Mao Zedong, he also admonished the party to study its mistakes, observing that "a party which is genuinely communist must learn from its mistakes and must correct them." (VOPB, 4 September; *FBIS*, 12 September.)

The attention given the integration of forms of struggle and the calls for learning from mistakes hint that the party is undergoing or considering a re-evaluation of the party's general strategy. Developments over the past year, including reversals on the battlefield (see below), have substantially altered the BCP's situation and must raise serious questions within the party about its future direction. The continued improvement in relations between Rangoon and Beijing and the apparently significant reduction of Chinese material support for the BCP seems to have provoked debate over the congruence between BCP and Chinese policies (*Asiaweek*, 18 May). The gradual improvement in Burma's economy during the year also undercut a central BCP propaganda concern of the past (see *YICA*, 1979, p. 224). Both the party's and the chairman's anniversary statements sought to discredit the validity of the government's socialist programs, characterizing them as a mask for the three "Isms"— feudal landlordism, imperialism, and bureaucratic capitalism.

Domestic Activities and Alliances. The party radio called for continued building of party institutions within controlled areas, but it carried no announcements of new party programs. Citing the importance both Marx and Mao Zedong attached to intellectuals and their role in revolutionary movements, the VOPB exhorted students to join the struggle. It praised the students' past activities, particularly the "December 1974 struggle" at Rangoon Arts and Science University and claimed that the government reaction to these demonstrations revealed to the people "the ogre which had donned the mask of the prince." (VOPB, 28 December 1978; *FBIS*, 3 January.)

The BCP repeated its wilingness "to unite with all forces that can be united with" (VOPB, 15 August; *FBIS*, 17 August). The BCP's troops collaborated with Kachin Independence Army forces in northern Burma; however, no mention was made in propaganda channels of the alliance forged between the two groups as early as August 1975. The VOPB also reported periodically on the military actions of the Shan State Progress (variously, Progressive) Party without referring to its role in the communist struggle. (VOPB, 6 February, 9 March, and 6 April; *FBIS*, 14 February, 13 March, and 17 April.) There were signs that the two-year-old alliance with the Shan group was under some strain, and one commentary noted that the Shan were cooperating with the BCP only east of the Salween River and were operating independently in areas west of the river (*Far Eastern Economic Review* [*FEER*], 15 June and 31 August). Since there is little common ideological ground between the BCP and its ethnic insurgent allies, these relations may become more contentious as Chinese material support for the BCP is reduced and the BCP is no longer able to provide Chinese-supplied arms and equipment to its erstwhile allies.

Faced with a loss or reduction of Chinese material support, the BCP may become more deeply involved in Burma's lucrative opium trade as a way of financing its insurgency. The area under BCP control produces nearly 40 percent of Burma's opium (upwards of 200 tons). The Burmese government charged that the BCP was already working closely with "economic insurgents," Rangoon's label for the nominally insurgent warlord armies in the Shan state that are deeply involved in narcotics trafficking (Rangoon Domestic Radio, 9 May; *FBIS*, 11 May). Although its propaganda once inveighed against opium cultivation and narcotics trafficking, this year the BCP made no mention of its activities in this area. It did, however, attack the government as responsible for Burma's drug problem (VOPB, 1 November; *FBIS*, 6 November).

Armed struggle remains the central element of the BCP's strategy, but it was apparent this year that the military dimension of the strategy has undergone considerable change. The multi-battalion operations that characterized the struggle in 1977 and 1978 and led to heavy casualties on both sides in battles at Hopong and Kunlong have given way to smaller-scale guerrilla operations (VOPB, 16 March and 12 July; *FBIS*, 22 March and 20 July). No doubt because of the troop losses of the previous year and the likely reduction in Chinese support, the BCP forces largely restricted their operations to ambushes of government patrols, raids on Burmese army outposts, and the mining of roads, especially the key routes west and north of Keng Tung. Both the casualty figures claimed by the BCP and those acknowledged by the government are substantialy lower than last year. (VOPB, 21 September; *FBIS*, 26 September; *FEER*, 31 August.)

The government staged several large operations against the communists, but its own party journal considered the most notable actions were those directed against the KIA and Shan State Army and not the BCP (*Lanzin Thadin*, 31 August; *Botataung*, 10 September; *Kyemon*, 10 October). The government also battled the so-called Arakan BCP, but this group's activities appeared insignificant (*Myanma Alin*, 17 January; *FBIS*, 31 January; *Botataung*, 10 September and 15 October).

International Views and Contacts. The BCP has long drawn its ideological inspiration from the "glorious and correct Chinese Communist Party" under the leadership of Mao Zedong (VOPB, 2 October; *FBIS*, 26 October). Despite the implications of a reduction in Chinese material support for the insurgency, BCP propaganda in 1979 showed no signs of wavering in its commitment to the Chinese line. Nowhere was this more evident than in the anti-Vietnamese, anti-Soviet themes continually broadcast over VOPB following the Vietnamese invasion of Democratic Kampuchea (Cambodia) and the subsequent Sino-Vietnamese war. Vietnam was excoriated as the "little hegemonist" of Asia and variously labeled as the "Asian Cuba," "Angola," and "Zaire." In one hard-hitting editorial, Vietnam was named "the root cause of all regional wars in Southeast Asia." (VOPB, 25 February; *FBIS*, 28 February). The BCP radio railed against Vietnamese fascism and its colonialism in Laos (VOPB, 9 and 12 August; *FBIS*, 12 and 13 August).

The BCP, echoing China, warned of the threat of "Vietnamese expansionist ambitions in Southeast Asia." An article entitled "After Phnom Penh, Who?" noted that "only when all the people of Southeast Asia . . . combine as one to collectively attack and prevent the big and small hegemonists' aggression and expansionist moves can regional and global peace and stability be assured" (VOPB, 26 April; *FBIS*, 5 May).

The BCP's propaganda closely followed Chinese shifts on support for Pol Pot's Democratic Kampuchean regime. In February the BCP sent a message to the Kampuchean Communist Party (KCP) expressing its resolute support for the KCP's war against Vietnamese aggression (VOPB, 7 August; *FBIS*, 8 August). In August, however, the BCP lauded "the resistance of the Kampuchean people under the leadership of the government of Democratic Kampuchea" and made no mention of the role of the KCP (VOPB, 7 August; *FBIS*, 8 August).

If Vietnamese aggression was the proximate concern of the BCP, other statements made it abundantly clear that the larger enemy lurking behind Vietnam was the Soviet Union., No opportunity was missed to score the dangers of Soviet hegemony and Soviet social-imperialism. The party's 40th anniversary statement called for "attacks against the imperialism of today—the two superpowers, U.S. imperialism and Soviet social-imperialism—and particularly the hegemonism of Soviet social-imperialism." (VOPB, 15 August; *FBIS*, 17 August.) Party Chairman Thakin Ba Thein Tin called Soviet imperialism more rampant than ever (VOPB, 4 September; *FBIS*, 12 September). An article broadcast by the BCP equated Soviet support for Vietnamese aggression in Kampuchea with Soviet actions in Prague a decade earlier and argued that this was at the heart of the Brezhnev doctrine (VOPB, 25 March; *FBIS*, 29 March). The BCP also saw nothing but the darkest designs behind the proposed Soviet-Japanese treaty (VOPB, 16 January; *FBIS*, 18 January).

Radio Moscow, in a Burmese-language broadcast, counterattacked with its own anti-Chinese arguments. It blamed China for all of Burma's insurgency. Commenting on rumors of a reduction in Chinese support to the BCP, Radio Moscow (26 December 1978) claimed that there was "not one chance in a million China will reduce its support" (*FBIS*, 27 December 1978). Repeating an international theme, Radio Moscow (20 September) subsequently accused the United States of colluding with China in supporting the BCP (*FBIS*, 21 September).

The BCP's 40th anniversary provided the occasion for other fraternal communist parties to send their greetings and endorse the Burmese struggle. In addition to a message from the Central Committee of the Chinese Communist Party, the BCP received greetings from the communist parties of Thailand, Malaysia, Indonesia, and the Philippines, as well as the Spanish Workers' Revolutionary Organization. The messages uniformly stressed the importance of the ideological leadership given by Mao Zedong, and all contained warnings of the threats posed by the hegemony of Soviet social-imperialism (VOPB, 15–16 August; *FBIS*, 16, 17, and 28 August).

Publications. The only firsthand information on the BCP comes from the VOPB, which has broadcast since 1971 from a communications facility near Kunming, China.

U.S. Department of State
Washington, D.C.

Jon A. Wiant

(Note: Views expressed in this article are the author's own and do not necessarily represent those of the State Department.)

China

The Chinese Communist Party (Zhongguo gongchan dang; CCP), founded in July 1921, is the largest communist party in the world. The CCP claimed "more than 35 million" members at its Eleventh Party Congress in August 1977; present membership is estimated at 37 million. As the only legal party, the CCP provides "absolute leadership" for all other organizations in the PRC (Eleventh Party Constitution, II: 14).

Organization and Leadership. According to the party constitution, the "highest leading body" of the CCP is the Party National Congress, to be convened every five years, which under "special circumstances" may be convened early or postponed. Actually each congress to date has been called under such circumstances. The last Party National Congress, the eleventh, met in August 1977. The congress elects the Central Committee, which acts when the congress is not in session. The Central Committee elects the Politburo, the Standing Committee of the Politburo, and the chairman and the vice-chairman or vice-chairmen of the Central Committee. The Eleventh Central Committee has had four plenary sessions: August 1977, February and December 1978, and September 1979. The Politburo and its Standing Committee exercise the functions and powers of the Central Committee when the latter is not in plenary session.

The Eleventh Central Committee (elected in August 1977) has 201 full and 132 alternate members. The committee is dominated by older, experienced cadres, a great many of whom were purged or criticized in the Cultural Revolution. The first secretaries of all 29 major administrative divisions—provinces, autonomous regions, and municipalities—are full members. There is strong military presence in the committee as a whole, as there is in the Eleventh Central Committee's Politburo.

The officers, members, and alternate members of the Politburo are:

Chairman: Hua Guofeng

Vice-Chairmen: Ye Jianying, Deng Xiaoping, Li Xiannian, Wang Dongxing, Chen Yun (added December 1978)
(These six comprise the Standing Committee of the Politburo.)

Members of the Politburo:

Wei Guoqing

Ulanfu

Fang Yi

Deng Xiaoping

Ye Jianying

Liu Bocheng

Xu Shiyou

Ji Dengkui

Su Zhenhua

Li Xiannian

Li Desheng

Wu De

Yu Qiuli

Wang Dongxing

Zhang Tingfa

Chen Yonggui

Chen Xilian

Geng Biao

Nie Rongzhen

Ni Zhifu

Xu Xiangqian

Peng Chong

Added in December 1978:

Chen Yun

Deng Yingchao

Hu Yaobang

Wang Zhen

Added in September:

Zhao Ziyang

Peng Zhen

Alternate Members of the Politburo: Chen Muhua, Saifudin

Below the Central Committee and its Politburo extends a network of party committees at the provincial, special district, county, and municipal levels. A similar network exists within the People's Liberation Army (PLA) from the military region to the regimental level. Primary party organizations or party branches are located in factories, mines, and other enterprises, and people's communes, offices, schools, shops, neighborhoods, PLA companies, and elsewhere as required.

According to the state constitution adopted 5 March 1978, the highest organ of state power in the PRC is the National People's Congress (NPC). The NPC is elected for a term of five years and holds one session each year, although both of these stipulations are subject to alteration. The first session of the Fifth NPC was held 24 February to 8 March 1978; the second session met from 15 June to 1 July.

The permanent organ of the NPC is its Standing Committee, which it elects and is composed of a chairman, vice-chairmen, a secretary general, and other members. The NPC Standing Committee exercises various functions and powers. It conducts the election of NPC deputies; convenes NPC sessions; interprets the constitution and laws and enacts decrees; supervises the work of the State Council, the Supreme People's Court, and the Supreme People's Procuratorate; changes and annuls inappropriate decisions adopted by organs of state power at various levels; decides on appointment and removal of State Council members on the premier's recommendation when the NPC is not in session; appoints and removes Supreme People's Court vice-presidents and Supreme People's Procuratorate deputy chief procurators; decides on the appointment and removal of plenipotentiary representatives abroad; decides on ratification and abrogation of treaties; institutes state titles of honor and decides on their conferment; decides on the granting of pardons; decides on the proclamation of a state of war "in the event of armed attack on the country" when the NPC is not in session; and exercises other functions and powers as may be vested by the NPC.

The officers and members of the Fifth NPC Standing Committee were elected on 5 March 1978. The officers are:

Chairman: Ye Jianying

Vice-Chairmen:

Song Qingling	Zhang Dingcheng	Added 1 July:
Nie Jongzhen	Cai Chang	Peng Zhen
Liu Bocheng	Deng Yingchao	Xiao Jingguang
Ulanfu	Saifudin	Zhu Yunshan
Wu Deh	Liao Chengzhi	Shi Liang
Wei Guoqing	Ji Pengfei	
Chen Yun	Ngapo Ngawang Jigme	
Guo Moro (died 12 June 1978)	Zhou Jianren	
Tan Zhenlin	Xu Deheng	
Li Jingquan	Hu Juewen	

Secretary General: Ji Pengfei (replaced by Peng Zhen, 29 November)

There are also 175 regular members of the NPC Standing Committee.

Under the NPC Standing Committee and responsible to it is the State Council, which, according to the constitution, is the central people's government and the highest organ of state power and of state administration. The State Council exercises several functions and powers. It formulates administrative measures, issues decisions and orders, and verifies their execution in accordance with the constitution; submits proposals on legal and other matters to the NPC or its Standing Committee; exercises leadership over the ministries and commissions; exercises leadership over the local organs of state administration at various levels; draws up and implements the national economic plan and the state budget; protects the interests of the state, maintains public order and safeguards the rights of citizens; confirms the administrative divisions (autonomous prefectures, counties, autonomous counties, and cities); appoints and removes administrative personnel according to law; and exercises such other functions that might be vested in it from above.

Officers of the State Council since the First Session of the Fifth NPC in March 1978 are:

Premier: Hua Guofeng

Vice-Premiers:

Deng Xiaoping	Chen Yonggui	Added 1 July:
Li Xiannian	Fang Yi	Chen Yun
Xu Xiangqian	Wang Zhen	Bo Yibo
Ji Dengkui	Gu Mu	Yao Yilin
Yu Qiuli	Kang Shien	
Chen Xilian	Chen Muhua	Added 13 September 1979:
Geng Biao		Ji Pengfei

Secretary General (re-established 12 June): Jin Ming
Minister of Foreign Affairs: Huang Hua
Minister of National Defense: Xu Xiangqian
Minister in Charge of the State Planning Commission: Yu Qiuli
Minister in Charge of the State Economic Commission: Kang Shien

Minister in Charge of the State Capital Construction Commission: Gu Mu

Minister in Charge of the State Scientific and Technological Commission: Fang Yi

Minister in Charge of the State Nationalities Affairs Commission: Yang Jingren

Minister in Charge of the State Agricultural Commission (established 23 February): Wang Renzhong

Minister of Public Security: Zhao Cangbi

Minister of Civil Affairs: Cheng Zihua

Minister of Foreign Trade: Li Qiang

Minister of Economic Relations with Foreign Countries: Chen Muhua

Minister of Agricultural Machinery (established 23 February): Yang Ligong

Minister of Agriculture and Forestry (renamed Ministry of Agriculture, 23 February): Huo Shilian (relieved Yang Ligong, 23 February)

Ministry of Forestry (established 23 February): Lo Yuchuan

Minister of Metallurgical Industry: Tang Ke

Minister of the First Ministry of Machine-Building: Zhou Zijian

Minister of the Second Ministry of Machine-Building: Liu Wei

Minister of the Third Ministry of Machine-Building: Lu Dong

Minister of the Fourth Ministry of Machine-Building: Qian Min

Minister of the Fifth Ministry of Machine-Building: Zhang Zhen

Minister of the Sixth Ministry of Machine-Building: Chai Shufan

Minister of the Seventh Ministry of Machine-Building: Zheng Tianxiang (relieved Song Renqiong, 23 February)

Minister of the Eighth Ministry of Machine-Building (Established 13 September): Jiao Ruoyu

Minister of Coal Industry: Xiao Han

Minister of Petroleum Industry: Song Zhenming

Minister of Chemical Industry: Sun Jingwen

Minister of Water Conservancy and Power (separated into the Ministry of Power Industry and the Ministry of Water Conservancy, 23 February): Qian Zhengying (Water Conservancy) and Liu Lanbo (Power Industry)

Minister of Textile Industry: Qian Zhiguang

Minister of Light Industry: Liang Liangguang

Minister of Railways: Guo Weicheng

Minister of Communications: Zeng Sheng (relieved Ye Fei, 23 February)

Minister of Posts and Telecommunications: Wang Zigang

Minister of Finance: Wu Bo (replaced Zhang Jingfu, 13 September)

President of the People's Bank of China: Li Baohua

Minister of Commerce: Wang Lei (relieved Yao Yilin, 23 February)

Director of the All-China Federation of Supply and Marketing Cooperatives: Niu Yinguan (relieved Chen Guodong, 12 June)

Minister of Culture: Huang Zhen

Minister of Education: Jiang Nanxiang (relieved Liu Xiyao, 23 February)

Minister of Public Health: Jiang Yizhen

Minister in Charge of the State Physical Culture and Sports Commission: Wang Meng

Minister of State Farms and Land Reclamation (re-established 12 June): Gao Yang

Minister of Food (re-established 12 June): Chen Guodong

Minister of Justice (established 13 September): Wei Wenbo

Minister of Geology (established 13 September): Sun Daguang

The 1978 state constitution provided for people's congresses and revolutionary committees in the provinces, the municipalities directly under the central government, counties, cities, municipal districts, people's communes, and towns and stated that these were the organs of self-government of the national autonomous areas. The constitution also referred to the people's congresses and revolutionary committees in the communes as organizations of political power at the grass-roots level and as leading organs of the collective economy. Local revolutionary committees at various levels were said to be the executive and administrative organs of local people's congresses at corresponding levels. Local people's congresses were to elect and recall members of revolutionary committees at corresponding levels.

This was the pattern of local governance well into 1979. However, the second session of the Fifth NPC made significant changes, amending the state constitution accordingly. Beginning in July, the following changes were to be implemented "speedily." Standing committees are now to be established for people's congresses at and above the county level as permanent organs at their respective levels. Local revolutionary committees at various levels are to be changed into local people's governments, and the titles of officers of local governments are to be changed to governor and deputy governors (of a province), chairman and vice-chairmen (of an autonomous region inhabited in compact communities by minority nationalities), mayor and deputy mayors (of a city), head and deputy heads (of a county), and director and deputy directors (of a commune administrative committee). (*Beijing Review* [*BR*], 13 July.) "Revolutionary committees," one of the last remaining vestiges of the Cultural Revolution, were eliminated.

The second session also changed the 1953 electoral law so that deputies to county people's congresses are to be elected directly instead of indirectly.

The Supreme People's Court is the highest judicial organ. Its president, re-elected at the Fifth NPC, is Jiang Hua.

The chief procurator of the Supreme People's Procuratorate (abolished in 1975 but re-established in 1978) is Huang Huoqing, also elected at the Fifth NPC. The second session in July changed the relation between higher and lower people's procuratorates "from that of supervision to one of leadership" (ibid., 13 July).

The People's Political Consultative Conference (CPPCC) is the official organization of the united front policy. The CPPCC is organized into a National Committee (the Fifth National Committee at its second session, 15 June–1 July, had 2,015 members, 1,734 of whom attended the opening ceremony), which holds plenary sessions and elects its Standing Committee. Deng Xiaoping is chairman of the CPPCC's National Committee. The CPPCC also has local committees at the provincial, autonomous region, municipal, and other levels. (For a description of the tasks of the CPPCC, see *YICA*, 1979, pp. 232–33.)

The PLA, which includes the navy and air force, has over 3.9 million members. According to the 1978 state constitution, the command of the PLA continues to be the responsibility of the chairman of the CCP, Hua Guofeng. The chief of the general staff is Deng Xiaoping. The defense minister is Xu Xiangqian. The PLA remains influential in CCP affairs, as its heavy representation on the Central Committee and Politburo suggests.

Mass organizations have played an important role in the organizational life of China, although they have for certain periods of time fallen into desuetude. Such was the case during the Great Proletarian Cultural Revolution. Following a period of resurgence that began just before the Tenth Party Congress in 1973, they again declined with the fall of the "gang of four" in 1976. However, in 1978 all three of the major mass organizations were reactivated and held congresses late in the year: the All-China Women's Federation in September 1978; the Communist Youth League of China (CYL) in October 1978; and the All-China Federation of Trade Unions (ACFTU) in October 1978. Central Committee member Han Ying is first secretary of the Central Committee of the CYL. Politburo member Ni Zhifu is president of the ACFTU.

Domestic Affairs. The year under review was characterized by important party and government meetings at which decisions of fundamental significance were made. Most important was the decision to scale down the ambitious economic development program announced in 1978. Also of significance was the promulgation of new laws and the adoption of amendments to the 1978 constitution. A number of prominent rehabilitees, especially associates of Deng Xiaoping, were highlighted in the course of these developments. Also of importance was the continuation of dissent and criticism in wall posters, underground publications, and protest demonstrations. Toward the end of the year, however, wall poster criticism was curtailed, and the familiar Democracy Wall was abolished (*San Jose News*, 6 December). In its place, carefully screened posters, with a number of prohibitions, are allowed in another part of Beijing. Criticism of the Cultural Revolution continued unabated; the late Chairman Mao Zedong was given scant direct positive attention. Beginning on 1 January, the Chinese phonetic alphabet (*pinyin*) officially superseded other forms of romanization in PRC publications. This change-over has generally been accepted by the international media and is followed in this work.

The basic direction for 1979 was established at the third plenary session of the Eleventh Central Committee, held 18–22 December 1978. Its Third Plenum further consolidated Deng Xiaoping's position, rehabilitating a number of his comrades and placing some in prominent positions. The plenum "solved a number of important questions left over from history," including the formal reversal of the "gang of four's" charge that the political line of 1975 (Deng's) was a "right-deviationist wind to reverse correct verdicts." Also, the Tian An Men events of 5 April 1976 were now adjudged to be "entirely revolutionary actions." The Third Plenum called for a revamping of the economic development program in order to emphasize agriculture.

In a 1 January speech, Deng Xiaoping noted that this New Year's Day was unusual. First, it marked the shift of the nation's work to the "four modernizations." Second, it marked the normalization of U.S.-PRC relations. And third, the cause of reunifying Taiwan to the mainland "is now on the agenda." Also on 1 January, Defense Minister Xu Xiangqian announced that the shelling of Jinmen (Quemoy) and other offshore islands held by the Nationalists would cease.

The new Central Commission for the Inspection of Discipline, established by the Third Plenum of the Central Committee in December 1978, held its first plenary session in Beijing, 4 to 22 January. It is made up of 100 members, headed by Chen Yun. This first session adopted an outline of the tasks, functions, and structure of the commission (*BR*, 9 February).

On 24 January the Central Committe's United Front Work Department announced that bank deposits and other properties confiscated from the national bourgeoisie were to be returned to them (ibid.). Similarly, on 28 January, the New China News Agency announced a recent decision that "all landlords, rich peasants, counterrevolutionaries, and bad elements" who have behaved well over the years "shall be considered as members of the people's communes." All those whose "class origin is that of landlord or rich peasant shall have the class status of commune member and the class origin of their children shall be commune member and no longer that of landlord or rich peasant." The same principle is to apply to urban areas. (Ibid., 9 February.)

The second session of the Fifth NPC was held in Beijing 18 June–1 July. The session heard and approved Premier Hua Guofeng's report on the work of the government; the 1979 national economic plan and Vice-Premier Yu Qiuli's report; the 1978 final state accounts; and the 1979 budget and Minister of Finance Zhang Jingfu's report. It also adopted a resolution on amendments to the 1978 state constitution; passed seven important laws; elected Peng Zhen, Xiao Jingguang, Zhu Yunshan, and Shi Liang vice-chairmen of the NPC Standing Committee and endorsed the nominations of Chen Yun, Bo Yibo, and Yao Yilin as vice-premiers of the State Council and Fang Yi as president of the Chinese Academy of Sciences; adopted a resolution on the reports of the work of the NPC Standing Committee, the Supreme People's Court, and the Supreme People's Procuratorate; elected a Nationalities Committee of the Fifth NPC, composed of 81 deputies of various nationalities with Tibetan Ngapo Ngawang Jigme as chairman; and approved a report by the Committee for Examining Motions. Ye Jianying, chairman of the session, gave the closing speech. (Ibid., 6 July.)

Meanwhile, the second session of the Fifth National Committee of the CPPCC was held concurrently with the second session of the NPC in Beijing, 15 June–2 July. Its chairman, Deng Xiaoping, gave the opening speech, said to be "a programme of action for the united front and the people's political consultative conference during this new period." The session elected Liu Lantao, Lu Dingyi, Li Weihan, Hu Yuzhi, Wang Kunlun and Tibetan Banqen Erdini Quoigyi Gyancan as additional vice-chairmen of the CPPCC National Committee. (Ibid., 6 July.)

Premier Hua's report on the work of the government was delivered to the NPC on 18 June. He first summarized the political, then the economic situation in China, which for the latter basically meant scaling down the ambitious targets set in 1978. The readjustment, which was to begin in 1979 and take three years, said Hua, should enable China to expand its agriculture, light and heavy industries, and various other branches of industry in a harmonious way, and to maintain a rational proportion between accumulation and consumption. Hua indicated that agriculture and the light, textile, coal, petroleum, and power industries and transport and communications services still lagged. He decried the many imbalances within and among industrial departments. In capital construction, he said that far too many projects were being undertaken at the same time. Finally, he mentioned the "obvious short-comings in the management of the economy and enterprises."

According to Hua, "Both in the three-year period of economic readjustment and in future years, China would take energetic steps to develop foreign trade, expand economic cooperation and technical exchanges with other countries, and adopt various reasonable practices now being used internationally to absorb foreign funds. This was a firm and important policy of the Chinese government."

Hua also spoke of the need to strengthen socialist democracy and the legal system, saying that political democracy was essential to the four modernizations. He said that "it was essential to implement the 'principle of the three nots,' i.e., not picking on people for their faults, not putting labels on people and not using the big stick, and [to] forbid the practice of repression and persecution against people who voiced different opinions." But cadres and the masses must "correctly understand and handle the relationships between democracy and dictatorship, democracy and centralism, and freedom and discipline."

On 21 June Vice-Premier and Minister in Charge of the State Planning Commission Yu Qiuli gave a report on the 1979 national economic draft plan, and the Minister of Finance Zhang Jingfu reported on the 1978 final state accounts and on the draft 1979 state budget. The reports were remarkable because this was the first time since 1959 that the Chinese government had made public its overall budget data. Also of significance were indications that the longtime practice of avoiding deficit spending was being abandoned. (Party Vice-Chairman Li Xiannian had already disclosed a week earlier that there had been a U.S. $6.5 billion deficit; *NYT*, 21 June.) Yu Qiuli listed production figures for 1978. Agricultural output value totaled 145.9 billion yuan; grain output was 304,750,000 tons. Cotton output was 2,167,000 tons. Total industrial output value was 423.1 billion yuan. Total capital construction investment was 39.5 billion yuan. The total value of imports and exports was 35.5 billion yuan ($22.6 billion), a 30.3-percent increase over 1977, with a slight surplus in the foreign-exchange balance.

The 1979 national economic plan called for a 4-percent increase in agriculture over 1978; an 8-percent increase in industrial production (8.3 percent in light industry, 7.6 in heavy industry) to be funded by 36 billion yuan ($22.9 billion) from the state budget for capital construction plus another 4 million yuan from loans; and the value of exports and imports was expected to reach 44 billion yuan ($28 billion), an increase of 24 percent. Yu said that investment in agriculture would increase from 1978's 10.7 percent to 14 percent; light industry investment would increase from 5.4 percent to 5.8 percent; but investment in heavy industry would decrease from 54.7 percent to 46.8 percent, with much of the funding given to the coal, petroleum, electric power, and building material industries. The allocation of such large outlays to heavy industry and the comparatively small figure for agriculture were surprising in view of Chinese talk over the past two decades about the priority of agriculture.

Yu spoke of specific important measures that would be adopted to boost agricultural production. The price of grain was to rise by 20 percent, and those who sell surplus grain over and above state quotas are to receive an additional 50-percent increase in the purchase price. Similarly, the purchase prices of eighteen major farm and sideline products are to increase by an average of 24.8 percent. Taxes, too, are to be reduced or remitted in rural areas.

Yu also stressed development in light industry and the need to complete a number of key projects as quickly as possible. With regard to wages, he said that from late 1977, 40 percent of the work force had received a wage grade advancement, while another 20 percent had their wages upgraded "to some extent." The average annual wage of workers and staff in units owned by the whole people (i.e., fully socialized) rose from 602 yuan in 1977 to 644 yuan in 1978, an increase of 7 percent. Yu said that per-capita income of peasants in the collective economy in 1978 rose 13.7 percent over 1977. The increase of purchase prices and tax adjustments would enable communes and peasants to increase their earnings by a further 7 billion yuan in 1979, and with developing production total income was expected to rise by 13 billion yuan.

Minister of Finance Zhang said that total revenues for 1978 were 112.1 billion yuan ($71.4 billion) and total expenditures were 111.1 billion yuan ($70.8 billion), with a favorable balance of 1 billion yuan ($600 million). Compared with 1977, revenues increased by 28.2 percent, expenditures by 31.7 percent. He said that the revenue and expenditure figures ($71.3 billion) for 1979 were expected to remain the same as for 1978. However, the actual income figure, without certain deductions (higher purchase prices for agriculture, wage and tax adjustments, etc.) would actually be $81.5 billion. (BR, 29 June; WP, 21 June; for Zhang's full report, see BR, 20 July.)

The above figures were supplemented on 27 June in a communiqué issued by the State Statistical Bureau on the fulfillment of China's 1978 national economic plan. The communiqué showed that national income for 1978 was 12 percent above the 1977 figure, which had risen 8 percent over the 1976 figure. It revealed that as of the end of 1978 China had a population of 975.23 million, including the population of Taiwan, or 958 million for mainland China. The natural population growth rate was said to be 12 per 1000 (BR, 6 July).

In June, however, the Hong Kong newspaper Ming Bao published other statistics of significance. Reportedly drawn from a speech given at a party meeting in April by Vice-Premier Li Xiannian, these indicated that China was facing an economic crisis, with a government deficit of $6.5 billion, 20 million people unemployed, and 100 million not getting enough to eat. The monthly grain ration of about forty pounds, with little additional nonstaple food such as meat and vegetables, was said to be inadequate for people doing heavy labor. Some observers have estimated that China's agricultural production has increased only 0.7 percent annually in the last three years, which is below the officially given population growth rate of 1.2 percent (Manchester Guardian, 24 June). Scenes reminiscent of pre-1949 China were reported in October, including stories of beggars, some of whom even snatched food from the plates of visiting foreigners in drought-beset Gansu province (Los Angeles Times [LAT], 21 October). Such unofficial supplementary statistics and such candid reports make the current concern for agricultural development and the raising of peasant income levels particularly understandable. The measures being taken, however, are inflationary. Indeed, on 1 November prices of perishable foods in Beijing were increased by as much as 33 percent, the first such price hike since 1949. The State Council concurrently announced that 100 million low-income people would be given wage increases of about 12.5 percent.

On 26 June Peng Zhen, the recently rehabilitated former mayor of Beijing and one of the principal targets of the Cultural Revolution, gave an explanation to the NPC of the seven draft laws that it was to approve. Peng spoke as director of the Commission for Legal Affairs of the NPC's Standing Committee. The new laws were: (1) the Organic Law of the Local People's Congresses and the Local People's Governments, which removed the term "revolutionary committees" from administrative nomenclature in China; (2) the Electoral Law for the National People's Congress and the Local People's Congresses, which extends direct elections to the county level and provides for secret ballots, a choice among candidates for the same office, and the right to supervise and recall officials; (3) the Criminal Law, which notably prohibits "extortion of confessions through torture," assembling crowds for "beating, smashing, and looting," "unlawful incarceration," and "frame-ups on false charges"; (4) the Law of Criminal Procedure, which notably provides that the accused has the right to counsel, either a lawyer or some other person, to plead on his behalf and that the duty of the advocate is to defend the "legitimate rights and interests of the accused" and further stipulates that "stress should be laid on evidence, investigation, and study," that "one should not be too ready to believe confessions," and that "the accused shall not be convicted and sentenced without evidence other than his confession"; (5) the Organic Law of the People's Courts; and (6) the Organic Law of the People's Procuratorates. These six laws were to take effect 1 January 1980. The seventh, the Law on Joint Ventures with Chinese and Foreign Investment, was drafted "for the purpose of absorbing foreign investments and expanding economic cooperation and technological exchange" and became effective on 8 July when it was promulgated (*BR*, 13 and 20 July).

Peng Zhen's political star seemed on the rise. On 1 July he was appointed vice-chairman of the Fifth NPC Standing Committee. Then in September he became a member of the Politburo, and in late November he was chosen to serve concurrently as the secretary general of the same committee.

Along with Peng Zhen, the appointment of Wang Guangmei (Mme. Liu Shaoqi) in June received worldwide attention. She was 1 of the 109 new members of the Fifth National Committee of the CPPCC. On 28 June Wang even appeared on television, recounting her story of twelve years of deprivation of freedom and of the right of political participation (*Da-Gong-Bao*, Hong Kong, American edition, 29 June). Although her rehabilitation was generally viewed as an exoneration of her husband, Liu Shaoqi, there was no mention of his fate.

The third anniversary of Mao Zedong's death on 9 September received considerably less attention than had the same anniversary for Zhou Enlai in January. The *People's Daily* and other publications did, however, front-page a talk that Mao had given to musicians on 24 August 1956. Mao's talk had underscored the need "to critically assimilate useful elements from the West on our own Chinese foundation" (*BR*, 14 September). De-Maoization proceeded apace. In August, three more prominent early Cultural Revolution targets were rehabilitated—Wu Han, Deng Tuo, and Liao Mosha, of whom only the last remains alive. These three had written the essays criticizing Mao known as the "Three Family Village" between 1961 and 1964. Meanwhile, Wu Han's play *Hai Rui Dismissed from Office*," the critique of which started the Cultural Revolution, was staged in 1979 (Reuters, Beijing, 3 August).

The fourth plenary session of the Eleventh Central Committee was held in Beijing, 25–28 September. It was attended by 189 full and 118 alternate members. According to the communiqué issued at the conclusion of the meeting on 28 September, the main task of the session was to discuss and approve the speech that Ye Jianying was to make during the celebration of the 30th anniversary of the founding of the PRC and to endorse decisions on "some questions concerning the acceleration of agricultural development." The draft of these decisions had been approved in principle by the Third Plenum in December 1978, and they were studied and put into trial use throughout the country during the intervening nine months. The Fourth Plenum made necessary revisions on the basis of this period of discussion and experimental implementation (*BR*, 5 October).

The Fourth Plenum elected twelve additional persons to the Central Committee: Wang Heshou, Liu Lanbo, Liu Lantao, An Ziwen, Li Chang, Yang Shangkun, Zhou Yang, Lu Dingyi, Hong Xuezhi, Peng Zhen, Jiang Nanxiang, and Bo Yibo. Zhao Ziyang, an alternate member of the Politburo, and Peng Zhen were elected full members of the Politburo.

The principal celebration of the 30th anniversary of the founding of the PRC was held in the Great Hall of the People in Beijing on 29 September. Party Vice-Chairman Ye Jianying gave the principal speech. His lengthy address reviewed the achievements of the PRC over the past three decades, criticized the "ultra-left line" of Lin Biao and the Gang of Four, and pointed out the direction for future efforts. Ye indicated that the Central Committee held that "at an appropriate time a formal summing up should be made of the history of the last 30 years, and especially of the 10 years of the Cultural Revolution, at a meeting convened for this purpose." Ye nevertheless went ahead with "a preliminary basic assessment" on this anniversary occasion.

Ye acknowledged that in the first seventeen years of the PRC certain serious mistakes had been made. But, he said, these were generally rectifiable through criticism and self-criticism in accordance with democratic centralism. However, since correct principles were not always applied "we had to pay a very bitter price, and instead of avoiding errors which could have been avoided, we committed even more serious ones." Consequently, from 1966 to 1976 China underwent "a fierce struggle between revolution and counterrevolution." Ye conceded that while it was necessary for the party to be vigilant against revisionism, "the point is that, at the time when the Cultural Revolution was launched, the estimate made of the situation within the party and the country ran counter to reality, no accurate definition was given of revisionism, and an erroneous policy and method of struggle were adopted, deviating from the principle of democratic centralism." Lin Biao and the gang exploited these errors, pushed things to the extreme and pursued an ultra-left line. "Their conspiratorial activities were entirely different in nature from the errors committed by our party. They were the most vicious enemies of the entire people, and it was impossible to settle their case through inner-party struggle."

Ye averred that now that the two conspiratorial cliques have been dealt with, "we must lay stress on analyzing and criticizing their ultra-left line and conscientiously sum up our experience in the struggle against them in order to prevent the recurrence of similar counterrevolutionary incidents." Ye then systematically described the "main characteristics of the ultra-left line" in the spheres of ideology, politics, economics, culture, and organization. Following this cataloging of specifics, Ye indicated that there were four main lessons to be drawn from the negative examples of Lin Biao and the Gang of Four:

> First, for socialism to replace capitalism, we must liberate the productive forces and achieve a constantly rising labour productivity to meet the people's material and cultural needs . . . Second, it is necessary to make a scientific analysis—one which conforms to objective reality—of the internal class situation and class struggle after the establishment of the socialist system and adopt correct policies and measures accordingly . . . We must strictly distinguish between the two different types of contradictions and never mistake contradictions among the people for those with the enemy . . . Third, we must have a correct understanding of the interrelationship between the masses, classes, political parties and leaders . . . Leaders are not gods . . . Fourth, we must further improve both party discipline and the socialist legal system, ensure democratic rights to all party members and citizens, and see to it that inner-party democracy and socialist democracy are institutionalized and guaranteed by law. (*BR*, 5 October.)

Strains among political leaders were apparent during 1979, but care was taken to preserve an appearance of political stability. Wang Dongxing, for example, continued to be criticized on wall posters from time to time but as late as the Fourth Plenum in September still appeared to rank sixth in the Politburo. In fact, Wang may have been removed from effective power, giving way to recently rehabilitated Chen Yun and Peng Zhen. Wang had been identified with a faction called the "whateverists" (implying that whatever Mao said was right), in opposition to Deng Xiaoping's faction of "realists," and these factions struggled, particularly at the Third Plenum (see David Bonavia, *Far Eastern Economic Review* [*FEER*], 8 June). Wang has been accused repeatedly of corruption, including the charge of having spent $4.3 million to build a new house in Zhongnanhai where Beijing's top leaders reside (*LAT*, 22 August).

Critical wall posters and dissident underground publications continued to capture considerable attention during the year, as did occasional protest demonstrations. Some posters and publications were particularly outspoken. One poster even attacked both Hua Guofeng and Deng Xiaoping personally, in this instance for having neglected the plight of hundreds of thousands of lower-ranking cadres who had been persecuted while only the few hundred top-level former officials were actually rescued. This poster also alleged that several long-suffering grievants had committed suicide (*WP*, 23 September). Many wall posters and demonstrations appeared to have government or party (or some faction thereof) sponsorship. But for those critics without such powerful backing, the authorities began to narrow the scope of permissible criticism and took sterner repressive measures, including the arrest of several dissidents. Among those arrested was Wei Jingsheng, the editor of the outspoken underground magazine *Tansuo* (Explorations). His trial was televised in October, and he was given a fifteen-year jail sentence. This sentence resulted in some controversy, even in the official press, since critics feared it would deter "independent thought" (*WP*, 26 October). Despite the severity of Wei's sentence and other repressive measures, *Tansuo* was continuing publication under a new editor; other underground publications similarly continued throughout the year.

Beijing municipal authorities issued a tough, detailed edict in late spring that prohibited all but officially approved contacts and friendships with foreigners. The edict reflected an official concern for safeguarding "national" secrets, expressed in the media in late May (*FBIS*, 31 May). But the regulation was not based on a specific Chinese law and, since it is not, may have had a deleterious effect on the credibility of the new emphasis being given law and legal processes (see, e.g., John Fraser, *CSM*, 5 June). Frederic A. Moritz, among others, noted: "The new emphasis on the 'rule of law' is designed at least as much to enforce conformity and order as to protect the individual . . . from the very beginning the government of Hua Guofeng and Deng Xiaoping has stressed implementing order" (*CSM*, 26 October). Earlier, A. Doak Barnett had appropriately cautioned against undue expectations in the West as a result of the ferment centering on Beijing's "democracy wall," reminding readers that "there is no social basis in China today for pluralistic political democracy in the Western sense" (*NYT*, 12 December 1978).

There were a number of demonstrations in Beijing and elsewhere. On 15 March in Shanghai about one hundred young people protested living conditions of youth sent to the countryside and demanded jobs and housing for those who had returned to the cities. This demonstration took place outside the theater in which the Boston Symphony Orchestra was giving its first concert in China (ibid., 16 March). Students at People's University in Beijing went on strike and held demonstrations, including one in which 2,500 went to party headquarters, to protest the continued presence of PLA troops on campus. Students at Beijing University reportedly applied pressure to have Zhou Lin, the vice-minister of education, removed from his post as administrative officer of the university (United Press International [UPI], Beijing, 14 October). As many as an estimated 20,000 petitioners demonstrated in Beijing from August into October about personal injustices they suffered in the past. Many of these often shabbily dressed protesters had come to Beijing repeatedly but were often ignored. In response, the government announced that one thousand officials were being assigned to look into the grievances (*NYT*, 15 September).

Economic and political difficulties continued to be reflected in the extent of illegal emigration to Hong Kong. Hong Kong authorities estimated that 80,000 immigrants from China arrived in the first six months of 1979. In late June, however, Chinese authorities acted to stem the flow, moving troops to the border from the wound-down Vietnam war and threatening to execute anyone caught for the third time trying to escape (ibid., 4 July).

On 7 October at a press conference for correspondents from the European countries Hua Guofeng was about to visit, Hua announced that the trial of the Gang of Four "probably won't be too far off," adding "we will not sentence them to death" (*BR*, 12 October).

The Fourth National Congress of Writers and Artists met in Beijing from 30 October to 16 November, nineteen years after the Third Congress. Deng Xiaoping gave a speech at the opening ceremony, and it was reported that Hua Guofeng met all 3,200 participants. (Ibid., 9 and 23 November.)

It was reported in November that an important change was made in the program of sending urban educated youth to the countryside. Instead of being settled in commune production teams scattered throughout rural areas, the young people are now being sent to "collectively owned farms specially set up for them" (ibid., 23 November).

International Views and Positions. China's foreign relations remained vigorous in 1979. Both Hua Guofeng and Deng Xiaoping made important trips abroad, just as they had done the previous year. Various other Chinese leaders and delegations also made trips, and a steady succession of important visitors appeared in Beijing. Relations with both the United States and the Soviet Union saw significant changes. With the former, diplomatic relations were finally established, and with the latter, even though relations remained cool important talks began between the two sides. Relations with Japan remained strong, but the smoldering differences with Vietnam finally resulted in a brief but bloody and inconclusive war. Despite the readjustment of the national economic development program, the emphasis on promoting foreign trade relations remained strong. The total volume of imports and exports for 1978 rose by 39 percent over 1977, with exports increasing 28.6 percent and imports 50 percent. By the end of 1978, China had trade relations with 167 countries or regions and had signed 80 trade agreements or protocols (ibid., 27 April). Foreign trade continued to rise during the first half of 1979, with total imports and exports registering a 43.2-percent rise over the same period in 1978. Exports during this six-month period increased by 26.8 percent, while imports increased 59.9 percent over the equivalent 1978 period (ibid., 27 July). Vice-Premier Gu Mu later revealed that imports continued to grow rapidly, with imports for the first seven months of 1979 increasing by 70 percent over the equivalent 1978 period. However, this percentage does not take price rises into account. Gu Mu also made clear China's determination to attract more foreign capital. Notable agreements and progress were made with the United States and Japan in this regard. The Bank of China signed loan agreements with nongovernment banks and corporations in the United States, France, Italy, Canada, Sweden, and Japan. Gu said that China was considering joining U.N. financial organizations and accepting loans from the World Bank and other international financial organizations. He gave assurances that China could repay such loans, referring to the country's rich mineral resources. He also said that foreigners are "welcome to invest in China, either as partners in joint ventures or as sole owners of enterprises . . . They will not get less returns from their investments in China than in other countries. We shall create favorable conditions so that their management experience and technical expertise will be brought into full play." (Ibid., 12 October.)

In November it was reported that China had sent 2,230 scholars and students to 33 countries in the preceding 22 months. Of these, 1,600 were researchers or scholars, 180 were postgraduates, and 420 were undergraduates. About 1,800 were in the natural sciences, while 400 were in the social sciences and language programs. They were distributed as follows: 500 in the United States, 300 in Britain, 200 each in France and West Germany, and 100 in Japan, with smaller numbers in Algeria, Australia,

Belgium, Canada, Denmark, Italy, North Korea, Kuwait, Mexico, the Netherlands, New Zealand, Norway, Romania, Sweden, Switzerland, and Yugoslavia. (Ibid., 23 November.)

Four countries extended formal diplomatic recognition to China during the year: the United States on 1 January, Djibouti on 8 January, Portugal on 8 February, and Ireland on 22 June. The PRC currently has formal diplomatic ties with 118 nations. Only twenty countries continue to have such relations with Taiwan. (For complete listings, exclusive of changes made after 1977, see *YICA*, 1977, pp. 277–78.)

Relations with the USSR. The year 1979 saw important developments in Sino-Soviet relations, as well as the usual acrimonious exchanges.

On 7 January a PRC official statement declared that "it is to serve the Soviet Union in its expansionist strategic plan that the Vietnamese authorities have invaded Kampuchea [Cambodia] so recklessly" (*BR*, 12 January). On 19 January a *Beijing Review* article said that "Soviet strategy in Asia is to put down a strategic cordon around the continent, stretching from the Mediterranean . . . to Haishenwei (Vladivostok), and using the 'Cuba of Asia,' Vietnam, as its hatchetman, seize the whole of Indochina to dominate Southeast Asia and South Asia and so edge the United States out of the continent." Deng Xiaoping, during his visit to the United States in February, attacked the Soviet Union and called for a "common understanding" of hegemonism, disclaiming, however, the need for "any kind of pact or alliance" (ibid., 16 February).

The Chinese invasion of Vietnam on 17 February was justified by the PRC as a counterattack against armed incursions into China by Vietnam, which was "emboldened by the support of the Soviet Union" (ibid., 23 February). On 23 February, China's permanent representative to the United Nations, Chen Chu, told the Security Council that Vietnam's expansionism and armed incursions into China "suited very well the needs of Soviet greater hegemonism" (ibid., 2 March). On 5 March Chinese troops began to withdraw from Vietnam. This relieved the tense situation that existed during the hostilities because of uncertainty over the Soviet Union's actions as a result of the treaty with Vietnam signed in November 1978.

On 3 April the Standing Committee of the Fifth NPC formally announced that the treaty of friendship, alliance, and mutual assistance with the Soviet Union would not be renewed. This treaty, which was originally signed in Moscow on 11 February 1950 and went into force on 11 April 1950, is scheduled to lapse on 11 April 1980. The Chinese asserted that nonrenewal was justified "in view of the fact that great changes have taken place since 1950 and that the treaty has long ceased to exist except in name, owing to violations for which the Chinese side is not responsible." At the same time, however, the Chinese proposed to the Soviet Union that "negotiations be held . . . for the solution of outstanding issues and the improvement of relations between the two countries" (ibid., 6 April). This action drew a critical response from the Soviet Union by means of an I. Aleksandrov commentary of 4 April, published in *Pravda* on 7 April, and other articles. The Chinese in turn responded with a *People's Daily* commentary on 17 April entitled "What Reason Is There for Moscow to Fly into a Rage?" (see ibid., 20 April).

Nevertheless, in a most significant development, the Soviet Union agreed to the Chinese overture. The Soviets even expressed willingness to include the antihegemonist principle in the negotiations. Premier Hua in his report on the work of the government on 18 June asked, however, if "this changed the essence of the matter" and stated: "Whether one is genuinely against hegemonism can only be judged by one's deeds. No ambiguity is permissible on this important issue of principle" (ibid., 6 July). Also of significance, however, is the fact that the Chinese did not insist upon preconditions that have been unacceptable to the Soviets in the past.

On 16 July there was a publicized border incident on the Xinjiang frontier. The Chinese formally lodged a protest with the Soviet embassy in Beijing on 24 July, claiming that twenty-odd Soviet soldiers lying in ambush on the Chinese side of the border killed one Chinese cadre and wounded a minority-nationality veterinary. The cadre's body and the wounded veterinary were then taken into Soviet territory. For their part, the Soviets had already protested verbally to the Chinese embassy in Moscow on 17 July that Chinese personnel had trespassed the boundary (ibid., 27 July).

Despite this incident and the continued polemics and what appeared to be intensified anti-China propaganda in the Soviet Union in September, both sides remained willing to enter into negotiations. Vice-Minister Wang Youping arrived in Moscow for this purpose on 23 September (*NYT*, 24 September). The talks began on 17 October, both sides agreeing to alternate the site for negotiations between the two countries each session. By mid-November the talks reached an impasse, but there was an agreement to continue them in 1980 in Beijing. The Soviets apparently wanted to end the prolonged feud and place relations on a new basis. They proposed a joint statement endorsing the principles of peaceful coexistence. The Chinese were reportedly amenable to such a declaration but set conditions, including Soviet military withdrawal from Mongolia, reduction of the concentration of Soviet military strength along the border, and an end to Soviet support of Vietnam (*CSM*, 16 November).

The new Sino-Soviet talks seemed to promise at least a limited settlement; the alternative remains costly at best and could result in a disastrous confrontation. One intriguing and well-publicized book serving Soviet purposes suggested a threatening scenario. The *Coming Decline of the Chinese Empire* by Soviet journalist and alleged KGB agent Victor Louis (published initially in the United States in 1979 by Times Books with a novel "dissenting introduction" by Harrison Salisbury) speaks of restiveness among China's minority peoples and suggests a pretext for a Soviet-backed dismemberment of China, a situation that appears plausible to some observers, at least if enacted in Xinjiang (see, e.g., Stephens Broening, *Baltimore Sun*, 5 August).

Relations with the United States. Full diplomatic relations were finally established between the PRC and the United States for the first time on 1 January, ending an almost 29-year period of mutual nonrecognition. Even the process of normalization, which began with the Kissinger-Nixon visits to China in 1971 and 1972, had taken an unusually long time to complete, primarily because of Taiwan. But 1979 saw developments move much more quickly. On 1 March the erstwhile liaison offices in each capital officially became embassies. Leonard Woodcock, who had been chief of the Liaison Office in Beijing, became the American ambassador. Chai Zemin was appointed China's ambassador to the United States.

There were prominent and numerous mutual visits during the year. Vice-Premier Deng Xiaoping and his wife and party visited the United States for nine days beginning 28 January. His highly publicized and successful visit included meetings with the president and other American government leaders. The itinerary also included Atlanta, Houston, Seattle, and Los Angeles. He saw an offshore oil rig, space facilities, Ford Motor and Lockheed factories, and Disneyland. Deng gave an interview to television commentators on 31 January in which he called for collaboration between China, the United States, and Western Europe (*BR*, 16 February). Five-year agreements on science and technology and cultural exchange were signed on the same day. On 1 February a joint American-Chinese communiqué condemned "hegemony" (ibid., 9 February). On 5 February the Chinese agreed to buy a high-energy particle reactor for $100–200 million and a communication satellite system for $500 million. Both sides agreed to the opening of consulates in Guangzhou (Canton) and Shanghai, and in Houston and San Francisco. By mid-November the two Chinese consulates were in operation.

Prominent American visitors to the PRC included Secretary of the Treasury Michael Blumenthal in March to facilitate the normalization of financial relations. The Bank of China was invited to establish a branch in the United States, and a joint Sino-American economic trade committee was established (UPI, Beijing, 2 March). Delegations of members of the House Armed Services Committee, the House Committee on Government, and the Senate Foreign Relations Committee met Deng Xiaoping on different days in April. A House Committee on Education and Labor delegation met Vice-Premier

Li Xiannian on 22 April. Secretary of Commerce Juanita Kreps visited China for ten days beginning 5 May. She initialed a trade agreement and signed an agreement on the settlement of claims and several protocols on cooperative ventures. Secretary of Housing, Education, and Welfare Joseph Califano visited the PRC in June. Bob Hope spent two months in the PRC taping a three hour special TV program for broadcast in the United States in late June. Senator Henry Jackson met Hua Guofeng on 24 August during his seventeen-day visit. Vice-President Walter Mondale began an eleven-day visit on 24 August. Mondale agreed to extend $2 billion in credit to China over a five-year period. The vice-president gave a talk that was televised throughout China (*WP*, 27 August). It was announced that President Jimmy Carter and Premier Hua Guofeng would exchange visits in 1980. Mondale signed accords on electrical plants and on cultural exchange. He also pledged that the PRC would be given most-favored-nation status by the end of the year (UPI, 28 August); the action was announced by President Carter on 23 October (*WP*, 24 October). Former President Nixon visited China for the third time as an invited private citizen on 17 September.

The Chinese punitive invasion of Vietnam in February did not affect the warming in relations with the United States. The United States called for the Chinese to withdraw, but on 20 February President Carter made it clear that "we will not get involved in conflict between Asian communist states." He also affirmed that the normalization of relations with China "will not be reversed" (*FEER*, 16 March).

On 28 May the PRC gave permission to four American newspapers to open offices in Beijing: the *New York Times*, the *Wall Street Journal*, the *Washington Post*, and the *Los Angeles Times.*

On 17 October a federal judge ruled that the president had violated the Constitution by abrogating the U.S.-Taiwan Mutual Defense Treaty, but this decision was reversed by an appellate court (*WP*, 1 December), and the U.S. Supreme Court subsequently refused to hear an appeal.

Relations with Indochina. On 24 December 1978 the Chinese Ministry of Foreign Affairs handed a note to the Vietnamese embassy in Beijing strongly protesting the "frequent dispatches of armed personnel to encroach upon Chinese territory and make armed provocations against China" (*BR*, 29 December 1978). The following day Vietnamese forces invaded Kampuchea and by 7 January 1979 had occupied Phnom Penh and threatened to eliminate the PRC-supported Pol Pot regime. Thus, Sino-Vietnamese relations, which had deteriorated badly in 1978, reached the brink of war. During Deng Xiaoping's trip to the United States and Japan, he spoke of the possibility of the use of military force to "punish" Vietnam. Soon after Deng's return to China, the Chinese went over the brink and on 17 February launched their invasion of Vietnam. The invasion lasted less than a month, and by 16 March the Chinese completed the withdrawal of troops from Vietnam (ibid., 23 March). The Chinese claim to have suffered 20,000 casualties. This figure accorded with Vietnamese estimates. According to General Wu Xiuqian, the Chinese deputy chief-of-staff, China had deployed 200,000 troops against 100,000 Vietnamese defenders (*NYT*, 2 May).

Most observers doubted that China had succeeded in achieving its objective of punishing Vietnam or of teaching it a lesson. Vietnamese occupation of and operations in Kampuchea continued throughout the year. Ethnic Chinese in Vietnam continued to be harshly treated and forced to migrate. The Vietnamese alliance with the Soviet Union remained viable, even though Soviet assistance to Vietnam was calculated and limited. The Chinese and Vietnamese entered into talks even before the Chinese completed their troop withdrawal. These talks continued throughout the year, and succeeded only in bringing about prisoner exchanges. Han Nianlong, the leader of the Chinese delegation to the talks, claimed that "hegemonism is the root cause for the deterioration of Sino-Vietnamese relations and for the worsening situation in Indochina and Southeast Asia" (*BR*, 11 May). By late summer the Chinese were warning that Vietnam would be taught another "lesson" (see, e.g., Frederick A. Moritz, *CSM*, 4 August). By September there were reports of a buildup in Chinese troop concentrations near the Vietnam border.

Relations with Other Countries. China's relations with Japan continued to grow during 1979, although there were difficulties early in the year over the issue of financing (whether loans would be made in yen or dollars) and over the freezing of joint ventures while modernization priorities were being reconsidered. The financing issue was settled on 15 May in an agreement that would provide China roughly $2 billion worth of long-term yen-denominated credits through the official Export-Import Bank of Japan. On 18 May a consortium of 22 Japanese commercial banks reached an agreement with a visiting Bank of China delegation on dollar-denominated long-term commercial credits of $2 billion. An additional arrangement was made for other banks to join these banks to provide a short-term loan package amounting to $6 billion. These agreements were viewed as supporting a $20 billion bilateral trade agreement that had been signed in February. (Tracy Dahlby, *FEER*, 1 June.) In September, Vice-Premier Gu Mu, in Tokyo, asked the Japanese for a loan in yen equivalent to $5.5 billion to finance eight projects (*Asian Wall Street Journal*, 5 September). In December Japanese Prime Minister Masayoshi Ohira visited Beijing. A joint communiqué announced that Japan had agreed to finance and construct six high-priority projects in China, including rail lines and a hydroelectric power complex. The low-interest loan amounted to $1.5 billion (*San Jose News*, 6 December).

Aside from Deng Xiaoping's visit to the United States and Japan early in the year, the most important trip abroad was taken by Hua Guofeng, who visited France, West Germany, Britain, and Italy between 15 October and 6 November. According to a *People's Daily* editorial of 11 November, Hua "exchanged views with leaders of four West European countries on bilateral relations and major international issues of common interest. An extensive consensus of views and positive results were achieved." (*BR*, 16 November.)

Comprehensive statements of Chinese foreign policy were made by Hua Guofeng in his report on the work of the government to the second session of the Fifth NPC in Beijing on 18 June (for full text, see ibid., 6 July) and by Vice-Foreign Minister and Delegation Chairman Han Nianlong to the 34th session of the U.N. General Assembly on 27 September (for excerpts, see ibid., 12 October.)

Publications. The official and most authoritative publication of the CCP is the newspaper *Renmin Ribao* (People's Daily), published in Beijing. The theoretical journal of the Central Committee, *Hongqi* (Red Flag), is published approximately once a month. The daily paper of the PLA is *Jiefangjunbao* (Liberation Army Daily). The weekly *Beijing Review* (known until 1 January as *Peking Review*), published in English and several other languages, carries translations of important articles, editorials, and documents from the three publications mentioned above, as well as from other sources. The official news agency of the party and government is the New China News Agency (Xinhua; NCNA).

University of Hawaii   Stephen Uhalley, Jr.

India

The Communist Party of India was formed in 1928 and from the beginning was divided in social character, base of support, and ideological stance. These factional cleavages were difficult to contain, and the party split in 1964. The Communist Party of India (CPI) laid claim to the party's heritage and charged that the secessionist party, the Communist Party of India–Marxist (CPM), was heretical. Moreover, the Sino-Soviet split and the 1962 border war between India and China helped precipitate the rift. The CPI remained loyal to the international goals of the Soviet Union, while the CPM adopted a position of "equidistance" between the two communist powers. Besides these two groups, a number of small Maoist groups are committed to revolution.

The ruling Janata Party, which displaced Mrs. Indira Gandhi's Congress Party in 1977, split in July after several months of intraparty squabbles among factional leaders. The government of Morarji Desai lost its parliamentary majority and resigned rather than face a confidence vote that it would have lost. The CPM, which had supported the Janata Party in the 1977 parliamentary elections, was initially undecided whether to continue backing Desai but finally withdrew its support and voted for the no confidence motion.

Following Desai's resignation, the major contenders for the prime ministership scrambled to put together a coalition commanding a parliamentary majority but without success. Charan Singh, the leader of the dissident Janata Party (later to be known as the Lok Dal) was asked by the president to be caretaker prime minister until the parliamentary elections on 3–6 January.

This series of events created a fluid set of alignments among the major political parties. The two communist parties both agreed to form an electoral alliance with Singh's Lok Dal and Y. B. Chavan's Congress (U), a splinter group from Mrs. Gandhi's Congress Party, although some state units of this combine paid scant attention to the arrangement. Ranged against this loose coalition was Mrs. Gandhi's Congress (I); the remnants of the Janata Party under the leadership of Jagjivan Ram, the deputy prime minister during Desai's tenure; and several regional parties.

The erosion of party organizations over the past few years made it extremely difficult either to predict a likely election scenario or to speculate on the cohesiveness of the government that may emerge after the elections. The two communist parties clearly anticipated increasing their parliamentary representation and playing a more influential role in the formation of the new government.

On the international level, India's foreign policy was put to the test by the waves of instability that swept over the southern tier of Asia. New political actors playing different roles have complicated New Delhi's efforts to advance key foreign policy goals. The escalating insurgency against the Marxist regime in Afghanistan has generated tensions with Pakistan and threatens to upset the structure of regional cooperation that India has been attempting to build. Further, the collapse of the Pahlavi dynasty in Iran removed a government that since 1974 had sponsored programs to draw the South Asian states closer together. Conflicts in Indochina have stalled the Sino-Indian normalization process and blocked New Delhi's efforts to serve as a bridge between Vietnam and the members of the Association of Southeast Asian Nations. Inter-Arab disputes have made it difficult for India to preserve good ties with the various sets of antagonists.

The pro-Moscow CPI has reacted to these developments by taking stands consistent with those of the USSR. It advocated Indian recognition of the Heng Samrin regime in Kampuchea (Cambodia), opposed Foreign Minister Vajpayee's February visit to China, blamed China for the instability in Southeast Asia, and opposed the Egyptian-Israeli agreements. The CPM has maintained a more independent stance.

The Communist Party of India–Marxist: Organization and Strategy. The 1977 general elections left the CPM politically the pre-eminent communist party in India. It had vigorously opposed the 1975-1977 Emergency and reaped the benefits of its stance in its areas of strength — West Bengal and Kerala. It won 22 seats (4.3 percent of the popular vote) in the 542-member parliament. The CPI, which had initially backed the Emergency, won only 7 seats and 2.8 percent of the vote. In subsequent state elections, the CPM won large majorities in the state assemblies of West Bengal and Tripura. Outside this northeast Bengali-speaking base, however, the party fared poorly.

At the party's Tenth Congress in 1978, the CPM laid the foundation for expanding its support outside its regional bases. This desire was reflected in the congress's decision to expand the Central Committee from 31 to 44 members and the Politburo, its highest policymaking body, from 9 to 12 members. The party's leadership structure was left largely intact, however. E. M. S. Namboodiripad was retained as general secretary, and all sitting members of the Politburo were re-elected. The party establishment, however, is aging. Only 33 of the 572 delegates at the Tenth Congress were 33 years or younger, and only a fourth had joined the party since 1964.

Party membership, estimated at some 100,000 in 1978, has remained stable for over a decade. It is concentrated in Kerala (40,000) and West Bengal (30,000), with smaller contingents in Tamil Nadu, Punjab, Andhra Pradesh, and Assam. Membership is low in the strategically important Hindi-speaking states, although the expansion of the party's national bodies underscores its intention to enroll new members there. The party has focused attention on increasing the membership of its affiliated groups, particularly the Centre of India Trade Union (900,000 members), the Students' Federation of India (160,000), and its peasant front, the All-India Kisan Sabha (1.1 million).

Delegates at the Tenth Congress affirmed the adoption of the "support and opposition" line with the ruling Janata Party, even while labeling that party a representative of the "bourgeois-landlord" class and calling for a consolidation of the "progressive" forces. This "support and opposition" approach was grounded on two considerations. The CPM-controlled government in West Bengal could govern more effectively if relations with the center remained good. Second, the CPM viewed the Janata as the major bulwark against Mrs. Gandhi's political comeback.

Although the Tenth Congress paid lip service to a national left alternative that would eventually replace the "bourgeois" parties, few moves were taken to implement this objective until the Janata collapsed in mid-1979. As late as March, General Secretary Namboodiripad advised the CPI, which attacked the CPM for its ties with the Janata, to "stop the talk of policy unity [among the parties of the left] till the political differences are settled to our mutual satisfaction." Further, he warned his CPI counterparts that "you have to re-establish your credibility as a leftist party by living down the shame that has fallen on you for nearly a decade [through support of Indira Gandhi]" (*People's Democracy*, 4 March).

The CPM, nevertheless, became increasingly outspoken against the Janata in early 1979. It was especially critical of the influential Rashtriya Swayamsevak Sangh (RSS), a Hindu voluntary association with close ties to the Jana Sangh faction of the Janata Party, and the inability of the Janata leaders to decide whether RSS members could participate in the activities of the ruling party. In a frontal attack on the RSS, the Politburo declared on 1 July that the RSS had been instrumental in fomenting a series of communal riots that had resulted in considerable loss of life and destruction of property. Moreover, CPM leaders declared that the RSS tarred the Janata with a communal brush and thus weakened the capacity of the Desai government "to fight the forces of authoritarianism [i.e., Mrs. Gandhi]" (*New Age*, 22 July). Given the factional divisions within the ruling party, this approach was eventually to place the CPM on the side of Charan Singh's dissident Janata group, which viewed the Jana Sangh as its major factional enemy.

When the Janata split, CPM leaders disagreed with the party's West Bengal unit over continued support for Desai. The West Bengal unit, which had worked out a relatively amicable relationship with the central government, favored backing Desai in the vote of confidence. The national leaders, on the other hand, supported Singh. This internal debate forced the party to postpone a decision on the confidence motion. However, the national leaders ultimately prevailed when it became clear that Desai might lose. The outcome rested essentially on national strategic considerations. Singh was not perceptibly more "progressive" than Desai, but an alliance with Singh, who commanded a powerful rural-oriented bloc of seats from the Hindi-speaking states, would give the CPM a better opportunity to expand its influence. Singh might provide critical support for the CPM in rural areas of India's Hindi-speaking heartland. Moreover, his faction had stronger ties with the Muslim community, and the CPM saw an opportunity to pick up support there as well.

Singh himself had to face a vote of confidence on 20 August. His only hope of surviving that vote depended on constructing a broad coalition in which the CPM bloc of votes was an important part. Both the CPM and CPI, as well as several small socialist parties, had decided to work together in the fluid political situation to enhance the bargaining power of the left. They decided to support Singh. Nevertheless, their backing was insufficient, and he too resigned. After his resignation, the loose left alliance agreed to work out electoral adjustments with Singh's Lok Dal and Chavan's Congress (U) for the January parliamentary elections.

Despite the decision to work closely with the party's "progressive" allies, the wide personality and ideological differences between the various parties backing Singh blocked efforts to allocate parliamentary seats in many states. The CPM had an additional problem. Its units in West Bengal, and to a lesser extent in Kerala, balked against giving up seats to the alliance partners. National leaders hoped that the two state units would be generous so that the CPM would be allocated seats in the Hindi-speaking states. However, the power of these two state units in the party councils prevailed, and the Politburo left it up to each state unit to devise its own electoral agreements. Responding to charges that the CPM units in Kerala and West Bengal were displaying a "big brotherly" attitude, Namboodiripad warned his "progressive" colleagues not to expect the CPM to concede seats where the party had a strong base (*Link*, 11 November). The CPM allocated only 3 of the 48 seats in West Bengal to the CPI, Even fewer were given to the Lok Dal and the Congress (U). In turn, the Lok Dal and the Congress (U) threatened to reduce the number of seats allocated to the CPM in the Hindi-speaking states.

Efforts to reconcile the CPM with the CPI were also difficult. Underscoring the pervasive CPM suspicion of the CPI, General Secretary Namboodiripad in late June criticized the CPI for participating in a "destabilization conspiracy" in West Bengal and for its "opportunism" in Kerala, where the CPI led a united front government (*Peoples' Democracy*, 1 July). The CPM backed efforts to bring down the Kerala government in October. In November General Secretary Namboodiripad, writing in a CPI-affiliated journal, notified his communist counterparts that CPM cadres, particularly those in West Bengal and Kerala, were still bitter over the CPI's participation in efforts ten years ago to topple CPM-led governments in those two states and over subsequent moves to harass party cadres (*Link*, 11 November).

Party journals continue to charge that the CPI might support Mrs. Gandhi in the postelection period. Indeed, there is a large CPI faction, led by former CPI Chairman S. A. Dange, that believes that the CPI should support the former prime minister since the CPI, or even the consolidated left, is too weak to operate alone. In the CPM's view, Mrs. Gandhi and her party are the major political threats to it, and its parliamentary representatives can be expected to take whatever steps are necessary to prevent her from returning to power. The CPM clearly hopes that it can win enough seats (i.e., 30 to 40) to play an influential brokering role in the next parliament. This strategy can work only if none of the major contenders for the prime ministership wins a majority or even a large plurality.

Attitudes on Internal and External Issues. The central leadership has concluded that socialism in one state (i.e., West Bengal) is unrealistic as long as the center is controlled by a "bourgeois" government. Consequently, the CPM government in West Bengal has sought to demonstrate that the CPM can provide good administration in its regional base while the party extends its influence elsewhere. Within this framework, it has called for labor peace in West Bengal and Tripura (although it has not hesitated to advocate strikes elsewhere). The West Bengal government promised the business community that the state would work for stability, administrative efficiency, and increased productivity. In late December 1978 Chief Minister Jyoti Basu called on large business houses to reinvest their profits in West Bengal. Further, he even welcomed investment from abroad. To mobilize mass support, particularly in the rural areas of West Bengal, the government embarked on a land reform program, though Jyoti Basu admitted in late 1978 that efforts in this direction were still inadequate. He also claimed his government was for the first time enforcing laws on minimum wages for the Bengali peasant.

In early 1979 CPM leaders stepped up their criticism of the policies of the Janata government in New Delhi. The party's official journal blamed the center for inadequately responding to communal rioting, for the deterioration of administrative efficiency, and for growing income differences (*People's Democracy*, 7 January). The West Bengal government, moreover, was among the most activist advocates of a substantial devolution of power and development resources to the states. The CPM's ability to achieve the objectives of its "govern and mobilize" line depends to a certain extent on increased state autonomy.

On the international scene, the CPM continued to demonstrate its low profile approach to foreign policy issues. Yet, the CPM was unusually critical of China for its military action against Vietnam. In late January the Politburo even proposed that India recognize the Heng Samrin regime. The official party organ meanwhile praised the USSR's "proved record" of "fighting revisionist trends in the world communist movement" (ibid., 15 April), a thinly disguised slap at the Chinese for their close relations with the West. Nevertheless, the CPM, unlike the CPI, was unwilling to read the Communist Party of China out of the world communist movement and even charged that the CPI was unthinkingly anti-Chinese (*New Age*, 13 May). The Communist Party of China, according to news reports, has made gestures to re-establish better relations with the CPM, which Beijing had disowned in 1968 for opposing the Maoist Naxalite movement of the Communist Party of India (Marxist-Leninist [CPI-MO]). The Soviets reportedly are also trying to establish better ties with the CPM. Yet, the CPM remains self-consciously independent. Basu in late 1978 asserted the standard party line: "We are not dependent on any other party outside our country" (*World Press*, 12 November 1978).

The Communist Party of India: Organization and Strategy. The CPI at its Eleventh Party Congress resolved that a mistake had been made when it supported the 1975–1977 Emergency. Yet, the delegates to the congress retained its aging leadership. S. A. Dange, who had been associated with the pro–Indira Gandhi faction, was re-elected chairman, and Rajeswara Rao, who took a hard line against the Emergency, remained the general secretary. Only two new members were elected to the eleven-member Central Secretariat. The two top CPI leaders continued to have major differences over strategy during the past year. This internal struggle came out into the open when Dange resigned as chairman in late November (to become effective after the elections in January 1980). He remains a member of the National Council and a potential rival of Rao if the CPI does poorly in the forthcoming elections.

Like the leaders of the CPM, the CPI leaders are urban, well-educated, and aging. The CPI claims 546,000 members, over half of whom are in Bihar (100,000), Andhra Pradesh (85,000), Kerala (80,000), and Uttar Pradesh (35,000). The party's major front groups are the All-India Student's Federation (105,000), the All-India Trade Union Conference (2.6 million), and the All-Indian Kisan Samiti (175,000), its farmers' affiliate.

The Eleventh Congress established the theoretical foundation for the party's strategy over the past year. It decided to distance itself from its earlier support of the Emergency and from Mrs. Gandhi. Second, it called for a consolidation of the leftist forces, particularly the CPI and CPM, in the country. Both steps were justified, according to a February National Council resolution, by "the crisis of the capitalist path," which "has deepened to such an extent that no bourgeois party can take it [the country] out of it or save our people from the danger of authoritarianism" (*New Age*, 11 March). In short, any "bourgeois" government would eventually have to resort to "authoritarianism," like that of the Emergency, to forestall violence on a massive scale. Yet, the CPI contains a strong faction, led by ex-Chairman Dange, which believes that the CPI's official tactical line is wrong. Dange does not think the time is ripe for "progressives" to strike out on their own against the "bourgeois" parties. To do so would isolate the left from the political mainstream. Rather, he advocates closer ties to the most "progressive" elements of the "bourgeoisie" who are, in his opinion, best represented by Indira Gandhi. Dange had angered his colleagues in late 1978 by congratulating Indira Gandhi on her parliamentary victory. He was formally censured for praising the defection of Finance Minister H. L. Bahuguna to Mrs.Gandhi in early November. His response, as indicated above, was to resign from the chairmanship of the party. If the CPI does poorly (i.e., wins only about ten seats in the parliamentary elections), Dange will be in a strong position to contest the party's present leadership and policy. If General Secretary Rao's tactics succeed (i.e., some twenty seats), the chances are good that the party might split.

The CPI found in the anti-RSS campaign an issue that could link together the various "progressive" forces. The CPI, which viewed the RSS as its major ideological competitor in the Hindi-speaking heartland, enthusiastically joined in the attack. Like the CPM, the CPI, or at least its dominant faction, refused to accept Mrs. Gandhi into its charmed circle of "progressives," although she was also an outspoken critic of the RSS. However, the CPI was more willing than the CPM to accept the notion that her party included "progressives" within it.

Nevertheless, the party expressed its opposition to Indira Gandhi with sufficient conviction to allay the misgivings of many CPM leaders over the CPI's attitudes toward the former prime minister. Indeed, the CPI adopted the CPM slogan that it was fighting "the twin evils of communalism [i.e., the RSS] and authoritarianism [i.e., Mrs. Gandhi]." Although the CPM proved a reluctant suitor during the first half of 1979, party leaders did agree that it was mutually advantageous for the front groups, particularly the labor and student affiliates, to cooperate with their CPI counterparts. A major stumbling block to closer political ties was the CPM's informal ties to the ruling Janata Party. This problem lost much of its salience with the collapse of the Desai government in July.

China's military action against Vietnam and the subsequent CPM criticism of China lowered another barrier between the two communist parties. Nevertheless, a residue of distrust among the cadres of both parties continues to hamper political cooperation. At the domestic level, the CPM is apprehensive that the CPI will support Mrs. Gandhi if she does well in the elections. On foreign policy issues, there remains in the CPM considerable sympathy for China. The CPM is also lukewarm toward the USSR in the Sino-Soviet conflict.

The Communist Party of India (Marxist-Leninist). The CPI-ML is not a united group but a number of contending groups with varying degrees of revolutionary fervor. A CPI journal noted early in 1979 that there are some eleven recognized factions. Although considerably weakened by government actions against them over the past several years, the groups apparently have some influence in the districts of northern West Bengal that border Nepal (*Link*, 4 March).

Two of the more prominent groups are the Santosh Rana group and the Vinod Misra group, each named after its leader. The two disagree over participation in the parliamentary elections. The former will apparently run candidates, although with no great enthusiasm. The more radical Misra group is generally opposed. It is unlikely that any CPI-ML candidate will win, although CPI-ML support for other candidates in certain constituencies may have some marginal influence on the outcome. The CPI, unlike the CPM, has been more willing to accommodate the CPI-ML groups. The West Bengal CPM government, which has had to confront CPI-ML radical activity, adamantly opposes any cooperation. On the foreign policy front, CPI-ML groups tend to take a pro-Chinese line. A large CPI-ML demonstration protesting the Vietnamese invasion of Kampuchea was reported outside the Soviet consulate in Calcutta in January. Still another 2,000 demonstrators reportedly marched in front of the Soviet embassy in March, again to protest the Vietnamese action (*Beijing Review*, 6 April).

Publications. The CPM's central organ is the weekly *People's Democracy*, published in Calcutta in English. The CPI publishes the weekly *New Age* and the fortnightly *Party Life*, both in English in New Delhi.

Arlington, Virginia   Walter Andersen

Indonesia

The Indonesian Communist Party (Partai Komunis Indonesia; PKI) is divided into pro-Soviet and pro-Chinese factions, both of which are outlawed and operate underground as well as from friendly foreign countries. Principal party leaders live abroad. The Indonesian government, despite the present shattered condition of the party following the abortive PKI coup attempt in 1965, officially continues to consider communism a potential threat to national security. The Suharto government has used a possible revival of the party as a pretext to maintain close control over public life in order to preserve domestic stability. Because of the close supervision of political activity in Indonesia today, the two PKI factions, apart from being limited to deep-cover proselytizing in the country itself, are largely confined to issuing periodic statements from abroad on domestic conditions, mutual criticisms, and congratulatory messages to friendly parties.

The pro-Chinese faction, led by Jusuf Adjitorop, a former PKI Politburo member now residing in Beijing, used to refer to itself merely as the "Delegation of the PKI" but more recently has claimed to be the "Communist Party of Indonesia." It has about 200 members and sympathizers, mostly in China. A few still live in Tirana, where the faction's principal journals, *Indonesian Tribune* and *API*, are published. Some members, because of the current strain in Sino-Albanian relations, have left Tirana, and this has affected the frequency of the group's publications.

Satiajaya Sudiman and Tomas Sinuraya have often acted as spokesmen for the pro-Moscow PKI faction, which has about fifty members. It appears not to have a single or official leader. Faction members reside mostly in Prague, Moscow, or other East European capitals, although some have reportedly found havens in Sri Lanka and India. The Moscow-oriented group usually calls itself the "Leadership of the Communist Party of Indonesia." Because of the gradual improvement in Soviet-Indonesian relations in recent years, the pro-Soviet PKI faction appears to have become less active, especially in publicly attacking the Suharto regime.

On 23 May Jusuf Adjitorop, on behalf of the "Central Committee of the PKI," issued a statement over the Voice of the Malayan Revolution (the South China–based transmitter of the pro-Beijing Communist Party of Malaya), commemorating the 59th anniversary of the party. Claiming that "people in all walks of life have become more aware of the consequences of Suharto's fascist rule," the statement asserted that the Suharto regime represented the "bureaucrat-capitalists, compradors, and feudal landlords," all "loyal servants of the imperialists." According to the statement, signs of a "growing resistance" against the government were evidenced by workers' strikes, student unrest, and even protest actions against traffic rules by cabdrivers. Deepening misery among the peasantry results from "feudal exploitation" by landlords who hold most of the land, compulsory labor services to be performed by peasants, renting of peasant land at low rates to sugar and tobacco estate corporations, food shortages, and "hunger." Because of the competition from modern fishing trawlers owned by foreign interests, Indonesian fishermen cannot compete effectively and therefore have suffered drastic losses. The widening opposition against the "Suharto fascist military regime" makes possible the formation of a "broad united front of democratic and patriotic forces." The PKI's policy is presumably designed to promote such a front, although this was not specifically mentioned in the Adjitorop statement.

As for international affairs, Adjitorop claimed that "the Indonesian communists and people" are opposed to the Vietnamese invasion of "democratic Kampuchea" (Cambodia), in which Hanoi was abetted by the "Soviet hegemonists." They also oppose the "anti-Chinese policy and action" of the Vietnamese government, reflected in Hanoi's armed "provocations and violations" of the Chinese frontier. Indonesian communists, it is asserted in the Adjitorop statement, continue to applaud the "great efforts of the Chinese people" led by the Communist Party of China in its program of modernization and "socialist development." The "Indonesian communists and people" also support the independence struggle of East Timor led by the Fretilin national independence movement there, and they oppose the "expansionist ambitions" of the Indonesian government, which is alleged to be threatening the neighboring country of Papua–New Guinea.

The Adjitorop statement concluded by reaffirming the Indonesian communists' commitment to *otokritik* (self-criticism") and the gradual improvement of "their organization and political awareness." There were no indications, however, of what specifically must be done to increase "awareness." (Voice of the Malayan Revolution, 21 June; *FBIS*, 6 July.)

Unlike the Adjitorop statement, pronouncements by representatives of the pro-Moscow PKI faction-in-exile during the year seldom if at all dealt with domestic Indonesian affairs but focused instead on international questions where the USSR also has taken a definite position. Virtual elimination of direct criticism of the Suharto government by PKI Moscow faction spokesmen probably reflects continuing Soviet efforts to improve relations with Indonesia, as part of the broader Russian drive for influence in Southeast Asia. The Chinese invasion of Vietnam elicited a brief formal condemnation by the PKI Moscow faction, which declared Beijing's leaders to "have long been traitors to the cause of the popular revolutionary liberation struggle" and added that the Communist Party of Indonesia joined other countries of the world in calling for "Hands off Vietnam!" (*IB*, no. 8, pp. 20–21.)

As in the past, PKI Moscow faction spokesmen regularly participated in general discussions of Marxist theory and strategy in such Soviet-controlled media as *World Marxist Review*, being careful, however, to avoid openly attacking the present Indonesian government. Tomas Sinuraya, described as a "representative, Communist Party of Indonesia," contributed an analysis of the "revolutionary process" to that journal. The "process" was seen as comprising both "national and international factors." Although Sinuraya held that the "internal factor" was the "more decisive one," he nevertheless urged paying careful attention to the need for "internationalism," e.g., by being aware that the advancement or retrogression of "the revolutionary movement" in one part of the world also affects the "revolutionary process" in other areas. In this connnection, Beijing was accused by Sinuraya of having entirely deviated "from the principles of internationalism in theory." (*WMR*, March, pp. 99–101.)

A similar note had been struck by PKI exiles in Moscow at the close of 1978, as Sino-Vietnamese relations steadily worsened. According to a Soviet report, the "Foreign Committee" of the PKI, after having held a "scientific-practical conference," condemned China's policies as a "threat to the cause of peace, socialism and nation liberation of the peoples." The PKI further voiced its "ardent solidarity" with the Vietnamese people since they were "directly confronting Chinese expansionism." (*Pravda*, 13 December 1978; *FBIS*, 20 December 1978.)

Domestic Developments. In keeping with frequent official warnings over the years that the communists have remained a persistent if "latent" danger to the country, the home affairs minister, Lt. Gen. Amir Mahmud, told a Thai Interior Ministry delegation visiting Djakarta that the PKI could stage a "comeback" by exploiting disputes over land. Therefore, Mahmud said, the Suharto government attached great importance to land reform measures as embodied in existing agrarian legislation. His statement came at a time when some observers believed that the Suharto government was abandoning its campaign of identifying the PKI as a continuing threat, while others thought that Mahmud's warning was perhaps intended to divert public concern from sharply rising prices and other domestic problems. (Agence France Presse [AFP], Djakarta, 15 May; *FBIS*, 15 May.)

Mahmud's statement regarding the potential danger of communism had been substantiated somewhat earlier, however. At the beginning of the year, the army announced that Indonesian military had exchanged fire in a jungle area in North Sulawesi (Celebes) with a group of communist guerrillas, who subsequently retreated. Documents and ammunition had been seized, according to the army, and it was reported that this had been the "first armed clash with communists" since the abortive PKI coup in 1965. (AFP, 9 January; *FBIS*, 10 January.) The location of this encounter with the guerrillas may have been a significant indication of a tactical shift by the communist underground since this region had not previously reported any PKI insurgent activity. No guerrilla movements along the Sarawak frontier were reported during the year. In June, following a warning by diplomatic sources that terrorists of the so-called Japanese Red Army organization had been sighted in various parts of Southeast Asia, an Indonesian police spokesman declared that the country's security forces had been put on alert to prevent possible disturbances by Red Army members. No incidents were reported, however.

In the opinion of some observers, a threat to the Suharto regime is less likely to come from communist quarters than from a broad range of social groups dissatisfied with the government's emphasis on economic development and modernization, which have aggravated corruption and brought little advance in the standard of living of the masses. The restiveness of the Muslim opposition to the Suharto government, backed by critical students and intelligentsia, has invited comparisons between the Indonesian situation and that in Iran under the shah (*NYT*, 17 June). Small underground Muslim extremist groups, some identified with a *Komando Djihad* ("Holy War Command"), have been organizing to overthrow the government. In early January, military sources announced the discovery of yet another "illegal underground movement," which was said to be based on "religion" (i.e., Islam) and to be operating in Central Java.

In accordance with previously announced decisions, the Suharto government continued releasing the so-called *tapol* (from *tahanan politik* ["political prisoners"]) — namely, those suspected of PKI affiliation or sympathies arrested after the 1965 coup attempt. The controversy over the number, arrest, treatment, and eventual release of these prisoners has been sharp. (See *YICA*, 1977, p. 299; ibid., 1978, pp. 254–55.) Early in December 1978, some 1,500 former PKI members were released as part of a planned amnesty, although a few presumably would not be freed and would face trial eventually. Subsequent releases involved several hundred prisoners. (*FBIS*, 13 December 1978, 27 April, and 3 May.) The process continues to be clouded, however, by the government's refusal to provide figures on prisoners still being held. This confusion is due partly to the large numbers involved (more than a half million persons were originally held in camps throughout the country after the 1965 coup) and partly because new arrests have taken place since that time (*Far Eastern Economic Review*, 18 May, p. 24). The prisoner problem has adversely affected Indonesia's relations with some of its principal foreign creditor and investor nations, and pressure to complete the release program has increased.

International Aspects. Indonesia's relations with the Soviet Union continued to improve. In April a Soviet industrial and trade fair opened in Djakarta. Perhaps more important was the USSR's announced readiness to postpone Indonesian repayment (originally scheduled for 1980) of the more than $800 million debt over a 30-year period, on terms similar to those levied by the Western creditor consortium (AFP, Djakarta, 22 April; *FBIS*, 23 April). In an interview with a visiting Soviet correspondent, Vice-President Adam Malik declared that "good relations" now prevailed between Moscow and Djakarta and further cooperation could develop "successfully" (*Pravda*, 2 May).

There were no changes in Sino-Indonesian relations during the year (diplomatic contacts were suspended in 1967). Suspicions concerning the loyalty of the 4 million ethnic Chinese and confusion about their citizenship or resident status continue. Trade Minister Radius Prawiro, in the interests of "safeguarding Indonesia's culture," banned import of all printed materials "written in Chinese with Chinese characters," except those intended for use by scientific or higher educational institutions (*Antara Daily News Bulletin*, 15 January). This announcement was widely understood to mean that the Suharto government would continue its campaign of compelling the Chinese to assimilate as much as possible.

Concern over Beijing's reported assistance to subversive movements in Southeast Asia increased after Vice-Premier Deng Xiaoping's remark to Malaysian leaders that the Communist Party of China would in effect continue to support the Malayan communists. However, Defense Minister Muhammad Jusuf, in a statement to the Indonesian parliament, declared that the armed forces were not troubled by Deng's comments since the military had been "trained to be always on the alert" and because the people, being religious, "would reject communism" (*FBIS*, 21 December 1978). Seven months later, authorities claimed that "many ethnic Chinese" in the West Java regency of Krawang, were in possession of firearms, mostly pistols, and that this had begun to worry government officials (AFP, Djakarta, 31 July; *FBIS*, 2 August).

Indonesian attitudes toward the Vietnamese occupation of Kampuchea (Cambodia) and the subsequent brief Chinese invasion of Vietnam developed primarily within the context of the Association of Southeast Asian Nations (ASEAN), to which Indonesia belongs. The meeting of ASEAN foreign ministers in Bangkok on 13 January called for withdrawal of all "foreign forces" from Kampuchea. Indonesia continues to recognize the regime of Pol Pot and Khieu Samphan of "democratic Kampuchea," not the Vietnamese-backed "People's Republic of Kampuchea" of Heng Samrin, as the legitimate government. Prior to establishment of the latter on 8 January, the Suharto government had moved cautiously toward some improvement in its relations with Hanoi.

The problem of Indochina, after the U.N. Security Council's failure to deal with the matter, also affected Djakarta's relations with Cuba, which hosted the summit meeting of nonaligned nations in

September. Cuban-Indonesian diplomatic relations were suspended after the 1965 coup, but on 24 July Deputy Premier Flavio Bravo Pardo arrived in Djakarta for discussions. Cuba reportedly preferred that neither Kampuchean faction appear at the Havana nonaligned meeting. Indonesia and Cuba reportedly agreed to resist expulsion of Egypt from the conference. Thanks were expressed for Cuba's noninvolvement with the problem in East Timor (see *YICA*, 1977, pp. 301–2). Pardo reportedly promised that his government would try not to have the East Timor question placed on the agenda of the nonaligned meeting. (Antara, Djakarta, 26 July; *FBIS*, 31 July.)

The fighting in Kampuchea remained a frequent topic of discussion, particularly in the media of the Chinese-oriented PKI faction. In March the Voice of the Malayan Revolution broadcast what was described as an editorial that had appeared in the February issue of the "Indonesian revolutionary magazine" *Suara Rakyat Indonesia* (Voice of the Indonesian People). The editorial sharply criticized the recent Vietnamese invasion of Kampuchea and charged that by "tying itself to the Soviet war carriage" the leaders of Vietnam were participants in a "new variant of the Soviet global strategy for world hegemony." It emphasized, however, that all Kampucheans had rallied together to oppose the invaders from Hanoi. (*FBIS*, 8 March.)

Publications. Publications of the two PKI factions are virtually uncirculated in Indonesia, where mere possession of them would be cause for arrest. During the year, circulation of these publications fell even among party members. The main journals of the pro-Beijing PKI faction, the English-language *Indonesian Tribune* (bimonthly) and *API* (*Api Pemuda Indonesia* [Flame of Indonesian Youth]; quarterly) are published in Tirana. The pro-Beijing group also claims distribution within Indonesia of *Suara Rakyat Indonesia*, but its distribution appears limited. The Voice of the Malayan Revolution station from time to time relays statements of the pro-Beijing PKI faction. Pro-Soviet Indonesian communist exiles in Prague and Moscow issue an irregularly appearing Indonesian-language journal, *Tekad Rakjat* (The People's Will). Reportedly, a few copies are confiscated from time to time in Indonesia by military authorities. Spokesmen for the pro-Moscow PKI faction occasionally issue statements in the two principal magazines for Soviet-oriented communist parties, *World Marxist Review* and its *Information Bulletin*.

University of Bridgeport   Justus M. van der Kroef

Japan

After serious setbacks in national elections in 1976 and 1977 and a bad year in 1978 because of criticism of the party by the press and the other parties for its militancy, its foreign connections, and party Chairman Kenji Miyamoto's involvement in a pre–World War II murder, the Japanese Communist Party (JCP) was due for a change. And 1979 was a better year for the JCP. Although there was no real progress in uniting with other "progressive" parties and the municipal and local elections held in the spring were not a clear victory for the JCP, the fall elections to the lower, more important house of the national Diet seemed to constitute a significant win for the party. The JCP regained the representation that it had lost in the House of Representatives in 1976 and increased by a small amount its percentage of the popular vote.

The other big event for the party was its reconciliation with the Communist Party of the Soviet Union (CPSU). The JCP had been at odds with Moscow over the 1963 Nuclear Test Ban Treaty and the Kremlin's support for the "Voice of Japan"—a faction of the JCP. Relations with China, however, remained cool, as they have been since a split at the onset of the Cultural Revolution in China in 1966.

New relations with the Soviet Union, however, have not altered the JCP's nationalistic stance. The party remains independent and still savors its ties with various European communist parties and a large number of other communist parties throughout the world, although it obviously tilted toward Vietnam and against the Pol Pot regime in Kampuchea (Cambodia) and favored Vietnam in its conflict with China early in the year.

While its line remained generally unchanged during the year, the JCP's pragmatism in the election campaigns thus paid off. Also contributing to the JCP's success at the polls were many of the party's traditional issues—welfare, taxes, and corruption—which seemed more important to the electorate than in past years. On the other hand, the party continued to oppose the U.S.-Japan Security Treaty and the Japanese Self-Defense Forces, positions not supported by Japanese public opinion.

The leadership of the party remained unchanged despite speculation following the electoral defeats of 1976 and 1977 that Chairman Miyamoto might be replaced. In fact, his leadership of the party seems more secure than ever, although his age (71) has invited more talk of a successor.

Party membership probably increased slightly during the year, with a claim of over 400,000 and a projected goal of 500,000 members. The former figure may have been slightly inflated, while the latter has been the party's target for some time. Subscriptions to the party's newspaper, *Akahata*, increased slightly.

Leadership and Party Line. Leadership of the JCP remained solidly in the hands of Chairman Miyamoto, despite the above-mentioned electoral defeats and the personal attacks on him by the press and by several of the other parties. His involvement in the murder of a party member (thought to have been a spy) before World War II got even more attention in 1978 following the expulsion of Satomi Hakamada, one of the old guard members of the party, who had testified to Miyamoto's personal involvement in the crime. In March a written complaint filed by a Liberal Democratic Party (LDP) member of the Diet against Miyamoto charged that he was unqualified to be a member of the Diet because of his involvement in this murder. The complaint did not, however, result in a formal move to disqualify Miyamoto. The JCP's reply to the charge was its oft-repeated one: the case had long ago been heard and settled. In March while Miyamoto was speaking in support of Kaoru Ota, a candidate in Tokyo's gubernatorial election, an unsuccessful attempt was made on his life by a member of a rightist political organization.

Miyamoto's leadership of the party seemed stronger than in the past year or two, particularly after the fall general election. There was increasing evidence that Tetsuzo Fuwa, the party's secretary general, was being groomed to succeed Miyamoto. Fuwa is in his early fifties.

The JCP's official line has remained that the party is a "Eurocommunist" party and will follow the "parliamentary road" to power in Japan. Party spokesmen have denied foreign control of the party and eschewed violence and any connection with radical leftist groups in Japan. The JCP's strategy of using election campaigns to educate the population, which in the past has meant that the party supported a large slate of candidates, changed somewhat in the interest of electing more candidates. The party's stands on the U.S.-Japan Security Treaty, corruption, women's liberation, and welfare remained about the same, and these continued to be its major issues. New issues of importance to the party were the "era names," or the old system of reckoning years in Japan based on the ruling emperor; the Japanese government's support of the Pol Pot government in Kampuchea; the government's proposed consumption tax; and the secrets preservation law.

The JCP's criticism of the U.S.-Japan Security Treaty focused on the "guidelines" passed by the seventeenth session of the Japan-U.S. Security Consultative Committee in November 1978. The JCP argued that the "guidelines" would "systematize" the Japan Self-Defense Forces, functionally tying them to U.S. security interests in East Asia. The party stressed the dangers in Japan's new role and protested that the Japanese Self-Defense Forces have become a real military force, carrying on war exercises rather than just training. Moreover, the party maintained that the United States, while withdrawing some of its forces, was in reality increasing its military power in the region. The JCP took this stand despite public opinion polls indicating that the great majority of Japanese perceived the treaty as benefiting Japan. The polls also showed that a large majority favored strengthening the Self-Defense Forces or maintaining them at their present strength rather than reducing them in strength or abolishing them. Thus, on these two issues the JCP was at odds both with public opinion and the other parties.

On the issue of China's support for the U.S.-Japan Security Treaty, the JCP criticized Beijing for "interference in Japan's domestic affairs" and for its "anti-Soviet preoccupations." Although supporting the U.S. decision to grant diplomatic recognition to China, the JCP took the opportunity to point out that China's major motive was to ally itself with the United States and Japan against the Soviet Union. In this context, the party pointed out that the United States retained the right to sell arms to Taiwan and that through the "Far Eastern provision" in the U.S.-Japan Security Treaty and the "Taiwan provision" in the 1969 U.S.-Japan joint communiqué, neither of which recognizes Taiwan as part of China or omits Taiwan from the list of areas to be defended, Japan has a responsibility for Taiwan's defense.

In January the JCP sent two of its representatives in the Diet to the United States to investigate McDonnell Douglas Corporation's alleged payments of bribes to Japanese politicians and officials. They were also to inquire about Grumman Corporation payoffs in Japan. Throughout the year the JCP continued to assail the LDP and the government generally on the corruption issue. The JCP also made a special point of protesting illegal contributions to political candidates before the national election in October, asserting that candidates were in effect buying election victories. Party spokesmen noted that losing candidates spent on the average U.S. $2.26 million during the election while winning candidates spent $3 million, while the average legal limit on spending is $50,000. The JCP, which reported an income of $71 million during 1978, is officially the richest political party in Japan. Because it does not rely on outside contributions to finance elections and has no subsidiary organization to depend on for financial support, the JCP is able to press the corruption issue with cleaner hands than the other parties.

The JCP's continued support for increased social programs also seemed to be in tune with greater support for more and better welfare programs. Business recovery and inflation were the most important issues, according to several public opinion polls, and the JCP talked a lot about inflation.

The JCP continued to support women's liberation in Japan; yet it was unsuccessful in getting women's rights organizations to support the party and in influencing women's groups. On the other hand, the JCP fielded more female candidates during the year than any other party, most noticeably in the national election in the fall. In that election the JCP supported 14 of the 22 female candidates and after the election was represented by eight of the eleven who were elected to the lower house.

On the special issue of using traditional "era names" in reckoning dates, the JCP strongly opposed new legislation that would promote their use because this might lead to changes in the constitution and would help promote the power of the emperor, militarism, and fascism. Public opinion polls indicated that the public supported the party's position two to one. In the same vein, the party also criticized the secrets preservation law (a piece of legislation carried over from 1978) and other emergency legislation that allowed trials without an attorney present for the defense. The JCP characterized such laws as representing a trend toward fascism.

Finally, on the issue of taxation, the party strongly criticized a government-proposed consumption tax as unfair and burdensome. It did not, however, propose any source of revenue to pay for its proposed welfare legislation.

Party Meetings. The JCP convened the sixth plenum of the Central Committee in February before the municipal and local elections. Party Chairman Miyamoto spoke on the issue of LDP corruption, stating specifically that Prime Minister Ohira should resign if government officials were implicated in the Grumman Corporation's allegedly unfair sales promotion tactics. Miyamoto also reiterated the party's position on the Soviet-held islands north of Hokkaido, saying that they should be returned, but that Japan was not in a position to demand their return as long as the San Francisco Peace Treaty remains in effect. He also called for cooperation with other "progressive" political parties, revealing that a joint agreement between the JCP and the Komeito (Clean Government Party) was not implemented because of obstruction from some of that party's leaders, but that the pact was not being repudiated. In this connection he continued to ask for that party's separation from its main base of support, the Buddhist Soka Gakkai (Value Creation Society). Miyamoto also appealed for cooperation with the Japanese Socialist Party (JSP) in fielding candidates in the upcoming elections.

On foreign policy issues, Miyamoto condemned the Pol Pot regime in Kampuchea as "antipeople" and pledged solidarity with the United Front for National Salvation and the new Vietnamese-backed government. He also expressed the JCP's support for Vietnam.

At the seventh plenum in August, Chairman Miyamoto discussed the political situation in Japan and the party's strategy for the elections. He assailed the government for excessive military spending and for tying Japan to a "U.S.–China–Japan–South Korea alliance" against the Soviet Union, pointing out that China and South Korea were not on friendly terms and did not even have diplomatic relations. He called for Japan to adopt a neutral foreign policy. Moreover, he scored the ruling LDP for its plans to introduce new taxes on consumer goods and generally to increase taxes on the population in the lower income brackets. In this context he called for halting price increases and inflation.

Elections. Local elections were held on 8 April, which included the governorships of 15 of the 47 prefectures, among them Tokyo and Osaka. In Tokyo the JCP-JSP–sponsored candidate was defeated, receiving only 35 percent of the vote, the first time in twelve years that a JCP-supported candidate lost this key post. In Osaka the JCP sponsored its own candidate. He lost by a narrow margin, receiving 48 percent of the vote; again it was the first loss for the JCP in this constituency in eight years. In Kyoto the JCP lost the governorship race in a prefecture that it had governed for 28 years. And in Okinawa the "reformist" candidate (one supported by the JCP) lost after a ten-year rule.

These defeats may be attributed to a number of factors. First, JCP-sponsored officeholders had resigned in both Tokyo and Kyoto and the party had to find new candidates. Second, the JCP split with the JSP on party platforms in the Tokyo and Osaka elections, resulting in the JCP alone supporting the "leftist" candidate in the latter election. Third, reformist governors in these cities, like a number of other cities in Japan, had in recent years overspent during a time of declining revenues. This created serious budgetary and fiscal problems necessitating new and higher taxes. Fourth, the ruling LDP realized that its strength was declining and that in order to win local elections it had to sponsor candidates jointly with other "moderate" or "rightist" parties. Thus, in most gubernatorial elections several parties joined to support candidates running against JCP- or reformist-supported politicians.

The losses mean that reformist parties control only three of the governorships and one of these is an independent who also has the support of the rightist parties. Furthermore, the losses in Tokyo and

Osaka, the two largest cities in Japan, and Kyoto (considered a JCP stronghold) may signal future political trends. Some analysts have viewed the defeats as an omen of the decline of the left at this level of government.

The same situation prevailed in mayoral races, also held in April. In the 24 cities where the JCP and the JSP united in a joint campaign, they won in only 4. Where the LDP and the moderate parties joined forces, they prevailed in 33 of the 44 contests.

Offsetting what otherwise appeared to be a major setback for the JCP, the party garnered a record 122 seats in local assemblies, while almost all other parties lost ground. In terms of total seats in local government, the JCP now holds 235 more than after the last nationwide election in 1975. The number of communist deputies in local government now totals 3,555 — putting the JCP in third place among the parties, behind only the LDP and the JSP.

Akahata described the local elections as a victory for the party, underscoring the victories of JCP candidates in 31 cities and 132 towns and villages where the party had not been represented before. It also pointed out that the communists increased their strength in 24 cities and 60 towns and villages. Meanwhile, the *Japan Times* described the election as a "decline for the left," pointing out that the strength of the Reformist Mayors Association, which helped elect JCP and other reformist party candidates, had steadily declined since 1972 and that the LDP's ability to ally with other parties, as the left had done in the past, plus the need for more fiscal responsibility in city government, reflected a trend favoring conservative candidates.

Japan's 25th general elections were held on 7 October. The JCP fielded a total of 128 candidates, the same number as in the 1976 election, trailing only the LDP and the JSP. Of these, 95 were new candidates, 17 were former candidates, and 16 were incumbents. Before the election the JCP ranked fifth in the House of Representatives, holding 19 seats, compared with 248 for the LDP, 116 for the JSP, 56 for the Komeito, and 28 for the Democratic Socialist Party. The New Liberal Club had 13, the Socialist Citizens' League 3, and the Conservative Reform Group 2. There were seven independents and nineteen vacancies.

The JCP campaigned on a number of issues: the removal of corruption-prone mechanisms created by the LDP in the government; a ban on political donations by commercial enterprises; the creation of a Japanese version of the U.S. Securities and Exchange Commission; financial rehabilitation without tax increases, with ¥3 trillion in new revenues to come from removing tax inequalities and cutting nonessential spending; direct deals with oil-producing countries to stabilize oil imports; the development of domestic coal and hydroelectric power and energy conservation; abrogation of the U.S.-Japan Security Treaty and a foreign policy of nonalignment; opposition to the hegemonistic alliance of the United States, China, and Japan; opposition to Japan's "interference" in Vietnam; restoration to Japan of Habomai and Shikotan islands, now held by the Soviet Union, with the eventual return of the entire Kurile Island chain; the founding of a new world economic order; the improvement of pension, medical insurance, and other social benefits through the creation of a long-term social security system that will include housing and job reforms.

When the votes were counted, the JCP clearly emerged the biggest winner in the election by more than doubling its representation in the House of Representatives. In the process it became the fourth largest party in the most important house of the Diet, led only by the LDP with 248 seats, the JSP with 107, and Komeito with 57. The JCP finished with 39 seats, plus the support of two independents. In terms of the popular vote, the JCP ranked third with 5.6 million votes, or 10.42 percent of the ballots cast; this percentage was not significantly different from that of the 1976 election.

A number of factors can explain the JCP victory. First, although the party fielded the same number of candidates as in the 1976 election, it was more selective in whom it supported with money and people. Second, the party was more careful in fielding candidates where it perceived it could win. Third, there were fewer efforts by the other parties and the press to "get the JCP." Fourth, voter turnout was small because of the typhoon-force rains that hit the country on election day, causing voter turnout to drop to 68.01 percent, second lowest in the post–World War II period. This helped the JCP because of its committed voters. Fifth, both the press and public opinion polls predicted a victory for the LDP, probably causing a sizable number of conservative voters to stay at home.

The JCP victory can also be explained in terms of its more popular campaign, more support for the party throughout the nation, and bad strategy and misfortunes on the part of the other parties. The JCP had clearly learned from its bad planning and poor platform in the last election. The party's stance on taxes was clearly more popular than it had been in the past, especially in the context of the prime minister's announcement before the election that taxes would have to be increased. Corruption became more of a real issue and so did welfare and a number of other long-established tenets of the JCP platform. The party simply had more support, which was also an important factor, but this was not as marked as its victory in the election.

After the election JCP spokesmen attributed the victory to broad support for the party's policies in defense of the people's interests and opposition to LDP's unpopular course. Specifically mentioned were the LDP's "arrogance toward the people" and the distrust fostered by the LDP's proposed general excise tax.

International Contacts and Views. The beginning of the year saw the first visit of a JCP Diet member to China in twelve years. Atsushi Hashimoto, a member of the House of Councillors, went to China for a week in January as part of a Diet goodwill mission. Members of the mission met with Vice-Premier Deng Xiaoping and other high Chinese officials.

The invitation may be read as an effort by China to improve relations with the JCP. In any event, the JCP continued to criticize Beijing on a number of issues and made no effort toward a rapprochement. While approving of U.S.-PRC diplomatic ties in principle, the JCP pointed out that the United States will maintain unofficial relations with and continue to sell arms to Taiwan. The JCP was also critical of the new change in relations between the United States and China in some other respects. Party spokesmen, for example, argued that although both sides condemned hegemonism, the United States was in the process of consolidating its military power in Asia by strengthening the U.S.-Japan military alliance and by continued deployment of troops in South Korea, Japan, and elsewhere in Asia. Party leaders pointed out that Beijing expressed approval of the U.S.-Japan alliance, citing this as evidence that China is encouraging the rebirth of Japanese militarism.

The JCP supported the invasion of Kampuchea by Vietnamese troops to overthrow the Pol Pot regime, and after the installation of Heng Samrin as head of state in Phnom Penh, it called on the Japanese government to recognize that government and break ties with the Pol Pot regime. Although the Japanese government has continued to recognize the Pol Pot government, the JCP has persisted in calling for recognition of the Heng Samrin government.

When China invaded Vietnam to "punish" the Vietnamese aggressors, the JCP condemned China's actions and called for a negotiated settlement, while unequivocally supporting Vietnam. Party officials had already remonstrated with the Japanese Foreign Ministry to try to persuade Deng Xiaoping, when he passed through Japan en route back to China from his U.S. visit, to stop pressuring Vietnam. Subsequently JCP leaders criticized the government's friendliness toward China in the context of the Sino-Vietnamese conflict.

In late June the JCP announced that a party delegation would tour the three Indochinese states of Vietnam, Laos, and Kampuchea. The delegation led by Central Committee Chairman Sanzo Nosaka left Japan on 28 June for a twelve-day visit. In all three countries Nosaka and other members of the delegation met with top government officials to discuss the situation in Indochina. In all three nations the JCP delegation was received warmly and the JCP was praised for its policies on Indochina. In July, after the delegation returned to Japan, the party launched a campaign to raise funds for the Kampuchean people. At the same time it criticized the Japanese government's policy of continuing to recognize the Pol Pot regime and its cutting of economic aid to Vietnam.

In August Tsutomu Hoshino of the party's Foreign Affairs Committee and Genichi Masuda, deputy chief of JCP's International Department, attended the American communist party congress in Detroit. In the past, JCP delegates have been denied U.S. visas on the basis of the McCarran-Walter Act. In September party Politburo member Shiro Matsui visited Albania at the invitation of the Albanian Party of Labor. Friendship and mutual support were expressed during his meeting with Albanian communist officials.

Relations with the Soviet Union. A very important event for the JCP in 1979 was its reconciliation with the CPSU after a fifteen-year period of alienation.There were hints of a thaw after meetings between top members of both parties during 1978, particularly in December when a *Pravda* article referred to the JCP as playing a "vanguard role." On 17 January a Soviet envoy to Japan met with JCP officials at their headquarters, and a subsequent secret meeting of the JCP Central Committee led to final approval of a rapprochement. Following this meeting both the JCP and the CPSU announced on 14 April that the Kremlin regarded the JCP as the sole party representing the communist movement in Japan. In May JCP Chairman Miyamoto announced that he would visit top Soviet leaders in Moscow, including General Secretary Brezhnev, in August.

Moscow's decision to abandon its policy of supporting the "Voice of Japan," a faction of the JCP, seemed to be the key to the JCP change of attitude. The issue that engendered the 1964 split was the Nuclear Test Ban Treaty, which the JCP refused to support, calling it an effort by the United States and the Soviet Union to maintain their nuclear monopolies (the JCP advocated the complete destruction of all nuclear weapons). At that time Yoshio Shiga, a ranking member of the JCP, supported Moscow and, after being expelled from the party, formed his own faction called the Voice of Japan, which Moscow subsequently supported.

The Soviet Union apparently changed its policy toward the JCP in an effort to win friends and support in Japan in the context of improved relations between Japan and China and what the Kremlin saw as a U.S.-China-Japan alliance against the Soviet Union following the signing of the Sino-Japanese treaty in 1978 and the U.S. recognition of Beijing in January. Moscow may also have sought a reconciliation to reverse some of the adverse publicity in Japan concerning the Kremlin's intransigence over the Kurile Islands. The JCP had been a strong advocate of Japan's claim to the islands and may have been seen by the Soviet Union as a possible mediator in the conflict. Most other leftist parties in Japan had also criticized Moscow in recent months on the issue, and the populace in general had developed a more hostile attitude toward the Soviet Union because of the issue, especially when Moscow announced early in the year that it was augmenting its military presence on one of the islands.

The JCP was motivated to seek better relations with the Soviet Union because of its continuing bad relations with the Chinese Communist Party (CCP). Improved Sino-Japanese relations, however, seemed to lead to a worsening of the JCP's relations with the CCP. The JCP no doubt felt slighted when leaders of other parties were invited to China and JCP leaders were not. Moreover, Deng Xiaoping ignored the JCP during his visits to Japan. Party leaders no doubt believed that relations between Japan and the USSR had to improve and when that happened, they could claim some credit. In fact, they may have felt that they would be able to negotiate a return of some or all of the northern islands claimed by Japan. Reconciliation with the Soviet Union was also consonant with the JCP's policy of opposing the government's support of the Pol Pot regime and its cutting of economic aid to Vietnam.

In July *Pravda* carried a long article reviewing the history of the JCP and praising its stands on Indochina, the invasion of Vietnam by China, and the U.S.-Japan Security Treaty. In August two Soviet delegations were sent to Tokyo to discuss relations with the JCP. In November, Tomio Nishizawa, a ranking member of the JCP, visited Moscow and subsequently announced that a summit meeting between the JCP and the CPSU was scheduled for mid-December in Moscow. He also revealed that the territorial issue would be discussed at that meeting and that a joint statement would be issued by Brezhnev and Miyamoto. Nishizawa further stated that he felt the Soviet leaders would be flexible on a number of issues of disagreement between the Soviet Union and Japan.

Publications. See *YICA*, 1978, p. 268.

Splinter Parties and Other Leftist Groups. The Voice of Japan, a pro-Moscow splinter group of the JCP, was shocked by Moscow's admission of error in splitting with the JCP and by its decision to reconcile with the JCP. This group, however, took no specific action vis-à-vis Moscow's decision. A number of other Marxist and communist parties in Japan also remained at odds with the JCP, and the latter made every effort to repudiate these groups. Most of these parties, in addition to other leftist parties and organizations, showed their displeasure with the JCP's decision to seek a reconciliation with the Soviet Union, and most voiced their feelings by loudly supporting China and the Pol Pot regime in Kampuchea.

Southwestern at Memphis   John F. Copper

Kampuchea

During 1979 the Vietnamese Communist Party asserted control over large portions of Kampuchea (Cambodia) after a successful invasion of the country by the Vietnamese army, which expelled Pol Pot's Khmer Communist Party (KCP) regime from Phnom Penh. At year's end, nearly 200,000 Vietnamese troops continued to occupy the main urban centers and highways and were expected to launch a dry-season offensive to try to eliminate Pol Pot's remaining guerrilla units, estimated to number between 25,000 and 50,000.

In December 1978, shortly after signing a new friendship treaty with the Soviet Union, Vietnam organized a Kampuchea National United Front for National Salvation (KNUFNS), in which Kampuchean supporters of the Vietnamese Communist Party played the dominant role. On Christmas 1978, Vietnam launched a massive invasion, and on 9 January Hanoi announced the victory of its forces over Pol Pot's KCP regime. The KNUFNS group proclaimed a People's Democratic Kampuchea and were promptly recognized by Vietnam and a number of Soviet bloc countries.

However, Pol Pot and some of his KCP colleagues who survived the invasion continued to receive arms and supplies from China, enabling them to continue to harass Vietnam's army of occupation. China and the Association of Southeast Asian Nations (ASEAN) also took the lead in building support for Pol Pot's effort to retain the Kampuchean seat at the United Nations. Meanwhile, throughout the year, Prince Norodom Sihanouk tried to persuade Beijing, Hanoi, and other powers that only he could lead a neutral and independent Kampuchea—and that it would be in their interest to help him do so. Sihanouk refused to consider any role in either the Pol Pot or the KNUFNS organization.

Meanwhile, the Vietnamese and the KNUFSN have contributed to additional destruction of the population. Of the estimated 7 to 8 million people living in the country in 1975 when Pol Pot came to power, up to one-third may have died because of the savagery of that regime (U.S., Department of State, Bureau of Public Affairs, "Kampuchean Relief: US Policy," November). During the Vietnamese invasion, both sides resorted to crop destruction and denial tactics, resulting in the loss of most of the rice crop. The extent of the famine is not known, but toward the year's end it was estimated that close to a half-million starving Kampucheans had crossed into Thailand, with more to come (*Far Eastern Economic Review*, 16 November, p. 25).

Leadership and Organization. The Vietnamese Communist Party evidently dominates the KNUFNS, which formally governs the urban centers and other areas under the control of the Vietnamese army. However, some reports indicate that much of the actual administration of these areas is carried out by Vietnamese army personnel. They, in turn, probably take orders from Vietnamese communist officials in southern Vietnam and ultimately from Hanoi. (Le Duc Tho may be directly in charge of policy for Kampuchea.) If Vietnam should find it expedient to withdraw some or all of its forces, Vietnamese communist influence would probably be exercised through well-indoctrinated Kampucheans in the KNUFNS (whose present role seems to be limited to providing a facade of Khmer self-government for domestic and foreign consumption). In addition to persons directly under Vietnamese Communist Party control, the KNUFNS front contains a dozen or more Khmer personalities, including members of the royal family and former diplomats, who are probably not members of any communist organization. The front also contains a fairly predictable array of "representative" Buddhist monks, soldiers, peasants, factory workers, and "intellectuals" who probably have neither communist orientation nor power in the organization.

Of the various individuals who appear to play a role in KNUFNS activities, Heng Samrin is invariably given the place of honor. Believed to be a deserter from Pol Pot's KCP forces, he holds the titles of KNUFNS president, president of the Kampuchea People's Revolutionary Council (KPRC), which has functioned throughout 1979 as the only formal government apparatus in Phnom Penh, and president of the KNUFNS Central Committee. Samrin also represented the Vietnamese-controlled regime abroad during the year, notably at the nonaligned conference in Havana (where neither he nor Pol Pot's representative was seated).

The KNUFNS regime, as reported at the time of their Second Congress in September 1979, included the following:

Heng Samrin: president of the KPRC and the KNUFNS Central Committee

Chea Sim: KNUFNS and KPRC vice-president and minister of interior

Say Bon Thang: chairman of the Organizing Committee of the KNUFNS Central Committee and a member of the KPRC

Ros Samay: KNUFNS secretary general and KPRC member

Hun Sen: KNUFNS Central Committee and KPRC member and minister of foreign affairs

Pen Sovan: vice-president of the KPRC, KNUFNS Central Committee member, and minister of national defense

Keo Chandra: KPRC and KNUFNS Central Committee member and minister of information, press, and culture

Nu Beng: KPRC and KNUFNS Central Committee member and minister of health

Chan Ven: KPRC and KNUFNS Central Committee member and minister of education

There are probably additional members of the KPRC, who would also be members of the less exclusive KNUFNS Central Committee. The latter group contains, according to Radio Phnom Penh, fourteen intellectuals, seventeen party cadres, three Buddhist monks, six women, and four ethnic minority leaders, for a possible total of 44 members. Among the Central Committee members, the following personalities (who may not be communists) were listed at the Second KNUFNS Congress: Vandy Kaon (Ph.D. in sociology), Khieu Kanharith (B.A. in international law), Mrs. Sisowath Sothivong Monovong (probably a member of the royal family), Princess Chem Snguon (former ambassador to Algeria), and Hor Nam Hong, another former ambassador. Sarin Chhak, who served as foreign minister of Sihanouk's exile government in the early 1970s, was also reportedly living in Phnom Penh, but he was not featured at the Second KNUFNS Congress.

As for the Pol Pot group, most of the personalities who ruled the country from 1975 to early 1979 are believed to have survived the Vietnamese invasion. (See list in *YICA*, 1979, p. 227). However, Son Sen and Vorn Vet may have been killed in the invasion. The New China News Agency (26 December) reported that Pol Pot had been killed and Khieu Samphan had replaced him. Ieng Sary and Khieu Samphan attended various international meetings during 1979. Ieng Thirith, Thiounn Prasith, and Chan Youran were reportedly seen at the 34th U.N. General Assembly along with Ieng Sary. Thiounn Thioeunn was reportedly seen in western Kampuchea in October by Jan Myrdal. There was no information about the status of Nuon Chea, a former leading figure of the Pol Pot regime.

Auxiliary and Mass Organizations. Pol Pot's guerrilla forces enlisted the support, voluntary or involuntary, of Khmer peasants in their areas of operation, but they were too hard pressed by the Vietnamese army to be much concerned about the niceties of mass organizations.

Heng Samrin's puppet government, on the other hand, made extensive use of mass organizations during 1979 in an attempt to enlist the support of the ethnic Khmer population and to make the Vietnamese army occupation more palatable to them. Radio Phnom Penh frequently mentioned the activities of women's, peasants', minorities', Buddhist, and other mass organizations under the KNUFNS umbrella. These groups and a new labor union were among the features of the Second KNUFNS Congress in September 1979. Reportedly, the adult male population is much smaller than the adult female population following a decade of war, disease, and political atrocities. This may partly account for Heng Samrin's apparent failure to raise any substantial Khmer forces to fight alongside the Vietnamese occupation army against Pol Pot's guerrillas. In the absence of a loyal puppet army, the mass organizations under KNUFNS control probably play an important part in the consolidation of Vietnamese communist control over Kampuchea and in the substantive work of national reconstruction.

Domestic Party Affairs. As mentioned above, 1979 witnessed the replacement of the ruthless KCP regime by a puppet administration under the control of the Vietnamese Communist Party. There appears to be little or no prospect for reconciliation between these two communist groups. At least until about 1960 (when a domestic Khmer communist movement began to emerge), the Vietnamese Communist Party dominated the leftist movement in Kampuchea. However, Vietnamese communists and their Khmer fellow travelers have always had to be careful to hide their allegiance as much as possible from the Khmer people, who automatically hate anything that smacks of Vietnamese imperialism.

International Views and Politics. The KCP continued to receive arms and supplies from China, and China led the coalition of U.N. members that voted to keep Pol Pot's brother-in-law in the U.N. seat reserved for Kampuchea. However, there were signs at the end of 1979 that China might be re-thinking its political support for Pol Pot's group. For example, in a 4 December speech to the World

Affairs Council of Norfolk, Virginia, the Chinese ambassador to the United States acknowledged that Pol Pot had a poor record on human rights and had "made mistakes"; the ambassador also sounded a shade more optimistic than ASEAN diplomats about Prince Sihanouk's chances of forming a nationalist government. At year's end, the KCP continued to enjoy the support of China and ASEAN, however. Unless Sihanouk could repair his relations with Bangkok, neither China nor the other ASEAN states were likely to drop the KCP and support him.

The KNUFNS group in Phnom Penh were wholly dependent on a Vietnamese army of occupation numbering between 150,000 and 200,000. They had neither military forces nor a political base of their own. They were politically linked to the communist regimes in Vietnam, Laos, and the Soviet Union by treaties, and they enjoyed the direct patronage of Moscow and most of its East European and Third World satellites.

In addition to these two communist groups, Prince Sihanouk and his followers were also active in a worldwide game to line up diplomatic support. At year's end, the KNUFNS group had succeeded only in persuading the Havana conference of nonaligned states (September) not to seat any Kampuchean delegation. This could be claimed as a victory for Prince Sihanouk's "third force," which urged the conference to take this stand. Heng Samrin's group failed dismally in its attempt to dislodge Pol Pot's group from its U.N. seat. On 21 September a group of 71 nations voted to keep Pol Pot's regime in the Khmer seat. China, the ASEAN states, Japan, and the United States led the coalition (though the U.S. role was muted). Many Third World countries that had recently been annoyed at Castro's high-handed tactics at the Havana nonaligned meeting voted to seat Pol Pot. The majority of Asian nations voted for Pol Pot, as did most of the Latin Americans and Western Europeans and more moderate Africans, while Heng Samrin had the support of 35 nations led by the Soviet Union, Cuba, and Vietnam. France and 33 other nations abstained, and 12 nations were absent. The long-term implications of the U.N. vote, however, were not clear, but it seemed evident that the East Asian–Pacific region had been newly polarized by the military alignment of Vietnam and the Soviet Union.

Publications. Radio broadcasts continued to provide the main medium for the propaganda duel between Pol Pot's KCP and the Vietnamese-supported KNUFNS. The latter group controlled Radio Phnom Penh. The KCP made use of a radio station located outside the country (perhaps in Thailand or southern China) called the Voice of Democratic Kampuchea.

Old Dominion University   Peter A. Poole

Korea: Democratic People's Republic of Korea

Leadership and Organization. The Democratic People's Republic of Korea (DPRK) has a typical communist administrative structure. The center of decision making is in the Korean Workers' Party (Choson Nodong-dang; KWP), and the government merely executes party policy. All important leaders hold concurrent positions in the party and government. The KWP's membership is currently estimated at 2 million, and the population of the DPRK is now slightly over 18.5 million.

The cult of the North Korean dictator and his family members continued unabated in 1979. North Korean media constantly stressed that loyalty to Kim Il-song and his ideology of *chuche'* ("self-identity" or "national identity") should continue from generation to generation, and the program of perpetuating his ideology and policies was given further institutional muscle. It is of interest that in his recently published two-volume memoirs, Albania's Enver Hoxha called Kim Il-song "a pseudo-Marxist and a vacillating, revisionist megalomaniac."

On 28 December 1978 Kim Ryo-jung, 76, a member of the KWP Central Committee and of the Central Committee of the Democratic Front for the Reunification of the Fatherland, died.

In early September O Guk-ryol, a member of the KWP Central Committee, assumed the post of chief of the general staff of the North Korean army, previously held by O Chin-u, a member of the all-powerful KWP Politburo and minister of national defense. During the same period, Ro Tae-sok, a member of the KWP Central Committee, was promoted to deputy premier.

In late June, Hyun Jun-kuk, vice-chairman of North Korea's External Cultural Liaison Association, disclosed in an interview with Japan's Kyodo News Service that Kim Chong-il, 39-year-old son of Kim Il-song and political heir apparent, remained very much alive and active in controlling Pyongyang's ruling party apparatus, contrary to past rumors (see *YICA*, 1979, pp. 256–57). Several long-time foreign residents claimed to have seen him during the 30th anniversary celebration of the founding of the DPRK, walkie-talkie in hand and obviously in command.

Domestic Attitudes and Activities. North Korea issued new currency that was exchanged "one for one without limits" for the old *won*. The official Korean Central News Agency did not say, however, why the exchange of currency was made.

From 25 April through 6 May, the DPRK hosted the 35th World Table Tennis Championships, and nearly 2,000 foreigners from more than 70 nations (including the United States) were allowed to enter. South Korea and Israel were barred from participating in the games.

The North Korean domestic economy, while certainly austere, did not seem to be in quite the state of disarray often supposed. The DPRK seems to have developed a basic domestic economy that meets its needs. The country is largely self-sufficient in food production. It now builds its own heavy machinery, machine tools, tractors, and other industrial equipment. The basic materials for clothing and shelter come from North Korean cotton fields, mines, and quarries. (See *Far Eastern Economic Review*, 17 August.)

In foreign trade, however, North Korea posted a miserable economic record. During the early 1970s, the nation ignored the *chuche'* philosophy and began to acquire foreign equipment and technology, contracting for it on a deferred payment basis. When world commodity markets softened after the oil crisis of 1973–1974 and North Korea could not sell its raw materials overseas, dozens of countries were left holding IOUs that so far have been worthless. The DPRK's debts in 1979 were estimated at about U.S. $2 billion; the Japan External Trade Organization offered the following breakdown: $360 million to Japanese creditors, $500 million to Westerners, and between $1 and $1.2 billion to other communist countries. North Korean officials said that by the end of the present seven-year plan (1984), their exports of cement, ferrous and nonferrous metals, fertilizer, and other products would allow them to pay off all their external debts. Kim Sok-jin, vice-minister of foreign trade, said in a recent interview with Westerners that the total export value would be much higher than $4 billion by 1984.

A top North Korean economist, Ryong Gon-san, who is head of the country's Economic Research Institute and professor of economics at the People's Economics College, indicated recently that the DPRK would in the immediate future look to Southeast Asia to expand its trade. This may be the result of the noncommunist industrial nations' reluctance to trade with North Korea in recent years due to Pyongyang's failure to pay its debts.

According to military sources in Washington in June, the two-year reassessment of the Defense Intelligence Agency and the Central Intelligence Agency detected a sharp rise in North Korean military strength. The reassessment placed the size of Pyongyang's army at up to 600,000 men and 2,600 tanks, a boost of 25 percent over the last U.S. estimate.

In late March the semi-annual session of the DPRK Supreme People's Assembly decided to earmark 15.2 percent of its $8.1 billion budget this year for defense spending. The actual defense expenditure is no doubt higher because the Pyongyang regime makes it a rule to hide defense expenditures in other sectors.

South Korea. During 1979 relations with South Korea continued to deteriorate. The DPRK intensified its violent propaganda attacks on the Republic of Korea, and tension between the two Koreas was at its highest level since the end of the Korean War in 1953. Nevertheless, early in the year Pyongyang agreed to talks with Seoul in response to a proposal by South Korean President Park Chung-hee on 19 January for bilateral talks "without any precondition, at any time, at any place, and at any level." On 17 February delegates sat down for the first time since 1973 in the truce village of Panmunjom to discuss possible unification. Little was achieved because both sides had different basic conceptions of the nature of the meetings. The North wanted to have large sessions attended by what they called widely representative groups from both sides, while the South preferred to use the mechanism set up in 1972, a small North-South coordinating committee, and to proceed on a step-by-step basis toward the ultimate aim of reunifying the divided peninsula. Pyongyang wanted the committee replaced by the larger Democratic Front for Reunification of the Fatherland, an organization already in existence in the DPRK, and a counterpart body to be set up in Seoul, where no such organization existed. But South Korea did not regard the Democratic Front as representative of the North. As in 1972-1973, both sides were so far apart in their pronounced goals that a serious dialogue seemed impossible. The Pyongyang regime had shown no change in its intransigent attitude in dealing with the issue of national unification, merely reiterating its opposition to any "cross-recognition" of Seoul and Pyongyang by outside countries, especially the great powers, and to simultaneous admission of the two Koreas to the United Nations.

In early July North Korea rejected the joint American and South Korean proposal for tripartite talks to "promote a dialogue and reduce tensions" on the divided peninsula, which was the highlight of President Carter's summit talks with South Korean President Park in Seoul on 1 July. The DPRK

Foreign Ministry said that the problem of Korean reunification should be solved through a "dialogue" among the Koreans themselves without any foreign interference. The question of withdrawing U.S. troops from South Korea and replacing the 1953 Korean armistice agreement with a peace agreement was a matter between Pyongyang and Washington, the actual parties to the armistice agreement, its statement said.

The first direct official reaction from North Korea to the assassination of South Korean President Park on 26 October came two days later. *Nodong Shinmun*, the KWP newspaper, commented that the struggle against "fascist rule" had intensified rapidly in the South and that the shooting of President Park proved the seriousness of the political crisis and the existence of social chaos in South Korea.

International Views and Positions. During 1979 Pyongyang tried to undermine the international position of its rival regime in South Korea and to develop world support for its own policies. Parliamentary, trade, and other goodwill missions were dispatched abroad and invited to North Korea. Moreover, numerous friendly diplomatic gestures were made, especially to Third World countries, whose bloc has increasingly dominated actions at the United Nations. In particular, the DPRK sought to prevent recognition of "the two Koreas" concept by the world community, to isolate South Korea from both the Third World and the communist bloc, and to drum up diplomatic support for the annual U.N. debate on the withdrawal of U.N. (actually U.S.) forces from South Korea.

During the year the DPRK denounced Vietnam for its invasion and occupation of Kampuchea (Cambodia) but stopped short of blaming either side in the Sino-Vietnamese border war. In mid-May Kim Il-song expressed Pyongyang's support for the ousted Khmer Rouge Pol Pot regime of Kampuchea, saying that the Kampuchean people now experiencing a severe trial would surely see the bright future of liberation and independence (Radio Pyongyang, 21 May).

In mid-June North Korea and the Palestine Liberation Organization established a friendship and solidarity committee.

Shortly before the sixth summit conference of the nonaligned countries in Havana in September, the Cuban hosts, with Soviet and East European support,promoted the thesis that the essence of non-alignment was the fight against imperialism and that the countries of the Soviet bloc were therefore the "natural allies" of the nonaligned. The Yugoslav thesis—that the nonaligned must take a stand not only against imperialism and neocolonialism but also against hegemonism and new forms of domination—received strong backing from the DPRK through a manifesto published as a three-part advertisement in the French newspaper *Le Monde* (2, 3, and 4 August). Criticizing the efforts of "outside forces" to dominate the nonaligned countries, the Pyongyang regime stressed that the nonaligned movement must remain "an autonomous political force outside blocs."

Relations with the Soviet Union and China. During 1979 Pyongyang continued to balance its relations carefully between the Soviets and Chinese and refused to favor either camp. Moscow and Beijing still sought to preserve the status quo on the Korean peninsula and gave verbal and material support in an attempt to gratify North Korea and to draw it closer to each of their sides. The Soviet Union and China both urged the prompt withdrawal of American troops from South Korea and supported both Pyongyang's stand against tripartite talks on Korea and the North Korean proposals for reunification.

On 31 December 1978 North Korea and the Soviet Union concluded an agreement governing mainly the increased cargo transportation between the two countries through Najin, the DPRK's northernmost east-coast port. In early January Pak Song-chul, North Korean vice-president, made a surprise visit to Moscow. There was no official explanation of the purpose of the visit, but according to U.S. State Department officials, Pak went to the Russian capital for talks with Soviet leaders on situations arising from the normalization of U.S. diplomatic relations with China.

In early March a Soviet foreign affairs journal indicated Russian displeasure with North Korea over Pyongyang's attitude toward the border conflict between China and Vietnam. The weekly *New*

Times, in a review of communist comment on the fighting, said that neither press, radio, nor television in North Korea had so far reported "China's aggression against Vietnam."

In a press interview held on 6 June at the East-West Center of the University of Hawaii following a lecture on "Communist China's role in Asia," Prof. Robert Scalapino of the University of California at Berkeley said that Moscow had suspended oil supplies to North Korea over its pipeline and that China was assuming the role of oil supplier for Pyongyang. Scalapino declined to name his sources for this information, which he had obtained six weeks previously, but stressed that they were very reliable. He went on to say, however, that the information had yet to be confirmed.

The U.S. journal *Foreign Policy* disclosed in its spring edition that Soviet military assistance to North Korea during the 1970s had declined sharply in both quantity and quality. The journal said that in current U.S. dollars, total North Korean arms imports from the Soviet Union fell from $249 million in 1973 to $32 million in 1976. Moreover, there had been no evidence of any major introduction of high-technology equipment into the DPRK over the past several years, although other Soviet allies had been given such weaponry.

In late December 1978, *Nodong Shinmun* welcomed the normalization of Sino-American diplomatic relations. In early February China and North Korea concluded an agreement on border river transport. In late May Deng Yingchao (Mme. Zhou Enlai), a member of the Politburo of the Chinese Communist Party and a vice-chairman of the National People's Congress, made a friendly visit to North Korea.

A March report prepared by the Library of Congress for the House Foreign Affairs Subcommittee on Asian and Pacific Affairs noted that the Chinese leaders' increased interest in improved contacts with the United States and Japan over the past year had coincided with some unusually moderate Chinese statements on the issue of Korean unification. The report went on to say that instead of firmly supporting North Korea's demands as in the past, Chinese spokesmen, including Vice-Premier Deng Xiaoping, had implied that China was unconcerned about Korea's status and was prepared to wait patiently for Korean reunification.

On the broader issue of Chinese involvement in Korean talks, U.N. Secretary General Kurt Waldheim, who went to Pyongyang from Beijing in May, said that Chinese Vice-Premier Deng made it clear that Beijing formally supported Pyongyang's stand in the North-South talks but was itself unwilling to become involved in the negotiations (although Beijing was a party to the Korean armistice). But Deng said that the United States would have to play a role.

A smouldering border dispute was reportedly continuing between North Korea and China because the latter had long urged Pyongyang to give up 250 square kilometers of land near Mt. Paiktu, located on the border of the two countries, in return for military aid given during the Korean War. The DPRK, wary of Beijing's current anti-Mao leaders and its invasion of Vietnam in February, was said to have fortified its border with China. (*Ming Pao Daily*, Hong Kong, 30 March; *Korea Herald*, 1 and 22 April.)

Since the announcement of the Washington-Beijing normalization, China has reduced its critical attitude and comments against South Korea, perhaps to check Seoul's approach toward Moscow. At the same time, Beijing has also refrained from excessive praise of North Korea. South Korea's consul general in Houston, in his capacity as acting dean of the consular corps in that city, officially greeted visiting Chinese Vice-Premier Deng at a welcoming ceremony there on 2 February, eliciting no objections from the Chinese, although they knew that he was a South Korean diplomat.

During the year, China seemed desirous of expanding its nongovernmental contacts with South Korea. In mid-April, for example, China issued entry visas for the first time to three South Korean citizens who were permanent residents of the United States. In May Beijing was believed to be discussing possible means of repatriating nine Koreans living in Manchuria with a Tokyo-based civilian organization representing the Seoul government. In the summer China was said to be negotiating for the first time a separate commercial transaction with South Korea through intermediaries in Hong Kong.

During 1979, on the other hand, Moscow, unhappy over the Washington-Beijing normalization of relations, intensified its anti-Seoul propaganda, criticizing domestic political events in South Korea. The Soviet Union's hard-line propaganda against Seoul seemed to be aimed at inducing North Korea to favor its side in the Sino-Soviet rift.

On the other hand, the Soviet Union continued to increase its nongovernmental contacts with South Korea, as it did in 1978. Moscow issued entry visas to two South Korean sports editors to attend the 43rd congress of the Association of International Sports Press in the Soviet capital in May. Sixteen South Korean scholars attended the International Political Science Association meeting in Moscow in August, and four South Korean delegates, including two government officials, participated in the International Social Security Association's Asia and Oceania regional conference in Tashkent, Uzbekistan, in late September. It is expected that a South Korean team will participate in the Moscow Olympic Games in 1980.

A formal international telephone link was established between Seoul and Moscow in late April through the offices of the British government. In mid-May Soviet Minister of Culture Piotr N. Demichev visited the "Five Thousand Years of Korean Art" exhibition at the Asian Art Museum in San Francisco.

Relations with Japan. The first visit by a top Japanese defense official, Ganri Yamashita, to Seoul in July was harshly denounced by the Pyongyang regime, which saw a new military alliance being formed against the DPRK. At the end of October, however, the DPRK Foreign Trade Bank signed an agreement with a Japanese trade delegation to repay its trade debt of $360 million to Japanese creditors by 1989. According to the agreement, North Korea will repay 60 percent of accumulated overdue interest, amounting to about $42 million, by the end of 1979, with the remaining 40 percent to be paid in June 1980. The principal is to be paid in equal annual installments between 1980 and 1989. In early September Japan's splinter communist party scathingly criticized the personality cult created by Kim Il-song and his despotic rule. This was the first major open criticism of the DPRK by a foreign communist party.

Relations with the United States. After the normalization of Sino-American relations, Pyongyang visibly relaxed its attitude and eased its tone toward Washington, apparently in a bid to create an atmosphere conducive to the ongoing U.S. troop pullout in South Korea. But the DPRK began stepping up its invective against the United States after President Carter's South Korean visit in the summer and his subsequent announcement that, at least temporarily, any further withdrawals of American forces from South Korea would be suspended on the grounds of "security considerations" (i.e., a sharp increase in North Korea's military strength in recent months). The DPRK charged that President Carter's recent visit to Seoul was an attempt to rationalize the U.S. military presence in South Korea. Calling the president "a vicious political mountebank and shameless hypocrite," it accused him of mouthing peace while in actuality intensifying the threat of war by reaffirming his intention to reinforce military coperation with South Korea, particularly through the continued U.S. military presence.

At the time of South Korean President Park's assassination on 26 October, the United States reaffirmed its commitment to the security of South Korea and warned that it would "react strongly" to any North Korean attempt to exploit the uncertain situation in the wake of the slaying of President Park. At the same time, all U.S. military units in South Korea were placed on a higher state of alert. The Pentagon also sent the aircraft carrier *Kitty Hawk* toward a South Korean port and rushed two airborne warning and control planes to the area to monitor North Korean military movements.

The Carter administration rejected the DPRK's reiteration of its proposals for direct talks with the United States and urged it instead to resume direct discussions with the South Korean government.

The United States repeatedly stated that the Carter administration would be prepared to improve relations with North Korea, particularly in the trade and cultural areas, provided China and the Soviet Union took similar steps toward South Korea.

A 42-member U.S. table tennis delegation—the first American group to visit North Korea since the Korean War ended in 1953—arrived in Pyongyang in late April for the 35th World Table Tennis Championships. State Department spokesmen were quick to deny any "political significance" in the American team's travel to North Korea.

During the latter half of 1979, the DPRK invited a number of U.S. congressmen to Pyongyang for the purpose of discussing the Korean question directly with the United States, but only one, Stephen J. Solarz, indicated that he might accept the invitation. In late October, in response to the North Korean invitation, Hodding Carter, spokesman for the U.S. State Department, declared that the department has no right to tell any Americans, including congressmen and senators, to travel or not to travel to any country. He emphasized that the Carter administration had removed all travel restrictions to foreign countries. He further noted that even if the congressmen accepted the invitation and visited the DPRK, that in no way would represent a signal of any change in U.S. policy on the Korean question.

United Nations. On 8 June the governing council of the U.N. Development Program unanimously authorized program administrator Bradford Morse to start talks on a program of technical cooperation with North Korea for mid-1979 through 1981 to be paid for with $8.85 million taken from funds reserved for "future participants."

Secretary General Waldheim visited both Seoul and Pyongyang in May in an effort to revive the Korean talks. In late August the DPRK formally rejected Waldheim's offer to act as intermediary in resuming the dialogue. The Korean question did not appear on the agenda of the 34th U.N. General Assembly session, which began 18 September.

Publications. The KWP publishes a daily, *Nodong Shinmun*, and a journal, *Kulloja*. The DPRK government publishes *Minju Choson*, the organ of the Supreme People's Assembly and the cabinet. The *Pyongyang Times, People's Korea*, and *Korea Today* are English-language weeklies. The official news agency is the Korean Central News Agency (KCNA).

Washington College   Tai Sung An

Laos

For Laos, 1979 was the year in which China officially became the "main threat" to the country's security. This threat was perceived by the Laotian leaders to be so great that they talked publicly for the first time about the stationing of Vietnamese troops in Laos, something in which they had tacitly acquiesced for seventeen years. The state of tension prevailing along the China-Laos border, coupled with continuing warfare in neighboring Kampuchea (Cambodia), to say nothing of sporadic domestic resistance to the communist takeover of 1975, meant that in 1979 peace for the people of Laos seemed far away.

In 1975 the country's governing party, the Lao People's Revolutionary Party (Phak Pasason Pativat Lao; PPPL) had an estimated membership of 15,000 (*NYT*, 5 October 1975). The estimated population of Laos is 3.6 million.

Leadership and Organization. The PPPL has a Political Bureau of seven members: Kaysone Phomvihan (general secretary), Nouhak Phoumsavan, Phoumi Vongvichit, Phoun Sipaseut, Khamtai Siphandon, Sisomphon Lovansai, and (former Prince) Souphanouvong. The Central Committee was apparently enlarged during 1979 to 29 members.

Little is known about these people and their roles in the PPPL leadership. Although the PPPL has moved into the open, its procedures and deliberations are still kept secret.

Auxiliary and Mass Organizations. At a national conference held from 16 to 20 February, the Lao Patriotic Front (Neo Lao Hak Xat), which was founded in 1956 and served as the PPPL's principal mass-mobilizing instrument during the long years of war to overthrow the royal government, was declared to have completed its historic task and was superseded by a new front organization, the Lao Front for National Construction (LFNC). The conference appointed a 76-member Central Committee. As the chairman, Souphanouvong, stated in his closing address: "The LFNC is a front of all Lao patriots who support socialism. It has affirmed the leading role of the PPPL—the organizer and leader of all victories of our people. The front has affirmed that it will base itself on the worker-peasant alliance and accept the various revolutionary mass organizations as its main members." (Radio Vientiane, 23 February; *FBIS*, 27 February.)

Party Internal Affairs. Few details of the PPPL's internal affairs are known, although it does provide the leaders of the Lao People's Democratic Republic (LPDR) and controls all important government positions. An unconfirmed report, quoting diplomatic sources, said an unidentified PPPL Central Committee member and four of his aides had fled to China and sought political asylum (Agence France Presse, Bangkok, 16 August; *FBIS*, 17 August). Another unconfirmed report said two leading PPPL members were sent to Vietnam for re-education because of their anti-Vietnamese views. A Laotian official who defected identified the two as the chairman of the Vientiane Provincial Administrative Committee and the minister of production, agriculture, forestry, and irrigation (*FBIS*, 29 August).

Domestic Attitudes and Activities. In an editorial marking the 24th anniversary of the PPPL, the party newspaper *Siang Pasason* said of the role of the party that "the PPPL is the vanguard of the Lao working class. It has inherited the great cause of the former Indochinese Communist Party and is a product of the combination of Marxism-Leninism and the young patriotic and workers' movement in our country. For this reason, the PPPL is sincerely and boundlessly loyal to the interests of the nation and our people." (Radio Vientiane, 22 March; *FBIS*, 27 March.)

The PPPL, in orthodox fashion, views the class struggle as a necessary feature of the transition to socialism in Laos. For instance, Kaysone told a visiting Mexican journalist:

The Lao revolution is now in the period of transition toward socialism . . . Apart from the fact that our country has become an outpost of socialism in Southeast Asia, it also has become the center of an intense and unrelenting struggle between the imperialist and reactionary forces on the one hand and the forces of peace and national independence on the other, and between capitalism and socialism in very diversified forms. This is a harsh and uncompromising class struggle. (Khaosan Pathet Lao [KPL], 31 August; *FBIS*, 5 September.)

The party faces difficult tasks on both the economic and security fronts. The results achieved so far, in this the middle year of a three-year plan, are reportedly not encouraging. The government has proceeded with its drive to establish agricultural cooperatives and now places the number of these at over 2,500 (Radio Vientiane, 2 August; *FBIS*, 3 August). One result has been the exodus of refugees, which continues unabated; thousands are still in re-education camps.

A graphic account of the extent to which the PDR government has come to rely on foreign assistance in coping with its problems was provided by an account of an interview with a high-ranking defector from an unidentified ministry in Vientiane published in the *Far Eastern Economic Review* (24 August). Aside from the 50,000 Vietnamese troops, which diplomatic sources believe are permanently stationed in Laos (some were reportedly used in the invasion of Kampuchea and others are apparently ready to counter a Chinese thrust into Laos), Vietnam's presence in Laos appears to be all-pervasive. There are reportedly 6,000 Vietnamese civilian officials, including 1,000 directly attached to Vientiane ministries. In addition, 800 Vietnamese secret police reportedly arrived in Laos at the end of 1978; their mission is to monitor the movements of foreigners and to identify dissidents in the army, government, and among the civilian population. Perhaps more significant as far as Vietnam's longer-term ambitions in Laos go, an estimated 100,000 Vietnamese civilians have been settled in the border regions of Laos, particularly in Saravane, Attopeu, Khamouane, and Sam Neua provinces, and occupy over 3,100 square miles. Large-scale cooperative projects are reportedly under way on the Bolovens Plateau and on the eastern edge of the Plain of Jars. Besides the Vietnamese, there are over a thousand Soviet personnel in Laos, including one hundred who act as ministry advisers and another one hundred attached to the air force. The Soviet advisers also handle police training. The report said that about 2,500 party cadres have been purged for their anti-Vietnamese views since 1975 and sent to re-education camps. Another 200, most of them soldiers, have been jailed, and at least 100 more have been killed. Between 2,000 and 3,000 soldiers have crossed into Thailand or joined the internal resistance.

The task of publicly justifying the presence of Vietnamese troops in Laos fell to Souphanouvong, who is not considered one of the PPPL's "pro-Vietnam" leaders. He declared in a speech at the non-aligned conference in Havana:

> The presence of Vietnamese troops in our country is necessitated by the common task of defending the independence and security of Laos and Vietnam, which are faced with the danger of aggression by the Chinese expansionists and the imperialists. The presence of Vietnamese troops in Laos, which is not a threat to any country and which stems from the friendship and cooperation treaty between the governments of Laos and Vietnam, conforms with the U.N. Charter and the spirit of the nonaligned principles, particularly Paragraph 119 of the Lima Declaration. This question will disappear as soon as the Chinese threat against my country is brought effectively to an end. (Radio Vientiane, 21 September; *FBIS*, 25 September.)

International Views and Policies. At the Havana summit, Laos faithfully echoed Hanoi's view of the world. The "Beijing reactionaries" were blamed for disrupting the "trend of peace and security" that had prevailed in Indochina after the 1975 communist takeovers. Kampuchea was said to be the scene of a mass uprising of the people against the "Pol Pot–Ieng Sary clique." In the version of Souphanouvong's speech initially released by the KPL, however, the Pol Pot government was described as having launched an armed conflict against Vietnam, which then "led to the complete victory of Vietnam over the Pol Pot–Ieng Sary forces, creating favorable conditions for the general uprising of the Kampuchean people against the tyrannical regime" (KPL, 18 September; *FBIS*, 19 September).

Following China's attack on Vietnam in February, Lao-Chinese relations all but broke down completely. In an interview with *Pravda*, Kaysone made the point that China was to blame: "The main threat to our revolutionary gains now comes from China, which is pursuing a policy of expansion and great-power chauvinism. The situation on the Lao-Chinese border remains tense. Beijing is continuing its subversive activity and is dispatching subversive spy groups to the LPDR's territory." (*Pravda*, 22 September; *FBIS*, 26 September.)

The government made known its views on the international ramifications of the refugee problem by distributing a circular at the Geneva conference on refugees in July, which, while disclaiming responsibility "for the difficulties encountered by those who have voluntarily fled Laos and for the problems they have created in the international community," promised cooperation with the U.N. High Commission for Refugees (Radio Vientiane, 28 July; *FBIS*, 31 July).

International Activities and Contacts. Close coordination at the top between the PPPL and its most important foreign contact in Hanoi is assured by Kaysone's regular and frequent trips there, which were confirmed in the *Far Eastern Economic Review* interview cited above. Kaysone also traveled to Moscow in September to confer with Leonid Brezhnev. In April he paid a friendship visit to Thailand.

A PPPL delegation led by Central Committee member Chanmi Douangboutdi visited Moscow in August at the invitation of the Communist Party of the Soviet Union "in order to exchange views, particularly on the task of cadre training and party building, and to further strengthen the solidarity and cooperation between the two parties" (Radio Vientiane, 2 August; *FBIS*, 2 August).

Souphanouvong paid an official visit to Kampuchea in March, a visit that was returned by Heng Samrin in August. Souphanouvong's delegation was described as being both a party and a government one. A delegation of the Communist Party of Japan led by Chairman Sanzo Nosaka paid a visit to Laos in July.

A Soviet economic delegation signed an aid protocol with Laos on 18 April, and a Laotian government delegation attended the 30th anniversary conference of the Council for Mutual Economic Assistance in Moscow during June.

Publications. The central organ of the PPPL is the newspaper *Siang Pasason* (Voice of the People), published in Vientiane. There is also an army newspaper. Official news is released by the Pathet Lao News Agency (Khaosan Pathet Lao; KPL), which has daily Lao and French transmissions for internal consumption and a daily English transmission intended for foreign listeners.

Radio Vientiane broadcasts 22 hours a day. Apart from broadcasting news in Lao and the languages of indigenous ethnic minorities, Radio Vientiane broadcasts in Vietnamese, Khmer, Thai, French, and English. Local transmitters are located in provincial capitals, and there are loudspeakers in district towns.

Bethesda, Maryland   Arthur J. Dommen

Malaysia

There are four communist parties in Malaysia, three in West Malaysia (the peninsula of Malaya) and one in the East Malaysian state of Sarawak. Each has its own guerrilla "army" and claims affiliated organizations for youth, women, farmers, and other special interests. Active in West Malaysia are the Communist Party of Malaya (CPM), established in 1930, and two smaller competitors: the Communist Party of Malaya/Revolutionary Faction (CPM-RF), organized in 1970, and the Communist Party of Malaya/Marxist-Leninist (CPM-ML), founded in 1974. (For origins of the CPM-RF and CPM-ML, see *YICA*, 1976, pp. 334–36.) In Sarawak during the 1950s, the North Kalimantan Communist Party (NKCP) developed from a number of communist front groups of farmers and youths, but no official founding date can be ascertained. (Kalimantan is the local name for Borneo.) There is no single Malaysian communist party because adherents to the three communist parties in West Malaysia believe that the establishment of the Malaysian Federation in 1963 was illegal. All three urge creation of an independent peninsular "Malaya" (which would include Singapore). The NKCP is formally committed to an independent Sarawak. Communist activity in Sabah, the other Malaysian state on Borneo, is minimal, and no separate party exists.

The CPM's military units are called the Malayan National Liberation Army (MNLA); those of the CPM-RF and CPM-ML are both referred to as the Malayan People's Liberation Army. The main political fronts and proselytizing organizations of the CPM include the Malayan National Liberation League (MNLL) and the Malayan National Liberation Front (MNLF), whose memberships and cadres largely overlap. The CPM-RF's main political tool is the Malayan People's Liberation Front (MPLF), while the CPM-ML has a similar group named the Malayan People's Liberation League. Among the NKCP's taproot organizations is the Sarawak Farmers' Association, which has largely been absorbed by the NKCP, however, and there is no special NKCP political front. The NKCP's military units are known as the North Kalimantan People's Guerrilla Force (NKPGF).

The CPM has between 2,000 and 3,000 cadres and full-time members. It is Malaysia's largest communist organization and additionally has the latent support of about 1,000 persons (including some in the MNLL and MNLF). These comprise mostly villagers along the Thai-Malaysian frontier and in southern Thai border regions where many members of the MNLA, CPM-ML, and CPM-RF have encampments, as well as ethnic Chinese students in the towns. The CPM-ML is thought to have about 300 followers, virtually all in its guerrilla force, and the CPM-RF about 700, including some 50 cadres in the MPLF. Little is known about internal party organization and structure of the communist movement in Malaysia.

Party media regularly mention only two leaders: Chin Peng, secretary general of the CPM for over thirty years, and Chairman Wen Ming-chuan of the NKCP, who is concurrently chief commander of the NKPGF. Wen has held both posts since 1974. Politburos and central and local party committees are claimed to exist. Except for those of the CPM, however, they appear to be largely paper organizations. CPM media regularly mention the Islamic Solidarity Party (Parti Persuadaraan Islam or "Paperi"), the Malayan Peasants' Front (Barisan Tani Melaya), and the Malayan Communist Youth League. The CPM has developed a fairly consistent, covert, proselytizing network and program among such groups as Chinese urban youths and rubber planters and tappers on both the Malaysian and the Thai sides of the frontier. The ideological affiliation of all but one of the communist parties in Malaysia is pro-Beijing. The exception is the CPM-ML, which has been described as "pro-Soviet," but its scant literature gives little indication where it stands on the Sino-Soviet conflict. The degree of its pro-Moscow orientation is unclear, since the bulk of members in all parties remains predominantly ethnic Chinese (*Far Eastern Economic Review* [*FEER*], 8 June, p. 20).

The CPM has perhaps no more than 300 Malays and a score of ethnic Indians. Rather than ideology, the conflict between the CPM and the rival CPM-ML and CPM-RF appears to revolve primarily around leadership quarrels and suspicions, although establishment of a "Democratic Socialist Malaya" is the formal aim of all three. The small, underground NKCP has a loosely structured following, including about 150 guerrillas, but it has no organizational or tactical connection with the West Malaysian parties. Even informal contacts appear to be minimal. No major organizational or leadership changes in the four parties occurred during the past year.

Through a clandestine radio transmitter, the Voice of the Malayan Revolution (Suara Revolusi Melaya; VOMR) in Hengyang in southern China (ibid., p. 21), the CPM continues to claim that a widespread revolutionary movement has made significant advances against the "Hussein Onn and Lee Kuan Yew cliques" (i.e., the Malaysian and Singapore governments) and their "fascist rule." A late 1978 VOMR broadcast claimed that the CPM's MNLA had engaged in "230 various kinds of military operations and battles" and had "wiped out" almost 900 "of the enemy" (60 percent more than the 577 allegedly killed during the previous year). The same broadcast also claimed a new "upsurge" in the party's "mass movement," declaring that all manner of workers, including clerks and those in various trades and professions, persisted in opposing "oppression" through "strikes, picketing, demonstrations, and other activities." Peasants and fishermen, it was said, refused to pay their taxes, and farmers "used violence" or otherwise resisted the "henchmen of the reactionary government" who were trying to take over their lands. Among students and intellectuals, the struggle in defense of "democratic rights and freedoms" similarly went on, and even small businessmen were becoming more engaged in the struggle against imperialism and bureaucrat capitalism." (VOMR, 31 December 1978; *FBIS*, 11 January.)

Although the CPM's MNLL has been considered mainly a political and proselytizing front for the party, it was noteworthy that the CPM continued to stress the primacy of the guerrilla struggle. Hence, on 20 January the MNLA and the MNLL Central Committee issued a joint statement on what was called the 30th anniversary of the army *and* of the league, suggesting that both were established simultaneously. (Previously it had been believed that the MNLL had first appeared in February 1965.) From this anniversary statement, the military aspects of "Malaya's national liberation" and the "mass struggles" of the MNLL appear to be mutual extensions. The statement declared that the objectives of both organizations include development of "the people's armed forces," expansion of the "national democratic united front" and the "revolutionary mass movement," and continuation of the "fight" against the Hussein Onn and Lee Kuan Yew regimes. The statement reaffirmed the policy of holding high the great red banner of "Marxism–Leninism–Mao Zedong Thought" and urged the seizure of political power through armed struggle by "surrounding the cities from the countryside." (VOMR, 27 January; *FBIS*, 1 February.)

Subsequently, the VOMR issued a special 30th anniversary message celebrating the MNLA "Tenth Regiment," which is believed to be composed primarily of ethnic Malays and Muslim Thais. It usually operates from bases located across from Kelantan state of Malaysia in Narathiwat province of Thailand. This message asserts that "from [its] commanders down to its fighters," the regiment "is composed entirely of people of the Malay nationality." Under its political commissar, Abdullah Siddi, the regiment is also said to have engaged in major encounters with the enemy, killing and wounding "thousands" during the past three decades. Thanks to the regiment, "the flames of the people's war" are now "raging more furiously in the border area and in Kelantan." (VOMR, 19 May; FBIS, 25 May.)

As is customary, on 28 April the VOMR commemorated the anniversary of the CPM (the 49th) with a commentary and "editorial." This statement emphasized the importance of guerrilla warfare, establishment of close bonds between the armed forces and the masses (especially workers and peasants), improvements in food supplies, and full utilization of the advantages afforded by "our jungles." The statement referred to a CPM Central Committee directive of 15 June 1978 urging concentration on "secret and illegal work" and noted that such work demands "well-selected cadres" and close ties with the masses. Workers, peasants, and petite bourgeoisie were identified as the "motive" force of "our revolution," and attention was called to the need "to solve the land question." In the latter connection, reference was made to the CPM's earlier agrarian reform program (see YICA, 1977, pp. 341–42).

The anniversary statement called on the CPM to "rally more closely" around its Central Committee, "headed by Comrade Chin Peng," and to persevere in achieving "the revolutionary task" set forth in its directives. The basis of the latter is described as "a war of the masses," and hence, success in revolutionary struggle can be achieved only through mobilizing the masses. (VOMR, 28 April; FBIS, 4 May.) The same theme of the joint need to develop a "mass movement" based on a united front and an armed struggle to seize "political power by armed force" appeared in a subsequent commemorative VOMR broadcast marking the 31st anniversary of the "national liberation" struggle against English colonial control in Malaya and of a supposedly new phase in Malaya's "democratic national revolution" (VOMR, 19 June; FBIS, 22 June).

On the thirteenth anniversary of the founding of the CPM front Islamic Solidarity Party, the party issued its customary commemorative message, which lauded the struggle of "Islamic patriots" against "imperialism, bureaucratic capitalism, and neocolonialism." As in the past, this statement sought to link Islam with poverty by playing simultaneously on the ethnic Malay's sense of religious identity and on his lower economic status in relation to other population groups in the country, such as Chinese and Indians. Government leaders, including Premier Hussein Onn, are not good Muslims but "hypocrites and selfish persons" who favor their relatives and harm the people so that the rest of the Muslim community has become "more and more miserable." (VOMR, 16 November 1978; FBIS, 1 December 1978.)

Domestic Developments. Intermittent guerrilla strikes carried out by small units of the CPM, CPM-ML, and CPM-RF continued during the year, while the NKPGF suffered from defections and reduced the level of its activities. An idea of the scope of recent insurgent activity can be gleaned from the November 1978 report by Deputy Police Inspector General Tan Sri Mahmood Yunus. Since 1976, a total of 225 "communist terrorists" (party faction unidentified) have been killed, while 56 have surrendered; 120 of the 225 were shot in the Malayan peninsula, 45 in Sarawak, and 60 in southern Thailand (Sarawak Tribune, 14 November 1978).

The MNLA's main operational areas remained much as in previous years (the Twelfth Regiment occupied major encampments in the Betong salient of Yala province in Thailand; the Tenth Regiment operated mainly along the Kelantan state border; and the Eighth Regiment was headquartered at the southwestern border of Songkhla province in Thailand). On 27 December 1978, the Malaysian field police had a brief skirmish with some MNLA guerrillas in the Thai border district of Padang Terap shortly after insurgents had struck at a police command post at Beranang, south of Kuala Lumpur, and escaped with a number of weapons. These two encounters came after several months of comparative quiet, a period that had Malaysian army commanders concerned that CPM units had eluded the military containment and patrol network established in such regions as the Ayer Kala area of Perak state and along the Pahang-Selangor border (FEER, 12 January, p. 16).

In subsequent weeks there were fire fights with officially described "communist terrorists" (party faction unidentified). In January combined Malaysian artillery and air strikes led to capture of a guerrilla camp in Gopeng, near Ipoh, and the killing of two insurgents. The following month it was decided to intensify joint Thai-Malaysian military action, particularly in the Betong border region where intermittent counterinsurgency operations had been under way for several years. In connection with this intensified drive, the Malaysian government disclosed that seven communist guerrillas had been killed and four others had surrendered. All were former secondary school students from the Muar and Batu Pahat districts of Johore. About seventy others in this category from the same districts were detained by security agencies. Malaysian sources claimed that through informal activities, such as picnics, students had been gradually drawn in and recruited by the communists (*Sarawak Tribune*, 2, 4, and 6 February).

It should be noted that concern over communist recruitment in the schools had already been expressed by Education Minister Datuk Musa Hitam in November 1978, when he claimed that several schools had been infiltrated by communist elements. A former student at Tunku Abdul Rahman College confessed that he had been recruited into the MNLF through communist infiltration of traditional Chinese festivals, sports, student outings, and other informal gatherings. According to this confession, after the initial recruiting contacts had "showed good progress," students became members of a party indoctrination cell. They began ignoring schoolwork and adopted attitudes that were "antisocial, antiparents, and antigovernment." (Ibid., 7 and 22 November 1978.) According to Chief Minister Tan Sri Haji Othman of Johore state, students involved in "communist activities" had been warned to surrender. Those who failed to do so would be arrested, he said, as the authorities were aware of their identities. Campaigns in Johore to make teachers and students more aware of the danger of communism had been satisfactory, the chief minister claimed. Seventy students in Johore had been arrested in 1978 (Radio Kuala Lumpur, 14 February; *FBIS*, 15 February). Home Affairs Minister Ghazali Shafie reported the arrest of 297 students for "involvement in communist activities in schools" since 1970, but only 13 remained in detention. The schools involved were in Johore, Negri Sembilan, Malacca, Perak, Penang, Kedah, Pahang, and the Federal Malaysian Territory. (*Sarawak Tribune*, 11 April.) The Johore area schools appear to have become special targets of CPM infiltration (*FEER*, 31 August, p. 48).

Throughout the year the government reported continuing clashes with "communist guerrillas" (party faction unidentified) in Thai border areas. In February a 4,000-man combined Thai-Malaysian military force supported by Thai fighter bombers struck at suspected guerrilla strongholds in the Sadao district of southern Thailand, capturing a guerrilla camp but not making contact with the estimated 300-member guerrilla force operating in the region (*Straits Times*, 8 February). The Sadao region is said to be heavily infiltrated by the CPM-RF faction (*FEER*, 8 June, p. 21). But it is not known whether the captured guerrilla camp belonged to this faction. In March some twenty insurgents ambushed a military supply convoy on the Kroh-Betong road along the Thai-Malaysian frontier. Five guerrillas and two Malaysian military were reportedly killed. In early June four "communist terrorists" were reportedly killed in the Perak-Kelantan border area along a principal communist route of infiltration. (*Sarawak Tribune*, 10 March; Radio Kuala Lumpur, 2 June.)

After sources in the Internal Security Operations Command of Thailand had noted that "activities of the Malayan Chinese communist bandits" had been continuing (collecting food supplies and money and obtaining intelligence information) in the Malaysian border region, the chief minister of the Malaysian state of Perak, Datuk Sri Haji Wan Mohamed, announced that six guerrillas had been killed in the Perak-Kelantan border area and that government planes had dropped some 100,000 leaflets into the jungle calling on the remaining insurgents to surrender. (Radio Bangkok, 21 April; *FBIS*, 26 April; *New Straits Times*, 28 June; *FBIS*, 3 July.) Perak state officials announced that attempts by unidentified "communist terrorists" to establish strongholds at the base of the Keledang Saiong mountain range near Menglembu and Buntong had been thwarted (*Straits Times*, 31 May; *FEER*, 31 August, p. 48). On 23 July, Malaysian government sources reported that a communist guerrilla ambush of an army convoy had led to six military deaths and wounding of an equal number of others, the highest number of casualties inflicted by insurgents in a single engagement that year (Associated Press, Kuala Lumpur, 23 July).

The CPM's interaction with supporters in Thailand reportedly continued. A senior Thai security official calculated that in the southern Thai provinces of Yala, Pattani, and Narathiwat, CPM extortionist practices were costing the economy as much as 200 million baht (U.S. $10 million); he claimed that rubber estate owners, miners, and merchants in the three provinces were paying "protection money" to the CPM (*Sarawak Tribune*, 9 January). Concern was expressed by both Malaysian and Thai officials that the fighting in Cambodia might inspire an increase in CPM guerrilla insurgency, and they reportedly agreed that Thai-Malaysian security cooperation therefore would be strengthened (ibid., 7 February).

The Indochinese refugee problem also was considered a potential new danger to Malaysian security in some quarters. It was reported that Malaysia had held "urgent talks" with Thailand in the wake of intelligence information that illegal Vietnamese immigrants (the so-called "boat people") landing on Malaysian shores were smuggling in small quantities of weapons that might find their way to the Thai-Malaysian border area (*StraitsTimes*, 12 December 1978). Thailand's difficulties with Cambodia also aroused concern over the future of joint action against the Malayan communist insurgents. However, Home Affairs Minister Tan Sri Ghazali Shafie declared that the Bangkok government's "preoccupation" with problems along the Cambodian border, precipitated by the movement of Cambodian refugees into Thailand, would not affect continuation of combined security efforts against the border guerrilla insurgents (Agence France Presse, Kuala Lumpur, 8 June; *FBIS*, 8 June).

In Sarawak, intermittent clashes between NKPGF guerrillas and government security forces continued. A police spokesman announced that during 1978 ten "communist terrorists" had been killed and 25 guerrilla weapons of various types seized in the state (*Sarawak Tribune*, 1 January). Security forces in the Matang Sempadi Forest Reserve area shot three insurgents, all Chinese in their late twenties and, according to the government, affiliated for eight or more years with the Sarawak communist underground. According to the chief minister, only 22 "communist terrorists" were operating in the state's First Division (ibid., 29 March).

Although the Sarawak government has continued its program of periodic public appearances by self-confessed and "self-renewed" (rehabilitated) former communist activists, who lectured audiences on the folly of identifying with the communist cause, Sarawak and Malaysian officials claimed that communism in the state was on the rise again. Malaysia's deputy defense minister, Datuk Mokhtar Hashim, declared that following a recent government amnesty program the communist guerrillas were renewing their ties with erstwhile supporters in an effort to establish themselves once again in their former strongholds (ibid., 7 April; *New Straits Times*, 12 April).

In its campaign against communist insurgents and suspected sympathizers, the Malaysian government is continuing to experience legal and constitutional difficulties in connection with the sweeping security laws under which it operates. In December 1978, the Privy Council in England, the supreme appeals court for Commonwealth countries, held that the Essential Security Cases (Amendment) Regulations of 1975, passed by the Malaysian parliament and promulgated by the government, were ultra vires, i.e., outside the scope of the Malaysian constitution (*FEER*, 29 December 1978, pp. 16–17). The 1975 regulations (see *YICA*, 1976, pp. 343–44) which allow secret testimony, provide for mandatory death penalties in certain cases, and permit minors to be treated as adults in security cases, had aroused sharp criticism among Malaysian lawyers. None of the 44 persons, including a fourteen-year-old boy, sentenced to death under the regulations has been executed thus far (*FEER*, 29 December 1978, pp. 16–17). The Hussein Onn government has announced that it will introduce a new "permanent" law, under constitutional provisions, designed to combat "subversive and other activities" against the public safety, including abuse of and dealing in drugs (*Sarawak Tribune*, 8 December 1978). Whether the proposed new legislation would in effect repeal the 1975 Essential Security Cases Regulations is not apparent. Nor is it clear if by linking drug abuse to other unspecified "subversive" activities, the government is seeking to mitigate the impression of its preoccupation with communist subversion in security matters.

Toward midyear, government supporters in the Malaysian lower house defeated a motion proposed by the opposition Democratic Action Party that in effect would have abolished all special emergency regulations adopted since 1964. The government had strongly opposed the motion. Home Affairs Minister Tan Sri Ghazali Shafie declared during the debate over the motion that existing emergency regulations needed to remain on the books. First, because in its joint effort with other members of the Association of Southeast Asian Nations to create a "zone of peace, freedom, and neutrality," no external intervention in local affairs could be permitted. Second, recent events in Indochina could give an impetus, including material assistance, to the CPM and to the Communist Party of Thailand. According to Ghazali, the government had been able to maintain parliamentary democracy and the rule of law despite the several crises that had endangered the country and "the way of life of the people." (Radio Kuala Lumpur, 30 June; *FBIS*, 3 July.) The London-based Amnesty International urged the Malaysian government to repeal its Internal Security Act, the foundation of its antisubversion powers (*FEER*, 7 September, p. 5).

International Aspects. As the conflict in Kampuchea (Cambodia) intensified, the CPM, as expected, denounced the Vietnamese invasion of that country in December 1978 and what it termed the establishment of a "puppet government" led by Heng Samrin. Over the VOMR, it also attacked "Soviet social-imperialism" for attempting to make Indochina a "beachhead for dominating the Asia-Pacific region" as part of Moscow's alleged strategy for world control. The November 1978 treaty between the USSR and Vietnam was viewed as part of a conspiracy to occupy Kampuchea, with Vietnamese becoming mere "pawns" in Soviet hands. (VOMR, 20 January; *FBIS*, 24 January.) This broadcast confirmed that the CPM remained firmly allied with Beijing in the developing Indochina "proxy" war between the USSR and China. Although the CPM-ML is sometimes described as pro-Soviet, thus far there has been no indication that it sided with Moscow in the Indochina conflict (*FEER*, 8 June).

The VOMR also commented on the January 1 establishment of diplomatic relations between the United States and the People's Republic of China. The broadcast considered these diplomatic ties a victory for the thought and policy of the late Mao Zedong and for his dictum that "friendly relations with all countries" should be established on the "principle of equality." The commentary also portrayed conclusion of Washington-Beijing diplomatic relations as a defeat of American postwar "imperialist" foreign policies. (VOMR, 21 December 1978; *FBIS*, 29 December 1978.) No significant developments in Sino-Malaysian relations occurred during the year, and both Beijing and Kuala Lumpur appear to have accepted the Chinese principle that while government-to-government relations can be officially cordial, this in no way affects continuing Chinese support for the CPM (*FEER*, 8 June, p. 21).

Premier Datuk Hussein Onn spent seven days in the USSR, visiting several cities. A joint communiqué issued at the end of his tour expressed concern over the "unstable" condition of Southeast Asia and expressed the hope that peace and stability in that area could be achieved on the basis of the principles of peaceful coexistence, respect for sovereignty, independence, territorial integrity, noninterference in internal affairs, and avoidance of force. Both countries declared that they were opposed to the arms race and agreed on the need for Israel to withdraw from all Arab territories occupied since the 1967 war. (*FBIS*, 27 September.)

Yugoslav Vice-President Fadil Hodza had previously visited Kuala Lumpur. After discussions with Premier Hussein Onn, a press statement announced that both leaders agreed on the "necessity of the withdrawal of all foreign forces" from Kampuchea. They also agreed that the movement of "non-aligned" countries (of which both are members) should adhere to its original objectives, and they voiced the hope that the forthcoming nonaligned conference in Havana would overcome existing differences between member states so that common objectives could be achieved. (Agence France Presse, Kuala Lumpur, 4 July; *FBIS*, 5 July.)

Media. The CPM's VOMR, a clandestine radio transmitter situated some 1,900 miles from the Malaysian capital in Hengyang, south of Changsha in the People's Republic of China (*FEER*, 8 June, p. 21), is the principal communications medium of Malaysian communism. In the past two years, it also has relayed statements by the pro-Chinese factions of the Indonesian and Philippine communist parties as well as of the NKCP. Most broadcasts are in Mandarin; a few have been in Malay. The CPM-ML's clandestine transmitter, which calls itself the Voice of the People of Malaya, was rarely heard during 1979, probably because of the weakness of its signal. Its location is uncertain. All factions of Malaysian communism make use of poorly printed or stenciled leaflets. Dissemination of these appears to be quite limited, and mere possession of them can bring official action under security regulations. British sympathizers of the CPM publish an infrequently appearing newsletter, *Malayan Monitor and General News*, which is highly critical of the Malaysian government. Chinese media, including those in foreign languages, currently devote less space to activities of the CPM insurgents than was the case a few years ago. Soviet publications and broadcasts are virtually silent on the nature and extent of Malaysian communist or guerrilla activity, although some do emphasize the extent of Beijing's alleged attempts at subversion by using overseas Chinese throughout Southeast Asia.

University of Bridgeport   Justus M. van der Kroef

Mongolia

A fusion of two revolutionary groups produced the Mongolian People's Party in 1921. The party held its First Congress in March of that year at Kyakhta, on Soviet territory. It became known as the Mongolian People's Revolutionary Party (MPRP) in 1924. Fiftieth anniversary celebrations in November 1974 commemorated this shift to "socialism" in 1924, but Russian dominance had already been established in 1921. The designation of the country as the Mongolian People's Republic (MPR) was adopted in 1924, as was the name of the capital, Ulan Bator (formerly Urga). At that time a noncapitalist and anti-bourgeois line was announced by the party's Third Congress and the First Great Khural (the structural equivalent of the USSR's Supreme Soviet).

In 1976 the MPRP claimed 67,000 members. The population of the MPR in 1979 was 1.64 million.

Organization and Leadership. Two new secretaries of the Central Committee were named in April: D. Damdin and G. Ad'yaa. S. Sosorbaram was removed as a party secretary, but the rest of the Secretariat continued unchanged, with four of the eight Politburo members and one of the two candidate members concurrently serving as party secretaries. Damdin (born 1931) published articles on Mongolian industry in 1959 and 1961 and was appointed minister of industry in April 1960. He served as minister of light and food industries from 1968 until his present appointment. Ad'yaa (born 1934) has been chief of the Central Committee's Department for Party Organizations since 1972 and before that was deputy chairman of the Commission for Information and Broadcasting and an editor of the party newspaper.

Ts. Molom (born 1932), minister of finance since 1969, was named a deputy prime minister in June, and E. Byambajav (born 1939) assumed the Finance Ministry post. Both men hold advanced degrees in economics from Soviet educational institutions.

Domestic Attitudes and Activities. Production began at Mongolia's largest economic project, Erdenet. The first trainload of copper and molybdenum concentrate left for the USSR in mid-December 1978, just five years after construction started. Fifteen thousand Mongolian and Russian construction workers had been involved in the project. Production of coal began at new mines at Baganur in January. This is supposed to double the country's total coal production, to 4 million tons. Agricultural acreage was again increased, but this failed to increase the grain harvest. Livestock production continued essentially unchanged. Manpower shortages persist, but the birthrate is high and the population is increasing. Construction by Soviet Red Army and some East German labor units is reported in the country.

The Mongolian-Soviet Joint Intergovernmental Commission held its seventeenth meeting in Ulan Bator in December 1978 and the eighteenth meeting in Moscow in June. Mongolia attended the Council for Mutual Economic Assistance meetings in Moscow in January and June. In mid-July, a deputy chairman of Gosplan was in Ulan Bator for coordination of the Soviet and MPR five-year plans for 1981 to 1985. Direct connection of the Soviet and Mongolian statistical bureaus was announced, continuing the trend of the last few years toward more direct contact between the two countries' ministries and governmental offices.

The trade imbalance, which represents a Soviet subsidy to the MPR, increased over the preceding year, following the pattern of over two decades. The copper and molybdenum from Erdenet is supposed to improve the situation significantly, and the trade figures for 1979 may tell a different story. But the available 1978 statistics show an imbalance.

International Views and Contacts. Ever closer integration and convergence of the MPR with the USSR proceeds. Prime Minister Tsedenbal referred to "economic and political fusion . . . abolition of national state barriers . . . no state frontiers . . . no national distinctions." Contradictions between claiming substantive independence for the Mongols while continually draining it away and between allegedly protecting Buddhism while propagating atheism are simply unresolved. But the unifying theme and the higher consistency of Mongolia's apparently contradictory policy is opposition to China. The escalation of the Sino-Soviet dispute due to the Vietnam-Kampuchea (Cambodia) situation and the USSR's aid to Vietnam in effect opened a second Soviet front against China. Moreover, the opening of Sino-Soviet talks with the possibility, however remote, of Sino-Soviet détente, caused repercussions in Mongolia and sharpened the inherent contradictions in the single unified policy of the USSR and the MPR.

Two moves by the USSR in Mongolia and countermoves by China illustrate the contradiction and the escalation. The Mongolians announced elaborate plans for memorials and museums at Nomonkhan and Ulan Bator to commemorate the 1939 victory over Japan and Russia's architect of that victory,

Marshal Georgi Zhukov. The memorial complex is to record "the theme of the combat fraternity of the Soviet and Mongolian armies." Its purpose is to emphasize Soviet resolve to defend Mongolia militarily against any invader, and it has been made amply clear that China in 1979 is equated with Japan in 1939. One of China's preconditions for the Sino-Soviet talks was withdrawal of Soviet troops from the MPR. The USSR has no intention of withdrawing.

A touch of verisimilitude was added to an otherwise unbelievable book by Victor Louis, who is commonly assumed to be a voice of the Soviet secret police, when the Dalai Lama visited Moscow and Ulan Bator in June. The book had made the fantastic suggestion that the Dalai Lama settle in Ulan Bator, establishing the capital of the MPR as the center of Buddhism. In Louis's words, "the appearance of the Dalai Lama in Mongolia . . . would be an event that could become the turning point in the history of that nation . . . it would result in a resurgence of religion in the MPR . . . Mongolia is fast becoming the sole heir of [Tibet's] spiritual functions."

China, which has been making overtures to the Dalai Lama to return to Lhasa, permitted a delegation representing him, including his brother, to visit Tibet for over a month. Beijing obviously hopes that the delegation's report will encourage the Dalai Lama to return. The reawakening in 1979 of a Mongolia–Tibet–Dalai Lama–Buddhist political connection as a factor in Russian-Chinese relations and the offering of Ulan Bator as a center of Buddhism have powerful historical justifications, but the present political rulers in Moscow, Beijing, Lhasa, and Ulan Bator hardly seem likely to call for that kind of re-creation of the past.

China now praises Genghis Khan and has reinstated the original boundaries of the Inner Mongolian Autonomous Region, which had been greatly reduced by administrative decree in 1969. Beijing charges that the USSR plans to annex the MPR and that forced russification is robbing the Mongols of their cultural identity. The Russians and Mongols reply that the truth is just the opposite: that China refuses to accept the independence of the MPR and wants to annex it and that forced sinicization is robbing the Mongols in China of their cultural identity. Victor Louis carried this theme further by seemingly calling for Soviet "liberation" of the oppressed minorities of China.

Soviet and Mongolian integration and pro-Buddhist policies conflict, but both are aimed against China. China's de-emphasis of Maoism and condemnation of the Cultural Revolution mean that the official policies of China and the USSR toward ethnic minorities are much the same. No significant ideological differences exist any more. But the nationalistic, territorial, and border questions nonetheless grow more serious as Sino-Soviet relations polarize. The genuine and substantively important part of Soviet policy is to maintain the total separation of the MPR from China and to integrate the MPR ever more closely with the USSR, whether that integration is ever formally confirmed by actual annexation. The genuine and substantively important part of Chinese policy is, minimally, to weaken Soviet military power in Mongolia and, maximally, to restore predominantly Chinese influence there.

The Soviet policy of encouraging religious expression and sympathy for genuine Mongolian independence may be artificial and propagandistic. China's current tolerance of religion and encouragement of minority ethnic groups may also be hypocritical. Thus, there is ultimately a contradiction in Russian and Chinese policies toward Mongolia and Tibet. The Sino-Soviet conflict is the key. The USSR systematically continues on all fronts to strengthen its total control, while offering tactical concessions that only appear inconsistent with the underlying policy.

Foreign policy activities in 1979 were more important and potentially more dangerous than previously, not only because of the escalation of the Sino-Soviet conflict because of Vietnam and Kampuchea but also because population movements, development policies, and military deployments place more ethnic Chinese closer to more ethnic Russians. At the same time buffer states, peoples, and cultures weaken and disappear so that there is less and less of a barrier to keep the Chinese and Russians apart.

More than ever before, there is no significant Mongolian foreign or domestic policy apart from the question of Sino-Soviet relations. This situation did not begin in 1979, but it emerged so much more starkly than before and was expressed in such unprecedented ways that it justifies marking 1979 as a decisive and exceptionally important year.

Among 300 representatives from fifteen countries attending the Fifth Asian Buddhist Peace Conference, which opened in Ulan Bator on 16 June, were for the first time representatives of Bhutan and Kampuchea. For Bhutan this small step away from complete Indian control placed it within the maneuvering over the Dalai Lama and the Sino-Soviet dispute. Reportedly the only Buddhist lama to survive the Pol Pot annihilation campaign attended the Ulan Bator conference. His presence added drama to the resolution of the meeting that called for recognition of the Heng Samrin government and condemnation of the Khmer Rouge.

Publications. The MPRP issues *Unen* (Truth), *Namyn Amdral* (Party Life), the Russian-language *Novosti Mongolii* (News of Mongolia), *Ediyn Dzasag* (Economics), and *Shine Hodoo* (New Countryside). The MPR assigns a reprsentative to the editorial board of *Problems of Peace and Socialism.* Radio broadcasts are made in Mongolian, Russian, English, Chinese, and Kazakh. Television broadcasting began in 1970.

University of North Carolina at Chapel Hill   Robert A. Rupen

Nepal

Developments in Nepal have raised the possibility that the Communist Party of Nepal (CPN) and other banned parties may be able to operate legally for the first time since 1960. Membership in the openly divided CPN is estimated at 4,000 to 5,000. Nepal's population is estimated at about 14 million.

Leadership and Organization. B. B. Manandhar has succeeded Keshar Jung Raimajhi as general secretary of the CPN moderate faction. Raimajhi now holds the post of president. In the leadership struggle among the extremist CPN elements precipitated by Pushpa Lal Shrestha's death in 1978, Man Mohan Adhikari appears predominant so far.

Domestic Attitudes and Activities. When B. P. Koirala, outspoken advocate of democratization and leader of the Nepali Congress Party, met King Birendra in October 1978, prospects for political liberalization appeared to increase. As part of the stepped-up political debate in 1978, four politicians, including Raimajhi, issued a declaration demanding abolition of the nonparty *panchayat* system, establishment of a constitutional monarchy, legalization of parties, and restoration of human rights. In any revival of political parties, the Nepali Congress Party (considered the country's strongest political group) and the CPN are expected to be major contenders.

The Bista government was increasingly criticized for corruption and ineffectiveness, and frequent cabinet changes occurred. Apparently in response to this criticism, the government decided to crack down. In early 1979 two Nepali Congress activists, convicted of treason several years earlier, were executed. These executions, the first in fifteen years, were widely condemned, even among government supporters.

A student demonstration in early April began a series of developments leading to a political crisis with a dramatic climax. Police broke up a demonstration protesting the execution of Pakistani Prime Minister Ali Bhutto, and students at numerous campuses reacted by going on strike. Universities were closed. Sporadic police-student clashes reportedly resulted in about thirty deaths. During this period terrorist incidents, attributed to radical Naxalites, also occurred in eastern and southern Nepal. Politicians, including B. P. Koirala and B. B. Manandhar, were detained for nearly two weeks. Others, including K. J. Raimajhi, went into hiding. Although some reports alleged Soviet instigation of the student actions, it is not believed that Soviet influence was sufficient. Moreover, the student movement seemed to include Nepali Congress and pro-Chinese elements as well as pro-Soviet students.

Opposition to the government's handling of the situation intensified, even in the national assembly. On 23 May a huge student demonstration criticized two government newspapers and demanded a direct dialogue with King Birendra. The following day the government resigned, and the king announced a referendum would be held at an unspecified time "in order to understand what our countrymen desire." The people were to choose between the existing *panchayat* arrangement with reforms and a multiparty system. (*FBIS*, 24 May.)

Restrictions on public meetings, speech, and the press were lifted, and political groups began organizing for the referendum. In June CPN extremist leader Man Mohan Adhikari addressed a meeting at which he called for swift dissolution of the *panchayat* system and the formation of a non-controversial interim government to ensure an impartial poll. He also urged that all political prisoners and exiles take part in it, reportedly expecting the *panchayat*'s defeat. (*Far Eastern Economic Review*, 29 June.)

K. J. Raimajhi also believes the Nepalese will reject the system which "minimizes the public" and has "no sympathy for the landless, the poor, and the downtrodden." Concerned about the strength of conservatism, he wants the voting age lowered to eighteen. At the same time, he warned against extremism, which he said "inevitably benefits right reactionaries." (*Asiaweek*, 20 July.) At one of several communist rallies held in September, K. B. Shrestha claimed that all leftists were united in several demands: lowering of the voting age, release of political detainees, withdrawal of political charges against political workers, and formation of a neutral government to conduct a free referendum (*FBIS*, 14 September).

International Views and Policies. The moderate CPN is supported by the USSR. Adhikari's extremist faction receives some Chinese support.

Publications. The weekly *Samiksha* reflects the views of the moderate CPN.

Alexandria, Virginia   Barbara Reid

New Zealand

The Communist Party of New Zealand (CPNZ) was founded in 1921. During the Sino-Soviet dispute of the sixties, it aligned itself with Mao Zedong, but in 1978 it broke with China and declared its support for Albania as the "socialist fatherland." Today the Albanian link is also severed, and the CPNZ is truly nonaligned.

Soviet supporters split off in 1966 to form the Socialist Unity Party (SUP), which soon eclipsed the CPNZ in size and influence. Various splinter groups that left the CPNZ in more recent years maintain their support for China. The main Trotskyist group is the Socialist Action League (SAL), founded in 1969.

These parties and groups all function legally. None publishes membership figures, although the SUP claimed a 40 percent increase in membership (*New Zealand Tribune*, 29 October). The combined membership of all Marxist organizations can be estimated at 500, of which the SUP might have 200, leaving up to 100 each for the CPNZ, the SAL, and the various Maoist groups. The population of New Zealand is 3 million.

Membership and Organization. The CPNZ held a national conference—its first since 1966—in Auckland from 26 to 28 January. The 34 delegates present gave "a resounding rebuff to the local followers of the new revisionist leaders of the Chinese party and all other revisionists and opportunists who have tried to disrupt and divert the CPNZ from its Marxist-Leninist line and make it collaborate with the class enemies of the New Zealand working people—the imperialists or social-imperialists who all collude and contend for world control and plunder" (*People's Voice*, 5 February). The conference approved a new draft constitution for the CPNZ and elected a Central Committee (previously called the National Committee). This committee in turn elected R. C. Wolf as chairman and H. Crook as secretary of the CPNZ, thus confirming the leadership that had ousted the long-term general secretary, V. G. Wilcox.

The SUP also held a national conference, its fifth triennial conference, during the year when 30 delegates met in Auckland from 19 to 21 October. The conference condemned the Chinese invasion of Vietnam and the Camp David agreements, expressed support for the SALT II treaty and New Zealand's withdrawal from the ANZUS (Australia–New Zealand–United States) pact, and sent greetings to the Central Committee of the Communist Party of the Soviet Union. Delegates re-elected G. H. Andersen as president, Ella Ayo as vice-president, and G. E. Jackson as national secretary.

Four Maoist groups—the Wellington Marxist-Leninist Organisation (WMLO), the Northern Communist Organisation (NCO), Struggle, and the Preparatory Committee for the Formation of the Communist Party of New Zealand (Marxist-Leninist)—held discussions during the year aimed at establishing a combined party. All four agreed on a joint letter to the government and people of Kampuchea (Cambodia) and on joint statements on the "Chinese counterattack against Vietnam's incursions on Chinese territory" and on "Soviet social-imperialism."

Two of these groups, the WMLO and the NCO, went further and decided to "merge in the near future to form a nationwide preparty organisation with one centre, one central committee and one central organ" (*Unity*, June). *Unity*, the monthly journal of the WMLO, became the joint organ of both groups in June, and in October a joint committee of the WMLO and the NCO decided that a founding conference would adopt the program, constitution, and name of the new organization.

The SAL announced that its sixth biennial conference would be held in Masterton from 28 December to 1 January 1980.

Auxiliary Organizations. The Democratic Youth Front, associated with the SUP, changed its name to Young Workers Alliance (YWA) and held its first annual conference in Auckland in June. The YWA played host during the year to a delegation from the Komsomol. The Young Socialists, who are linked with the SAL, held their fifth national conference in Wellington in June. They decided to maintain a presence in the universities—hitherto their main field of activity—but to concentrate future work among young workers in big factories.

The Union of New Zealand Women, in which the SUP has some influence, remained active, as did the Chile solidarity committees and the friendship societies working in support of the Soviet Union, China, and the Democratic People's Republic of Korea.

Domestic Attitudes and Activities. Nineteen seventy-nine was a year of much industrial unrest and saw New Zealand's first general strike since 1913. The SUP, which is strongly anchored in the trade union movement, took an active part in these events. K. G. Douglas, the Wellington SUP leader who was the only communist on the national executive of the N.Z. Federation of Labour, was elected secretary-treasurer of the federation in June in a postal ballot of affiliated unions. The federation, with a membership of almost 500,000 workers, is New Zealand's central trade union body, and the secretary-treasurer is the most important post next to the presidency. Douglas's success, by a narrow margin of votes, was undoubtedly helped by the strong attacks against him and the SUP launched by the prime minister and the deputy leader of the opposition Labour Party. G. H. Andersen, the national president of the SUP, was re-elected president of the Auckland Trades Council, and other SUP militants gained office on the Wellington and Otago Trades Councils.

The other communist groups are also seeking to gain influence among industrial workers. The Maoists in particular see the SUP as their main opponent in the unions, but they failed to prevent the Federation of Labour from passing a resolution condemning China's military aggression in Vietnam.

The SAL held a special conference in June 1978 that decided to base the party more firmly in industry by asking members to transfer to factory jobs. A National Committee meeting three months later decided to concentrate on the meat freezing industry (among the country's largest), which has strong and militant unions and a significant proportion of Polynesians in the work force. As a result of this campaign, at least half the members of the SAL took work in meat freezing during the year, and the League's journal, *Socialist Action*, began to devote regular pages to reports from this industry, including interviews with union leaders and other activities.

International Activities and Contacts. In November 1978 the CPNZ had hailed the "steadfastness, courage and resolution" of the Albanian Party of Labor as "an example and inspiration for Marxists-Leninists everywhere" (*People's Voice*, 13 November 1978). A year later Albania was no longer mentioned. The breach has not been publicly acknowledged, but a major contributing factor seems to have been Enver Hoxha's characterization of Mao Zedong as a longtime revisionist. Without mentioning Hoxha or Albania, a writer in the *N.Z. Communist Review* dismissed as subjective "dogmatic assertions, unsupported by facts, that Mao was a lifelong revisionist who opened the Party to bourgeois factions and supported the bourgeoisie in the Party and state" (*N.Z. Communist Review*, October).

In March the CPNZ used the occasion of the visit of Chinese Vice-Premier Chen Muhua for counterdemonstrations with placards reading: "Communist party of NZ condemns China's invasion of Vietnam! Oppose U.S.-China-Soviet imperialist wars" (*People's Voice*, 26 March).

G. E. Jackson led an SUP delegation to Hungary in August, while G. H. Andersen attended the 22nd national convention of the Communist Party, U.S.A. that same month. A fraternal delegate from the Socialist Party of Australia attended the SUP national conference in October.

The SAL held an educational conference in Auckland over the New Year holidays, which was attended by Mary-Alice Waters of the U.S. Socialist Workers Party. Later in January the SAL sent representatives to the convention of the Australian Socialist Workers' Party in Sydney.

Publications. The CPNZ weekly journal *People's Voice* has been published regularly since 1943. The party also produces a monthly theoretical organ, *N.Z. Communist Review*. The SUP publishes the fortnightly *New Zealand Tribune* (since 1966) and an irregularly appearing theoretical journal, *Socialist Politics*. The SAL's fortnightly journal *Socialist Action* celebrated its tenth anniversary with well-attended dinners in Auckland and Wellington. The SAL also began publication of a quarterly supplement, *Socialist Action Review*, during the year.

Unity, now the joint organ of the WMLO and the NCO, is published monthly in Wellington. The NCO bulletin *Class Struggle* is to become a joint theoretical organ of the two groups. The pro-Chinese theoretical journal *Struggle* has continued to appear bimonthly, and the Preparatory Committee for the Formation of the CPNZ (M-L) has brought out several issues of its *Bulletin* at irregular intervals.

No circulation figures are available, but *Socialist Action* has probably the largest circulation (up to 3,000 copies), followed by the *New Zealand Tribune* (which claimed a 26 percent increase in sales) and the *People's Voice*.

University of Auckland   H. Roth

Pakistan

As of late 1979 the illegal Communist Party of Pakistan (CPP) reportedly posed no direct threat to the government of Pakistan. The CPP, an offshoot of the Communist Party of India, was formed shortly after Pakistan became independent in August 1947. In 1954 the government banned the CPP as a subversive and illegal organization under the provisions of the Criminal Law (Amendment) Act of 1908. The Political Parties Act of 1962 prohibits the formation or functioning of any party that the government defines as detrimental to "Islamic ideology" or the "integrity and security of Pakistan." Moreover, on 16 October 1978 Pakistan's martial law government promulgated an ordinance amending the 1962 act to specify that no political party that received aid from or was associated in any way with a foreign country or its nationals would be allowed to exist. The amendments stipulated that officers of parties that had been dissolved by the government may not engage in any political activity for seven years from the date of dissolution.

Foreign observers speculated that in the late 1970s the CPP had a few hundred members, a minuscule fraction of the country's estimated 80.2 million (mid-1979) population. Intelligence officials of the U.S. government professed not to know even an approximate number but suggested that although formal membership in the CPP was undoubtedly extremely small, a large and growing number of workers, students, intellectuals, and ethnic and regional dissidents privately espoused variations of communist doctrines and were members or supporters of various small, clandestine, little-known communist organizations. Among these organizations were the Awami Jamhurriya Ittehad (United People's Democratic Party) and the Baluch Awami Azadi Mahaiz (Baluch People's Liberation Front); the former was viewed as generally pro-Soviet, and the latter described itself as a Marxist-Leninist organization. In the past foreign observers believed that most Pakistani communists or communist sympathizers were pro-Soviet, but in 1979 several observers conjectured that most Pakistani communists were concerned more with ethnic, regional, and national political issues than with adherence to ideological purity as defined either in Moscow or Beijing.

Events throughout 1979 favored the creation and expansion of dissident antigovernment groups. On 4 April the martial law regime, which had deposed the government of Zulfiqar Ali Bhutto in a military coup d'etat on 5 July 1977, executed Bhutto after the Pakistani Supreme Court, in a split decision (four to three), upheld a lower court decision that Bhutto was guilty of a charge of conspiracy to commit murder. The execution evoked deep and bitter anger and resentment not only within Bhutto's Pakistan People's Party but also among numerous other groups, some of which had been apolitical. Shortly after the execution, President Mohammad Zia ul Haq, the chief martial law administrator, chief-of-state, and head of the government, again promised to hold parliamentary elections. He had made a similar promise immediately after the 1977 coup. On 30 August, however, he promulgated numerous legal obstacles to participation in the election by the extant legal parties and on 16 October postponed the scheduled 17 November election for "an indefinite period." He also banned all political activities, dissolved all political parties, closed various newspapers and journals, and imposed censorship on all newspapers and mass media.

It was at first assumed that the censorship applied only to domestic publications, but on 14 November the police arrested Salamat Ali, a Pakistani citizen employed as a correspondent by the Hong Kong–based *Far Eastern Economic Review*. He was charged with "creating hatred among the people," and on 29 November a military court found him guilty as charged and sentenced him to one year in prison.

Some analysts, both foreign and Pakistani, suggested that under General Zia's increasingly harsh and authoritarian rule, opponents of his regime would be attracted to extremist groups at either end of the political spectrum. Because of Zia's several pronouncements that the letter of Islamic law (*sharia*) should be observed and imposed throughout the society, he has preempted the far right, leaving the communists on the far left as a major alternative center of opposition. These analysts therefore believe that communist or communist-affiliated groups will increase in size and influence in the early 1980s.

The American University   Richard F. Nyrop

Philippines

Communism in the Philippines is divided between a pro-Beijing and a pro-Moscow party. The latter and older of the two, the Philippine Communist Party (Partido Kommunista ng Pilipinas; PKP), was established on 7 November 1930. Larger and more active is the Communist Party of the Philippines/Marxist-Leninist (CPP-ML), organized on 26 December 1968. It has a guerrilla force called the New People's Army (NPA), formally established on 29 March 1969. Both parties are illegal under the antisubversion law of 17 June 1957 (Republic Act 1,700). Because of the more moderate position adopted by the PKP, which has sometimes praised reform measures of President Ferdinand Marcos, active counterinsurgency is directed primarily against the NPA and CPP-ML. Under Secretary General Felicisimo Macapagal, the main PKP cadres surrendered in 1974 and were granted amnesty. They enjoy some freedom of movement (*Bangkok Post*, 5 August).

Former PKP Secretary General José Lava has become affiliated with the *World Marxist Review* and recently praised Vietnam's national development effort (*WMR*, April, pp. 121–30), in keeping with the party's pro-Soviet position. The PKP has a membership of about 250, with several scores of covert sympathizers among intellectuals and in labor groups. The CPP-ML's strength is estimated at about 2,000 members, most of whom are active also in the NPA. The principal leaders of both parties are in prison, with the CPP-ML and NPA especially dependent on dispersed and decentralized commands. Both parties claim to have functioning central committees. The PKP program stresses nationalistic themes of "liberation" from foreign, especially American "imperialist" domination of the economy and foreign relations. It holds out the possibility of achieving better living conditions through agrarian reform, if possible through peaceful and constitutional means. The CPP-ML emulates Maoist principles and is committed to "liberation war," encircling cities from the countryside, and establishing a broad-based national front. It would combine all those, including workers, peasants, national bourgeoisie, students, and ethnic minorities, who are opposed to the government. The threat posed by the NPA was cited by Marcos in his proclamation of martial law on 22 September 1972, the basic provisions of which continue in force. Various CPP-ML sympathizers belong to such organizations as the National Democratic Front, which also has foreign supporters. (For a fuller discussion, see *YICA*, 1976, pp. 362–65, and *YICA*, 1977, pp. 363–65.)

Domestic Developments. During the year it was reported that the NPA, after a comparative lull in activity following capture on 10 November 1977 of its chief commander, CPP-ML Chairman José M. Sison, began staging new attacks against military units and exploiting alleged repression by the Philippine military in various rural areas. This new upsurge, marking what NPA sources define as taking the "strategic defensive," followed a preparatory period in which guerrilla recruiters and propaganda units first infiltrated an area. NPA units, some as large as 200 men, now appear to be seeking combat in northern Luzon, on Samar island in the Visayans, and in Davao province on the southern island of Mindanao. The overall objective appears to be to create a widespread pattern of confrontation with the government, immobilizing and confining the latter to cities, while a coalition mass movement, which would include leftist-oriented elements of the Roman Catholic Church, pressed for Marcos's downfall. (*Far Eastern Economic Review*, 29 June, pp. 24–25.)

In mid-February the constabulary reported from Pampanga province that 50 NPA guerrillas had surrendered following the killing of their commander. On 20 May military sources claimed to have "smashed the backbone" of the insurgent movement on Negros island in the central Philippines after a series of raids on Bacolod city. Efren Gerardino, a high-ranking "communications director" and several of his followers were seized in this operation. Vicente Clemente, identified as head of the "explosives unit," reportedly was captured on 29 May in the town of Paranaque in Samar province. Thirty-seven NPA guerrillas were reportedly killed during the course of sixteen battles with the constabulary in that same province within two months. The regional constabulary commander for the Western Visayans announced that 29 guerrillas had been killed, another 166 captured, and 243 NPA sympathizers had "returned to the government fold" during 1978. Most of the foregoing action occurred in Panay and Negros Occidental provinces.

Other counterinsurgency successes, according to Philippine military sources, involved aborting a supposed conference of guerrilla commanders near the town of Asuncion on Mindanao and the killing of two guerrilla leaders in April. At mid-year, an NPA training camp in the town of Tinglayan, Kalinga-Apayao province, was captured and training equipment destroyed. At about the same time, the military reported the capture of a "death squad" member sent to kill three Filipino "landowners" near the town of Gapan in Nueva Ecija province. (*FBIS*, 16 February, 2 March, 23 April, 22 May, and 18 June.)

Despite such reverses, the government admits that NPA activities continue. In mid-May, for example, the military reported that guerrillas had killed fourteen persons, including four militiamen, in various raids and ambushes throughout Davao del Norte and Samar provinces. Insurgents even took over a town hall in western Samar, disarming local police, raising the NPA flag, and compelling inhabitants to gather for a meeting. Regional elections in the southern Philippines were interrupted by guerrilla raids, including attacks on Diplog and Cotabato cities. At mid-year, "an eight-hour blazing gun battle" took place in the Tarlac province town of Capas, with other fighting in the provinces of Misamis Occidental, Camarines Sur, and Kalinga-Apaya. Results included the killing and capture of a score of guerrillas. The military also clashed with "heavily armed" insurgents in Iloilo, Ifugao, and Agusan del Sur provinces, which again resulted in the killing of nearly a dozen communists. On 14 July, a government medical team was attacked near the town of Manukan on the coast of Mindanao. During the same week, sources said that 15 insurgents had been killed and 72 others captured, mostly in the Samar area. (Ibid., 8 and 18 May, 13 and 21 June, 18 July; *NYT*, 15 April and 15 July.)

In the fall, it was announced that the constabulary had begun a new "massive operation" against the NPA in the provinces of Agusan del Norte, Agusan del Sur, and Misamis Oriental. The aim of the operation was to capture a major stronghold, believed to contain some 600 insurgents. (*FBIS*, 14 September.) Eleven guerrillas were killed and others wounded and captured when constabulary forces raided NPA camps in Laping township in northern Samar and on Leyte (ibid., 27 September).

Intensified activity on the island of Samar prompted increasing official concern, as it became apparent that allegedly unjust treatment of the local population by local officials was helping communist insurgents. Also, by dispensing a Robin Hood style of justice for the benefit of Samar peasants oppressed by local officials and cattle rustlers, the NPA personnel had secured some confidence among local inhabitants. After a visit to the area, Defense Minister Juan Ponce Enrile ordered the "immediate transfer" of local military and constabulary units because of misconduct. At this time, Enrile was reportedly informed that the capital of Catarman on Samar was in NPA hands and that local insurgents were described as "farmers by day and soldiers by night." Government reform measures on Samar, however, came only after several clashes in preceding months on the island had indicated that NPA guerrillas were entrenched in the region. (*Asiaweek*, 15 June, p. 20; *FBIS*, 30 March and 4 June.)

United front antigovernment activity instigated by the CPP-ML continued even as Marcos persisted in efforts to present a more democratic and humane face both at home and abroad. A street demonstration involving 100,000 persons in Manila on 13 May organized by leftist students' and workers' groups was dispersed by police. In a press release, organizers claimed that the event had shown the "solidarity of the people against the U.S.-imperialist–dictated Marcos fascist regime." Prominent among demonstrators, as in the past, were leftist-oriented members of the Roman Catholic clergy.

The following month, Defense Secretary Enrile criticized what he called "religious radicals" and propagandists of the "Christian left" for their antigovernment campaign. Jaime Cardinal Sin, primate of the Roman Catholic Church, responded that such allegations represented an attempt to justify continuation of martial law in the country. He admitted that a growing number of priests had attacked the government's denigration of human rights and revealed himself among the critics. In a BBC interview he warned that civil war would result unless Marcos ended martial law. (*FBIS*, 7 September.)

Divisions within the Moro National Liberation Front (MNLF), the secessionist Muslim insurgent organization operating in Mindanao, continued and probably precluded more active cooperation with the NPA. (On the MNLF, see *YICA*, 1978, p. 308.) There was no persuasive evidence of active or continuous collaboration during the year between MNLF elements, which seek to establish an independent "Moro republic" in the southern Philippines, and the NPA. However, evidence of such cooperation in the past has been claimed in official quarters. As in Samar, rough treatment of the local population by military forces fighting against MNLF insurgents on Mindanao has been of concern to the central government (*Far Eastern Economic Review*, 16 March, pp. 21–28).

International Aspects. Developments in Indochina found the CPP-ML, not surprisingly, on the side of Beijing and highly critical of both Hanoi and Moscow. The publication of the National Democratic Front, *Liberation*, in its 1 February issue branded "Soviet social-imperialists and the Vietnamese leaders" as "aggressors in Indochina" and noted that the USSR has been aiding Hanoi economically and with weapons in order to make it part of the designs of "Kremlin hegemonists" (Voice of the Malayan Revolution, 3 July; *FBIS*, 13 July). Articles in *Ang Bayan* (The People), the CPP-ML's main publication, charged the Soviets with responsibility for masterminding the military campaign of the Vietnamese against the Pol Pot regime in Cambodia. The USSR's aim was to "gain a foothold" in Southeast Asia for Muscovite "social-imperialism." According to the CPP-ML, Vietnam should sever all connections with Russia's ambitions in the region, abrogate its friendship treaty with the USSR, and realize that the "contradiction" in the Indochina area is between "Soviet social-imperialism" and the "interests of socialism" in both Cambodia and Vietnam. Despite attacks on the Soviets and Vietnamese, the CPP-ML has not weakened its opposition to U.S. "imperialism," because the alleged American stranglehold on the Philippine economy and political life remains the country's principal problem (*Far Eastern Economic Review*, 8 June, pp. 21–22).

The new agreement signed between Washington and Manila on 7 January providing both for Philippine sovereignty and control over military bases, as well as American operational use, has come in for sharp criticism (*NYT*, 15 April). Sources sympathetic to the CPP-ML have called the formal recognition of Philippine sovereignty merely "cosmetic." Moreover, since the new agreement provides for at least $500 million in U.S. military sales, grants, and credits, Washington allegedly is further strengthening the "Marcos dictatorship" and intervening in domestic policy. The new agreement provides that American military forces may become involved by mutual agreement in "security activities" even outside U.S. bases (*Philippine Liberation Courier*, Oakland, Calif., 23 February, pp. 2–3).

No notable developments have occurred in Soviet-Philippine relations since the two countries established formal diplomatic relations in May 1976. In connection with NPA resurgence during the year, one Soviet comment charged that Beijing leaders were being formally friendly toward the

Philippine government, but in fact were making use of "local Chinese moneybags" to assist NPA guerrillas (Tass, 13 April; *FBIS*, 17 April). The alleged use of overseas Chinese resident in Southeast Asia as conduits for local aid to communist guerrillas has been a common theme over the years in Soviet commentaries.

Relations between Manila and Beijing were strengthened with a new trade agreement on 11 July. Imelda Marcos signed the seven-year treaty, which provides for an estimated $2 billion turnover between the two countries. The exact nature of Chinese exports is not clear, although there has been speculation that they might include oil in addition to the 1.2 million tons currently being received. (*Antara Daily News Bulletin*, 16 July, p. 2.)

Within the context of military cooperation between members of the Association of Southeast Asian Nations, the government has intensified regional counterinsurgency cooperation. Rear Admiral Romulo Espaldon, chief of the armed forces' southern command, has declared that the Philippines, Malaysia, and Indonesia were preparing a joint border defense agreement on security measures. The new agreement was to provide for hot pursuit across frontiers against insurgents and "other threats to the region's stability." (*The Indonesia Times*, 26 October 1978.)

Formally, and despite its close economic and military cooperation with the United States, the government seeks to maintain friendly relations with all countries, including communist-ruled ones. Deputy Foreign Minister Manuel Collantes revealed a proposal by North Korea to exchange ambassadors. This suggestion came through Mrs. Marcos while she was visiting Beijing via the North Korean embassy. (Agence France Presse, 11 July; *FBIS*, 12 July.)

Publications. The PKP's main newspaper is *Ang Kommunista* (The Communist), appearing irregularly in stenciled form in both English and various Philippine languages. At times the international journals of the pro-Moscow communist parties, *Information Bulletin* and *World Marxist Review*, carry statements by PKP leaders. The CPP-ML has a much broader spectrum of publications, including occasional access to the South China–based clandestine radio transmitter, Voice of the Malayan Revolution, and to the *Indonesian Tribune*, published in Tirana, the main journal of the Maoist wing of the underground Communist Party of Indonesia. The bimonthly *Ang Bayan* (The Nation), in both English and various Philippine languages, is the CPP-ML's principal organ. The less frequently appearing *Liberation* is published by the pro–CPP-ML organization, the National Democratic Front. CPP-ML sympathizers also claim to have their own "news agency," BMP (Balita ng Malayang Pilipinas; Free Philippines News Service), which is said to provide reports to a number of anti-Marcos "underground newspapers" and "progressive publications." One of these, *Dangadang* (Fight), is in the Ilocano language of northwestern Luzon; another, *Silyab* (Flame), appears in the Bicol area; and *Ang Gerilya* (The Guerrilla) is issued "in the hills of Samar." (*Philippine Liberation Courier*, 27 April, p. 5.)

University of Bridgeport   Justus M. van der Kroef

Singapore

No distinctive communist party as such exists in Singapore, and communists in this island republic are viewed formally as members of the Communist Party of Malaya (CPM) or of its front groups. The reason for the absence of a separate organization is that both Malayan and Singapore communists regard establishment of the Malaysian Federation in 1963 (at that time including Singapore) and the subsequent departure of Singapore from the federation in 1965 to become an independent republic within the Commonwealth to have occurred unlawfully and undemocratically. Open CPM activity or affiliation with its fronts is illegal in Singapore, although the government considers the small 250-member opposition Barisan Sosialis Malaya (Malayan Socialist Front; MSF) to be communist-infiltrated and/or sympathetic to the CPM cause. The MSF, founded on 26 July 1961 and led since then by its chairman, Dr. Lee Siew Choh, has over the years been permitted to participate in general elections. But like other opposition groups, it has found it impossible to break the dominance of Premier Lee Kuan Yew's People's Action Party (PAP) over the past two decades (see, for example, *YICA*, 1978, pp. 313–15). The MSF has frequently complained that it cannot obtain the necessary government permits to publish literature or to hold rallies except during short periods before elections. According to government sources, these allegations are but excuses for the MSF's lack of popular support. Like the CPM, the MSF has since 1962 continued to favor the so-called "merger," i.e., a unification of peninsular Malaya and Singapore, permitting the Malaysian Federation's states of Sarawak and Sabah on Borneo to achieve independence, if they desire.

Domestic Developments. In mid-June the Home Ministry announced that it had broken up a procommunist unit within the University of Singapore Chinese Society (USCS). Tan Peng Lim, a 33-year-old lecturer in mathematics at the Singapore Polytechnic Institute, previously had been arrested along with eight other past or present USCS members. The eight subsequently "recanted" and were set free, but Tan was held under a detention order for engaging in "procommunist activities" and efforts to "overthrow the government through armed struggle." The Home Ministry statement alleged that the USCS had been "infiltrated and manipulated" by persons connected with a front group of the pro-Soviet Communist Party of Malaya/Marxist-Leninist called the Malayan People's Liberation League. These persons, it was charged, "through publications and discussions" with USCS members had been advocating violent resistance to the government. Tan Peng Lim, according to the statement, had become increasingly Marxist-oriented when he was engaged in graduate work at the University of Auckland. He established contact with other Singapore students in Sydney who had similar "procommunist" leanings. Tan and another member of this latter group decided on their return to Singapore to carry on proselytizing activities among certain target groups—namely, the intelligentsia and the professionally trained, including students, cultural groups, and workers. (*Sunday Times*, Singapore, 17 June; *FBIS*, 19 June.)

With the arrest of Tan and his followers, the procommunist infiltration of the USCS presumably has been stopped. But the incident has tended to underscore past charges made by the Lee Kuan Yew government that certain Australian and New Zealand universities have been sources of Marxist influence on Singapore students. The Voice of the Malayan Revolution (VOMR), the South China–based clandestine radio transmitter of the CPM, noted the arrest of Tan Peng Lim and his associates. It claimed that those apprehended had been active in promotion of the USCS biannual essay contest and in dissemination of literature, efforts that had "received broad support from the public." The VOMR declared that the USCS had published an "open letter" in connection with the arrests, noting that it was a legitimate and properly registered student group, that its publications appeared under a government permit, and that the arrests would have a chilling effect on the essay contest. The "open letter," according to the VOMR, pleaded for public support and called on the government either to bring those arrested to public trial or else to release them "unconditionally" (VOMR, 24 July; *FBIS*, 31 July.)

The government's use of preventive arrest and detention of prisoners for political reasons under the Internal Security Act has continued to arouse concern from various quarters. Some forty persons are estimated to be held under the act. Instead of a trial, the government frequently appears to offer a choice to the accused: either confess alleged misdeeds or be expelled from Singapore. (*Amnesty International Report 1978*, London, pp. 185–87.)

In November 1978 the government conditionally released from prison Lim Hock Siew and Said Zahar, identified as "prominent leaders of the communist united front" in Singapore, who had been arrested and held without trial since February 1963 on grounds they had "planned and organized pro-communist agitations against the government." Lim and Zahar, though released from prison, were confined to the small island of Ubin. Both reportedly refused to promise they would cease work on behalf of the CPM or other front groups. The Home Affairs Ministry also noted in connection with their conditional release that the CPM planned to continue its united front activities in Singapore and that its intention to do so had been reaffirmed in a broadcast. (Radio Singapore, 17 November 1978; *FBIS*, 29 November 1978.)

In late 1978 the VOMR also accused the government of recruiting Gurkhas to serve as prison guards over political detainees. It further charged that political prisoners were badly treated and that the population "will never submit." (VOMR, 30 November 1978; *FBIS*, 6 December 1978.) Despite the VOMR claims, there remains little doubt that the government is firmly in control. In the February by-elections, the PAP won all seven seats at stake and 71 percent of the votes in five districts where opposition candidates ran (*Far Eastern Economic Review*, 23 February).

International Aspects. Developments in Indochina during the year were of paramount concern to the government. According to the veteran PAP leader and acting premier, Dr. Goh Keng Swee, "the most important event in the last twelve months was the invasion of Kampuchea [Cambodia] by the Vietnamese army," while the second most important occurrence was the Chinese incursion into North Vietnam a few weeks later. These developments demonstrated that communist forces had no regard for international borders and that the fighting in Indochina had permitted the USSR to expand its influence in the area. Dr. Goh also asserted that the conflict in Indochina was being aggravated by the "great human tragedy" of the Vietnamese refugees, which had produced many problems for the Southeast Asian nations. He predicted that "the Vietnamese will in due course learn that they will have to conduct their relations with other countries according to rules accepted by the international community." (Radio Singapore, 8 August; *FBIS*, 9 August.)

Somewhat earlier, Premier Lee Kuan Yew, in an interview, declined to describe the Vietnamese as performing a similar role to that of Cubans in Africa ("the Vietnamese are people much more inclined to be serious than the Cubans"), but he conceded that the USSR "probably had approved the Vietnamese plans to invade Cambodia" and that "the situation has changed in the Soviet Union's favor." Lee added that in Singapore itself "the appeal of communism has never been as insignificant as it is now." (*Le Figaro*, Paris, 30 July). The premier has, however, been especially critical of Hanoi when among colleagues in the Association of Southeast Asian Nations (ASEAN). During a visit to Bonn, he charged that the Vietnamese by means of their refugee policies were practicing "pitiless, cruel, barbaric methods of political blackmail" on their Southeast Asian neighbors, which were already confronted with serious racial difficulties of their own (*Far Eastern Economic Review*, 22 June).

The Singapore government has been in the forefront among ASEAN states in accusing Hanoi of attempting to "destabilize" the Southeast Asian region through the Vietnamese "boat people." It has emphasized the racial element, i.e., the fact that so many of the recent refugees are ethnic Chinese. All Southeast Asian countries have sizable minorities (some 75 percent of Singapore's 2.5 million population are Chinese). This together with Hanoi's expropriation of refugee properties, in Premier Lee's opinion, would lead to increased anti-Chinese sentiment from which only the Soviets would benefit (ibid., 10 August). Partly because of the Indochina fighting, Singapore today seems further than ever from establishing regular diplomatic relations with mainland China, while official relations with the USSR and Eastern Europe remain warily correct.

Publications. Because of the alleged inability to obtain government permits, the publications of the MSF, especially its journal *Plebeian*, have virtually ceased to appear. At election time, handbills and leaflets are often the MSF's only means of printed communication. From time to time the government has claimed discovery inside Singapore of publications issued by the Malayan National Liberation Army or other front groups of the three branches of the communist movement in peninsular Malaya, but their contents have not been made public. No avowedly Marxist organ is published in Singapore, where the press is careful to practice self-censorship. From time to time the VOMR has broadcast criticisms of the Lee Kuan Yew government. Neither the media of the People's Republic of China nor such Soviet-oriented organs as *World Marxist Review* publish critical analyses of Singapore government policies.

University of Bridgeport   Justus M. van der Kroef

Sri Lanka

In 1979 the Sri Lanka Communist Party (SLCP) and other leftist parties continued their search for ways to regain influence in the absence of parliamentary representation and may have made some progress toward overcoming divisions among themselves. Communist party membership is estimated at 6,000, mostly in the pro-Soviet SLCP. Pro-Chinese splinter groups apparently wield little influence. Sri Lanka's estimated population is 14.5 million.

Leadership and Organization. New SLCP officers were elected after the party's Tenth Congress in 1978. Dr. S. A. Wickremasinghe remains president. In July longtime General Secretary Pieter Keuneman was removed and appointed to the less influential post of vice-president. The reason for Keuneman's ouster is unclear, but his relatively moderate policies had long been criticized by the hard-line party faction headed by Wickremashinghe. The new general secretary is K. P. Silva, also associated with this faction. Other members of the Politburo include M. G. Mendis, A. Vaidialingam, H. G. S. Ratnaweera, L. W. Panditha, Sarath Muttettuwegama, J. A. K. Pererz, D. W. Subasinghe, D. E. W. Gunasekera, Leslie Gunawardena, Jayatillaka de Silva, and Peter Jayasekera.

Domestic Attitudes and Activities. The SLCP is still pursuing unity of the "progressive" forces, and the past year has seen overtures between the old left—the SLCP and the Trotskyist Lanka Sama Samaja Party (LSSP)—and the new left represented by the Janatha Vimukthi Peramuna (JVP). In late 1978 Keuneman indicated measures were being taken to strengthen his party's and the LSSP's United Left Front (ULF) and stated that the ULF was establishing committees in various provinces (*FBIS*, 22 December 1978). He also continued to attack the United National Party government for "repressive" measures, such as a ban on strikes and the revival of capitalism.

Local elections in May provided some gauge of popular opinion toward competing political parties. The United National Party, which had made politically risky welfare cuts, nevertheless did as well as expected (its prospects were enhanced by the urban composition of the electorate and the proportional representation system). The SLCP and the LSSP, which contested on a joint platform, fared poorly and, in fact, were outpolled in the Colombo area by the JVP. Before the elections, Keuneman had claimed that the system was rigged against the left but asserted that this "will in every way be a good thing, encouraging the people to rely mainly on their united actions." The communists' electoral failure thus could lead to extra-parliamentary measures, one of the themes of the SLCP's 1978 congress. The party's journal, *Forward*, had also reiterated that "the main struggle lies in building up an extra-parliamentary mass movement." (*Far Eastern Economic Review* [*FEER*], 11 May.)

The leftists have not been able to play much of a role in the major communal problem facing the government, the resolution of the deep-seated grievances of the Tamil minority. Continued terrorism by young Tamil militants in northern Sri Lanka prompted the government to introduce new anti-terrorist laws and to order the area cleared of agitators by the end of December. President Jayewardene had earlier called for a conference to address the communal problem but excluded the leftists from any deliberations. Keuneman has met at least once with the Tamils' parliamentary leader, but the SLCP did not comment on the meeting; the party is believed to be sympathetic to Tamil demands. (Ibid., 18 May and 17 August.)

In the trade union field, where the leftist parties have significant influence and have previously cooperated, left-wing unions launched a campaign in September against the government's draft of the Essential Public Services bill, claiming it would prevent union action in certain public sectors. Employees of government offices, banks, and mercantile firms began picketing, and protest rallies were held. At the same time, however, a pro-Soviet communist union leader has indicated some of the problems facing leftist union organizers. He pointed out that many workers belong to several unions, including that of the governing party, and stated that a long, hard struggle lies ahead. In terms of strategy, he advised that it was important to rely first on concrete economic demands characteristic of the particular sector and then gradually add political demands. (*WMR*, August.)

Finally, on 2 October five leftist parties exhibited at least a temporary show of unity at a rally to protest the Essential Public Services bill and government "oppression." The parties represented were the SLCP, the LSSP, the JVP, the new Sama Sarnaja Party formed by LSSP rebel V. Nanayakkara, and the Revolutionary Marxist Party of veteran trade unionist Bala Tampoe. According to JVP leader Rohan Wijeweera, whose party apparently made the strongest showing, the five parties had agreed on a common action program a month earlier. A joint statement at a reportedly large rally demanded the withdrawal of the public services bill, abolition of the antiterrorism law, and the end of the state of emergency in the northern Tamil area.

International Views and Policies. The pro-Soviet SLCP has issued resolutions applauding the USSR-Vietnam treaty of friendship and cooperation and supporting Vietnam against Chinese "aggression" (*FBIS*, 27 November 1978 and 4 May; Tass, 3 May). A delegation headed by General Secretary Silva visited Hungary in October. Earlier in the year Politburo member D. W. Subasinghe warned against new imperialist counteroffensives in the form of a human rights campaign against the socialist countries and allegations of a "Soviet threat." He also attacked China more harshly, calling it a "monstrous" partner of imperialism. (*WMR*, March.)

The Soviet Union is believed to support leftist unity in Sri Lanka. At the same time, relations between the two countries remain cordial, and the Soviets will undoubtedly continue working with the incumbent establishment (*FEER*, 31 August).

The pro-Chinese communists have shown few signs of activity. They did issue several statements directed mainly against the USSR and Vietnam. The Communist Party (Marxist-Leninist), for example, has declared the Soviet-Vietnam treaty a threat to Asian peace and has extended support to the Pol Pot regime in Kampuchea (Cambodia). (*FBIS*, 21 November 1978 and 7 May; *Peking Review*, 15 December 1978.)

Publications. The SLCP publishes *Aththa*, *Mawbima, Deshabimani*, and *Forward*.

Other Leftist Groups. Of the various Marxist parties, the JVP has appeared the most active during the year, showing organizational ability (noted by Sri Lanka's president before the May elections) and probably gaining strength (*FEER*, 18 May). The LSSP elected a new president, Athauda Seneviratne, following the death of N. M. Perera on 14 August.

Alexandria, Virginia   Barbara Reid

Thailand

Nineteen seventy-nine proved extremely significant for the Community Party of Thailand (CPT). Previously the CPT had tried to stay on good terms with both China and Vietnam despite their widening differences because it depended on both for material support in its revolutionary struggle. However, the invasion of Kampuchea (Cambodia) by Vietnamese troops, the establishment of a Vietnamese-backed regime led by Heng Samrin, and continued Chinese support for Pol Pot and his guerrilla resistance produced a situation in which the CPT could no longer avoid taking a stand. By early January, CPT cadres based in Laos were privately critical of Vietnam's military action against the Pol Pot government and of the presence of Vietnamese troops in Laos (*CSM*, 25 July). This criticism resulted in the Central Committee of the Lao People's Revolutionary Party issuing an order in January forcing most of the CPT guerrillas to leave their long-established sanctuaries in Laos (*Far Eastern*

Economic Review [*FEER*], 27 July). Almost simultaneously the Vietnamese forced the CPT to close its guerrilla bases in Kampuchea because the CPT refused to recognize the Heng Samrin government (*Soviet Analyst* [*SA*], 27 September). In May, the clandestine China-based Voice of the People of Thailand (VOPT) began a series of broadcasts of published statements from around the region criticizing Vietnam for its refugee policies, the invasion of Kampuchea, and for supposedly acting as a surrogate of the Soviet Union (*FEER*, 27 July). On 7 June the VOPT directly attacked Vietnam for the first time, accusing it of planning an invasion of Thailand (*SA*, 27 September). Subsequently the CPT reportedly offered to cooperate temporarily with the Thai government in resisting Vietnamese expansionism (*Le Monde*, 26 June). On 10 July the VOPT called on the Thai people to resist the "new aggressor"—a clear reference to the Vietnamese. The next day, a VOPT broadcast dealt with what was called "the tragedy of hegemonism created by Vietnam." (*FBIS*, 18 July.)

The impact on the CPT of this decision to oppose Vietnam and its attendant developments was considerable. Loss of CPT bases in Laos and Kampuchea forced many CPT insurgents to relocate under less secure circumstances in Thailand, and it cut most of the CPT supply lines into northeast Thailand from Laos and Kampuchea. Bunyen Wothang and Therdphum Chaides, two prominent members of the Committee for Coordinating Patriotic and Democratic Forces (CCPDF), a front organization of the CPT, broke away to form a new, pro-Vietnamese group. They were joined by a small number of low-level CPT cadres and guerrillas. The new group, based in Laos, operates its own radio transmitter from Vientiane. Known as the Northeast Thai National Liberation Movement, it is led by and consists mostly of ethnic Thais and at present is reported to be directing its activities mainly at the sixteen provinces of northeast Thailand (ibid., 21 September). Evidence of a further schism within the CPT seemed forthcoming when the VOPT announced on 11 July that it was temporarily suspending operations as of that date, thus ending sixteen years of broadcasts. It had not resumed broadcasting by December. Some observers believe that China silenced the broadcasts as a gesture of goodwill toward Thailand (*WP*, 20 July). However, most observers concluded that the closure was due to opposition by middle- and lower-level cadres to the increasingly anti-Vietnamese content of VOPT editorials (*FEER*, 27 July).

Organization and Strategy. The top leaders of the CPT, consisting of Politburo and Central Committee members, are mostly Sino-Thai; i.e., they are entirely or partly of Chinese ancestry. They were responsible for moving the party into an anti-Vietnamese stance. In particular Chang Yuan, alias Virat Angkathavorn, whom some identify as the real power in the CPT (rather than Mitr Samanant, alias Charoon Wanngarm, the secretary general of the CPT), is thought likely to have played a prominent role in this decision. He reportedly has exercised tight control over the VOPT (*Voice of the Nation*, 18 July). There was no sign of a rift among these top leaders over the anti-Vietnamese posture taken by the party. Nor was there any evidence that these leaders have shifted away from their reliance on the basic Maoist line. However, they were forced to take account of unrest among middle-level cadres and jungle soldiers of the CPT.

This unrest stems from several factors. First, the loss of crucial training and logistic facilities in Laos and Kampuchea as a result of the party's pro-Beijing stand severely handicapped CPT insurgents in Thailand. Supplies were much harder to obtain, especially in northeast Thailand. And no longer were there sanctuaries to which insurgents operating near the borders in northeast Thailand could retreat when pressed by the Thai military. Second, the insurgents had failed to establish a "liberated area" anywhere in Thailand after fourteen years of armed struggle (*Asiaweek*, 28 September). Third, there was a marked increase during the year in the number of insurgents who surrendered to Thai authorities. Fourth, the breakaway of a faction meant the establishment of a competing communist movement in Thailand, contributing to the near disintegration of the CCPDF. The break also resulted from the difference in overall viewpoints between the CPT hierarchy and many of the former students, labor activists, and intellectuals who constitute this front organization (*FEER*, 10 August). In part the difference lies in the unwillingness of these urbanized and educated types to accept blindly the use of Chinese dogma in a Thai context. Moreover, these relatively new converts to communism have not been fully integrated into the party hierarchy. And they, as well as some other party cadres, have resented their inability to influence party decisions.

Party leaders, sensitive to the dissatisfaction at lower levels, scheduled the Fourth Party Congress for October. Originally it was to be held in northern Thailand in Nan province, but lack of security reportedly forced a change in location to South China. In acknowledgment of its awareness that in the past party leaders had not had sufficient contact with the general membership, the Politburo called on the regional committees to launch extensive discussions on possible policy changes and to incorporate these into reports to be reviewed by the central committees before or during the Fourth Congress (ibid.). This apparently was done, although the results of this process and of the congress had not been revealed as of December.

Some Thai government officials were worried that one result might be a shift in policy to permit a CPT campaign of urban terrorism. They recognized that such a campaign would run counter to the rural-oriented nature of a Maoist-inspired revolutionary movement such as the CPT insurgency. Also, they admitted that at this stage the insurgents required the urban population to remain neutral, and therefore they were not likely to risk alienating the population through terrorist acts. But these officials contended that the failure of the CPT to establish a "liberated area," the serious logistic problem now facing the insurgents, and the urban background of many of the new CPT recruits had led to a deepening sense of frustration among many insurgents and a corresponding wish to carry the war to the cities. The officials pointed to South America where frustrated rural guerrillas had turned to urban terrorism. Moreover, the officials suspected that if the CPT leaders refused to allow urban terrorism, a splinter group intent on taking the insurgency to the towns might emerge. (Ibid.). This possible new strategy has been referred to as "linking the jungle with the cities" (*FBIS*, 6 August).

The Anticommunist Law. In February the National Assembly passed an amendment to the anticommunist law, making it tougher. Under the new version, a communist suspect can be detained for up to sixteen months for interrogation. Directors for communist suppression, commissioned military and police officers, and grade-three local administration officials are empowered to arrest any person suspected of communist activities or conduct a search without a warrant for communist-related materials. Provincial directors for communist suppression are given the power to ban public gatherings, advertisements, or movies suspected of instigating the public to offend the anticommunist law; to order gun owners to surrender their arms temporarily to the authorities; to impose a curfew; and to summon any person for questioning or for undergoing a fifteen-day orientation course. Greater powers are assigned to the regional directors. They are allowed to censor letters, telegrams, documents, news, parcels, or any materials believed to be used for contact among communist suspects. They also can censor newspapers, advertisements, and novels and ban the publication of such printed material (*Bangkok Post* [*BP*], 2 February; *FBIS*, 2 February).

The New Constitution and the Elections. A new Thai constitution was approved in December 1978. It provides for a parliament consisting of a Senate with 225 appointed members and a House of Representatives with 301 members elected by universal suffrage. The two houses are to meet in joint session to appoint the prime minister, act on motions of confidence, and adopt the budget. The prime minister and the ministers do not need to be members of the House of Representatives or of any political party.

The first elections under the new constitution were held on 2 April. Politically conservative parties dominated the elections, and parliament appointed Gen. Kriangsak Chamanan as prime minister. The VOPT strongly criticized the new constitution because the members of the Senate, most of whom were military and police officers, were appointed and because the prime minister is selected by both houses acting in a joint session. It was argued that since General Kriangsak had appointed the members of the Senate, he was assured of their support. The VOPT also condemned the election results, noting that only 25 percent of eligible voters participated. The VOPT claimed that the electorate boycotted the elections since they were considered meaningless, given the foregone conclusion that General Kriangsak would be selected prime minister. (VOPT, 27 April; *FBIS*, 8 May.)

Insurgency. Armed, full-time guerrillas of the CPT, who are called the Thai People's Liberation Armed Forces, were estimated at the beginning of the year to number between 10,000 and 12,000. They were supported by an estimated 10,000 to 15,000 militia, whose main role is to protect villages where the communists have gained some degree of influence. Another estimated 60,000 to 70,000 persons were considered CPT sympathizers (*WP*, 20 January). The insurgent growth rate has been estimated at 6 to 10 percent per year (*NYT*, 23 January). It was considered doubtful, however, whether growth was comparable during 1979, given the developments in Laos and Kampuchea and the resultant difficulties encountered by the CPT in supplying the guerrillas. The reduction in supplies, plus other factors, led to an increase in defections from the insurgents—approximately 600 during the first six months of the year, double the number of defectors for the whole of 1978 (*FBIS*, 12 September). A large number reportedly surrendered between May and July in the two provinces of Ubon and Sri Saket along the Kampuchean border (*Keesing's Contemporary Archives*, 7 September).

Guerrilla warfare, employing Maoist tactics, continued in rural border areas in the north and northeast, although the number of incidents declined markedly in areas near the Kampuchean border. The insurgency continued in parts of the south but did not extend to the Central Plains region, in large measure because of unsuitable terrain. Communist guerrillas operated in 46 of the 72 provinces during 1979.

The Northeast. Communist guerrilla activity fell off sharply in the part of Thailand adjacent to the Kampuchean border. For example, the insurgents carried out four operations in March in contrast to nineteen in December 1978 (*FBIS*, 12 April). The significance of this decrease in activity is even more apparent when it is realized that from November 1977 through December 1978 fighting between the insurgents and the Thai military accounted for 25 to 30 percent of the Thai army casualties. The decline was due primarily to the ouster of CPT insurgents from their Kampuchean bases, which, combined with the fighting between the Vietnamese and Pol Pot forces, greatly reduced the flow of supplies from Kampuchea to CPT guerrillas in neighboring Thai provinces. Another factor was the presence of sizable Thai security forces near the Kampuchean border, stationed there to handle the massive influx of refugees and to prevent the fighting in that country from spreading across the border. It became increasingly difficult for CPT insurgents to operate under such conditions.

When the CPT insurgents based in Kampuchea were ordered to leave or when their bases were overrun during the fighting, most of them—about 1,200—tried to return to Thailand (ibid., 12 February). A few of them failed, but the majority did cross safely into Thailand. Some surrendered to Thai authorities on or shortly after their arrival. Others have either moved into existing CPT guerrilla bases or have established new bases, mainly in the mountains along the Prachin–Buriram provincial border or in neighboring Surin province (*FEER*, 8 June).

In other parts of the northeast, the supply situation for the CPT guerrillas worsened when Laos ordered CPT insurgents based in Laos to leave and when it ceased supporting the CPT. Some of the guerrillas who had been based in Laos fled to adjoining provinces in northeast Thailand, particularly Nakhon Phanom and Loei (*BP*, 4 September; *FBIS*, 6 September). The severity of some of the communist attacks in this region increased. For instance, in late May a large band of heavily armed CPT guerrillas ambushed a Thai army patrol unit in Udon Thani province, killing 25 soldiers and seriously wounding several others (*BP*, 2 June; *FBIS*, 6 June). This was the heaviest loss ever suffered by government forces in a single action against CPT insurgents in Thailand (*Bangkok World* [*BW*], 31 May; *FBIS*, 31 May). However, the number of incidents did not increase appreciably, while the number of defections did.

The North. Many of the CPT insurgents who fled Laos moved to Chiang Rai and Nan provinces (*BP*, 4 September; *FBIS*, 6 September). Although they initially suffered from a lack of food and other supplies, new supply lines passing through the remote northwestern part of Laos (where Laotian authorities do not exercise effective control) and through northeastern Burma (where Burmese officials similarly exercise little or no control) were opened up from China. These lines, along with others already in existence, attempt to supply both the newly armed guerrillas and those already in north Thailand. It was estimated that there were about 2,000 armed communist insurgents, including some from the hill tribes, operating in several northern provinces during the year (*BW*, 21 April; *FBIS*, 26 April).

Although the insurgents attacked several isolated police and military outposts, the main thrust of their activities was obstructing road construction in remote areas of such provinces as Nan, Chiang Rai, Phayao, and Tak (*FBIS*, 28 February). For example, a series of attacks were made in Chiang Rai along a 103-kilometer stretch of road linking the Terng district with the Chiang Khong district on the Laotian border. In March more than one hundred insurgents armed with automatic rifles and rocket-propelled grenades assaulted a construction camp; three persons in the camp were killed, and U.S. $100,000 worth of equipment was destroyed. A similar incident took place in mid-July, involving a 30-minute attack on a construction site; six guards were killed. Two weeks later, another attack left nineteen guards dead and 41 wounded. Periodically, construction workers and guards were killed or injured by mine explosions along portions of the road. Another example is the Mae Sot–Umphang highway in Tak, where more than one hundred guards were killed and 1,150 wounded in attacks by communist insurgents between September 1978 and July 1979 (*Asiaweek*, 4 September). The CPT justified these efforts on the grounds that these roads are to be used to facilitate the transport of troops and police to suppress the rural people (VOPT, 19 May; *FBIS*, 22 May). However, other observers pointed out that strategic roads in remote areas permit security forces to react more quickly, to take the offensive, and to wrest control over the local population out of insurgent hands (*Asiaweek*, 21 September).

Thai authorities feared that CPT insurgents in the north would become even more active during the next year or so. Because the major supply lines for external aid have been relocated from the northeast to the north, they believed that most of the CPT insurgents in the northeast would eventually be forced to shift to the northern provinces. In order to prevent the development of guerrilla base areas, government forces undertook several fairly large offensive actions against strategic heights where the potential for base areas existed. Their greatest success came in Chiang Rai when one such location fell to government forces on 25 July after a series of assaults over a three-week period. Over a thousand ground troops, supported by artillery and aircraft, were involved. Government casualties numbered 20 dead and 103 wounded, while those of the insurgents were reported as 90 dead and about 100 wounded (*BP*, 4 August).

The South. Communist insurgents carried out several attacks in the southern provinces of Thailand during the year. Some incidents involved ambushes of government officials and military, while others took the form of attacks on village defense units and rural police stations (VOPT, 31 March; *FBIS*, 4 April). The most spectacular incident occurred on 26 December 1978 when about one hundred insurgents attacked a train carrying an entire provincial payroll, getting away with $60,000 according to the official version and $300,000 according to the unofficial version (*Los Angeles Times*, 9 April). Encouraged by their earlier success, the insurgents attacked another payroll train in July. This time they were beaten off by police and military forces, although there were several casualties among the police (*BP*, 11 July).

Despite these activities, CPT insurgents in the south appeared to be in a state of partial disarray. Defections were at an all-time high. For instance, Chit Chongchit, the leader of CPT insurgents in Nakorn Si Thammarat province, surrendered to authorities in March (*FBIS*, 12 April). Another insurgent leader, identified only as Sombun, also gave himself up. He was said to have controlled all CPT insurgents in Trang, Patthalung, and Satun provinces (*BW*, 7 April; *FBIS*, 11 April). At about the same time, eighteen insurgents in Nakorn Si Thammarat, all of them former students, were executed by other insurgents when they tried to defect (*BW*, 28 March; *FBIS*, 30 March). And a total of 46 insurgents in the southern region surrendered to government authorities (*FBIS*, 9 August).

Insurgents belonging to the Communist Party of Malaya and its offshoots continued to operate on both sides of the Thai-Malaysian border, although most of them were based in Songkhla, Yala, Pattani and Narathiwat provinces of Thailand. Most of their activities were directed against targets in Malaysia. However, they did try to obstruct road construction in the remote areas of southern Thailand where their bases are located. In February, Malaysian and Thai security forces began joint operations on the Thai side of the border against these insurgents. These operations, known as Operation 792 Alpha and Operation 792 Beta, continued into June. Several insurgent camps were captured and supplies confiscated. However, all but a handful of the insurgents escaped unharmed.

Northern Illinois University   M. Ladd Thomas

Vietnam

For a brief history of the Vietnam Communist Party (VCP) and the communist movement in Vietnam under its various names in the 1930–1975 period, see earlier editions of *YICA*, especially 1976 and 1977.

For the Socialist Republic of Vietnam (SRV) and the ruling VCP, the year 1979 was one of extraordinary difficulty, bordering at times on the catastrophic. Major events of the year included a seventeen-day border war with China (which meant that for a period Vietnam was fighting a two-front war) that left in its wake a continuing all-out cold war struggle between these two one-time allies; a bogged-down campaign to pacify Kampuchea (Cambodia), where war combined with anarchy and widespread famine turned the countryside into a holocaust; a massive exodus of Vietnam's citizens, both as boat people and as expelled Chinese; further isolation of Vietnam on the world scene, marked by loss of status and influence, alienation from its Association of Southeast Asian Nations (ASEAN) neighbors, with no friends in the region and few elsewhere; destruction of most of the genuine goodwill for Vietnam left in the world, manifested by loss of almost all economic aid from noncommunist countries; signs of strain in Soviet-Vietnamese relations, as the price Moscow paid for supporting Vietnamese enterprises steadily increased, although officially the two remained close; ever worsening hardships for the Vietnamese people, with a precipitous economic decline marked by fiscal chaos, spreading poverty, and food shortages so serious as to begin to affect the nation's health; and leadership disarray, characterized by the first Politburo-level defection in party history, as Hoang Van Hoan fled to China.

Party Leadership and Organization. For Vietnam's rulers—the seventeen men of the Politburo who run the country—it was a year of ruined expectations. They had expected quick military success in Kampuchea without Chinese retaliation. They had expected a bountiful harvest from the communes and at least moderate advances in other economic sectors. They had expected economic aid from outside sources to continue to increase and relations with Southeast Asia and the United States to improve. Each of these expectations was unfulfilled at year's end.

Yet the Politburo maintained control and its members remained united. They aged a year, of course, to an average of 71 (that of the Central Committee is about 69). They became a bit more calcified in their world view, and even more rigid in implementing their various internal programs and external strategies. Vietnam's gerontocracy was characterized by implacability, absence of creative problem-solving abilities, and an inability to acknowledge the cause, extent, or often even the existence of its many problems. It continued to single out a scapegoat, that one evil villain responsible for all of Vietnam's ills. Currently, this is China, which Politburo members charge is, and always has been, Vietnam's chief enemy.

Some personnel changes were reported at the sub-Politburo level. Death claimed Vice-President Nguyen Luong Bang, 75, on 20 July, a party member since the 1920s, longtime Central Committee member, and first ambassador to the USSR. An early associate of Ho Chi Minh, Bang used "Red Star" as his revolutionary name and was closely identified with the USSR.

The most dramatic, although probably not the most significant, party leadership event during the year was the defection to China of party veteran and ex–Politburo member, Hoang Van Hoan, 74. While at the Karachi airport en route to Berlin for medical treatment 3 July, Hoan feigned illness, deplaned, and the following day boarded a plane for Beijing. A week later he appeared, wearing a Mao cap, at a press conference where he called on the Vietnamese to overthrow the "Le Duan clique because it has turned Vietnam into a Soviet satellite and conducted a pogrom against ethnic Chinese by dumping them into the sea." Hanoi stripped Hoan of his various posts and honors and announced he would be tried for treason in absentia. A polemic against him concentrated on his Chinese connections—the years he spent in China in the 1930s, and his position as ambassador to Beijing (1950–1957). His defection was more embarrassing than significant to the Hanoi government. Hoan had been purged in 1976 during the general weeding out of party officials deemed "pro-Chinese" and had been under virtual house arrest since 1977. The Hanoi media focus on his pro-Chinese proclivities was simply part of a more general propaganda campaign. Actually Hoang Van Hoan's behavior over the years was no more pro-Chinese than was Ho Chi Minh's. His defection did trigger a new crackdown on those considered sympathetic to China. Press reports told of the detention or house arrest of four upper-level officials, all believed to be at least part Chinese: Ly Ban, former vice-minister of foreign trade and economic aid negotiator with China for many years; Tran Dinh Tri, a Hoan protégé and National Assembly Standing Committee member who worked in various ethnic Chinese programs; Gen. Chu Van Tan, a Nung (an ethnic minority also found in China) and one of the founders of the People's Army of Vietnam (PAVN); and Gen. Le Quang Ba (part Nung), former chairman of the State Nationalities Commission, which handles Chinese ethnic minority affairs.

Before the invasion of Kampuchea (December 1978), reliable reports from Hanoi told of a doctrinal dispute at the Politburo level over the question of how best to handle the Pol Pot challenge. It was part of a broader question involving the idea of a federation of Indochina. Essentially the dispute was technical, not over the objective of federation itself but over the best methods and pace to achieve it and, within this, the best means of dealing with the Kampuchean problem. By the time the invasion was launched, however, SRV leaders reportedly agreed that lesser means had been tried and failed and that the only remaining alternative was a full-scale military attack followed by an all-out pacification effort.

Out of these reports, however, came persistent rumors that a major power struggle was under way between those labeled pro-Soviet hard-liners and the more moderate and pragmatic centrists. Predictions were made that moderate Premier Pham Van Dong was about to lose power and be promoted to the largely ceremonial post of president, with a hard-liner, Defense Minister Vo Nguyen Giap, replacing him as premier, and another hard-liner, Gen. Van Tien Dung, replacing Giap as defense minister. Presiding over and approving this shuffle was the supposedly new hard-liner, VCP Secretary General Le Duan. None of these changes had taken place by 1 December, and by all appearance the balance of power in the Politburo was the same as it had been for the past decade. If anything was clear about a decline in political power in Vietnam during the year, it was the final eclipse of the so-called southern faction of Nguyen Huu Tho, Huynh Tan Phat, and Mme. Nguyen Thi Binh, all of whom have been relegated to obscurity or to the task of "barbarian manager," i.e., a guide for credulous, sympathetic foreign visitors to Vietnam.

It appears that leadership in the VCP and the SRV is increasingly dominated by the more proletarian-minded (less educated, working-class background) Marxists, rather than by the more elitist gentry Marxists that ruled in the Ho Chi Minh era. Some have attributed this to Soviet influence, while others see it as an inevitable generational change.

Much attention was paid during the year to military figures—Generals Giap, Dung, and Chu Huy Man, as well as to the more praetorian civilian Politburo figures such as Tran Quoc Hoan—but this may simply have been due to the recurrence of war. Assuming a somewhat increased prominence during the year were the economic czars, Do Muoi and Le Thanh Nghi, as well as such party faithfuls as Le Van Luong and Vo Van Kiet. Also, at a lower level, Mai Chi Tho appears to have become the party's virtual dictator of Ho Chi Minh City affairs.

During the year there were the usual diplomatic cocktail party stories about individual leaders: that Pham Van Dong had developed throat cancer (and that he had had a pacemaker installed in Moscow); that Nguyen Duy Trinh had become senile; that Gen. Tran Van Tra had been fired for bungling the Kampuchean campaign; that Le Duan had had a stroke (he was absent without explanation for all of May and June); and that several high-ranking generals had been killed in Kampuchea.

Nguyen Co Thach's star rose during the year while that of his superior, Foreign Minister Nguyen Duy Trinh, declined. The post of foreign minister was in effect vacant, and Thach, acting under the title secretary of state (a new term apparently for chef de cabinet) became de facto foreign minister. Thach, a Pham Van Dong protégé, long had been regarded as the number-two man in the Foreign Ministry.

The size of the VCP officially remained at 1.5 million (6 percent of the adult population), although this figure may be out-of-date. Party officials recently told visitors that in the past two years some 160,000 members had been removed from party rolls in "moral purification drives." Although recruiting is actively pursued, it is doubtful that 160,000 new members have been added.

This reduction in party membership is not a purge in the usual Soviet sense, but rather a perennial effort to weed out the incompetent, the unreliable, and the corrupt, as well as (said the party journal) "the halfhearted, the old, and the tired." In the past five years, however, this has amounted to an annual quasi-purge. In 1975 it was directed against "party uneducated," apparently meaning illiterates who had found their way into the party and in some instances into positions of responsibility. In 1978 the campaign singled out "superstitious party members," i.e., those southerners sympathetic to religion (Buddhism). In 1977 most ethnic Chinese were expelled, as were those ethnic Vietnamese married to Chinese or with other close Chinese ties. The 1978 campaign was part of a broader state drive against corruption and malfeasance in office. Within the party it was launched under a Politburo resolution entitled "Revolutionary Standards," dealing with "the curbing of negative manifestations," and directed against those who "misuse their office or regard office as a reward." It was alleged that many party officials (or their wives used as fronts) misappropriated state property, fenced stolen goods, and ran black markets in everything from razor blades to electricity.

Thus, in one form or another the party has been purging its membership continually since 1974. The annual purge appears to have lost much of its original meaning and purpose and largely become a ritual conducted with standardized rhetoric of castigation. The party cadre, overworked and under-appreciated, and generally the person to be credited with such successes and accomplishments as the regime has achieved over the past generation is made responsible for party ills, society's shortcomings, and the leadership's mistakes. Rather than improving the quality of the party, these annual purges merely offer up a scapegoat. Party members realize that each year in order to mollify Politburo ire and dampen public complaints, some party members and cadres are thrown to the wolves.

A new party recruiting drive was ordered in 1979 with instructions to concentrate on the young. The average age of VCP members at the time was 40, compared with 25 some twenty years ago. Instructions were to reduce the average age to 30 through recruiting.

Late in the year party members were ordered to begin preparations for a lavish observance of the party's 50th anniversary on 3 February 1980.

Domestic Attitudes and Activities. A grim, no-nonsense mood dominated day-to-day life for the average Vietnamese during the year. Daily, the corps of agitprop cadres drummed home the single message—Vietnam was beset by problems, surrounded by enemies, facing a battle for survival. Once again the golden word *dau tranh* ("struggle") permeated official rhetoric.

Typical of this martial appeal was a *Quan Doi Nhan Dan* editorial on 3 February dealing with the Kampuchean invasion, which declared that all party members, military and civilian alike, "must struggle to become a powerful force of skilled fighters, always combat-ready and always struggling to fulfill the tasks of the party."

Visitors to Vietnam who know the country from the past were struck by the deterioration in material life. Poverty in the north seemed worse than during the war years. There was enormous economic chaos, marked by severe shortages of all items, particularly food. The average middle-aged Hanoi resident got less food in 1979 than at any time in his memory. A visiting Dutch doctor said in November that Vietnam was on the borderline of famine, with signs of malnutrition visible everywhere. Travelers also reported widespread grumbling and discontent.

Vietnam's economic sector—as described by foreign visitors, including international funding agency officials—was a chaotic mix of interrelated problems, in which one sector's difficulties fed on all others. Generally this was the scene:

—Economic development, that is nation building, slowed or virtually halted. Vietnam was first drained of its resources by the Kampuchean war and then badly dislocated by the Chinese attack. Also, there was a marked failure to capitalize on existing economic potential.

—Economic planning and problem solving were neglected. This, combined with lowered industrial production and exacerbated by maldistribution of such goods as were produced, resulted in wide-spread economic suffering, particularly in rural areas.

—Technical and managerial levels were gutted by the demands of war, resulting in diminished administrative capacity, lack of qualified personnel, bureaucratic ineptitude, a sharp increase in incompetency, and manifestations of such negative national traits as chauvinism and obstinacy in leadership.

—Economic corruption rose, which further debilitated the economic sector and engendered passive resistance to various state economic programs.

—Economic discontent led to muted but steady pressure, not a revolution of rising expectations exactly, but a universal desire for an end to economic woe and a desire for a more prosperous life. In the face of the regime's failure to provide these postwar benefits, there was growing cynicism and a generally depleted spirit.

—Isolated from the world's economic system (marked by loss of some U.S. $300 million in non-communist foreign economic aid during the year), Vietnam became more dependent on the socialist world, particularly the USSR, and was subsidized at the rate of more than $2 million a day.

One of the few redeeming facts Hanoi could salvage from this bleak condition was that somehow these economic ills failed to affect foreign affairs, such as the war in Kampuchea.

Food, getting it and paying for it, was probably the average Vietnamese's chief concern during the year. Supposedly the fourteen necessary staple items were available through rationing, but the shelves of state stores were often bare. The rice (or grain) ration was cut 20 percent in January "to support the freedom fighters in Kampuchea," and indeed much of the food shortage was due to diversion of stocks there. The ration was cut again in May, "on a voluntary basis," following the Chinese incursion. At year's end, the official monthly rice/grain ration was about 13 kilograms per individual in Hanoi and 9 in Ho Chi Minh City. Within this, rations vary according to work performed. But no one received a full ration of rice. Generally the allotment was about 10 percent rice and 90 percent other grains, chiefly wheat or pasta made from wheat flour. Other rationed goods, such as meat, fish, sugar, and cooking oil, were either in short supply or unavailable.

Once found, the problem of paying for the food remained. Since the state market was often bare, Vietnamese were forced into the "free" (uncontrolled) or the black market, where food prices averaged ten times those of the official market. This was due both to shortages and to galloping inflation. Prices have increased by 600 percent in Hanoi in the last three years and about 400 percent in the south. In 1979 the average Vietnamese spent about 85 percent of his salary on food. With a salary range of VN $50–100 (average VN $60), an urban Vietnamese found that with his monthly salary he could buy only two kilos of pork, five kilos of fish, two kilos of sugar, seven tins of sweetened condensed milk (used as baby food), or one liter of gasoline. Prices in the rural areas averaged about 25 percent lower. In Ho Chi Minh City they were kept artificially high as a means of driving urban residents out to the New Economic Zones. Many Vietnamese augmented their income by moonlighting, selling furniture and other possessions, or with help from abroad—an estimated one out of five families in Vietnam receive regular remittances from relatives and friends in the United States and elsewhere.

Without enough food money, a Vietnamese family was reduced to eating a cheap but unappetizing mixture of sorghum and cassava (roughly molasses and tapioca), which is universally known in Vietnam by an unprintable name meaning excrement. In the midst of this, Hanoi Agricultural Ministry official Mai Luong told a *Japan Times* reporter (27 August) that the Vietnamese eat too much rice anyway.

There was a sharp drop in protein consumption during the year. A Hanoi resident in 1979 ate one-third less meat than at any time during the war. The official explanation for this was the devastation caused by the invading Chinese, who allegedly destroyed or stole 157,000 cattle and 244,000 swine (*Japan Times*, 27 August). More serious perhaps was the drop in availability of fish, normally Vietnam's chief source of protein. The official reason for this was that 5,000 fishing boats—half the nation's total fleet—had been stolen by departing refugees. Late in the year U.N. health officials estimated that Vietnam needed a 30 percent increase in protein to meet minimal nutritional needs. Foreign advisers reported that many workers, deprived of adequate protein, were able to work only about five hours a day, further reducing productivity.

The 1979 farm harvest probably will prove better than average, certainly better than the 1978 crop, which was 15 percent lower than 1977. In 1978, officials reported, some 3.4 million hectares of rice were planted; a third of these were damaged by flooding and insect infestation, leaving a grain shortfall of about 4 million metric tons (MT). Not only bad weather but also poor central planning and serious transportation and farm supply shortage problems reduced the size of the yield.

In 1979 an additional 100,000 hectares were planted. Production for the year had not been determined as of this writing (1 December) but was estimated abroad at 11.5 million MT, which, after adjusting for population growth, left a 3.7 million MT shortfall over the minimum daily nutritional standard of 1,500 calories per person (or, as calculated by Hanoi officials, a shortfall of about 2.5 million MT). This meant Vietnam had to obtain the needed grain abroad at a cost (to the SRV, or the USSR) of about $175 million for each million tons required.

The first of the year's two rice crops—the fifth-month harvest—was exceptionally high (2 percent over target), leading officials to hope that the entire year would break production records. However, transplanting was behind schedule for the tenth-month crop, and other difficulties arose, which reduced the year's harvest to the estimated 11.5 million MT figure.

Added to Vietnam's food shortfall was the famine in Kampuchea, and although there was no indication Hanoi sent food to civilians there, it did feed the 175,000 PAVN troops in their war against Pol Pot and his government of Democratic Kampuchea.

In any event, for another year Vietnam could not feed itself and had to depend on aid from abroad, chiefly from the USSR. By July Moscow had already sent over a million tons of wheat through the port at Haiphong.

Elsewhere in the economic sector, these conditions prevailed during the year:

—Planning. The SRV Five-Year Plan (1976–1980) was for all practical purposes scrapped (if, in fact, it ever had been implemented) as the basis for administering the economy. The heart of the plan had been quick industrial development, a goal now questioned because of the vulnerability of Vietnam's factories located near the Chinese border. Also, the plan was based on the assumptions of much noncommunist foreign assistance, of a slow pace for collectivization in the south, and of the intensive use of military manpower in economic development (as well as reduced military spending). None of these conditions obtained. There is a need, Vietnamese officials indicated, to overhaul the plan or produce a new one to take into consideration these changed conditions. Thus, during 1979 the planners' objective was simply to devise ways to meet minimal subsistence needs for the next several years.

—Economic Growth. There has been none in Vietnam during the last five years of peace. The slight growth in GNP has more than been wiped out by population increases. Per capita income in Vietnam is estimated by Hong Kong bankers at $150, but most Hanoi watchers think this is unrealistic since it is based on averaging the prewar per capita incomes of the two parts of Vietnam ($90 in the north and $220 in the south) and clearly economic conditions in the north remain worse than in the south. Even if the $150 figure is accepted, it is the lowest in the region.

—Industry. This sector generally was stagnant, with manufacturing reduced because of lack of raw materials, spare parts, and labor. Petroleum products were particularly short. Previously Vietnam's yearly need of 1.5 million tons of petroleum came from China; now its chief source is the USSR, with small amounts coming from Iran, Iraq, and Libya.

—Money Availability. Vietnam suffered a lack of financial reserves and a shortage of hard currency, which affected its credit rating among Japanese bankers and others. Its chronic trade deficit continued to run at about $700 million per year and was expected to reach $1 billion by the early 1980s. Exports during the year totaled about $50 million, half of them to the socialist world, which also furnishes about 70 percent of imports.

—Economic Aid. This assistance continued to keep Vietnam afloat economically during the war. It totaled well over $1 billion, with almost all coming from socialist nations. It is estimated that 70 percent of the SRV national budget is supplied by its communist allies, the administration of which has been supervised since 1970 by Soviet and East German fiscal advisers. Vietnam still reeled from China's mid-1978 cancellation of 80 aid projects valued at more than $0.5 billion and also from the $300 million loss during the year from noncommunist countries, who canceled aid programs to protest the Kampuchean invasion or as pressure to end the refugee flow. Hanoi's hope that the World Bank and other international lending agencies would take up this economic slack proved unrealistic. Still, bloc aid continued. The East Germans began construction of a food market in Hanoi and several 50-unit apartment buildings; the Poles began work on a 500-bed hospital; the Cubans a factory and a hotel.

—Construction Work. Building lagged, chiefly because of the lack of skilled workers and building materials. Vietnam continues to suffer from a serious housing shortage. Even planned construction is hardly adequate; new housing is calculated on the basis of 75 square feet per person, the same criterion used in the construction of U.S. federal prisons.

—Labor. The labor shortage was particularly crucial during the year. The lack of skilled workers was due in part to the demands of the armed forces and in part to the loss of ethnic Chinese as a labor source. Vietnam's industrial labor force apparently has diminished over the past several years. Figures released this year offered this breakdown: agricultural labor 82 percent, industry 7 percent, and services 11 percent. (During the war, the respective percentages for the north were 80, 10, and 10. The difference cannot be explained simply by calculating in the southern labor force.) More labor went into the armed forces during the year; the PAVN had at least 500,000 persons under arms, with nearly an equal number involved in economically unproductive quasi-military or military support work. This was a serious drain on the labor pool, estimated at about 11 million males and 11.5 million females. A forced labor directive—Politburo Directive 97/CT.UB—was implemented during the year. It established a form of conscripted, or corvée, labor for "areas far from the city" (the highlands) and for "front-line areas" (the provinces adjacent to Kampuchea). The directive established a category of persons subject to forced labor: "persons whose antisocial behavior is not so bad as to warrant re-education or legal prosecution." A person was "sentenced" to this forced labor for periods of 6 to 24 months, with a "parole board" reviewing his sentence every 6 months. (*Tin Sang*, 4 July.) Labor trouble was reported during the year. The Bach Dang shipyard in Haiphong was the scene of a summer-long labor dispute witnessed by foreign seamen, and there were several wildcat strikes at the Mai Lam Steel Plant in Hanoi.

—Transportation. Public transportation was virtually nonexistent for a period since all rolling stock was being used in the two-front war. Nor was the situation helped by an order banning all motorcycles and motor scooters from urban areas, an order that was apparently largely ignored.

—Private Investment. Foreign business interest in Vietnam was limited because of the war and the new opportunities opening in China. As far as could be determined, only one foreign company, a French pharmaceutical firm, has taken advantage of the 1977 SRV Investment Code and established a joint-stock company (with a Vietnamese governmental corporation holding 51 percent of the stock).

—New Economic Zones (NEZs). Apparently the steam went out of the drive to create the NEZs. No longer were there mass movements into the rural areas as in 1977 and 1978. Increasingly the NEZ has become a form of rural house arrest rather than an experimental economic institution. The program seriously affected southern agriculture, drawing as many as one-third of the residents from some farming villages and some 2 million from the cities.

—Agricultural Collectivization. Officially an all-out collectivization drive, scheduled to be completed by the end of 1980, was launched during the year for southern agriculture. Since collectivization involves three levels or stages (production brigade, low-level commune, and high-level commune/state farm), apparently the order meant that all southern agriculture had to be in at least the first stage by the end of 1980. There has been much passive resistance to this collectivization effort, resulting in a reduced production rate in the south. Much of the trouble in 1979, Le Duan said in a 12 July speech, resulted because the cadres implementing the program "failed to consider the spirit and mentality of the peasant." A Hanoi report (Vietnam News Agency, 7 April) said that 17 percent of the farmland in the twelve provinces of southern Vietnam had been collectivized into 210 low-level communes. Refugees say most of these were formed from land confiscated from those who fled or from nationalized foreign holdings. The remaining 83 percent of the land, said the Hanoi report, was in the initial collectivization stage.

Northern Vietnam has some 12,000 communes (about a third less than a decade ago when a consolidation program was ordered and the 18,000 communes then existing were reduced to the present figure) and some 250 state farms.

Outside of the economic sector, life was equally grim during the year for the average Vietnamese, particularly in the south where the "purification campaign" continued unabated.

The society was put back into wartime harness by the 3 March general mobilization order. This was not, as was widely reported, a response to the Chinese invasion. Rather it was the culmination of a social mobilization campaign launched six months earlier. Actually the order was promulgated after the Chinese had announced withdrawal of their military forces.

The general mobilization order set "three great tasks" for the society: build national defense, increase production, and develop the socialist managerial system. The emphasis was on the youth of the nation, for whom there were five separate great tasks: "annihilate the enemy, develop the paramilitary system, do productive labor, ensure internal security, and perform necessary ideological tasks." The order required all ablebodied persons to work ten hours a day, eight in productive labor and two in military training. It required universal participation in civil defense exercises and unleashed a massive emulation and motivation campaign employing the most purple language—for example, the Hanoi poster said of the Chinese: "The horrible animal ferocity of these feudal pillagers and invaders, driven by lust and barbaric ambition . . ."

The main theme in implementing this general mobilization order was the "doctrine of collective self-mastery," which deals with the use and control of power. The dominant ideological concept during the year, it was portrayed as a development or an adaptation of standard Marxist dogma. The doctrine is thought of as a process and implemented with a combination of social reorganization efforts and emulation and motivation campaigns. It is anti-individualistic and makes individualism and spontaneity the two major social sins. Collective self-mastery advocates and justifies total concentration of power at the center. At the same time it authorizes allocation (or "dispersion") of power down the chain of command in order to fix responsibility.

The general mobilization order apparently had other secondary purposes or results. It was used to justify the further transfer of resources from civilian to defense uses. It was cited as reason for greater tightening of the bonds with Laos and for the Kampuchean adventure. It was the rationale for making new demands for support on Moscow and the Council for Mutual Economic Assistance. Apparently it had strong anti-Chinese overtones since the great exodus of Chinese from the north began then and not earlier when China attacked.

Refugees continued to flow out of Vietnam during the year, an estimated 300,000 total. This meant that since the end of the Vietnam war over 1.8 million persons have fled Indochina, by land into Thailand and China and by boat to the entire Pacific region from Japan to Australia, although chiefly to Thailand, Malaysia, Indonesia, and the Philippines. At least 60 percent of these came from Vietnam.

The exodus increased sharply in late 1978 and the first six months of 1979, then dropped off after the Geneva meeting. The rough totals of known arrivals abroad for the year are December 1978

(11,000), January (18,000), February (12,000), March (23,000), April (31,000, May (64,000), June (60,000), July (34,000), August (12,000), September (14,000), and an actual or estimated 9,000 or fewer per month for the rest of the year.

About two-thirds of these, or 200,000, traveled by boat. If the U.N. estimate is correct—that half of all departing boat people die at sea—then an additional 200,000 persons were lost at sea. Some of the departing Vietnamese left with governmental assistance, i.e., in government-supplied vessels with passage paid in gold. Many, perhaps more than half, were ethnic Chinese who had been expelled.

The expulsion of ethnic Chinese was launched in 1977, with a census of all *hoa* (Chinese) in Vietnam. The census listed names, occupations, and property held and asked a series of questions about the interviewee's desire to leave Vietnam. On the basis of this, all Chinese were put into one of three categories: the first generation, or "pure" Chinese; potential "regroupees," i.e., those who indicated they wanted to leave; and others, chiefly part Chinese. Only the third group received citizenship cards; the first two were considered transients. For all Chinese, there was constant pressure during 1977 and 1978 to leave the country. After the Chinese border war in February, the pressure increased to outright expulsion. But this simply accelerated a trend of events and a policy direction begun several years earlier. The original Chinese population of Vietnam was about 1.1 million (850,000 in the south and 250,000 in the north). About 400,000 departed in the past five years. (The Chinese population in Hanoi has been drastically reduced from about 175,000 to an estimated 10,000, but apparently many of these are now in NEZs). Hanoi gives every evidence of wanting to rid itself of virtually all ethnic Chinese, although some observers believe it simply wants to reduce the number to a "manageable" level of perhaps 150,000.

The massive midyear flow of refugees to Southeast Asia culminated in angry demands by the nations of the region that Hanoi curb the exodus. An international meeting on the matter was held in Geneva in June. Vietnam attended reluctantly and pledged to control the outflow. Hanoi announced in late August that 4,000 persons had been arrested and faced trial "for engaging in the refugee escape racket."

Resistance against the regime and other antigovernment activity continued sporadically during the year, according to departing refugees. The resistance, now universally termed *phuc quoc* or "restoration" (usage dating from turn of the century opposition to the French and with high emotive value), is described as widespread, low-level, mostly passive and generally ineffectual. Possibly as many as 100,000 South Vietnamese, in at least a half-dozen distinct *phuc quoc* organizations, consider themselves in a resistance underground. However, they are poorly organized and badly led and engage in little guerrilla war (most of their armed attacks are token gestures or to advertise their particular *phuc quoc* group). Most observers agreed that there is no serious armed resistance in Vietnam, although some observers believe that there is more potential than is apparent and that the *phuc quoc* groups are inactive to avoid calling attention to themselves and are waiting for the proper moment to rise (though the two-front war in 1979 would seem to have been an ideal time for such an antigovernment underground to strike). Some Vietnamese observers abroad believe that the *phuc quoc* movement is waiting to be energized by China and that Beijing will stage some sort of palace coup d'etat in Hanoi and replace the present Politburo with a new one, possibly headed by Hoang Van Hoan.

Vietnam continued to hold several tens of thousands of political prisoners (by Amnesty International definition) in re-education camps, prisons, and in the more remote NEZs. Foreign Ministry official Nguyen Co Thach told newsmen in midyear that 90 percent of all re-education center inmates had been released. Since earlier the regime had said that 1.5 million had been ordered into re-education, presumably 150,000 were still being held. Some observers accepted this figure, but most regarded it as high. A more conservative estimate was 50,000.

Religion suffered in Vietnam during the year. The number of Buddhist pagodas and adherents declined sharply. Only one Buddhist center—the An Quang Pagoda in Ho Chi Minh City—remained an operating Buddhist institution. The number of practicing Buddhists was fixed at 50 percent of the number at the end of the war. Other pagodas continue some activities but were harassed, constantly under surveillance, and frequently limited in the number of days each week they could be open. Thich Tri Quan reportedly was under house arrest, and two Buddhist figures—Thich Thien Chau and Nun Man De La—were expelled by the An Quang Pagoda when they announced their public support for the SRV.

In October the regime widely disseminated the text of the SRV law on counterrevolution (promulgated in 1967 and published by *Nhan Dan* on 16 October), which defined counterrevolution as "opposition to the fatherland and the people's democratic administration" and produced a long list of specific acts for which the death penalty could be imposed: treason, revolution ("overthrow of the administration"), espionage, border crossing, rebellion, banditry or murder for counterrevolutionary purposes, desertion or defection, sabotage, theft of military equipment, spreading of poison, disruption of the monetary system, "intentional bungling," refusal to do defense work, inciting to riot, "undermining of the people's solidarity or . . . national religious policy," "opposition to implementation of state laws," disturbance of public order and security, jail breaking, or freeing of prisoners.

The draft of the new SRV constitution—the product of nearly five years work by the National Assembly—was released in September. It is to replace the 1959 constitution. Aside from incorporating South Vietnam and more candidly acknowledging the centrality of the VCP in all of the society's affairs, the new document's importance lies in changes in the state's governing institutions. Under the National Assembly, theoretically the highest state organ, previously there were five institutions: (1) the Council of Ministers, which was composed of the Standing Committee, the Office of the Premier, five superministers or "czars," and beneath them, the regular cabinet of 23 ministries; (2) the National Defense Council, the highest military command structure; (3) the Office of the President, which included three vice-presidents, all largely honorific or ceremonial; (4) the Supreme Court, the nation's highest court; and (5) the Supreme Procuratorate, or the state prosecutor. In the new constitution, the Office of the President has been absorbed (or in effect abolished) into the Council of Ministers, and the new structure is known as the State Council. The new arrangement more closely parallels the party structure at the highest levels. The full significance of the changes will not be known until the names of the new officeholders are revealed.

International Views and Attitudes. In foreign affairs, it was a year of enormous alienation for the SRV and the VCP. Both suffered significant loss of status and prestige among communist governments and parties around the world. The strike into Kampuchea drew sharp attacks from many noncommunists whom Vietnam once counted as friends. The Chinese attack won back some sympathy but further polarized attitudes toward Vietnam within the communist world. The expulsion of ethnic Chinese, with its highly racist overtones and finally Hanoi's callous attitude toward the famine in Kampuchea had at year's end virtually destroyed what was left of genuine goodwill for Vietnam in the world.

China loomed large in Vietnamese external affairs during the year. Tensions between Beijing and Hanoi increased sharply after the Vietnamese invasion of Kampuchea in late 1978. For the Chinese this was the final intolerable action by a Vietnam guilty of a long string of unconscionable moves—intimacy with the USSR, brutality toward ethnic Chinese in Vietnam, "imperial dreams" in Southeast Asia, and provocative and insulting behavior toward China. The Chinese response in January was some sharp brinkmanship, saber rattling, "stern warnings," and a military buildup on the border. Vietnam replied in kind. The situation grew tense, then ominous, and then exploded in the seventeen-day Vietnam-China border war.

The Chinese attack came at dawn on the morning of 17 February and employed infantry, armor, and artillery but no air power (which did not appear at any time during the war). Within a day the

Chinese army had advanced some five miles into Vietnam along a broad front. Then the advance slowed and nearly stalled, apparently because of heavy Vietnamese resistance and serious supply difficulties for the Chinese. On 21 February the advance resumed against Cao Bang in the far north, the important city of Lang Son, and the lesser targets of Dong Dang and Soc Giang. Cao Bang was entered 27 February and was under complete Chinese control by 2 March. Lang Son and Lao Cai were captured two days later. By 5 March the Chinese, apparently having decided that Vietnam had been sufficiently chastised, announced that the incursion was over and Chinese forces were withdrawing. However, the withdrawal was slow and Carthaginian, with the departing Chinese army destroying as it went. Withdrawal was completed on 16 March. The central residual fact of the war was its inconclusiveness. It settled little between the Vietnamese and the Chinese, for all of the contending issues that triggered it remained.

Negotiations were one of China's preconditions for withdrawal. During the remainder of the year, nearly a dozen sessions were held by the two sides to discuss the issues involved. But the negotiators (Han Nianlong for China and Dinh Nho Liem for the SRV) accomplished little. The meetings were highly acrimonious and the exchanges full of polemics. China's essential posture at the meetings was that it had been forced into the role of protector of Southeast Asia against Vietnamese aggression, a task it took so seriously that if necessary it would be willing to strike again. Vietnam, it was charged, was guilty of hegemonistic dreams and of plotting to create a federation of Southeast Asia that would "extend from Sri Lanka to the Philippines . . . with Hanoi as its core and master," as Han Nianlong expressed it at the 28 July meeting. He added that Vietnam's cold war against Thailand and its policy of flooding Southeast Asia with refugees was part of this hegemonistic effort. Vietnam replied that China's true objective in its military attack on Vietnam (and Laos) was territorial annexation, that it had always wanted to assimilate the two peoples. Liem charged that China was actively backing antigovernment elements in both countries "in alliance with imperialism for whom it seeks to subjugate ideologically the two countries."

Some of the exchanges contained revealing information. For instance, in the 30 July meeting, China castigated Vietnam for being ungrateful. The spokesman said that during the Vietnam war, China sent more than 300,000 Chinese troops to Vietnam to man antiaircraft batteries and maintain logistic and transportation centers. More than a thousand had been killed and several thousand wounded. In August there was an exchange of prisoners of war, but this was not the result of the talks. It began as a unilateral release of all Vietnamese prisoners by China, and Vietnam reciprocated. Border incidents increased in July and again in November but no new action was taken against Vietnam.

Kampuchea represented the second major concern for Vietnam during the year. The war there had been launched during late December 1978 with a highly visible Soviet-type attack: tank-led infantry plunging suddenly across the border, fanning out and within days occupying if not controlling all of Kampuchea, including the capital of Phnom Penh. Pol Pot and his followers of the Democratic Republic of Kampuchea fled to the Cardamom Mountains between Battambang and the Gulf of Siam, there to continue the war. They were given full assurances of support by China. Meanwhile, Prince Sihanouk began a yearlong effort to organize a Kampuchean third force as well as an international conference on Kampuchea. Visitors in Hanoi at the beginning of the Kampuchean war said that there was at the time much genuine optimism among Vietnamese officials. But by March these same officials were admitting to serious difficulties. And by the end of the year almost all of the initial enthusiasm had dissipated.

Heng Samrin and some 300 Khmer cadres were installed as the new government of the People's Republic of Kampuchea. Pham Van Dong led a high-level delegation to Phnom Penh and on 18 February signed a treaty of peace, friendship, and cooperation similar to the one Vietnam signed with Laos a year earlier. The two treaties further delineated the "special relationship" existing among the three Indochinese communist nations and, critics charged, further advanced conditions for the eventual creation of a federation of Indochina.

The SRV (and USSR) campaign launched early in the year to legitimize the Heng Samrin government triggered an extensive doctrinal dispute in the socialist world and divided the nonaligned movement. Pro-Chinese and independent-minded communist governments and parties took sharp exception to the Hanoi-Moscow effort. China, Yugoslavia, and North Korea condemned it. This led to something of a confrontation between Yugoslavia and Cuba at the nonaligned movement summit meeting in Havana later in the year. Albania also condemned the Vietnamese invasion but placed the blame on the two communist superpowers. The communist parties of Malaysia, Thailand, and Burma all took an anti-Vietnamese position.

The continuing war in Kampuchea kept Vietnam's relations in the region at the freezing point. At year's end no ASEAN nation had recognized the Heng Samrin government as Hanoi had asked. All expressed distaste for Pol Pot but insisted that the Vietnamese action was unjustified. As Singapore's Lee Kuan Yew expressed it: "When Hanoi subverts a noncommunist nation, it is called 'liberation,' and when it subverts a communist nation, it is called 'salvation.' "

When the rains stopped in early summer, the PAVN launched a major pacification drive, using some 20,000 of its 170,000 troops in Kampuchea. The press billed this as an all-out offensive, but it proved to be only a limited operation. Possibly Hanoi had decided to restrain its military effort for a combination of reasons: the uncertainty of conditions, pressure from Moscow, fear of Chinese retaliation, economic trouble at home, and Politburo-level differences of opinion. In any event, the military struggle continued with no indication that it was near resolution.

In retrospect, the Vietnamese invasion of Kampuchea appears to have been a disastrous mistake. Apparently it was a decision hastily taken in the belief that a quick, successful takeover would force the Chinese to accept the new situation. Also, it was apparently based on the estimation that Pol Pot had neither political depth nor military staying power and that a traumatic assault would shatter his capability to resist and cause the Khmer people to rally to the new government overwhelmingly. Past strategy had been the slower but more dependable tactic of protracted conflict. But the enterprise was misbegotten from the start. The assumptions proved wrong. The strategy didn't work. The attack did not solve the Pol Pot problem; it merely bogged Vietnam down in a costly war. It badly tarnished Hanoi's image abroad, tarring it with the aggressor brush. It totally ruined relations with China that might otherwise have been salvaged. It drained the economy and unleashed a host of other problems domestically.

All of this meant increased agony for the people of Kampuchea. Although the holocaust of war and anarchy continued and the famine worsened, the Vietnamese remained intransigent on any compromise political settlement or even on cooperation with outside governmental and private relief agencies attempting to help the starving Khmer. The Vietnamese strategy against the Pol Pot forces involved using food as a weapon, and Hanoi saw no reason to alter it. A trickle of relief supplies was allowed into Kampuchea as a means of heading off the worst of the international criticism. Later in the year the ever worsening famine in Kampuchea engendered a massive influx of Khmer into Thailand, nearly 700,000 by early December. Thailand, after first trying to stem the flow, reversed its policy and accepted all. Together with others, Bangkok moved to implement what was called the Danzig solution, that is the creation of an internationalized "free city," if possible flying the U.N. flag, that would be neither Thailand nor Kampuchea. As an internationalized zone, it was hoped that it would be free of attacks from Vietnam and would put the responsibility for the care of the refugees less on the Thais and more on the United Nations and outside nations.

During 1979 Vietnam grew increasingly dependent on the USSR for some 20 percent of the food it consumed, for virtually all of its military hardware, and for such vital commodities as oil, chemical fertilizers, and spare parts for the transportation system. The Soviet response was adequate.

The most tenuous movement of the year in Hanoi-Moscow relations came at the start of the Chinese attack on Vietnam. Moscow's policy, which it maintained throughout the seventeen days, was to take only minimal action and to label its every move clearly so as to eliminate ambiguity. The USSR did nothing that could be interpreted as being militarily hostile towards China. This required considerable skill. Moscow's pronouncements on the war, particularly at the start, were so generalized as to be virtually meaningless, and deliberately so. At no time during the seventeen days did the USSR make any move in the direction of China. A Moscow call-up of reserve forces for training was clearly labeled an annual affair of no greater magnitude than in years past, which was true. Nor were there any military buildups along the Sino-Soviet border.

In short, the Soviet Union judiciously did nothing in military terms. It did immediately generate a crash program of military assistance. A special airlift flew in needed light cargo, such as medicines, and some heavy cargo in small amounts, chiefly for show purposes. The war was over before new supplies could make any significant contribution, but they did demonstrate Soviet support.

Moscow's fundamental calculation apparently was two-fold: first, China would not make an all-out war against Vietnam but rather a shallow and brief incursion; and second, Vietnam was capable of handling this limited threat. Thus, Soviet officials reasoned that quite soon the situation would solve itself as far as the USSR was concerned. Both calculation and conclusion proved correct.

During 1979 the USSR and the SRV moved closer to a systematic military arrangement, if not an alliance, but the pace was measured. Soviet warships called at Vietnamese ports, and the USSR provided various kinds of military assistance for the war in Kampuchea. But many observers were of the opinion that Moscow's closeness to Vietnam had hurt its relations in Southeast Asia and had prevented improved relations with China and consequently concluded that in all probability the limits of intimacy between Vietnam and the USSR had about been reached. Privately Vietnamese diplomats and other officials complained that the USSR had sent wheat not rice, that it "dumped" goods but did not send critical supplies when asked, that Hanoi was "disappointed in" the Council for Mutual Economic Cooperation, and that Moscow's economic ties with the West inhibited it from aiding Vietnam fully. This sort of complaining, however, is virtually standard for Hanoi.

Thailand moved to center stage in Vietnamese affairs during the year because of the war in Kampuchea and renewed overtures from China. Bangkok was wooed by both of the contenders in Kampuchea as well as by the USSR. Vietnam conducted a yearlong war of nerves against Thailand, with the reiterated threat that it would "teach Thailand a lesson" because of its softness on Kampuchea.

Laos threatened to become Vietnam's pressure point once again amid reports of Chinese plans to create an insurgency or set in motion other plans to make life difficult for the Vietnamese there. Vietnamese-Lao relations appeared to cool slightly, engendering some political instability among the ruling Pathet Lao hierarchy. Bangkok, Paris, and others sought without much success to encourage more Lao "independence" from Vietnam.

Hanoi engaged in some pro forma wooing of the United States during the year and in August launched a power play to induce diplomatic relations. However, it did not appear that Hanoi's heart was in the effort. It seemed clear that for the moment diplomatic recognition would not be achieved, but some way was sought to ensure American "neutrality" in the event of another attack by China, apparently in the belief that a U.S.-Chinese military collaboration against Vietnam was an actual possibility.

Publications. No new publications appeared in 1979. (See *YICA*, 1978, p. 330.)

Washington, D.C.   Douglas Pike

THE AMERICAS

Argentina

The Communist Party of Argentina (Partido Comunista de Argentina; PCA) originated from the Internationalist Socialist Party, a splinter from the Socialist Party. It was established in 1918 and took its present name in 1920. Presently, the PCA is the Argentine representative of the pro-Soviet wing of international communism.

Since all parties are illegal in Argentina, the PCA's membership is unascertainable. In the PCA's most recent, short period of legality (1973–1976), it claimed more than 125,000 members, although noncommunist sources put its membership at a considerably lower figure. One U.S. government source estimated PCA membership in 1978 at 70,000. The population of Argentina in 1979 was estimated at 26.8 million.

The substantial majority of PCA members are certainly manual workers, although the leaders are principally middle class. Early in 1979 Athos Fava, a member of the PCA Central Committee, reported that 80 percent of all new members were young workers who had been Peronistas (*WMR*, January).

Other communist parties in Argentina include the Revolutionary Communist Party (Partido Comunista Revolucionario; PCR), the Communist Vanguard (Vanguardia Comunista; VC), and the Marxist-Leninist Communist Party (Partido Comunista Marxista-Leninista de Argentina; PCMLA) all of which are Maoist. Trotskyism is represented by several rival groups, one of which resorted to guerrilla activities in the early 1970s, and was largely liquidated by the military regime after 1976.

Leadership and Organization. The PCA's secretary general is Gerónimo Arnedo Alvarez. Other leading figures include Rodolfo and Orestes Ghioldi, Rubens Iscaro, Alcina de la Pena, and Hector P. Agosti. The PCA is organized pyramidally from cells, neighborhood committees, and local committees on up to provincial committees, the Central Committee, the Executive Committee, and the Secretariat. Since the outlawing of all parties by the military government of Jorge Videla, all levels of the PCA have had to function illegally, although persecution of the communist party by military leaders has not been very severe.

The PCA youth movement, the Communist Youth Federation (Federación Juvenil Comunista) is organized along the same lines as the party. Before illegalization, it claimed some 40,000 members and sent 50 of the 510 delegates to the PCA's last legal congress in 1973.

The PCA is still weak in the labor movement despite the presence of party units in many unions. The military regime has removed the leaders of many of the country's principal unions, and the central labor organization, the General Confederation of Labor, has been unable to function. Hence it is difficult to measure communist influence in organized labor, compared with that of the Peronistas, who have dominated the trade union movement for more than a generation. The PCA has for 25 years controlled the Movement for Trade Union Unity (Movimiento de Unidad y Coordinacion Sindical;

MUCS), which has had some small regional unions, mostly in Córdoba and Mendoza, associated with it. Rubens Iscaro, MUCS secretary general, has long had a leading role in the World Federation of Trade Unions, the Moscow-oriented world labor movement. The communists professed during the year to see a movement away from Peronism on the part of the workers. Athos Fava wrote in January that "moving further and further to the left, worker Peronists reject capitalism although they have yet to make a resolute enough step toward socialism." He claimed that "it is not a question of replacing Peronist leaders by communists. We favor the formation at all levels, from top to bottom, of a leadership committed to unity and expressing the working people's militancy and interests. This is a feasible if very difficult task." (Ibid.)

Although most peasant organizations belong to the noncommunist Argentine Agrarian Federation, the PCA has claimed to be active in the Union of Agrarian Producers of Argentina, formed in 1969, which is composed of farmers with small- and medium-sized holdings.

Most PCA fronts, such as the Argentine League for the Rights of Man, the Union of Argentine Women, and the Argentine Peace Council, have been illegal for many years, except during the second Peronista regime (1973–1976). Since establishment of the military government, there has been little evidence of activity on their part.

Domestic Attitudes and Activities. In spite of the war to the death against extreme leftist guerrilla activists, the military government has maintained relatively friendly relations with the USSR and Cuba. This has undoubtedly been a major factor in determining the PCA's cautious attitude toward the regime.

The communists professed to see conflicting tendencies within the Videla regime. Arnedo Alvarez commented that the political process

> is not uniform, nor should one expect it to be. We should not be surprised or disconcerted by the growing internal contradictions and struggles, which are due to the magnitude of the forces involved and the grave problems to be faced and solved . . . Two currents are struggling in the armed forces and this struggle will become much more complex and much more open. It is one of our duties as well as a duty of all democratic forces at this crucial hour to defeat "Pinochetism" and pave the way for a renewed democracy, with the active participation of the workers and people. (*IB*, no. 4.)

He urged President Videla to establish "specific and early deadlines so as to guarantee the achievement of the democratic objectives" and added that the people want to "express their opinion and take part in decision-making. Otherwise promises may become a boomerang torpedoing such goals as democratization and a civilian-military convergence" (ibid.).

However, the PCA was very critical of the Videla government's economic policies, presided over by Minister of Economy José Martínez de Hoz. Arnedo Alvarez objected very strongly to his reappointment in a cabinet reorganization early in the year. He claimed that "the whole country emphatically rejects the economic plan" and said that the PCA was developing its own economic plan as an alternative to the Martinez de Hoz program, which was "applauded only by U.S. bankers." (Ibid.)

A few months later, Fernando Nadra, PCA Politburo member, took much the same line in an interview with the Cuban paper *Granma* (24 June). He said that the PCA still supported a "civilian-military democratic convergence . . . and agreement between democratic civilians and members of the armed forces around a program of national liberation." He reported that the PCA was cooperating with other political parties to bring about such a dialogue and urged the government to create an appropriate atmosphere for discussions by explaining the whereabouts of the political prisoners who were claimed to have "disappeared."

The PCA supported the Videla government in its controversy with the Chilean government over the international border in the Beagle Channel. It was reported in December 1978 that "the Argentine

Communist Party declared itself in favor of the government's just position in the southern border dispute which this country has with Chile. At the same time, the PCA launched a call for a large civilian assembly which, together with the armed forces, would analyze the problem and draft a collective and national position." (Agence France Presse, 21 December 1978.)

International Views and Contacts. During the year the PCA maintained close relations with the pro-Soviet international communist tendency. Central Committee member Julio Laborde served as a member of the Editorial Board of the *World Marxist Review*. He took part in a conference on "The Agrarian Question in Latin American Countries," along with representatives of communist parties from fourteen other Latin American countries, as well as from Czechoslovakia, East Germany, and the USSR (*WMR*, May).

The PCA strongly supported the Soviet Union and Vietnam against China in Southeast Asia. Arnedo Alvarez sent a message of congratulations to Heng Samrin, head of the Vietnamese-imposed government of Kampuchea (Cambodia), when it was placed in power in January (*FBIS*, 16 January). The PCA also issued a strong denunciation of the Chinese attack on Vietnam, which began: "Following in the footsteps of the U.S. imperialists, 400,000 Chinese have invaded the territory of the glorious homeland of Ho Chi Minh. This is outright betrayal." (*IB*, no. 9.)

Several PCA delegations visited Cuba, Eastern Europe, and the USSR during the year. Arnedo Alvarez was in Cuba in December 1978. In July Argentine Politburo member Fernando Nadra visited Bulgaria on the invitation of that country's party leaders. In August Arnedo Alvarez was in the Soviet Union, where he was received by B. N. Ponomarev, a secretary of the Communist Party of the Soviet Union.

Publications. The military regime does not allow the legal publication of PCA periodicals. However, the weekly *Nuestra Palabra*, the theoretical journal *Nueva Era*, and other PCA publications continued to appear.

The Revolutionary Communist Party (PCR). The PCR (originally the Communist Party of Revolutionary Recovery) was created in January 1968 by dissidents from the PCA, especially its youth organization, who criticized the alleged "class conciliation" and "conciliation with imperialism" of the PCA. Its principal figures are Cesar Otto Vargas and Guillermo Sanchez. The PCR is a Maoist party and over the years has received recognition as such from Beijing through invitations to its leaders to visit China and friendly references in the *Beijing Review*. Although the PCR has officially favored armed insurrection, particularly urban guerrilla activities, there is little evidence of its ever having engaged in them. The PCR has functioned illegally since the coup of March 1976. Its activities did not gain public attention during 1979.

The Communist Vanguard (VC). The VC, probably founded in 1964, is also pro-Chinese and reportedly had some influence among student and worker groups in the early 1970s. It has shown little evidence of activity since the advent of the Videla military dictatorship.

The Marxist-Leninist Communist Party (PCMLA). The third Maoist party in Argentina, the PCMLA, broke away from the Argentine Socialist Party (PSA), taking the name Vanguard Socialist Party before changing its name in the mid-1970s to PCMLA. Its principal leaders are Elias Seman and Roberto Cristina, its secretary general. In December 1978 the PCMLA issued a joint statement with the Communist Party (Marxist-Leninist) of the United States, charging that "the USSR today constitutes the main source of a new world war. Of the two superpowers, the USSR is today the rising, more aggressive and most dangerous superpower." The statement also said that "both our parties support the just struggle of the Kampuchean people headed by the Communist Party of Kampuchea and its leader, Comrade Pol Pot, for sovereignty, national independence and socialism, and against the Vietnamese aggression which is carried out at the instigation of the Soviet social-imperialists." (New China News Agency, 13 December 1978).

The People's Revolutionary Party. This group, otherwise unidentified, issued a statement in January signed by its secretary general, Luis Mattini, congratulating Kim Il-song and the Korean Workers' Party on the 30th anniversary of the establishment of the communist regime in North Korea (Radio Pyongyang, 17 January).

The Trotskyists. Trotskyism is represented in Argentina by several groups. The Socialist Workers' Party (Partido Socialista de Trabajadores; PST) is affiliated with the United Secretariat of the Fourth International. The Revolutionary Workers' Party (Partido Revolucionario de los Trabajadores; PRT) broke from the United Secretariat in the early 1970s and concentrated its efforts on the work of its paramilitary wing, the People's Revolutionary Army (Ejército Revolucionario del Pueblo; ERP). The Trotskyist Labor Party (Partido Obrero, Trotskista; POT) is aligned with the International Secretariat of the Fourth International headed by J. Posadas, an Argentine. Politica Obrera is a group without international affiliation. Another element of Trotskyist origins, the Socialist Party of the National Left (Partido Socialista de la Izquierda Nacional; PSIN) has formally foresworn allegiance to Trotskyism, while still revering Trotsky.

The Workers' Socialist Party (PST). PST was formed in 1971 by a merger of the faction of the PRT opposed to guerrilla activities, headed by the veteran Trotskyist Nahuel Moreno, with a faction of the PSA headed by Juan Corral. It became the Argentine affiliate of the United Secretariat. The PST ran its own candidates in the two presidential elections of 1973. The party has strongly opposed the military dictatorship since 1976. In October 1979 it was reported that "dozens of members" of the PST were held as political prisoners, including the party's onetime vice-presidential candidate, the autoworker José Francisco Paez. (*Intercontinental Press*, 15 October.)

The Revolutionary Workers' Party/People's Revolutionary Army (PRT/ERP). During the early 1970s, the PRT's ERP carried on extensive guerrilla activities, both in the cities and the countryside. It refused to accept President Juan Perón's demand, after his return to power in 1973, that leftist guerrillas give up their activities. Their continued guerrilla war was a major factor in precipitating the coup of March 1976. Thereafter, the armed forces carried out an intensified campaign against ERP guerrillas. A few months after the advent of the Videla government, the ERP attempted to seize control of a part of Tucumán province, concentrating almost all of their paramilitary units there, with the result that they were overwhelmingly defeated, the army being able to kill or capture virtually all of the guerrillas. By 1979 there was little indication that the ERP was able to carry on any effective guerrilla activity.

The Trotskyist Labor Party (POT). The POT of J. Posadas has tended to concentrate its activity on publishing and distributing a periodical, *Voz Proletaria*, consisting principally of speeches of Posadas. There is no indication whether it has been able to publish this illegally since the advent of the military dictatorship.

The Socialist Party of the National Left (PSIN). The PSIN was founded in the 1950s by a group of Trotskyists who favored the Perón regime. It continued thereafter to be aligned with the Peronistas. In the 1973 elections it organized a broader grouping, the Popular Leftist Front (Frente de Izquierda Popular; FIP), which supported Perón for president. Since then, the party has functioned under the name of the FIP. It has been able to continue some activity under the dictatorship. In May the party's major figure, Jorge Abelardo Ramos, and eight other party members were arrested in the city of Resistencia "for violating a ban on political activities" (*NYT*, 7 May).

Peronista Extremist Elements. During the early 1970s several paramilitary groups were formed by Peronista elements. The most important of these was the Montonero Peronista Movement (Movimiento Peronista Montonero; MPM), which absorbed most of the others. During the second Peronista government (1973–1976), the MPM largely ceased guerrilla activities, although shortly before the overthrow of President Isabel Perón, it announced that its members were resuming armed resistance to the government, which they charged had betrayed Peronista principles. Their activities helped provoke Isabel's ouster by the military in March 1976. Thereafter, the military carried on a ruthless campaign against the MPM and succeeded in killing, capturing, or driving into exile virtually all of them.

In February 1979 two top leaders of the Montoneros, Adolfo Galimberti and Juan Gelman, announced that they were breaking with the organization so as better to carry on "the revolutionary struggle against the dictatorship and for the liberation of the Argentine people." They accused the Montonero leaders of being out of contact with events in Argentina because of living in exile. (*Le Monde*, 25–26 February.) In March, Fernando Vaca Narvaja, reported to be deputy chief of the Montoneros, was sentenced to prison for three years by an Italian court for possessing weapons and forged identity papers (EFE, 15 March). However, some months later, Vaca Narvaja was interviewed in Nicaragua. He denied that the Montoneros had fought with the Sandinistas against the Somoza dictatorship but admitted that they had a medical brigade at Masaya and that "we have also given material support to the Sandinista front, particularly to finance the war in its last stages." (Agence France Presse, 22 July.) Meanwhile, Mario Firmenich, principal leader of the Montoneros, who had also been in Nicaragua during the last phase of the civil war there, announced from Santiago, Chile, that "the Montoneros are not dead. The struggle is resuming, and this year we will launch an offensive over the whole territory." (Ibid., 22 July.) By the end of the year there was little evidence that the Montoneros had been able to make good on Firmenich's boast.

Rutgers University   Robert J. Alexander

Bolivia

The far left in Bolivia is exceedingly splintered. Virtually all of the parties and tendencies originated in one of five original groups: (1) the heirs of the pro-Stalinist Party of the Revolutionary Left (Partido de Izquierda Revolucionaria), established in 1940, including the pro-Moscow Communist Party of

Bolivia (Partido Comunista de Bolivia; PCB) and the pro-Chinese Marxist-Leninist Communist Party of Bolivia (Partido Comunista de Bolivia Marxista-Leninista; PCB-ML); (2) the Trotskyist Revolutionary Workers' Party (Partido Obrero Revolucionario; POR), also organized in 1940, which has given rise to at least five parties, most still using the name POR; (3) the National Liberation Army, (Ejército de Liberación Nacional), Ernesto "Che" Guevara's guerrilla group organized in 1966, which in 1975 established the Revolutionary Party of Bolivian Workers (Partido Revolucionario de los Trabajadores de Bolivia); (4) the middle-of-the-road Christian Democratic Party (Partido Demócrata Cristiano; PDC) gave birth to the Movement of the Revolutionary Left (Movimiento de Izquierda Revolucionaria; MIR) in 1971; and (5) the center-left Nationalist Revolutionary Movement (Movimiento Nacionalista Revolucionario; MNR), a dissident left-wing group, which formed the Socialist Party (Partido Socialista de Bolivia) in the early 1970s. The total membership of these communist factions does not exceed 2,000 or 3,000. The population of Bolivia is estimated at approximately 5.2 million.

Leadership and Organization. The first secretary of the PCB is Jorge Kolle Cueto. Others prominent in the party include Mario Monje Molina, a former secretary, and Central Committee members Simón Reyes, Arturo Lanza, Carlos Alba, and Luis Padilla, the last a frequent international spokesman for the party. The PCB's youth organization is the Communist Youth of Bolivia (Juventud Comunista de Bolivia). Reyes, head of the PCB's miner activists, has been a leading official of the Mine Workers' Federation (FSTMB) since the early months of 1978.

Domestic Attitudes and Activities. The PCB greeted the coup d'etat of 24 November 1978 with cautious optimism. Party Secretary General Kolle commented on 20 December 1978 that "two promises are being received favorably by the majority of democratic forces; the organization of free elections in the course of the first six months of 1979 and the implementation of measures favorable to the true democratization of the country" (*L'Humanité*, 20 December 1978).

The new president did carry out his promise to call new presidential and congressional elections on 1 July. The PCB, as it had done in 1978, endorsed the candidacy of Hernán Siles Suazo, nominee of the Union Democratica y Popular (UDP). The Central Committee, in a statement in March announcing its position, proclaimed that "the historic achievement of the Bolivian people embodied in the UDP maintains all its vigor and continues to be a possible victorious option, to the extent that it is capable of consolidating its identification with a people's democratic program already proposed in its original documents—an anti-imperialist plan of genuine national liberation . . . Therefore, we call on all the comrades of the front, with whom we are helping to crystallize this instrument and with whom we are confident that we will culminate this great plan, to strengthen the UDP's platform, organization, and unity." The PCB statement strongly attacked Siles Suazo's principal opponent, Victor Paz Estenssoro. It alleged that "the political philosophy espoused by Paz Estenssoro is the principal choice of imperialism, though not the only one . . . The offensive of Social Democracy and Carterism has had some impact on the UDP's unity." (*Presencia*, 20 March.)

When the July election resulted in an impasse, the PCB reiterated its support of Hernán Siles and the UDP. It was reported that the PCB "believed that Hernán Siles Suazo's victory has not yet been consolidated, and the process of democratization is not yet irreversible. The danger of a fascist threat, of a conspiracy to sabotage the institutional normalization and impose a reactionary dictatorship, still looms over the Bolivian people. Therefore, the masses and their unions and political organizations must remain perpetually alert." (Radio La Paz, 30 July.)

The National Congress. In April the PCB held its Fourth Congress, the first held legally in eight years. Four hundred delegates attended, as did fraternal delegations from the Argentinian, Peruvian, and Uruguayan communist parties. Delegates from parties in communist-controlled countries were denied visas by the Bolivian government. The congress confirmed PCB participation in the UDP.

Relations with Organized Labor. Since the PCB's inception in 1950, it has sought influence in organized labor. It has had to face the competing influence of the Partido Revolucionario de Izquierda Nacionalista of Juan Lechín, head of the FSTMB and the Bolivian Labor Central (COB), as well as the influence of the MNR, the Maoist PCB-ML, and various Trotskyist groups. At the Fifth Congress of the COB in May, all these groups were represented, and the struggle among them was intensified by the support given competing candidates in the 1 July elections by the different parties. Lechín was re-elected executive secretary, but there was little agreement on other issues. The PCB gained more representation in the new Executive Committee of the COB than might otherwise have been the case because of the withdrawal of members of the PCB-ML the day before the choice of a new committee. (*Latin*, 8 May.)

International Views and Contacts. The PCB remained a member of the pro-Soviet bloc of communist parties throughout the year. Luis Padilla was the PCB representative on the editorial board of *World Marxist Review*. In December 1978 Kolle Cueto visited Eastern Europe and the Soviet Union. He was received in the USSR by Communist Party of the Soviet Union (CPSU) Politburo member Boris Ponomarev and in Berlin by East German Politburo member Hermann Axen. In March the PCB sent a message to Le Duan, general secretary of the Vietnam Communist Party, condemning the Chinese invasion of Vietnam. It said: "We condemn the invasion carried out by the Chinese Communist Party leaders and consider it a clear indication of their ideological deterioration following their collusion with the North American imperialists and other international reactionary forces" (Radio Hanoi, 2 March).

The CPSU Central Committee sent a message of congratulations to the PCB's Fourth Congress, reaffirming the CPSU's "staunch solidarity with the Bolivian communists' courageous struggle against the forces of imperialism and reaction and for the strengthening of national sovereignty, the democratization of sociopolitical life, and the rights of working people" (*Pravda*, 22 April.)

The Marxist-Leninist Communist Party of Bolivia. The PCB-ML was founded as a result of a split in the PCB in 1965. It has long been torn by dissension. The faction headed by Oscar Zamora has given its blessing to Hua Guofeng and continued to be recognized by the People's Republic of China. It was the only pro-Chinese group that was registered for the 1978 and 1979 elections and is thought to have several hundred members. The PCB-ML announced in March in a statement signed by Zamora that it was going to support Victor Paz Estenssoro in the 1 July election: "The Central Committee . . . fully supports the resolution unanimously approved by the Central Committee of the Revolutionary Front of the Left [FRI] to participate in a political alliance with the MNR, the PDC, and the Authentic Revolutionary Party . . . The FRI and especially the PCB-ML assume within this alliance the commitment to defend the interests of the working class and peasant masses, as well as those of vast sections of the small bourgeoisie." (*Presencia*, 15 May). The support of the Maoists for Paz Estenssoro served as the excuse for the right-wing Socialist Falange (FSB) to claim that his victory would result in Chinese control over the Bolivian government. The FSB also argued that this would mean that the Pinochet government in Chile would be able to impose its will on Bolivia since the Chinese were supporting the Pinochet regime. (Ibid., 11 June.)

Relations with the Labor Movement. Since its inception, the PCB-ML has had some influence in the labor movement, particularly among the miners. The party sent 175 delegates to the Fifth Congress of the COB, which met on 1 May. There was a physical clash between Maoist and Trotskyist delegates on the first day, and on 7 May the PCB-ML delegates abandoned the sessions of the Congress, to the advantage of the PCB, as noted above.

The Movement of the Revolutionary Left. The MIR was established by members of the youth section of the PDC in the late 1960s. Its members launched guerrilla activities but were disastrously defeated. They subsequently returned to legal political activity and obtained legal recognition when political parties returned to open activity in 1978. The MIR formed part of the UDP and supported Siles in both the 1978 and 1979 elections.

The Trotskyists. The Trotskyists were the second largest political element in the labor movement in the 1950s. However, they subsequently split into at least five factions. The POR headed by Hugo Gonzalez is affiliated with the United Secretariat of the Fourth International. The Communist Vanguard of the Revolutionary Workers' Party (Vanguardia Comunista del Partido Obrero Revolucionario), led by mine workers' leader Filemon Escobar, which split away from the Gonzalez party, held its first congress in 1979, attended by Hugo Blanco, leader of the United Secretariat's Peruvian affiliate. On the other hand, the POR faction led by Guillermo Lora is affiliated with a Fourth International faction based in Paris, and the Posadista POR is the Bolivian affiliate of the Fourth International faction led by the Argentinian J. Posadas. All the Trotskyist factions except the Guillermo Lora group supported the candidacy of ex-President Hernán Siles in the 1979 elections.

Rutgers University   Robert J. Alexander

Brazil

The original Communist Party of Brazil (Partido Comunista do Brasil; PCdoB), founded in March 1922, remains the most important Marxist-Leninist organization in the nation. Several small groups that broke away or were expelled from the party in its first decade formed a Trotskyist movement that subsequently split into several factions. At least two of these still maintain a precarious existence. In 1960, in a bid for legal recognition, the original pro-Soviet party dropped all international slogans from its statutes and changed its name to Brazilian Communist Party (Partido Comunista Brasileiro; PCB). A pro-Chinese element broke away the following year and in February 1962 adopted the original party name, Communist Party of Brazil. This group has since abandoned allegiance to China and become pro-Albanian. Another source of far-leftist groups was Popular Action (Acão Popular), which originated in the Catholic student movement in the late 1950s. In the following decade, a segment of the AP identified itself as the Marxist-Leninist Popular Action (Acão Popular Marxista-Leninista).

The communist movement has been illegal in Brazil throughout most of its existence, although it has at times operated with varying degrees of freedom. The military regime that came to power in March 1964 drove the PCB and other far-left groups deeply underground and banned existing communist-influenced organizations. However, with the advent to power in 1979 of the fifth of the military presidents, this situation began to change. Many exiled leftists were allowed to return to Brazil, and the various far-left parties were able to operate in somewhat more open circumstances, although they did not obtain legal status.

The PCB and PCdoB combined do not have more than a few thousand members, most of them in the former. Little is known of the numerical strength of the other Marxist-Leninist groups. The population of Brazil is estimated to be 124.4 million.

Organization and Leadership. The PCB apparatus is supposed to include a 23-member Executive Commission, a Central Committee, state committees, municipal committees, and local cells in residential districts and places of employment. However, government persecution has made it impossible for the party to maintain a full panoply of organization.

In a March 1978 article, PCB General Secretary Luiz Carlos Prestes, an exile since 1964 and Moscow resident since 1971, explained the situation of the party after the 1964 military coup. He noted that despite "long experience and the efforts made by our Central Committee, by the whole party, to maintain vigilance and use new methods of illegal work, the truth is that these methods, adopted by various sections of the party, beginning from the CC, were not adequate to the new devices employed by the repressive agencies." He added that "in the face of repression and violence aimed at physically destroying the party's leaders, the PCB Central Committee passed a decision that the most prominent members of the party leadership should leave the country." (*WMR*, March 1978.) PCB leaders who returned to Brazil after the amnesty included ex-deputy Gregorio Bezerra, Hercules Correia, and communist ex–trade union leaders Luis Tenorio and Lindolfo Silva (*WP*, 1 October).

Domestic Activities and Attitudes. The PCB is an orthodox pro-Soviet party that seeks to mobilize and manipulate the masses to achieve power. It long ago recognized the impossibility of achieving power in Brazil by violence and thus advocates popular front tactics. Within its limited possibilities, the PCB seeks to identify with—and to claim responsibility for articulating—the legitimate grievances and aspirations of broad sectors of Brazilian society. The total failure of the "reckless adventures" of extremist left-wing guerrilla organizations during the last decade has reinforced the belief of PCB leaders in the correctness of the party's domestic line.

This attitude was reinforced by Brazilian political developments during 1979. Before leaving office, the last Brazilian president abolished most of the repressive legislation that the military dictatorship had imposed since 1964, particularly Institutional Act No. 5, which had allowed the president to cancel the civil rights of Brazilian citizens and arbitrarily remove members of the country's legislative bodies.

After being inaugurated in March, the current president continued and expanded the liberalizing policies of his predecessor. He allowed a series of strikes a month after his inauguration without taking any reprisals. Later in the year, he issued an amnesty for most political prisoners and exiles. On this occasion, the exiled leaders of the PCB stated that despite the amnesty's limitations, it represented a popular victory because it would become "a positive motivation to intensify the struggle for a general amnesty" (Agence France Presse, 24 July).

Throughout 1979 the PCB continued to support the "popular front" policy. A Central Committee plenum in November 1978 declared that "our activity must be directed at expanding and strengthening the unity of the opposition, at organizing these forces in the struggle for democratic freedoms. Thus our key task is to fight for the mobilization, organization and permanent participation of the working classes and other population strata in the present political process." (*IB*, no. 3.)

Throughout 1979 the PCB continued to support the legal opposition, the Brazilian Democratic Movement (MDB). Interviewed in March, Prestes insisted that "it is our endeavor to keep the MDB united, although we are not opposed to the organization of new parties. We advocate, though, a struggle for democratic freedom, including the freedom to organize political parties of all shades, including a communist party." (*Die Wahrheit*, West Berlin, 16 March.)

A party plenum early in 1979 reiterated these positions. Its political resolution argued that "there is dissatisfaction with the situation, not only among the forces of the opposition, including the MDB whose role in the fight against the dictatorship is increasing." It added: "In the present situation, first-priority attention must be attached to the struggle for democratic freedoms. In this very objective, all forces must now be united, regardless of their economic interests and their political views, for all want to put an end to the existing regime." (*Horizont*, East Berlin, 11 November.) In November the PCB was reportedly still supporting the MDB as the united center of the opposition. Consequently it was opposing attempts to establish a workers' party despite the desires of some of the new labor leaders who had come into prominence in 1978–79 as a result of widespread strikes. (*Intercontinental Press*, 5 November).

International Views and Contacts. The PCB remained a loyal member of the pro-Moscow group of communist parties. Prestes continued to live in Moscow, although he visited other European countries during the year, including France in April, where he had extensive discussions with officials of the French Communist Party (*L'Humanité*, 25 April), as well as East Germany and Czechoslovakia, where he was received by top party officials.

In conformity with its pro-Moscow position, the PCB strongly opposed the Chinese Communist Party during the year. Prestes published an article in the *World Marxist Review* (March) in which he alleged that "reactionaries backed by Peking have launched fierce ideological attacks against the socialist countries, particularly the Soviet Union . . . The reactionary offensive calls for the resistance on our part. The Chinese leaders' activity and their obsession with anti-Sovietism are undoubtedly the biggest trump-card of bourgeois policy and propaganda against the people's struggle for international security and social progress."

Publications. The PCB paper *Voz Operaria* was published abroad by the party's exiled leaders. It undoubtedly circulated illegally within the country.

The Communist Party of Brazil (PCdoB). The organizational structure of the PCdoB, which was founded in 1961 by men who had long held leadership positions in the PCB, is believed to be patterned after that of the parent party. Little is known about the number or distribution of currently functioning units. Although the PCdoB originated as a pro-Chinese party, it broke with Chinese leaders after the death of Mao Zedong and the purge of the extremist Chinese leaders, the so-called "gang of four." The PCdoB became associated with the Albanian party and regime of Enver Hoxha.

In April, João Amazonas, PCdoB secretary general, headed a delegation that visited Albania and was received by Hoxha (Radio Tirana, 14 April). In September, Hoxha, in a message sent in the name of the Albanian party to the Seventh National Conference of the PCdoB, proclaimed: "We send our warmest revolutionary greetings . . . to the invincible militants of the Communist Party of Brazil, the militant proletariat and the Brazilian workers" (ibid., 5 September). In September João Amazonas again visited Albania and was received by Hoxha (ibid., 20 September).

The PCdoB was reported in November as being opposed to any move to form a new labor party (*Intercontinental Press*, 5 November).

Other Organizations. Few of the numerous extremist and terrorist organizations that operated in Brazil in the late 1960s and early 1970s seem to have survived into 1979. It is interesting to note, however, that Luiz Carlos Prestes sought in 1979 to rehabilitate Carlos Marighella, the former PCB leader who broke with the party in the mid-1960s to launch urban guerrilla activities. In March a group said to be associated with the MR-8 Revolutionary Movement was arrested in Minas Gerais and accused of "crimes coming under the National Security Law" (*O Estado de São Paulo*, 16 March).

The Trotskyists also continued active. The principal Trotskyist organization during the year was Socialist Convergence, launched in Rio de Janeiro in March 1978, principally by students. The "national coordinator" was Julio Tavares. It reported in May that it had groups in the states of São Paulo, Rio de Janeiro, Rio Grande do Sul, Minas Gerais, and Paraíba (*Jornal do Brasil*, 13 May). In March, 25 members of the group were brought to trial by the military regime. Socialist Convergence was associated with the United Secretariat of the Fourth International.

Rutgers University   Robert J. Alexander

Canada

Several parties and groups with a Marxist-Leninist orientation function legally in Canada, the oldest and largest being the Communist Party of Canada (CPC), which has been continuously pro-Soviet since its founding in 1921. Throughout the 1970s it has attempted to cooperate with nonrevolutionary organizations on the left in an effort to produce a broad "antimonopoly alliance." There have been various Trotskyist organizations in Canada since the 1930s; currently most active is the Revolutionary Workers League (RWL), which was formed in 1977 by a merger of three existing Trotskyist groups (see *YICA*, 1979, pp. 318–19). More prominent have been several Maoist groups that began appearing in 1963 as part of the new left student movement and subsequently broadened to include minority groups and some workers. At present, the two most important are the Communist Party of Canada (Marxist-Leninist) (CPC-ML), which emerged in 1970 and has since repudiated its initial Chinese orientation to become pro-Albanian and avowedly Stalinist; and the Workers Communist Party (Marxist-Leninist) (WCP), which was organized this year from the Canadian Communist League, a preparty formation. It is pro-Chinese, as is another small Maoist group, the Alive Production Collective. In addition to these, with no apparent international affiliation, is the Marxist-Leninist Organization of Canada en Lutte!/in Struggle! (MLOC), which has been active in the 1970s, initially in Quebec but increasingly in English Canada as well. It has received some support from a small group in Toronto called the Bolshevik Union. The estimated total membership of these parties and groups is between 5,000 and 8,000, out of a total Canadian population of approximately 23.8 million.

In 1979 Marxist-Leninist political activity in Canada continued to be characterized by disunity. The parties and formations listed above expend considerable energy disputing each other's claims and have been unable to cooperate despite a recognized need for a more integrated political left. These groups are also characterized by their relative insignificance in Canadian politics. There has been no noticeable growth in membership or popular support despite the existence of economic and political crises in Canada. Growing voter dissatisfaction with high unemployment, wage controls, inflation, and the status of Quebec within Canada did not translate into electoral gains in the 22 May federal elections. The combined total vote for all Marxist-Leninist candidates was only 0.2 percent. In contrast, the three main Canadian political parties dominated the election, with the Progressive Conservatives forming a new minority government under Prime Minister Joe Clark. A notable feature of the election was the "parallel campaign" of the 2.3 million member Canadian Labour Congress (CLC) to win greater working class support for a moderate socialist party, the New Democrats (NDP). The CLC itself, however, has been faced with some growing militancy and opposition in its own ranks. It is noteworthy that the emergence of widespread and significant Marxist scholarly activity in Canadian universities, described by one of Canada's leading political scientists as "one of the most remarkable developments in Canadian intellectual history," has had no discernible impact on Marxist-Leninist political formations (John Meisel, *Canadian Forum*, May).

Leadership, Organization, and Internal Affairs. It is estimated that the CPC has about 2,500 members. Many of the candidates who ran in the federal elections were young, reflecting a recruiting effort begun in 1974 that has somewhat offset the party's elderly image. William Kashtan, 70, continues as CPC general secretary, a position he has held since 1965. Alfred Dewhurst is executive secretary of the Central Committee, and Bruce Magnuson is labor secretary. Provincial party leaders include William Stewart in Ontario, William Ross in Manitoba, Maurice Rush in British Columbia. Sam Walsh continues as president of the semiautonomous Parti communiste du Québec. The Young Communist League has centers in seven Canadian cities and is led by Mike Gidora. The CPC was to hold its 24th convention on 5–7 January 1980. The convention was to be based on a draft policy resolution prepared by the Central Committee in June.

Domestic Attitudes and Activities. The CPC regards Quebec and the rest of Canada as two distinct nations but rejects separatism in favor of a united Canada based on a new constitution. It has advocated "a constituent assembly with equal representation from both nations" to work out a constitution (*Communist Viewpoint*, no. 1). It also sees constitutional reform as a means of bringing Canadian energy resources, which are presently largely under provincial jurisdiction, under greater federal control. It has also argued that "the only way to energy self-sufficiency and stable energy prices is through the development of an all-Canadian energy policy based on public ownership" (*Canadian Tribune*, 19 November).

Throughout 1979 the tactical position of the CPC was to promote a broad "antimonopoly alliance" which, in addition to workers, would include small businessmen, farmers, intellectuals, Quebec nationalist elements, and native peoples, as well as the trade union movement and elements of the NDP. It has attempted, with limited success, to pursue this alliance strategy in elections at the local level, most notably in the British Columbia and Toronto municipal elections in November 1978. In British Columbia, the CPC ran twenty candidates, electing four, and now asserts that it has "matured into a serious civic political force in B.C." In the Vancouver elections it pursued a united front with the Committee of Progressive Electors, which, while losing, gained 23 percent of the vote and emerged as a second force in Vancouver politics. (*Communist Viewpoint*, no. 1.) In the Toronto elections, the party pursued a "united approach" as a part of the Reform Metro movement. It was unable to obtain NDP and Toronto Labour Council support, but it did succeed in electing two of its eight candidates, while three others were runners-up. It was the first time in 28 years that a communist had been elected to city office (ibid., no. 6, 1978). The CPC places special emphasis on its activity at the municipal level in the belief that "as we break through on the municipal front, so conditions are created to break through also in the provincial and federal fields" (ibid., nos. 4–5).

Despite this and the ailing Canadian economy and the Quebec crisis, which provided issues around which to rally dissatisfied voters, the CPC was completely unsuccessful in the 22 May federal elections. The party ran candidates in 69 of the 264 ridings. Not one was able to garner as much as 1 percent of the vote cast in any riding. Nationwide, out of 11.5 million votes cast in the election, the CPC received 9,134, or 0.08 percent.

International Attitudes and Activities. The CPC consistently supports the position of the Communist Party of the Soviet Union on international issues. It claims to do so out of solidarity rather than subservience, regarding the Soviet Union as decisive in the struggle against "imperialism" and therefore condemning anti-Sovietism among socialists as disruptive to unity. In this regard, it has been critical of Eurocommunism (*WMR*, April) and has strongly condemned Chinese leaders for committing aggression against Vietnam. It views the Chinese incursion as part of a deal with the United States made during Deng Xiaoping's visit to Washington (*IB*, no. 9). The CPC also applauded "the rapid collapse of the reactionary pro-Beijing regime of Pol Pot" (*FBIS*, 16 January) and urged Canadian recognition of the People's Revolutionary Council in Kampuchea (Cambodia) as the sole representative of the Khmer people.

The CPC regards "détente and its extension into the military field" as the first priority in international affairs (*Communist Viewpoint*, no. 1). In July, Kashtan visited the Soviet Union and together with Soviet leaders B. N. Ponomarev and A. S. Chernyayev issued a joint statement stressing the importance of the SALT II treaty and the resolution of both parties to struggle against the arms race. The CPC has been vocal in urging the ratification of the SALT II agreements and is suspicious of possible U.S. backtracking. It has been especially critical of NATO and the neutron bomb. In the federal elections, the CPC platform included a promise to cut the Canadian arms budget by 50 percent and to withdraw from NATO and U.S.-Canadian defense arrangements. The CPC regards the new Islamic government in Iran as a progressive development that will establish friendly relations with the Soviet Union and counter U.S. influence in the Persian Gulf. It believes that the pace of events in Iran is being set by industrial and office workers and by students and intellectuals among the urban youth. (Ibid., no. 2.)

Communist Party of Canada (Marxist-Leninist). The CPC-ML has an estimated membership of between 500 and 2,000. Its national headquarters is in Montreal. It also has a headquarters in Toronto and maintains contact points in 23 other Canadian cities. In May it held a week-long consultative conference in Toronto, to which the Albanian Party of Labor sent a delegation. The Albanian delegation also attended a rally in Montreal to conclude the conference and reported that 1,500 were in attendance (Albanian Telegraphic Agency, 29 May; *FBIS*, 11 June). The CPC-ML's leader continues to be Hardial Bains. The party was particularly active in the federal elections, fielding 139 candidates under the banner of the Marxist-Leninist Party of Canada to distinguish it from the CPC. In this respect it was more prominent than the CPC (which fielded 69 candidates), and its total of 14,386 votes outpolled the CPC, although no single candidate received more than 200 votes. Its election campaign was conducted under the slogan "Make the Rich Pay!" and its program, more militant than that of the CPC, included the abolition of Parliament and the establishment of a centralist workers' and small farmers' government. It would also grant self-determination to Quebec and "expropriate monopoly capital and imperialist property without any compensation." In international affairs, the party continues its orientation towards Albania, condemning "U.S. imperialism" and both Soviet and Chinese "social-imperialism." In August a delegation led by Bains visited Albania.

Workers Communist Party (Marxist-Leninist) of Canada. The WCP was founded at a congress held in Quebec on 1–2 September. Simultaneously the Canadian Communist League (CCL), a preparty formation that had worked for four years to launch a new party, was dissolved. At its first meeting, the WCP Central Committee elected Roger Rashi chairman and Ian Anderson vice-chairman (New China News Agency [NCNA], 14 September). The WCP has contact points in thirteen cities across Canada and distributes publications through Norman Bethune bookstores in Montreal, Toronto, and Vancouver. It is currently conducting a fund-raising campaign and claims to have attained more than three-quarters of its stated goal of Canadian $100,000. Its domestic orientation emphasizes combining a working class movement with oppressed nationalities in Canada, and it is active in recruiting native Black and French-speaking Canadians (*Forge*, 16 November). Its international position is strongly allied with China. The WCP upholds the three-worlds theory, condemns Soviet influence in Vietnam, and strongly supports the beleaguered Pol Pot forces in Kampuchea as an obstacle to Soviet imperialism in Southeast Asia. At the end of December 1978, Roger Rashi led a delegation of the CCL to Phnom Penh (NCNA, 31 December 1978). The Alive Production Collective, located in Guelph, Ontario, which is also strongly pro-Chinese, has so far held back from fully endorsing the WCP. This group disagrees with the WPC's analysis of Canada, but supports its international position (*Alive*, 22 September).

Marxist-Leninist Organization of Canada en Lutte!/in Struggle! The MLOC adopted its current name and a new constitution at its Third Congress in September 1978. It is led by its secretary general, Charles Gagnon, and has organized readers' circles and other activities in 23 Canadian cities and towns, mostly in Quebec. It also runs bookstores in Montreal, Quebec City, Toronto, and Vancouver. In the latter half of 1979, it organized meetings across Canada to celebrate its sixth anniversary on 8 December and to discuss the Quebec issue, which it regards as the heart of Canadian political life. Its position is to unify the Canadian proletariat on the basis of "absolute equality of languages and nations." It recently achieved some national notoriety when it was attacked by Dennis McDermott, the moderate president of the CLC, for its militant activities among the Canadian Union of Public Employees, which represents 250,000 workers (*Toronto Globe and Mail*, 5 November). It is currently engaged in a campaign to influence workers to "dump McDermott" (*In Struggle*, 13 November). Its international position is not tied to any foreign communist party, but the party has been critical of both Chinese and Soviet positions and is particularly militant against the United States.

Revolutionary Workers League. The RWL is a Trotskyist party and belongs to the Fourth International. Its Central Committee includes Bret Smiley, and its Political Committee consists of Steve Penner, Michel Prairie, John Steele, and Art Young. The RWL held a convention in April and voted to continue a campaign, initiated by its Central Committee in January, to enlist its members in unions, particularly in industry, transport, and communications. It claims that 28 percent of its members have industrial jobs. The RWL believes that class polarization is increasing in Canada, and its present strategy is to radicalize the rank and file of the trade union movement against present union leaders and the leadership of the NDP, thereby "building our Trotskyist tendency in the unions and the NDP and laying the basis for the mass class-struggle of the future" (*Socialist Voice*, 10 September). It has criticized the CPC for class collaboration. The RWL supports Quebec's national rights and emphasizes the importance of "binational" campaigns in the Canadian labor movement. It also regards ties with U.S. unions as important and is working to build international fractions in these unions in collaboration with the Socialist Workers Party of the United States.

Publications. The CPC publishes a theoretical journal, *Communist Viewpoint*, six times a year and two weekly newspapers, the *Canadian Tribune* (Toronto) and the *Pacific Tribune* (Vancouver). Its youth organization publishes *New Horizons* ten times a year. The CPC-ML publishes a daily newspaper, the *People's Canada Daily News*, and also a French edition, *Le Quotidien du Canada populaire*.

The WCP produces a weekly newspaper, *The Forge*, in French and English editions. The MLOC publishes a weekly bilingual newspaper, *En Lutte!/In Struggle!* The fortnightly *Socialist Voice* serves as an organ of the RWL. The Alive Production Collective publishes a weekly, *Alive Magazine*, which resumed in 1977 after a six-month interruption due to internal factional struggles. The Bolshevik Union produces *Lines of Demarcation* in English and French six times a year. The North American editions of the Prague-based *World Marxist Review* and its companion publication, the fortnightly *Information Bulletin*, are published in Toronto.

University of Waterloo   David Davies

Chile

The Communist Party of Chile (Partido Comunista de Chile; PCCh) was first established as the Socialist Workers' Party in 1912. The name PCCh was adopted in January 1922 following the party's decision in 1921 to join the Communist International. The party was illegal between 1948 and 1958. A Maoist party, the Revolutionary Communist Party of Chile (Partido Comunista Revolucionario de Chile; PCRCh), was founded in May 1966, primarily by a group of communists expelled from the PCCh in 1963. The Movement of the Revolutionary Left (Movimiento de Izquierda Revolucionaria; MIR) brought together several leftist groups in 1965 and soon developed an affinity for the form of armed revolutionary struggle advocated during the mid- and late-1960s by Che Guevara and Fidel Castro. All these groups have been illegal since the military coup of September 1973.

The PCCh claimed 200,000 members in early 1973. Many party leaders have been killed, imprisoned, or forced into exile since September 1973, but most of the present party members in Chile are free, although banned from political activities. The PCCh acknowledges that its membership has decreased since the coup, but the PCRCh maintains that its membership, estimated at several hundred in 1973, has increased. The MIR, which probably had some 10,000 active members in 1973, has been greatly reduced, and most of its top pre-coup leaders are dead, in jail, or abroad. Some communists and other leftists were reportedly returning openly to Chile in 1979 (*WP*, 19 May).

Popular Unity Movement. Since 1969 most Chilean Marxists have been members of the Popular Unity (Unidad Popular; UP), an alliance of leftist parties that enabled Salvador Allende to win a narrow plurality in the September 1970 presidential elections. During 1979 the most important UP members—all of them illegal—were the PCCh, the Socialist Party (PSCh), the Radical Party (PR), and several leftist Christian splinter groups, essentially the composition of the original 1969 alliance.

During the Allende period, the unity of the UP was weakened by internal dissension over the best strategy and tactics of revolution and by disputes with non-UP groups that adopted a more militant revolutionary line, particularly the MIR. Since the coup, the PCCh has led the drive to build a broader and more secure leftist front, ranging from the Christian Democrats (PDC) in the center of the political spectrum to the MIR and other organizations on what the communists have long considered the political "ultra-left."

During 1979 UP members sought to strengthen the alliance, particularly through closer cooperation with the PDC. To this end, they held meetings abroad, organized and attended international Chile "solidarity" conferences, and issued statements on the development of "antifascist unity." The move toward cooperation with the PDC made some progress, and Socialist Clodomiro Almeyda, head of the UP movement abroad, and others even expressed a willingness to work with former Chilean president and PDC leader Eduardo Frei, long anathematized by the Marxist left. At the same time, the PSCh split on this and other issues, the Almeyda wing remaining in the UP mainstream, while the Socialists following longtime party General Secretary Carlos Altamirano (removed from that position at the PSCh plenum in May) refused to authorize a reconciliation with Frei. (*Hoy*, Santiago, 13 and 20 June; Agence France Presse, 24 May.) "We are certain that the UP and the PCD will be able to achieve a basic consensus," Almeyda said, one "that will offer Chileans a viable and stable political and governmental formula" (*Hoy*, 13 June).

Leadership and Organization. The PCCh's general secretary, Luis Corvalán, has been in exile since December 1976 when he was released from a Chilean prison in exchange for the freedom of a Soviet political prisoner. Political Commission members and alternate members who are active in exile include Orlando Millas, Rodrigo Rojas, Volodia Teitelboim, José Cademártori, Jorge Insunza, Americo Zorrilla, Manuel Cantero, and Gladys Marín, who is also general secretary of the Communist Youth (Juventud Comunista de Chile; JCCh). The JCCh, a powerful force in university and secondary school politics before the overthrow of Allende, is outlawed, although JCCh members won positions in the May elections of student delegates at the University of Chile in Santiago. The once-powerful communist-dominated Single Center of Chilean Workers (CUT) has been illegal since 1973 but operates underground through unions that the government permits to exist. Both the JCCh and the CUT are active abroad, the latter in particular getting strong support from such international labor organizations as the World Federation of Trade Unions.

The PCCh carried out numerous covert actions during 1979; it participated in May Day rallies and other antigovernment activities among workers, students, and members of the armed forces. In a document released at the end of the year, the party claimed to be the largest, best organized, most active, and most united party operating in Chile, the "main force in the development of the struggle of the popular masses" (*Pravda*, 23 September).

Positions on Domestic Developments and Responsibilities. The party's three main goals, according to a document signed by Corvalán, are unity of action to end the dictatorship, a search for common ways to form a new constitutional system, and the conclusion of an agreement to form a government that would include representatives of the UP and the PDC. The document, circulated underground in Chile, calls for a new people's democratic system that will ensure changes directed toward achieving social progress. The objective conditions for this are to be created by a broad antifascist movement. (Ibid.) An earlier PCCh document stated: "We are convinced that mutual understanding between the UP and Christian Democracy and their striving for common goals is the decisive factor in working out a democratic alternative . . . We are convinced that it is possible and necessary to reach a minimum of accord which would involve the broadest democratic forces and put an end to the dictatorship . . . The opposition should propose a clear option to the Chilean people, presupposing not only the creation of a provisional government, but a real opportunity for the emergence of a stable and firm regime, enjoying universal support." (*IB*, no. 3.) In early September the Chilean government accused the communists of trying to involve the PDC in a subversive plan to disturb public order through street demonstrations and hunger strikes, a charge the PDC said was unfounded.

The minimal common program for the opposition forces, presented many times during the year in slightly varying forms, included such points as a guarantee of full respect for human rights and democratic freedoms; eradication of "fascism"; clarification of the fate of "missing patriots"; punishment of perpetrators of crimes; the return of exiles; a wage increase; adoption of measures against unemployment, inflation, and corruption; housing, education, and health programs; expropriation of monopolies; a new land reform; convocation of a legislative assembly that would draft a new constitution; and broad participation by workers and all people in the organs of public administration and management of enterprises (*Rudé právo*, Prague, 19 May).

The PCCh charges that the present Chilean government "rejects every thought which does not unconditionally coincide with its ideas," that Chilean "fascism practices violence and crime with blind fanaticism, above all against Marxism" (*Political Affairs*, March). The military government's draft constitution aims at "legalizing the fascist, autocratic system" and "would provide broad guarantees for the monopoly circles of the big bourgeoisie while at the same time excluding from public life all those who profess leftist convictions" (*IB*, no. 3). "The fascist dictatorship keeps itself in power with the help of terror and the support of North American imperialism, the financial oligarchy, and military circles," says a manifesto allegedly circulated in Chile in May (*Rudé právo*, 19 May).

The PCCh planned a major effort to work with members of the armed forces to "put an end to fascism, to work out and introduce in practice a new state system envisaging the transformation of the armed forces, bearing in mind all that they can do tomorrow to strengthen a correctly understood national security and to rehabilitate the country." Therefore, says a PCCh statement, "we establish contacts with the officers, NCOs and men. Junta propaganda seeks to depict us as proponents of revenge and liquidation of the armed forces. The truth is different. We see the armed forces as a factor of primary importance in defending sovereignty and genuine national security. We know that the overwhelming majority of officers, NCOs and men are affected by the sharp crisis . . . We know they have no desire to serve some caste or the money moguls . . . that they do not want to see their country artificially split into camps, in which the working people live on the brink of poverty." And the document concludes: "It is essential that a movement should emerge in the armed forces which would make its contribution to overthrowing Pinochet and the dictatorship." (*IB*, no. 3.)

International Positions. The PCCh adopted international positions akin to those of the Soviet Union, arguing that "recent revolutions in other continents of the so-called Third World, like the Ethiopian and the Afghani, prove that the locomotive of history has not halted its progress" (*Political Affairs*, March). The party praised the Soviet Union and its allies for their role in "the struggle against imperialism and all forms of oppression" (*Pravda*, 23 September) and attacked the "adventurist and expansionist policy of the Chinese leaders," who have "aligned themselves with imperialism and encouraged the activities of the most openly reactionary forces" (*Avante*, Lisbon, 1 March). Cademártori said the threat of war between Argentina and Chile was encouraged by "chauvinistic cliques, the international corporations that covet the resources of the region, and the arms traffickers" (*Tribuna Popular*, Caracas, 16 February). Corvalán stated in a letter to the Chilean people that the fall of Somoza in Nicaragua "will bring closer the victory of our own people," and while visiting Mongolia in October, he added that now the other "tyrannical regimes nurtured by American imperialism will without fail also fall" (*Ercilla*, Santiago, 11 July; *Montsame*, Ulan Bator, 4 October).

The Revolutionary Communist Party of Chile. The PCRCh was led by David Benquis until his death last year of natural causes. The party now finds its chief spokesman in Secretariat member Jorge Palacios. Under Palacios's leadership, the group has become increasingly active, both domestically (where its role in strikes, demonstrations, and agitation is still limited) and especially abroad. Palacios toured the United States in late 1979, speaking on college campuses, sometimes under the joint sponsorship of university departments.

Domestic and International Positions. On its objectives, the PCRCh proclaims: "To achieve the unity of all antifascist forces in a broad mass movement of national scope and national importance organized in a single great front is a task that the proletariat must accomplish in order to advance to the conquest of power." The party believes that progress is being made in this endeavor despite temporary setbacks: "The people's antifascist forces follow a rising curve and grow stronger, while the antipopular fascist forces follow a downward curve and grow weaker." (*A.N.Ch.A.,* May.) But the unity and united front sought by the PCRCh are not those cultivated by the "false" communist party, whose "long-term plan is to implant in Chile a pseudo-socialism, a regime of state capitalism, such as exists in the Soviet Union." (*Causa M-L*, September-November.) The PCRCh repeatedly warns that the policies of the PCCh and the mainline UP will lead Chile to the same impasse confronted in 1973. Groups at present issuing statements with the PCRCh include splinters from the PSCh, the PR, and the PDC—the Seccional Suecia del PSCh(CNR), the Organización del Tercer Congreso de la Juventud Radical Revolucionaria de Chile, and the Dirección Política Frente Exterior del MAPU. (Ibid., January-March, September-November.) At midyear the party condemned the government's "labor plan" as one serving the interests of the monopolies, reactionaries, and proimperialists (*El Pueblo,* July).

In its international policy, the PCRCh adopts positions in accord with Maoist principles. In particular it supports the Revolutionary Communist Party, USA, and other like-minded groups, and condemns the Soviet Union as well as the People's Republic of China. Chinese leader Deng Xiaoping, according to the PCRCh, is the "ideologue and representative of the revisionist clique in China" (Statement of International Commission, dated 25 September, passed out at Palacios's appearances in the United States). Its detailed analysis of the international situation, formulated in September 1978 with Maoist groups from Colombia, Ecuador, and Venezuela, was published in *Causa M-L* (January-March).

Movement of the Revolutionary Left. The MIR has been particularly hard hit by government security forces since September 1973, one exiled leader estimating that some 5,000 members were killed through mid-1978 (*Caretas*, Lima, 18 September 1978). Throughout 1979 the government continued to report clashes with and arrests of party members. Prominent MIR leaders include Víctor Toro and Andrés Pascal Allende, the latter said to have returned to Chile early in the year after several years abroad. Chilean security officials charged in August that Pascal was organizing a meeting of the Revolutionary Coordinating Committee, an organization of guerrilla leaders from Chile, Argentina, Bolivia, and Uruguay that was formed in 1974.

Publications. The illegal Marxist and Marxist-Leninist parties and organizations of Chile circulate irregular clandestine papers and leaflets domestically and publish limited circulation but legal newspapers abroad. These include *Unidad Antifascista* and *Principios* (PCCh), *Liberación* (JCCh), *El Rebelde* and *Chilean Resistance Courier* (MIR), *La Chispa* (PSCh), *Frente Antifascista* (UP), *El Pueblo* and *Causa M-L* (PCRCh), and three publications of the ultra-leftist factions of the PDC, *Resistencia Democrática, Venceremos,* and *Pueblo Cristiano.* Other statements are carried by *Chile Newsletter* and *Agencia Noticiosa Chilena Antifascista (A.N.Ch.A.).* Pro-Soviet statements circulate most widely in the regular journals of individual pro-Soviet communist parties around the world, as well as in the Prague-based *World Marxist Review* and its *Information Bulletin.*

Hoover Institution   William E. Ratliff

Colombia

The communist movement in Colombia has undergone various transformations in both name and organization since the party's initial formation in December 1926. The Communist Party of Colombia (Partido Comunista de Colombia: PCC) was publicly proclaimed on 17 July 1930. In July 1965 a schism within the PCC between pro-Soviet and pro-Chinese factions resulted in the latter becoming the Communist Party of Colombia, Marxist-Leninist (PCC-ML). Only the PCC has legal status. It has been allowed to participate in elections under its own banners since 1972.

The PCC took part in the 26 February 1978 general elections as a member of the leftist coalition National Opposition Union–National Popular Alliance–Independent Liberal Movement (UNO-ANAPO-MIL). The coalition won one seat in the 112-member Senate and two seats in the 199-member Lower Chamber. At the state assembly level, the UNO maintained the same number of deputies (twelve) as in the 1976 elections. The PCC elected 173 municipal councilmen in 1976 but lost at least 23 seats in 1978. The presidential candidate endorsed by the PCC in the 4 June 1978 elections, ex-ANAPO congressman Julio César Pernía, received less than 2 percent of the popular vote, while the total vote for all leftist candidates was less than 4 percent.

According to U.S. intelligence estimates, the PCC has 12,000 members. Although the party contends that its ranks have increased in recent years, the 1978 elections provide compelling evidence that the party's growth has been less than its leaders had hoped, especially in the large cities. The PCC continues to exercise only marginal influence in national affairs. The population of Colombia is 26.1 million (1979 estimate).

Guerrilla Warfare. Although not a serious threat to the government, guerrilla warfare has been a feature of Colombian life since the late 1940s; the current wave began in 1964. The four main guerrilla organizations are the Revolutionary Armed Forces of Colombia (FARC), long controlled by the PCC; the pro-Chinese People's Liberation Army (EPL), which is the guerrilla arm of the PCC-ML; the Castroite National Liberation Army (ELN); and the M-19, a predominantly urban guerrilla organization that claims to be the armed hand of ANAPO. A fifth group, the Movement for Workers' Self-defense (MAO), first surfaced in September 1978 when it claimed credit for the assassination of former Government Minister Rafael Pardo Buelvas. Specializing in urban kidnappings and assassinations, the MAO is considered by Colombian authorities to be Trotskyist in orientation and linked to the Fourth International.

Serious ideological and tactical differences continued to divide Colombia's guerrilla movements in 1979 despite periodic appeals for unity. In a communiqué released on 3 April, the ELN and the M-19 announced their decision to unite for the purpose of "gaining power for the people." The message voiced strong criticisms of the FARC, accusing it of splitting the masses of other revolutionary movements by "intimidation through the sacrifice of hundreds of peasants" (*Alternativa*, 9 April). However, in a bulletin sent to communications media on 26 April, the ELN urged other insurgent groups to unite "in a common struggle to reach the final objective of attaining power through revolution" (*El Tiempo*, 27 April). On 1 June the EPL claimed credit for several bank robberies for the purpose of obtaining funds to unify the guerrilla movements. The M-19, for its part, is believed to act as a coordinator to increase unity among the country's various subversive groups. On 8 May it announced that all Colombian extremist movements had initiated a joint struggle "to enforce respect for human rights in the country" (Agence France Presse, 9 May). According to the Seventh Brigade's commander serving in Villavicencio, by August guerrilla groups had begun responding to efforts aimed at unifying their activities in rural areas: "What the leftist front FIRMES [see below] is trying to do politically by seeking to unite the left, the M-19 is trying to do militarily by seeking to unite the guerrilla movement" (El Siglo, 10 August).

The spectacular theft by the M-19 of over 5,000 arms from the Usaquén military arsenal north of Bogotá on 31 December 1978 prompted security forces to intensify their actions against all subversive groups. The army detained over a thousand people in January in massive nationwide raids. The action produced widespread charges of violations of human rights and concern over the military's role in Colombia's democracy. Alternativa (5 February) wrote that the military authorities "are concerned not just with recovering weapons and destroying the underground movement that stole them, but with making the most of the operation to settle scores with all kinds of left-wing groups." On 29 January Government Minister Germán Zea Hernández announced that the country had been saved from the "terrorism that recently has been the scourge of Uruguay and Argentina" (El Tiempo, 30 January). Military spokesmen claimed that the armed forces had succeeded in dismembering the M-19, "one of the most dangerous and powerful subversive groups that ever existed in the country" (El Espectador, 5 February). On 7 April a spokesman for the Military Institutes Brigade (BIM) announced that the country's largest military operation against subversion had resulted in the arrest of 946 persons allegedly linked with the M-19, the FARC, or the MAO. Of the 630 suspected members of the M-19 arrested between 2 January and 7 April, all but 93 had been released (La República, 8 April). Despite the military's apparent success, by August officials were once again expressing concern over the increase in guerrilla activity and issuing appeals to the public, particularly the peasantry, to cooperate in investigations to eradicate subversion. On 19 August BIM commander Gen. Miguel Vega Uribe admitted that leftist guerrilla groups "have been shaken, but they are not through" (El Siglo, 20 August). On 5 October President Julio César Turbay Ayala conceded that although the government had "smashed subversion," it had not managed to eliminate it by implementing severe security measures. He said that the repression of subversion would continue "unabated" and that the continued acts of violence carried out by guerrilla groups were "an unmistakable demonstration that the struggle for legal order must continue" (Agence France Presse [AFP], 5 October).

Leadership and Organization. The PCC is headed by its 12-member Executive Committee and 54-member Central Committee. The highest party authority is the Congress, convened by the Central Committee at four-year intervals. The PCC held its Twelfth Congress on 5–9 December 1975. Gilberto Vieira is general secretary of the PCC. The party operates several types of indoctrinational schools at the district and national levels for the education of cadres. It also maintains the Center of Social Studies, with branches in several cities. Apart from research, these facilities circulate Marxist-Leninist classics and run courses on social subjects. (WMR, June.)

A major source of the PCC's influence lies in its control of the Trade Union Confederation of Workers of Colombia (CSTC), which claims a membership of 300,000. The CSTC was granted legal status by the Colombian government in August 1974 and is a member of the World Federation of Trade Unions. The president of the CSTC is Pástor Pérez. The CSTC has succeeded in recent years in achieving an unprecedented degree of cooperation among Colombia's four major labor centrals and the creation of a National Labor Council (CNS; see YICA, 1979, p. 328). However, the Turbay Ayala administration has cultivated the leaders of the more moderate Union of Workers of Colombia (UTC) and the Confederation of Workers of Colombia (CTC) in an effort to divide the trade union movement. In April the national plenum of the UTC harshly criticized the attitude of the communist labor unions and warned the country that "the left has not learned to uphold union pacts." A representative of the metalworkers claimed that "the Marxist leaders cannot teach us trade unionism, nor shall we allow them to compromise us in the eyes of the nation." In an obvious reference to the CSTC a delegate from El Valle stated that the "democratic unions have some associates who are not playing fair with us." (*El Tiempo*, 21 April.) President Turbay Ayala met with officials from the UTC and CTC and indicated a "conciliatory" attitude toward their economic demands (*Intercontinental Press*, 21 May). By recognizing the "legitimacy" of these federations, the government is attempting to isolate the CSTC and prevent the formation of a single, united labor federation. The PCC tries to influence peasants through the National Federation of Agrarian Syndicates, which functions as a part of the CSTC.

The PCC's youth organization, the Communist Youth of Colombia (JUCO), has an estimated membership of 2,000. The JUCO has its own National Directorate, Executive Committee, and Central Committee. The general secretary is Jaime Caycedo. As a militant adjunct of the PCC, the JUCO plays an active role in promoting party policy among university and secondary school students. As part of military actions aimed at destroying the urban networks of various groups suspected of seditious activities, the "operations unit" of the BIM raided JUCO headquarters in Bogotá on 28 January. The PCC denounced the violation of JUCO archives and announced that it would sue those responsible for the raid for allegedly removing 10,000 pesos of the organization's funds (*El Espectador*, 29 January). Party leaders subsequently released a communiqué condemning the raids carried out by the military and alerting the country to the possibility that a "fascist-type dictatorship" may be established (*Voz Proletaria*, 1 February).

The PCC has controlled the peasant guerrilla FARC since 1966. Party leaders have maintained an ambivalent attitude in recent years toward the use of armed struggle in furthering the revolutionary process. Although the political resolution adopted at the Twelfth Congress in 1975 affirmed that the rural guerrilla movement has "always been a notable factor in the general popular struggle," the general position of the party is that armed struggle cannot yet be the chief means of resistance. The FARC's supreme commander, Mario Marulanda Vélez, formerly served as a member of the PCC's Central Committee. According to Gilberto Vieira, the FARC is not the armed branch of the PCC but "of the Colombian peasants against their oppressors, the big landowners, and against military men who place themselves in the service of the big landowners or who want to become landowners" (ibid., 27 September).

According to intelligence estimates, in 1975 the FARC had fewer than 300 men operating in five fronts with units of 40 to 90 men. Their areas of influence were centered in municipalities in the departments of Huila, Caquetá, Tolima, Cauca, Boyacá, Santander, and Antioquia. By the end of 1979, the FARC had expanded its areas of influence to include portions of El Valle, Meta, Cundinamarca, and the territory of Arauca (*El Tiempo*, 25 May). Estimates of the FARC's current membership range from 700 to 1,000 armed men, with approximately a third of them scattered throughout the Magdalena basin. Its general headquarters is located somewhere in the border zone between Caquetá and Huila. Each FARC unit is in essence a communist cell. The minimal guerrilla unit consists of twelve men. The leadership mechanisms and general policy of the FARC are determined by the PCC's bylaws and political resolutions emitted at various congresses and plenums and presumably transmitted to the various fronts through Marulanda's directives.

The FARC was the most active of Colombia's guerrilla movements in 1979. Its dominance in rural areas has reduced the effectiveness of the ELN and forced the EPL to limit its operations primarily to urban areas. In recent years FARC units have systematically killed peasants for collaborating with military forces. Although there are no precise statistics for this type of FARC activity, the Defense Ministry asserted in March that the FARC killed 35 peasants in 1977 and 60 in 1978 (*El Siglo*, 17

March). A spokesman for the Colombian army had previously stated that the FARC's fourth front killed 69 peasants in 1978 in the middle Magdalena region alone (*El Tiempo*, 6 December 1978). During the first five months of 1979, over 50 peasants were reportedly "executed" either as informants or for refusing to collaborate with the guerrillas (ibid., 25 May). During the year FARC units carried out major attacks against more than a dozen towns, seizing money, arms, and supplies and distributing propaganda. In September intelligence services reported that 30 FARC guerrillas had returned secretly to Colombia after taking a four-month course on weapons and military tactics in specialized camps in the Soviet Union and Czechoslovakia (*El Siglo*, 21 September). In response to the increase in guerrilla activity, the military launched a major counterguerrilla operation in the Uraba region between Antioquia and Córdoba departments and also in Santander. On 24 October troops reportedly captured 25 members of a FARC unit that had earlier ambushed an army convoy near Puerto Berrío (ibid., 24 October). On 31 October General Gonzalo Forero announced "a struggle without truce against the guerrillas." At a meeting of American army commanders held to discuss subversion in Latin America, the general said that "communism has advanced not only in Colombia but in the rest of the Latin American countries as well" (AFP, 31 October). Further FARC operations in mid-November included attacks on two towns in Tolima, suggesting the continued intensification of guerrilla warfare.

Domestic Attitudes and Activities. In analyzing the 1978 congressional election returns in which the combined forces of the left received approximately 4 percent of the vote, the PCC's Central Committee reaffirmed the "correctness" of pursuing a policy of broad popular unity. According to this interpretation, the 4 June presidential election established the popular coalition consisting of the PCC-ANAPO-MIL as "the country's third political force" and "the nucleus of a broad front vital to Colombia." It concluded that the main lesson to be drawn from the June election was that "we must continue our policy of popular unity and of alliances now, not waiting until 1980 or 1982 to resume joint leadership throughout the country" (*Voz Proletaria*, 22 June 1978). Despite the party's official position, the initiative for creating a single opposition front appears to have been seized by the FIRMES movement, which grew out of a pre-election campaign organized by the weekly *Alternativa* to channel discontent into a unified left-wing party. Much of the intellectual inspiration behind the movement is provided by the Colombian writer Gabriel García Márquez. In October spokesmen for the PCC, ANAPO-UNO, the MIR, FIRMES, and the pro-Chinese Independent Revolutionary Workers' Movement (MOIR) agreed to lay the groundwork for a joint electoral campaign for the 1980 assembly and municipal elections and later to present a democratic opposition front. The representatives agreed that FIRMES would draft a joint declaration to be submitted at the group's first "convention" (Cadena Radial Super, Bogotá, 31 October). On 11 November spokesmen for the organizing nucleus of the front announced that "an understanding has now been achieved that will definitely lead to the birth of a true and strong opposition to confront Colombia's traditional parties" (AFP, 11 November). It remains to be seen if the PCC will be able to make the ideological accommodation necessary to participate in such a heterogeneous group. In the past, Vieira has repeatedly affirmed that the PCC would seek no coalition with any group that opposed Cuba or the CSTC, precisely the two points that the party has made use of in its struggle with the MOIR to achieve control of the left.

The PCC expressed concern early in 1979 over the Turbay Ayala government's escalation of "brutal reprisals against the working people." It condemned the security statute issued on 6 September 1978, which provides for military jurisdiction over activities connected with terrorism and subversion. The party termed the statute "a new offensive against the people's rights, giving the ruling reactionaries a free hand to strangle the forces of the left." The party called for support for new initiatives in 1979, including a national forum against reprisals, a signature drive against the "security statutes," solidarity with political and trade union prisoners, struggle against "military-penal justice," the liquidation of "security" organizations, and support for the CSTC (*Voz Proletaria*, 18 January). In March the

Executive Committee issued a statement denouncing "the wave of repressions unleashed in the country by the reactionary military." The document charged the government with the arrest and torture of many citizens in Bogotá, Medellín, and other cities, including a member of the editorial board of *Voz Proletaria* and several trade union leaders belonging to the CSTC (Ibid., 22 March). On 27 October Alvaro Vásquez, a member of the party's Executive Committee, was released after spending seven months in prison awaiting trial on a charge of supporting and guiding guerrilla movements (EFE, Madrid, 27 October).

Writing in the *World Marxist Review* (April), Ramón Tovar Andrade, PCC alternate member to the Central Committee, affirmed the party's "unfailing loyalty" to Marxism-Leninism. According to Tovar, the party evolves its strategy and tactics according to the principles asserted by the October Revolution, emphasizing working-class hegemony in the socialist revolution, the dictatorship of the proletariat, and proletarian internationalism. He added that the party recognizes the experience of the Communist Party of the Soviet Union (CPSU) as an ideological source but also takes "maximum account of the national characteristics and revolutionary and democratic traditions of the Colombian people." This has enabled the PCC to work out its own tactics that combine diverse forms of mass struggle, ranging from electoral campaigns to guerrilla warfare. Tovar indicated that the latter is now entering a new stage, "that of a qualitative upswing as part of our struggle for power." Tovar's remarks are consistent with the intensification of the FARC's actions during 1979.

According to Vieira, recent years have seen Colombia's working class gradually winning vanguard positions in the popular movement to achieve power. The main slogan of the PCC in the labor movement is "unity of action." The alternative proposed by the "ultra-leftists" is "ideological unity" on the basis of their sectarian Maoist or Trotskyist concepts. Vieira believes that proletarian solidarity has increased with the formation of the CNS. He recognizes, however, that there is presently no consensus on political problems in the CNS that will support the unified program of political action championed by the CSTC. (*WMR*, May.)

International Views and Positions. The PCC faithfully follows the Soviet line in its international positions. American "imperialism" is the chief enemy of the Colombian people (*Voz Proletaria*, 24 August 1978). The struggle against imperialism requires exposing the role of Maoism, which, according to Vieira, is "a reactionary, chauvinist ideology that is counterposed to Marxism-Leninism and against world peace" (ibid., 8 March). After Deng Xiaoping's visit to the United States, the PCC accused China's leaders of attempting to create a Washington-Beijing-Tokyo axis directed against the Soviet Union and other socialist countries, while simultaneously urging the imperialists to "punish Vietnam and Cuba" for their consistent anti-imperialist stand (*IB*, no. 9). Throughout 1979 the PCC continued its unwavering support for the principles of internationalism as interpreted by the Soviet Union and as represented in the western hemisphere by Cuba.

Party Contacts. A delegation of the PCC headed by Gilberto Vieira visited Cuba in February. Vieira visited Panama in March. Members of the Executive Committee headed by Hernando Hurtado visited Romania and other Eastern European countries in October.

Publications. The PCC publishes a weekly newspaper, *Voz Proletaria* (reported circulation 40,000), a theoretical journal, *Documentos Políticos* (5,000), and the Colombian edition of *World Marxist Review* (7,500). The FARC publishes a clandestine bulletin, *Resistencia*.

The Maoists. The PCC-ML is firmly pro-Chinese. Its present leadership hierarchy is not clearly known, although Arturo Acero was cited by the Chinese press in September 1977 as the political secretary of a group referred to as the Marxist-Leninist League of Colombia. The PCC-ML has never recovered from the setback it received in July 1975 when its general secretary, Pedro León Arboleda, was killed by police in Cali. The PCC-ML has an estimated membership of one thousand. Unlike the PCC, it has not attempted to obtain legal status. Its impact in terms of national political life is insignificant. Its official news organ is *Revolución*. The Marxist-Leninist League of Colombia has a monthly publication, *Nueva Democracia*. Statements of the PCC-ML are sometimes found in Chinese publications and those of pro-Chinese parties in Europe and Latin America.

The basic form of struggle adopted and approved by the PCC-ML is rural guerrilla warfare, peasant indoctrination, and the creation of a popular liberation army that will eventually achieve revolutionary victory. The PCC-ML's guerrilla arm, the EPL, was the first pro-Chinese group to attempt to stage a revolutionary "people's war" in Latin America. The EPL has limited its operations primarily to urban areas since 1975, although several rural attacks and kidnappings were attributed to the group in 1979.

In response to an appeal by the government in February for all guerrilla groups to cease fighting, the PCC-ML and the EPL issued a communiqué affirming their decision to "continue fighting until the final defeat of imperialism, social-imperialism, and the oligarchy and all its lackeys." Despite the EPL's relative weakness, the statement proclaimed that "we are carrying out a revolutionary war against a system of economic exploitation and political oppression . . . which can end only with the destruction of that brutal and bloodthirsty system" (AFP, 21 February). The EPL claimed responsibility for a series of actions carried out in several cities in March, including the occupation of radio stations in Pereira and Armenia. On 12 April police sources reported the arrest of more than twenty guerrillas belonging to the "Pedro León Arboleda" urban command attached to the EPL (*El Tiempo*, 13 April). On 1 May an urban command claimed credit for bombing the residence of U.S. marines assigned to the American embassy. In a communiqué sent to news media in Bogotá on 1 June, the EPL claimed responsibility for the February attack on the town of Acevedo in Huila. Although the movement obtained money, arms, and supplies, the leader of its "Ernesto Che Guevara" front was killed in the attack (*El Espectador*, 2 June). Military circles reported on 14 June that sixteen members of an EPL urban command had been arrested in Bogotá (*Latin America Political Report*, 22 June). The EPL's leadership was further weakened in 1979. In April the army arrested Jorge García Sánchez, regarded as the founder of the "Pedro León Arboleda" command. In September Rafael Vergara Navarro, considered by Colombian intelligence sources to be one of the EPL's principal leaders, sought asylum in the Mexican embassy. The EPL has rejected on ideological grounds any attempt in recent years at unified guerrilla action. It is perhaps a sign of the movement's growing weakness that in June it announced its intention to unite with the country's other rebel groups (*El Tiempo*, 2 June).

The MOIR, established in 1971, aspires to become the first mass-based Maoist party in Latin America, with leadership and organization independent from those of the PCC-ML. Its general secretary is Francisco Mosquera. The MOIR did poorly in the 1978 elections and is unlikely to strengthen its political position except as a member of the opposition front currently being organized.

The M-19. The M-19 first appeared in January 1974 as the self-proclaimed armed branch of the opposition wing of ANAPO. It takes its name from the contested presidential election of 19 April 1970, although ANAPO leaders have disavowed any connection with the movement. Until 1976 the group's only noteworthy action was the theft of Bolívar's sword from the Liberator's estate in Bogotá. However, on 18 February 1976 the M-19 kidnapped and subsequently killed José Raquel Mercado, president of the CTC (see *YICA*, 1977, p. 424). Since then the M-19 has been actively involved in Colombia's urban guerrilla movement, pursuing "a popular revolution of national liberation aimed toward socialism." Before the M-19's spectacular theft of weapons on 31 December 1978, little had been known about the movement's size, leadership, or organization. As late as November 1978, the secretary general of the presidency gave assurances that the M-19 had "never existed" and was only "a ghost organization" whose symbol was being used by common criminals to disguise their illegal activities (Radio Cadena Nacional, 15 November 1978). After December, army circles stressed that the M-19 had stopped being "a completely phantom movement." Evidence gathered in January clearly established the fact that the M-19 is now considered "an extremely dangerous organization" whose activities include kidnapping, robbery, assault, and murder (El Siglo, 31 January). In a bulletin released to news media in February, the M-19 admitted that the army had dealt it "serious blows" during the government's massive raids in January. It also admitted to tactical errors in the arms robbery but claimed to still possess enough weapons for its internal needs (La República, 13 February). Ex-ANAPO congressman Carlos Toledo Plata identified himself as a member of the M-19's supreme command, explaining that the time had come to bring an end to the mystery surrounding the organization and provide it with a human dimension (Alternativa, 19 February). On 7 March the French embassy granted asylum to Marco Antonio Velandia, identified by police as one of the main leaders of the M-19 and a participant in the murder of Raquel Mercado (El Tiempo, 8 March). In July the military released its assessment of the leadership hierarchy of the M-19, which it said consisted of twenty officers. On 5 October the army claimed to have captured the movement's second-in-command, Carlos Villamil Franco (Latin America Political Report, 12 October). Intelligence sources subsequently identified former law student Jaime Beteman as the M-19's top leader. According to the report, Beteman was originally a member of the FARC but became disillusioned with that movement's failures (El Siglo, 20 October). On 21 October National Defense Minister Gen. Luis Carlos Camacho Leyva admitted that a member of the M-19 had succeeded in infiltrating the military intelligence service and had been able to obtain "extremely valuable information about army activities against urban guerrillas" (El Tiempo, 22 October). By mid-November some 200 alleged M-19 guerrillas had been brought to Bogotá for trial. Military operations to break up the M-19 and other urban guerrilla groups were carried out with unprecedented intensity during 1979. It cannot be stated at this time how successful they have been.

The National Liberation Army. The ELN was formed in Santander in 1964 under the inspiration of the Cuban revolution. It undertook its first military action in January 1965.

Once recognized as the largest and most militant of the guerrilla forces operating in the country, the ELN has never recovered from the toll exacted on its leadership and urban network in recent years by government forces, including the defection in 1976 of its principal founder and maximum leader, Fabio Vásquez Castaño. In a leaflet sent to news media on 26 April, the ELN admitted that ten of its top leaders have been killed in its fifteen yeares of existence. The movement disclaimed government reports of its elimination and said it would renew the guerrilla struggle after completing new plans of action and reorganization of its leadership. The statement included an appeal for unity among Colombian guerrillas and rejected the government's proposed amnesty (Alternativa, 30 April).

According to another clandestine bulletin distributed in Bucaramanga on 16 May, twenty ELN guerrillas negotiated with the military for their surrender. The bulletin branded the guerrillas as "traitors" and reaffirmed that the ELN would continue its fighting from the mountains in Santander. At a news conference held in Bogotá the same day, President Turbay Ayala confirmed that the government would consider the possibility of decreeing amnesty "as long as it contributes to the pacification of the country" (El Tiempo, 17 May).

In September the ELN claimed to have achieved reunification with the appointment of a priest, Manuel Pérez Martínez, as its top leader. In a bulletin the group indicated that Pérez had assumed leadership of the movement after another of its principal leaders, José Vera, was arrested in Medellín in August (El Siglo, 11 September). By late 1979 the ELN had been reduced to operating in the middle Magdalena region. Military authorities report that the movement has now been practically destroyed.

The capture of Elias Awad in late October, depriving the ELN of one of its few remaining leaders, gives more credibility to the military's assessment than at any point in recent years.

Washington College   Daniel L. Premo

Costa Rica

The Communist Party of Costa Rica (Partido Comunista de Costa Rica) was founded in 1931, under the leadership of Manuel Mora Valverde, who still remains the secretary general. It was accepted as a full member of the Communist International in 1935. In 1943, in conformity with the "Browderite" policy accepted by several Latin American communist parties, the Costa Rican communists changed their name to the Popular Vanguard Party (Partido Vanguardia Popular; PVP). It remains the country's pro-Moscow communist party. The PVP is estimated to have about 3,000 members. The population of Costa Rica is about 2.2 million.

The PVP was illegal between 1948 and 1974, although during much of that period it functioned quite openly, only being banned from running candidates under its own name. Since 1974 it has participated in a coalition with two other far-left parties (see below), under the name of United People's Party (Partido Pueblo Unido; PPU). In the 1978 election, the PPU presidential candidate got 2.7 percent of the total vote, while its congressional nominees received 7 percent, electing 3 members to the 57-member Legislative Assembly.

Other far-left groups include the pro-Cuban Socialist Party (Partido Socialista; PS) and the Revolutionary Movement of the People (Movimiento Revolucionario del Pueblo; MRP), the latter in theory at least an advocate of violent revolution. The PVP, PS, and MRP make up the PPU coalition. There is also an anti-Soviet far-leftist group, the Costa Rican People's Front (Frente Popular Costarricense). International Trotskyism is represented by the Socialist Organization of Workers (Organización Socialista de los Trabajadores; OST), a "sympathizing" group of the United Secretariat of the Fourth International.

Leadership and Organization. In addition to its 70-year-old lifetime Secretary General Manuel Mora Valverde, PVP leaders include Assistant Secretary General Eduardo Mora Valverde (brother of Manuel) and organizational secretary and former national deputy, Arnoldo Ferreto Segura.

The PVP is active in the labor movement through the General Confederation of Costa Rican Workers (Confederacion General de Trabajadores Costarricenses; CGTC), the country's largest central labor organization, which it controls. The communists have long been influential among the banana workers on the Pacific coast. They also have considerable influence among university students, particularly in the National University in Heredia.

Domestic Activities and Views. Three strikes during the year presented serious problems for the national government. The communists were involved in all three. In February a walkout of banana workers near Golfito on the Pacific coast resulted in a visit to the area by the Costa Rican president to urge the strikers to return to work. Two communist deputies, Mario Devandas and Humberto Vargas Carbonel, also went to the strike zone, where they denounced the president's appeal, threatening that violence against the strikers would be met by violence on their part (Radio Reloj, San José, 20 February). The workers finally returned to their jobs after a government offer of mediation.

In March, a strike at the Tempisque sugar mill resulted in a television speech by the minister of labor in which she said that "the promoters of the movement are a group of communist agitators who are not seeking to improve the social and economic conditions of the workers but rather to establish a communist system in our country." Devandas then went to the presidential palace, seeking an interview with the chief executive. He told reporters: "I came to talk with the president because if the labor minister wants to see some bloodletting, she will." He added that his party would not enter into a general dialogue until the labor minister withdrew her remarks. (Ibid., 16 March.)

In August, a general strike involving port, railway, hospital, oil refinery, and banana workers, took place in the Puerto Limon area on the Atlantic coast. Although the leaders of the strike were not communist, the CGTC threatened a general strike in solidarity. Communist deputies Devandas and Rodrigo Ureña Quiros went to the area and helped organize roadblocks to prevent the bringing in of strikebreakers.

When police fired on a group of strikers, injuring several of them, communist ex-Deputy Arnoldo Ferreto Segura went on the radio to denounce the president and the civil guard commander, saying that although the communists supported the walkout, it was being led by the anticommunist Confederacion Costarricense de Trabajadores Democraticos (ibid., 20 August). The president declared two staff members of the Soviet embassy persona non grata, charging that they had been involved in the Puerto Limon strike (*WP*, 21 August).

Throughout the year the communists reiterated their desire to form "a broad national alliance of democratic forces." Manuel Mora noted that "in calling for the creation of this alliance for participation in the elections scheduled for February 1982, we are guided by our passionate desire to make democratic changes as painless as possible for our people" and added: "We believe that in our country there are considerable possibilities for this because Costa Rica is famous for its deep-rooted democratic traditions and our people are strong enough to direct the struggle into a peaceful channel" (*WMR*, March).

After noting communist participation in the Pueblo Unido coalition, Ferreto Segura told a Hungarian interviewer in May: "We would like to develop, in close collaboration with the other two left-wing parties, an alliance based on wide mass support, which would encompass the working class, the peasantry, and the middle class more than before. Similarly important tasks of ours are the creation of a larger and more influential union center that would rally all progressive forces and the strengthening of youth organizations." (*Népszabadság*, 11 May.)

International Affiliations and Contacts. Throughout the year the PVP maintained close relations with the pro-Soviet faction of international communism. In April and May Ferreto Segura and Mario Silis Porras visited Poland, East Germany, the Soviet Union, Bulgaria, Romania, Hungary, Czechoslovakia, and Cuba. In each country, the Costa Rican delegation was received by officials of the local communist party, although in no case by the top leader. In August, Leonid Brezhnev of the Soviet party and Gustav Husák of the Czech one sent greetings to Manuel Mora on his 70th birthday. The Bulgarian government awarded Mora the Georgi Dimitrov Order on the same occasion. Early in the year there was a meeting in Costa Rica of the pro-Soviet parties of the Caribbean area.

The PVP continued to be strongly anti-Chinese. In an interview in July, Manuel Mora recounted his 1964 visit to China when he "had serious differences with Mao Zedong on both theoretical and practical issues." Mora added: "Our party has always opposed the imperialist trends of the Chinese Communist Party." (Radio Sofia, 20 July.)

The Trotskyists. The Trotskyist movement is represented in Costa Rica by the OST, headed by Alejando Calderon. It remained active during 1979. In January two of its leaders were arrested in Puerto Limon for helping to organize a local demonstration against the state of public utilities in the city (*Intercontinental Press*, 22 January). It indicated strong support throughout the earlier months of the year for the struggle of the Sandinistas against the dictatorship of General Anastasio Somoza in Nicaragua.

Rutgers University   Robert J. Alexander

Cuba

The Communist Party of Cuba (Partido Comunista de Cuba; PCC) is the country's ruling party, the only one permitted under the 1976 constitution. At the end of 1979, PCC membership was estimated at over 200,000, an overall increase in ranks, according to Havana. The country's population was approximately 9.9 million.

Leadership and Organization of State Authority. In 1979, called in Cuba the "twentieth year of victory," the leadership and organization of the PCC did not change, even though there were indications of intraparty frictions and tensions. Late in December 1978, the Central Committee of the PCC approved the 1979 budget of about U.S. $12 billion. One Central Committee member, Raúl García Peláez, was "released" from the Central Committee and named ambassador to Afghanistan. Presumably the rest of the members of the Central Committee and the PCC Politburo were confirmed in their posts. At the same time, the Politburo met in Havana, adopting measures concerning the growth and the "social composition of party ranks," according to Havana's daily *Granma* (31 December 1978), which reported that a "substantial number of workers directly related to production joined the PCC in 1978." Serious problems within the ruling party were revealed in July by President Fidel Castro, first secretary of the PCC Central Committee. In a lengthy, nationally televised speech, Castro not only criticized "indiscipline, softness, the buddy system, and tolerance" within governmental and party bureaucracies but also conceded that these were "the shortcomings of our system, of our socialism." He also spoke about a "problem of consciousness of our cadres, our leaders, administrators, and workers . . . We are naive in our thinking, transforming spontaneity into a philosophy. We must go deeper into the issue [of work indiscipline] and ask ourselves to what extent there exists political, revolutionary, and social consciousness." Citing a specific example, Castro said that "discipline on the railroads has collapsed . . , We must go into the heart of the matter and must put an end to the tendency to shirk problems, to favored treatment for friends, to tolerant attitudes toward indiscipline. This must be done at the state and administrative national levels." The Cuban president complained that although there are "thousands of cadres" willing to go to Angola and Ethiopia, few are willing to perform daily productive chores diligently. Among the shortcomings of the Cuban system, Castro also singled out the judiciary: "We have set up what we can call a paradise for the offender. We have naively created all sorts of safeguards for the offender. I think we have set up a system of safeguards that for all intents and purposes favors the offender, forcing the police department to reveal to him, even before his arrest, the [incriminating] information it has on him." (Ibid., 15 July.)

Several months later, General of the Army Raúl Castro, the party's second secretary, referred to the same problems in a more alarming tone: "I note in the conduct and expression of certain diverse elements of present-day society signs of that same weakness, of the poverty of spirit and timid psychology of the fainthearted, that flourishes in times of trouble . . . We have sufficient evidence to say that some party and state cadres are shying away from coming to grips with those who have made a habit of lack of labor discipline, lack of discipline vis-à-vis society, lack of respect for social property, and lack of respect for socialist norms of conduct; we know of party members who do not battle against those who have interpreted freedom from exploitation as freedom from work." Even more significant was an admission by Raúl Castro that younger Cubans, apparently members of the party, openly question the wisdom of the actions of the older generation of leaders now in power. "Nor are we unaware," he said, "of certain gatherings at which the allegedly well-informed, who have no firsthand experience of the misery of capitalism, take on the role of prosecutors and strategists, coming up with instant solutions for every possible problem." Raúl Castro promised tough measures against the critics, although he did not make them specific. "We must be demanding in a calm and mature way," he stated, "and especially settle accounts, regardless of hierarchy, with those who violate labor discipline, tolerate wrongdoing, are arbitrary, and have a petit-bourgeois view of criticism and self-criticism." (Ibid., 11 November.) No indication was given by Havana as to the scope of what Raúl Castro called "settling accounts" with internal dissidents.

In another action, the PCC Politburo created the National Control Committee in May, with organs at the provincial level. The committee has been put in charge of reviewing PCC finances and assets. In addition, it has to act on appeals of persons who are denied party membership and of party members sanctioned for infringements of party rules. Announcing the creation of the new body, the Presidium said that the PCC had to set "the example of dedication, tenacity, firmness, morality, and audacity given to us every day by our leader and chief comrade Fidel Castro." (Ibid., 27 May.)

Mass Organizations. There was practically no change in 1979 in the functioning and size of Cuba's mass organizations. The Federation of Cuban Women (Federación de Mujeres Cubanas) increased its membership by about 50,000 to 2.3 million. The organization also credited itself with the increase to 30 percent of the participation of women in the country's work force. The Committees for the Defense of the Revolution (Comités de Defensa de la Revolución) were engaged primarily with internal problems, a task that Havana called a "struggle against features of antisocial behavior inherited from the past." The Pioneer Movement (Movimiento de Pioneros) comprised nearly 2 million Cuban children in 1979, or 99.3 percent of all children from the first through the eighth grades. There are two levels of Pioneers: Moncadistas, for children in grades 1 to 4, who are organized in groups of six called Stars (Estrellas) headed by a pioneer from grades 5 through 8 who plays with them and prepares them for entry into the José Martí Pioneers when they reach the fifth grade. The José Martí Pioneers have class-room-size groups. They elect leaders and a schoolwide council that controls, under the guidance of an adult, pioneer activities: study, work, sports, culture, and "international solidarity." (Ibid., 19 June.)

The Revolutionary Armed Forces: Foreign Involvement and Soviet Troops in Cuba. Although there were reports early in 1979 that Cuba had withdrawn some troops from Africa, specifically about 2,500 from Ethiopia, there was no indication at the end of the year that such a pullout had taken place. Cuban military units appeared to have bogged down in a seemingly endless struggle in both Angola and Ethiopia, where they were estimated to have, respectively, 20,000 and 15,000 soldiers. (*NYT*, 21 October.) According to the same reports, Cubans in Angola have developed a "base mentality," not unlike the French and American troops in Vietnam. Prolonged stationing of Cuban troops has affected their morale, according to the same story, which, quoting "government analysts," said that Cuba had about 50,000 troops in twenty countries of Africa and the Middle East.

According to Havana, the country's 1979 military budget was about $1.1 billion, but this apparently did not include the cost of weapon replacements that Cuba continues to receive free of charge from the Soviet Union. After the death of President Agostinho Neto of Angola, the situation of Cuban troops became more delicate in view of the intensified antigovernment guerrilla activities there. Also in 1979, a small contingent of Cubans who had helped to maintain the dictatorship of Nquema Biyoto Masie in Equatorial Guinea did little to defend him when he was overthrown.

The Cuban Revolutionary Armed Forces (Fuerzas Armadas Revolucionarias; FAR), according to the latest available estimates by Western experts, were organized as follows: army, 150,000 men in fifteen infantry brigades and three armored regiments with some 600 tanks and 90,000 reserves; navy, 9,000 men, several subchasers and torpedo boats and one diesel attack submarine; air force, 20,000 men, including air defense units, two fighter-bomber squadrons with 30 MIG-17s and some MIG-23s, seven fighter squadrons with a total of 118 MIG-21s and MIG-19s.

The presence of Soviet troops in Cuba, for almost eighteen years a permanent feature of Cuban-Soviet military ties, became an issue in Washington-Havana relations in 1979 when the Carter administration announced that a part of the Russian military personnel on the island had become a "combat brigade," comprising three infantry battalions and one tank ballation. On 5 September Secretary of State Cyrus R. Vance stated that the "presence of a Soviet combat unit in Cuba is a matter of serious concern." Two days later, President Carter escalated the controversy by declaring that the unit's existence could affect U.S.-Soviet relations and that "the status quo is not acceptable." (Ibid., 8 September.) Havana and Moscow denied that a Russian combat unit existed in Cuba. Both said that since the end of the October 1962 missile crisis, neither the size of the Soviet contingent in Cuba (estimated by Washington at between 10,000 and 13,500) nor its training purpose has been changed. On 1 October after a series of discussions between Vance and Soviet Ambassador Anatoli F. Dobrynin and an exchange of messages between the White House and the Kremlin, President Carter indicated that the Soviet combat unit was a manageable problem. At the same time, the president ordered a series of countermeasures to the Soviet presence in Cuba, among them intensification of intelligence surveillance of Cuba; resumption of SR-71 spy plane overflights of the island; establishment of a Caribbean task force headquartered in Key West, Florida; military maneuvers in the region, including the Guantánamo Naval Base; and an increase in economic assistance to Caribbean countries. At the year's end, the presence of Soviet troops in Cuba ceased to be an issue that seriously concerned Washington.

Domestic Affairs. Underlying repeated official disclosures of intraparty and intragovernment tensions was a worsening economic situation. Cuba's dependence on Soviet economic aid increased in 1979. To keep its Caribbean ally afloat, Moscow had to pour in an estimated $3 billion (or about $8 million a day), almost one quarter of the country's gross national product. In 1979 Cuba produced almost 8 million tons of sugar, 600,000 more than in 1978. But according to President Carter, who announced this high sugar output — the second highest ever — because of low world market prices, the value of the entire harvest would not be sufficient to pay for the petroleum Cuba consumes if it had to buy oil in hard currency. For the past several years, the Soviet Union has supplied Cuba with over 95 percent of its consumption of about 220,000 barrels a day, charging it less than the world price and less than Moscow's European allies have to pay — which reportedly is causing problems within the Council for Mutual Economic Assistance. On the other hand, possibly for bookkeeping purposes, Russia pays Cuba several times more than the world market price for its sugar. The Soviet Union alone accounted for over 60 percent of Cuba's trade in 1979, and economic relations included technical cooperation between 26 ministries and over sixty scientific organizations in both countries. Among some forty Soviet projects under construction in Cuba are power-generating units, a cane-harvesting combine plant, an oxygen factory, and others that require higher consumption of petroleum.

Late in 1978, Cuba abolished the previously much praised "microbrigades," construction crews recruited from unskilled office and factory workers to supplement the few available professionals. About 16,500 housing units were completed in 1978, but at the same time 26,000 units were torn down for lack of repairs, aggravating the already serious housing shortage. In virtually every segment of the economy in 1979, Havana acknowledged widespread deficiencies in organizational planning, supply, and the execution of governmental directives. In November Raúl Castro sounded an ominous note regarding the economic future: "Climatic and natural phenomena," he said, "have recently adversely affected crop yields and have considerably reduced the quality of cane available for the next sugar harvest, all of which will inevitably be reflected negatively in 1980 and even in 1981." (*Granma*, 11 November.) In a "state of the country" report, the Eighth Plenum of the PCC Central Committee was equally pessimistic: "Economic growth envisioned by the First PCC Congress in 1975 has been seriously affected by grave and inevitable consequences of external objective conditions. The drop in the price of sugar in the world market and inflation . . . have reduced Cuba's purchasing power. Productivity has increased [during the 1975–1978 period], although in the past three years there has been a series of serious problems in the implementation of the socialist principle of the distribution [of rewards] according to work . . . Oil consumption by the sugar industry has been on the increase, there are manifest problems concerning the quality of production and services. There is a negative situation in tobacco production, coffee output suffered a notable decline, the quality of work in the cattle industry is poor, and losses in hog rearing due to indiscipline have been considerable. Bus service, especially in Havana, has declined significantly . . . State agencies must struggle against shortcomings, negligence, and irresponsibility that affect us all . . . as well as against crimes against property that are basically theft." (Ibid., 27 March.)

International Positions. Aside from direct military involvement in various parts of the world, Cuba worked hard, and at a great expense to its depleted treasury, to improve its position abroad, especially among the Third World nations. Havana was the site of the Sixth Summit Conference of the Organization of Nonaligned Countries. As the conference host, Fidel Castro became president of the 94-member organization and will be its spokesman for the next three years. The next meeting of the grouping is scheduled for Baghdad in 1982.

Even before the Havana gathering, many nonaligned countries voiced their concern that the Cuban leader would try to use his new position to convert the organization into a tool of Soviet international policy. A draft of the conference's statement, prepared by Cuba, corroborated the neutrals' apprehension, and so did Castro's speech opening the gathering. In his address, Castro assailed the United States, China, Israel, and Egypt (which he proposed be expelled from the movement) and was full of praise for the Soviet Union, which, according to him, was a "natural ally" of the nonaligned bloc. Castro attributed major ills in the world to the United States and Washington's allies and new friends (meaning China). He charged that the United States was engaged in "dirty scheming" and "feverish diplomatic contacts" aimed at weakening the conference's impact. Castro defended Cuba's international policy and said that Cuban soldiers were fighting and dying abroad for "just causes." He added: "We don't try to impose radicalism on anyone, much less on the nonaligned movement." (Ibid., 5 September.)

Before the Cuban draft became the conference's final declaration, it was considerably watered down, and some delegates expressed bitterness and even anger at Cuban manipulation of the meeting. Among the heads of state urging evenhandedness in the group's dealing with the great powers was President Tito of Yugoslavia. Outside Havana and most nonaligned capitals, the Havana declaration was less than a success. It "sets a record for woolly silliness," said the *New York Times* (11 September), adding that it was "composed under the bullying tutelage of Fidel Castro." Shortly afterwards, Fidel Castro addressed the U.N. General Assembly as president of the nonaligned organization. His brief visit to New York turned Manhattan into a policeman's nightmare, but his U.N. speech was slightly more conciliatory than the one he had given at the Havana conference. At the United Nations Cuba was unsuccessful in the attempt to expel the Pol Pot regime as the Kampuchean (Cambodian) representative and had difficulty in obtaining the two-thirds majority needed for a Security Council seat.

In 1979 Cuba re-established relations with Ecuador, Iran, and Nicaragua and established ties with the new nation of St. Lucia. Havana promised to send doctors and civilian technicians to help civil-war–torn Nicaragua, whose revolutionary regime was praised by the Castro government. Cuba's strong anti-Israel and anti-China policies continued unchanged.

International Contacts. In January, U.N. Secretary General Kurt Waldheim visited Cuba. In February, Agostinho Neto, president of Angola, met with Fidel Castro in Havana in the last Cuban visit for the African leader, who died of cancer in September. The same month Raúl Castro traveled to Eastern Europe. In Moscow he was awarded the Order of Lenin and decorated Premier Alexei Kosygin with the José Martí National Order. Ivan V. Arkhipov, vice-president of the Soviet Council of Ministers, Ros Samay, secretary general of the Kampuchean National United Front for National Salvation, and Bachir Mustafa, leader of the Polisario movement, visited Cuba in March. The following month Piotr Jaroszewicz, chairman of the Council of Ministers of Poland, visited Cuba, as did Todor Zhivkov, first secretary of the Bulgarian Communist Party. In May Fidel Castro flew to Mexico for a two-day visit with the Mexican president. Back home, Castro received a visit from Dr. Taha Muhyiddin Ma'rouf and Dr. Sadoon Hemmadi, vice-president and foreign minister, respectively, of Iraq. The same month Cuban Politburo member Blas Roca traveled to Romania, Czechoslovakia, and Bulgaria. In July several leaders of the revolutionary junta of Nicaragua visited Havana. In August Felipe González, leader of the Spanish Socialist Workers' Party, and Michael Manley, prime minister of Jamaica, met with Castro. The Summit Conference of Nonaligned Nations drew a large number of chiefs of state and leading figures from the 94 countries and movements represented at the gathering. In October Castro traveled to New York to speak to the U.N. General Assembly. Later that month Raúl Castro attended the celebration of the 26th anniversary of the Algerian revolution in Algiers, heading a large delegation. In November, four Puerto Rican terrorists, released from prison in the United States, visited Cuba and were decorated with the Playa Girón National Order.

Publications. The official organ of the PCC Central Committee is *Granma*, published in Havana six times a week, with an average circulation of 600,000. Central Committee member Jorge Enrique Mendoza is the publisher of *Granma*, which also appears in weekly Spanish, English, and French editions, circulated mostly free of charge abroad. The Central Committee's secretarial publication, *Militante Comunista*, is a periodical with news about PCC activities. The Union of Young Communists publishes the daily *Juventud Rebelde* in Havana, whose 200,000 circulation makes it the country's second largest newspaper. National weeklies are *Verde Olivo*, the organ of the FAR, and *Bohemia*, a general news magazine whose circulation is 300,000. There are seven provincial dailies. The largest, *Sierra Maestra*, published in Santiago de Cuba, has a circulation of close to 50,000. Since 1959, Cuba has operated its own news agency, Prensa Latina (PL), which views its staffers as performing their "duty as journalists and revolutionaries." In 1979 the PL had 34 offices or branches around the world and two satellite channels of communications with Moscow, two with East Berlin, and one with Warsaw. It transmitted on its wires a daily average of 300 stories edited in Havana. It had 400 employees in Cuba and abroad.

University of Miami   George Volsky

Dominican Republic

Leftist forces in the Dominican Republic continued to be fragmented in 1979. If anything, their influence has diminished, and the freedom to operate openly has accentuated intramural differences that became open squabbles.

By the end of 1979, there were about fifteen different Marxist groups in the country, among them the Dominican Communist Party (Partido Comunista Dominicano; PCD), whose secretary general is Narciso Isa Conde and which follows the Moscow-Havana line; the Dominican People's Movement (Movimiento Popular Dominicano), a pro-Beijing group, which in turn is divided into two factions, one led by Onelio Espaillat and Jorge Puello Soriano and the other by Rafael Chaljub Mejía; the Nucleus of Communist Workers (Núcleo de los Trabajadores Comunistas, led by Rafael (Fafa) Taveras; the Dominican Liberation Party (Partido de Liberación Dominicana), whose leader is former President Juan Bosch; the Patriotic Anti-Imperialist Union (Unión Patriótica Antiimperialista), led by Franklin Franco; the Camilo Torres Revolutionary Committee (Comité Revolucionario Camilo Torres); the Marxist-Leninist Path (Via Marxista-Leninista), headed by Fidelio Despradel; the Dominican Liberation Movement (Movimiento de Liberación Dominicana), presided over by Agustín Alvarez; the Trinitarian National Liberation Movement (Movimiento de Liberación Nacional delos Trinitarios), led by Juan Bautista Castillo Pujols; the Communist Party of the Dominican Republic (Partido Comunista de la República Dominicana), whose leader is Luis Montás (Pin); the New Republic Revolutionary Movement (Movimiento Revolucionario Nueva República, headed by Rafael Gamundy Cordero; and the Popular Socialist Party (Partido Socialista Popular), led by Félix Servio Ducouray.

In 1979 the Red Line of the 14 June Movement (Movimiento Línea Rosa del 14 de Junio), and the Proletarian Banner (Bandera Proletaria) decided to merge to "consolidate the irreversible march toward the unity of Dominican Marxist-Leninists" and were planning to found a new Dominican workers' party. Another new group was the Revolutionary Leftist Movement (Movimiento de Izquierda

Revolucionaria; MIR), which adopted as its slogan the phrase "Always toward victory," a battle cry of Ernesto Ché Guevara. In its first statement, the MIR—led by Fernando Paniagua and Enrique Cabrera Vázques (El Mellizo)—said that another group, previously unknown in the country, called the Armed Forces of National Liberation (Fuerzas Armadas de Liberación Nacional), would merge with it.

There were no estimates of the membership of the Dominican Marxist groups, but their total strength was believed not to exceed 5,000. In the 1978 presidential election, the entire left received only 3 pecent of the vote (*WMR*, December 1978). There are reports that both the Soviet Union (through Cuba) and China subsidize the activities of several of the groups, which contributs to the balkanization of the country's extreme left because old and new Marxist groups demand a share of the available funds.

The principal reason for the weakness of the leftist forces appears to be the liberal policies of President Antonio Guzmán, elected in August 1978, and the ruling Dominican Revolutionary Party (Partido Revolucionario Dominicano; PRD), associated with the social democratic parties of Western Europe. The PRD's secretary general, José Francisco Peña Gómez, a popular and charismatic leader, is secretary of the Socialist International's Latin American Bureau. Stealing the revolutionary thunder from the extreme left, the PRD supported the struggle against the Anastasio Somoza regime of Nicaragua. The Dominican government permitted the publication of an anti-Somoza periodical by a Sandinista Committee in Santo Domingo.

As a result, the activities of most extreme leftist groups have been principally aimed at widening the narrow base of their support. But in 1979, it appears that any shift in membership was from one leftist organization to another.

In March 1979 the PCD, which was founded 35 years ago, held its Second Congress, which was attended by over 400 delegates and representatives of foreign communist parties. Isa Conde, re-elected as secretary general, stressed his group's allegiance to the Soviet Union and Cuba and strongly attacked the government of China. Internally, the PCD is committed to participation in the political process, and its goals are relatively modest: nationalization of some foreign enterprises; a far-reaching agrarian reform, with the distribution of land among landless peasants; and the strengthening of the public sector of the economy. It also wants to "frustrate attempts to impose a two-party system" in the Dominican Republic.

As Isa Conde conceded in a *World Marxist Review* article (December 1978), his party has not been successful in reaching its goals despite "greater opportunities for free political activity." After the victory of President Guzmán and the PRD, Isa Conde wrote: "Our point of view now coincides with the country's public opinion, but we still lack proper political leverage. The force of the party's ideas and proposals can influence some events and actually has, but the party is not yet in a position to lead the masses. Our goal is to become a real and effective force . . . our principal object today is to become a mass organization, win over the rank and file that follows the PRD and conclude a practical alliance with them." (Ibid.)

Publications: Since 1978 the PCD has published the weekly *Hablan los Comunistas.*

University of Miami   George Volsky

Ecuador

Ecuador has experienced constant division and factionalism among its Marxists since 1931. In that year the Communist Party of Ecuador (Partido Comunista del Ecuador; PCE) came into existence alongside the Ecuadorian Socialist Party. Both organizations underwent periodic internal divisions, feuds, and reorganizations. During the 1960s the panorama was further complicated by creation of both Maoist and Fidelista groups. The former took the name Marxist-Leninist Communist Party of Ecuador (Partido Comunista Marxista-Leninista del Ecuador; PCMLE), and the latter became the Ecuadorian Revolutionary Socialist Party (Partido Socialista Revolucionario Ecuatoriano; PSRE). By the 1970s the PCE numbered some one thousand official members, with those of the PCMLE and PSRE estimated at no more than 500 each.

In August 1979 Jaime Roldós Aguilera was inaugurated as Ecuador's 44th president. Thus, nine years of dictatorship drew to a close, and the armed forces returned to the barracks. For the country's Marxist organizations, the restoration of democracy and civil liberties promised enhanced opportunities to develop and advance their interests. Yet their political strength was minimal, and over the half-century since the 1926 founding of the original Ecuadorian Socialist Party, relatively few inroads into the society and politics of the republic had been made. Ricardo Paredes Romero, prime founder of the Marxist movement, died at age 81 late in 1979 (*FBIS*, 13 September) after years of political inactivity.

The Marxists and Electoral Politics. Three stages of elections led to the ultimate re-establishment of elected government in Ecuador. First was the 15 January 1978 referendum to choose a new constitution. This was followed on 16 July by the first round of presidential elections, as well as by local and municipal races. The process was completed on 29 April 1979 with the presidential runoff and congressional elections. Marxist participation in these contests centered on two organizations: the PCE with minuscule leftist allies, and the Democratic Popular Movement (Movimiento Popular Democrático; MPD), which emanated from the earlier PCMLE.

The PCE, which had extended partial and qualified support to the military government during much of the 1972–1979 period, was among the majority of political parties to favor a new draft constitution for the January 1978 plebiscite. The electorate approved the new draft by a margin of 43 to 32 percent over a revised version of the 1945 constitution, with the remaining votes either nullified or spoiled. Consequently the PCE initiated efforts to create a Marxist coalition for the forthcoming July race. Participating as senior partner of the coalition, it directed the Broad Front of the Left (Frente Amplio de la Izquierda; FADI). The Revolutionary Socialists and five other tiny Marxist groups— none of which were officially recognized by the Supreme Electoral Tribunal (Tribunal Supremo Electoral; TSE)—joined to support the presidential candidacy of René Maugé Mosquera, 40, one of the second generation of PCE leaders from the party's Central Committee.

More radical Marxists, predominantly followers of a pro-Chinese line, created the MPD as an alternative to the moderate FADI and René Maugé. The rector of the Central University in Quito, Camilo Mena Mena, was named the MPD nominee and began an active campaign. However, the government-controlled TSE soon barred his candidacy and the participation of the MPD. Consequently the Maoists called for the casting of a no vote in the July elections. It remained for the FADI to seek support for a "socialist, democratic Ecuador that is free from any dependency," while proposing such policies as expanded state activity in the economy and the nationalization of business, banks, and the oil industry (ibid., 26 April 1978).

Maugé and his vice-presidential running mate, Anibal Muñoz of the PSRE, campaigned vigorously and displayed considerable organizational skills despite minimal financing. However, the ticket finished last in a field of six, polling barely 5 percent of the vote and trailing all competitors in fourteen of the twenty provinces. Meanwhile, Jaime Roldós and Osvaldo Hurtado won a victory for their alliance of the former's Concentration of Popular Forces (Concentración de Fuerzas Populares) and the latter's Popular Democracy (Democracia Popular). Despite military reluctance to accept the outcome and a four-month delay in recounting and revalidating the vote, the Roldós-Hurtado duo was eventually declared the victor with 27 percent. Finishing second and therefore qualifying for the runoff was Sixto Durán Ballén for the rightist coalition Constitutionalist National Front (Frente Constitucionalista Nacional).

Regulations for the April 1979 elections prohibited the participation of electoral alliances. Consequently the FADI was dissolved and the PCE ran on its own. Adopting as its customary electoral front the name Popular Democratic Union (Union Democratica Popular; UDP), it placed its veteran secretary general, Pedro Antonio Saad, at the head of the slate competing for the twelve congressional seats contested on a national basis, and Maugé was relegated to a secondary position in the 1979 campaign. Meanwhile the MPD had succeeded in winning official recognition as a party and thus undertook a new struggle with the PCE for domination of the Marxist sector. Labor lawyer Jaime Hurtado González headed its ticket in the "national" congressional race.

The Marxists and Constitutional Government. The elections provided an unexpected victory for the MPD over the PCE. In the race for the twelve national members of the unicameral Chamber of Representatives, the MPD ran ninth among twelve parties, with 4.8 percent of the vote. Hurtado was subsequently named to the Chamber. The Communists' UDP finished tenth with 3.2 percent, which was insufficient for Pedro Saad to receive a seat. The total also reflected a drop from the July 1978 elections. Application of proportional representation in the race for province-based congressmen produced one member of the UDP, Jorge Chiriboga, from Esmeraldes on the northwestern coast. With the installation of the new legislature in August, then, there were two elected representatives of Ecuadorian Marxism—one apiece for the MPD and for the PCE (*El Comercio*, Quito, 10 August).

In the wake of President Roldós's inaugural address, the PCE announced support for his message. While approving his criticisms of the mismanagement of the preceding military dictatorship, the PCE also praised his pledge to pursue progressive reformism within a spirit of freedom, liberty, and national sovereignty (*FBIS*, 22 August). A few weeks later, the party also announced its agreement with the natural resources minister in an extended critical analysis of oil policy under the military government (ibid., 3 September).

The PCE was also strongly critical of the authoritarianism of the congressional majority headed by Roldós's rival, Chamber President Asaad Bucaram (*Nueva*, September-October), and his pact with the Conservative Party that allowed him to gain a congressional majority (*El Tiempo*, 19 July). During the early sessions of the Chamber, it was unclear whether the MPD's Hurtado would play an active role (*El Telégrafo*, 9 September).

Organization and Leadership. The PCE continued to be dominated by Secretary General Saad, who also remained a central figure in the communist-dominated Confederation of Ecuadorian Workers (Confederación de Trabajadores Ecuatorianos; CTE), which he founded in 1944. Although the choice of René Maugé in 1978 as presidential candidate had been regarded as an indication that leadership would be shared with the rising younger generation, Saad subsequently reasserted his control. The Central Committee of the CTE held a plenary meeting in Guayaquil late in January 1979, at which Saad was named head of the electoral slate (*IB*, February). At the same time, Maugé and others who had been central to his presidential campaign were moved to positions of less prominence.

The CTE, long affiliated with the communist-front World Federation of Trade Unions, remained the largest and best organized of the country's three national labor federations. Yet it continued to be challenged by the Ecuadorian Center of Classist Organizations (Central Ecuatoriana de Organizaciones Clasistas) and by the Ecuadorian Confederation of Free Workers' Organizations (Confederación Ecuatorian Organizaciones Sindicales Libres; CEOSL), while fully half of Ecuador's organized workers were members of independent groups.

There was considerable apprehension over the Roldós government's attitude toward the working class. Labor leaders found its 21-point program insufficiently precise and generally unresponsive to labor's nine-point joint declaration of 20 August 1975, the "Platform of Struggle for the Labor Federations." Only José Chavez of the CEOSL was willing to concede conditional support to the government. Bolivar Bolaños, acting president of the CTE, announced that the organization would be independent of the government and judge its performance on the basis of the earlier joint declaration (*Nueva*, August).

The initial actions of the new government appeared sympathetic to the workers. A land invasion by urban squatters in Guayaquil in August was met by a personal visit from President Roldós and key cabinet members. Instead of repression, special commissions were established to consider wage increases, while public employees were paid the four months' back salaries withheld by the outgoing military leaders. In view of the partial support extended by the PCE through the CTE to the military government, it was uncertain how the policies of the new administration would be viewed in the long run.

Domestic Views. In contrast to the 1978 electoral process, the PCE made few explicit policy statements during the 1979 campaign. In 1978, Maugé had used the revival of party politics to articulate communist views (*YICA*, 1979, p. 345). The lackluster PCE performance in 1979 was largely devoted to attacks and counterattacks against the MPD. Similarly, the MPD devoted more time and attention to its Marxist competitors than to specific national problems. Most of the exchanges were couched in ideological rhetoric and did not address national policy issues.

International Views. Ecuador re-established consular and trade relations with Cuba on 16 July, thanks to insistent demands by then president-elect Roldós on the outgoing military government. The PCE's leaders praised the action and urged full diplomatic relations (*FBIS*, 22 July). They expressed gratification a few weeks later when the Roldós administration announced the exchange of ambassadors with Cuba.

Greater enthusiasm, however, was generated in connection with the Sandinista overthrow of Nicaragua's Anastasio Somoza Debayle in July. For months before the eventual denouement, Ecuadorian leftists in general and Marxists in particular had followed Nicaraguan events closely. A week-long solidarity visit to Quito in late 1978 by a member of the Sandinist National Liberation Front produced a spate of excitement (ibid., 29 November 1978). The PCE and MPD both issued triumphant communiqués when Somoza ultimately fled Managua. They also rejoiced when two members of the Sandinista government attended the presidential inauguration of Roldós. Yet it was in a sense an exercise in futility for the Marxist parties since the new president had effectively stolen their thunder.

As president-elect, Roldós had helped convince the military junta to extend a form of partial recognition to the Sandinistas before their victory. When the latter occurred during Roldós multination pre-inaugural trip abroad, he adroitly expanded his itinerary to include Managua. He also devoted time to the Sandinista leaders attending his inauguration, as did Rosalynn Carter and Cyrus Vance of the U.S. delegation (*WP*, 10 and 11 August). Consequently, both PCE and MPD leaders had little opportunity to meet with the Nicaraguans, let alone gain political mileage from the situation. This was a symbolically meaningful commentary on the activities and accomplishments of Ecuadorian Marxists in 1979. In a year of considerable importance to the republic, the role and involvement of the PCE, the MPD, and the several Marxist miniparties can only be regarded as negligible.

The Pennsylvania State University   John D. Martz

El Salvador

The Communist Party of El Salvador (Partido Comunista de El Salvador; PCES) was founded in 1930 and currently has about 225 members. Since the communist-led uprising of 1932, the party has been illegal and has taken no part in government. After the coup of 15 October, the military-civilian junta that replaced President Carlos Humberto Romero and the ruling Party of National Conciliation (Partido de Conciliación Nacional) in this nation of 4.6 million persons announced its intentions to legalize the PCES. It later appointed a PCES member as minister of labor. In the early 1970s, members of the PCES organized a terrorist movement known as the People's Revolutionary Army (Ejército Revolucionario del Pueblo; ERP), but this group broke with the PCES in 1975. Since then, the ERP has divided into a number of guerrilla and terrorist factions.

The PCES. Jorge Shafik Handal was re-elected PCES secretary general at the Seventh National Congress, held in San Salvador in May. Following this meeting, there was a major shift in party attitudes. Until this time, the party had been moderate and almost passive in its attitude toward the growing disintegration and violence in El Salvador. The official line had been that the PCES opposed terrorism and did not believe in violent revolution. In August, however, Handal reportedly declared: "It is often maintained that a victorious revolution is impossible in a small country such as El Salvador . . . But the Salvadorian communists vehemently oppose such a view because it is false and is aimed at paralyzing the upsurge of progressive forces. We are firmly convinced that the revolution will be [as] victorious in our country as in all of Central America." (*Horizont*, no. 33; *FBIS*, 17 August.) This change on the part of the PCES was due partly to the victory of the Sandinista movement in Nicaragua and partly to the growing strength of the more radical Marxist-Leninist movements in El Salvador, which far outstripped the Moscow-oriented PCES in popular support.

Other Marxist Groups. There are two important Marxist mass movements in El Salvador, the larger of which is the Popular Revolutionary Bloc (Bloque Popular Revolucionario; BPR), whose general secretary, Facundo Guardado y Guardado, recently declared: "We abide by Marxist-Leninist ideology adjusted to El Salvador's specific conditions" (*Jornal do Brasil*, 21 May; *FBIS*, 25 May). The BPR consists of a number of peasant, labor, and student groups and commands an activist following of perhaps 30,000. Although illegal, it operated in open defiance of the previous government and during the course of the year made a number of dramatic gestures, including the seizures of the Venezuelan and French embassies and the occupation of the Cathedral of San Salvador on 4 May. These actions led to violence, and 23 BPR supporters were shot down at the Cathedral on 8 May. Then, on 22 May, fourteen BPR members were killed outside the Venezuelan embassy. Toward the end of the year, the BPR formed ties with the terrorist group known as the Popular Liberation Forces (Fuerzas Populares de Liberación; FPL), which carried out a number of assassinations during the year (victims included the mayor of Santa Ana, El Salvador's second largest city, in March, and the minister of education and a Swiss diplomat in May).

The other major Marxist group is the Unified Popular Action Front (Frente Acción Popular Unificada; FAPU), which seized the Mexican embassy and the headquarters of the Red Cross in January. The FAPU is linked to the terrorist Armed Forces of National Resistance (Fuerzas Armadas de Resistencia Nacional; FARN), the group specializing in kidnapping foreign businessmen and holding them for ransom that killed the Israeli consul in March. The FARN has criticized the PCES for its timidity, declaring in a manifesto that the PCES "each day increases its decadence and loses its influence in the popular movement" (*NYT*, 2 December 1978). The PCES countered by declaring that the terrorist tactics of FARN were "bound to fail" (ACAN, Panama City, 24 December 1978). In addition to these two main Marxist blocs, a number of minor terrorist bands, including the ERP, exist. All radical Marxist groups were active in the six weeks of violence that preceded the coup of 15 October. In this violence, the most dramatic acts were the FPL's assassination on 6 September of the brother of the then president and the BPR's seizure of the National Assembly building in mid-September.

Although the leaders of the new junta promised reforms, the Marxist groups remained suspicious, the BPR calling the junta only "a change of face" (*Time*, 29 October). On 25 October the BPR seized the ministries of economics and labor, along with the ministers themselves and many employees. The assassinations also continued with the FPL gunning down the inspector general of the army on 19 October and the ERP shooting the chief of investigations of the National Guard on the 29th. That same day a group of leftists known as the 28 February Popular League attempted to storm the United States embassy and two were killed, while near the occupied ministries more than thirty persons died in clashes between the BRP and security forces.

Eastern Connecticut State College   Thomas P. Anderson

Guadeloupe

The Communist Party of Guadeloupe (Parti communiste guadeloupéen; PCG) was founded in 1944. In 1979 it agreed with the Martinique Communist Party (PCM) and the French Communist Party (PCF) that autonomy rather than independence or further integration is best for the overseas departments, that racism is increasing in France and in the Caribbean, and that a sense of national identity is increasing in Martinique, Guadeloupe, Guyane, and Réunion. Severe economic problems overshadowed these issues, however. The PCG differed sharply with the PCM and the PCF over the issue of Caribbean ties with the European Economic Community (EEC).

Leaders and Organization. At the beginning of the year party Secretary General Guy Daninthe called 250 delegates to a national conference at which the Central Committee pointed to the need to renew the party. Delegates discussed means of appealing to Guadeloupans in order to recruit new members and examined the role of elected communist officials, publicity, and the meaning of democratic centralism. The members analyzed the failures of the alliance with the Socialists and decided to form PCG cells in every business establishment with at least five communist employees. The Union of Guadeloupañ Communist Youth also met in its own first national conference. Sixty participants denounced the Paris government and multinational corporations. The young men and women pledged to fight for national liberation.

Evidence of party success came in the cantonal elections held on 18 March and 25 March. In mid-February the Central Committee formulated a program, subsequently published in the party newspaper, *L'Etincelle*. Seven communist candidates ran; two won on the first round, one being Dr. Henri Bangou, the popular mayor of Pointe-à-Pitre, and one was victorious during the second round. Since only half the 36 General Council seats are renewed once every three years, the four other PCG incumbents did not run for reelection. The total of seven communists in the General Council did not change, but the party claimed success because of a slight increase in the popular vote. It also celebrated the victory of a noncommunist ally and a socialist who often votes with the PCG in the General Council.

Domestic Attitudes and Activities. After the elections, General Council debates became so disorderly and noisy—partly because of the presence of citizens in the galleries—that the Council decided, over communist objections, to restrict entry. On 6 August PCG members and others marched on the Council building to protest. Soldiers kept guard, and PCG councillors refused to attend sessions as long as the restrictions and guards continued.

The party expressed concern about another form of disorder—namely, the reports of growing racism in metropolitan France and Guadeloupe. On 15 February fights broke out between black islanders and white metropolitans at the Baimbridge lycée. In the shouting that accompanied the melee, racial comments showing the deepening antagonism between the races in Guadeloupe were made. Authorities closed the school for a few days, and a temporary peace prevailed. On the university campus unknown persons attacked students, and the Union of Guadeloupan Women held a study session on the growing problem of prostitution in the islands.

The PCG supported or led strikes by social service employees, teachers, and electrical workers. The last, led by the communist General Confederation of Labor, demanded all benefits that metropolitan electrical workers receive, including retirement at age 55 and application of all social laws concerning unemployment and health.

Inflation, unemployment, and the threat of a further decline in the sugar industry mobilized the party. The prefect of Guadeloupe, the highest administrative official, announced the probable closing of three large sugar mills, with the loss of over 2,000 jobs. The PCG called for a meeting of the General Council to protest this action and the low price for sugarcane set by the administration each year. The destruction caused by Hurricane David brought new problems, although neighboring islands suffered more than Guadeloupe.

The Central Committee again demanded autonomy for the department as the only way to solve these economic and social problems. The secretary of the French Socialist Party, François Mitterand, visited Guadeloupe and publicly disagreed with this goal. The PCG denounced Mitterand in particular and the Socialists in general.

International Attitudes and Activities. Although the PCG maintained its close ties to the PCF (delegates attended the PCF Congress, for example), the PCG separated itself from the French party over the issue of elections to the European parliament. Unlike the PCM, Guadeloupe refused to support the communist candidate list headed by Georges Marchais, head of the PCF, and Paul Vergès, head of the Communist Party of Réunion. It advised its members and supporters to abstain from the 10 June vote because, it said, the EEC operates against the interests of Guadeloupe. The PCB blamed the EEC for the decline in sugar, for example, with the resulting unemployment. Although about 80 percent of the voters did abstain, over 4,000 Guadeloupans still voted for the PCF list and 5,500 for the Giscard list.

The PCG also denounced meetings between President Valéry Giscard d'Estaing and other Western European leaders and President Carter. The first meeting of the year took place in Guadeloupe itself, and the party led demonstrations in Pointe-à-Pitre and Saint François. The party fully supported the Soviet Union, Cuba, and Vietnam. It praised the overthrow of the Cambodian government and denounced China for its attacks on Vietnam and for normalizing relations with the United States, actions it labeled "attacks on détente."

The PCG continued to deepen the cultural ties between Guadeloupe and Cuba. A Cuban delegation, headed by its ambassador to Guyana, arrived in Pointe-à-Pitre to plan for the annual Caribbean cultural meeting, Carifesta, which takes place in Havana.

Publications. The party newspaper, *L'Etincelle*, celebrated its 35th anniversary at its annual party, 16–17 June. It currently has a weekly press run of 12,000 copies. This year it ran a series of articles on East Germany.

Howard University   Brian Weinstein

Guatemala

The communist party in Guatemala, which since 1952 has been called the Guatemalan Party of Labor (Partido Guatemalteco del Trabajo; PGT), originated in the predominantly communist-controlled Socialist Labor Unification, founded in 1921. The PGT operated legally between 1951 and 1954, playing an active role in the administration of Guatemalan President Jacobo Arbenz. Outlawed in 1954 following the overthrow of Arbenz, it has since operated underground. Although the party has some influence among students, intellectuals, and workers, it does not play a significant role in national affairs.

According to U.S. intelligence sources, the PGT is estimated to have 750 members. The population of Guatemala is about 6.8 million (1979 estimate).

Guerrilla and General Violence. Various guerrilla groups have operated in Guatemala in recent years, including the Revolutionary Armed Forces, which is the military arm of the PGT, and the Rebel Armed Forces (Fuerzas Armadas Rebeldes; FAR), at least some of whose members have claimed affiliation with the PGT. The Revolutionary Armed Forces and the FAR probably have fewer than one hundred members each, with several hundred sympathizers. A third leftist guerrilla group calling itself the "29 May Guerrilla Movement" announced its formation in commemoration of the Panzós "massacre" of 1978 (see *YICA*, 1979, p. 355). Dedicated to "waging socialist revolution," the new organization claimed no credit for guerrilla activity during 1979 and appears to have no discernible structure. On 20 September the self-styled Armed People's Organization (Organización del Pueblo en Armas; ORPA) announced the beginning of its military actions in Guatemala. In a communiqué sent to news media, the ORPA noted that "after several years of preparation in which our organization has been set up in total secrecy, we emerge today publicly to join our efforts with those of the general struggle of the people" (*Diario El Gráfico*, 21 September). The ORPA reported in November that it had occupied four hamlets and a village in Sololá Department. It also reported that some 600 villagers had attended an ORPA rally in Guineales, an important commercial center in Santa Catarina municipality (Agence France Presse [AFP], 7 November).

The largest and most active of the guerrilla organizations operating in 1979 was the Guerrilla Army of the Poor (Ejército Guerrillero de los Pobres; EGP). The EGP began operations in November 1975 when it assumed responsibility for the murder of an anticommunist leader and proclaimed "a war to the death on U.S. imperialism and its local representatives." Its membership is believed to contain remnants of leftist guerrilla groups that succumbed to the effective counterinsurgency tactics of the Guatemalan military during the late 1960s and the "law and order" administration of Gen. Carlos Arana Osorio (1970–1974). The EGP does not claim any direct affiliation with the PGT, nor is there any compelling evidence on which to base such an inference. (For further discussion of this significant guerrilla movement, see below.) The guerrilla situation is complicated by the continued existence of nonideological groups of common criminals who engage in kidnapping, extortion, robbery, and other acts of violence.

Politically motivated killings involving leftist groups and right-wing paramilitary organizations have been a common feature of Guatemalan daily life in recent years. Right-wing terror was initiated by the clandestine Secret Anticommunist Army (ESA), evidently the successor to such similar right-wing paramilitary organizations as the White Hand and the Eye for an Eye that were active in the early 1970s. The director of police stated in April that common and political crimes have increased in recent years. On 28 April he reported that 68 persons had been murdered during the previous week, "some the result of struggles between criminal gangs, but most common criminals stabbed or shot by the death squads" (*Prensa Libre*, 29 April). Government Minister Donaldo Alvarez Ruíz stated in May that security forces had established total control over the nation's territory except for leftist guerrilla centers located in the country's northwest region (*El Imparcial*, 9 May).

On 10 June the army's chief of staff was assassinated in Guatemala City. Although no group claimed responsibility for his murder, an army communiqué attributed his death to members of "clandestine extremist organizations, which the army will continue fighting" (*Diario El Gráfico*, 11 June). In early July government spokesmen accused Cuba of promoting communist subversion in Central America and intensifying its efforts to provoke an uprising in Guatemala by exhorting leaders of the various guerrilla groups to merge. The presidential press secretary stated on 9 July that the government had the outbreaks of political subversion "under control." Foreign guerrillas and agitators were reported to have entered the country to engage in acts of sabotage and terrorism, but the government was prepared, he said, "to smash any attempt at communist interference" (*El Imparcial*, 10 July). On 13 July police revealed that two socialists who had participated in the organization of the Social Democratic Party (PSD) had been murdered in an apparent resumption of the execution of leftists by the ESA. In a communiqué to the local press, the ESA warned that it would continue killing leftists and "not allow Guatemala to become another Nicaragua" (*Prensa Libre*, 14 July).

A constant focus of popular opposition to the government in 1979 was the Democratic Front Against Repression. Established in February, the Democratic Front is a loosely organized movement consisting of the PSD, the United Revolutionary Front, and various peasant, trade union, student, and church groups. Its principal activities involved the denunciation of the arrest and disappearance of opposition leaders and the promotion of public demonstrations against the government. On 8 November the staunchly anticommunist National Liberation Movement (MLN) announced the creation of the Antisubversion Guatemalan Front (Frente Guatemalteco contra la Subversión) "to restore peace in Guatemala." A MLN deputy, Leonel Sisniega Otero, stated that "Guatemala does not need an antirepression front, but it needs a front against subversion" (Agencia Centro Americano Noticias [ACAN], Panama City, 8 November). The systematic persecution of left-wing political and labor leaders in what appears to be a campaign aimed at dissolving those organizations that are not rightist has led to the increasing radicalization of political life in Guatemala. Threatening positions have been adopted by both the extreme left and the extreme right. Many observers are fearful that the growing polarization between the two large antagonistic fronts may eventually lead to an armed confrontation. Amnesty International reported in September that "a wave of political murder and repression" had taken 2,000 lives in the previous sixteen months. The group published a chronological list of abductions and killings since May 1978, with over a thousand bodies found in the first four months of 1979. Apart from criminals killed by various death squads, victims have included leading opposition politicians, labor and student leaders, journalists, priests, lawyers, and members of the Indian population (*Los Angeles Times*, 14 September). There is no indication that this alarming rate of political violence has diminished since the first of the year or that security forces responsible for maintaining public order have been any more effective in controlling it. The resignation of the vice-president on 27 November added a further dimension of instability to the political situation in Guatemala. Although the resignation was not unexpected, the vice-president attributed his decision to the government's failure to fulfill its political program and "an increase in repression" (ACAN, 27 November).

Leadership and Organization. Little information is available on the present leaders of the PGT or on the party's structure. Since 1972, two general secretaries and nineteen ranking members of the Central Committee have "disappeared," apparently the victims of assassination. Following the murder of Humberto Alvarado Arrellano in December 1975, Isías de León became general secretary. Other prominent members of the Central Committee are Otto Sánchez, Jorge Muñoz, A. Bauer Pais, Antonio Fuentes, and Pedro González Torres.

The PGT has a youth auxiliary, the Patriotic Youth of Labor (Juventud Patriótica del Trabajo). Student agitators are active at the secondary and university levels, although direct affiliation with the PGT is disclaimed. Student leaders supported by the PGT have been unsuccessful in recent years in their efforts to gain control of the influential Association of University Students (AEU), although the AEU's statements on domestic issues tend to be strongly critical of the government and its inability to control right-wing paramilitary violence. Members of student movements and university officials have been the frequent victims of political violence. In February the adviser to the rector of San Carlos University was murdered by "persons unknown." On 23 April the president of a high-school student association, who also served as a coordinator of secondary students, was killed by unidentified assailants (*El Imparcial*, 24 April). Two University of San Carlos students were kidnapped and killed in May. Spokesmen for the AEU demanded that the university "adopt measures of defense and denounce the policy that seeks to impose terror on the students and the rest of the popular forces" (*Prensa Libre*, 23 May).

The PGT also controls the clandestine Guatemalan Autonomous Federation of Trade Unions, a small and relatively unimportant labor organization. The federation became an affiliated member of the communist-front World Federation of Trade Unions in October 1974. The National Committee for Labor Unity (CNUS), which includes some seventy unions, has become the most important voice for organized labor in Guatemala. Some observers believe that its militant activities in recent years have been the result of increasing PGT influence within its ranks. Names of union leaders and organizers figure prominently on the hit lists distributed by the ESA. Violence has been directed especially against members of the union for the local Coca-Cola bottling company, which has become the acknowledged leader of the Guatemalan labor movement. The secretary general of the Guatemala Bottling Union was assassinated in late December 1978. His successor fled the country in January after two unsuccessful attempts on his life, and his successor was murdered in March. At a meeting convoked by the CNUS in April, the Democratic Front denounced the tyranny headed by Lucas García that "maintains the privileges of the dominating classes and U.S. imperialism's exploitation in Guatemala." The document added that more than 600 persons had been killed thus far in 1979, "most of them murdered by the ultra-rightist groups that act openly with the support of the government" (Havana International Service, 23 April).

Domestic Attitudes and Activities. It is difficult to determine whether the PGT's Central Committee met on a regular basis during 1979, or where. Similarly, there are few data that reveal the content of any political resolutions that may have been adopted. In order to characterize the PGT's attitudes on domestic and foreign issues, it is necessary to rely on statements of party leaders made in foreign publications or in occasional interviews. Clandestine bulletins attributed to the PGT appear occasionally in Guatemala, but their authenticity is questionable.

The Political Commission of the PGT published a statement of party policy in late 1978 on the 29th anniversary of the party's foundation. From the party's point of view, the upsurge in the mass struggle in recent years results from the growing level of consciousness and mass organization of the popular masses and from working class unity against a regime of "social decomposition and corruption" dominated by a system of capitalist exploitation (*IB*, no. 23, 1978). In a declaration dated 28 January, the Political Commission condemned the "irrational and inhuman" repressive policy conducted by the government: "Mass murders in the northern regions of the country, the expulsion of thousands of peasants from their lands, the assassination of outstanding leaders of the opposition, and the intensive campaign to intimidate the population characterize the coincidence of interests between the local bourgeoisie and U.S. imperialism." The document also denounced the government for "false accusations" against the PGT for actions in which it took no part and which "are obviously intended to mislead the people and isolate our party." (Ibid., no. 7.)

The PGT's secretary general claimed in April that communist influence among Guatemala's masses is growing, despite the oppressive tactics of paramilitary gangs and auxiliary police formations "all of which are in the service of the government or of other reactionary groupings in Guatemala." He noted that the PGT's newspaper *Verdad* and other publications are distributed illegally throughout the country and serve as the principal means of distributing the party's program. Basic demands in the program are the people's right to organize freely, wage increases and cuts in the cost of living, the elimination of the apparatus of oppression, respect for human rights, and the defense of independence and sovereignty, especially "the termination of the national sellout of Guatemala's wealth and natural resources" (*Horizont*, East Berlin, 23 April).

The party has expressed its support for establishing a broad alliance of forces to create the conditions for revolution and the election of a people's government responsible for implementing structural changes. The working class and its closest ally, the peasantry, are expected to form the backbone of this alliance. The PGT viewed the creation of the Democratic Front as "an initial great success of the progressive forces." To achieve its goals, the party is prepared to use both legal and extralegal means of struggle. Precisely to what extent the PGT was responsible for the instigation of violent acts in 1979 is difficult to ascertain. In a communiqué released in March, the FAR blamed the government for the assassination of Colóm Argueta and announced its decision to "apply revolutionary justice to the perpetrators and masterminds of the Guatemalan people's repression" (AFP, 29 March). Earlier the FAR had claimed responsibility for the killing of a Guatemalan industrialist whom leftist groups accused of being responsible for the death of a labor leader (ibid., 2 March). On 18 July the FAR kidnapped the deputy foreign minister, who was released unharmed on 3 August after the government permitted the publication in local media of a lengthy manifesto justifying the guerrilla struggle.

The PGT believes that a violent revolution is the only realistic way to resolve the situation in Guatemala in favor of the masses. This assumption was stated in a press release issued in Mexico City by the Political Commission to coincide with the party's 30th anniversary. The declaration appealed to all guerrilla and civic groups to unite in a single front against repression and government terror (ibid., 26 September). In reviewing the conditions for revolution, the PGT stated that the party had been "purged" in 1979 of a trend that would have led to the party's liquidation or to the party's becoming a "militarist, aggressive organization." No further information on the precise nature or extent of possible dissension among the party's leaders was available. However, an EGP communiqué issued in October alleged that most of the worker and peasant rank and file and the party's intermediate cadres have disavowed the PGT's pro-Soviet leaders and have sought a more militant and revolutionary line (ibid., 16 October).

Although the revolutionary movement in Guatemala is presently divided, the PGT contends that conditions are being created for a unified people's struggle (EFE, Madrid, 28 September). The party undertook an intensive propaganda campaign in September to commemorate its founding. Leaflets were distributed in both the capital and the interior calling on the people to "unite in organized popular struggle" and "to follow Nicaragua's example" (ACAN, Panama City, 18 September). In response to the PGT's propaganda campaign, anticommunist sectors launched their own campaign in October. Anticommunist slogans accused San Carlos University of being under PGT control. Slogans also attacked the EGP, although most observers are no longer inclined to believe that any organizational or ideological connection between the two movements exists.

International Positions and Contacts. The PGT's positions on international issues follow closely those of the USSR. According to Otto Sánchez, Guatemalan communists view their international duty primarily as strengthening the party's solidarity with the Soviet Union and other countries of the socialist community. The party maintains that by steadfastly supporting the USSR, the international working class "strengthens its solidarity with all the peoples fighting for political emancipation, economic independence, democracy, peace and socialism" (*WMR*, April). The PGT adheres to a firm position with respect to the "aggression" and "Maoist subversion" of Chinese leaders. According to a party communiqué, the Chinese leaders are distinguished by "chauvinistic policy" and their "proclivity for divisive hegemonism" (*IB*, no. 23, 1978).

The party opposes the "chauvinistic slogans" adopted by the Guatemalan military "on the pretext of recovering Belize." The PGT has repeatedly accused the government of stirring up conflict with Great Britain over Belize in order to divert the people's attention from the country's pressing social and economic problems. In a September statement, the party greeted the triumph of the Nicaraguan revolution and expressed its solidarity with Vietnam, Laos, and Kampuchea (Cambodia). It also reaffirmed its support for Cuba and Puerto Rican nationalists (ACAN, 28 September). A high-level delegation of the PGT visited Cuba in January to attend events celebrating the twentieth anniversary of the Cuban revolution. Numerous congratulatory messages were received from communist parties around the world on the occasion of the PGT's own anniversary.

Publications. The party's clandestine newspaper, *Verdad*, appears irregularly.

The Guerrilla Army of the Poor. The EGP made its initial appearance in 1975. The guerrillas are believed to have increased in number from about 300 to an estimated 800 in 1979. They are divided into four independent commands, three in the countryside and one in Guatemala City. They have been most active in propagandizing and organizing in El Quiché, a mountainous region in northern Guatemala, near Esquintla along the tropical Pacific coast, and to a lesser extent in the department of Zacapa, where the guerrillas had their strongest support a decade ago. Guatemalan intelligence reported in late 1976 that the EGP's principal leader is César Montes, who was a member of the Revolutionary Armed Forces until that group was crushed with U.S. support in the late 1960s.

American and Guatemalan officials agree that the guerrillas are not under the direct command of the PGT, although a large percentage of urban guerrillas are believed to be party members. César Montes was at one time a member of the PGT's Central Committee, but he reportedly resigned in 1968 to protest the party's failure to support the guerrilla movement fully. A similar split may have occurred within the PGT's leadership hierarchy in response to the EGP's efforts in 1979 to unify Guatemala's revolutionary organizations.

By the end of July, the EGP claimed to have occupied some sixty towns in 1979, delivering political lectures and leaving behind Marxist propaganda. To increase its public support and offset its relatively poor military strength, the movement has adopted a policy of avoiding armed confrontation and increasing its efforts at indoctrination, especially among Guatemala's large Indian population (*Asian Wall Street Journal*, 27 July). According to news reports, the EGP has staged a number of attacks with units numbering up to 150 well-armed guerrillas, composed primarily of Indians and mestizos. Young Indians of western Guatemala are said to have left their farms and communities to join the guerrillas operating in the area of El Quiché (*Prensa Libre*, 5 May). Increased Indian participation is believed to be significant since "the Guatemalan left has traditionally considered the Indians as a highly conservative force among the local peasantry" (*Latin America Political Report*, 17 August). Many members of the EGP's main guerrilla group are believed to have fought with the Sandinistas. According to an EGP bulletin issued in July, the first lesson to be learned from the fall of Somoza is that "revolutionary armed struggle, in any of its forms, is the only path by which poor, hard-working, and exploited people can destroy the power of the rich and establish their own political, social, economic, and military power" (AFP, 19 July).

On 10 October the EGP claimed responsibility for kidnapping a businessman, who is the nephew of Guatemala's president. As one of the demands to be met for the ransom, local and foreign newspapers published a lengthy communiqué on economic conditions in Guatemala. According to the EGP, in its new stage of armed struggle "social and labor organizations have multiplied, while the Indian masses are awakening and beginning to rise." The movement defended guerrilla warfare and stated that it did not believe that social changes were authentic unless there was an in-depth transformation of the society. The EGP further revealed that efforts to achieve revolutionary unity were being made in conjunction with the FAR and the PGT (*NYT*, 26 October). According to a communiqué delivered to the press on 16 November, the EGP claimed responsibility for the serious wounding of the chief of the narcotics section of the National Police, a man charged with the torture and murdering of citizens. The communiqué also claimed credit for the occupation of two villages in the Huehuetenango mountains on 7 November and in San Juan Ixcoy on 5 November (AFP, 17 November). As of late November, the businessman was still being held for ransom.

Washington College   Daniel L. Premo

Guyana

The People's Progressive Party (PPP) was founded in 1950. At its First Congress (1951), it declared itself a nationalist party committed to socialism, national independence, and Caribbean unity. During most of the following two decades, the leaders of the PPP were predominantly Marxist-Leninist, but party followers in general were not knowledgeably so. In 1969 party leader Cheddi Jagan moved for the first time to align the PPP unequivocally with the Soviet Union, and in turn, the PPP was recognized by Soviet leaders as a bona fide communist party. Party leaders say that the process of transforming the PPP into a Leninist party began in 1969.

The PPP is a legal organization and represents the major opposition to the ruling People's National Congress (PNC), a party led by onetime PPP member and present Guyanese prime minister, Forbes Burnham. Particularly since Burnham's break with the PPP in the mid-1950s, Guyanese politics have been heavily influenced, at times determined, by ethnic differences in the population—roughly 50 percent of the population is of East Indian descent (traditionally supporting the PPP), some 40-odd percent of African descent (generally supporting the PNC), and the remainder assorted Amerindians, Portuguese, Chinese, and racial mixtures. In 1973 Burnham was re-elected for his third term, while the PPP, still claiming to be the majority party in the country, received only 26 percent of the vote (and 14 of the 53 seats in Parliament). Jagan with good reason protested that fraud and illegal maneuvers had prevailed. The PPP boycotted Parliament in protest until May 1976. The PPP accused the government of large-scale fraud in a July 1978 referendum that authorized Parliament to postpone general elections for fifteen months and ordered the creation of a constituent assembly to draft a new constitution. In protest, the PPP again boycotted full assembly proceedings and loudly condemned Burnham's decision in late October 1979 to put off elections for another year.

Two other Marxist-Leninist parties in Guyana are the Working People's Vanguard Party (WPVP), formed in 1969, and the Working People's Alliance (WPA), established as a formal party in 1979.

The membership of the PPP is unknown, though the number of active and influential Marxist-Leninists is probably no more than 500. In the past few years, a number of blacks have joined the PPP, while many East Indians have drifted into the PNC. Neither the WPVP nor the WPA is close to the size and significance of the PPP, although the WPA is said to be growing rapidly, particularly among intellectuals. The population of Guyana is approximately 850,000 (estimated 1979).

Leadership and Organization. At its Twentieth Congress in August, the PPP elected a Politburo, Secretariat, and 32-member Central Committee. The Politburo (Executive Committee) consists of Cheddi Jagan (general secretary), Janet Jagan (secretary for international affairs), Ramkarran (secretary for labor), Ralph Ramkarran (secretary for membership), Feroze Mohamed (secretary for education), Pariag Sukhai (secretary for mass organizations), Clinton Collymore (secretary for propaganda), Narbada Persaud (secretary for finance), Isahak Basir, Rohit Persaud, Cyril Belgrave, Reepu Daman Persaud, and Harry Persaud Nokta. (Personal correspondence from Narbada Persaud, dated 9 October 1979.)

The Progressive Youth Organization (PYO), traditionally a source of strong personal support for Cheddi Jagan, is headed by First Secretary Navin Chandarpal. The PYO's propaganda secretary, Clement Rohee, said at a "Youth Week" ceremony in May that the most basic right of the Guyanese people—to elect a government of their own choosing, a right guaranteed by the constitution—had been taken away by the PNC. Young people, he said, have the sacred responsibility to struggle to regain that right by taking to the streets and, with all other progressive and revolutionary forces, call for the government to resign. (*Mirror*, Georgetown, 25 May.)

The PPP-controlled Guyana Agricultural and General Workers' Union (GAWU), based in the sugar industry, claims to be the largest trade union in the country, with some 20,000 members. Ramkarran is president and Sukhai is secretary general. The GAWU is a member of the Guyana Trade Union Congress (TUC), but frequently criticizes TUC administration and policies, which it charges serve the PNC government rather than the people of Guyana.

The PPP sponsors the Women's Progressive Organization (WPO). Its main leaders are Janet Jagan (president), Arai Thantony (general secretary), Nalini Narine, and Merlin Rahman. The WPO blamed the PNC government for the "exploitation, unemployment and poverty to which our women and children are condemned." The organization also charged the government was responsible for worsening the "poverty, homelessness, degradation and crime" oppressing the people. (Ibid., 31 May.)

Party Internal Affairs. The PPP held its Twentieth Congress in Georgetown during the first week of August (The event had been preceded by regional conferences.) Besides electing party officers (see above), it adopted a new program and rules, although the shortage of newsprint forced on the PPP by the PNC government made it difficult to print copies of the documents. The congress was attended by representatives of communist and workers' parties of the Caribbean, South America, Soviet Union, and Soviet-bloc countries. According to *Pravda* (7 August), the congress "demonstrated the unity in the PPP's ranks." The leaders of the PPP have been shaken on several occasions since Jagan's 1969 decision to become affiliated with the Soviet-bloc parties. The most important defectors have been Lalbachan Lalbahadur, Ranji Chandisingh, and Vincent Teekah. The last two were appointed ministers in the PNC government. Teekah, who became a member of the Guyanese Parliament in 1969 as a representative of the PPP, was assassinated on 25 October on a street in Georgetown.

Domestic Attitudes and Activities. The PPP is committed to Marxism-Leninism, scientific socialism, proletarian internationalism, and the creation of a national patriotic front government consisting of what it calls all left and democratic forces with an anti-imperialist, socialist-oriented program. In February Jagan warned: "What we are coming to here is a dictatorship, a terroristic state, a semi-police state" (*Los Angeles Times*, 9 February). Several months later, in his May Day address, Jagan said "never in living memory have things been so bad and life so hard." Some of the problems, he said, were "lack of democracy, bureaucratic-administrative and police-military methods of rule, denial of human rights and civil liberties, militarization of politics and industrial relations, refusal to establish democratic management and workers' control at state enterprises, non-recognition of truly democratic mass organizations, political and racial discrimination in the allocation of jobs, lands, credit, houses and consumer goods at state outlets, political patronage, corruption and extravagance." (*Mirror*, 6 May.)

Since mid-1978 the PPP has been actively calling for the resignation of the Burnham government. Amid political and social agitation, including extensive strikes in the bauxite, rice, and sugar industries, the PPP in August 1979 again demanded that the government step down because "it has shown its incapacity to govern," because "its commitments and promises have been dishonored," and because it "resorts to terror and thuggery" (Agence France Presse, 20 August). It demanded "free and fair elections, under electoral procedures agreed on by the government and the opposition, supervised by international observers" (Kingston Domestic Service, 20 August). Near the end of the year, Jagan warned: "We of the PPP do not want it, the people of Guyana do not want it, but if the government continues in the way it is going, then civil war in the country is inevitable" (*Daily Gleaner*, Kingston, 30 October).

The Jonestown massacre of 18 November 1978 remained an issue in Guyanese politics. An editorial in the *Mirror* (6 May) charged that the government had allowed Jonestown to import drugs and weapons without license and that the community had become a "state within a state." As early as 3 December 1978, the *Mirror* accused the Burnham government of using the People's Temple commune (Jonestown) and another largely black cult, the House of Israel, to "prop up the PNC."

International Views and Contacts. The PPP's international views parallel those of the Soviet Union: socialism is the principal force in the world today, the SALT II treaty is a good thing, the People's Republic of China is hegemonic and expansionist. At the August congress, the party stated that "the overthrow of the reactionary regime in Grenada and the creation of progressive governments in Dominica and Saint Lucia are evidence of the Caribbean people's reluctance to tolerate the rule of the stooges of neocolonialism and foreign monopolies" (*Pravda*, 7 August). "We are not anti-American," Jagan said early in the year. "We see two Americas—one America of the people, and another America of the multinational corporation, which in the end not only impoverishes countries like ours but leads them toward dictatorships and fascism" (*Los Angeles Times*, 9 February). On foreign investment, Jagan said in his May Day speech: "Once and for all, private investment from abroad is welcome in specific fields in consortium with government and/or the cooperatives, provided that in each case government and/or the cooperatives hold majority equity and real control" (*Mirror*, 6 May).

A highly publicized issue arose in January regarding the PPP's international ties when a government parliamentarian reminded Jagan that the Georgetown *Daily Chronicle* had called the PPP leader "a Moscow puppet." Jagan replied: "Called me a Moscow puppet? I am glad for that. I'm not ashamed of being a Moscow puppet, if you want to put it that way, because Moscow stands for socialism, for democracy, for proletarian internationalism. It helps liberation movements, not like you puppets of the CIA, of imperialism." Several days later, in a letter to the *Chronicle*, he expanded on his response to heckling by government supporters: "Let me say that neither the PPP nor I take orders from Moscow. We can state categorically that at no time has any attempt been made to give us orders." (*Daily Chronicle*, 9 and 14 January.)

Publications. The PPP's newspaper is the *Mirror*, edited by Janet Jagan and published in Georgetown. A daily until late August, it was thereafter reduced to a short edition on Sundays by the government's denial of newsprint. The party's theoretical journal is *Thunder.*

The Working People's Vanguard Party (WPVP). The WPVP was founded in 1969 by Brindley Benn, a former leader of the PPP who broke with Cheddi Jagan over the latter's interpretation of Marxism and his willingness to take part in the electoral process. The WPVP adopted a pro-Chinese position. It was part of the WPA (see below) for several years but pulled out in 1977. It maintains its staunch antigovernment stance and publishes a periodic tabloid, which is said to change its name after each issue to evade government laws regulating publications. Several members of the WPVP were arrested in August.

The Working People's Alliance (WPA). The WPA, which came into existence in the mid-1970s, chiefly as a pressure group and critic of the PNC government, became a political party at the end of July 1979. It consists of the African Society for Cultural Relations with Independent Africa (ASCRIA), the Indian Progressive Revolutionary Associates (IPRA), and RATOON. An earlier member of the WPA, the WPVP, withdrew in 1977 (see above). The organization published a 30-page program entitled "For a Revolutionary Socialist Guyana" and announced a fourteen-member "collective" executive, with a rotating chairmanship and no permanent officers such as secretary general. The first chairman of the executive, considered provisional until the first WPA congress at some future date, is Eusi Kwayana (formerly Sydney King), who heads ASCRIA. Other members of the executive are Moses Bhagwan (head of IPRA), university professor Clive Thomas (head of RATOON), university lecturers Maurice Odle and Joshua Ramsammy, and other political activists. (*Daily Gleaner*, 2 August.) Three WPA members, including historian Walter Rodney and university lecturer Rupert Roopnarine, were charged with arson at midyear after the burning of government and PNC buildings. Hamilton Green, Guyanese minister of health, labor, and housing—against whom an unsuccessful assassination attempt was made in August—stated that the WPA "consists of a small group of the lunatic fringe whose only objective is to disrupt and to destroy" (*NYT*, 13 October).

The WPA program pledges to use Marxism-Leninism to create "a classless society in which human exploitation, coercion and want are at an end." Thomas says that the Alliance is "definitely leftist and as socialist as the PPP, but not linked to any international bloc, as they are." The WPA wants a two-year transitional government that will redistribute income, undertake land reform, renegotiate the foreign debt, define the economic role of the public sector, and stop the growth of the public sector as a way to end the economic crisis. Thomas adds, "We believe the government will never change through elections, which Burnham will continue to postpone in any case." He denied that the WPA had committed arson or that it was arming its members. "But," he concluded, "if the government drives us underground, that would change the ground rules." (Thomas interview with Lew Wheaton, Associated Press, 4 November.)

Hoover Institution   William E. Ratliff

Haiti

The United Party of Haitian Communists (Parti unifié des communistes Haitiens; PUCH) was formed in 1968 by the merging of several smaller leftist parties. The membership of the PUCH is unknown but estimated at less than 300 persons, most of whom are underground, in jail, or in exile. The population of Haiti in 1979 was approximately 5.5 million.

All political parties have been outlawed in Haiti since 1949. In April 1969 a law was passed declaring all forms of communist activity crimes against the state, the penalty for which is confiscation of property and death. Most PUCH activities have been carried on outside Haiti among exiles in Europe, the Soviet Union, and Cuba. The main PUCH spokesmen in the past year have been Jacques Dorcilien, elected general secretary at the party's First Congress (in late 1978 or early 1979), and Gesner Briard.

Domestic and International Positions. The "Final Declaration" of the First Congress stated that mass resistance is increasing in Haiti and is seen in numerous strikes by workers, peasant actions, and the move for general elections and the end of the lifetime Duvalier presidency. The party demanded: (1) an end to imperialist plunder of the country's wealth; (2) abrogation of the 1969 anticommunist law and other similar legislation; (3) an end to the lifelong and hereditary presidency; (4) publication of the names of all political prisoners and their immediate release; (5) a general amnesty, including the right to unconditional return of all political exiles; and (6) the right to free organization of political parties and the holding of general elections at all levels. (*IB*, no. 3.) It branded the February National Assembly elections a "trick" (Havana Domestic Service, 12 January). Several points in the "Final Declaration" were elaborated on by Briard in the *World Marxist Review* (April). The big bourgeoisie, the bureaucratic elite, and a segment of the middle strata in collusion with foreign companies are plundering the nation's wealth, while "the poverty of the masses is reaching appalling proportions." The dictatorship is consolidating its "repressive machine" and "clinging to power by coercion." Although worker, peasant, and student actions are scattered, they "comprise the basis on which the People's Unity Front is being set up." The PUCH claims it "bears the brunt of the struggle against the dictatorship." The government seeks to isolate the party, Briard stated, but the PUCH continues to work to broaden its actions with the objective of setting up "a broad alliance of popular forces capable of overthrowing the dictatorship and setting up a regime that would ensure democratic freedoms and satisfy the day-to-day requirements of the people." Party leaders hail international support for their efforts, laud the policies of the Soviet Union, and condemn the United States.

Hoover Institution   Lynn Ratliff

Honduras

The Communist Party of Honduras (Partido Comunista de Honduras; PCH) was organized in 1927, destroyed in 1932, and reorganized in 1954. A dispute over strategy and tactics in 1967 led to the expulsion of one group and the division of the PCH into rival factions. Since 1971, a self-proclaimed pro-Chinese Communist Party of Honduras/Marxist-Leninist (PCH-ML) has functioned, but little is known about its leaders and membership. Since most statements by the PCH-ML have emanated from Beijing, there is a strong possibility that it is little more than a paper organization.

The PCH has been illegal since 1957 but has operated openly in varying degrees under recent governments. The prospects for legal status for the PCH are doubtful since the coup of August 1978 brought in a more conservative regime.

Membership in the PCH is estimated at 650. The population of Honduras is about 3.6 million (1979 estimate).

Leadership and Organization. After an apparent reorganization of the party's top leadership in late 1978, Rigoberto Padilla Rush, Central Committee secretary, emerged as the new PCH secretary general, replacing Dionisio Ramos Bejarano, whose current party status is not known. Emerging with increased status—manifested in participation with Padilla in talks with East European and Soviet leaders—was Longino Becerra, a propaganda spokesman in the 1960s who resurfaced in April 1977 after five years of unexplained absence. In early January, when Becerra emerged as a member of the Political Commission of the Central Committee, he denied there had been a purge. He said that there had only been an "internal reorganization to make room for the party's cadres, giving new members an opportunity to participate." Becerra said Ramos Bejarano "continued to be a member of the Political Commission and to perform other duties." (Agencia Centro Americano Noticias [ACAN], Panama City, 5 January.) Interestingly enough, opinion articles on hemispheric themes by Ramos appeared fairly regularly in October in the San Pedro Sula newspaper *Tiempo* (e.g., 15 and 18 October) but without any mention by himself or the newspaper of his former position or affiliation.

Milton René Paredes, a Central Committee member in recent years, apparently retained his position in the shakeup. He, however, was subjected to public criticism in September and October by Roger Isaula, a teacher at the National Autonomous University (*La Tribuna*, Tegucigalpa, 18 October). Little was heard in 1979 of either Mario Sosa Navarro, a member of the Political Commission for the past ten years, or Rigoberto Luna, who had been active among north coast labor unions from 1970 to 1977.

On 10 April Erich Honecker, secretary general of the East German Socialist Unity Party, sent a message of "fraternal greetings" on the 25th anniversary of the reorganization of the PCH in 1954. But the event was not marked in Honduras or elsewhere with public statements, perhaps because the new leadership under Padilla may not have felt confident enough to issue any statements or to publicly celebrate the event. (*Neues Deutschland*, East Berlin, 10 April.) At the PCH's Third Congress, held in May and June 1978, there had been no hint of an impending leadership crisis or change.

The party has been active in recruitment and organizational work among secondary and university students. The PCH sponsors the Socialist Student Front (FES) and the Federation of Secondary Students (FESE).

Although elections were held for the Executive Committee of the Honduran University Student Federation in July, not enough is known about the winners to determine the extent of FES influence vis-à-vis that of the conservative United Democratic University Front, which has dominated political activities on the Tegucigalpa and San Pedro Sula campuses of the university. Before the election, however, the July issue of *Tribuna Sindical*, organ of the Union of National University Workers, carried an article by Matías Funes urging students to support "the progressive sectors of the university community." From 1973 to 1976, Funes was director of the PCH newspaper *Vanguardia Revolucionaria*; it is not known if he is still affiliated with the PCH, especially since the leadership change in December 1978–January 1979. In addition, the same issue carried a reported interview by Roger Isaula with a fourteen-year-old Nicaraguan peasant who had been fighting with the Sandinista Liberation Front.

The FESE was the principal organizer of the strikes in October that immobilized four secondary institutions in Tegucigalpa and neighboring Comayaguela for several days (*Tiempo*, 15 October). The FESE was unable to obtain support from the 130 other secondary schools that it asked to join the strike. On 25 October, however, some 2,000 students of the Vicente Caceres Central Institute demonstrated near and occupied offices of the Ministry of Public Education (*La Tribuna*, 26 October), although neither the FESE nor another secondary student group, the Revolutionary Action Front, claimed any responsibility for or role in the vandalism.

The PCH was active in the several trade union elections and strikes in 1979. Perhaps the most dramatic was the conflagration on 6 March that resulted in three deaths, an undetermined number of burned and wounded, and millions of dollars' worth of damage to the Bemis Handal Textile Factory in San Pedro Sula (*La Prensa*, San Pedro Sula, 7 March; *Tribuna Sindical*, July). An undetermined number of workers, including several who were reported to be "known members of the communist party," were arrested and held for investigation and trial (*Tribuna Sindical*, July).

Although the PCH lost much of its influence in the north coast region as a consequence of the 1977 defeat of Napoleon Acevedo Granados in elections for the leadership of the Union of the Standard Fruit Company, the PCH spent a lot of effort in early 1979 to influence the outcome of elections for the Federation of Workers of the Capital District (FECESITLIH), the most important trade union federation in the Tegucigalpa and central regions of the country. Mario N. Flores, secretary general and a postal-telecommunications leader, had become acting president in January with the departure for Cornell University on a scholarship of Gustavo Zelaya, the longtime FECESITLIH president. When elections were held on 29 July, challenges were made over the legality of the credentials of delegates from nine organizations that had not paid their 1979 dues to the federation. However, these dissidents reportedly said that Flores and the incumbents refused to accept their unpaid dues. As of late October, the Ministry of Labor had not decided between the "losing" slate headed by Flores or the "winning" slate headed by Emílio Gonzales—a former FECESITLIH auditor—who had the support of unions of rural teachers, sawmill workers, and employees of the university and banks. (Ibid.; *Tiempo*, various issues.)

Domestic Events and Views. Most political party activity in Honduras in 1979 centered around elections to be held 20 April 1980 for the Constituent Assembly, which is to elect a new president to replace the current junta. There was some apathy in the early part of the year, attributed by some to a feeling that the National Party (PN) had so rigged the National Electoral Tribunal with its members and registered so many fraudulent names that an honest election could not be held (*Tiempo*, 13 October; *La Tribuna*, 25 October). By November many members of the Liberal Party (PL) and the Christian Democrats (PDCH) were so irritated with the alleged fraudulent registrations that they threatened to abstain from the elections unless the armed forces took measures to purify the voter registration lists (*Tiempo*, 18 October). Perhaps foreseeing the charges of voter registration fraud, the PCH Political Commission issued a statement on 22 November 1978 calling for a "free and democratic election," charging that the more traditional PL and PN "no longer express the vital aspirations of the popular masses" and that the "revolutionary forces are not advancing a democratic alternative capable of arousing the people, mobilizing their enthusiasm, selflessness, and fighting capacity." These remarks about the "revolutionary forces" may have been veiled criticisms of Ramos Bejarano. In August, Isaula, previously unknown as a PCH international spokesman, told a Mexican newspaper correspondent that the PCH had joined the left wing of the PL headed by Roberto Reina, the PDCH, the Revolutionary Party, the Party of Innovation and Unity, and the Socialist Party in abstaining from the 1980 elections unless the registration irregularities were stopped (*Excelsior*, Mexico City, 15 August). Formation of a socialist party on 3 January by a well-known National University professor, Marco Virgilio Carias, was billed as a "popular alternative to achieve the unity of peasants, workers, students, intellectuals, and professors" (ACAN, Panama City, 3 January). Some days later, when Becerra announced the new leadership of Padilla Rush, he praised the establishment of the new party. However, there were no future public commentaries by the PCH during the year about the new group.

The Central Committee noted that "any democratic solution" to the crisis of transferring power from the military to a presumably civilian regime "must take account of the role of the army, which over the past thirteen years has turned into a political arbiter in the country." However, there appears to be something of a shift in the PCH's view of the divisions among the top leaders of the army. In March and April 1978 and again in July 1979, Padilla spoke favorably of "reformists within the pre–August 1978 administration who "elaborated a progressive social reform program, including an agricultural reform plan in 1974" and "reformists" within the 1979 regime who "have won the support of the masses and the communist party" (*Latinskaya Amerika*, Moscow, March-April 1978; *Népszabadság*, Budapest, 20 July). But in speaking of conservative or reactionary groups within the military, there appears to be something of a shift. In November 1978, the Political Commission identified the 1979 regime with "the interests of a bourgeois-landowner oligarchy and imperialism." In July, Padilla Rush told a Hungarian newsman that the government was allied with "representatives of reactionary estate owners and the middle bourgeoisie allied with imperialism." They "are opposed by a group of moderates, representatives of the nationalist-minded industrial bourgeoisie, who by virtue of their progressive initiatives, enjoy the support of the democratic forces, the workers, peasants, and students." (*Népszabadság*, 20 July.) A statement of the shift of multinational corporation support from the former to the now dominant Paz Garcia faction came in Isaula's statement to *Excelsior* on 15 August that United Fruit and Standard Fruit were continuing to manipulate the Honduran economy and military through "close links" to the "ultra-rightist" head of military intelligence, who was linked to the 1979 military leader and others involved in a 1978 drug-smuggling scandal that led to the 1978 coup.

International Activities and Contacts. Rigoberto Padilla and Longino Becerra spent at least ten days during July in Eastern Europe and the Soviet Union, meeting with officials of the communist parties of Czechoslovakia, Hungary, and the Soviet Union. Although little was said of their discussions in Czechoslovakia, extensive coverage was given to their comments on the overthrow of Anastasio Somoza's government in Nicaragua by the Sandinista forces as well as to PCH support for détente and the SALT II treaty. In an extensive interview in Budapest, Becerra noted that:

> Somoza's downfall is a defeat of the political model forced on the countries of our continent by imperialist power. This model, which can be characterized economically as being capitalism in a position of dependence and politically as being the establishment of so-called governments of national security, has failed completely in both these respects.

The reason it has failed economically was because it was unable to attain an even development within the Latin American countries, and necessarily in a state of stagnation, it was unable to resolve the problems of the masses. Its failure politically was the result of its inability to transplant even the most modest middle-class reform into practice.

In response to a question why there was "no direct foreign military intervention" preceding Somoza's fall, Becerra said:

The intervention was thwarted, for instance, by the Costa Rican parliament's decision and the protest demonstrations by the Costa Rican people that forced the U.S. military aircraft and helicopters deployed near the Nicaraguan border to withdraw. However, what is essential is that U.S. imperialism was not able to repeat the 1965 Dominican intervention because the present international situation—the changed balance of power and world public opinion . . . did not make this possible. (Ibid.)

Of a 27 July meeting in Moscow with Boris Ponomarev, Tass (27 July) noted that "the representatives of the Communist Party of the Soviet Union [CPSU] and the PCH warmly welcomed the victory of the Nicaraguan people over the forces of internal reaction and imperialism. The unswerving support of the CPSU for the struggle of the democrats and patriots of Latin America for their freedom and happiness of their people was stressed."

Milton René Paredes indirectly criticized Soviet dissidents and U.S. efforts on behalf of human rights in a March *World Marxist Review* article on the efforts of different socialist countries to build socialism and the efforts of "bourgeois ideologues" to discuss developments in "socialist countries."

Publications. The PCH's principal publication is *Patria*, which has appeared only sporadically and clandestinely since it replaced *Vanguardia Revolucionaria* in 1976. *El Trabajo*, a theoretical and informational journal, has not circulated publicly in the past six years and has not been mentioned in international communist publications. Party statements are often found in the *World Marxist Review*, that journal's *Information Bulletin*, and in occasional press conferences or articles in Honduran newspapers.

Texas Tech University   Neale J. Pearson

Jamaica

Two communist parties have been formed in Jamaica during the past four years: the Jamaican Communist Party (JCP) and the Jamaican Workers' Party (JWP).

The JCP was founded in 1975 and is led by its general secretary, Chris Lawrence. The party is active in the Independent Trade Union Action Council, a federation of small units affiliated with the

World Federation of Trade Unions. The JCP has given critical support to the ruling People's National Party (PNP), led by Prime Minister Michael Manley. It has called for the unity of all "progressive" forces to avert what it considers the "fascist threat" posed by the Jamaican Labor Party (JLP). To this end it has called on the prime minister to pull together the nation's political, social, and labor organizations to halt the advance of "reactionary" forces. The JCP condemned the JLP for urging the overthrow of the Manley government and called instead for the PNP to fulfull the mandates given it by getting rid of the International Monetary Fund (IMF), rolling back prices, introducing an anti-layoff law, and providing jobs so that people will be encouraged to support the government and smash what the JCP calls the "fascist offensive." The JCP rejected JLP charges of Cuban subversion of the nation. (Kingston Domestic Service, 23 February, 20 March; *Intercontinental Press*, 19 November.) The party charges in return that the United States is meddling in the affairs of Jamaica and of Grenada, among other countries.

The JWP was formed in December 1978 when the Workers' Liberation League (WLL) transformed itself into the JWP at its first congress. According to Trevor Munroe, WLL founder and JWP general secretary, the new party will be a full member of the international community of communist and workers' parties. Among the party's leaders are John Haughton and Barry Chevannes. A representative of the Communist Party of the Soviet Union attended the founding congress, and the JWP has adopted a pro-Soviet stance. (*Granma*, Havana, English ed., 31 December 1978; *Canadian Tribune*, 4 December.) The WLL exercised some influence on students, teachers, and intellectuals, in addition to workers. Munroe claims WLL members were elected to positions of leadership at the University of the West Indies, where Munroe is a senior lecturer, and in the more than 800 Jamaica youth clubs. It is on speaking terms with the JCP.

The JWP maintains its position of critical support for the PNP government. In May Munroe issued a statement announcing that the JWP would enter candidates in the next elections, defend the Manley government, and "seek an electoral alliance with the People's National Party" (*Daily Gleaner*, Kingston, 22 May), an alliance that the prime minister declined to accept. In July the JWP instructed its lawyers to investigate the possibility of court action to allow more than the two major parties to have referees during vote counting. In May Munroe reiterated his opposition to IMF operations in the country but acknowledged the JWP's failure to have the IMF expelled. "Our movement has to suspend the struggle for the time being to reject the IMF agreement and continue to educate the working people." (Ibid., 22 May.) The JWP rejected JLP charges of Cuban subversion in the country and in particular denied that Munroe was a link between Prime Minister Manley and the Soviet KGB. The party does welcome the development of relations between Jamaica and the Soviet Union and applauded the prime minister's visit to Moscow during the year.

Hoover Institution   William E. Ratliff

Martinique

The Martinique Communist Party (Parti communiste martiniquais; PCM) was founded in 1921. In 1979 it stepped up its attacks on the central government in Paris, but tended to downplay its usual calls for autonomy. Rather, it emphasized the island's difficult economic situation and, sensing heightened racial feeling, denounced whites for discriminating against blacks. Without giving up its support for the idea of autonomy within France, the party, in speeches by leaders and in newspaper articles, nonetheless accepted the idea of Martiniquan nationhood. Cantonal elections brought no new strength or losses.

Leadership and Organization. At its first national conference, held on 16 and 17 December 1978 at Lamentin, the PCM called for a strengthening of the party, particularly through an intense membership campaign. By the end of April 1979, leaders claimed success with a reported 20 percent increase in membership, and new adherents met for a series of classes.

Armand Nicolas, secretary general of the PCM, continued his very active role. His book on the slave revolt of 22 May 1848 was widely read by party members, and he spoke frequently in the towns of the island. In May he organized a study session for communist town council and General Council members around the theme "The Role of Communist Elected Officials in the Struggle for Short-Term Goals and for Democratic and Popular Autonomy." The commmunist-led Union of Women of Martinique met under its president, Solange Fitte-Duval, and in July the Union of Communist Youth of Martinique held a meeting to discuss unemployment.

The only elections this year were at the cantonal level. Half the seats in the 36-member General Council were filled. Because most of these cantons had shown little support for the party in the past, the PCM ran candidates in only seven. The party was able to return the only communist incumbent, the councillor of Macouba. Thus, communist representation in the General Council, which votes the budget of the department, did not change. Out of 36 members, the PCM still had 3, while neo-Gaullists and Giscardians controlled the majority of seats. On the other hand, the party's popular vote increased in these cantons from 2,353 to 2,827 between 1973 and 1979. As usual, the PCM asked the Martinique Progressive Party (PPM) to cooperate, but the PPM refused. (The PPM retained its three seats.)

Domestic Attitudes and Activities. The difficult economic situation and the increasing incidents of racial conflict occupied party members this year. Threats to close a major sugar mill, a planned decrease in banana production, a rate of inflation around 12 percent, a rise in social security taxes, and other factors threatened to drive the rate of unemployment above 40 percent. The ravages of Hurricane David made the situation worse, although aid from the metropole arrived. A 2.2 percent increase in the minimum wage was too low to affect worker welfare significantly. The PCM thus made several declarations denouncing government policy and the island's economic situation.

The several annual strikes of teachers, factory workers, and others won the party's support. During these events, the racial issue seemed to become sharper. The arrival of white metropolitan teachers in the lycées was denounced. The reported 7,000 French police and military stationed in

Martinique were labeled racist. This year a corporal who last year shot a high school student was sentenced to nine years of prison, a sentence the PCM said was too light. Demonstrations this year led to some beatings, and one person was killed in a demonstration on 14 July. The party newspaper, *Justice*, gave considerable attention to the trial of a white accused of killing a black youth in Guadeloupe.

On 22 May the PCM celebrated Martinique's national day, which commemorates the anniversary of a slave uprising in 1848 that contributed to the end of slavery. *Justice* ran a series of historical cartoons written in the Creole language about the uprising, thus contributing to a growing sense of special identity in the island.

To help the economy, the PCM proposed mixed private and public enterprises in the sugar industry and offered the public a general "plan for survival," originally drawn up 8 December 1978 but published at the beginning of January 1979. Among other suggestions, the PCM called for a local planning body, a new agreement with the European Economic Community (EEC) that would give Martinique the right to raise or lower tariffs on imports from Europe, and lower transport costs. The party generally denounced French economic policies under which sugar production is declining and Martinique is being further integrated with the EEC.

International Views and Policies. Criticism of the EEC did not prevent the PCM from participating in the elections to the European parliament created by the EEC. In the 10 June elections it fully supported the French Communist Party (PCF) list headed by Georges Marchais and Paul Vergès, secretary general of the Réunion Communist Party, who visited Martinique in 1979. At a press conference Armand Nicolas explained that Martinique voters should participate in the elections so that the PCF could represent Martinique's interests in Europe. Only 29 percent of the electorate voted, however, and the communists received 5,500 votes compared with about 25,000 for the Giscard-supported list.

True to its pro-Russian posture, the PCM supported the Vietnamese invasion of Kampuchea (Cambodia), calling it a force of liberation, denounced the rapprochement of China and the United States as treason, and condemned Chinese attacks on Vietnam as a "crime against socialism." The PCM supported SALT II and promoted close ties with Cuba, particularly in cultural matters. Martiniquans traveled to Havana to participate in ceremonies organized by the Cuban La Casa de las Américas honoring French-language writers in the West Indies. The PCM sent representatives to Carifesta, the cultural meeting held in Havana between 16 and 22 July. The meeting of nonaligned states was hailed, and the communist countries were praised as the true friends of the Third World.

Party members followed events in Saint Lucia, which became independent, and in neighboring Dominica, which underwent an internal crisis.

Publications. *Justice*, published for almost sixty years, had a weekly press run of 8,000 copies. On 4 January it issued a supplement called "Le Plan de survie" and distributed it widely throughout the year as the PCM's answer to Martinique's economic problems. The "Fête de justice" was held on 8 and 15 July.

Howard University   Brian Weinstein

Mexico

Founded under a different name in 1919, the Mexican Communist Party (Partido Comunista Mexicano; PCM) has maintained its present name since 1920. Although the PCM is a legal party, it had not been able to participate in elections since 1946. According to the electoral law in effect until 1977, a party had to meet a membership requirement of 65,000 to enter registered candidates in national elections. It also had to provide lists to the government with data on all members. The PCM had been unable or unwilling to provide this information. The electoral reform of 1977, however, granted the PCM conditional registration, thus enabling the party to participate in the 1979 elections for the Chamber of Deputies and seven state governorships. According to the new law, if the PCM candidates received at least 1.5 percent of the popular vote, the party would not need to demonstrate a membership of 65,000 in order to be registered for future elections. Party leaders hoped to win much more than 1.5 percent, enabling the PCM to become the largest of the parties to the left of the Popular Socialist Party (PPS). In addition to allowing the PCM to participate in the elections, the reform enlarged the Chamber of Deputies to 400 members, 100 to be filled through proportional representation and 300 to be elected directly. The population of Mexico is 66.5 million (1979 estimate).

At the end of the PCM's national convention on 25 February, it and several smaller parties presented a joint list of candidates and a common platform for the 1 July elections. The four-party coalition included the PCM, the Mexican People's Party, the Revolutionary Socialist Party, and the Socialist Unity and Action Movement. Although the PCM complained about fraud and lost ballots in some districts, party leaders were generally satisfied with the election results. The Institutional Revolutionary Party (PRI) won 68 to 70 percent of the votes and received 296 of the 300 seats contested by direct election; the National Action Party (PAN) won 13 percent of the vote and the four remaining seats (*Latin America Political Report*, 13 July). The PCM exceeded the minimum required for definitive legal registration by a substantial margin; the electoral commission estimated the coalition vote at 5 percent, and the PCM estimated it at 5.7 percent. Although the PCM failed to win any of the 40 seats it contested in the Federal District, it surpassed the PPS and became the second opposition party after the PAN. In the electoral commission's allocation of the additional 100 seats reserved for the six opposition parties under the system of proportional representation, the PAN was expected to receive 40 to 50 seats. The communists received 18.

Party Internal Affairs. According to PCM Secretary General Arnoldo Martínez Verdugo, the party has 103,000 enrolled and affiliated members. In addition to Martínez Verdugo, prominent party members during 1979 included Valentín Campa, María Elena Morales, Antonio Franco, Marcos Leonel Pasadas, Linomedina Salazar, Samuel Meléndrez Luevano, Gilberto Ricón Gallardo, José Encarnación Pérez, Pablo Gómez and José María Zerero. Arturo Martínez Nateras, a member of the Central Committee and Executive Committee, resigned in December 1978. His letter of resignation criticized the lack of democratic procedures within the party.

Domestic Attitudes and Activities. The PCM is attempting to develop mutual understanding between communists and Catholics. According to Martínez Verdugo, the party is working alongside Catholics and Jesuits in the urban slums and among the peasants. "Hence there has been a decline in anticommunism. We note greater understanding even among the (church) hierarchy, and we find that our influence is increasing." (*L'Unità*, Rome, 28 February.) Martínez Verdugo believes the Mexican constitution's restrictions on the church are inappropriate today, and the PCM has called for full political rights for priests.

The PCM secretary general also believes that communists can win power through democratic evolution leading to socialism; thus the PCM is working to improve the conditions for democratic development in Mexico. Furthermore, the party sees democratic and social transformations as the way out of the crisis Mexico is experiencing. The PCM's "assumption is that democratic and anti-oligarchy acts such as the abolition of dependence on imperialism, elimination of big capitalist property in land and its transfer to the peasants, together with encouragement of collectivization in agriculture, establishment of democratic political power and nationalization of the monopolies, have, apart from their general democratic content, also a definite anticapitalist orientation." (*WMR*, April.)

The PCM sees the government's electoral reform as an effort to revitalize and modernize the system without changing its substance. According to Martínez Verdugo, the reform maintains the status quo so that the PRI and the government can manipulate election results. Nevertheless, the reform is a result of the persistent struggle for democracy that the masses have been conducting. Although it is very limited, it is the most the democratic movement could accomplish at the time. At present the communists and their allies could not go further because of the weakness of the mass movement.

In seeking allies, the communists are emphasizing unity among those groups opposed to the PRI. They want to join forces with workers, peasants, elements of the middle class, and other groups that are democratic, anti-imperialist, and antimonopolistic. They hope to build on their electoral coalition and ultimately create a democratic and popular bloc to replace Mexico's present political leaders. In accord with these tactics, the PCM wants to cooperate with the Trotskyists, whom they see as a trend within the labor movement rather than as a band of assassins, spies, and imperialist agents as in the Stalinist view. Although the Trotskyists did not join the PCM in the electoral coaliton, the two groups have formed alliances in the universities. Trade union unity is also consistent with this tactic. The PCM maintains that trade union freedom is practically nonexistent and that only a unified effort of all workers, regardless of their membership in this or that trade union center or sectoral union or political party, will enable the working class to achieve its goals. Thus, the PCM maintains close ties with the recently formed 50,000-member University Workers' National United Trade Union (*Latin American Political Report*, 19 October).

The PCM continues to criticize government repression. "Repressive practices became widespread from the start of the conflict between guerrilla groups [which appeared in 1965] and the police who, using this struggle as a pretext, introduced systematic arrests, torture, and organized disappearances among the peasant, labor, and student sectors. We demand a full explanation for these actions and punishment of the guilty. So far the replies have been evasive, and government policy continues to exhibit glaring contradictions." (*Mundo Obrero*, Madrid, 4 March.) The PCM also claims that there are still 120 guerrillas in jail, 363 persons who have disappeared, and nine activists in exile.

International Views and Positions. When Pope John Paul II visited Mexico early in the year, PCM representatives were among those who greeted him at the airport. The party joined right-wing pressure groups in demanding that diplomatic relations be established with the Vatican. Party leaders also met with Romanian officials in Bucharest. During the visit, the Romanian and Mexican communists stated that relations between communist and workers' parties should be grounded on the principles of equal rights, noninterference in internal affairs, and observance of the right of each party to work out its revolutionary strategy and tactics autonomously according to the specific historical, social, and economic conditions in its own country. The PCM considers Eurocommunism a way to resolve the specific problems of European societies and developed countries but insists that it would be a mistake to think that this concept could be used to resolve the problems of Latin American revolutionary movements. The Romanian and Mexican communists also called for the strengthening of cooperation between communist and socialist parties and among all progressive, democratic, and anti-imperialist forces in the general struggle for the consolidation of world peace and security. At a subsequent meeting in Yugoslavia, PCM officials praised President Tito and the Yugoslav communists for seeking ways to strengthen the nonaligned movement and called on Mexico to advance from its observer status and play a more active role in that movement. The Mexican communists were critical of President Carter during his visit to Mexico. They stated that he wanted "to perpetuate the relations with the home of the transnationals and to establish new shackles to keep Mexico inferior" (EFE, Madrid, 13 February). They claimed that he was trying to turn Mexico into a huge oil well for the benefit of the United States. The PCM called on Mexico to join the Organization of Petroleum Exporting Countries in order to break the economic chains of imperialism and to fight the price battle alongside the other petroleum producers. PCM official Valentín Campa, upon returning from a trip to the United States, his first since 1939, called for a labor convention that recognizes the U.S. need for migratory workers and grants them union rights. He contended that Mexico, with its migrants, is financing the U.S. economy, which finds cheap labor for which it is not required to provide social security and whose children it does not have to educate, even though these workers pay taxes to the U.S. government. In contrast to criticizing President Carter and the United States, the PCM supported certain actions of the Mexican government, such as the cool reception of the U.S. president, the visit of Cuban President Fidel Castro, and the severing of diplomatic relations with the Somoza government of Nicaragua.

Publications. The primary PCM organ continues to be *Oposición*, a weekly newspaper.

Guerrillas and Terrorists. During November and December 1978, some guerrilla groups carried on limited activities. These included the Armed Forces of Liberation in Guerrero, initially led by Lucio Cabañas, who was killed in 1974; the People's Union, one of whose leaders, Eladio Ramírez Castillo, was killed by police; and the People's Armed Revolutionary Branch, who released kidnapped businessman Raúl Garza Cantú for 10 million pesos. In 1979, police captured two members of the Revolutionary Organization of the Proletariat, whose main objective was to assassinate agrarian officials and leaders whom they accused of delaying and hindering the distribution of land. The police said they were investigating alleged branches of the organizations in order to disband it completely. Compared with recent years, the activities of the 23 September Communist League (Liga Comunista 23 de Septiembre) were not frequently reported. The league—which takes its name from the date of an attack on an army garrison in Chihuahua in 1965—has participated in or been accused of many bombings, kidnappings, and assassinations in recent years. In the spring, one league member was killed in a shootout with the police at the National University. League members were surrounded by police in a parking lot where they went to pick up U.S. $880,000 in ransom for Mónica Pérea, whom they had kidnapped. Police reported that the arrest of other league members involved in the shootout had not yet led to her release.

Grand Valley State Colleges   Donald L. Herman

Nicaragua

The fall of the Somoza dynasty in July marked a major turning point in Nicaragua, with the Marxist-leaning Sandinist Liberation Front (Frente Sandinista de Liberación Nacional; FSLN) emerging as the dominant force in the new government. The nine-member Directorate of the FSLN became the ultimate authority in Nicaragua following the collapse of the government of Gen. Anastasio Somoza Debayle. In late June, the FSLN had established a government-in-exile in Costa Rica headed by a five-member junta. That junta immediately took power as organized resistance to the Sandinista guerrillas collapsed and Somoza fled the country to exile in the United States.

The FSLN, founded in 1961, was essentially a small guerrilla organization until 1978 when its ranks were swelled by hundreds of Nicaraguans. By the time General Somoza fled the country, it is estimated there were 5,000 Sandinistas under arms and another 15,000 in noncombatant roles.

There are three other leftist parties. The Socialist Party of Nicaragua (Partido Socialista Nicaragüense; PSN) is a pro-Soviet group founded in 1937. It was declared illegal a year later and has been a clandestine organization ever since. Its membership is estimated at 250, some of whom are linked with the Sandinist guerrillas. The Communist Party of Nicaragua (Partido Comunista Nicaragüense; PCN) is an anti-Soviet group formed in 1967 when an internal struggle in the PSN resulted in the expulsion of six party leaders. These six established the PCN but have had limited success in attracting members to their cause. The PCN's present membership is estimated at under 160, although it claims to have 1,200. A third group, the Popular Action Movement (Movimiento de Acción Popular emerged in 1967, declaring itself a Maoist group and embracing a sharply leftist Marxist-Leninist philosophy. Its membership is thought to be less than 25. Its newspaper, *El Pueblo*, was more widely read, however, although it was closed down by both the Somoza and the Sandinista governments. The population of Nicaragua is about 2.5 million.

The Sandinistas. Founded in 1961 by the late Carlos Fonseca Amador and several others, the Sandinist Liberation Front consistently maintained the necessity of direct action against the Somoza government. During the 1970s, the movement split into at first two and then three different tendencies. One favored the concept of protracted warfare and generally included people who were involved in the founding of the movement or joined it soon thereafter. Where this tendency concentrated on rural activities, a second favored urban warfare and also sought a quicker victory. Both of these groups were decidedly Marxist, while a third tendency was leftist but included many non-Marxist elements as well and like the second group urged a more active struggle. The majority of Sandinist adherents belong to this group, and it became apparent in 1979 that this *tercerista* ("third") force often mediated between the other two tendencies.

The first group is headed by Tómas Borge Martínez, the only founder of the movement still alive, and includes Henry Ruiz and Bayardo Arce Castaño; the second group is nominally headed by Jaime Wheelock Román and includes Carlos Nuñez Téllez and Luis Carrión Cruz. Finally, the *tercerista* group includes Daniel Ortega Saavedra, his brother Humberto, and Víctor Manuel Tirado López.

During the year, these leaders mapped their battle strategy for what they called "the final offensive" against the Somoza government. Meeting in a five-day session in Panama during mid-May, they planned to bring down the Somoza government by August at the earliest. When they began their offensive on 28 May Borge told his fellow commanders by radio: "I'll see you in Managua in three months." But it did not take three months. By 19 July Sandinist military strategy had worked so well that General Somoza was in Miami in exile, and the black and red banner of the Sandinist Army, now Central America's most battle-seasoned military force, flew over all of Nicaragua. The government that took over was a collegial affair with the Sandinist Directorate setting the tone and offering guidance, the five-member junta in charge of the day-to-day operation of government, and a Cabinet that included many Sandinist commanders as well as non-Sandinist leaders. The junta also included a political mix — Sandinist Directorate member Daniel Ortega; Moisés Hassán Morales, a Sandinist leader; Sergio Ramírez Mercado, a lawyer-writer who leaned to the Sandinist cause; Alfonso Robelo Callejas, a businessman who had been active in the non-Sandinist opposition to General Somoza; and Violeta Barrios de Chamorro, the widow of assassinated newspaper editor Pedro Joaquín Chamorro Cardenal, whose murder in January 1978 was probably the single most important catalyst in the mushrooming buildup of opposition, Marxist and non-Marxist, to General Somoza.

The FSLN army, obviously well-organized and well-equipped, operated mainly as a guerrilla force until the launching of the final offensive. It engaged the pro-Somoza National Guard in numerous skirmishes, many of them simply hit-and-run raids. When these skirmishes became real battles, the FSLN would fade away to do battle elsewhere, having learned that the superior firepower of the National Guard could usually be counted on to win the engagement. In May, with the major offensive under way and the FSLN equipped with improved firepower, the engagements became battles in which the FSLN was able to defeat the guard on many occasions, such as the encounters in June in Metagalpa, León, and Rivas. The FSLN used Costa Rican territory as a haven for training, rest, recuperation, and regrouping; it received a variety of new, semisophisticated weapons from Panama, Venezuela, the Middle East, and elsewhere. It was estimated that the value of the military hardware received by the FSLN during 1979 alone amounted to more than U.S. $20 million.

Use of Costa Rica by the FSLN army was paralleled by the use of this neighbor country as the site of the government-in-exile established in June. The five-member junta met regularly in San José, the Costa Rican capital, and drafted a plan of government that provided for political pluralism and a mixed socialist-capitalist economy. But both the odd nature of the collegial government and this diverse political-economic system raised questions about the viability of the new government once it took over on 19 July. Moreover, it was evident that the ultimate authority was the Sandinist Directorate, composed of self-professed Marxists. Yet Wheelock, who early became minister of agrarian reform, a post that made him responsible for administering Somoza's extensive property, was able to say in late July that the new government not only wanted private enterprise and would respect private property but also guaranteed such property.

The new government inherited a bankrupt economy with more than $1.6 billion in foreign debts. About 50,000 people were killed in the eighteen months of civil war between January 1978 and the fall of Somoza in mid-July 1979, while another 150,000 were injured or wounded and upwards of 1 million were made homeless. Many industries had been destroyed in the fighting, agriculture was set back considerably by the disruption of planting and harvesting cycles, and the country was "flat on its back with almost nothing of a hopeful quality," as Borge said in July.

The Marxist connection of the FSLN was not hard to pinpoint, although Sandinist leaders kept insisting that the government was not simply Marxist. To many observers, however, there were tendencies in this direction — the attendance of two members of the junta at the 26 July celebration in Havana, the subsequent visit to Cuba of top FSLN members to attend the nonaligned meeting, the arrival between September and November of approximately one thousand Cuban teachers to work in

Nicaraguan schools and 600 Cuban medical personnel to work in hospitals, the dispatch of 800 Nicaraguan teenage children to Cuba for study, and other contact with Castro's government in Havana. On the other hand, the Sandinist Directorate took firm action against elements within the FSLN that sought a total Marxist state in Nicaragua. It adopted a moderate tone toward its former enemies and followed the line enunciated by Borge that the Sandinists "were implacable in war, but generous in peace." Further, the FSLN arrested a number of Sandinist soldiers who violated the human rights of some of their captives and openly reported these developments to the world press. Moreover, Sandinist leaders ordered a halt to pro-Marxist propaganda on government-run radio and television stations. Such propaganda continued to be heard, however, although clearly at a lower level. The government took over the presses of the Somoza newspaper *Novedades* and began publishing *Barricada*, a newspaper that looked somewhat like Cuba's *Granma*, the official organ of the Central Committee of the Cuban Communist Party. The new paper became less strident toward the end of the year, and while it continued to put forward a somewhat Marxist line, this was also at a lower level.

The tendency of observers in Nicaragua as the year ended was to feel that Sandinist leaders were still deciding the nature of the government they wanted to establish in Nicaragua and that much would ultimately depend on factors outside the immediate sphere of their influence—the role Cuban teachers and doctors would play, the amount of aid that the United States would offer (the United States sent a group of diplomats to Managua, to help the new leaders), and the pressure put on the new government by neighboring countries. Also important in the eyes of observers was the evident lack of experience in governing, which the FSLN freely admitted was one of its problems. The FSLN said in an August communiqué: "We are starting almost from scratch, for the country is bankrupt and we are inexperienced."

At the same time, it was clear that the Sandinist movement would ultimately dictate the future of Nicaragua. Having defeated General Somoza and enjoying massive popular support, the FSLN was in charge and could begin with a clean slate. It was generally believed that the direction of the new government might well be signaled in 1980 as FSLN leaders settle into their new role as governors rather than guerrillas.

Other leftist political groups were largely inactive during the year and supported the Sandinist movement. They were expected to be jockeying for position during 1980.

Christian Science Monitor   James Nelson Goodsell

Panama

The Communist Party of Panama (Partido Comunista de Panamá) was founded in 1930 but dissolved in 1943 in favor of the People's Party of Panama (Partido del Pueblo de Panamá; PPP). Since political activity in Panama has largely concentrated on the Panama Canal issue and the PPP generally supports the government of President Arístedes Royo, the communist apparatus has enjoyed continuing freedom of action in recent years. In 1979 it formally requested legalization under a new law that went into force during the year. For the PPP, the opportunity to become fully legal continued a process begun in 1975 when the government of strongman Gen. Omar Torrijos Herrera began tolerating leftist political activities. During these years, the PPP operated with considerable caution, and it is expected that the party will be extremely careful in the immediate future in order not to ruffle the political climate too much and thus incur the wrath of the government.

The PPP's membership is difficult to ascertain, but it is generally thought to be between 500 and 600. The population of Panama is about 1.9 million.

Other leftist groups in Panama include the Revolutionary Unity Movement (Movimiento de Unidad Revolucionario), the National Action Vanguard (Vanguardia de Acción Nacional), the Panamanian Revolutionary Union (Unión Revolucionaria Panameña), and the National Liberation Movement of 29 November (Movimiento de Liberación Nacional de 29 de Noviembre). These groups have been largely inactive in recent years and showed little evidence of any change in 1979. Many of their members are either in prison or in exile. In 1976, the Revolutionary Socialist League (Liga Socialista Revolucionaria; LSR) emerged, replacing the Revolutionary Socialist Faction (Facción Socialista Revolucionaria). In January a splinter group from the LSR, named the Socialist Revolutionary Movement (Movimiento Socialista Revolucionario), was formed.

Domestic Attitudes and Activities. Rubén Darío Sousa is secretary general of the PPP, a post he has held since 1951. In addition to its own activities, which include publication of the monthly newspaper *Unidad* and a new journal, *Síntesis*, the PPP works through trade union and student groups. Its labor affiliate, the Trade Union Federation of Workers of the Republic of Panama (Federación Sindical de Trabajadores de la República de Panamá), was disbanded by the Torrijos government in 1968 along with other labor organizations. But it has managed to keep some of its cadres together, and occasional rumblings of discontent with the hiatus in labor activities were heard from the PPP in 1979. "It is time for a truly effective labor movement," Secretary General Sousa declared in March. "This is our goal and this is the goal of all democratic forces in the republic." In the education sphere, the PPP worked through the Federation of Students of Panama (Federación de Estudiantes de Panamá; FEP), which is active on the campus of the University of Panama. Numerous FEP leaders are either members of the PPP or close to PPP leaders.

Much of the PPP's activities throughout 1979 focused on the Panama Canal issue and the 1 October end of the Panama Canal Zone when 58 percent of the zone's 521 square miles were turned over immediately to Panama. "This is not enough," said Secretary General Sousa in a June statement.

"All of the zone should revert to Panama immediately. Thus, while we may applaud the step toward return of what is rightfully Panamanian, we must demand and do so most energetically that all this occupied land be restored to its rightful owner immediately. There can be no delay, and the government should demand this with every device it possesses for otherwise Panama remains tied to the imperialist monster." Felix Dixon, a member of the PPP Central Committee, called the new Panama-U.S. treaties on the future of the Panama Canal "the beginning of a new stage of the Panamanian revolution." In a June article in the *World Marxist Reivew*, he wrote that the treaties make it possible for the Panamian people "to complete their territorial and political liberation." The PPP made a number of similar statements on the changing situation regarding the Panama Canal.

But the PPP had other things on its mind. Secretary General Sousa tried through the year to get the party fully legalized; on 15 May the party officially filed its request for registration with the electoral tribunal in keeping with Law 81 of 1978. On the occasion, Sousa said the PPP could easily register 30,000 members but will "have to be selective." He added that 1980 will be the year of registration for the party and indicated that "national liberation" will be the theme of the party's activities during the 1980s. "In legalizing the party of the Panamanian working class, we are also strengthening one of the pillars of this national liberation process."

International Attitudes and Contacts. Along with other leftist groups, the PPP supported the Sandinista movement in Nicaragua, and it was reported that several PPP members were part of the Simón Bolívar Brigade, a Panamanian group that fought in Nicaragua alongside the Sandinistas from early in 1978 until July 1979, when the government of Gen. Anastasio Somoza Debayle was overthrown.

Top leaders of the PPP, including Secretary General Sousa, visited several East European countries in June and in each country signed joint communiqués with their hosts pledging support of world socialist goals. In Hungary, for example, the communiqué pledged "unswerving support for the goals of the progressive parties in Panama against imperialist interference and for the true liberation of the peoples of Panama." In late May the PPP took a swipe at the leaders of the Communist Party of China, saying they were "slipping to the positions of imperialism" and accusing them of "discarding the principles of Marxism, Leninism, and proletarian imperialism." The statement took a pro-Soviet stance and was echoed in September when a PPP comment on the Havana meeting of nonaligned nations said that "only by living up to the standards of Marxism and Leninism, as enunciated by Moscow, can the peoples of the world truly achieve their liberation."

Christian Science Monitor   James Nelson Goodsell

Paraguay

The Paraguayan Communist Party (Partido Comunista Paraguayo; PCP) was founded in 1928 but did not hold its First Congress and adopt a party platform until 1941. The party has been illegal throughout its existence, except for a period between August 1946 and January 1947. Former Secretary General Oscar Creydt formed a rival PCP in 1965, after being ousted from the main body of the party, and has maintained an essentially pro-Chinese stance since that time.

The membership of the Paraguayan communist movement, including factions and sympathizers, has been estimated at approximately 3,500. Many are exiles in various Latin American and European countries. The population of Paraguay was approximately 3.1 million in 1979.

Organization and Party Positions. The PCP is led by Antonio Maidana as first secretary and Obdulio Barthe as president. Its minimum program for Paraguay provides for protecting the country's sovereignty; ending the activities of foreign monopolies; ascertaining the whereabouts of the patriots reported as missing; releasing all political prisoners; lifting the state of siege; abrogating "repressive fascist acts"; giving full freedom to all political parties and other public organizations; meeting the vital needs of the working class, the peasants, and the students; and providing better living and working conditions for the people (*WMR*, July).

The party maintains that "some headway has been made in uniting the forces opposing Stroessner's fascist dictatorship"; i.e., the coalition formed by the four main opposition parties in the country, which does not include the communists. Although the PCP sees this as "an important step toward the formation of a broad national anti-dictatorial front," the absence of the communists is seen as a boon to the government and "imperialism." The party calls for a front of the working class, the peasants, the petite bourgeoisie, and the middle sectors of the urban population, with the eventual participation of portions of the national bourgeoisie and even some latifundists and big intermediary bourgeoisie who have differences with the government and foreign powers. Still, the PCP warns that no cooperation with bourgeois sectors must be made at the expense of the "main alliance, the alliance of workers, peasants and the middle strata, to say nothing of doing this at the expense of the proletariat's class independence." The PCP further warns that "Stroessner's regular election farces will never bring about a democratic change, so that our people have only one way of ending the political oppression and the economic crisis — by overthrowing the dictatorship in a common effort by the masses, employing all the necessary forms of struggle." (Ibid.) On the PCP's 51st anniversary, it reiterated its call for a "broad coalition of all forces — without exception — that are opposed to the dictatorship," arguing that such a coalition "would be an instrument capable of creating the conditions for the overthrow of Stroessner's corrupt fascist dictatorship, for its replacement by a provisional civilian-military government of democratic and patriotic unity" (*Granma*, Havana, English ed., 4 March).

Maidana hailed the overthrow of the Somoza government in Nicaragua, saying that "the victory in Nicaragua shows that however powerful it may look, imperialism and its puppet governments cannot forestall the victory of the people when they rally and heroically fight with the support of the great force of international solidarity (Bulgarska Telegrafna Agentsiya, Sofia, 21 July). He emphasized the importance of proletarian internationalism in an article in the *World Marxist Review* (March), insisting that "anti-Sovietism . . . is the main danger threatening the vital need to strengthen mutual international solidarity."

The underground PCP paper is *Adelante*.

Hoover Institution   Lynn Ratliff

Peru

The Peruvian Communist Party (Partido Comunista Peruano; PCP) took its present name in 1930 as a result of orders from the Communist International. Since 1964 the movement has been divided into a pro-Soviet party and several pro-Chinese splinter groups, some of which use the PCP name. The party experienced a further division in January 1978 when the PCP separated publicly into two factions, the PCP-Unidad and the PCP-Mayoría, named after their respective newspapers (see *YICA*, 1979, pp. 378–79).

There are also various Marxist-Leninist and Trotskyist parties and coalitions to the left of the PCP. These include various factions of the Castro-oriented Movement of the Revolutionary Left (MIR); the Revolutionary Vanguard (VR); the Popular Democratic Union (UDP), an eighteen-group coalition that includes the majority of the miners' federation leaders, some Trotskyists, and Maoists; and the Workers', Peasants', Students', and Popular Front (FOCEP), a thirteen-group coalition that at the beginning of 1979 contained various Trotskyist organizations, including a faction of the Socialist Workers' Party (PST), the Revolutionary Workers' Party (PRT), and the Revolutionary Marxist Workers' Party (POMR).

American intelligence estimates place the current hard-core membership of the pro-Soviet PCP at 3,200 and that of the pro-Chinese PCP groups at 1,500. Other Marxist-Leninist and Trotskyist groups are smaller, with the PRT, POMR, and VR believed to have the largest memberships. The population of Peru is about 17.3 million (1979 estimate).

Elections were held in Peru in June 1978 for the first time since the military assumed power in October 1968. At stake were 100 seats for the Constituent Assembly that in 1979 drafted a new constitution in preparation for general elections and the transfer of power to civilians in 1980. For the first time in its history, the PCP was permitted to participate openly in an election. It won 5.9 percent of the vote, entitling it to six seats in the Assembly. The combined leftist vote reached almost 30 percent of the popular vote, displaying surprising strength in Lima and in Peru's mining and coastal cities. Although PCP spokesmen expressed general satisfaction with the election results, viewed more objectively the elections represented a serious defeat for the PCP and those parties that supported the policies of former president Juan Velasco Alvarado (1968–1975).

Leadership and Organization. The highest organ of the pro-Soviet PCP is officially the National Congress, which is supposed to meet every three years. The Seventh Congress, the most recent, met in Lima from 31 October to 4 November. This congress was the first since the PCP threw its support behind the military regime of General Velasco in 1973. Jorge del Prado, who has led the PCP for nineteen years, was re-elected general secretary, and Raúl Acosta Salas was elected undersecretary general. The Central Committee was increased from 53 to 57 members, the Political Commission from 13 to 15 members. The Political Commission members elected by the congress were Jorge del Prado (chairman), Raúl Acosta Salas, Isidro Gamarra, José Martínez, Guillermo Herrera, Mario Ugarte, Pedro Mayta, Gustavo Espinoza, Alfredo Abarca, Eduardo Castillo Sánchez, Guillermo Castro, Manuel Díaz, Andrés Paredes Luyo, Manuel Miguel de Priego, and Carlos Bonino Nieves. Attending the congress were 350 delegates; workers constituted 30 percent, peasants 8 percent, employees 35 percent, professionals 20 percent, and others 7 percent. The average age of the delegates was 32. Thirty-one percent had been with the party from 1 to 3 years, 37 percent from 4 to 10 years, 21 percent from 10 to 20 years, 4 percent from 20 to 30 years, 4 percent from 30 to 40 years, and 3 percent from 40 to 50 years. (*Unidad*, 9 November.) The congress approved the political report (ibid., 15 November), the social program (ibid., 9 November), and the economic program (ibid., 25 October). Commenting on the elections, del Prado said that "they demonstrate once again the unity and combative militancy that exist in the party at this difficult moment in Peruvian history" (*El Comercio*, 5 November).

The PCP is organized from cells upward through local and regional committees to its Central Committee. Regional committees exist in at least 22 cities. Lima has the largest number of local committees, concentrated in low-income neighborhoods and slum areas, which the government refers to as "new towns." The PCP employs around sixty paid officials including leaders and rank-and-file cadres. The party's expenditures include subsidies for the General Confederation of Workers of Peru (Confederación General de Trabajadores del Perú; CGTP), the Peruvian Communist Youth (Juventud Comunista Peruana; JCP), and specific regional committees of the party. Raúl Acosta Salas serves as undersecretary of the party. Jaime Figueroa is head of the party's National Propaganda Committee, and Mario Ugarte Hurtado serves as head of the Finance Committee. Other prominent members of the Central Committee are Isidro Gamarra, Guillermo Herrera, Eduardo Castillo Sánchez, Alejandro Olivera Vila, Juliano Sierra Corrales, Eteldrita Humala Aybar, Gustavo Espinoza, José Martínez, Vicente Ramírez, and José Reccio. According to del Prado, the oldest members in terms of active membership in the party besides himself are Raúl Acosta and Isidro Gamarra. The other members of the Political Committee and the Central Committee have been active for "only twenty years or less."

In February the PCP expelled Luis Alberto Delgado from the party and asked the National Elections Board to disqualify him as a representative to the Constituent Assembly. Delgado, considered one of the party's ideologues, resigned in early February and registered with the FOCEP, reducing the PCP's representation in the Assembly from six to five. The party told the Elections Board that Delgado had committed "disciplinary errors" and that during the elections he was guilty of "deceit and political fraud" (Agence France Presse, Paris, 21 February).

The PCP's youth group is relatively small and operates mainly at the university level. Carlos Bonino is the group's general secretary. In recent years the JCP has actively competed with Maoist and Trotskyist groups for control of the university student movement. According to del Prado, "The students have always been allies of the workers' movement, but in Latin America, Yankee imperialism has set in motion a strategy aimed at dividing the left, and it has succeeded in separating the student movement from the anti-imperialist struggle" (*Oiga*, Lima, 10 June 1977). Dissension within the PCP has had repercussions among the JCP's National Executive Committee, a faction of which was openly critical of the party's "revisionist elements" in 1978 (see *YICA*, 1978, p. 376). In November the JCP actively supported demonstrations in Lima and other cities protesting an increase in transportation fares. The government accused "professional agitators, some professors, and left-wing deputies of the

Constituent Assembly" of inciting the students to stage disturbances (EFE, Madrid, 10 November).

A major source of the PCP's influence lies in its control of the CGTP. The CGTP, headed by PCP members Isidro Gamarra, president, and Eduardo Castillo Sánchez, secretary general, claims a membership of 700,000 workers. The CGTP was formed in 1968 after unions of miners, metalworkers, and bank workers had broken from the Peruvian Workers' Confederation (CTP), long controlled by the Peruvian Aprista Party. From its inception, the CGTP has been dominated by the pro-Soviet faction of the PCP. It gained government recognition in 1971 and is today the principal trade union federation in Peru. Other important unions, especially those like the United Federation of Educational Workers of Peru (SUTEP) in which Maoist forces gained influence, also broke with the old CTP but have not entered the CGTP. The CGTP held its Fifth National Congress in Lima from 26 to 30 September 1978, bringing together 300 delegates from some sixty unions. General secretary Eduardo Castillo attacked the "ultra-left" as the main enemy of the workers' movement and called for the removal of the PCP-Mayoría leaders from their CGTP posts in order to "purify" the federation. Castillo also attacked the government more sharply than CGTP leaders had done in previous years. He characterized the Morales Bermúdez regime as "the faithful servant of the International Monetary Fund" and extolled the militancy of the Velasco era. The pro-Soviet faction consolidated its control over the CGTP apparatus by electing a 45-member National Council consisting entirely of PCP-Unidad stalwarts. An opposition slate—reportedly the first in the federation's history—received one-third of the votes cast (*Intercontinental Press*, 27 November 1978).

On 19 December 1978 CGTP leaders called for a general strike 9–11 January to protest low wages, an annual inflation rate of about 70 percent, government austerity measures, and price increases of up to 35 percent on such items as bread, sugar, milk, and gasoline. The government's labor minister charged the CGTP with adopting a position "in compliance with foreign plans" and "fruitlessly trying to set the country on a path that is contrary to national sentiments and traditions" (*El Comercio*, 28 December 1978). Representatives of the CGTP denounced the "treasonable attitude" of the Maoist leaders of the SUTEP, along with other unions, for not endorsing the call for the work stoppage (*Unidad*, 4 January). On 5 January the government proclaimed a national state of emergency and declared the strike to be "politically subversive" (*NYT*, 7 January). The government responded quickly by arresting over one hundred leftist labor leaders and politicians before the strike could effectively get under way. On 10 January the CGTP announced the suspension of the strike "in order to continue the struggle under more favorable conditions." Although Castillo admitted that the strike call had been heeded "a little less than in May 1978," he claimed that the strike had developed successfully, "despite the violent repression unleashed by the government" (Agence France Presse, 10 January).

The CGTP held its National Assembly on 10 May, with 205 delegates representing 21 federations and 63 unions from all parts of the country. In the annual report, Castillo observed that since the Fifth Congress "intense mass struggles in defense of the legitimate rights of the workers" had occurred. In his estimation, the January strike had served "to expose clearly the reactionary and repressive policy of the government" and also to reveal the "antiworker, opportunist, and adventurist role of the ultra-leftists, Maoists, and Trotskyists of various stripes" (*Unidad*, 17 May). On 19 July the CGTP held a "fairly successful" work stoppage in Lima to protest price increases. Government repression was "restrained" compared with the January strike, although some 300 persons were arrested, including Castillo and Isidro Gamarra (*Intercontinental Press*, 6 August).

In September a group of leftist political leaders including Jorge del Prado, Antonio Meza Cuadra of the Socialist Revolutionary Party (PSR), and Víctor Cuadros of the UDP, proclaimed a hunger strike in support of SUTEP teachers, who had begun a strike on 4 June. The Lima hunger strike briefly united most left-wing tendencies, from the pro-Soviet PCP to the Trotskyist PST, led by Enrique Fernández Chacón. Hugo Blanco, the popular Trotskyist leader, was in Nicaragua when the strike started but began his own hunger strike when he returned. There appears, however, to be little possibility of his agreeing to join forces with the PCP or the PST in any united electoral front. Such a coalition is still the objective of all political groups, at least at the rhetorical level. There are those who believed that practical solidarity with SUTEP would help to overcome ideological differences (*Latin America Political Report*, 21 September). The organization of another strike in support of SUTEP might have been an important step in the construction of such a front. However, SUTEP called off its strike on 2 October with the government still refusing to negotiate with its leaders.

The PCP attempted to exert influence in the peasant sector through its participation in the National Agrarian Confederation (CNA) until the CNA's abolition by the government in 1978. Like SINAMOS before it, the CNA, established in 1974, was an uncomfortable remnant of the Velasco government (see *YICA*, 1979, p. 378). In accordance with resolutions of the CGTP's Fifth Congress, the CGTP held its first peasant congress in March 1979. Attended by sectors of the Peruvian peasantry, the congress founded the General Confederation of Peasants of Peru (CGCP; *Unidad*, 17 May).

The PCP's principal opposition in the peasant sector comes from several Chinese-oriented parties belonging to the Confederation of Peruvian Peasants (CCP). According to Raúl Acosta Salas, one faction of the CCP is under the direction of the "Bandera Roja," and the other follows the dictates of the Revolutionary Vanguard. Spokesmen for the CCP reacted bitterly to the creation of another peasant central, accusing the PCP leaders of being "traitors and divisionists." Andrés Luna Vargas, secretary general of the CCP, said that the objectives pursued at the peasant congress were "alien to peasant interests" and "another betrayal" by the CGTP and the PCP "in the long history of betrayals of the Peruvian workers and people" (*El Comercio*, 27 March).

Party Internal Affairs. The PCP has been forced to redefine its domestic position by the gradual erosion of the image of revolutionary development in Peru and the impending return to civilian government in 1980. The PCP gave virtually uncritical support to the government and the armed forces during the years of Velasco's rule. When General Morales Bermúdez replaced Velasco in August 1975, the PCP hailed the move as a "deepening of the revolution." As the Morales government became more openly conservative, the PCP vacillated, on some occasions supporting workers' and peasants' struggles and at other times seeking a "dialogue" with the military to create a more orthodox political role for the party. The result has been rather widespread disillusionment in recent years with both the party's leaders and its policies. This is reflected not only in the growing influence of currents to the left of the PCP, as indicated by the relatively strong showing of the FOCEP, the PSR, and the UDP in the 1978 Assembly elections, but also in the evidence of existing differences within the party itself (see *YICA*, 1979, pp. 378–79).

Domestic Attitudes and Activities. According to Jorge del Prado, the Peruvian communists remain true to the principles of Marxism-Leninism and are "consistently fighting to overcome the country's economic and social backwardness." The basis for this struggle is an alliance of "the working class, the peasantry, the urban middle strata, and the patriotic elements among the local bourgeoisie." For del Prado, the first stage of structural reforms associated with the Velasco regime has passed. The party now perceives a weakening of the anti-imperialist, anti-oligarchic posture of the government in the early 1970s. It believes that the Morales Bermúdez government has turned Peru toward "a capitalist road of development" and increased the country's dependence on "U.S. imperialism" (*IB*, no. 23, 1978). The party's position in 1979 was to work through the Constituent Assembly for a constitutional reform that would consolidate the structural transformations put into effect before the revolutionary process was "forcibly discontinued." Early in the year del Prado defined the party's major responsibility as one of leading the working class in carrying on the day-to-day struggle against the "selfish electoral ambitions" of the right-wing parties, the government's policy of repression, and the economic measures of the International Monetary Fund (*WMR*, March).

The realignment of sociopolitical forces since 1975 has persuaded del Prado that "no halfhearted revolution is possible in our day." He also believes that a nation cannot eliminate its dependence on imperialism "without making a break with the capitalist system." (Ibid.) During the Constituent Assembly's debate on drafting a new constitution, del Prado enunciated the PCP's major economic proposals: (1) to expand the sphere of influence of state-run enterprises to the basic-industry sector; (2) to emphasize the priority role of the public and social property sectors; (3) to provide state-run enterprises with the financial and technological resources necessary to plan and promote the economic development of the country; and (4) to legalize the participation of workers in all levels of management. He added that for the media to serve a social purpose it would be necessary for the state to take control of them (*Unidad*, 17 May and 25 October).

The PCP favors an alliance of all parties and fronts that represent the masses. In the recent past, the party has proposed the formation of a popular, anti-imperialist and anti-oligarchic coalition consisting of the Communist, Socialist Revolutionary and Christian Democratic parties, together with the FOCEP and the UDP. With the prospective transfer of political power in 1980, unification of the left was considered an "urgent necessity" in 1979. However, the party has established certain conditions for unity that emphasize that political solidarity and consistency are not simply a matter of number. "Quality" is the most important thing, which to the party means that any front must give greater importance to a common program than to individuals. It also means that the coalition "not practice pseudo-leftist anticommunism along with those who craftily attack true socialism and the PCP with the same arguments of McCarthyism and imperialism." Finally, it means that within the framework of agreement on a single program each party's political independence must be respected. (Ibid., 14 June.) A fundamental task of the PCP is the ideological struggle to the death against Maoism and Trotskyism, whose activities objectively favor the plans of imperialism (ibid., 15 November).

At a press conference on 28 August, spokesmen for the PCP, the FOCEP, and the PSR announced a joint program for achieving leftist unity. Del Prado defined it as a "programmatic alliance" open to all forces of the left. It would involve the formation of a government "capable of dealing with Peru's pressing social problems and of moving towards socialism." The joint program guarantees the inviolability of democratic rights, a higher standard of living for the people, and a popular government based on the unity of rural and urban workers. The document further states that Peru will follow a nonaligned foreign policy; broaden its diplomatic, economic, and cultural ties with other countries; and develop active solidarity with all peoples fighting against imperialism. (Ibid., 30 August.) In October Genaro Ledesma explained that there is no political pact among the FOCEP, the PCP, and the PSR. He stated that the only thing these three organizations have in common is "a draft program for the 1980 electoral process, and we want this draft to represent the entire left wing." He added that the FOCEP has no commitments with the other parties with whom he prepared the left-wing program draft (*El Comercio*, 23 October).

For his part, del Prado has said that if the left runs a single slate, it will win the 1980 elections and obtain 40 percent of the vote (*Granma*, Havana, English edition, 28 October). The PCP chose del Prado as the party's presidential candidate at the conclusion of its Seventh Congress. However, del Prado's candidacy will most likely be withdrawn if the PCP enters an electoral coalition with the FOCEP, the PSR, and other parties of the moderate left. Ledesma's name, along with that of Antonio Meza Cuadra, has been mentioned as the coalition's probable candidate. By November it appeared unlikely that the more radical factions of the left would join the proposed coalition. During the PCP's congress, harsh attacks were made against Hugo Blanco, who has proclaimed his own presidential candidacy and is actively promoting unity among Peru's major Trotskyist parties (*Lima Times*, 9 November). The PCP also strongly criticized the Maoist groups loosely allied within the UDP, whose principal spokesman, Alfonso Barrantes Lingán, has initiated his campaign for the presidency. On balance, the PCP finds itself in an embarrassingly weak position in its efforts to establish control over the policy and movements of the Peruvian left. Disunity among leftist groups is likely to be exacerbated as leaders representing divergent ideological views attempt to strengthen their positions with respect to the 1980 national electoral process. For any viable electoral coalition to be achieved, it may be necessary for the PCP to compromise its long-standing principle that "in the sphere of ideology there can be no agreement between us and elements of the Maoist and Trotskyist ultra left" (*IB*, no. 23, 1978).

International Views and Positions. The PCP continues to follow the Soviet line closely in its international positions. In response to conservative criticism that the PCP is simply a tool of international communism, del Prado has stated that "the PCP is in fact playing the role of the vanguard of the Peruvian working class and is a recognized detachment in the struggle against imperialism and the oligarchy and for socialism on Peruvian soil" (*Unidad*, 30 March 1978).

The party has taken an active part in calling for the strengthening of the world communist movement, especially through its condemnation of the provocative activity of Chinese leaders. Party statements criticize Beijing's "subversive activities" in Latin America, Africa, and Asia. In 1979 the party condemned China's attempts to improve its image in the United States and its continued hostile policy toward the Soviet Union. Del Prado stated that "those who are aware of the real danger posed by China's general political line will fully understand the Peruvian communists' solidarity with the Soviet Union and the socialist camp" (*WMR*, March). During a visit to Hanoi in September, Gustavo Espinoza stated that the PCP "values highly the Vietnamese people's struggle for independence, freedom, and socialism." He also welcomed the militant solidarity and friendship between the Vietnamese and Kampuchean (Cambodian) peoples "in their struggle against Chinese expansionist schemes and acts" (Vietnam News Agency, Hanoi, 13 September). In expressing its solidarity with the USSR, party statements periodically reaffirm the PCP's steadfast adherence to Marxism-Leninism and consistent implementation of proletarian internationalism. The party continues to attach great importance to the expansion of trade, as well as scientific and technological cooperation between Peru and the socialist countries.

The PCP maintained a variety of international contacts in 1979. In September a delegation headed by Espinoza visited Kampuchea and North Vietnam. Fraternal greetings and support for the PCP were declared by foreign delegates from numerous countries during the party's Seventh Congress in November, including representatives from the Soviet Union, East Germany, Cuba, and Vietnam.

Publications. The PCP weekly organ is *Unidad*, which claims a circulation of over 10,000. *Unidad* was among ten newspapers and magazines suspended by the government in January for supporting the general strike. It was authorized to resume publication on 24 April.

Other Parties. The pro-Chinese groups have experienced continuous internal dissension and splits from their inception in the 1960s. As many as twenty Marxist political organizations have been identified in the past, many of which, strictly speaking, no longer exist.

In recent years two major factions of the pro-Chinese PCP have existed. The one that enjoys more or less official recognition from the Chinese Communist Party is known as the Peruvian Communist Party, Marxist-Leninist (PCP-ML), headed by Antonio Fernández Arce. Its members are affiliated with the Peru-China Cultural Institute. A second pro-Chinese faction is headed by Saturnino Paredes Macedo and, from its somewhat sporadic periodical, *Bandera Roja*, is generally known as the PCP–Bandera Roja.

The PCP-ML, popularly known as the Red Fatherland faction because of its periodical *Patria Roja*, is believed to have the largest following of all pro-Chinese groups among students and labor. It reportedly exercises control over several national labor organizations with memberships in excess of 100,000, the most important of which is SUTEP. On the other hand, the Bandera Roja faction heads only local organizations with fewer than 100,000 members. The PCP-ML also controls one of the labor "unification organizations" that has engaged in fierce competition with a similar unifying organization controlled by the CGTP.

The Red Fatherland boasts that it has a military and paramilitary apparatus "duly prepared and trained to face any major emergency in the struggle for the conquest of power" (*Gente*, Lima, 6 December 1978). Statements appearing in *Patria Roja* in February censured Vietnam for its "Soviet-backed aggression against Kampuchea" and pointed out the Soviet Union's use of Cuba "as a tool for its social-imperialist expansion" (New China News Agency, Beijing, 9 February). On 30 May the government accused the Red Fatherland organization of "using young students in disturbances aimed at frustrating the transfer of power to civilians and the country's economic recovery" (Agence France Presse, 31 May). In June PCP-ML leader Rolando Brena announced that the Red Fatherland would participate in the 1980 elections as part of a "great revolutionary front" uniting Peru's Maoist organizations (ibid., 8 June). In late October a spokesman for the Castro-oriented MIR announced that talks had been held with the PCP-ML, the Revolutionary Communist Party-Working Class, the VR–Proletarian Communist, and the Bandera Roja to form the Single Revolutionary Leftist Front. Assuming that some form of coalition can be created from groups operating with such diverse ideological and political bases, it would presumably seek to join with other Maoist-oriented groups, such as the UDP (*El Comercio*, 13 November).

Factionalism also plagued the FOCEP in 1979. As early as March, significant differences of opinion surfaced between the popular Trotskyist leader Hugo Blanco and "independent" Genaro Ledesma (*Opinión Libre*, Lima, 23 March). By midyear the FOCEP had expelled the PST for promoting Blanco's presidential candidacy and creating "insurmountable differences" between the Trotskyists and the center-left parties, such as the Christian Democrats and the PSR, headed by Meza Cuadra and retired Gen. Leonidas Rodríguez Figueroa. Blanco, considered by many observers the left's most compelling electoral figure, continues to occupy himself in trying to create a single party from the various Trotskyist groups. It is doubtful that Blanco's personal ambitions or his ideological inclinations will permit him to become a member of either the electoral coalition formed by the predominantly Maoist parties gathered under the UDP's umbrella or the coalition that appears to be emerging between the pro-Soviet PCP, the PSR, and the Ledesma faction of the FOCEP. The final configurations of party coalitions and their respective presidential candidates are not likely to occur until the last possible moment before the May elections.

Washington College   Daniel L. Premo

Puerto Rico

Puerto Rico's extreme left is numerically small. Only one leftist group participates openly, hoping to persuade the population to vote for independence; others have embraced the strategy of violence. For years, violence has been just behind the facade of apparent tranquility of the island, whose 3.3 million inhabitants have been oscillating between two major options for its political future: the continuation of its present Commonwealth status, advocated by the current opposition, the Puerto Rican Peoples Democratic Party; and statehood, whose proponents are members of the New Progressive Party. Governor Carlos Romero Barceló is the leader of the Progressives. Without exception, the extreme left—as well as other non-Marxists—supports independence for Puerto Rico. In 1976 the "independentistas" polled about 6 percent of the vote.

The Puerto Rican Socialist Party (Partido Socialista Puertorriqueño; PSP) is the largest and best organized Marxist group on the island. It was founded in November 1971 at the Eighth Annual Assembly of the Pro-Independence Movement. It participated in the 1976 gubernatorial elections, and its candidate, Juan Marí Bras, received 11,000 votes. Marí Bras has been a frequent visitor to Cuba for years and is regarded as Fidel Castro's "man in San Juan."

Organization and Leadership. The PSP has an organizational structure that follows the Soviet party's pattern: Central Committee, a Secretariat, and Political Commission (or Politburo). The Party Congress (the first was held in 1971 and the second in 1979) charters long-range policies for the group. Marí Bras is the PSP's secretary general. Other leaders are Julio Vivres Vásquez, president; Carlos Callisá, first deputy secretary general; Pedro Biagés, second deputy secretary general; and Lucia Romero, organizing secretary. The PSP publishes the daily newspaper *Claridad*.

Policy and Activities. The group believes that Puerto Rico is a U.S. colony. The only solution to this condition is independence and the creation of a sovereign Republic of Puerto Rico, according to Marí Bras. At the present time, PSP actions are aimed at promoting unity of all forces opposed to what Marí Bras calls Governor Barceló's policy of annexation to the United States. The PSP's secretary general has voiced these views in his country, in Havana, which he visits periodically, at the United Nations, and in many capitals around the world. His reliance on assistance from Cuba is also evident, and the PSP has an office in Havana. "The existence [of the Cuban revolution] has the added significance of having been the inspiration and example that helped revive the spirit of the Puerto Rican people's struggle for independence during the 1960s," said Marí Bras. "It is not a coincidence that the Pro-Independence Movement, historically antedating our party, was founded on 11 January 1959, only a few days after the triumph of the revolution in Cuba and that during the past twenty years this movement has followed the interesting course of changing from a pro-independence organization without a clear class content to a Marxist-Leninist party." (*Bohemia*, Havana, 11 May.) The PSP has also been active in protesting the use by U.S. naval forces of the island of Vieques, east of Puerto Rico, as a firing practice area. As a result of his protests in connection with the Vieques issue, Marí Bras was arrested and later released by federal authorities.

Evidencing Cuba's continuing and active interest in Puerto Rican affairs, Fidel Castro invited to Havana four Puerto Rican nationalists who were released from prison in the United States on President Carter's order. The release of the three men and one woman—Rafael Cancel-Miranda, Lolita Lebrón, Irving Flores Rodríguez, and Oscar Collazo—cleared the way for the release of four Americans imprisoned in Cuba. The four freed Puerto Ricans were unrepentant in their statements in Havana and San Juan. (Collazo attempted to assassinate President Truman in 1950, and the other three opened fire at congressmen from the spectators' gallery of the House of Representatives, wounding five members. The fourth Puerto Rican who took part in the shooting in Congress in 1954, Andrés Figueroa Cordero, was released from prison in 1977 and died of cancer in San Juan in March.)

Renewed Violence. On 3 December a band of armed men ambushed a busload of U.S. navy personnel outside San Juan. Gunmen then strafed the bus with automatic fire, killing two sailors and wounding ten others. In a "communiqué" left on a San Juan street corner, three groups claimed responsibility for the attack and declared themselves at war with "Yankee imperialism." They were the Volunteers of the Puerto Rican Revolution; the Boricua Popular Army, also known as the Macheteros; and the Armed Forces of Popular Resistance. The three clandestine terrorist groups released a similar joint communiqué on 17 October after bombings in San Juan and New York. On that occasion, the statement was also signed by the Armed Forces of Puerto Rican National Liberation (Fuerzas Armadas de Liberación Nacional Puertorriqueña; FALN). Although the police had no evidence that the Puerto Rican terrorists have been receiving financial or logistical support from abroad, some investigators have contended that PSP members traveling to Cuba receive guerrilla training there. Castro, for years an outspoken advocate of Puerto Rican independence, an issue which he mentioned in his October U.N. General Assembly speech, has not discouraged violence as a tactic in Puerto Rico.

Other Leftist Groups. The Puerto Rican Communist Party (Partido Comunista Puertorriqueño) has long been closely associated with the Communist Party, U.S.A. and is likewise pro-Soviet and anti-Chinese. It was founded in 1934, dissolved in 1944, and revived in 1946. It has under 200 members and publishes the newspapers *El Pueblo* and *El Proletario*. The FALN is an underground revolutionary group with a handful of members. It is said to have been responsible for over sixty bombings in the past decade in both Puerto Rico and the U.S. mainland. The International Workers' League (Liga Internacional de los Trabajadores) is said to be associated with the Fourth (Trotskyist) International. The Puerto Rican Socialist League (Liga Socialista Puertorriqueña; LSP), founded in 1964, is reported to have ties with the Progressive Labor Party of the United States. The LSP is led by Secretary General Juan Antonio Corretjei, a former aide to the late Pedro Albizú Campa, leader of the independence movement. The Armed Commandos of Liberation (Comandos Armados de Liberación) is a small group that was active in the late 1960s and early 1970s and claimed responsibility for several bombings and fires in the New York area. There are said to be other obscure terrorist groups whose activities and membership are little known.

University of Miami   George Volsky

United States

The Communist Party, U.S.A. (CPUSA) remains the largest and most influential Marxist-Leninist organization in the United States. It is descended from the Communist Labor Party and the Communist Party, both formed in 1919. At various times the CPUSA has also been called the Workers Party and, for a brief period of time during World War II, the Communist Political Association. The CPUSA is a legal party. Restrictive laws that hindered access to the ballot in some areas have been removed. In 1976 the party's presidential ticket of Gus Hall and Jarvis Tyner was on the ballot in nineteen states and the District of Columbia and received about 59,000 votes. The party's 1978 gubernatorial candidate in New York received 11,279 votes. At present the party has no representation either in Congress or any state legislature.

Hall has claimed that the party has between 15,000 and 20,000 members, but a party spokesman claimed there were between 30,000 and 80,000 (*NYT*, 25 August). The membership is concentrated in a few industrial states and believed to be largely middle-aged or older. Recruitment efforts are aimed at minority groups (blacks, Puerto Ricans, Chicanos) and young industrial workers. The population of the United States is around 220 million.

The Socialist Workers Party (SWP) is the leading Trotskyist party. Organized formally in 1938, it traces its origin to 1928 when James Cannon and several other CPUSA leaders were expelled for backing Leon Trotsky. The SWP has spawned numerous other small parties, including the Workers' World Party, the Spartacist League, and the Revolutionary Marxist Organizing Committee. Membership in the SWP is probably somewhere between 1,500 and 2,500. Like the CPUSA, the SWP runs candidates for office, usually in more localities, and usually receives more votes. Although concentrated in the industrial states, the SWP has established branches in areas of the South and Southwest where the CPUSA has no presence. The Workers' World Party has a few hundred members.

The two most important Maoist groups are the Communist Party (Marxist-Leninist; [CP (M-L)]) and the Revolutionary Communist Party (RCP). The Communist Labor Party has moved in the direction of Stalinism. There are dozens of other Maoist organizations including the Proletarian Unity League, the Bay Area Communist Union, the Communist Party of the United States of America (Marxist-Leninist), which supports Albania, the Central Organization of US Marxist-Leninists, the Revolutionary Wing, the Philadelphia Workers Organizing Committee, the Workers Party for Proletarian Socialism, El Comite–M.I.N.P., the August 29th Movement, and I Wor Kuen. The CP (M-L) and the RCP have no more than a few thousand members; the others are much more limited and, occasionally, all but invisible. The Progressive Labor Party, also small, is Stalinist.

The CPUSA and the SWP are active in a wide variety of organizations and causes, particularly those relating to civil rights, peace, and labor issues. The smaller Maoist sects, many of which sprang out of the campus upheavals during the 1960s, no longer seem capable of attracting more than a handful of students and, while receiving occasional publicity, have little influence.

Leadership and Organization. There were few changes in CPUSA leadership during 1979. Gus Hall and Henry Winston remain general secretary and national chairman. Arnold Bechetti is organizational secretary, Sid Taylor treasurer, and Betty Smith national administrative secretary. Directors of party departments include Alva Buxenbaum (chairwoman, National Women's Rights Section), George Meyers (chairman, National Labor and Farm Department), Roscoe Proctor (secretary, National Labor and Farm Department), James Jackson (education director), Helen Winter (chairwoman, International Affairs Department), Si Gerson (chairman, Political Action and Democratic Rights Department), Tom Dennis (chairman, Nationalities Department), Daniel Rubin (chairman, Economic and Social Rights Department), Victor Perlo (chairman, Economics Section), Lorenzo Torres (chairman, Chicano Section), Alex Kolkin (chairman, Jewish Section), Carl Winter (editor, *Daily World*), Carl Bloice (editor, *People's World*). Leaders in key states are Jarvis Tyner (New York), Jack Kling and Ishmael Flory (Illinois), Jim West (Ohio), Mike Boyer (Indiana), Matt Berkelhammer and Kendra Alexander (California), Helvi Savola (Minnesota), Ed Texieira (Massachusetts), B. J. Mangaoang (Washington), and Sam Webb (Michigan).

The CPUSA does not formally have any affiliated organizations, but the Young Workers Liberation League (YWLL), serves, in fact, as the party's youth arm. The YWLL has an estimated 3,000 members, apparently having not grown much since 1976. James Steele is chairman, Jay Schaffner organizational secretary, and Judith LeBlanc national educational director. Several other organizations, although not tied as directly to the CPUSA, are dominated by the party and controlled and led by its functionaries. The most prominent and successful of these united front groups continues to be the National Alliance against Racist and Political Repression. Charlene Mitchell, onetime CPUSA candidate for the U.S. presidency, is executive director. Other key figures include Angela Davis and Judge Margaret Burnham of Massachusetts. At its Fifth Convention in May, 226 delegates heard Congressman John Conyers and writer James Baldwin speak and decided to concentrate more on industrial problems.

The Trade Unionists for Action and Democracy (TUAD), founded in 1970, is the party's major vehicle for increasing its influence in that field. Rayfield Mooty and Fred Gaboury are TUAD leaders. Other party-dominated organizations include the Committee for a Just Peace in the Middle East, the National Council of American-Soviet Friendship, the Chile Solidarity Committee, the Metropolitan Council on Housing, and the National Anti-Imperialist Movement in Solidarity with African Liberation. The party's most important front for women is Women for Racial and Economic Equality (WREE). Among WREE leaders are Georgia Henning, Sondra Patrinos, and Vinnie Burrows. Carmen Teixidor is editor of *WREE View*.

Party Internal Affairs. The party held its 22nd convention in Detroit on 22–26 August. Guests representing communist organizations and parties from more than 30 countries attended. Some 385 delegates and alternates were present from 39 states. Among them were 154 women and 231 men, 96 blacks, 77 Jews, 15 Chicanos, and 134 trade unionists; 108 of the delegates were under 30 years old, a larger representation of the young than ever before. (*Daily World*, 28 August.)

The Central Committee urged that industrial concentration be made the main focus of the whole party, laying the blame for weaknesses on inadequate attention to the whole economic arena. Although reporting some progress in the work of party clubs, it noted that they remained "a weak link in the work of the party," charging that many failed to "get down to the nitty-gritty of guiding and leading movements and struggles." Clubs were instructed to raise the socialist consciousness of neighbors, build the party press, study theoretical issues, and be involved in mass struggles. Their purpose had to be recruiting since "we have to face the truth that with the present size of the party there are limitations on what we can do or contribute." In line with this comment, the Central Committee noted that opportunities were numerous: "The party is not isolated from mass movements and developments. Today the doors are wide open." (*Political Affairs*, June.)

Domestic Attitudes and Activities. The CPUSA sees a continued deterioration of American imperialism, leading to an increasingly serious domestic crisis. "Class relations, class division and the class struggle continue to sharpen." As a result of increasing worker militancy, the communists foresee closer alliances between left and center forces in the trade union movement. Before this unity can be fully effective, however, the Central Committee of the party foresees the need for "left unity," an important component of which involves isolating the "phony left sects" that "are disruptive of working-class unity" and serve as a "launching pad for the agents of the FBI." The draft of the party's main political resolution also called for full equality for women workers and an alliance with independent and family farmers on an antimonopoly platform. (Ibid., April.)

The party hopes to develop a broad antimonopoly coalition outside of the two-party system but does not reject the idea of supporting "progressive" candidates while running communists for office. Because of their isolation, however, "where possible," communists should consider running as part of an antimonopoly ticket. On racial issues, the party urged "real affirmative action programs with quotas" in all private and public employment, "all hiring through government hiring offices," and massive governmental aid to blacks, financed by a 50-percent cut in military spending. (Ibid., June.)

One of the rare times when public disagreement among party officials broke out occurred over the issue of nuclear energy. Victor Perlo supported the peaceful use of atomic energy in the *People's World*, drawing a mild dissent from editor Carl Bloice when the Three Mile Island accident occurred (*Militant*, 31 March). The *Daily World* (30 March) later supported nuclear power with adequate safeguards. Soon after, however, Gus Hall called for the closing of all plants until "peoples' committees" could supervise them (ibid., 11 April).

The CPUSA nominated its national ticket for the 1980 election: Gus Hall for president and Angela Davis for vice-president. Hall received nearly 59,000 votes in 1976. (*NYT*, 20 November.)

International Views and Policies. The CPUSA is one of the most consistently pro-Soviet parties in the world. It faithfully follows all Russian views on foreign policy. The draft resolution of the Detroit convention charged that anti-Soviet campaigns are designed to bolster American imperialism (*Political Affairs*, April). The CPUSA vigorously supported Vietnam in its conficts with Kampuchea (Cambodia) and China and denounced Joan Baez's condemnation of the Vietnamese by asserting that their revolution was one of the "most tolerant, even gentle" in history (*Daily World*, 2 June). The party's strong support for the Palestine Liberation Organization and hostility to Israel continued. The Egyptian-Israeli peace treaty was condemned as a plot of American imperialism to weaken Arab national liberation movements. Jack O'Dell, a former member of the Central Committee under the name of Hunter Pitts O'Dell and an editor of *Freedomways*, served as foreign policy adviser to PUSH and accompanied its director, Jesse Jackson, on his trip to the Middle East. When a May Day speaker hailed the Middle East peace accord, the march organizer took the microphone and denied that this was the position of the event's sponsors (*Guardian*, 16 May). Until the Soviet Union began to denounce Iran's Islamic Revolution, the *Daily World* was effusive about Ayatollah Khomeini, one of its columnists going so far as to call his stand on women "egalitarian, humane, and democratic" (*Daily World*, 6 April). The party was briefly touched by the fallout from the People's Temple mass suicide: cult leader Jim Jones's will left his property, if none of his family survived, to the CPUSA (*WP*, 9 February).

Publications. The *Daily World*, appearing five times a week in New York, is the CPUSA's major publication, with a claimed circulation of 30,000 copies. *Political Affairs* is a monthly theoretical journal. Other party-linked papers are *People's World*, a San Francisco weekly; *Freedomways*, a black quarterly; *New World Review*, a bimonthly newsletter; *Cultural Reporter; African Agenda; Labor*

Today; Korea Forum; and *Black Liberation Journal.* International Publishers has long been identified as the CPUSA publishing outlet.

The Socialist Workers Party. There was little change in the leadership of the SWP during the past year. Jack Barnes is national secretary and Barry Shepard organizational secretary. Other party leaders include Steve Clark (editor, *Militant*), Peter Camejo (national field organizer), Linda Jenness, Bruce Levine, Lew Jones, Ed Heisler, Malik Miah, Cindy Jaquith, Larry Siegle, Susan Lamont, Maceo Dixon, and Betsy Stone. Mary-Alice Waters became editor of *Intercontinental Press.*

The SWP's most important auxiliary is the Young Socialist Alliance (YSA). Cathy Sedwick is national chairperson, Betsy Farley organizational secretary, and Chuck Petrin national secretary. The YSA decided in December 1978 to move its largely student membership into industry, following the example set last year by its parent organization. By August more than 40 percent of its membership of about 500 were supposedly in industry. A small minority wanted to retain the emphasis on campus organizing but lost (*Militant*, 7 September). Other party organizations include the Political Rights Defense Fund, the National Student Coalition against Racism, and the U.S. Committee for Justice to Latin American Political Prisoners.

The SWP's 30th National Convention was held 5–11 August with 1,550 people, virtually the whole party, present. More than 46 percent of its members are industrial workers with 170 in the steelworker and 142 in the auto workers unions. The convention considered and decisively defeated a proposal to reverse the turn to industrial work. Its National Committee is now 24 percent black, 8 percent Latino, and 31 percent female. The convention "unanimously" defeated Tim Wohlforth's effort to label the Cubans "counterrevolutionary Stalinists" and to adopt the same attitude toward them as toward the Russians. (Ibid.) The SWP is vehemently opposed to nuclear power. It has mounted a major campaign to save several Iranian Trotskyists imprisoned by the new regime and has supported the Vietnamese in Indochina. The party has called for a new labor party to fight the growing offensive of capital and nominated Andrew Pulley, a black, and Matilde Zimmerman for national office in 1980. The party is critical of the Soviet Union. During the year Joseph Hansen, a longtime SWP and Fourth International leader, died. Hansen, editor of *Intercontinental Press*, had served as a secretary to Leon Trotsky in Mexico.

The SWP publishes the weekly *Militant*, the monthly *Young Socialist*, and the Spanish-language biweekly *Perspectiva Mundial.*

Other Groups. The numerous splinter sects spent this year arguing with each other about events in Indochina. Despite unity stirrings among some, there were more splits and new groups formed. The CP (M-L) led by Michael Klonsky, holds the Chinese government franchise. In line with the Chinese three-world theory, the CP (M-L) urges unity between the Third World and advanced capitalist nations against the superpowers, with the main enemy being the Soviet Union. The party's journal, *The Call*, vigorously supported the Chinese invasion of Vietnam and the Pol Pot government in Kampuchea.

The RCP, which defended the "gang of four" (see *YICA*, 1979, p. 391), spent the year denouncing the Chinese government as "revisionist." Some 400 members protesting the visit of Deng Xiaoping to Washington battled police in Lafayette Park; 50 were injured and 69 arrested. Party chairman Bob Avakian and sixteen others face felony charges that could bring them 100 years in jail. Deng was attacked as a "posturing boot-licking and sawed-off pimp" (*WP*, 26 January). Although critical of China, the RCP also attacked Vietnam for serving as a "pawn of the Soviet Union" (*Revolution*, July-August). The RCP publishes the *Revolutionary Worker*, a weekly, and *Revolution*, a bimonthly journal.

The Revolutionary Workers' Headquarters, led by Mickey Jarvis, is an offshoot of the RCP. It publishes *Workers Voice* and has been exploring unity with the CP (M-L). The *Guardian*, which represented an independent Maoism, was convulsed this year by feuds. Wilfred Burchett, its longtime correspondent, resigned in February when the paper withheld its judgment on the Indochinese invasions. Burchett supported Hanoi; the *Guardian* (28 February) condemned China and the Soviet Union, criticized Vietnam, and deplored the Kampuchean government. It also blamed the whole episode on American imperialism, "even though it is not yet directly involved." Irwin Silber, associated with the newspaper for many years, launched a National Network of Marxist-Leninist Clubs, with five chapters, which hoped to "rectify" a communist line to begin the process of party building (ibid., 18 April). Silber was soon denounced by his former associates.

A new "party" was created—the CPUSA (Marxist-Leninist). Formed by the formerly pro-Chinese Marxist-Leninist Organizing Committee, the new party, which publishes *Unite*, is competing with the Central Organization of US Marxist-Leninists, which publishes *Workers Advocate*, for the honor of representing Enver Hoxha's Albania in America (ibid., 21 February). The Spartacist League, a small Trotskyist sect, distinguished itself from other groups by adopting a pronuclear stance and attacking "clamshells, abalones, shads and other organizations similarly located on the evolutionary scale that argue that nuclear power is intrinsically more unsafe than other methods of producing energy under capitalism" (ibid., 16 May). The Progressive Labor Party, which publishes *Challenge/Desafio*, is unabashedly Stalinist. Its major front group is the Committee Against Racism.

The Workers Viewpoint Organization changed its name to the Communist Workers Party and achieved notoriety when, at the beginning of a Death to the Klan Rally in Greensboro, North Carolina, five of its members were killed in an attack by Klansmen and Nazis. Three of the five dead were medical doctors; several had abandoned medicine for textile organizing (*Greensboro Daily News*, 6 November).

Emory University   Harvey Klehr

Uruguay

The Communist Party of Uruguay (Partido Comunista del Uruguay; PCU) dates from September 1920. The National Liberation Movement (Movimiento de Liberación Nacional), better known as the Tupamaros, was formed in 1962. These parties remained outlawed in 1979. The PCU's membership, estimated in the early 1970s at 30,000, may have fallen to less than a third of that in 1979. The population of Uruguay is approximately 2.9 million.

Party Organization and Leadership. The PCU's first secretary, Rodney Arismendi, continued to reside in Moscow and issued communications from various locations in Europe. The PCU Central

Committee has 48 members and 27 alternates when every position is filled. The five-member Secretariat consists of Arismendi, Enrique Pastorino, Jaime Pérez, Enrique Rodríguez, and Alberto Suárez. Prominent PCU leaders imprisoned during the year included José L. Massera, Pérez, Gerardo Cuesta, Vladímir Turiansky, and Alberto Altesor. Pastorino remains president of the pro-Soviet World Federation of Trade Unions; Julia Arévalo, in jail since 1976, is a vice-president of the Women's International Democratic Federation. Pérez, in jail since 1974, was sentenced to ten years in prison in January. The Uruguayan government launched its third major campaign against the communists since 1973 in February and March (the first two occurred in late 1973 and in late 1975). The party, already much weakened by government repression, claimed that hundreds of party members were jailed and tortured, adding that in order to intimidate the population, terrorist acts were openly committed in the streets. Rodríguez wrote at midyear: "There is no need to pretend that the blow was not a heavy one" to both the PCU and its youth group, the Young Communist League. The new wave of repression coincided with the appointment of an "extremely reactionary" general as commander of the army, according to Rodríguez. The PCU leader asserts that the party is now reforming its ranks even faster than it did after the 1975 repression. (*WMR*, July.)

Domestic and International Positions. Although an occasional PCU member states that "the dictatorship will be ousted and ousted soon" (*Guyana Chronicle*, Georgetown, 18 May), most leaders acknowledge the long, hard efforts that will be needed to defeat the military enemy. "The country's sharp economic and social contradictions were eroding the dictatorial regime and creating conditions for a new stage in the struggle against fascism," wrote Eduardo Viera early in the year. "However, they should not give rise to the illusion that changes will be easy." Conditions for "a vast national movement, including the adoption of higher forms of mass struggle, would be provided if the parties reach agreement and took the initiative of raising it to the level of a great national alignment so as to shape further development." (*IB*, no. 10.)

Alberto Suárez outlined three basic prerequisites for the success of the antimilitary struggle: "the level of the people's struggle must be raised; there must be joint action by the whole of the democratic opposition; and a policy of principle must be pursued with respect to the army in order to increase dissent within the armed forces" (*Mundo Obrero*, Madrid, 8 February). Arismendi stressed the existing "crisis in the army" between the "ultra-reactionary wing, which advocates intensified terror and repressions," and those within the armed forces who "speak of the need for political liberalization and want to contact and negotiate with political parties" (*IB*, no. 1). The PCU's leaders are not impressed by the government pledge of elections by 1981, charging that this is "nothing but an attempt to embellish the regime." Since the military leaders realize it will be difficult to retreat from the promised elections, Rodríguez wrote at midyear, they launched the new wave of repression in early 1979 hoping to "prevent the truly popular forces and their vanguard from having any influence on political developments." (*WMR*, July.)

Specific domestic goals of the PCU include the release of all "political prisoners," information on the fate of persons who have disappeared, a repeal of the ban on political parties, and a restoration of the civil rights of the thousands of people affiliated with political parties. In an effort to achieve its goals, the PCU is said to continue contacts with traditional bourgeois parties and church circles and to publish its analyses of conditions in its illegal newspapers—*Carta Semanal*, organ of the PCU; *Liber Arce*, the Youth League paper; and the theoretical journal *Análisis y Orientación* (*IB*, no. 1).

Hoover Institution   Lynn Ratliff

Venezuela

Founded in 1931, the Communist Party of Venezuela (Partido Comunista de Venezuela; PCV) is the oldest but no longer the most important Marxist force in the country. Participation in the guerrilla warfare of the 1960s undermined the PCV's once strong popular base. At the same time, its rigid adherence to the Moscow line alienated many of the party's most promising leaders. Disenchanted with old-guard intolerance, a large group broke away in 1970 and founded the Movement toward Socialism (Movimiento al Socialismo; MAS). The MAS rapidly took first place among leftist parties. Still weak from this massive desertion, the PCV suffered another split in 1974, with part of the old guard itself leaving to form the Communist Vanguard (Vanguardia Comunista; VC), later renamed the United Communist Vanguard (Vanguardia Unitaria Comunista; VUC). Another Marxist-Leninist group, the Movement of the Revolutionary Left (Movimiento de Izquierda Revolucionario; MIR), grew significantly during the past few years but now seems unavoidably headed for a split. The MIR originated from a division within the Democratic Action Party (Acción Democrática; AD), which has controlled the government for three of the last five administrations. An AD splinter, the People's Electoral Movement (Movimiento Electoral del Pueblo; MEP) does not call itself Marxist, but it must be included in any evaluation of leftist strength in Venezuela. The Socialist League (Liga Socialista; LS) was the only Trotskyist movement recognized as a national political party but lost that status after it failed to receive 1 percent of the vote in the 1978 presidential election. Guerrilla activity has been minimal this year, characterized chiefly by the return to legality under the terms of the government's pacification program of several prominent leaders. All communist factions combined are estimated to have some 10,000 members. The population of Venezuela is estimated at 14.5 million.

The 22 leftist votes in the 195-member Chamber of Deputies have occasionally assumed a crucial importance as neither the AD nor the governing Social Christian Party (COPEI) won a controlling majority in the December 1978 congressional elections. No formal bloc has materialized, however, and AD threats of a pact with the left never reached the state of concrete proposals. The most significant and immediately productive achievement of the left this year was the presentation of a unified ballot in the 3 June municipal elections. The six leftist parties mentioned above, plus the Revolutionary Action Group (Grupo de Acción Revolucionario; GAR) and a regional party, The People Advance (El Pueblo Avanza; EPA), together received 18.5 percent of the vote and representation in all but a very few of the country's municipal councils. These results obviously cannot be transferred automatically to future presidential elections, but the leftist claim that the AD-COPEI polarization has been broken is not without substance. The COPEI won overwhelmingly in the municipal contest, but the left, particularly the MAS, scored some fairly impressive gains at the expense of a humiliated AD.

The Communist Party of Venezuela. *Organization and Leadership.* The top leadership of the PCV is its eighteen-member Politburo. This body includes President Gustavo Machado, Secretary General Jesús Faría, Radamés Larrazábal, and ex-presidential candidate Héctor Mujica. Mujica has been mentioned as a "renovation" candidate to succeed Jesús Faría (*El Nacional*, 16 September).

Until the December 1970 split, the PCV's Venezuelan Communist Youth (Juventud Comunista Venezolana; JCV) was the largest political group in the student movement. The split deprived it of its leaders and members, and signs of recovery, apart from some successes in secondary schools, are few. In the November Central University (Universidad Central de Venezuela; UCV) elections, the JCV joined a slate supporting one of the MIR candidates for president of the Federation of University Centers (Federación de Centros Universitarios; FCU). The ticket ran second, but the JCV again failed to receive a seat on the Executive Committee of the FCU or the University Council.

The principal center of PCV influence in the labor movement is the United Workers' Central of Venezuela (Central Unitaria de Trabajadores de Venezuela; CUTV), established in the early 1960s when the PCV lost virtually all influence in the majority Confederation of Workers of Venezuela (Confederación de Trabajadores de Venezuela; CTV). The CUTV has little ascendancy on the local scene but gained favorable publicity this year from its joint sponsorship with the CTV of a wage increase bill. (The bill was passed after several days of demonstrations, riots, and threats of a general strike.) President Cruz Villegas and Secretary General Hemmy Croes of the CUTV made numerous statements applauding the unified action of the labor confederations. The PCV will nonetheless continue efforts to increase its representation in the CTV through participation in unity slates for labor union elections.

Domestic Attitudes and Activities. The PCV maintained its status as a national party with just over 1 percent of the vote in the presidential election, a share that did not increase perceptibly in the municipal elections. A resolution of the Seventeenth Central Committee Plenum attributed this poor performance to "deficiencies in political organization, lack of contact with the masses, and the scarcity of funds noted at the Sixteenth Central Committee Plenum" (ibid., 24 June). The same text recommended that "members and friends . . . actively work with the masses in order to spread the communist ideology and to develop unity of action with the other leftist forces."

The Chamber of Deputies paid tribute to Gustavo Machado on the occasion of his retirement from that body in June. The homage was sharply criticized by a former army commander, Gen. Arnaldo Castro Hurtado, who had resigned shortly before amid rumors of an AD-inspired military coup. (The rumors persisted, with varying intensity, throughout most of the year.) Disagreement with the government's pacification program figured largely among the causes of his resignation. Castro Hurtado accused Machado of responsibility for "the death and sacrifice of almost an entire generation" in the guerrilla warfare of the 1960s (ibid., 13 July). The PCV's reply defended the pacification program and Machado and promised that in the unlikely event of a coup, the "PCV will fight with more energy than ever at the side of the people—including democratic (army) officers—for the victory of true democracy in our country" (ibid., 17 July). Machado will continue as president of the PCV.

International Views and Positions. Jesús Faría condemned the Chinese "aggression against the heroic and long-suffering Vietnamese people . . . It is not a matter of differences between socialist countries, as some circles are saying, but of foul aggression by a powerful ally of imperialism against a much smaller socialist country." (*Tribuna Popular*, 20 February.) Gustavo Machado was honored at the World Conference of Solidarity with Nicaragua (Caracas) in memory of his struggle at the side of Augusto César Sandino. The PCV expressed solidarity with Nicaragua and opposed attempts of the Andean Pact to "democratize" the dictatorships of Guatemala, El Salvador, and Honduras (*El Nacional*, 16 September). The Politburo hailed the Sixth Conference of Nonaligned Countries as a victory of "progressive forces, ratifying the principles that serve as solid bases and adding new contributions, such as the recognition of the friendly conduct of socialist countries and the repeated and militant rebuff to the imperialists" (ibid., 11 September). The Seventeenth Central Committee Plenum praised the signing of the SALT II treaty in Vienna as a contribution to world peace (ibid., 24 June).

Publications. The PCV publishes the weekly *Tribuna Popular*.

The Movement Toward Socialism. The MIR was formed late in 1970 following the first major PCV split. Teodoro Petkoff led the rebellion against old-guard dogmatism and gained the support of Politburo member Pompeyo Márquez. Together they took with them a large part of the leadership cadres of the PCV, a majority of the PCV rank and file, and virtually all of the JCV. Márquez and Petkoff are now secretary general and assistant secretary general, respectively, of the MAS. There are two under-secretaries, Freddy Muñoz of the Petkoff faction and Eloy Torres, who supports Márquez. (See below.)

The MAS youth organization, originally called Communist Youth–MAS (Juventud Comunista–MAS) but now called Youth-MAS (Juventud MAS), initially dominated most of the student bodies of Venezuelan universities. It was displaced by the MIR in 1977 but regained the presidency of the FCU in the November 1979 election as a result of the MIR split. (See below.) The MAS's proposals for a unified left slate including the two MIR factions was rejected, and it ran alone to avoid taking sides in the dispute. Party candidate Eladio Hernández won by a very slight margin over the MIR–Eduardo Semtei ticket, which was supported by the LS and other groups. The MAS will have four places on the FCU Executive Committee and a seat on the university council.

At its inception the MAS had some influence in the CUTV trade union. Those who went with the MAS first formed the "CUT Clasista" as a rival organization. In 1974 the MAS Central Committee decided to have its followers enter the CTV, and the MAS now has one seat on the CTV Executive Committee. The MAS will participate in unified left slates for labor union elections preceding the May 1980 CTV congress. Jesús Urbieta, MAS representative on the CTV Executive Committee, said that other leftist parties have followed the MAS lead in creating a bloc capable of challenging the two predominant ideologies in the labor movement, social democracy and Christian democracy" (ibid., 22 August). With the rest of the left, the MAS supported the wage increase bill and condemned police brutality in the repression of the labor demonstration on 25 October. Petkoff and former MAS presidential candidate José Vicente Rangel received slight wounds in these riots.

Internal Dissension. According to Senator Márquez, the "Petkoff-Márquez match is a championship bout, which some people have been waiting eight years to see" (ibid., 20 November). He promises, however, that the March 1980 national convention will not provide that spectacle. To date, Márquez is the only candidate for secretary general, and Petkoff's aspirations seem to be centered on the 1983 presidential nomination. Speculation exists that Márquez may also be interested in the nomination; if not, he would again back the candidacy of Rangel. Petkoff reportedly controls the powerful sections of the Federal District and the state of Miranda and maintains a slight edge in the National Directorate, while Márquez controls most of the interior sections and dominates the mass organizations. Regional leaders in the mining-industrial zone of Guyana denounced a "climate of terror" imposed by followers of Petkoff (ibid., 1 September). Rangel, a seasoned left-wing independent with prestige and followers in many sectors, would be a more appealing candidate for a coalition ballot than Petkoff. Petkoff is charismatic but is intimately identified with the MAS and has engaged in bitter disputes with his ideological neighbors over the years. Some minor polemics between Rangel and Petkoff this summer were seen as a premature beginning of the struggle for the nomination (ibid., 6 June and 14, 18, and 19 July).

Domestic Attitudes and Activities. Ideological debate has been almost entirely removed from the conflicts discussed above, and both factions seem comfortable with the definitions of democratic socialism. The internal power struggle thus did not impede unification experiments, with encouraging results in the 3 June elections. Unity also carried over into some parliamentary activity and caused some alarm when the left agreed to vote with the COPEI for a public debt bill that had previously been blocked by the AD. The AD's president, Gonzalo Barrios, subsequently suggested an AD-MAS alliance to control congress as of next March, with a member of the AD as president of the Senate and a member of the MAS, perhaps Independent-MAS deputy D. F. Maza Zavala, as president of the

Chamber of Deputies. Rangel was clearly intrigued with the possibility, but Márquez called the suggestion a "publicity stunt to blackmail the COPEI" since no follow-up contacts were forthcoming. He added that the MAS will not make pacts with either the COPEI or the AD: "The MAS will emphasize an independent, autonomous line, although coincidences with one or the other party from time to time are not discounted." (Ibid., 28 August.) The MAS consistently held this policy in its insistence on pursuing investigations of administrative corruption in the armed forces, investigations that the AD opposed and the COPEI would have preferred to ignore.

International Views and Positions. In a trip through Romania, Yugoslavia, Italy, and Spain, Márquez found many areas of agreement between the MAS and the communist parties of those countries. They all advocate pluralistic, democratic socialism independent of any international center of power; find the USSR-China conflict a negative factor; condemn the interventions in Vietnam and Kampuchea (Cambodia) equally; and reaffirm the Marxist inspiration of parties, while recognizing that Marxism has no monopoly on the truth (ibid., 28 April). The secretary general of the Communist Party of Galicia visited Venezuela for conversations with MAS leaders: "I will also meet other groups, but the links of the Spanish communists are with the Venezuelan socialists" (ibid., 23 June). Teodoro Petkoff was received by Li Xiannian during a visit to China to "strengthen friendly relations between China and the MAS." Petkoff said, "They will have understood that we are friends, but not of the same family." (Ibid., 23 September.)

Publications. The principal MAS organ is the newspaper *Punto.*

The United Communist Vanguard. Following a split in the PCV old guard in 1974, two of the party's traditional leaders, Eduardo Machado (brother of Gustavo) and Guillermo García Ponce, left to form the VC, later renamed the VUC. The VUC's First Congress, held in 1974, elected Machado president and García Ponce secretary general. It also proclaimed the new group to be a Marxist-Leninist party, faithful to the traditions of international solidarity. The VUC supported Rangel in the presidential election but did not win the 1 percent of votes necessary to maintain its status as a national political party. On the unified left ticket, the VUC elected some six municipal councillors on 3 June. García Ponce complained that "faulty formulas of alliance" permitted the MAS to absorb a "considerable number of votes of the other parties," a situation that particularly affected his party. (Ibid., 9 June.) Mario Márquez, a member of the National Policy Committee of the VUC, suggested the integration in one single party of the VUC, LS, GAR, EPA, Causa Radical, and other groups (ibid., 13 August).

The Movement of the Revolutionary Left. The MIR was established in 1960 by AD dissidents unhappy with President Betancourt's policy of economic austerity. These included some members of the Executive Committee, led by Domingo Alberto Rangel, and virtually all of the youth movement. A number of splits preceded both the MIR's formal decision to enter the armed struggle in 1964 and its official withdrawal in 1969. Domingo Rangel, opposing continued guerrilla participation, left the party in the mid-sixties and now leads a small group of independent leftists who boycott elections. The MIR's 1978 presidential candidate, Américo Martín, won 0.98 percent of the vote, and the party's congressional slate polled 2.35 percent, electing four deputies. In 1978 the MIR controlled the FCU and had begun to make some inroads in the labor movement. This recuperation—from a group totally disbanded eight years earlier to the fourth political party in the country—was not sufficient to prevent a new schism that now seems irreversible.

Secretary General Moisés Moleiro and Américo Martín are disputing control of the party, or what will remain of it. A third faction led by Rigoberto Lanz, a member of the National Directorate and director of the UCV School of Sociology, has demanded the resignation of the National Directorate. Moleiro is in the United States for heart surgery, and his Marxist-Leninist group is headed by acting

Secretary General Héctor Pérez Marcano. Other supporters include Carlos Flores, Julio Estévez, Segundo Meléndez, and Pedro Pérez. Jesús Vethencourt, Estanislao González, and Hely Saúl Puchí are among the followers of Martín's line, which is usually called renovationist or simply socialist. The Marxist tendency of Lanz is supported by Freddy Lovera, Ramón Mendoza, and Ramón Alvarado, but it is not in the running for party control.

Regional conferences in preparation for the Eighth National Conference were interrupted in early November by the Moleiro group, and the National Conference was postponed. Martín continued with parallel conferences, and two national conferences will probably be held in December. It is impossible at this time to discriminate between the mutual accusations of illegality. Documents from both factions had already been forwarded to the Supreme Electoral Council, and a decision as to which faction would retain the party name was expected in January 1980. But this judgment may not be exempt from political influence. The Electoral Council is composed of representatives of the political parties, and the new COPEI secretary general is a close friend of Martín.

The People's Electoral Movement. Inclusion of the MEP may be disputed, as noted above. The MEP was founded by Luis Beltrán Prieto Figueroa. One of the founders of the AD, Prieto left the party in 1968 when convention maneuvers deprived him of the presidential nomination. As an MEP candidate the same year, he won almost 20 percent of the vote, which contributed decisively to the AD defeat. With its strongest base in the labor unions, the party moved to the left, espousing national liberation and democratic socialism. Most of its supporters returned to the AD. Prieto ran for president again in 1978, receiving 1.11 percent of the vote. The MEP elected four deputies, including Salom Mesa, who was released from prison as a result of the election. Secretary General Jesús Angel Paz Galarraga will defend his post against Carlos Torres Bracho at the March 1980 national convention. Torres Bracho maintains that alliances with the middle-class MAS are depriving the MEP of its image as a workers' party (ibid., 15 July).

The AD controls roughly 50 percent of the CTV; second place is disputed by the COPEI and the MEP. If MEP delegates to the 1980 congress exceed those of COPEI, a MEP candidate supported by the COPEI and the left might displace the AD in the leadership. In the preliminary elections, the MEP has participated singly or in alliance with the left, joining the COPEI only where neither option is viable, i.e., in labor unions or federations with no leftist representation other than the MEP. If the COPEI's delegation to the congress is stronger than that of the MEP, a pact with the COPEI will be considered. (Ibid., 4 September.) A MEP director, Isaac Oliveira, president of the Venezuelan Federation of Teachers, led the teachers in a controversial strike that produced bitter confrontations with the COPEI government.

Prieto Figueroa was the first recipient of the Inter-American Education Prize awarded in April by the Organization of American States. In July, he presided over the World Conference of Solidarity with Nicaragua in Caracas (ibid., 14 July). Romesh Chandra, president of the World Peace Council, addressed the conference. The MEP expressed great satisfaction with the results of the Sixth Conference of Nonaligned Countries and the "failure of all the maneuvers of U.S. diplomacy and espionage services" to sabotage the conference (ibid., 14 September).

Trotskyists. The Venezuelan Trotskyist Group made its appearance in 1972 and in 1973 took the name of Socialist Workers' Party (Partido Socialista de los Trabajadores; PST). This merged in 1974 with the LS, which is the Venezuelan section of the United Secretariat of the Fourth International. The PST in 1973 and the LS in 1978 supported Rangel's candidacy for president. A very small PST still exists and is active at the university level. The International Secretariat is represented by the Revolutionary Workers' Party, Trotskyist-Posadist, which supported the PCV presidential candidate in 1978 but seems otherwise inactive.

David Nieves was released from prison as a result of his election to the Chamber of Deputies. The LS leader had been held in connection with the 1976 kidnapping of William Niehous, vice-president of Owens Illinois in Caracas. Niehous was rescued in July, but subsequent investigations have not shed much light on this puzzling affair. Responsibility for the kidnapping had been claimed by the unknown "Revolutionary Command Argimiro Gabaldón," generally believed to be part of the Organization of Revolutionaries (OR, see below), a guerrilla group closely identified with the LS. In 1976 LS founder and Secretary General Jorge Rodríguez was arrested as a presumed courier for the kidnappers and tortured to death by the intelligence police. Former OR militants deny any connection with the kidnapping, and the LS denies that it is the "legal face" of the OR. Of the ex-guerrillas who have accepted presidential pardons, three well-known commanders of the OR—Julio Escalona, Marcos Gómez, and Fernando Soto Rojas—joined the LS. Escalona is now secretary general. The LS announced that death threats received by Escalona, Nieves, and others came from "AD paramilitary squads controlled by David Morales Bello." Nieves and others have accused Morales Bello of involvement in the Niehous case because of his alleged role as government go-between for Owens Illinois. (Ibid., 11 July and 12 November.)

Maoists. The most important Maoist groups are the Party of the Venezuelan Revolution (Partido de la Revolución Venezolana; PRV), Ruptura, and the Committees of Popular Struggle (Comités de Lucha Popular; CLP). Both the PRV and Ruptura are experiencing internal dissension, but a merger between the two may be in the offing. Ruptura and its breakaway faction Tendencia Revoluciónaria appeared separately on the MIR-Semtei ballot in the UCV election. A paid announcement signed by five persons expelled from the PRV maintains that Politburo rigidity and intolerance were responsible for the resignation of Politburo members Alí Rodríguez and Julio Chirinos and for the expulsion of numerous middle-level leaders. The Politburo attributed failure of the 1973-1978 "nueva línea táctica" to "incomprehension and faulty implementation " of party militants. The resulting "rebellion" of the mid-echelon leadership was repressed "without discussion" and its "assemblies declared illegal." (Ibid., 11 August.) This is the only published information available so far. The PRV originally rejected the government's pacification program, holding out for a broad amnesty (ibid., 7 July). Charges against PRV leader Douglas Bravo, however, were stayed on 24 September, and he ended eighteen years of hiding on 24 November in Coro where his insurrection began. Shortly before, Diego Salazar, another PRV returnee now with Ruptura, had said that the PRV and Ruptura were discussing unification of the two movements (ibid., 2 November). Fifteen thousand persons reportedly attended Bravo's PRV-Ruptura welcome rally in Coro. In his speech, Bravo said that "the desperation in which the people lived a few years ago has begun to be shaken by the mobilization of the workers . . . by student participation in the struggle . . . A new stage has been initiated in our country . . . The people have been reincorporated into the struggle." (Ibid., 25 November.)

José Demetrio Bonilla, on behalf of the National Committee of the CLP, signed a declaration attacking the pacification program and named the MIR and the PCV, "now wallowing in the filthy mire of opportunism," as examples of the dangers of a policy of conciliation (ibid., 3 May). At the time of the Chinese invasion of Vietnam, Bonilla led a campaign in the UCV in which he affirmed that the only socialist country in the world is Albania. The CLP has had some limited success in university elections.

The Guerrillas. The Red Flag Party (Partido Bandera Roja; PBR) maintains that "the only way to seize power is by revolutionary people's war, the cornerstone of our strategy." The scene of the long-term struggle will be in the countryside, where the revolutionaries have the tactical advantage over the government forces. An extended analysis of the origin of the PBR and its place in the Venezuelan revolutionary struggle by National Political Committee members elaborated on the party's rejection of the revisionist PCV and other so-called revolutionary groups. Party leader Gabriel Puerta Aponte insisted that PBR members are not "violence fanatics," but simply recognize the realities of Venezuela's current needs. (*Causa Marxista-Leninista*, Paris, September-November.) The Americo Silva Front (FAS) of the PBR held a press conference somewhere in Monagas in July to announce its rejection of the pacification program. The FAS was created in 1977, one year after the division of the Antonio José de Sucre Front. The split was caused by the expulsion of Carlos Betancourt who took "most of the men, 65 in all" to form the PBR-Marxista Leninista. According to FAS commanders Puerta, Faustino Lugo, Pedro Rincón, and Pedro Véliz, the "prospects of the revolutionary movement are broad. After the defeat in 1960 of a plan to seize power immediately, we imposed the thesis of the prolonged struggle, in which the armed element has a strategic value, but the emphasis is on ties with sectors of the masses: workers, peasants, and students." The leaders admitted that they had provided technical aid and funds to the Argimiro Gabaldón Front but had lost all contact with the group after the Niehous kidnapping. They refused to name another organization that they said took part in the operation. (*El Nacional*, 4 July.)

In an interview with *El Nacional* (12 June), Carlos Betancourt announced his imminent return to legality. One day later, his brother Argenis, also an ex-guerrilla, was killed by police. Carlos Betancourt has not appeared publicly. Both the PBR and the OR were formed in 1969 when the MIR split over the question of abandoning armed resistance. Betancourt accused MIR leaders Martín, Moleiro, and others of withholding Cuban funds from the guerrilla fronts. He said that the PBR had never had any relations with Cuba or other socialist countries. (Ibid., 12 June.)

A national guardsman was killed in El Pao in the state of Bolivar by presumed guerrillas. Police believe that cells of the Antonio José de Sucre Front are operating in the region. Américo Silva was killed in El Pao in 1972. (Ibid., 20 March.)

Police have intimated that extreme-left subversives were responsible for the disruption of the 25 October labor demonstration and ensuing riots in Valencia and Caracas. The LS accuses the extreme right of similarly attempting to create a propitious atmosphere for a military coup (ibid., 12 November).

Caracas, Venezuela   Carole Merten

Document: Latin America

STATEMENT BY SEVEN SOUTH AMERICAN COMMUNIST PARTIES

The Latin American peoples are extremely concerned over the growing threat of a military conflict between Chile and Argentina in connection with the Beagle Channel territorial dispute. Such a conflict would run counter to the traditional fraternity between the two peoples forged in the battles for their independence, as symbolically reflected in the strong handshake of solidarity of San Martin and O'Higgins, the heroes of our liberation struggles . . .

U.S. imperialism stands behind all these territorial disputes. It is intent on strengthening its domination there and ultimately to lay its hands on the areas rich in oil, ore and sea products and the strategically important areas stretching to the Antarctic . . .

At the same time they are fanning chauvinism, instigating anti-national, anti-popular coups or creating new seats of military tension.

These forces are the enemies of our peoples. They seek to revive disputes between Bolivia and Chile, Peru and Ecuador, Brazil, Argentina, Paraguay and Argentina, etc.

In this uncertain time the communist parties of the southern cone of the American continent urge all the peoples of the region, all champions of peace, democracy and national independence to raise their voice in protest and to join in the struggle to avert a military catastrophe with its inevitable toll of lives, destruction of the fruit of the people's labor, imperilling the very existence of our nations.

It is essential to launch a struggle against the chauvinist instigators of war, against the preparations for a military conflict. In these circumstances, U.S. imperialism, the forces of fascism and reaction intend to hamper the peoples' struggle for democracy and social progress and to establish or impose regimes that trample on liberties, to strengthen the domination of imperialism and the most reactionary forces.

The struggle for peace is thus closely linked with the struggle for democracy, national sovereignty and the social progress of our peoples.

Luis Corvalán, General Secretary, Communist Party of Chile

Gerónimo Arnedo Alvarez, General Secretary, Communist Party of Argentina

Luiz Carlos Prestes, General Secretary, CC, Brazilian Communist Party

Rodney Arismendi, First Secretary, CC, Communist Party of Uruguay

Jorge del Prado, General Secretary, CC, Peruvian Communist Party

Jorge Kolle Cueto, First Secretary, CC, Communist Party of Bolivia

Antonio Maidana, First Secretary, CC, Paraguayan Communist Party

Sources: Tass dispatch from Buenos Aires, in *Pravda*, 15 January; full text in *IB*, no. 5, pp. 5–6.

AFRICA AND THE MIDDLE EAST

Egypt

The Communist Party of Egypt (al-Hizb al-Shuyu'i al-Misri) was founded in 1921. It has been proscribed since its inception. In 1972 the party re-emerged clandestinely as the Egyptian Communist Party (ECP), attending international communist conferences and publishing articles in communist journals with full Soviet approval. Under the new Egyptian policy of liberalization and democratic pluralism that began in 1976, Egyptian leftists formed a faction within the Arab Socialist Union that subsequently developed into a legitimate party, the National Progressive Unionist Party (NPUP), embracing Marxists, Nasserites, trade unionists, and intellectuals, under the leadership of Khalid Muhyi al-Din. The NPUP began to publish a weekly newspaper, al-Ahali, which by May had a circulation of 135,000. Before the dissolution of parliament in April 1979, three members of the NPUP held seats in the 375-member People's Assembly: Khalid Muhyi al-Din, Qabbari 'Abdallah, and Abu al-'Izz al-Hariri. The NPUP has maintained close, unofficial ties with the five proscribed Egyptian communist parties: the ECP, the Egyptian Communist Workers' Party, the Revolutionary Current (Maoist), the Revolutionary Egyptian Communist Party, and the Eighth of January Organization. In June Egypt held its first multiparty elections in over 25 years. However, laws that emerged from a May 1978 referendum explicitly proscribed political activity by communists, religious extremists, and those who held office before 1952.

Political Positions of the NPUP. In a public meeting celebrating the third anniversary of the foundation of the NPUP, Khalid Muhyi al-Din declared that the NPUP "has in its ranks all patriotic and democratic forces of the country" and has struggled since its inception "for the preservation of the gains of the July revolution of 1952, for the deepening of socio-economic progressive transformations, for a democratic and free Egypt" (FBIS, 16 April). On 21 April Egyptian President Anwar Sadat dissolved parliament, ostensibly as part of his campaign to broaden democracy through the holding of new multiparty elections. According to Khalid Muhyi al-Din, the parliament had unconditionally supported all decisions of the government, but the emergence of an organized opposition to the government within the parliament precipitated the dissolution of parliament to prevent any further development of that opposition. He called on "all national progressive forces" to form a united front to face the 7 June elections (Tass, 27 April; FBIS, 30 April). Muhyi al-Din, who was not re-elected to parliament, asserted that the elections were "held in an atmosphere of repression and suppression of the Egyptian's democratic rights and freedoms unprecedented throughout the country's history." He deplored the opposition's lack of access to the mass media, the limitations on its campaign strategy, the detention of opposition party candidates, and the rigging and falsifying of ballots. While advocating greater political freedom, however, the NPUP charged that economic "liberalization" had caused great damage in Egypt. (Tass, 11 June; FBIS, 12 June.)

The Egyptian-Israeli Peace Treaty. According to the NPUP, one of its leaders, Muhammad Isma'il Amir, was arrested on 29 March for expressing opposition to the visit to Egypt of Israeli Premier Menachem Begin. A few weeks later, Egyptian security officials allegedly raided the Cairo headquarters of the NPUP, confiscating documents and party funds. In a subsequent party statement, the NPUP called "on all honest Egyptians to say a resolute 'no' in the forthcoming referendum on the separate treaty with Israel" and termed it "nothing more than a blatant infringement of Egypt's sovereignty" (*FBIS*, 17 April). Khalid Muhyi al-Din, who is regarded as the core of opposition to the treaty, declared on 18 April: "We consider the treaty as a large step back in the Arab people's struggle for liberation of the occupied lands and for ensuring the legitimate national rights of the Arab Palestinian people for a genuine, all-embracing, and fair peace in the Middle East." He charged that the aim of the treaty was the furtherance of "imperialist-Zionist plans" in that region, "the formation of a new military bloc," and the "suppression of the Arab people's struggle for economic and social progress" (Tass, 13 April; *FBIS*, 16 April). In May the Egyptian government started an investigation of Muhyi al-Din, who lost his parliamentary immunity with the dissolution of parliament. He was accused of working closely with representatives of the Iraqi government in opposing the treaty. During the election campaign in May and June, the Egyptian government banned discussion of the treaty with Israel. Nevertheless, the government interpreted the defeat of almost all candidates known to be strongly opposed to the treaty, particularly Muhyi al-Din, as a reaffirmation of the public's endorsement of President Sadat and the treaty.

The Egyptian Communist Parties. The five communist parties mentioned earlier have small but active memberships. Their operations consist almost exclusively of clandestine organizing on campuses and in factories. They rarely surface to issue public statements or participate in conferences. In late December 1978, the ECP, which is recognized by the Soviet Union as Egypt's official communist party, did attend the last regional communist party meeting, which attacked the Ba'thist regime in Iraq for its persecution of communists.

Political Bureau member, Nagib Kamal, who is the ECP's representative to the *World Marxist Review*, published two articles in that journal during the year. In the March issue he condemned "the capitulatory accords with Israel," calling them "the result of seven years' unremitting preparation . . . for an open and irrevocable defection to the camp of the counterrevolution." Kamal gave the ECP's historical account of the changes made by Sadat that undo what the party views as the progressive social achievements made under Gamal 'Abd al-Nasser. The changes he listed were the passing of laws to encourage foreign and Arab (non-Egyptian) investments, the granting of tax benefits to the Egyptian bourgeoisie equal to those granted to foreign investors, the gradual undermining of the public sector, and the promulgation of amendments to existing labor legislation that restrict and repress union activity. Kamal further charged that the Egyptian regime, in collaboration with U.S. imperialists, used the hardships of the working class, the decline in their living standards, and their desire for peace, as well as the mistakes of some national forces in the Arab world, to create an atmosphere in Egypt willing to accept a capitulatory settlement of the Middle East crisis. Kamal reasserted that the ECP considers its prime objective the overthrow of "the power of the parasitical bourgeoisie."

The ECP advocates a number of temporary and partial alliances and agreements on tactical issues with all forces opposed to the policies of the present government. In his article in the April issue of *World Marxist Review*, Kamal offered to the Arab mass democratic movement the "coherent and clear-cut revolutionary alternative offered by the Arab communist parties." According to Kamal, these parties advocate a full and fundamental solution to the Palestine problem, genuine democracy, freedom of speech and criticism, freedom to establish legislative bodies and political and trade union organizations, an alliance of the national progressive forces, and an end to the anticommunist and anti-Soviet campaign. On the economic level, the ECP advocates balanced and independent economic development, struggle against imperialist monopolies, and ties with world revolutionary forces led by the socialist community. He noted that this revolutionary alternative can be achieved, provided that it is carried on under the leadership of the working class and its vanguard communist party equipped with the theory of Marxism-Leninism.

Government Repression of Egyptian Communists. In late May sources in Cairo reported that eight Egyptians, including two journalists and two leftist candidates for parliament, were being interrogated on charges of forming an underground cell and spying for an embassy of a communist state. In August the prosecutor, Gen. Salah Rashidi, declared that 56 people had been arrested in a series of predawn raids. He asserted that the action was taken in conjunction with the uncovering of an alleged plot to overthrow President Sadat and replace him with a communist ruler. The official declared that those arrested were members of the ECP and included six lawyers, four journalists, and a former member of parliament. Officials of the Interior Ministry asserted that all ECP members would be rounded up if there were evidence of their complicity in the plot to set up a communist government in Egypt (*Arab Report*, 5 September; *NYT*, 20 August). In November the government arrested 35 persons for belonging to the Workers' Communist Party (*FBIS*, 14 November). The ECP and the four other communist parties are clearly not a significant threat to the Egyptian government. In association with the NPUP, however, they serve as a focal point for opposition to the Sadat government and to the Egyptian-Israeli peace treaty.

Stanford University   Patricia Mihaly

Iran

The most important, traditional communist party of Iran has been the Tudeh Party (Party of the Masses), formed in 1941. Between 1941 and 1953, its membership swelled significantly. When the party was suppressed in 1953 by the shah's government, it reorganized itself in East Germany, where it remained active until 1979 when the shah's government collapsed. After sixteen years of exile and activity abroad, the party returned to Iran following the revolution early in the year. It is the only communist organization recognized and permitted to operate openly by the new regime.

Despite the revolution and the return of the Tudeh, the party's membership has not increased significantly since Pahlavi days. Its estimated numbers remain at a few thousand members. The party has suffered from the sudden appearance of numerous new Marxist-Leninist organizations since the revolution. The Tudeh Party itself has witnessed splintering and has seen defections. The traditional Tudeh alliance with the Soviet Union has been the major ideological reason for many of these defections. Several more nationalist-oriented communist groupings have formed in its wake. The nationalist-religious complexion of the Iranian revolution has lessened much of the appeal of the Tudeh Party. There is evidence, for example, that the post-Pahlavi regime tolerates Tudeh activity precisely because it is perceived as a force of very limited attraction.

Organization and Leadership. The most dramatic change in Tudeh Party leadership in many years occurred in early January. Iradj Eskandari, first secretary of the party since 1971, was suddenly replaced by his deputy, Noureddin Kianouri. The reason for the change concerned Eskandari's misreading of the fundamentally important role played by the Shi'ite religious leaders in the revolution. Soon after this change, Kianouri returned to Iran, where he remained active throughout the year. In the process, the new first secretary consistently reiterated the Tudeh's support for Ayatollah Khomeini and for the concept of an Islamic republic. Although small in numbers, the party is well organized and highly disciplined.

Domestic Issues. The party calls for an "anti-imperialist democratic revolution" that will unite the working class, the peasantry, the petite bourgeoisie, the national intelligentsia, and even the substantial part of the national bourgeoisie that does not have close links with imperialist capital. It asks support for Ayatollah Khomeini, who fought against the "antinational" shah regime, and promises that it will respect the social doctrines of Shi'ism, the branch of Islam prevalent in Iran. (Interview with Noureddin Kianouri, *IB*, 15 April, pp. 21–23.) According to the party, Shi'ite social doctrines have a "positive significance" and are in harmony with popular and revolutionary movements. According to the party's first secretary, within the national democratic movement, the working class—led by the workers in the oil industry—now constitutes an organized and politically conscious force numbering over 3 million people. Moreover, the peasantry is beginning to join the working class, partly because of the efforts made by patriotic Shi'ite clergy. (Noureddin Kianouri, *WMR*, April, pp. 105–9.) The party calls for a peaceful settlement of the Kurdish issue, but the "legitimate and just demands of the Kurdish people . . . cannot be identified with the subversive activity of the counterrevolutionary forces" (*FBIS*, 26 October). The party looks to immediate measures designed to eliminate unemployment, halt price increases, aid the "oppressed strata of the population," and maintain government control over oil exports (ibid., 1 May), but downplays for the moment the Tudeh Party's wider revolutionary objectives.

Foreign Policy. The Tudeh Party considers U.S. imperialism Iran's archenemy. American machinations contrast with the "unselfish policy" of "our great and good friend, the Soviet Union," which has "held out a helping hand to the Iranian people." In contrast, "the Maoist leadership of China has failed to show the slightest sympathy with the Iranian people's movement," having in effect supported the shah "in alliance with U.S. imperialists." The party also supports the cause of the Arab Rejection Front and of the Palestine Liberation Organization (PLO) against Israel and condemns what it considers to be the schemes of international Zionism. (*WMR*, March, pp. 87–91.)

Other Marxist Organizations. Following the Iranian revolution, many Marxist organizations of widely diverging ideologies came into being. At least three of these groupings were direct offshoots from the Tudeh Party. The most important of these is the Communist Union of Iran, a group that defected because its members felt the Tudeh was discredited by its connections with Moscow.

The two most significant radical political organizations that have surfaced since the revolution are the Fedayan-e Khalq (Devotees of the People) and the Hezb-e Kargaran-e Sosialist (Socialist Workers' Party; HKS). During 1979, these two groups exhibited considerably more influence and appeal in Iran than did the Tudeh Party.

The Fedayan is a well-organized militant group with impeccable revolutionary credentials. Formed in 1971, this organization fought the shah's military and police apparatus relentlessly for almost a decade. In the process, it developed a fairly sophisticated guerrilla style and saw several hundreds of its members killed by the old regime. In mid-February, the Fedayan played a crucial role in the urban fighting that in the end defeated the shah's Royal Guardsmen. This group has approximately 5,000 members. Although it has maintained a relatively low profile since the revolution, it is well armed and dedicated. In the beginning, the Fedayan cooperated with Ayatollah Khomeini and national religious leaders. By the summer, however, this alliance had crumbled and the Fedayan found themselves heavily outnumbered and outflanked by the masses of Iranian peoples who supported the religious leaders. As a result, this Marxist group has been relatively quiet on the Iranian political scene throughout the year. The Fedayan are advocates of an Iranian form of scientific socialism and call for a people's militia and people's committees to direct all levels of the Iranian social and economic scene.

The HKS was formed in Teheran on 22 January. This Trotskyist party calls for government by the workers and peasants, full equality for women, cultural and political autonomy for the various nationalities and tribes, and a socialist state without religious overtones. The leader and one of the major theoreticians of this party is Babak Zahraie. The membership of the HKS consists largely of members of the intelligentsia, although an effort has been made to gain support from the lower classes. This kind of recruitment has been difficult because of the strong influence of Shi'ite religious leaders among the masses. Despite this and the relative newness of the organization, this party exhibited intellectual dynamism and a growing appeal among the intelligentsia as the latter became increasingly disenchanted with the religious domination of the revolution. The party belongs to the Fourth International and calls for a militant revolutionary policy. Fifteen of it leading members were imprisoned during the year for allegedly inciting the Arabs, forming a fifth column, and other offenses.

Publications. The Tudeh Party's paper, *Mardom* (Masses), now circulates freely in Teheran, as does *Donya* (World). The HKS publishes *Kargan*.

Communism and the Iranian Revolution. The Iranian revolution of 1978–1979 pitted the population against the shah and his circle of family and friends, who were protected by a modern military shield. After thirteen months of mass opposition in which over 20,000 Iranians were killed and casualties totaled more than 100,000 persons, the absolutist Pahlavi monarchy collapsed. The depth and breadth of this revolution were unique in recent world history. Since the various communist groups had long opposed the old regime and had fought the Pahlavis for decades, it might have been expected that they would be among the major beneficiaries of the revolution. The events of 1979 demonstrated that this was not to be the case.

The primary role played by Shi'ite Islam in the revolution (best represented in the words and activities of Ayatollah Ruhollah Khomeini) has been the key factor retarding the growth of communist influence in Iran. Throughout 1979, an overwhelming percentage of the masses of the Iranian people constantly indicated their total support for the leading ayatollahs. Khomeini himself repeatedly warned against the communist danger, while condemning the United States and Western imperialism. When necessary, the *pasdaran* ("revolutionary guards") moved forcefully against the communist groups. Even the Tudeh Party was attacked and its newspaper *Mardom* suspended for several weeks in the middle of the year. After months of praising the revolution and its leaders, the Soviet Union slowly and indirectly began criticizing it in the early fall. Through 1979, Khomeini and other front-line leaders continually proved their own revolutionary credentials by speeches and actions favoring the downtrodden and poor classes of Iranian society (the *mostazefin*). The visit of PLO leader Yassir Arafat to Iran just after the revolution must also be viewed in this light.

The Iranian revolution represented a dramatic landmark in that country's history. It provided a rare opportunity for the expansion of communist influence in Iran, and a number of Marxist-Leninist and Trotskyist groups did take root in the country following the collapse of the Pahlavis. But owing to a combination of religious, cultural, and political factors, these organizations failed to exert any significant political influence vis-à-vis the heavily Shi'ite-oriented postrevolutionary leadership.

University of Texas at Austin   James A. Bill

Iraq

The Iraqi Communist Party (ICP), subjected to persecution and arrest of its leaders ever since it was founded in 1934, suffered further losses in 1979. Its membership has been essentially confined to minority groups—ethnic and religious—and to intellectuals and hardly exceeds 2,000 in a country whose population is over 12 million. Formally, the ICP is still allied with the ruling Ba'th Party and operates within the framework of the Progressive National Front (PNF); since April, however, the ICP representatives have not attended PNF meetings, although they have not formally withdrawn from the PNF. Only one ICP member, Mukarram al-Talabani, is still in the cabinet. 'Amir 'Abd-Allah, another ICP member, was relieved of his cabinet post while on leave abroad in April.

Domestic Attitudes and Activities. In December 1978, eight members of the ICP Central Committee, including the activist Majid 'Abd al-Rida, were arrested, and a wave of arrests of other communists was carried out throughout the country. In January eighteen members of the ICP were executed. In February it was reported in the foreign press that over 4,000 ICP members and sympathizers had disappeared from the country (*Le Monde*, 23 February). In March the number of persons arrested, according to the foreign press, exceeded 10,000; presumably most of them were communist sympathizers, who were subjected to torture and persecution. Some like 'Aziz Muhammad, secretary general of the ICP, and 'Amir 'Abd-Allah, ICP representative in the PNF and the cabinet, had already left the country to escape arrest or other punitive measures. By April more ICP members had been executed.

On 31 March the ICP celebrated its 45th anniversary in straitened circumstances. In a message to congratulate the ICP Central Committee, the Communist Party of the Soviet Union encouraged Iraqi communists to continue their "selfless struggle" for freedom.

Controversy over Ideological and National Issues. The ICP has fully supported the ruling Ba'th Party's denouncement of the Camp David and the Egyptian-Israeli agreements. It also backed Iraq's policy toward the Palestine Liberation Organization and Palestinian rights to self-determination and the establishment of a Palestinian state (in this respect, the ICP has perhaps demonstrated more solidarity with the Ba'th than any other Arab communist party has with its government).

However, Soviet activities in Afghanistan, South Yemen, and the Horn of Africa have not only aroused Ba'thist concern about increasing Soviet influence in Arab lands, but also prompted criticism of Soviet leaders for their support of Ethiopia's and South Yemen's opposition to Somalia, Eritrea, and North Yemen. The Ba'th leaders also made public statements supporting Saudi Arabia and the Gulf states against possible Soviet threats. In response, ICP leaders expressed alarm about a possible rapprochement between the Ba'th Party and the West, especially in view of Iraq's increasing trade with the United States and the purchase of weapons from France and perhaps other European countries.

Meanwhile, the ruling Ba'th Party, in an effort to demonstrate its independence from foreign pressures, moved to curb communist activities inside the country. The ICP leaders who escaped conducted a campaign in the foreign press and in communist countries, in particular against the arrest and persecution of ICP members inside the country. In December 1978, the representatives of ten Arab communist parties met and issued a manifesto criticizing the Iraqi regime for its "oppressive police methods" (*IB*, no. 4, pp. 12–13). In the Arab and European press, ICP members published reports about the wave of arrests and persecutions of thousands of communists and unknown numbers of others who had disappeared. In the *World Marxist Review* (March), Naziha al-Dulaymi, a former communist cabinet minister under the Qasim regime, published an article in which she appealed to communists all over the world to stop the government's persecution of Iraqi communists.

To counteract the ICP propaganda campaign abroad, a new communist party called the Organization of the Iraqi Communist Vanguard, designed to support the ruling Ba'th Party and to oppose the pro-Soviet stance of the ICP, was established in May. Like an earlier right-wing dissident group under the Qasim regime, the new organization is made up of a small group encouraged by the regime to demonstrate that it is not opposed to communism in principle but to communist leaders who proved to be subservient to foreign influence and opposed to cooperation with the Ba'th Party.

Relations with Other Communist Parties. Although the action of the ruling Ba'th Party has considerably undermined the position of the pro-Soviet ICP, the Soviet Union refrained from criticizing or reproaching its Iraqi ally. *Pravda* (10 January), however, reproduced a couple of articles published by the ICP organ, *Tariq al-Sha'b*, in which the editor called for reconciliation between the Ba'th and ICP leaders. Indeed, Na'im Haddad, secretary general of the PNF, said on behalf of the Iraqi authorities that there was no change in Soviet-Iraqi relations and affirmed the friendship between the two countries.

In December 1978, Saddam Husayn, then vice-president of the Revolutionary Command Council (in July he succeeded Ahmad Hasan al-Bakr as president) led an official delegation to the Soviet Union. Iraqi leaders pointed out that their disagreement with the ICP leaders was purely domestic and could not affect Soviet-Iraqi cooperation in political and economic affairs. No sooner had Saddam Husayn returned to Baghdad, however, than the arrest of ICP members was resumed. Relations between Iraq and the Soviet Union seem to have been seriously strained as the Soviet leaders reproached Iraq for increasing its trade relations with the West. The official Soviet reaction to the arrest of ICP members was reflected in Radio Moscow broadcasts expressing concern for "the patriotic forces in the Arab world" in the wake of widespread persecution of communists in Iraq (*FBIS*, 10 January). The broadcasts also stated that this campaign had been going on for over a year and that it had hurt the Iraqi revolutionary movement against imperialism, Zionism, and reaction. *Pravda* (31 March) continued to reproduce articles from *Tariq al-Sha'b* about the deteriorating relations between the Ba'th and the ICP. It stressed the need for cooperation and appealed for reconciliation in the interests of the revolutionary movement.

In an endeavor to avoid an open rupture between the two countries, Soviet leaders refrained from public criticism of Iraq. Since the Iraqi government has been paying for its purchases of Soviet weapons in hard currency, the Soviets seem to have accepted the Iraqi view that the Ba'th-ICP conflict was a domestic affair that should not affect or impair official relations in foreign affairs between the two allies. Nevertheless, official visits by Soviet and Iraqi leaders, which had been quite frequent only a year ago, have been virtually discontinued. Instead, ICP leaders—especially 'Aziz Muhammad, secretary general, 'Amir 'Abd-Allah, ICP representative in the cabinet, and Zaki Khayri, Central Committee member—made their way to Moscow, where they began a propaganda campaign against Ba'th leaders. In April, Mukarram al-Talabani, the only communist left in the government, went to Moscow and tried to persuade the ICP to cooperate with the Ba'th within the framework of the PNF. He met with 'Aziz Muhammad and others, but no agreement seems to have been reached and he returned empty-handed. The ICP leaders continued their campaign and visited other socialist countries in Europe and elsewhere to explain their disagreement with the ruling Ba'th Party.

Publications. Publication of the ICP organ, *Tariq al-Sha'b* (Peoples' Road), was suspended for one month on 5 April, and it has been discontinued owing to strict censorship. In August it reappeared as a clandestine publication. Earlier, another secret publication, *Risalat al-Iraq* (Iraq's Message), was circulated inside and outside the country as part of the campaign against the ruling Ba'th Party.

The Johns Hopkins University   Majid Khadduri

Israel

The communist movement in Palestine dates back to 1920. Two years later, a Palestine Communist Party (Palestinische kommunistische Partei; PKP) was established, and it joined the Comintern in 1924. Following the periodic appearance of factional divisions, the PKP split along ethnic lines in 1943. In October 1948, with the new state of Israel in control of most of Palestine, both groups reunited to form the Israeli Communist Party (Miflaga Kommunistit Isra'elit; MAKI).

The movement split again in 1965, partly along ethnic lines. The New Communist List (Reshima Kommunistit Hadasha; RAKAH)—pro-Moscow, strongly anti-Zionist, and drawing a majority of its members from the Arab population—gained international recognition as the communist party in Israel. The MAKI, which became an almost completely Jewish organization and moderate in its opposition to government policies, was eclipsed. In 1975, the MAKI disappeared as a separate organization after merging with the MOKED (Focus), a Zionist socialist organization moderate in attitude toward the Arabs. In 1977 the MOKED united with other noncommunist groups in the "peace camp" to form Peace for Israel (Shalom le-Israel; SHELLI). By this time, some former (post-1965) MAKI members had joined or at least supported the RAKAH as the country's only communist party.

In keeping with Israel's competitive political party system, communists have been free to organize and participate in public life. The prevailing system of proportional representation has facilitated election of candidates from small parties, including the communists, to the Knesset (parliament).

Although RAKAH membership is about 80-percent Arab, many of its leaders (including a majority on top party organs) are Jews. The party presents itself as a model for Arab-Jewish cooperation. In September its membership was estimated at about 1,500 out of an Israeli population of 3.8 million (not including occupied territories).

However, the RAKAH is isolated from the mainstream of Israeli politics. No communist party has ever participated in the cabinet. Since the December 1977 election, the RAKAH-led coalition, the Democratic Front for Peace and Equality (DFPE) has held five seats in the Knesset, two of which belong to the two noncommunist coalition partners: the Black Panthers (an Afro-Asian Jewish group protesting against alleged discrimination by Jews of European origin) and the Arab Local Council Heads. The less radical SHELLI, with two seats, sometimes votes with the DFPE but rejected the RAKAH's 1978 proposal to form a common electoral list in Tel Aviv's local elections.

Local elections in November 1978 brought major gains for DFPE candidates in Arab towns. Tawfiq Zayyad, the communist mayor of the largest Arab town, Nazareth, was re-elected by a large majority (62.7 percent), while DFPE candidates won eleven of the seventeen seats on the Nazareth council. The DFPE obtained 112 seats on 37 municipal councils and now heads 20.

Leadership and Organization. Meir Vilner is general secretary. The fifteenth plenary session of the Central Committee met on 15 March. (For additional details, see *YICA*, 1979, p. 410; for names of leading personalities, see *YICA*, 1978, pp. 434–35).

Auxiliary and Mass Organizations. The RAKAH dominates the DFPE at the local and national levels. It sponsors the active Young Pioneer children's movement and a youth organization, the Young Communist League. The RAKAH also participates in the Democratic Women's Movement, the Israeli Association of Anti-Fascist Fighters and Victims of Nazism, and the Israeli-USSR Friendship Movement.

Domestic Attitudes and Activities. The RAKAH's leaders continued to stress the adverse economic effects of Israeli militarism. Vilner estimated that the price index had increased 500 percent since 1972 (*WMR*, April, p. 44). The DFPE also opposed "the policy of national discrimination" against the Arab minority and resolved "to fight for equal rights" and for "energetic public action against the demolition of houses in Arab villages" (ibid., February, pp. 105–6). The RAKAH played a leading role in organizing peaceful demonstrations in several Arab towns during the annual Day of the Land (30 March).

International Activity and Contacts. Political Bureau member David (Sasha) Khenin was in Sofia in November 1978. During the same month, a delegation of Israeli public figures, including Political Bureau members Tawfiq Tubi and David (Uzi) Burnstein traveled to Moscow on the invitation of the Soviet Peace Council. Vilner visited East Berlin in June and received the Order of Karl Marx. Vilner also went to Bucharest and Sofia in July. A RAKAH delegation, including David Burnstein, visited the USSR in August, while a DFPE delegation was in Bulgaria and Hungary during September.

International Views and Policies. Reflecting a continuing pro-Moscow and anti-Beijing position, Vilner praised the USSR as "a bastion of peace, national liberation, democracy, and socialism" and called "anti-Sovietism . . . the most terrible poison in our country" (ibid., April, pp. 3–4). Vilner also declared his support for the Soviet "struggle for détente" and "the signing of the SALT II treaty" (*FBIS*, 15 June). He condemned "Eurocommunism" as being "non-class, anti-Marxist" and for sowing "discord among working class contingents" (*WMR*, April, p. 5). In a letter to the Vietnamese Communist Party Central Committee, he denounced "China's war of aggression against Vietnam" (*FBIS*, 28 March).

Party statements reaffirmed support for the withdrawal of Israeli forces from all occupied territories, independence for both Israel and an Arab Palestine, and a reconvened Geneva Conference, with the participation of the Palestine Liberation Organization (PLO) as the sole representative of the Palestinian people. Vilner characterized the "colonial occupation of Palestinian and other Arab territories" as one of "brutal oppression" (*WMR*, April, p. 4). Israeli attacks on Lebanon were condemned by RAKAH leaders. Vilner described Israeli policy as being "completely subordinated to U.S. imperialism" (ibid., p. 45).

Party leaders condemned the Camp David accords and the Israeli-Egyptian peace treaty as an attempt to isolate the PLO and to exclude the USSR from the peace process. The five DFPE members of the Knesset voted against the peace treaty. Vilner proclaimed it a "step contradicting peace" and "the interests of the Arab peoples and the Israeli people" and said it provided Egyptian and U.S. consent for Israel's occupation of Arab territories. He alleged that the treaty was "based on the intensification of the arms race" in the Middle East, that it "planned to create U.S. military bases in Haifa, the Negev Desert, and on Sinai," and that it involved the "formulation of an alliance of Zionist and Arab reaction together with U.S. imperialism, with "Israel and Egypt . . . being assigned the role of gendarmes of U.S. imperialism" (*FBIS*, 4 April). Emile Tuma, a member of the Political Bureau, proclaimed that the treaty denies to "the Arab Palestinian people the right to existence, to self-determination and the establishment of an independent state of its own" and that it "enables Israel to carry on extensive colonization of the occupied Palestinian lands" (*WMR*, July, p. 52).

Publications. The RAKAH newspaper, *al-Ittihad* (Union), is an Arabic biweekly published in Haifa, edited by Tubi and Emile Habibi. A Hebrew weekly, *Zo Ha-Derekh* (This is the Way), is edited by Vilner in Tel Aviv. Other party publications are *al-Jadid* (The New), a monthly literary and cultural magazine published in Haifa by Samih al-Qasim; *al-Ghad* (Tomorrow), a youth magazine; the Yiddish *Der Weg* (The Way), published weeky by Vilner in Tel Aviv; the Bulgarian *Tovaye Putnam* (This is the Way), published every two weeks in Jaffa; the theoretical *Arakim: Be'ayot ha-Shalom ve-ha-Soatziyalizm* (Values: Problems of Peace and Socialism), published six times a year in Tel Aviv; and the sporadic English *Information Bulletin, Communist Party of Israel*, published in Tel Aviv by the Foreign Relations Department of the Central Committee.

Other Marxist Organizations. Several other groups exist in Israel, but none of them is comparable as a political force to RAKAH, whose leaders tend to dismiss them with contempt. Each consists of a handful of members, mostly young Jews but now including some Arabs as well. None offers its own list of electoral candidates.

The most radical trend is represented by the Israeli Socialist Organization (Irgun Sotziyalisti Isra'eli: ISO), formed by a group expelled in 1962 from the MAKI. Widely known by the name of its monthly Hebrew publication, *Matzpen* (Compass), issued from Tel Aviv, the ISO condemns establishment of Israel at the expense of Palestinian Arabs and its "open alliance with . . . imperialism and collusion with the most reactionary forces in the Arab world." The ISO recognizes the continued existence of a Hebrew nation in Palestine but calls for "de-Zionification" and "a socialist revolution," as well as "integration into a unified, socialist Middle East." It criticizes the USSR's policy of "peaceful coexistence," Soviet "bureaucracy," and the RAKAH's acceptance of the Soviet line. It also has censured Beijing's policies. The *Matzpen* viewpoint has received most attention outside Israel. Several splits in the organization occurred during the early 1970s. Breakaway splinter groups include the Revolutionary Communist League (Brit Kommunistit Mahapkhanit), which is associated with the Fourth (Trotskyist) International; the Workers' League (Brit ha-Po'alim), also Trotskyist (Lambertist section), which publishes *Avant-garde* and tends to emphasize opposition to capitalism more than to Zionism; and the Maoist-oriented Revolutionary Communist Alliance (Brit Kommunistit Mahapkhanit), which publishes *Ma'avak* (Struggle).

The Israeli New Left (Smol Yisrael Chadish; SIAH, or "Dialogue") was launched in 1968. It consisted of a few loosely organized youths, mainly students, previously associated with the MAKI and the United Workers' Party, formerly a far-left party but now a part of the Labor Alignment. The SIAH, which identifies with the radical student movement in Europe, professes devotion to Marxism and, in the case of the group in Tel Aviv but not the more radical Jerusalem branch, to Zionism. It calls for the creation of an independent Palestinian state to exist alongside Israel. Its publications include *Siah* (published irregularly in Hebrew) and *Israleft*, a biweekly English newsletter that disseminates statements by various leftist and peace groups.

Indiana State University
Terre Haute

Glenn E. Perry

Jordan

The Communist Party of Jordan (al-Hizb al-Shuyu'i al-Urdunni; CPJ) was officially established in June 1951 and has operated under the guise of various popular front organizations since that time. Its work has centered on the West Bank, where it has drawn support from students, teachers, professional workers, and the lower middle class.

The CPJ has been illegal since 1957, although the government's normally repressive measures have been relaxed on occasion. At present, communist party membership is punishable by jail sentences from three to fifteen years. Few other radical organizations are active in Jordan; however, various Palestinian groups, such as the Marxist-oriented Popular Front for the Liberation of Palestine (embittered by "repression" of the Palestinians during 1970–71), urge the overthrow of King Hussein. They appear to have little overt influence in Jordan. Beginning in 1972, Israel clamped down on the party in the West Bank because it had engaged in terrorist activities. More recently, West Bank communists have returned to more conventional political action, perhaps in preparation for Israel's implementation of an autonomy plan for the West Bank.

The CPJ has perhaps no more than 500 members, mostly Palestinians. Jordan's population of about 3 million includes more than 700,000 in Israeli-occupied East Jerusalem and the West Bank.

Leadership and Organization. The CPJ is said to be a tightly organized, well-disciplined network of small cells. (For details regarding the party's leadership, see *YICA*, 1979, p. 413.) There are two West Bank communist factions. The Palestine Communist Organization, an establishment-oriented group headed by Bashir Barghuti, a well-known Marxist from Ramallah, is reportedly the larger of the two. The Palestinian Communist Party is a small, militant organization affiliated with the Leninist Lodge, which seceded from the CPJ in the early 1970s because of ideological and personal differences. Both factions engage in organizational and propaganda activity and recruit from the five small West

Bank colleges. They have made their influence felt by penetrating municipalities, professional associations, trade unions, and welfare organizations. Recently they have become more open about their Marxist orientation. The communists are among the few groups with a political organization operating throughout the West Bank.

Auxiliary and Mass Organizations. The Palestine National Front (PNF) is composed of professional and labor union representatives and "patriotic personalities." It was established in August 1973 on the West Bank, evidently on CPJ initiative. The PNF generally follows the Palestine Liberation Organization (PLO) line and advocates an independent Palestinian state comprising the West Bank and the Gaza Strip. Its program includes mass political struggle and armed resistance in the occupied territories. The PNF's precise relation to the CPJ is unknown.

Party Internal Affairs. The CPJ has been described officially as the working-class party of two fraternal peoples—Jordanian and Palestinian. Despite its support of Palestinian statehood, the CPJ remains somewhat suspicious of the PLO, an attitude that is reciprocated.

Domestic Attitudes and Activities. The CPJ's leaders have consistently denounced the "reactionary regime" in Amman and its links to "imperialism." In a recent article, Central Committee member Na'im Ashhab emphasized that "Palestinian-Jordanian relations should be arranged in the light of . . . their joint struggle against imperialism and the Israeli occupation" (*WMR*, July). Secretary General Fayiq Muhammad Warrad has referred to CPJ efforts to rally all "progressive national patriotic forces" in Jordan to promote democracy and oppose imperialism (*FBIS*, 13 September).

The Palestine issue has vexed the party since its inception. As a generally pro-Soviet organization, the CPJ evidently has not been entirely free to take an independent stand. Consequently it has lost support to more committed and radical Palestinian liberation movements. The CPJ's basic position on Palestine is similar to that of the main Palestinian groups. The party recognizes the PLO as the sole representative of the Palestinian people and has urged all Palestinians to rally round the PLO against "renegades and traitors" (*WMR*, November 1978). It "advocates the establishment of an independent Palestinian state on the West Bank of the Jordan, in the Gaza Strip and in the Arab section of Jerusalem after their liberation (ibid., July). The Palestine Communist Organization has taken a similar position. It "vigorously rejects the 'conspiratorial' Camp David agreements," opposes the "autonomous administration" on the West Bank, and supports creation of an independent Palestinian state on the West Bank and the Gaza Strip based on the 4 June 1967 borders (*IB*, no. 23, 15 December 1978).

International Activities and Attitudes. Central Committee members Sulayman Mazhar and Majid al-Khatib met with the secretary of the Bulgarian Communist Party in Sofia on 20 February. They reviewed relations between the two parties, the world situation, and the international communist movement. They denounced China's aggression against Vietnam and announced their support for the "heroic struggle" of the Vietnamese people (*FBIS*, 22 February). In a statement in July Central Committee member Na'im Ashhab also condemned China's subversive activity against the international revolutionary movement, including the Arab national liberation movement, and its support of the Camp David accords and the Egyptian-Israeli peace treaty (*WMR*, July). Another CPJ delegation visited Bulgaria during 3–11 September.

The CPJ has accused the United States of attempting to strengthen its position in the Middle East by creating an Egyptian-Israeli alliance or front, possibly with other reactionary regimes. The party condemned the Camp David meeting and the "criminal accords" that resulted from it. The statement denounced President Sadat of Egypt, who had "totally capitulated" to Israel and ignored Palestinian rights. It called on "all patriotic and loyal forces of the Arab world" to foil the "Sadat-Begin-Carter plot" and urged all Arab countries to isolate Sadat and support the Egyptian people in an effort to remove the "traitorous regime." The statement viewed U.S. policy as an effort to "continue the plunder" of Arab natural resources. (*IB* no. 22, 30 November 1978.)

In an article coauthored with Emile Habibi, a member of the Israeli Communist Party, Na'im Ashhab asserted that the Geneva Peace Conference, chaired by the United States and the USSR, is still important as a mechanism to achieve peace in the Middle East (*WMR*, December 1978). Following the signing of the Egyptian-Israeli treaty, Ashhab declared that the treaty was directed against "real peace" in the area since it denied the Palestinians' national rights, making a "lasting peace" impossible (*FBIS*, 4 April). The treaty opened the way for Israel to commit aggression against neighboring states and, in the event of an Arab-Israeli war, placed Egypt's commitments to the Arabs on the same basis as those toward Israel. Ashhab wrote in the *World Marxist Review* (April) that Soviet involvement in settling the Middle East crisis was necessary "to promote international détente instead of aggravating tensions." He further noted that "communism is the greatest revolutionary movement in mankind's history." The need for communist party unity is greater than ever since U.S. imperialism and NATO are stepping up the arms race.

Publications. The CPJ publishes *al-Jamahir* (Masses) and the underground newspaper *al-Watan* (Homeland). Both appear once or twice a month, the former in Jordan and the latter on the West Bank. The party also issues a political and theoretical magazine, *al-Haqiqah* (Truth), distributed in Jordan and the West Bank. These publications are distributed clandestinely on both sides of the Jordan River, except for *al-Watan*, which is restricted mainly to the West Bank. In early 1978, *al-Taliyah* (Vanguard), an Arabic weekly published in East Jerusalem with the knowledge of the Israeli authorities, appeared on the West Bank. Its editor-in-chief and founder is Elias Nasralla, a member of the Israeli New Communist Left party; senior editor is Bashir Barghuti, a member of the Palestine Communist Organization. Shortly after its appearance, Israeli military authorities ordered *al-Taliyah* to cease publication because it did not have a permit. Another CPJ organ, *al-Shaab* (The People), appeared in 1978. The PNF publishes its own newspaper, *Filastin* (Palestine). News of CPJ activities also appears in the organs of the Lebanese Communist Party, *al-Akhbar* and *al-Nida'*. Many communist and communist-inspired pamphlets have appeared recently on the West Bank.

U.S. Department of State   Norman F. Howard
Washington, D.C.

(Note: Views expressed in this article are the author's own and do not represent those of the State Department.)

Lebanon

The Lebanese Communist Party (al-Hizb al-Shuyu'i al-Lubnani; LCP) was established in 1924. In 1965 it shed its policy of independent action and became an active member of the Front of Progressive Parties and National Forces under the leadership of the Progressive Socialists. It later became a member of the Lebanese National Movement. The LCP gained legal status in 1970. It has been an active participant in the civil strife that began in 1975. The party has an estimated 2,500 members and sympathizers. However, according to *Fiches du monde arabe* (May 1976), its ranks swelled to 15,000 during the civil war, and its composition changed from a Christian and primarily Greek Orthodox majority to 30 percent Christian, 50 percent Shi'a Muslim and 15 to 20 percent Sunni Muslim. The population of Lebanon is under 3 million.

Leadership and Organization. The Congress, which is supposed to be convened every four years, is the supreme LCP organ. Owing to the instability in Lebanon, the Fourth Congress was not held until 1979 and was characterized by complete secrecy. During the congress, Niqula al-Shawi was elected to the new post of party president, an honorary position created for the longtime LCP leader. George Hawi, who is the effective leader of the party, was elected secretary general. The new Central Committee includes Shawi,* Hawi,* Nadim 'Abd al-Samad,* Khalil al-Dibs,* 'Abd al-Karim Muruwwah,* Joseph Abu 'Aql,* Artin Madoyan, George Habr, Maurice Nahra, Suhayl Tawilah, Yusuf Khattar al-Hilu, Mustafa al-'Aris, Ilyas al-Bawariquk Husayn Muruwwah, Mahmud al-Wawi, Khalil Na'us, and Albert Farahat, as well as eight new members: Sa'dallah Mazra'ani,* Rashid Yusuf, George Jubran, Ilyas 'Atallah, Faruq Salim, Hanna Salih, Milhim Abu Rizq, and Mahmud Shaqra (*denotes known members of the LCP Secretariat). Some of the new members were elected to replace those martyred during the war, including Ahmad al-Mir al-Ayyubi, Kivork (alias Abu 'Ali), 'Adnan al-Dughaydi, Bahij al-Qatrib, and Shibli Haydar. These include younger party members who had been active in student and trade union circles. Between congresses, authority is vested in the Central Committee, which in turn elects the Political Bureau, five secretaries, a Central Control Commission, and a Financial Commission.

Domestic Views and Activities. On 26 April the LCP urgently appealed for solidarity against the five-day-old Israeli aggression that occupied a part of southern Lebanon, named the "State of Free Lebanon." The LCP declared that this was the beginning of a new stage of the U.S.-Israeli effort to "impose complete surrender on the Arab peoples; perpetuate the division of Lebanon; establish a sectarian, racist entity on its territory; strike at the Palestinian revolution; and exert pressure on Syria and other steadfast Arab forces to make them join the bandwagon of Sadat" (*al-Safir*, Beirut, 27 April). The LCP congress called for "a firm confrontation with the imperialist-Zionist-reactionary-isolationist plot in the Lebanese arena and of Israel's aggression and occupation of part of southern Lebanon through its agent Sa'd Haddad." It noted that this confrontation requires complete support for the national movement, which is leading the Lebanese national struggle in cooperation with the Palestinian resistance. The congress called for the establishment of a broad national alliance of all forces, parties, factions, and individuals who advocate maintaining Lebanon as a "united, independent, sovereign, free, Arab, and democratic country, regardless of their class origins, ideological differences, religious or sectarian affiliations, positions inside or outside authority, and differences in political views on other issues." Within this framework, the LCP calls for the development of a Christian national democratic current that supports a comprehensive national solution as a viable and positive alternative to the plan of the "fascist isolationist forces." The LCP sees as the nucleus of this national alliance the Lebanese National Movement comprising communists, Ba'thists, Nasserites, nationalists, and independent national and progressive personalities. The LCP has strongly criticized government leaders, especially President Sarkis, in the past. However, in a joint communiqué with the Soviet communist party published on 4 July, the LCP expressed full support "for any measures that may be taken by the legitimate Lebanese authorities in defence of Lebanon's sovereignty and territorial integrity" (*Arab Report*). In an interview in *al-Nahar*, published in late July, the new secretary general, George Hawi, warned that the United States is preparing to install a military dictatorship in Lebanon, recalling the lesson of the Greek junta in that regard. He urged a cessation of violence as a prerequisite for dialogue between the Lebanese parties.

The LCP and the Arab World. The LCP holds that the problem occasioned by the Palestinian presence in Lebanon cannot be resolved by liquidating the Palestinian resistance through violence. It asserts that the armed Palestinian presence in Lebanon has been imposed by the Israeli occupation of Palestine and could be liquidated only at the cost of the total destruction of Lebanon as an integral, free, and independent country (*FBIS*, 13 July). The LCP fully supports the Palestinians' struggle "for their national rights, including their right to establish their independent national state on their soil,support for the Palestine Liberation Organization, this people's only legitimate representative, and firm adherence to the historic Arab right in Palestine." The LCP congress called for strengthening and deepening the Lebanese-Palestinian national alliance in the interest of both peoples. It urged the "scrupulous implementation" of the Baghdad and other Arab resolutions calling for isolating the Sadat regime, expelling Egypt from the Arab League, ceasing economic, diplomatic, and cultural relations with Egypt, and stopping all economic and financial aid. The LCP also urged support of Egyptian efforts to overthrow Sadat.

In the April issue of *World Marxist Review*, Niqula al-Shawi asserted that "the Camp David agreement marked the Sadat regime's open defection to the enemies of the Arab peoples and the formation of a U.S.-Israeli-Egyptian alliance directed against the Arab national-liberation movement." In the June issue, he called the agreements "a logical outcome" of the policy Sadat has followed since coming to power: renunciation of the progressive changes that had been carried out in Egypt under former Egyptian President Nasser and unconditional surrender to imperialism. The LCP supports the reconciliation between Syria and Iraq. It asserts its solidarity with South Yemen's efforts to unite the two parts of Yemen and to withstand threats from imperialists and Arab reactionaries. Moreover, the LCP declares its support for the people of Sudan, Oman, Morocco, Saudi Arabia, and the gulf in their struggle against their ruling regimes. It also supports the struggle of the Western Sahara and al-Saquiyah al-Hamra for self-determination. The LCP congress advocated the building of fronts comprising the national and progressive forces in every Arab country and on the pan-Arab level. It also called for the revival of the Front of Steadfastness and Confrontation as a way, through a more advanced program and more drastic measures, to deal with imperialism, Zionism, and reaction. (Lengthy summaries of resolutions issued by the Fourth Congress of the LCP were published in *al-Safir*, Beirut, 21 July, and were reprinted in *FBIS*, 24 July.)

International Views and Activities. The LCP has maintained a consistently pro-Soviet posture. The Fourth Congress called for "consolidating the ties of friendship and alliance of struggle with the

Soviet Union and the other socialist bloc countries, which are a cornerstone of any successful confrontation of the imperialist design" (al-Safir, 21 July). This position was reaffirmed throughout the year by the frequency of visits by LCP delegations to Soviet bloc countries. These included visits by LCP leaders to the Soviet Union in January, June, and September and to Bulgaria in January, March, and August. Many of the Soviet bloc countries, including the Soviet Union, East Germany, and Romania, in turn expressed their recognition and support of the LCP through their messages of congratulations to the Fourth Congress. All the communiqués and communications expressed solidarity and an identity of views on all issues. In the perception of the LCP, the Arab struggles in Lebanon, Israel, Yemen, and elsewhere are "an integral part of the all-out world battle against U.S. imperialism and its allies." Thus, on 15 March the LCP issued a statement calling for "breaking off relations with the United States; nationalizing its assets, companies, and capital; cutting off oil supplies; withdrawing Arab funds from U.S. banks; and destroying the U.S. interests throughout the Arab homeland" (al-Nahar, 16 March). The second focus of LCP condemnation is the People's Republic of China. According to the LCP, "China's Maoist leadership" shares common principles and programs with the imperialists. In the June issue of World Marxist Review, Shawi noted that the Chinese supported the same type of politician in Angola, Chile, and Zaire and pointed to Beijing leaders' friendship with the ex-shah and their support of President Numayri's repression of Sudanese communists. He condemned the PRC's aggression against Vietnam and its threats against Laos. According to Shawi, imperialism and Beijing are one in their hatred for the Soviet Union and other countries of the socialist community. The LCP perceives the existence of a general imperialist offensive in the world, which has two parts. On the one hand is the imperialist-Zionist-Sadat campaign and on the other is China's aggressive and antagonistic posture against Vietnam, Laos, and the Soviet Union.

Publications. On 28 January a simple celebration marking the twentieth anniversary of the party's daily newspaper, al-Nida' (The Call), was held at LCP offices. The celebration, which was kept small in deference to the martyred Palestinian Abu Hasan, was attended by an array of high-level Palestinian leaders, including Yasir Arafat, members of the Central Political Council of the Lebanese National Movement, the dean of the Lebanese press syndicate, and the ambassadors of Arab and socialist bloc countries, including the Soviet ambassador in Beirut. Other publications of the LCP, distributed with varying degrees of regularity during the Lebanese crisis, are the weekly magazine al-Akhbar (The News) and the literary and ideological monthly al-Tariq (The Road). These LCP organs also serve as general information media for illegal communist parties in the Middle East.

The Organization of Communist Action (OCAL). The OCAL held its first congress in 1971. Its secretary general is Muhsin Ibrahim. Fawwaz Trabulsi is a member of its Politburo. The OCAL has consistently supported the Palestinian resistance and maintains close ties with the Democratic Front for the Liberation of Palestine (DFLP). Muhsin Ibrahim is secretary general of the National Movement, and as such he participated in the Palestinian, Syrian National, and Lebanese Nationalist Coordination Committee, which met in Damascus on 14 June. Since its first congress, the OCAL has moderated its strong support for China in the Sino-Soviet conflict. In recent years, the OCAL and the LCP have drawn closer. According to an OCAL official, this is "a new experience—it is unusual to have two communist organizations with very good relations. We now have the same tactical positions and view of the current situation" (Arab Report, 9 May). The OCAL publishes the weekly journal al-Hurriya in cooperation with the DFLP.

Stanford University   Michel Nabti

Lesotho

The Communist Party of Lesotho (CPL) was apparently founded in 1962 and was officially banned in 1970. It now operates clandestinely, and its membership remains small. During the year violence returned to Lesotho politics. The government attributed these outbreaks to exiled members of the Basuto Congress Party (BCP), a group described by the CPL as petit bourgeois in composition. There are no indications that the CPL has played any role in this violence.

Leadership and Organization. The latest information available mentions John Motloheloa as secretary, J. M. Kena as secretary general, and R. Matji as chairman. Jeremiah Mosotho continues to be the only member publishing materials on the party. Party structure consists of a Congress, a Central Committee, and district and village committees (*Free Africa Marches*, Prague, International Publishers, 1978, pp. 53–68).

Domestic Attitudes and Activities. The party derives its main support from workers, most of whom are migrant laborers in South Africa. The party is active among workers in South Africa and Lesotho and claims the leadership of several unions. A second target group is the "peasant-workers," employees of wealthier farm owners. Many of these peasant-workers have been employed in South Africa; experience in that developed country supposedly has caused the growth of a strong sense of class consciousness.

International Views and Positions. The CPL maintains close ties with the Communist Party of the Soviet Union, although attendance of CPL members at Soviet-sponsored conferences seems to have dropped off recently (*WMR*, February, p. 3). The party stands for a nonaligned foreign policy, but this does not mean equidistance from the two camps: "Nonalignment can only be anti-imperialist . . . We believe that the national-liberation movement is an inalienable part of the world revolutionary process, of which the socialist countries, the international working class, are the leading force, and that solidarity with the national liberation movement is an inalienable part of proletarian internationalism." (*Free Africa Marches*, p. 58.)

University of South Carolina   Mark W. DeLancey

The Maghreb

ALGERIA

The Algerian Communist Party (Parti communiste algérien; PCA) was founded in 1920 as an extension of the French Communist Party. It has existed independently since October 1936. The PCA participated in the nationalist struggle against France but was proscribed in December 1962, only five months after Algerian independence. Dissident left-wing elements of the legal National Liberation Front (NLF) joined with communists to form the Popular Resistance Organization, which in January 1966 was renamed the Socialist Vanguard Party (Parti de l'avant-garde socialiste; PAGS); this group, barely tolerated by the Algerian government, is recognized in the communist world as the official Algerian communist party. Membership is now estimated to be 400 to 500. The population of Algeria is estimated to be 18 million.

Leadership and Party Affairs. Sadiq Hadjeres is first secretary of the party. Other prominent members of the party in recent years are believed to include former PCA Secretary General Larbi Bukhali, Bashir Hadj 'Ali, Ahmad Karim, and 'Ali Malki. Both Sadiq Hadjeres and 'Ali Malki have contributed to the *World Marxist Review* and the *Information Bulletin* on behalf of the PAGS.

Domestic Views. Statements made by the PAGS early in 1979 praised Algeria's late President Houari Boumedienne, who died on 27 December 1978. On 23 January Sadiq Hadjeres sent a message to the Fourth Congress of the NLF "on behalf of the Algerian communists" asserting that "the death of our deeply mourned brother and comrade, President Houari Boumedienne, his heritage, lessons and experience of struggle demand a heightened sense of responsibility of every Algerian patriot and revolutionary" (*IB*, no. 7). In addition, the message reaffirmed the PAGS call for the formation of a broad political movement embracing all the forces of socialism, guided by a strong vanguard party. Ten days later the PAGS addressed the Algerian people prior to the national elections held on 7 February. The PAGS, a proscribed organization, expressed disappointment that representation at the executive level had not expanded consonant with the far-reaching changes being implemented in other areas. Despite this criticism, however, the PAGS endorsed both the NLF and its secretary general and presidential nominee, Benjedid Chedli. After the election, Sadiq Hadjeres sent a congratulatory message to Chedli in which he expressed PAGS support for the National Charter and rejected all forms of sectarianism. Hadjeres noted in particular that President Boumedienne had fought against anticommunism with courage and sagacity, viewing it as a divisive tool of imperialists and multinationals (ibid., no. 9). The PAGS is clearly seeking greater acceptance and a more active political role for itself as a participant in the broad political movement. The PAGS does not openly describe itself as the vanguard party needed by Algeria, but neither does it nominate the NLF for that role. The PAGS rather envisions such a party emerging as a synthesis of the most progressive elements of the proposed unified socialist movement. Apparently the PAGS hopes that its own ideological superiority will place its members in the forefront of this expanded NLF, assuring its preeminence in a popularly supported political institution without having to engage in an intense political struggle.

In a pre-election statement, the PAGS noted that price rises, Ramadan, and the long illness and death of Boumedienne had contributed to lethargy and disenchantment among the Algerian people during the preceding six months. The party called for united action to deal with such unresolved issues as the external debt and the dangerous situation on the frontiers. The PAGS wishes "to strengthen and extend the socialist management of enterprises"; to renew "people's assemblies and communes"; to "consolidate the gains of the agrarian revolution"; and to resolve the vital problems of "purchasing power, housing construction, education, public health, transport, national culture, and the vocational training and leisure of unemployed young people" (ibid., no. 8).

International Views. The PAGS reaffirmed its pro-Soviet orientation in an article by 'Ali Malki in the April issue of *World Marxist Review*. According to him, "the USSR is the best guarantee of world peace." He condemned the alleged coalition between U.S. imperialism and Chinese leaders, which is directed against the USSR and Vietnam. He charged them with supporting reactionary regimes in Africa and South America and exposed their alleged efforts to cause alienation between Japan and the USSR. The PAGS supports peaceful coexistence as "a framework for the class struggle between the two opposite socio-economic systems." The PAGS supports present Soviet proposals for peace in the Mediterranean and the Middle East and hails Soviet support for "the Palestinian people's struggle and the independence of the Arab peoples." Moreover, it condemns U.S. imperialists but distinguishes between them and the people and peace forces in the United States.

Publications. The PAGS has issued at infrequent intervals the clandestine journal *Sawt al-Sha'b* (Voice of the People).

MOROCCO

The Moroccan Communist Party (Parti communiste marocain), which was founded in 1943 as a branch of the French Communist Party, was banned by the French protectorate in 1952. After three years of open operations in independent Morocco, it was banned in 1959. Renamed the Party of Progress and Socialism (Parti du progrès et du socialisme; PPS), it was granted legal status in 1974. The PPS participated in the Moroccan national elections of November 1976, but won no offices. Membership in the PPS is estimated at about 700. Morocco's population is estimated to be over 19.8 million.

Leadership and Organization. The Second National Congress of the PPS was held in Casablanca from 23 to 26 February. 'Ali Yata was re-elected secretary general of the party. The newly elected Secretariat of the Central Committee consists of 'Abd al-Majid Douab, 'Umar Fasi, Thami Khiyar, and Simon Levy, in addition to the incumbent committee members: 'Ali Yata, 'Abd Allah Layashi, and 'Abd al-Salam Bourqia. The Politburo is composed of these seven members along with Isma'il 'Alawi, 'Aziz Bilal, Muhammad Ben Bella, Muhammad Shu'ayb Rif'i, Muhammad Musharak, and 'Abd al-Wahid Suhail. In addition to delegates from all PPS organizations in Morocco, the congress was attended by representatives of all major political parties and trade union organizations of Morocco, delegations of communist and workers' parties from socialist and other countries, national democratic organizations, and national liberation movements. On the ideological level, the PPS congress reaffirmed its commitment to the ideals of scientific socialism and the principle of proletarian internationalism and stressed the significance of strengthening the united front of all progressive forces in their struggle for peace and against imperialism, Zionism, and reaction.

Domestic Issues. The PPS's policy calls for the formation of a national democratic alliance of revolutionary and progressive forces, the working class, the poor peasantry, and the petite bourgeoisie. Such an alliance would include, along with the PPS, the Socialist Union of Popular Forces, the National Union of Popular Forces, the Moroccan Labor Union, and above all, the Istiqlal Party. In an address to the party congress, 'Ali Yata asserted that the government's economic policy, the country's close ties with the world capitalist economy, and its dependence on foreign monopolies had precipitated a deep crisis in Morocco. He outlined his party's proposals to end this crisis: "nationalize the key branches of the national economy, strengthen the state sector, impose restrictions on private property, end the one-sided orientation of foreign trade to the Western countries, and develop all-around economic ties with the socialist countries." Along with the criticisms leveled against the Moroccan political and economic system, the PPS congress recognized some of the positive political actions taken by the Moroccan government in recent years, such as the release of most political prisoners, the legalization of the PPS and the National Union of Moroccan Students, and the holding of local and parliamentary elections.

International Issues. The PPS leveled its strongest criticisms at Chinese leaders. It charged China with aggression against Vietnam and demanded the immediate withdrawal of Chinese troops from that country. In a report to the Central Committee of the PPS, 'Ali Yata labeled Chinese attacks on the Soviet Union as slanderous and condemned Chinese "collusion" with imperialist and reactionary forces, particularly the United States. In addition, the PPS leader attacked the Chinese positions on Chile, Angola, Ethiopia, Afghanistan, and South Yemen. (Ibid., no. 23, 1978; *FBIS*, 27 February.) Regarding the Middle East conflict, the PPS denounced the Camp David agreements and subsequent peace treaty as tools of imperialism, Zionism, and reaction. The PPS called for a comprehensive settlement based on withdrawal of Israeli troops from occupied territories and recognition of the legitimate rights of the Palestinian people, including self-determination and an independent state, reached within the framework of the Geneva conference and with the participation of all parties concerned, including the Palestine Liberation Organization. The PPS has broken from a consistently pro-Soviet posture over the issue of Spanish Sahara. Although it has officially proposed that the countries involved agree to respect each other's sovereignty and territorial integrity, 'Ali Yata became a member of the Defense Council which was formed by Morocco's King Hassan in March to assist him in formulating policy on the Western Sahara and to demonstrate the support of Morocco's claim to Western Sahara by the entire Moroccan political spectrum. (*NYT*, 1 May).

Publications. Since November 1972 the PPS has legally distributed in Rabat a weekly publication, *al-Bayan* (The Bulletin). It also publishes *al-Mukafih* (The Fighter), which appears in Casablanca daily in Arabic and monthly in French.

TUNISIA

The Tunisian Communist Party (Parti communiste tunisien; PCT) was founded in 1920 as a branch of the French Communist Party and became independent in 1934. The banning of the PCT in 1963 formalized a single-party state under the direction of the Destourian Socialist Party. It is believed that the PCT has about one hundred members. The population of Tunisia is estimated to be over 6 million.

Leadership. Little is known about the leaders of the clandestine PCT, but Muhammad al-Nafa' reputedly continues to be its secretary general and Muhammad Harmel its secretary. 'Abd al-Hamid ben Mustafa, Tahar 'Ali, and K. Tahar are also said to be among the leaders.

Domestic Issues. A statement issued by the PCT in late 1978 charged the Tunisian government with "disregarding the people's demands for the democratization of socio-political life." According to the PCT, the government's determination to follow the capitalist path of development has assured its failure to fulfill its promises of future economic prosperity and employment and thereby eliminate the backwardness inherited from colonialism. The PCT demands of the Tunisian government "an end to repression and the persecution of trade union figures; the release of political prisoners; and the insuring of really democratic freedoms, including legalization of democratic parties and organizations, including the PCT" (*FBIS*, 6 December 1978). The PCT advocates an alliance of all progressive, democratic, and patriotic forces. It continues, so far unsuccessfully, to appeal to the government to grant the party legal status.

International Views. The PCT has a consistently pro-Soviet orientation. It opposes the "American peace" in the Middle East and charges Egyptian President Sadat with following a capitulationist policy. It favors a comprehensive solution to the crisis that would include the establishment of the legitimate national rights of the Arab people of Palestine. (Ibid., 12 June.)

Publications. The PCT has had no official organ since the party was proscribed in 1963.

Stanford University   Michel Nabti

Réunion

The Réunion Communist Party (Parti communiste réunionnais; PCR) celebrated its twentieth anniversary as an independent communist party in 1979. Although the PCR became separate from the French Communist Party (PCF) in 1959, it maintains close ties to the PCF. Réunion is an overseas department of France, and the PCR is a legal party. Its membership has been estimated at 2,000 (*Témoignages*, 2 February 1977), but a dearth of recent figures, coupled with the party's mobilization of nearly 10,000 persons to greet Georges Marchais in April, would suggest that the party's membership is somewhat higher. The population of Réunion is approximately 503,000.

France has continued to emphasize a single-crop economy—sugar—in Réunion, and the consequent shrinkage of the nonsugar labor force, mounting unemployment (over 60,000 persons), and increased inflation have fueled the influence of the PCR and its labor union allies. By designating the PCR's secretary general, Paul Vergès, as its fourth-ranked candidate in the June elections for seats in the European parliament, the PCF provided a substantial boost to the PCR's demands for "democratic and popular autonomy within the framework of the French republic." Vergès was handily elected, and the communist list won 33.1 percent of the total vote in Réunion (*Le Monde*, 12 June), up slightly from the 32.8 percent showing in the 1978 legislative elections. The PCR lost two seats in partial departmental elections in March, returning four *conseilleurs généraux* while polling 35 percent of the total vote.

Party Organization and Internal Affairs. The PCR follows the cell and section organization of the PCF. Representatives of these smaller groups meet in monthly general assemblies to implement agenda items provided by the party's Central Committee. Paul Vergès leads the party. There were no reported changes in leadership during 1979. At the PCR's Fourth Congress in 1976, a Central Committee of 34 members and a Political Bureau of 11 members were elected. Members of the Central Committee include Laurence Vergès, Hippolite Piot, Roger Hoarau, Gervais Barret, Ary Payet, Elie Hoarau, and Lucet Langenier (*Témoignages*, 28–29 July). Other party leaders are Adrien Minienpoullé, Roland Robert, Bruny Payet, and Julien Ramin (ibid., 4, 5, and 17–18 February).

The PCR and its daily newspaper, *Témoignages*, coordinate several other leftist organizations on the island, including the General Confederation of Réunion Workers (Confédération général des travailleurs réunionnais; CGTR), led by Bruny Payet; the Youth Front for Autonomy; the party's Women's League; the General Confederation of Planters and Stock-Raisers, and the Christian Witness Movement of Réunion (*Africa*, London, June). The Anticolonialist Front for Réunion Autonomy (Front anticolonialiste pour l'autonomie réunionnaise) is an umbrella organization for these and other groups of the Réunion left.

Domestic Policies and Activities. The PCR's major goal, attainment of autonomy within the framework of the French republic, serves as the armature for the party's domestic and international policies. The PCR contends that Réunion's neocolonialist status is the cause of the island's social and economic problems. During the campaign for the European parliament, Vergès singled out the detrimental effect of European Economic Community (EEC) sugar quotas and import price regulations on Réunion's income from sugar and its cost of living (*L'Humanité*, 1 March). Through frequent public meetings, the columns of its daily newspaper, and in governmental bodies where the PCR has spokesmen, the party articulates a cohesive program criticizing maladjustments in the island's economy brought about by overspecialization in sugar, which occupies 87 percent of the island's arable land and has reduced production of other agricultural commodities, such as tobacco and vanilla, by as much as 90 percent of the 1946 figures (*Témoignages*, 17 September). This specialization, contends the party, leads to layoffs in the construction trades and among dockers at a rate of 2,000 persons a year (ibid., 21 August), pushing unemployment to over 60,000 persons, more than 25 percent of the labor force.

France's new unemployment compensation legislation went into effect on 1 July, but the new law has not been implemented in Réunion. The PCR made this issue its major domestic objective in 1979. Public meetings to rally support for the campaign were followed by a postcard campaign during the summer and autumn, when thousands of militants and supporters wrote to the central government urging application of the new legislation on the island.

In the face of governmental policies favoring emigration to France rather than diversification and retraining programs for the work force (*L'Année politique africaine*, 1978), the PCR has joined forces with the CGTR to resist technological innovations in cargo handling at the island's ports. At one point, the arrival of an automated ship provoked an eleven-day dock strike, and the dockers' union held a bulk-loaded ship hostage for several days in response to party and union directives (*Témoignages*, 24 July and 31 August). In collaboration with the CGTR, the PCR called for industry-by-industry strikes in October, culminating in general strikes throughout Réunion on 19 and 26 October (ibid., 15, 16, 20–21, and 23 October).

International Activities. The election of Vergès to the European parliament in June gave the PCR a prestigious sounding board for its autonomy proposals. Georges Marchais had come to the island to campaign for the PCR's slate in April, thus making the PCR's goals part of the PCF's platform. In his speeches in Réunion, Marchais endorsed the goal of autonomy within the framework of the French republic and advocated a separate regime for the overseas territories and departments vis-à-vis the EEC (ibid., 4 and 6 April). In addition to its ties with the PCF, the PCR has frequent meetings with left-wing organizations of other French overseas territories and with its regional counterparts. Vergès met with the leaders of the Guadeloupe and Martinique communist parties in February (ibid., 27 February) and attended meetings of the Progressive Party Association of the Southwest Indian Ocean in the Seychelles in May (ibid., 5–6 May). The PCR took a strong stand critical of the People's Republic of China during February over the Vietnam question.

Publications. The PCR's daily newspaper, *Témoignages*, has a circulation of between 5,000 and 10,000 copies. In November it doubled in size. The CGTR publishes the semimonthly *Travailleur réunionnais*.

Stanford University

Peter S. Stern

Senegal

Senegal has three communist-inspired parties. The only legally recognized party is the African Independence Party (Parti africain de l'indépendance; PAI), founded in 1957. In the 1978 legislative elections, the PAI did not enter candidates. In the wake of the elections, all three major Marxist-inspired parties have regrouped their forces. The PAI, directed by Majmout Diop, held its Second Congress in February and opened its ranks to the other leftist factions in November, when Diop announced formation of the Bok Sa Rew Front (*Le Soleil*, 7 November). In November 1978 the clandestine PAI, whose principal domestic political spokesman is Mamadou Dia, created the Coordination of the Unified Senegalese Opposition (Coordination de l'opposition sénégalaise unie, COSU) and the Association of Senegalese Democrats (Association des sénégalais démocrates; ASD) in an effort to unify the Marxist-Leninist and other leftist opposition to the regime of Léopold Senghor (*Andë Sopi*, November 1978; *FBIS*, 7 March). Cheikh Anta Diop's National Democratic Rally (Rassemblement national démocratique; RND) has launched a periodical, *Taxaw*, in order to increase its own membership (*Andë Sopi*, January). The only reported fruit of these efforts has been the rallying of the elitist Democratic League (estimated membership: 40) to the legal PAI early in the year (*FBIS*, 7 March). The legal PAI's membership is between 1,000 and 4,000, and that of the clandestine faction is estimated at 1,000 (*Africa*, London, February 1978). The population of Senegal is 5.4 million (*Le Soleil*, 7 June).

Party Organization and Internal Affairs. Majmout Diop is the secretary general of the legal PAI, which has a Central Committee and an eight-member Politburo, of whom five members are workers, but names were not immediately available (*Le Monde*, 20 February). There were 250 delegates at the party's Second Congress, held on 16–17 February (ibid.). The PAI has no representative in the legislature. It serves primarily to give credence to Senghor's acceptance of a multiparty regime, in which four parties are permitted, representing conservative, liberal, socialist, and communist tendencies. According to *Africa* (April 1978), the PAI was largely discredited as a political force by its poor showing in the 1978 presidential elections, in which Diop received less than 1 percent of the vote.

The clandestine PAI worked through the vehicle of the new COSU front in 1979, trying to obtain official representation as a legal party by forming the ASD. Seydou Cissoko is the secretary general of this faction. Amath Dansoko, a member of the Central Committee, is the group's principal spokesman on international issues. The faction's other leaders are Maguette Thiam, the secretary general of the influential United and Democratic Union of Senegalese Teachers (Syndicat unique et démocratique d'enseignants sénégalais), and Samba Diouidé Thiam, the editor-in-chief of *Andë Sopi* (*L'Année politique africaine*, 1978).

Other dissident Marxist-Leninist groups in Senegal include the Karebi-Andjeuf Group (Unity of Action for Struggle; Unité d'action pour la lutte) and the Trotskyist Workers' Revolutionary Group (Groupement ouvrier révolutionnaire) (*Le Monde*, 20 February).

Domestic Policies and Activities. The legal PAI works in cooperation with the Senghor regime; this tactic renders the PAI's legitimacy suspect in the eyes of the clandestine left. Majmout Diop defined the party's goals at a press conference held in November as follows: the development of unity among workers, the left, the nation, and eventually all African nations; the abolition of economic exploitation; and cooperation between Marxist and Islamic thought (*Le Soleil*, 7 November). Although vaguely critical of the regional organisms created by the Senghor regime for cooperation and economic development in Senegal, the PAI seems to articulate a program more marked by innocuousness than by aggressive opposition to the present regime.

The illegal parties have to contend with new legislation designed to prosecute their newspapers (*Andë Sopi*, January) and the threat of governmental action to impede their organizational efforts (*Le Soleil*, 13–14 October). Cheikh Anta Diop's RND and the clandestine PAI nevertheless continue to attack the "neocolonialist" foundations of the Senghor regime and criticize the government for refusing to allow them to operate as legal parties. The new COSU group, and its party appendage, the ASD, tried without success to gain recognition in November 1978 (*Andë Sopi*, November 1978). Mamadou Dia developed the basic policies of the clandestine PAI in a series of articles appearing in *Andë Sopi* (December 1978; June, July, and August). They include nationalization of French participation in Senegalese commerce and industry, estimated at 82 percent of the largest Senegalese companies; domestic control of the capital market; and an African rather than a European orientation to the economy.

International Activities. The legal PAI does not participate in the international communist movement; a Romanian Communist Party delegate was the only Eastern-bloc representative at its February congress. The clandestine faction enjoys the support of the Soviet Union and the French Communist Party (*Le Monde*, 20 February). Amath Dansoko is on the editorial board of the *World Marxist Review*. His essay on the revolutionary process in Africa appeared in *Free Africa Marches* (Prague) in 1978.

Publications. The legal PAI publishes a monthly, *La Lutte* (Struggle), and a weekly, *Monsarev* (Independence). The clandestine faction occasionally publishes its own edition of *Monsarev* and relies on the monthly *Andë Sopi* (Unite for Change), which has a circulation of about 7,000, to present its views. The RND publishes *Taxaw* at infrequent intervals.

Stanford University

Peter S. Stern

South Africa

Founded in 1921 as the Communist Party of South Africa, the party dissolved itself in 1950 under the threat of impending suppression. In 1953, the party was reconstituted as the South African Communist Party (SACP), an underground body working in alliance with the African National Congress (ANC), the South African Indian Congress, the Coloured Peoples Congress, the Congress of Democrats (for whites), and the multiracial South African Congress of Trade Unions (SACTU). Most SACP leaders, including the members of the Central Committee, now live and work in friendly African states and in Europe. But the SACP continues to maintain cadres, conduct propaganda, and participate in anti-government activities in South Africa, despite the government's efforts to suppress all radical opposition, including the SACP and the ANC. The SACP remains a nonracial body, but according to its chairman, it is "today almost exclusively a party of the black and coloured people" (*FBIS*, 13 June). It is impossible to estimate the size of its dispersed membership; very probably it is numerically small but heavily concentrated in the ANC and other organizations allied with it.

Leadership and Organization. Since 1972, the SACP's chairman has been Dr. Yusef Dadoo, a 70-year-old Indian medical practitioner. He remains the principal acknowledged spokesman for the SACP; other leaders are not publicly designated and write for party publications under noms de plume.

According to Dr. Dadoo, the SACP "has become completely integrated with the African National Congress, which is the rallying point of the national liberation movement in South Africa today" (ibid., 13 June). The ANC was founded in 1912 as the first countrywide African nationalist organization. It has, since its proscription in 1960, been forced like the SACP to operate underground within South Africa and in exile in facilities provided by friendly African states and sympathetic communist-ruled countries. Under the leadership of Oliver Tambo (president), Alfred Nzo (secretary general), and other leaders, the ANC directs its activities from abroad, including the planning and coordination of pamphleteering, demonstrations, strikes, and other semilegal mass-based activities, along with the training and infiltration of the guerrilla organization known as Umkhonto we Sizwe (Spearhead of the Nation). Since 1969, membership in the ANC has been open to all South Africans, regardless of race.

The closeness of the ANC both to its non-African supporters and to the SACP are symbolized in the person of Dr. Dadoo, who serves both as chairman of the SACP and as vice-chairman of the ANC's Revolutionary Council, the body charged with strengthening the underground organization of the ANC and Umkhonto we Sizwe. In Dadoo's characterization, "the Party's relations with the ANC are based on mutual confidence and mutual commitment and determination to overthrow the white minority regime. This has led to greater clarity and understanding on the part of both organizations on how to evolve the correct revolutionary strategic perspectives and tactical maneuvers in the revolutionary struggle." (*Free Africa Marches*, Prague, 1978, p. 18.) Yet the SACP also unequivocally asserts the "absolute right of our Party to exist as an independent organization and to continue to exercise its public role as the advance vanguard of the working class" (*African Communist*, no. 70, p. 44).

Domestic Activities and Attitudes. The SACP continues to adhere in all essentials to a program adopted in 1962 at an underground meeting in South Africa.

> the characteristic thing about our revolution is that it is developing in conditions of extreme national oppression, expressed in the system of racism and apartheid, which deprives the oppressed majority of the people, the creator of the wealth of the nation, of even the very minimum economic and political rights. Thus, the main content of our struggle is the national liberation of the African people from the yoke of racist and colonialist rule . . . The tasks of national liberation are closely linked with those of social liberation. Furthermore, the country has attained a social and economic level that provides objective material preconditions . . . for transition to an advanced social system. When free, the people of South Africa will be able to proceed towards socialism fairly rapidly. (*Free Africa Marches*, p. 17.)

Yet the achievement of revolutionary change "is not an easy task to accomplish. The revolutionary struggle in our country is a complex, immensely difficult and at times contradictory process. We shall utilise different forms and methods, armed and unarmed, illegal and legal, and planned mass actions, to strengthen the capacity and determination of the oppressed and exploited and to weaken the enemy's morale." (Ibid., pp. 16–17.)

Central to the internal strategy of the SACP is the mobilization of the African working class with its close links to the rural population. "To fulfil this task, the SACP and the ANC intend to encourage the African workers to create their own factory committees—legal, semi-legal and illegal—and use their collective strength to fight relentlessly for higher wages, better working conditions and free trade union rights" (ibid., p. 19). The SACTU is to be revitalized as the vehicle for black trade unionism, and particular attention is to be devoted to Indian and colored workers to thwart attempts to divide the black working class. Complementary efforts are to be made to mobilize the rural working population to assure appropriate support for guerrilla activities. A supporting role is also foreseen for the black middle class on the basis of their stance in favor of the students during the Soweto confrontations of 1976. Within the white segment of the population, the SACP continues its work among "democratic and progressive elements." (*WMR*, July 1978, pp. 30–31.)

The SACP unconditionally rejects the Bantustans and those Africans who have undertaken to work within them as a means to advance the African cause. Specifically, the SACP condemns Inkatha, the Zulu-based organization revived by Chief Gatsha Buthelezi and extended to urban areas, as a threat to the national unity of the oppressed (*African Communist*, no. 74, p. 97). "Black consciousness," as exemplified in the writings of the late Steve Biko, is criticized as a new form of liberalism, "an ideology tried, tested, found wanting and long since rejected by the conscious blacks as a dead-end in the road to change, leading nowhere but to pessimism and defeat." For the SACP, black consciousness is an important stage, but ultimately its supporters must recognize that it is a limiting ideology beyond which they must move toward the ANC. The party journal notes approvingly that a number of former adherents of black consciousness are presently serving in Umkhonto we Sizwe. (Ibid., no. 79, p. 30.)

The armed struggle conducted by Umkhonto we Sizwe is recognized as necessary, but difficult to organize logistically "since every single inch of the country's territory has felt the jackboot of fascist rule and enemy troops can very rapidly reach any point in the country." Thus, the illegal exodus of hundreds of African youths across the country's borders "to join the ANC and its military wing, Umkhonto we Sizwe . . . in order to acquire the political and military skills with which to confront the enemy" is readily welcomed as a step toward the day when "armed revolutionary struggle can not only be initiated, but also sustained." (*Free Africa Marches*, p. 20.) That time probably has not yet arrived, but the attack by a three-man squad of Umkhonto we Sizwe operatives on a police station in Soweto in May (in which one policeman was killed, five persons wounded, and essential records burned) provides evidence of new tactics to be utilized as efforts continue to be made to expand guerrilla activity, particularly in urban areas, using recruits trained outside of the country.

For inspiration, the leaders of the SACP turn to the experiences of the Front for the Liberation of Mozambique and the Popular Movement for the Liberation of Angola (MPLA). According to Dadoo, the successful armed struggles of both parties have "altered the geopolitical situation in Southern Africa and given an incalculable boost to the fighting morale and militant spirit of the oppressed toiling masses in Namibia, Zimbabwe and South Africa." The socialist politics pursued by both regimes have "brought into sharp focus the difference between people's power and that exercised by a privileged minority, the pawns of imperialism and neo-colonialism." (*WMR*, July 1978, p. 25). In more detailed analyses of the Angolan and Mozambican revolutions appearing in the *African Communist* (Nos. 73–75), Joe Slovo, a prominent party theoretician, pointed to the "many lessons of more general relevance [that] can be learned from a study of the Mozambican revolutionary experience" (ibid., no. 73, p. 20) and suggested that "the kaleidoscope of MPLA experiences reflects the widest variety of problems which are common to the revolutionary process in much of our continent. The answers you [MPLA] have found and are continuing to find to these problems are instructive for revolutionaries everywhere." (Ibid., no. 74, p. 10.)

International Views and Activities. The SACP undoubtedly continues its contacts with individual African radicals and socialists and their organizations on the continent in keeping with "A Communist Call to Africa," the document issued by the 1978 conference of "communist and workers' parties of Africa" (ibid., no. 75, pp. 5–33); such contacts have not, however, been publicly announced in the party press. Yet articles on developments elsewhere in Africa testify to the ongoing interest of the party in using its journal as a continent-wide forum.

In its stance on the policies of the Communist Party of China, the SACP has reiterated its harsh criticism of present Chinese leaders and has maintained its fervent identification with the Soviet Union and Cuba. The Chinese attack on Vietnam "plumbed the depths of degradation . . . the Chinese leadership have abandoned the principle of proletarian internationalism and substituted their own brand of petty-bourgeois nationalism" (ibid., no. 77, pp. 6–7). In contrast, articles in the party press have praised the direct support given by the Soviet Union and Cuba to Ethiopia and Angola as indications of true proletarian internationalism.

Publications. The most visible of the SACP's publications is the quarterly *African Communist*, which has appeared since 1959; it is presently printed in the German Democratic Republic and distributed from London. This journal circulates underground in South Africa, along with *Inkululeko-Freedom*, a theoretical journal that originates within South Africa. The SACP also clandestinely issues party proclamations and pocket-sized Marxist-Leninist classics. Its ally, the ANC, publishes a monthly, *Sechaba*, which is also printed in the German Democratic Republic and distributed from London; it is paralleled by *Workers' Unity*, a news sheet issued from London by SACTU. Both organizations issue underground publications and pamphlets in South Africa; the ANC complements its printed material with daily broadcasts on the state radio stations of Angola, Tanzania, and Zambia.

Duke University   Sheridan Johns

Sudan

The Sudanese Communist Party (al-Hizb al-Shuyu'i al-Sudani; SCP) traces its origins to 1946 when a group of revolutionary intellectuals and members of the working class founded the Sudanese Movement for National Liberation under the leadership of 'Abd al-Khaliq Mahjub. At its Third Congress in 1956, the movement was renamed the SCP. Having been implicated in an attempted coup, the party was banned in 1971 (see *YICA*, 1972, pp. 290–92). Numerous SCP leaders, including Mahjub, were executed, and thousands of party members were arrested and held without trial. The SCP has also been accused of participating in more recent plots against the government. No reliable figures exist on present SCP membership. Before the 1971 coup attempt, the party was estimated to have from 5,000 to 10,000 active members; more recent estimates put the figure at 3,500. An unknown number are continuing party activities in exile or clandestinely within Sudan. The population of Sudan is estimated to be almost 21 million.

Leadership and Organization. The secretary general of the SCP is Muhammad Ibrahim Nuqud. Ibrahim Zakariya, Sulaiman Hamid, Su'udi Daraj, 'Abd al-Majid Shakak, and Dr. 'Izz al-Din 'Ali 'Amir are known members of the Central Committee; Ahmad Salim is a member of the SCP Economic Commission. Other SCP leaders include Dr. Mustafa Khujali and Dr. Khalid Hasan al-Tum.

The SCP has always been active in establishing and participating in mass organizations—trade unions and youth, women's, and other associations. The party attempts to operate through local party branches established at places of residence and work and integrated within regional organizations. The party has held four congresses: 1950, 1951, 1956, and 1967.

Domestic Issues. In December 1978 the SCP issued a scathing attack on the Sudanese government, accusing it of directing an intensive campaign against the SCP with U.S., Israeli, Egyptian, and Chinese collaboration on the pretext of aborting a communist coup attempt supported by Cuban troops. The SCP labeled this campaign an effort to blame the communists for the serious political and economic crisis in Sudan and to crush growing opposition to the regime of President Ja'far Numayri. The SCP denounced what it called "Numayri's despotic rule based on absolute personal power and a military dictatorship." The party called for the creation of a mass movement and political strikes "for the liberation of our people and country from autocracy and dictatorship." (*IB*, no. 10.) The leader of the Muslim Brotherhood, Hasan Turabi, who subsequently was appointed attorney general of Sudan, stated on 4 January that the SCP was the only member of the National Front that had not accepted reconciliation, adding that this opportunity was still available to communists as individuals. His statement was in response to one issued in London by Sudanese communists, which declared that the SCP would only accept reconciliation if political parties were given legal status (*Arab Report*, 31 January).

On 8 August the Sudan experienced rioting instigated by students protesting against food shortages and price increases. The students were joined on 11 August by the Sudan Railway Workers' Union, the country's largest trade union. The crisis precipitated the dismissal of various government officials, the reorganization of the Sudanese Socialist Union, and the rescinding of some of the price increases. President Numayri admitted the existence of serious economic problems, but according to the London *Daily Telegraph*, also accused "communist forces" of "inciting the students to rebellion" (*FBIS*, 6 September). The SCP, which charges the Numayri government with responsibility for the country's economic difficulties, apparently participated in these demonstrations. During the height of the crisis, many Sudanese accused of membership in or sympathy with the proscribed SCP were imprisoned (*Financial Times*, 11 August). Whether the SCP in fact instigated the demonstrations and rioting, it clearly took advantage of the opportunity to strengthen opposition to the Numayri government, and there is evidence that Ethiopia provided assistance to the SCP in this regard (*Economist*, 25 August). The demonstrations in August were followed in September by a strike of Sudanese doctors. Clandestine sources reported that 300 doctors were protesting against the dismissal of 40 of their colleagues from their jobs. Although the Ministry of Health gave no reason for its action, the doctors reportedly were dismissed for being communists (*FBIS*, 25 September).

International Views. Early in 1979 the SCP issued a statement expressing solidarity with the revolution of the Iranian people against the government of the shah. It denounced the action taken by Sudan's "reactionary regime" on 22 July 1971 establishing close relations between Sudan and the shah's government. According to the SCP, the situation in Iran demonstrated the "objective law of the revolution" that when real conditions are created for a revolution, dictatorship cannot be maintained, despite repression or outside assistance, provided that the masses are adequately organized and led. The SCP claimed that the battle being fought by the Iranian people was part of the regional struggle against imperialism and Zionism as well as against dictatorial and reactionary regimes (*IB*, no. 10). The SCP rejected the peace treaty between Egypt and Israel as "Sadat's separate peace agreement and unconditional capitulation to the Zionist enemy" and denounced Numayri's tacit support of Egypt. In May the SCP joined the Arab People's Congress, an organization that seeks to isolate Sadat and calls for actions against American interests in the region. The SCP labels U.S. imperialism as the "main enemy of our peoples," charging that "it is intent on dominating our country in order to plunder our wealth and exploit out strategic position" (ibid., no. 5). The SCP consistently maintains a pro-Soviet posture, heralding it as the vanguard of the struggle waged by all progressive forces in the world. While asserting that the Chinese revolution was one of the greatest achievements of the communist and democratic movement after World War II, the party denounces Maoism as counterrevolutionary. It charges that Maoism has severed all links with Marxism and condemns it for assisting "imperialism and racism" in issues such as Angola. The SCP advocates the convening of a new international meeting of communist and workers' parties to decide on a new common stand in order "to repulse imperialist attacks" (*WMR*, April).

Publications. Because the SCP is severely repressed in Sudan, the party does not have a regular party organ, but rather publishes and distributes leaflets infrequently and clandestinely.

Stanford University   Patricia Mihaly

Syria

The Syrian Communist Party (al-Hizb al-Shuyu'i al-Suri; SCP) is an offshoot of the Lebanese Communist Party, which was established in 1924. Cooperation between the SCP and the Syrian government began after the Ba'th coup d'etat of 8 March 1963. The SCP has held two cabinet posts since 1971. In March 1972 the party gained de facto legality through its participation in the National Progressive Front (NPF) composed of the Ba'th Party, the SCP, and other nationalist forces. A dissident SCP faction, led by Riyad al-Turk, split from the party in 1973. It is not represented in either the Syrian cabinet or the NPF. Membership in the SCP is believed to be about 5,000, with another 10,000 sympathizers. The population of Syria is about 8.4 million.

Leadership and Organization. Khalid Bakdash, a Syrian Kurd, was re-elected secretary general of the SCP at its Fourth Congress in 1974. Yusuf Faisal is deputy secretary general. The Politburo consists of Bakdash, Ibrahim Bakri, Khalid Hammami, Daniel Ni'mah, Maurice Salibi, Dhahir 'Abd al-Samad, Ramu Shaikhu, 'Umar Siba'i, and Murad Yusuf. Siba'i is minister of communications and 'Abd al-Samad is minister of state in the Syrian cabinet. Bakdash and Ni'mah are the SCP representatives in the NPF. In August 1977 six SCP members were elected to the Syrian legislature, the People's Council.

Relations with the Syrian Government. Consistent with Soviet directives, the SCP is a strong advocate of and an active participant in the NPF, which is dominated by the ruling Ba'th Party of President Hafiz al-Asad. An assessment by Khalid Bakdash of the October meeting of the NPF noted that it had "adopted a number of important decisions intended to create favorable conditions, to ensure a further rise in the economy and living standards of the country's population." He noted that the implementation of these decisions "will help eliminate many problems of Syria's home policy." (Tass, 15 October; *FBIS*, 16 October.) SCP's support of and pride in the domestic policies of the present government can be seen in the analysis by Bakdash of "Israel's policy of permanent aggression against Arab countries." The SCP perceives that one aim of this policy is "to prevent progressive Arab countries, primarily Syria, from pursuing and stepping up independent economic development and social progress" (*WMR*, August). In July the SCP sent a cable of condolences to President Asad after the assassination of Zuhayr Muhsin, member of both the Ba'th Party's National Command and the Palestine Liberation Organization's Executive Committee. The cable expressed the party's solidarity with Asad and the Ba'th Party "against all colonialist schemes hostile to our people and homeland" (*FBIS*, 30 July).

International Views. The SCP considers the treaty between Egyptian President Sadat and Israel to be a "capitulationist 'peace' with the aggressor, betraying the national interests of the Egyptian people, the fraternal Arab people of Palestine and other Arab peoples" (*WMR*, August). The SCP supports efforts by the NPF to unify "progressive" Arab forces against what it perceives as a sinister conspiracy between the United States, Israel, and Sadat to obstruct independent economic development and social progress and to weaken the influence of the Soviet Union in the Arab world. The SCP's consistent reference to Sadat rather than to Egypt stresses its position that the actions taken by Sadat lack the support of the Egyptian people. The SCP calls for a comprehensive Middle East settlement based on Israel's total withdrawal from occupied territories and the securing of the legitimate national rights of the Arab people of Palestine, including the rights to return to their homeland, to self-determination, and to an independent national state.

While the SCP denounces anticommunist policies in various Arab countries, it labeled "particularly outrageous" the persecution of communists where the national leaders follow an anti-imperialist policy and a "progressive orientation." In 1978 the SCP expressed its staunch support for the joint national action charter between Syria and Iraq and stressed its "solidarity with the heroic Iraqi Communist Party" (ibid.), who have been the victims of persecution by the Iraqi government. The SCP takes every opportunity to praise Soviet support for Syria and all "progressive" forces in the Middle East and throughout the world.

Several SCP leaders met with Soviet Foreign Minister Gromyko in Damascus at the end of March, and in mid-June Bakdash led an SCP delegation to Moscow to meet with Soviet communist party leaders. In a *World Marxist Review* article in March, Daniel Ni'mah charged that Sadat has been used by imperialism to distort the truth about the Soviet Union. Ni'mah also denounced Chinese leaders for their anti-Sovietism, which "leads to undisguised treachery and the conversion of this leadership into a weapon of the most die-hard imperialists." In regard to other socialist countries, Khalid Bakdash met with party leaders in Poland in mid-September. On 11 January he also sent a congratulatory message to Heng Samrin on the occasion of the "total liberation of Kampuchea [Cambodia] from the Pol Pot–Ieng Sary regime," calling the ties of friendship between Kampuchea and socialist Vietnam and Laos "an important element in the consolidation of peace and stability in Indochina, Southeast Asia and the world" (*FBIS*, 13 January).

In the August issue of *World Marxist Review*, Khalid Bakdash analyzed the relations between West European social democratic parties (the Socialist International) and the national liberation movements in Asia, Africa, and Latin America. He accused the Socialist International of lacking concern for the welfare of the peoples of developing countries. He charged it is being used by imperialism to deradicalize and "pacify" progressive forces. "There is no doubt that in the developing countries, as elsewhere, one of the main objectives of the propaganda of 'democratic socialism' is to 'end' the growing influence of Marxism-Leninism."

Publications. The official SCP organ is the fortnightly newspaper *Nidal al-Sha'b* (People's Struggle), which is banned but has been circulating freely since the party joined the NPF in 1972.

Stanford University   Patricia Mihaly

International Communist Front Organizations

The international fronts operating since World War II are counterparts of organizations set up by the Comintern after the First World War. Their function today is the same as during the interwar period: to unite communists with persons of other political persuasions to support and thereby lend respectability to Soviet foreign policy objectives.

Moscow's control over the fronts is evidenced by their faithful adherence to the Soviet policy line as well as by the withdrawal of one group after another (e.g., certain Western-oriented affiliates after the cold war began, the Yugoslav ones following the Stalin-Tito break, and the Chinese and Albanian representation as the Sino-Soviet split developed). Similarly but less dramatically, in the 1977–1979 period, the Eurocommunist French gave up the secretary generalships of two of the most important fronts, the World Federation of Trade Unions (WFTU) and the World Federation of Democratic Youth (WFDY); the Eurocommunist Italians gave up the WFDY presidency and withdrew from the WFTU altogether; and the by now anti-Soviet Egyptians apparently directed the Egyptian secretary general of another important front, the Afro-Asian People's Solidarity Organization (AAPSO), to become inactive. (The first deputy secretary genral, an Iraqi leftist, has since served as acting secretary.)

The Communist Party of the Soviet Union controls the fronts through its International Department (ID). Presumably the ID is connected with those Soviets serving as full-time secretariat members at headquarters of seven of the major fronts considered here: World Peace Council (WPC); World Federation of Trade Unions (WFTU); Women's International Democratic Federation (WIDF); Afro-Asian Peoples' Solidarity Organization (AAPSO); International Organization of Journalists (IOJ); International Association of Democratic Lawyers (IADL); and Christian Peace Conference (CPC). The WIDF and the IOJ have Soviet vice-presidents as well. Three other fronts have a Soviet vice-president rather than a Soviet secretary: World Federation of Democratic Youth (WFDY); International Union of Students (IUS); and World Federation of Scientific Workers (WFSW). How the USSR exercises on-the-spot control in these last cases is not known. Vice-presidents traditionally reside in their home countries, and none of these three fronts is headquartered in Moscow.

In addition to apparent ID control, the WPC seems to function as a front coordinator. This makes sense when it is remembered that the Soviets consider the "peace movement" the most important joint action by the "anti-imperialist" forces and the most important of the movements "based on common specific objectives of professional interests" (*Kommunist*, no. 3, February 1974, p. 101). A glance at the nearly 150 members of the WPC Presidential Committee reveals that it includes, in addition to an ID deputy chief (V. S. Shaposhnikov), the past and present WFTU general secretaries, the WIDF president and secretary general, the presidents of the WFDY, IUS, WFSW, and CPC, and the secretary general of AAPSO (*New Perspectives*, no. 4). The organizations thus represented are certainly the most important fronts. Among the remaining 1,150-plus WPC members, moreover, are found the top leaders of the other fronts considered here: the IADL secretary general and both the president and the secretary general of the IOJ. Certain other fronts are also represented on the WPC, and some of these (the Berlin Conference of Catholic Christians in European States, the Asian Buddhist Conference for Peace, and the Arab Lawyers Union) are even represented on the WPC's Presidential Committee.

Another means of coordination are interfront meetings. Representatives of all fronts treated here plus the regional (European and Israeli) International Federation of Resistance Fighters, the International Institute of Peace (a WPC research appendage), and the Editorial Board of *World Marxist Review* (an outright Soviet organ) convened at Budapest in March 1979. The *World Marxist Review*'s editorial board includes representatives from almost sixty communist parties, but its editor-in-chief is the Russian Konstantin Zarodov (*WMR*, August, pp. 2, 127). The magazine's point of contact with the fronts appears to be its Problems of Peace and Democratic Organizations Commission, whose Soviet secretary, Aleksandr Didusenko, attended the February WPC session in East Berlin.

World Peace Council. The WPC has the largest geographical coverage of all fronts and presently claims affiliates in more than 130 countries. It was reportedly considered by Soviet officials in the mid-1970s to have about 400 million supporters (*Posev*, September 1978, p. 30). The WPC was formed at a series of conferences between 1948 and 1950. Headquarters have been at Helsinki since 1968, when it moved from Vienna, leaving behind the International Institute of Peace.

Although the WPC sponsors large conferences, congresses, and assemblies, these do not elect the next higher body, as do their namesakes in most other front organizations. Instead, the WPC reconstitutes itself every three years, reportedly after considering recommendations from affiliated national peace committees and other international organizations. The list of WPC members at its last regular meeting (Warsaw, May 1977) contained 1,333 names; the names of members from twenty countries were yet to be added (WPC, *List of Members, 1977–1980*).

The WPC elects a Presidential Committee, with a president (the Indian communist, Romesh Chandra), 23 vice-presidents, and 122 other members (*New Perspectives*, no. 4). This committee generally meets once a year and in turn elects a smaller Bureau and the permanent Secretariat. The former includes the president, a vice-president, and a limited number of representatives from national peace movements. The latter is headed by Chandra, assisted by John Benson, an Australian executive secretary (*Peace Courier*, April), and includes some twenty other full members (secretaries), allegedly providing the best possible geographical and political representation.

Three additional WPC secretaries are located abroad (New York, Geneva, Paris) to deal with appropriate U.N. agencies. The WPC has nongovernmental organization (NGO) status with the United Nations, occupies a vice-presidency in the Conference of NGOs, a vice-presidency on the Special NGO Committee on Disarmament and Security, and a secretarial position with the Bureau of the NGO Special Committee on Development. The WPC has consultative status "A" with UNESCO and general consultative status with UNCTAD, UNIDO, and ECOSOC. One of its representatives has addressed the U.N. General Assembly's Special Political Committee and its Fourth Committee (dealing with non–self-governing countries) every year since 1971.

The relative emphases given various subjects by the WPC over the past year can be measured by the size of its meetings. The largest of these was the special session of the WPC (outside the normal three-year cycle) held 2–5 February in East Berlin, which was concerned primarily with "problems of disarmament and détente." The WPC claimed that 600 delegates from 99 countries and 37 international organizations attended. The major conclusions were contained in a pamphlet called *Stop the Arms Race*, which attacked the Chinese communists for not participating in disarmament efforts and for allegedly supporting "the most reactionary forces" in Chile, Iran, and South Africa as well as the "militarists' maneuvers aimed at deceiving public opinion and introducing neutron weapons in NATO arsenals" (ibid., February). Neither the North Koreans nor Romanians were present, apparently because their ruling parties maintain relations with their Chinese counterpart.

The next largest meeting was the World Conference of Solidarity with Chile, held in Madrid 9–12 November 1978. Reportedly more than 500 delegates from 77 countries and nearly thirty international organizations attended. Their statement, "Act of Madrid for Liberty of Chile," called for, among other things, an embargo on shipments to Chile and an investigation by the ad hoc working group of the U.N. Human Rights Commission (ibid., December 1978).

The International Emergency Conference in Support of Vietnam, held 6–8 March at Helsinki, purportedly attracted 400 delegates from 103 countries and 30 international organizations. Their reaction to the Chinese invasion of Vietnam was published as a pamphlet entitled *Hands off Vietnam*.

Other major WPC-sponsored meetings included the following:

NAME	THEME	DATE	PLACE
Anti-Apartheid Continuation Committee (jointly with AAPSO)		December	Paris
Seminar on Nonalignment		March	Kingston
WPC Presidential Committee	30th anniversary of WPC	April	Prague
International Conference of Solidarity with Palestine	Self-determination and independent state	May	Basel
International Conference of Solidarity with Nicaragua	Support for the Sandinistas	July	Caracas
International Conference of Solidarity with the People of Afghanistan	Support for Taraki regime	August	Kabul
WPC Presidential Committee Bureau	Support for Panama on the canal issue	September	Panama

Despite the above, the main WPC emphasis was supposed to be on national campaigns and efforts to draw in an ever wider spectrum of domestic elements (*Programme of Action, 1979*). The annual meeting of national peace movement representatives was canceled, however, because of the WPC special session in East Berlin. Regional meetings as substitutes for the worldwide event appeared either to be behind schedule or not taking place at all. Another WPC "nonstarter" seems to have been a world conference of parliamentarians for peace.

The WPC publishes the bimonthly *New Perspectives* and the monthly *Peace Courier* news bulletin. It revealed more than usual during 1979 by publishing *The World Peace Council: What It Is and What It Does; Programme of Action, 1979;* and *List of Members, 1977–1980*.

World Federation of Trade Unions. The labor movement, especially as embodied in the WFTU, has been mentioned by a Soviet writer as the second most important area of front activity (*Kommunist*, February 1974, p. 101).

Although formed in 1945, it had an antecedent in the Red International of Labor Unions (Profintern), which functioned from 1921 to 1937. Its headquarters are in Prague. Over half the WFTU's claimed membership of 150 million is in its Soviet affiliate, the All-Union Central Council of Trade Unions, and the bulk of the remainder comes from other communist-ruled states (*YICA*, 1979, p. 444). Many of the non-bloc affiliates are communist-dominated trade unions. The WFTU, therefore, is less of a genuine front than the WPC and more of an outright communist organization. Since the number of delegates to the WFTU Congress from each affiliate is determined by the affiliate's membership, the Soviets and their clients obviously control the organization through sheer weight.

The WFTU's Congress meets every four years. The last one at Prague in April 1978 elected a General Council of 85 members and 87 candidate members. This Congress also chose a 28-member Executive Bureau and an 8-man permanent Secretariat. The Secretariat is headed by a Uruguayan communist, Enrique Pastorino, as secretary general. His deputy is a Sudanese communist, Ibrahim Zakariya. It includes six other secretaries. A Hungarian communist, Sándor Gáspár, is the WFTU president.

The WFTU maintains close relations with other international fronts and certain regional trade union federations. Pastorino is a WPC vice-president, and he signed a formal agreement of cooperation with the WPC on behalf of the WFTU (*Flashes*, 14 May). The WFTU sent delegations to the three largest WPC meetings of the year. The special WFTU session devoted to "solidarity with Vietnam" (April) paralleled the WPC International Emergency Conference held a month earlier. Similarly its cosponsorship of the Third International Trade Union Conference of Solidarity with Palestine (at Damascus in May) paralleled the WPC conference at Basel the same month. During March the WFTU signed formal cooperation agreements with the WFDY and the IUS. That same month a meeting of the WFTU/IADL Working Committee was held (ibid., 31 March and 28 May).

The WFTU has established close relations with the United Nations and several of its agencies. It has permanent representatives in New York (U.N. headquarters), Geneva (International Labor Organization; ILO), Paris (UNESCO), and Rome (Food and Agriculture Organization; FAO). It has consultative status with the three specialized agencies as well as with ECOSOC. Relations with the ILO are especially close.

The WFTU is also close to the Organization of African Trade Union Unity (OATUU), the International Confederation of Arab Trade Unions (ICATU), and the Permanent Congress of Trade Union Unity of Latin American Workers (CPUSTAL). These four organizations plus the General Federation of Palestinian Workers cosponsored the previously noted Third International Trade Union Conference of Solidarity with Palestine in May; the same four plus the United Workers' Centre of Chile continue to run an International Trade Union Committee of Solidarity with Workers and People of Chile. A joint WFTU/ICATU Standing Committee exists. Both the OATUU and CPUSTAL have, along with the WFTU, representation on the WPC. Working with and through these other trade union organizations, the WFTU can bring its message to an ever wider audience and thus perform a true front function.

In addition to the WFTU's concern with Vietnam, Palestine, and Chile, at its General Council session held in Sofia 10–13 April, resolutions were also passed against apartheid in South Africa and the Somoza regime in Nicaragua. At the same meeting, the WFTU admitted new affiliates from Afghanistan, Kampuchea (Cambodia), Namibia, and Puerto Rico and added Japan to its Bureau (ibid., 28 April). The WFTU's concerns resulted in two new bulletins, *Solidarity with Korea* (March) and *Dialogo Sindical* (for Latin America, in April), as well as in sponsorship of the Fourth World Conference on Working Women in Nicosia during October.

The WFTU increased its organizational efforts in Southeast Asia, an area where the communist movement has traditionally been dominated by pro-Chinese elements. The friendship treaty signed by Vietnam and the Soviet Union (November 1978) provided new opportunities, and the trade union movement appeared to be one of the mechanisms chosen by Moscow. That same month, a regional WFTU office under the direction of the Vietnamese communist trade union leader Ly Van was established in Ho Chih Minh City but was moved to Hanoi by January. Together with the WFTU's Asian secretary, Mahendra Sen, Ly conducted a trade union seminar in Manila during mid-December 1978 and later that same month spent two days in Bangkok conferring with Thai labor leaders. A WFTU seminar in New Delhi during March was attended by trade unions from Thailand, Singapore, and Malaysia (all without WFTU affiliates), as well as from the Philippines. Ly Van paid another two-week visit to Bangkok in August, where he saw government and U.N. officials and trade union leaders. Before his death in September, Ly attempted to secure invitations from trade union leaders in Malaysia as well. (*Far Eastern Economic Review*, 7 September, p. 15.)

The Trade Union Internationals (TUIs) affiliated with the WFTU comprise national federations devoted to a single craft, trade, or profession. Top officers of each of the eleven TUIs sit on the WFTU

General Council, and the WFTU has a special TUI Department. In January 1979 a "consultative meeting" between the WFTU and the TUIs convened at Prague. The TUIs claim to be independent, and the high number of Frenchmen in leadership positions may support this contention. Four TUIs held international conferences during the past year:

NAME	LEADERS	DATE	PLACE
Metal and Engineering Industries	Reinhard Sommer (GDR) elected president; Pierre Baghi (France) re-elected secretary general	November (1978)	Warsaw
Chemical, Oil, and Allied Workers	Ferenc Dajka (Hungary) elected president; Alain Covet (France) elected secretary general	May	Sofia
Agricultural, Forestry, and Plantation Workers	Andreas Kyriakou (Cyprus) re-elected president; Claude Billault (France) re-elected secretary general	May	Warsaw
Building, Wood, and Building Materials Industries		September	Moscow

Zdenek Spicka (Czechoslovakia), secretary general of the Textile, Clothing, Leather, and Fur Workers TUI, died in April 1979; his successor is not yet known.

The WFTU organization publishes a monthly magazine, *World Trade Union Movement*, and a weekly newsletter, *Flashes from the Trade Unions*.

World Federation of Democratic Youth. Founded in 1945, the WFDY is the de facto successor to the Comintern's Communist Youth International. Its headquarters are in Budapest. The organization has consultative status with ECOSOC, UNESCO, FAO, and ILO.

The WFDY claimed 150 million members in 210 affiliates (student groups are often members of both the WFDY and the counterpart youth organizations in their own countries) in 104 countries (*YICA*, 1979, p. 442). The WFDY's Assembly meets once every three years. Its last meeting in East Berlin (22 February–1 March 1978) was attended by 704 delegates, who elected an Executive Committee of 68 members. The WFDY appears to have a consolidated Bureau/Secretariat responsible for day-to-day operations. This organ when last elected consisted of a president (Ernesto Ottone of Chile), eight vice-presidents, a secretary general (Miklos Barabas of Hungary), two deputies, a treasurer, and seventeen secretaries (*WFDY News*, nos. 4–5, 1978). The consolidated Bureau/Secretariat may explain why the USSR finds a vice-president, rather than a secretary, sufficient for control over the organization. Vsevold Nakhodkin replaced Vladislav Kornilov as the Soviet vice-president in early 1979 (ibid., no. 7).

The main WFDY meeting of the year was that of its Executive Committee held at Dortmund 1–4 February, which passed resolutions on apartheid in South Africa, the Afghan revolution, Nicaragua, Chile, and Palestine, duplicating WPC and WFTU activities noted above. Not surprisingly, delegates from countries with relatively independent communist parties (Italy, France, Belgium, Great Britain,

Spain, Japan, North Korea, and Mexico) criticized the condemnation of Chinese foreign policy contained in several of the resolutions (*L'Unità*, 12 February). Soon after the Chinese attack, the WFDY bureau held an "extraordinary session" on Vietnam, paralleling the WPC Emergency Conference and the WFTU special session.

As mentioned above, the president of the WFDY sits on the WPC Presidential Committee, and its secretary general is also a WPC member. The chief front contact, however, is the IUS. (The IUS and WFDY cosponsor the large-scale World Youth Festival every five years.) In May the WFDY and the IUS cosponsored the Conference of Solidarity with Vietnam at Hyderabad, which attracted roughly one hundred participants (*Neues Deutschland*, 10 and 24 May).

The WFDY has established a degree of cooperation with its socialist counterpart, apparently unique for a communist front and doubtlessly facilitated by the association of many socialist youth organizations with the left wings of their respective parties. In November 1978, the WFDY cosponsored a seminar on disarmament at Budapest with the International Union of Socialist Youth. During the following May, both organizations, along with the IUS and two noncommunist European youth federations, conferred in Brussels on plans for future cooperation (*IUS News Service*, nos. 13–14, July).

The WFDY publishes the bimonthly *World Youth* and *WFDY News*, which appears about every three weeks.

Women's International Democratic Federation. The WIDF was founded in 1945 and has headquarters in East Berlin. Its president is Freda Brown from Australia and its secretary general the Finnish communist Mirjam Vire-Tuominen. Although no membership figures have been released since the 1966 claim of "over 200 million," the WIDF currently reports that it has 129 member organizations in 114 countries (*Women of the Whole World*, no. 3).

The WIDF's Congress meets every five or six years (the last time in East Berlin, 1975). It elects a Council, which in turn chooses a Bureau and permanent Secretariat. The Bureau consists of 30 members (president, eight vice-presidents, representatives of nineteen other affiliated organizations, chairman of the audit committee and, presumably, the secretary general) and last met in East Berlin 2–4 April. This meeting passed the usual resolutions on Palestine, apartheid, and disarmament (ibid., no. 2) and held an extraordinary session on Vietnam.

No other major meeting sponsored solely by the WIDF apparently occurred during the year. The Nicosia Conference on Working Women (October) seems to have been wholly a WFTU affair, even though there had been a joint WIDF/WFTU seminar on the same subject in Budapest during November 1978. Sponsorship of the WIDF's main effort in 1979, the International Conference on Children in Moscow, was shared with over twenty other organizations. This major event claimed nearly 800 delegates from 132 countries and 46 international organizations (*Peace Courier*, October).

On the other hand, the WIDF continues to exercise a notable degree of influence in other organizations. It is the only front whose president and secretary general are represented on the WPC Presidential Committee. The WIDF not only has consultative status with ECOSOC, ILO, and UNESCO, but its permanent representative to the latter (the Frenchwoman François Lafitte) was elected head of the Permanent Committee of NGOs with UNESCO in mid-1979. The WIDF's president, Freda Brown, chairs the executive of the multi-organizational International Committee for the U.N. Decade for Women, which organized the Moscow children's conference.

The WIDF publishes the bimonthly *Women of the Whole World*.

Afro-Asian Peoples' Solidarity Organization. Although only a regional organization, the scope of AAPSO is large enough to have broad significance. It is also the only front not completely dominated by the Soviets. The Egyptians have shared in its control from the very beginning, with other countries also exercising influence at various times. This latter factor appears to have weakened the organization perceptibly in recent years, as Soviet and Egyptian (and later, Iraqi) foreign policies diverged.

Founded in December 1957 as an offshoot from the WPC, with an anticolonial focus, AAPSO maintains headquarters in Cairo with an Egyptian government–selected president/secretary general, Abdul Rahman al-Sharqawi. Sharqawi never seems to have taken hold of the organization since his appointment in early 1978; rather the Iraqi first deputy secretary general, Nuri Abdul Razzaq Hussein, appears to have been the de facto leader as *acting* secretary general during the year (*Pravda*, 15 May). Hussein earlier had been the IUS's secretary general.

These two men are not known to be communists. Neither are the organization's other top leaders (the three vice-presidents, Aziz Sherif of Iraq, Vassos Lyssarides of Cyprus, and Vasco Cabral of Guinea-Bissau) nor its two other deputy general secretaries (Baren Ray of India and Facine Bangura of Guinea). However, AAPSO's orientatioan is usually pro-Soviet. The exact way this is manifested appears to vary with external pressures. For example, at the January meeting in Hanoi of its Presidium, AAPSO denounced the "hegemonic aspirations" of Chinese leaders and expressed support for the Kampuchean (Cambodian) National United Front for National Salvation (*Neues Deutschland*, 10, 11, and 16 January). However, at the April Conference in Support of African Liberation Movements at Lusaka, Soviet and Vietnamese attempts to adopt an anti-Chinese resolution were, according to Chinese sources at least, voted down by delegates from Somalia, the Sudan, Korea, Tanzania, Egypt, Sierra Leone, and Zambia, among others (New China News Agency, 19 April).

These two meetings apparently represented AAPSO's major efforts during the year. Its highest body, the Conference, had been scheduled to hold its sixth session in December 1977, but it did not take place. In view of the planned locale in Baghdad, it appears that postponement may have been related to deteriorating Soviet-Iraqi relations. Substitution of an Iraqi for an Egyptian as de facto leader of the organization may not have turned out to Soviet advantage.

The Conference elects a Council, which includes one representative from each national affiliate. The Council has not met since its twelfth session, held in Moscow during 1975. The ongoing policy-making body appears to be the Presidium. It met twice in 1976, but only once each year since then. The Presidium consists of a president, three vice-presidents, and representatives from between twelve and twenty of the national affiliates. The 1979 Presidium session, although not attended by Sharqawi, had 114 delegates from 37 countries and nine international organizations (*Neues Deutschland*, 10, 11, and 16 January). The permanent Secretariat in Cairo consists of a secretary general, three deputies, an assistant secretary general for technical affairs, and thirteen secretaries.

The Hanoi meeting illustrated AAPSO's external relations. The WFTU, WFDY, WIDF, IUS, IADL, and IOJ all sent representatives, and the meeting voted to install permanent representatives at Geneva, Paris, and New York for U.N. contacts (ibid.). The AAPSO has consultative status only with ECOSOC. Its closest relations appear to be with the WPC. At the top level, the president/secretary general sits on the WPC Presidential Committee, and Aziz Sherif is a vice-president of both organizations. Vice-President Cabral, First Deputy Secretary General Hussein, and Deputy Secretary General Ray are all members.

The size of the AAPSO is unknown. It has full-member affiliates in most African and Asian countries and associate-member affiliates in the Soviet bloc (*Baghdad Observer*, 24 April). Helmut Müller from East Germany even sits on the AAPSO Secretariat. The AAPSO's largest meeting of the year (in April at Lusaka) reportedly attracted over 300 delegates from 60 countries and a number of international organizations (*New Times*, no. 17, April). This was smaller than the three largest WPC meetings noted above but larger than those of the WFTU during the same period.

International Union of Students. The IUS claims over 10 million members in 103 affiliates, which places it in first place among the smaller fronts (*YICA*, 1979, p. 440). It was founded in 1946 and has headquarters in Prague. Its president is Miroslav Stepan from Czechoslovakia, and its secretary general, Fathi al-Fadl, comes from the Sudan. New affiliates in Afghanistan, Iran, Lebanon, and Turkey were admitted in December 1978 (*World Student News*, March).

The IUS's structure duplicates almost exactly that of the WFDY. The highest organ is the Congress (last held at Sofia in November 1977), where each affiliate is represented. It should meet every three years. The Congress elects an Executive Committee that convenes once a year (most recently at Nicosia in December 1978). The latter in turn elects the Bureau/Secretariat consisting of a president, twelve vice-presidents, a secretary general, at least eleven secretaries, and perhaps others.

The Executive Committee meeting in December 1978 concerned itself with Vietnam, apartheid and "national liberation" in Southern Africa, Palestine, and disarmament, all along predictable lines. Developing some of these issues, the IUS participated in the International Youth and Student Conference on South Africa held in February at Paris and the International Students Disarmament Conference in April at Prague. Just prior to the Nicosia Executive Committee meeting, the IUS cosponsored, with the Pan-Cyprian Federation of Students and Young Professionals, the Conference of Solidarity with Cyprus.

As this last meeting reflects, most IUS activity appears to take place in conjunction with other organizations, its connection with the WFDY being the closest. The IUS and WFDY cosponsored a Vietnam conference at Hyderabad in May. The meeting on South Africa was also a joint venture with the WFDY, although under the general auspices of the United Nations. Hence, a statement protesting China's attack on Vietnam came only from IUS and WFDY participants, not from the conference as a whole (*Neues Deutschland*, 21 February).

In contrast, the meeting at Prague on disarmament condemned Chinese "aggression" against Vietnam as well as the Israeli-Egyptian treaty and the neutron bomb. This came as a surprise since the conference was cosponsored by the International Student Movement for the U.N. and the World Student Christian Federation as well as the IUS, the Continental Organization of Latin American Students (OCLAE), and the All-Africa Students Union (AASU). The IUS's relations with the last two groups, plus the General Union of Arab Students (GUAS), appear especially close and parallel exactly the WFTU connection with three trade union federations covering the same geographical areas. Representatives of the IUS, OCLAE, AASU, and GUAS conferred together at Prague in January and again in June. At the latter meeting, Vietnam, South Africa, Palestine, Nicaragua, and Puerto Rico were discussed (*IUS News Service*, 12 June).

The president of the IUS, like that of the WFDY, sits on the WPC Presidential Committee, and the IUS secretary general is a member of the WPC. The IUS has consultative status with both UNESCO and ECOSOC.

The IUS publishes the monthly *World Student News* and the semimonthly *IUS News Service*.

International Organization of Journalists. The IOJ was founded in 1946. It currently maintains headquarters at Prague and at least three journalist training schools (Budapest, East Berlin, Havana) as well as two regional centers (Paris and Cairo). The organization claims membership of more than 150,000 in about one hundred countries. New affiliates from Ethiopia, Jamaica, Mexico, and the Western Sahara were admitted most recently (*Journalists' Affairs*, nos. 1–2).

The IOJ's highest body is its Congress, which meets every five years. The last one at Helsinki in 1976 elected a new Executive Committee and Presidium. The latter consists of an honorary president (ex-President Jean-Maurice Herman from France), president (Kaarle Nordenstreng of Finland), nineteen vice-presidents, apparently two commission chairmen, and a secretary general (Jirí Kubka of Czechoslovakia) and holds one annual meeting. The Executive Committee appears to meet only once between congresses and consists of the Presidium plus representatives from 29 national affiliates (*YICA*, 1979, p. 439). In addition there is a permanent General Secretariat, at least seven of whose members have been identified in IOJ publications (*Journalists' Affairs*, nos. 1–2, 11–12, 13–14).

The IOJ participated in meetings of other fronts during the past year but appeared to have held no major meeting of its own other than Presidium sessions in Mexico City during November 1978.

Themes stressed there were opposition to the neutron bomb and "repression" in Southern Africa as well as "persecution" of journalists in Latin America, especially Argentina, Chile, Nicaragua, and Paraguay. Later, with respect to the Chinese attack on Vietnam, the IOJ issued the usual condemnation and sent President Nordenstreng to the WPC-sponsored International Emergency Conference (which he addressed) at Helsinki (ibid., nos. 5–6).

Like APPSO, the IOJ maintains especially close relations with the WPC. It has four officers representing the organization on the WPC, more than any other conventional front: President Nordenstreng, Secretary General Kubka, Vice-President Ernesto Vera (Cuba), and one of the secretaries (Sergiuz Klaczkow of Poland). In April the IOJ conferred its highest award, the Julius Fucik Medal, on WPC Chairman Romesh Chandra (ibid., nos. 9–10).

Like the WFDY and the IUS, the IOJ maintains close relations with counterpart federations in Latin America and the Arab world. One of its vice-presidents, Saad Qasim Hamudi from Iraq, was elected chairman of the Federation of Arab Journalists in April. He is also a WPC member. Toward the end of 1978, the IOJ signed a cooperation agreement with the Federation of Latin American Journalists (FELAP). Gerardo Carnero Checa of Peru, FELAP secretary general, sits on the IOJ Executive Committee and serves as FELAP's representative on the WPC. The IOJ has consultative status with ECOSOC and UNESCO.

The IOJ publishes two journals, *Democratic Journalist* and *Journalists' Affairs.*

Christian Peace Conference. The CPC, founded in 1958, has headquarters at Prague. It has three regional subsidiaries: African CPC, Asian CPC, and Regional Committee for Latin America and the Caribbean. It claims members (churches, ecumenical bodies, and individuals) in 79 countries but provides no figures.

The CPC's highest body, the All-Christian Peace Assembly, last met at Prague during June 1978. This organ elected a Continuation Committee and a smaller (46-member) Working Committee (*CPC Information*, 21 February). The latter appointed an International Secretariat, composed of international secretaries from specified countries, not to be confused with the CPC permanent Secretariat in Prague. During the past year, the Working Committee met only once, with 78 foreign delegates plus an unspecified number of Finnish attending guests, at Helsinki in April. The usual statements on détente, disarmament, Southern Africa, and Vietnam appeared. The one on Palestine was unusually mild, however, merely reaffirming the "validity of the principles formulated by the U.N. Assembly" (ibid., 9 April). The International Secretariat met in January at Budapest, in June at West Berlin, and apparently during the Working Committee session at Helsinki. The CPC's leaders include President Karoly Toth (Hungary), Secretary General Lubomir Mirejovsky (Czechoslovakia), Continuation Committee Chairman Kiril V. V. Filaret (USSR), and Deputy General Secretaries Georgi Fomin (USSR) and Christopher Rosa (Sri Lanka).

The CPC's relations with the WPC are close. It sent a thirteen-member delegation (including four of the five officers mentioned above) to the WPC conference on Vietnam held at Helsinki in March, after which Toth, Mirejovsky, and a former CPC president, Tibor Bartha, conferred with WPC Chairman Chandra at Budapest (ibid., 16 and 27 March). At the CPC disarmament conference at Selm in the Federal Republic of Germany, Gerhard Kade, vice-president of the WPC's International Institute of Peace in Vienna, gave the main address (ibid., 24 May). The CPC also maintains relations with the Conference of Catholic Christians in European States, another organizational member of WPC. The CPC and this group held their fourth consultation in East Berlin during March. Not only does the CPC have consultative status with UNESCO and ECOSOC, but one of its leaders (Dr. Philip Oke) was elected chairman of the executive committee for the 331 NGOs represented at U.N. headquarters in New York (ibid.).

The CPC publishes the quarterly *Christian Peace Conference* and an irregular bulletin, *CPC Information.*

World Federation of Scientific Workers. The WFSW was founded in 1946, at the suggestion of the British Association of Scientific Workers. Headquarters are in London, and its president is a British subject (and a WPC Presidential Committee member), E. H. S. Burhop.

The WFSW's highest organ, the General Assembly, apparently last met in September 1976 at London. It elects an Executive Council of 30 to 35 members. A smaller Bureau, apparently elected by either the Assembly or the Executive Council, appears to be the most important organ of this not very active organization. It met at Warsaw in September 1977 and Paris in February 1979. At the latter meeting, it was announced that the organization's strength had grown to some 450,000 members. The Chinese attack on Vietnam was predictably condemned (Radio Sofia, 19 February).

The WFSW's permanent structure is geographically dispersed. Its secretary general, the French citizen J. M. Legay, resides in Paris, not in London. The organization has regional secretariats in Prague, Cairo, and New Delhi. It has consultative stataus with both ECOSOC and UNESCO. The WFSW publishes the quarterly *Scientific World.*

International Association of Democratic Lawyers. Apparently the least active of the international fronts, the IADL has not engaged in any notable activity since the October 1978 International Lawyers' Seminar on Disarmament held at Helsinki, where it claimed a participation of about one hundred lawyers from 30 countries. This meeting, sponsored jointly by the IADL and the Finnish Democratic Lawyers, predictably condemned the neutron bomb and expressed its support for Vietnam against China.

The IADL was founded in 1946, maintains headquarters in Brussels, and claims about 25,000 members in 65 countries. It has a congress-council-bureau structure, but even the last seemingly has not met since January 1978 (in Algiers). At that meeting, however, a program for the next two years was discussed, and it was announced that the organization's Eleventh Congress would be held somewhere in Western Europe during 1980. The IADL's president is Joe Nordmann of France, and its secretary general is Gerhard Stuby of West Germany. Nordmann represents the IADL on the WPC, and Stuby is a member of the West German delegation to that body. The IADL participates in a joint working committee with the WFTU. The organization has consultative status with ECOSOC and UNESCO. It publishes the *Review of Contemporary Law* (supposedly a semiannual).

Biographies of
Prominent International
Communist Figures

MIKHAIL SERGEEVICH GORBACHEV

Born in 1931, Gorbachev is the only top Soviet leader under fifty. As a young man, he worked as an assistant combine harvester operator at a machine tractor station in Stravropol *krai* (1946–1950). However, virtually his entire career has been in party work. He became a member of the Communist Party of the Soviet Union (CPSU) three years before graduating from Moscow State University in 1955. Gorbachev worked as first secretary of the Stavropol city Komsomol committee (1956–1958), advancing to become second and then first secretary for the Stavropol region (1958–1962). He then moved to party work as first secretary of the Stavropol Municipal CPSU Committee (1958–1962), during which time he received a correspondence course degree from the local agricultural institute. His next assignments were as second secretary and then first secretary of the Stavropol *Krai* CPSU Committee (1968–1970).

Gorbachev became a member of the Supreme Soviet of the USSR and served on its Youth Affairs Committee (1970–1974). Elected a member of the CPSU Central Committee in 1971, he was brought to Moscow seven years later as national CPSU secretary in charge of agriculture, replacing Fedor Kulakov, who had died earlier in the year. On 27 November 1979, he was named a candidate member of the Politburo. Gorbachev has led CPSU delegations to Belgium (1972), West Germany (1975), and France (1976).

Sources: Borys Lewytzkyj and Juliusz Stroynowski, eds., *Who's Who in the Socialist Countries*, Munich, 1978; *NYT*, 28 November.

HENG SAMRIN

Born in 1934 in the Ponhea Krek district of Prey Veng province in eastern Kampuchea (Cambodia), Heng Samrin was a member of a large family of poor peasants. He began his revolutionary activities in 1959, advancing to battalion and then regimental commander. When the Lon Nol government fell in 1976, Samrin became political commissar and commanding officer of the Fourth Division. At the same time, he was made assistant chief of the general staff and a member of the party's executive committee for the eastern zone.

In May, Samrin and Chea Sim led insurgent forces against their own Pol Pot–Ieng Sary communist regime. According to a German source, this attempted coup was betrayed, and both men were forced to cross the border into Vietnam.

In early December 1978, a congress of Samrin and Sim supporters allegedly met and founded the United Front for National Salvation. Samrin was elected president of the Front's Central Committee.

After the capture of Phnom Penh by Vietnamese invasion forces, Samrin was elected president of the National Liberation Council, the new administration of Kampuchea, on 8 January 1979.

Representatives of the Pol Pot regime portray Samrin, who they say is also known as Rin or Weuk, as a "traitor and lackey of the Le Duan–Pham Van Dong clique." They allege that in 1955 he became chief of the brigands who were stealing cattle from Kampuchea and trading them in Vietnam for goods that they smuggled back into the country. Moreover, they assert that during the 1960s Samrin worked for the Viet Cong, stealing supplies of rice as well as poultry and cattle, and delivering them to his masters. Subsequently, they contend that he even became a member of the Viet Cong armed forces and a member of the Workers' (communist) Party of Vietnam.

Sources: *Frankfurter Allgemeine Zeitung,* 22 February; Letter and Annex of Thiounn Prastith, Kampuchean (Pol Pot) representative, addressed to the president of the Security Council, U.N. Document S/13128, 28 February; *Novoe vremya,* June, p. 8.

BABRAK KARMAL

Born around 1929, the new communist leader in Afghanistan has been a Marxist since age twenty. After graduation from a German-language secondary school, Karmal became a law student at the University of Kabul. These studies were interrupted by five years in prison for radical activities. On his release, Karmal completed law school, served in the armed forces, and then worked for the Ministry of Planning (1957–1965). He next spent eight years as a representative in the lower house of parliament until the 1973 coup abolished the legislature and the monarchy.

The Parcham (Banner) communist faction, to which Karmal belonged, competed against the Khalq (Masses) group of Nur Muhammad Taraki and Hafizullah Amin. Both cooperated in the April 1978 coup that brought them to power. Karmal became vice-president and deputy prime minister, but two months later was sent to Czechoslovakia as ambassador. In September he was ordered home to face charges of plotting a coup but remained in Prague.

Karmal is believed to have married Anahita Ratebzad, his longtime political assistant. She was made ambassador to Yugoslavia but lost that position in the general purge of Parcham faction members. Karmal has the reputation of being a most enthusiastic supporter of the USSR.

On 27 December, Amin was ousted in a bloody coup and three days later Karmal seized power with the support of 5,000 Soviet combat troops airlifted into Kabul during the two days preceding the coup, which doubled the number of Russians in Afghanistan. He proclaimed himself president, prime minister, commander-in-chief, and secretary general of the communist People's Democratic Party. In a radio speech, Karmal called his predecessor the "bought tool of world imperialism, headed by United States imperialism." He also promised to follow a policy of nonalignment. At year's end, Soviet military units (already totaling "tens of thousands" throughout the country) were patrolling the streets of Kabul.

Source: *NYT,* 28–31 December.

NIKOLAI ALEKSANDROVICH TIKHONOV

Tikhonov was born on 1 May 1905 in Kharkov (Ukraine) into a professional family. He began his working career as an assistant locomotive engineer (1924–1930); was graduated from the Dnepropetrovsk Metallurgical Institute in 1930; and subsequently spent seventeen years as an engineer, department head, and chief engineer at various plants in that city or in Pervouralsk. He served as director of a pipe factory at Nikopol (1947–1950), when Brezhnev was CPSU party secretary of that region. He won two Stalin prizes for production of pipes.

From 1950 to 1955, Tikhonov next became head of the main board of the USSR Ministry of Ferrous Metallurgy (1950–1955) and then deputy minister (1955–1957). With abolition of the ministry, he was appointed chairman of the Dnepropetrovsk Economic Council (1957–1960) and in 1958 was elected a deputy to the USSR Supreme Soviet. In 1961 he became a candidate member of the CPSU Central Committee and a full member five years later. In 1960, he assumed the chairmanship of the Scientific Economic Council attached to the USSR Council of Ministers (1960–1963). Thereafter, appointed a deputy chairman of Gosplan, in 1965 he became a deputy premier. In 1970 he was made deputy chairman of the Council of Nationalities, USSR Supreme Soviet, and in 1976 first deputy premier. In 1978 he was made a candidate member of the Politburo, and on 27 November 1979 a full member.

Tikhonov has traveled widely with Soviet government delegations. In addition to two Stalin prizes, he is the recipient of the following decorations: two Orders of Lenin, Order of the Red Banner of Labor, Hammer and Sickle Medal in Gold, and Hero of Socialist Labor.

Sources: Lewytzkyj and Stroynowski, eds., *Who's Who in the Socialist Countries*; *NYT*, 28 November.

Select Bibliography 1978–79

GENERAL ON COMMUNISM

Adomeit, Hannes, and Robert Boardman, eds. *Foreign Policy-Making in Communist Countries.* Farnborough, Eng.: Saxon House, 1979. 164 pp.

Agger, Ben. *Western Marxism.* Santa Monica, Calif.: Goodyear, 1979. 353 pp.

Babris, Peter J. *Silent Churches: Persecution of Religions in the Soviet-Dominated Areas.* Arlington Heights, Ill.: Research Publishers, 1978. 531 pp.

Birnbaum, Karl E. *The Politics of East-West Communication in Europe.* New York: Saxon House, 1979. 180 pp.

Breitman, George, ed. *Writings of Leon Trotsky: Supplement (1929–33).* New York: Pathfinder, 1979. 428 pp.

Bronner, Stephen, ed. *The Letters of Rosa Luxemburg.* Boulder, Colo.: Westview Press, 1978. 259 pp.

Brown, Archie, and Jack Gray, eds. *Political Culture and Political Change in Communist States.* New York: Holmes & Meier, 1979. 289 pp.

Burton, Anthony. *Revolutionary Violence.* New York: Crane, Russak, 1978. 147 pp.

Butler, William. *A Source Book on Socialist International Organizations.* Alphen aan den Rijn: Sijthoff & Noordhoff, 1978. 1,143 pp.

Connor, Walter D. *Hierarchy and Change in Eastern Europe and the U.S.S.R.* New York: Columbia University Press, 1979. 389 pp.

Davis, Horace. *Toward a Marxist Theory of Nationalism.* New York: Monthly Review, 1978, 294 pp.

Eddy, William. *Understanding Marxism: An Approach Through Dialogue.* Totowa, N.J.: Rowman & Littlefield, 1979. 157 pp.

Ellman, Michael. *Socialist Planning.* London: Cambridge University Press, 1979. 300 pp.

Eveev, E. S., ed. *Sionizm: Pravda i vymysly.* Moscow: Progress, 1978. 278 pp.

Forman, James D. *Communism: From Marx's Manifesto to 20th-Century Reality.* New York: Watts, 1979. 151 pp.

Francisco, Ronald A., Betty A. Laird, and Roy D. Laird, eds. *The Political Economy of Collectivized Agriculture: A Comparative Study of Communist and Non-Communist Systems.* Elmsford, N.Y.: Pergamon Press, 1979. 250 pp.

Gandy, Daniel R. *Marx and History: From Primitive Society to the Communist Future.* Austin: University of Texas Press, 1979. 190 pp.

Gould, Carol C. *Marx's Social Ontology: Individuality and Community in Marx's Theory of Social Reality.* Cambridge, Mass.: MIT Press, 1978. 208 pp.

Grier, Philip T. *Marxist Ethical Theory in the U.S.S.R.* Dordrecht: Reidel, 1978. 276 pp.

Höhmann, Hans-Hermann. *Die Wirtschaft Osteuropas und der VR China, 1970–1980.* Stuttgart: Kohlhammer, 1978. 380 pp.

Howe, Irving. *Leon Trotsky.* New York: Viking, 1978. 214 pp.

Jacobs, Dan N., ed. *From Marx to Mao and Marchais: Documents on the Development of Communist Variations.* New York: Longman, 1979. 359 pp.

Kissin, S. F. *Farewell to Revolution: Marxist Philosophy and the Modern World.* New York: St. Martin's Press, 1978. 256 pp.

Kiva, A. V. *Strany sotsialisticheskoi orientatsii.* Moscow: Nauka, 1978. 288 pp.

Klepacki, Zbigniew M. *The Organs of International Organizations.* Warsaw: PWN, 1978. 137 pp.

Kolakowski, Leszek. *Main Currents of Marxism.* London: Clarendon Press, 1978. 3 vols.

Konrád, György, et al. *Intellectuals on the Road to Class Power.* New York: Harcourt Brace Jovanovich, 1979. 252 pp.

McMurty, John M. *The Structure of Marx's World-View.* Princeton, N.J.: Princeton University Press, 1978. 269 pp.

Maguire, John M. *Marx's Theory of Politics.* New York: Cambridge University Press, 1978. 251 pp.

Mandel, Ernest. *From Stalinism to Eurocommunism: The Bitter Fruits of "Socialism in One Country."* London: New Left Books, 1978. 223 pp.

Marcou, Lilly. *L'Internationale après Staline.* Paris: Grasset, 1979. 316 pp.

Miller, James. *History and Human Existence: From Marx to Merleau-Ponty.* Berkeley: University of California Press, 1979. 287 pp.

Mitin, M. B., ed. *Ideologiia i praktika mezhdunarodnogo sionizma.* Moscow: Politizdat, 1978. 272 pp.

Molyneaux, John. *Marxism and the Party.* London: Pluto Press, 1978. 192 pp.

Proektor, D. M., et al. *European Security and Cooperation.* Moscow: Progress, 1978. 405 pp.

Raddatz, Fritz J. *Karl Marx: A Political Biography.* Boston: Little, Brown, 1979. 335 pp.

Rakowska-Harmstone, Teresa, ed. *Perspectives for Change in Communist Societies.* Boulder, Colo.: Westview Press, 1979. 194 pp.

Sarup, Madan. *Marxism and Education.* London: Routledge & Kegan Paul, 1978. 224 pp.

Sayer, Derek. *Marx's Method.* Atlantic Highlands, N.J.: Humanities Press, 1979. 197 pp.

Schaff, Adam. *Structuralism and Marxism.* Elmsford, N.Y.: Pergamon Press, 1977. 205 pp.

Schwarz, Hans-Peter, and Boris Meissner, eds. *Entspannungspolitik in Ost und West.* Cologne: Carl Heymann, 1979. 307 pp.

Sementowsky-Kurilo, Nikolaus von. *Europa und das unsichtbare Russland.* Freiburg: Aurum, 1978. 190 pp.

Shlaim, Avi, and G. N. Yannopoulos, eds. *The EEC and Eastern Europe.* Cambridge, Eng.: Cambridge University Press, 1978. 251 pp.

Sivachev, Nikolai V., and Nikolai N. Yakovlev. *Russia and the United States.* Chicago: University of Chicago Press, 1979. 301 pp.

Skocpol. Theda. *States and Social Revolutions: A Comparative Analysis of France, Russia and China.* New York: Cambridge University Press, 1979. 448 pp.

Sobel, Lester A., ed. *Political Prisoners: A World Report.* New York: Facts on File, 1978. 285 pp.

———, ed. *Refugees: A World Report.* New York: Facts on File, 1979. 225 pp.

Solzhenitsyn, Aleksandr I. *A World Split Apart: Commencement Address Delivered at Harvard University, June 8, 1978.* New York: Harper & Row, 1978. 61 pp.

Staar, Richard F., ed. *Yearbook on International Communist Affairs, 1979.* Stanford, Calif.: Hoover Institution Press, 1979. 484 pp.

Taylor, Richard. *Film Propaganda: Soviet Russia and Nazi Germany.* London: Croom Helm, 1978. 265 pp.

Thalheim, Karl C. *Die wirtschaftliche Entwicklung der beiden Staaten in Deutschland.* Opladen: Leske Verlag, 1978. 142 pp.

Ulam, Adam B. *The Unfinished Revolution: Marxism and Communism in the Modern World.* Boulder, Colo.: Westview Press, 1979. 287 pp.

Ul'ianovskii, Rostislav A. *National Liberation: Essays on Theory and Practice*. Moscow: Progress, 1978. 396 pp.

Volodin, I. A., et al. *Mezhdunarodnyi Soiuz Studentov*. Moscow: Molodaia Gvardiia, 1978. 176 pp.

Zagladin, V. V., and B. I. Koval, eds. *Mezhdunarodnoe rabochee dvizhenie: Spravochnik*. Moscow: Politizdat, 1978. 408 pp.

SOVIET UNION

Adler, Alexandre, et al. *L'URSS et nous*. Paris: Editions sociales, 1978. 223 pp.

Allback, Steven. *Alexander Solzhenitsyn*. New York: Taplinger, 1978. 222 pp.

Anschell, Eugene, ed., *American Appraisals of Soviet Russia, 1971–1977*. Metuchen, N.J.: Scarecrow, 1978. 386 pp.

Avtorkhanov, Abdurakhman. *Sila i bessilie Brezhneva*. Frankfurt/M.: Possev, 1979. 327 pp.

Bacon, Walter M., Jr. *Behind Closed Doors: Secret Papers on the Failure of Soviet-Romanian Negotiations, 1931–1932*. Stanford, Calif.: Hoover Institution Press, 1979. 212 pp.

Bajanov, Boris. *Bajanov révèle Staline: Souvenirs d'un ancien secrétaire de Staline*. Paris: Gallimard, 1979. 300 pp.

Beamish, Tufton, and Guy Hadley. *The Kremlin's Dilemma: The Struggle for Human Rights in Eastern Europe*. London: Collins, 1979. 285 pp.

Bechtel, Marilyn, David Laibman, and Jessica Smith, eds. *Six Decades That Changed the World*. New York: New World Review Publications, 1978, 264 pp.

Begin, Menachem. *White Nights: The Story of a Prisoner in Russia*. New York: Harper & Row, 1978. 240 pp.

Bellis, Paul. *Marxism and the U.S.S.R.* Atlantic Highlands, N.J.: Humanities Press, 1979. 267 pp.

Bennigsen, Alexandre A., and S. E. Wimbush. *Muslim National Communism in the Soviet Union: A Revolutionary Strategy for the Colonial World*. Chicago: University of Chicago Press, 1979. 267 pp.

Berliner, Joseph, et al. *Doing Business with the Russians*. New York: Praeger, 1979. 166 pp.

Berner, Wolfgang, et al., eds. *The Soviet Union, 1976–77: Domestic, Economic, and Foreign Policy*. New York: Holmes & Meier, 1979. 270 pp.

Bötticher, Manfred von. *Industrialisierungspolitik und Verteidigungskonzeption der UdSSR, 1926–1930*. Düsseldorf: Droste, 1979. 571 pp.

Boim, Leon, and Glenn G. Morgan. *The Soviet Procuracy Protests, 1937–1973*. Alphen aan den Rijn: Sijthoff & Noordhoff, 1978. 603 pp.

Breslauer, George W., and Stanley Rothman. *Soviet Politics and Society*. St. Paul, Minn.: West Publishers, 1978. 347 pp.

Brezhnev, Leonid I. *Aktual'nye voprosy ideologicheskoi raboty KPSS*. Moscow: Politizdat, 1978. 2 vols.

_____. *Leninskim kursom*. Moscow: Politizdat, 1979. 672 pp.

_____. *Mir sotsializma-torzhestvo velikikh dnei*. Moscow: Politizdat, 1978. 665 pp.

_____. *Na strazhe mira i sotsializma*. Moscow: Politizdat, 1979. 662 pp.

_____. *Our Course: Peace and Socialism*. Moscow: Novosti, 1978. 214 pp.

_____. *Peace, Détente, and Soviet-American Relations*. New York: Harcourt Brace Jovanovich, 1979. 235 pp.

_____. *Vozrozhdenie*. Moscow: Politizdat, 1978. 146 pp.

Brook-Shepherd, Gordon. *The Storm Petrels: The Flight of the First Soviet Defectors*. New York: Harcourt Brace Jovanovich, 1978. 288 pp.

Bruchis, Michael. *Rossiia, Rumyniia i Bessarabiia, 1812, 1918, 1924, 1940.* Tel Aviv: Russian and East European Research Center, 1979. 310 pp.

Brym, Robert J. *The Jewish Intelligentsia and Russian Marxism.* New York: Schocken, 1978. 157 pp.

Bukovskii, Vladimir. *I vozvrashchaetsia veter . . .* New York: Khronika Press, 1978. 384 pp.

————. *To Build a Castle: My Life as a Dissenter.* New York: Viking, 1978. 438 pp.

Butler, William W., comp. *The Soviet Legal System: Selected Contemporary Legislation and Documents.* New York: Oceana, 1978. 733 pp.

Cameron, George D. *The Soviet Lawyer and His System.* Ann Arbor: University of Michigan, Graduate School of Business Administration, 1978. 198 pp.

Carrère d'Encausse, Hélène. *L'Empire éclaté: La Révolte des nations en U.R.S.S.* Paris: Flammarion, 1978. 314 pp.

Chalidze, Valery, comp. *SSSR-rabochee dvizhenie?* New York: Khronika Press, 1978. 166 pp.

Chernenko, K. U., ed. *V. I. Lenin: KPSS o rabote s kadrami.* Moscow: Politizdat, 1979. 703 pp.

————, ed. *V. I. Lenin: KPSS o rabote sovetov.* Moscow: Politizdat, 1979. 744 pp.

Clarkson, Stephen. *The Soviet Theory of Development: India and the Third World in Marxist-Leninist Scholarship.* Toronto: University of Toronto Press, 1978. 322 pp.

Clements, Barbara Evans. *Bolshevik Feminist: The Life of Aleksandra Kollontai.* Bloomington: Indiana University Press, 1979. 384 pp.

Colton, Timothy J. *Commissars, Commanders and Civilian Authority: The Structure of Soviet Military Politics.* Cambridge, Mass.: Harvard University Press, 1979. 365 pp.

Conquest, Robert. *Kolyma: The Arctic Death Camps.* New York: Oxford University Press, 1979. 254 pp.

Corrigan, Philip, Harvie Ramsey, and Derek Sayer. *Socialist Construction and Marxist Theory: Bolshevism and Its Critique.* New York: Monthly Review Press, 1978. 232 pp.

Davydov, Iurii P. *Mezhdunarodnaia razriadka i ideologicheskaia bor'ba.* Kiev: Politizdat Ukrainy, 1978. 144 pp.

Dawisha, Karen. *Soviet Foreign Policy toward Egypt.* New York: St. Martin's Press, 1979. 271 pp.

Debo, Richard K. *Revolution and Survival: The Foreign Policy of Soviet Russia, 1917–18.* Toronto: University of Toronto Press, 1979. 462 pp.

Dismukes, Bradford, and James M. McConnell. *Soviet Naval Diplomacy.* Elmsford, N.Y.: Pergamon Press, 1979. 450 pp.

Douglass, Joseph D., Jr., and Amoretta M. Hoeber. *Soviet Strategy for Nuclear War.* Stanford, Calif.: Hoover Institution Press, 1979. 138 pp.

Dunstan, John. *Paths to Excellence and the Soviet School.* Windsor, Eng.: NFER Publishing, 1978. 302 pp.

Dziewanowski, M. K. *A History of Soviet Russia.* Englewood Cliffs, N.J.: Prentice-Hall, 1979. 406 pp.

Ellsworth, Raymond. *The Soviet State.* New York: New York University Press, 1978. 462 pp.

Enteen, George M. *The Soviet Scholar-Bureaucrat: M. N. Pokrovskii and the Society of Marxist Historians.* University Park: Pennsylvania State University Press, 1978. 236 pp.

Erickson, John, and E. J. Feuchtwanger, eds. *Soviet Military Power and Performance.* Hamden, Conn.: Shoe String Press, 1979. 219 pp.

Fitzpatrick, Sheila, ed. *Cultural Revolution in Russia, 1928–1931.* Bloomington: Indiana University Press, 1978. 309 pp.

Friedgut, Theodor H. *Political Participation in the USSR.* Princeton, N.J.: Princeton University Press, 1979. 356 pp.

Garvey, Terence. *Bones of Contention.* London: Routledge & Kegan Paul, 1978. 203 pp.

Gill, Graeme J. *Peasants and Government in the Russian Revolution.* New York: Barnes & Noble, 1979. 233 pp.

Goldhurst, Richard. *The Midnight War: The American Intervention in Russia, 1918–1920.* New York: McGraw-Hill, 1978. 288 pp.

Gorschkow, Sergej G. *Seemacht der Sowjetunion.* Hamburg: Hoffmann & Campe, 1978. 427 pp.

Grey, Ian. *Stalin: Man of History.* Garden City, N.Y.: Doubleday, 1979. 547 pp.

Grier, Philip T. *Marxist Ethical Theory in the Soviet Union.* Dordrecht: Reidel, 1978. 276 pp.

Grimstead, Patricia K. *Archives and Manuscript Repositories in the USSR: Estonia, Latvia, Lithuania and Belorussia.* Princeton, N.J.: Princeton University Press, 1979. 436 pp.

_____ . *Archives and Manuscript Repositories in the USSR: Moscow and Leningrad.* Princeton, N.J.: Princeton University Press, 1979. 466 pp.

Gruzinov, V. P. *The USSR's Management of Foreign Trade.* White Plains, N.Y.: Sharpe, 1979. 243 pp.

Haselkorn, Avigdor. *The Evolution of Soviet Security Strategy, 1965–1975.* New York: Crane, Russak, 1978. 139 pp.

Harding, Neil. *Lenin's Political Thought: Theory and Practice in the Democratic Revolution.* New York: St. Martin's Press, 1978. 360 pp.

Heinzig, Dieter. *Sowjetische Militärberater bei der Kuomintang, 1923–1927.* Baden-Baden: Nomos, 1978. 339 pp.

Herman, Victor. *Coming Out of the Ice.* New York: Harcourt Brace Jovanovich, 1979. 369 pp.

Hough, Jerry F., and Merle Fainsod. *How the Soviet Union is Governed.* Cambridge, Mass.: Harvard University Press, 1979. 679 pp.

Hunczak, Taras, ed. *The Ukraine, 1917–1921: A Study in Revolution.* Cambridge, Mass.: Ukrainian Studies Fund, 1979. 432 pp.

Inozemtsev, N. N. *Leninskii kurs mezhdunarodnoi politiki KPSS.* Moscow: Mysl', 1978. 208 pp.

Irickson, John, and Feuchtwanger, E. J., eds. *Soviet Military Power and Performance.* Hamden, Conn.: Shoe String Press, 1979. 219 pp.

Jacoby, Daniel, et al., eds. *L'Affaire Chtcharansky: Procès sans défense.* Paris: Grasset, 1978. 248 pp.

Jahn, Egbert, ed. *Soviet Foreign Policy: Its Social and Economic Conditions.* New York: St. Martin's Press, 1978. 160 pp.

Jain, R. K. *Soviet–South Asian Relations, 1947–1978.* Atlantic Highlands, N.J.: Humanities Press, 1979. 2 vols.

Jelen, Christian, et al. *L'Occident des dissidents.* Paris: Stock, 1979. 231 pp.

Joennson, Christer. *Soviet Bargaining Behavior: The Nuclear Test Ban Case.* New York: Columbia University Press, 1979. 309 pp.

Jones, David R., ed. *The Military-Naval Encyclopedia of Russia and the Soviet Union.* Gulf Breeze, Fla.: Academic International Press, 1978. 247 pp.

Kapitonov, I. V., ed. *Voprosy organizatsionno-partiinoi raboty KPSS: Sbornik dokumentov.* Moscow: Politizdat, 1978. 599 pp.

Karcz, Jerzy F. *The Economics of Communist Agriculture: Selected Papers.* Bloomington, Ind.: International Development Institute, 1979. 494 pp.

Keep, John L. H., ed. *The Debate on Soviet Power: Minutes of the All-Russian Central Executive Committee of Soviets. Second Convocation, October 1917–January 1918.* Oxford: Clarendon Press, 1979. 465 pp.

Kirk, Grayson, and Nils H. Wessell, eds. *The Soviet Threat: Myths and Realities.* New York: Academy of Political Science, 1978. 182 pp.

Klimenko, I. E. *Partiinoe rukovodstvo voenno-patrioticheskim vospitaniem naseleniia.* Moscow: Politizdat, 1979. 104 pp.

Krotkov, Iurii. *The Red Monarch: Scenes from the Life of Stalin.* New York: Norton, 1979. 253 pp.

Krylov, Constantine A. *The Soviet Economy: How It Really Works.* Lexington, Mass.: Lexington Books, 1979. 252 pp.

Kulinchenko, V. A., ed. *Voprosy povysheniia urovnia partiinoi raboty na sovremennom etape.* Moscow: Mysl', 1978. 263 pp.

Kuznetskaia, Liudmila I. *Lenin: Great and Human.* Moscow: Progress, 1979. 205 pp.

Lane, Christel. *Christian Religion in the Soviet Union: A Sociological Study.* Albany: State University of New York Press, 1978. 256 pp.

Lavigne, Marie, and Pierre Lavigne. *Regards sur la constitution soviétique de 1977.* Paris: Economica, 1979. 163 pp.

Lenin, V. I., and Leon Trotsky. *Kronstadt.* New York: Monad Press, 1979. 159 pp.

Lersch, Edgar. *Die auswärtige Kulturpolitik der Sowjetunion in ihren Auswirkungen auf Deutschland, 1921–1929.* Frankfurt/M.: Peter Lang, 1979. 451 pp.

Lewytzkyj, Borys. *The Soviet Union: Figures-Facts-Data.* Munich: Saur, 1979. 614 pp.

Liber, George, and Anna Mostovych. *Nonconformity and Dissent in the Ukrainian SSR, 1955–1975.* Cambridge, Mass.: Ukrainian Studies Fund, 1979. 285 pp.

Levy, Bernard-Henri. *Barbarism with a Human Face.* New York: Harper & Row, 1978. 210 pp.

McAuley, Alastair. *Economic Welfare in the Soviet Union: Poverty, Living Standards, and Inequality.* Madison: University of Wisconsin Press, 1979. 389 pp.

McClellan, Woodford. *Revolutionary Exiles: The Russians in the First International and the Paris Commune.* London: Cass, 1978. 266 pp.

Mastny, Vojtech. *Russia's Road to the Cold War: Diplomacy, Warfare, and the Politics of Communism, 1941–1945.* New York: Columbia University Press, 1979. 409 pp.

Medvedev, Roy A. *On Stalin and Stalinism.* New York: Oxford University Press, 1979. 216 pp.

Medvedev, Zhores A. *Nuclear Disaster in the Urals.* New York: Norton, 1979. 214 pp.

Meerson-Aksenov, Michael, and Boris Shragin, eds. *The Political, Social and Religious Thought of Russian "Samizdat."* Belmont, Mass.: Nordland, 1978. 624 pp.

Meissner, Boris, George Brunner, and Richard Loewenthal, eds. *Einparteisystem und bürokratische Herrschaft in der Sowjetunion.* Cologne: Markus Verlag, 1978. 320 pp.

Murphy, Paul J., ed. *Naval Power in Soviet Policy.* Washington, D.C.: U.S. Government Printing Office, 1978. 341 pp.

Naik, J. A., ed. *Russia in Asia and Africa: Documents, 1946–1971.* Kolhapur, India: Avinash Reference Publications, 1978. 664 pp.

Nove, Alec. *Political Economy and Soviet Socialism.* London: Allen & Unwin, 1979. 249 pp.

O'Dell, Felicity Ann. *Socialization Through Children's Literature: The Soviet Example.* New York: Cambridge University Press, 1978. 278 pp.

Padover, Saul K., ed. *The Letters of Karl Marx.* Englewood Cliffs, N.J.: Prentice-Hall, 1979. 576 pp.

Parming, Toenu, and Elmar Jaervesoo, eds. *A Case Study of a Soviet Republic.* Boulder, Colo.: Westview Press, 1978. 432 pp.

Pejovich, Svetozar. *Politics and Economics of the USSR.* Dallas: Fisher Institute, 1979. 101 pp.

Pliushch, Leonid. *History's Carnival: A Dissident's Autobiography.* New York: Harcourt Brace Jovanovich, 1979. 429 pp.

Rigby, T. H. *Lenin's Government: Sovnarkom, 1917–1922.* New York: Cambridge University Press, 1979. 325 pp.

Ro'i, Yaacov, ed. *The Limits of Power: Soviet Policy in the Middle East.* New York: St. Martin's Press, 1979. 376 pp.

Rosenfeldt, Niels E. *Knowledge and Power: The Role of Stalin's Secret Chancellery in the Soviet System of Government.* Copenhagen: Rosenkilde & Bagger, 1978. 219 pp.

Ryavec, Karl W., ed. *Soviet Society and the Communist Party.* Amherst: University of Massachusetts Press, 1978. 256 pp.

Rzhevsky, Leonid D. *Solzhenitsyn: Creator and Heroic Deed.* University: University of Alabama Press, 1978. 124 pp.

Sakharov, Andrei D. *Alarm and Hope.* New York: Knopf, 1978. 200 pp.

Salisbury, Harrison E. *Russia in Revolution, 1900–1930.* New York: Holt, Rinehart & Winston, 1978. 284 pp.

Scherer, John L., ed. *USSR Facts and Figures Annual.* Gulf Breeze, Fla.: Academic International Press, 1979. 309 pp.

Schwartz, Morton. *Soviet Perceptions of the United States.* Berkeley: University of California Press, 1978. 224 pp.

Scott, Harriet Fast, and William F. Scott. *The Armed Forces of the USSR.* Boulder, Colo.: Westview Press, 1979. 439 pp.

Service, Robert. *The Bolshevik Party in Revolution: A Study in Organizational Change, 1917–1923.* New York: Barnes & Noble, 1979. 246 pp.

Shamalov, Varlam. *Kolymskie rasskazy.* London: Overseas Press, 1978. 895 pp.

Shershnev, Evgenii S. *On the Principle of Mutual Advantage: Soviet-American Economic Relations.* Moscow: Progress, 1978. 211 pp.

Shindler, Colin. *Exit Visa: Détente, Human Rights and the Jewish Emigration Movement in the USSR.* London: Bachan & Turner, 1978. 291 pp.

Shneidman, N. Norman. *The Soviet Road to the Olympics: Theory and Practice of Soviet Physical Culture and Sport.* Toronto: Ontario Institute for Studies in Education, 1978. 180 pp.

Shragin, Boris I. *The Challenge of the Spirit.* New York: Random House, 1978. 262 pp.

Skrjabina, Elena. *After Leningrad: From the Caucasus to the Rhine, August 9, 1942–March 25, 1945.* Carbondale: Southern Illinois University Press, 1978. 190 pp.

Smith, Gordon B. *The Soviet Procuracy and the Supervision of Administration.* Alphen aan den Rijn: Sijthoff & Noordhoff, 1978. 155 pp.

Solomon, Peter H., Jr. *Soviet Criminologists and Criminal Policy.* New York: Columbia University Press, 1979. 248 pp.

Stites, Richard. *The Women's Liberation Movement in Russia: Feminism, Nihilism and Bolshevism.* Princeton, N.J.: Princeton University Press, 1979. 464 pp.

Swearingen, Rodger. *The Soviet Union and Postwar Japan: Escalating Challenge and Response.* Stanford, Calif.: Hoover Institution Press, 1978. 340 pp.

Tarschys, Daniel. *The Soviet Political Agenda: Problems and Priorities, 1950–1970.* White Plains, N.Y.: Sharpe, 1979. 217 pp.

Taylor, Richard. *The Politics of the Soviet Cinema, 1917–1929.* New York: Cambridge University Press, 1979. 232 pp.

Todd, Emmanuel. *The Final Fall: An Essay on the Decomposition of the Soviet Sphere.* New York: Karz, 1979. 236 pp.

Toth, Zoltan. *Prisoner of the Soviet Union.* London: Unwin Books, 1978. 202 pp.

Tselishchev, N. N. *Velikaia sila proletarskogo internatsionalizma.* Moscow: Mysl', 1978. 182 pp.

U.S. Congress, Joint Economic Committee. *Soviet Economy in a Time of Change.* Washington, D.C.: U.S. Government Printing Office, 1979. 2 vols.

Ustinov, Dmitrii F. *Izbrannye rechi i stat'i.* Moscow: Politizdat, 1979. 518 pp.

Vardys, V. Stanley. *The Catholic Church, Dissent, and Nationality in Soviet Lithuania.* Boulder, Colo.: East European Quarterly, 1978. 336 pp.

Volchikhin, V. G., comp. *Organizatory molodezhi.* Moscow: Molodaia gvardiia, 1978. 256 pp.

Wolfe, Thomas W. *The SALT Experience.* Cambridge, Mass.: Ballinger, 1979. 405 pp.

Zwass, Adam. *Money, Banking and Credit in the Soviet Union.* White Plains, N.Y.: Sharpe, 1979. 233 pp.

EASTERN EUROPE

Aczél, György. *Instead of a Cancelled Debate: Paris Asks, Budapest Answers.* Budapest: Corvina Press, 1978. 203 pp.

Albania. *Letter of the Central Committee of the Party of Labour and the Government of Albania to the Central Committee of the Communist Party and the Government of China, July 29, 1978.* Tirana: 8 Nëntori Publishing, 1978. 56 pp.

Alexander, Stella. *Church and State in Yugoslavia since 1945.* Cambridge, Mass.: Cambridge University Press, 1979. 376 pp.

Altman, Franz-Lothar, ed. *Jahrbuch der Wirtschaft Osteuropas.* Vienna: Günther Olzog Verlag, 1979. 506 pp.

Amnesty International. *Rumänien: Zur politischen Verfolgung seit 1970.* Baden-Baden:Nomos, 1978. 80 pp.

Association of Polish Students. *Dissent in Poland: Reports and Documents in Translation.* London: A.P.S., 1977. 200 pp.

Bahro, Rudolf. *The Alternative in Eastern Europe.* New York: New Left Books, 1978. 460 pp.

Barthel, Horst. *Die wirtschaftlichen Ausgangsbedingungen der DDR.* East Berlin: Akademie Verlag, 1979. 191 pp.

Bromke, Adam, and Derry Novak, eds. *The Communist States in the Era of Détente.* Oakville, Ontario: Mosaic Press, 1979. 306 pp.

Buch, Günther, comp. *Namen und Daten wichtiger Personen der DDR.* Bonn: Dietz, 1979. 386 pp.

Burda, Andrzej. *Parliament of the Polish People's Republic.* Wroclaw: Ossolineum, 1978. 174 pp.

Comisso, Ellen Turkish. *Workers' Control under Plan and Market: Implications of Yugoslav Self-Management.* New Haven, Conn.: Yale University Press, 1979. 320 pp.

Czechoslovakia. *Jahrbuch des Aussenhandels der Tschechoslowakei, 1978.* Prague: Tschechoslowakische Handelskammer, 1978. 208 pp.

de Roeck, Jef. *Der Mann aus Polen: Papst Johannes Paul II.* Düsseldorf: Patmos Verlag, 1978. 128 pp.

de Weydenthal, Jan B. *The Communists of Poland.* Stanford, Calif.: Hoover Institution Press, 1978. 217 pp.

Dunn, Dennis J. *Détente and Papal-Communist Relations, 1962-1978.* Boulder, Colo.: Westview Press, 1979. 216 pp.

Eckhardt, Karl-Heinz. *Die DDR im Systemvergleich.* Reinbek bei Hamburg: Rowohlt, 1978, 332 pp.

Erbe, Günter, et al. *Politik, Wirtschaft und Gesellschaft in der DDR.* Opladen: Westdeutscher Verlag, 1979. 419 pp.

Faye, Jean Pierre. *Prague: La Révolution des conseils ouvriers, 1968–1969. Communiqués et présentés.* Paris: Seghers-Laffont, 1978. 285 pp.

Fischer-Galati, Stephen, ed. *The Communist Parties of Eastern Europe.* New York: Columbia University Press, 1979. 393 pp.

Friss, István, ed. *Essays on Economic Policy and Planning in Hungary.* Budapest: Corvina, 1978. 279 pp.

Gać, Stanisław. *Geschichte der polnischen Armee.* East Berlin: Militärverlag der DDR, 1978. 342 pp.

Gáspár, Sándor. *The Hungarian Trade Unions in the Building of Developed Socialism.* Budapest: Táncsics Publishing House, 1978. 232 pp.

German Democratic Republic. *DDR-CSSR Sozialistische Zusammenarbeit.* East Berlin: Staatsverlag der DDR, 1978. 247 pp.

_____ . *DDR: Das Manifest der Opposition. Eine Dokumentation: Fakten-Analysen-Berichte.* Munich: W. Goldmann, 1978. 270 pp.

_____ . *Dokumente und Materialien der Zusammenarbeit zwischen der Sozialistischen Einheits-partei Deutschlands und der Kommunistischen Partei Kubas 1971 bis 1977.* East Berlin: Dietz, 1979. 282 pp.

_____ . *Kampf um Einheitsfront. Dokumente zum 60. Jahrestag der Gründung der Kommunistischen Partei Deutschlands.* East Berlin: Dietz, 1979. 104 pp.

_____ . *On the 100th Anniversary of the Publication of August Bebel's Book "Women and Socialism."* Dresden: Zeit im Bild, 1978. 174 pp.

_____ . *Zur gesellschaftlichen Stellung der Frau in der DDR.* Leipzig: Verlag für die Frau, 1978. 376 pp.

Goma, Paul. *Le Tremblement des hommes: Peut-on vivre en Roumanie aujourd'hui?* Paris: Seuil, 1979. 329 pp.

Gorbanevskaia, Natalia. *Nous, dissidents: La Dissidence en U.R.S.S., Pologne, Allemagne de l'Est, Tchécoslovaquie.* Paris: Edition recherches, 1978. 254 pp.

Guikovaty, Émile. *Tito.* Paris: Hachette, 1979. 350 pp.

Hajdú, Tibor. *The Hungarian Soviet Republic.* Budapest: Akadémiai Kiadó, 1979. 172 pp.

Henrich, Wolfgang. *Wehrkunde in der DDR.* Bonn: Hohwacht, 1978. 168 pp.

Hoxha, Enver. *Imperialism and the Revolution.* Chicago: World View Publications, 1979. 460 pp.

_____ . *Reflections on China.* Tirana: 8 Nëntori Publishing, 1979. 783 pp.

_____ . *Yugoslav "Self-Determination": A Capitalist Theory and Practice.* Tirana: 8 Nëntori Publishing, 1978. 101 pp.

Huszár, Tibor, Kálmán Kulcsár, and Sándor Szalai, eds. *Hungarian Society and Marxist Sociology in the Nineteen-Seventies.* Budapest: Corvina Press, 1978. 280 pp.

Institut für Marxismus-Leninismus. *Dokumente und Materialien der Zusammenarbeit zwischen der SED und KPK, 1971–1977.* East Berlin: Dietz, 1979. 282 pp.

Jacobsen, Hans-Adolf, et al., eds. *Drei Jahrzehnte Aussenpolitik der DDR.* Munich: Oldenbourg, 1979. 945 pp.

Kádár, János. *Sotsializm i mirovoi revoliutsionnii protsess.* Moscow: Mysl', 1978. 352 pp.

Kaplan, Karel. *Dans les archives du Comité Central: 30 ans de secrets du bloc soviétique.* Paris: Albin Michel, 1978. 365 pp.

Kardelj, Edvard. *Democracy and Socialism.* London: Summerfield Press, 1978. 244 pp.

Köpeczi, Béla. *Kulturrevolution in Ungarn.* Budapest: Corvina Verlag, 1978. 404 pp.

Konrad, George, and Ivan Szelenyi. *The Intellectuals on the Road to Class Power.* New York: Harcourt Brace Jovanovich, 1979. 252 pp.

Konstantinov, Iu. A. *Den'gi v sisteme stran SEV.* Moscow: Finansy, 1978. 288 pp.

Korkisch, Friedrich. *Fragen des ost-mitteleuropäischen Rechts.* Basel: Horst Erdmann, 1979. 408 pp.

Kovrig, Bennett. *Communism in Hungary: From Kun to Kádár.* Stanford, Calif.: Hoover Institution Press, 1979. 525 pp.

Kregel, Bernd. *Aussenpolitik und Systemstabilisierung in der DDR.* Opladen: Leske, 1979. 153 pp.

Kreile, Michael. *Osthandel und Ostpolitik.* Baden-Baden: Nomos, 1978, 242 pp.

Krejcí, Jaroslav, ed. *Sozialdemokratie und Systemwandel: 100 Jahre tschechoslowakische Erfahrung.* East Berlin: Dietz, 1978. 250 pp.

Kuhn, Heinrich. *Von der Massenpartei zur Staatspartei: Die kommunistische Bewegung in der Tschechoslowakei von der Gründung der Republik 1918 bis zum Februar-Putsch 1948.* Cologne: Bundesinstitut für Ostwissenschaftliche und Internationale Studien, 1978. 3 vols.

Kuznetov, V. I. *SEV i obshchii rynok.* Moscow: Mezhdunarodnye otnosheniia, 1978. 192 pp.

Lamberz, Werner. *Ideologische Arbeit.* East Berlin: Dietz, 1979. 582 pp.

Lammich, Siegfried, et al. *Die Staatsordnung der Tschechoslowakei.* West Berlin: Berlin Verlag, 1979. 440 pp.

Legters, Lyman H., ed. *The German Democratic Republic: A Developed Socialist Society*. Boulder, Colo.: Westview Press, 1978. 304 pp.

Leptin, Gert, and Manfred Melzer. *Economic Reform in East German Industry*. Oxford: Oxford University Press, 1978. 200 pp.

Linden, Ronald H. *Bear and Foxes: The International Relations of the East European States, 1965–1969*. New York: Columbia University Press, 1979. 328 pp.

Liubskii, M. S., et al. *Valiutnye i kreditnye otnosheniia stran SEV*. Moscow: Nauka, 1978. 160 pp.

Loebl, Eugen. *Le procès de l'aveu*. Paris: France-Empire, 1977, 284 pp.

Loew, Konrad, Peter Eisenmann, and Angelika Stoll, eds. *Betrogene Hoffnung: Aus Selbstzeugnissen ehemaliger Kommunisten*. Krefeld: Sinus Verlag, 1978. 220 pp.

Lorenz, Peter. *Multinationale Unternehmen sozialistischer Länder*. Baden-Baden: Nomos, 1978. 187 pp.

Lundestag, Geir. *The American Non-policy Towards Eastern Europe, 1943–1947*. Oslo: Universitetsforlaget, 1978. 654 pp.

Magocsi, Paul R. *The Shaping of a National Identity: Subcarpathian Rus', 1848–1948*. Cambridge, Mass.: Ukrainian Studies Fund, 1979. 655 pp.

Martin, David, ed. *Patriot or Traitor: The Case of General Mihailovich*. Stanford, Calif.: Hoover Institution Press, 1978. 499 pp.

Mies, Herbert, and W. Gerns. *Wege und Ziel der DKP*. Frankfurt/M.: Marxistische Blätter, 1979. 163 pp.

Mints, I. I., and Ia. S. Grosul, eds. *Pobeda sovetskoi vlasti v Moldavii*. Moscow: Nauka, 1978. 295 pp.

Mitrofanova, N. M. *Tseny v mekhanizme ekonomicheskogo sotrudnichestva stran-chlenov SEV*. Moscow: Nauka, 1978. 176 pp.

Mlynár, Zdenek. *Nachtfrost: Erfahrungen auf dem Weg vom realen zum menschlichen Sozialismus*. Cologne: Europäische Verlagsanstalt, 1978. 366 pp.

Moreton, N. Edwina. *East Germany and the Warsaw Alliance: The Politics of Détente*. Boulder, Colo.: Westview Press, 1978. 267 pp.

Nawrocki, Joachim. *Bewaffnete Organe in der DDR*. West Berlin: Holzapfel, 1979. 206 pp.

Neugebauer, Gero. *Partei und Staatsapparat in der DDR*. Opladen: Westdeutscher Verlag, 1978. 238 pp.

Nitz, Juergen, and Fred Merkwitschka. *German Democratic Republic*. Leiden: Sijthoff, 1978. 128 pp.

Obradović, Josip, and William N. Dunn. *Workers' Self-Management and Organizational Power in Yugoslavia*. Pittsburgh: University of Pittsburgh, Center for International Studies, 1978. 448 pp.

Oesterreich, Tina. *Ich war RF (Republikflüchtling, DDR)*. Stuttgart: Seewald Verlag, 1978. 351 pp.

Otto, Elmer Dieter. *Nachrichten in der DDR*. Cologne: Wissenschaft und Politik, 1979. 190 pp.

Pachman, Ludek. *Was in Prag wirklich geschah: Illusionen und Tatsachen aus der Ära Dubcek*. Freiburg: Herder, 1978. 127 pp.

Park, Daniel. *Oil and Gas in COMECON Countries*. New York: Nichols, 1979. 240 pp.

Paul, David W. *The Cultural Limits of Revolutionary Politics: Change and Continuity in Socialist Czechoslovakia*. New York: Columbia University Press, 1979. 361 pp.

Piekarski, Adam. *The Church in Poland*. Warsaw: Interpress Publishing, 1978. 237 pp.

Pilon, Juliana Geran. *Notes from the Other Side of the Night*. South Bend, Ind.: Regnery, 1979. 147 pp.

Poklad, B. I. *Vneshniaia politika narodnoi Pol'shi*. Moscow: Mezhdunarodnye otnosheniia, 1978. 256 pp.

Precan, Vilém. *Die sieben Jahre von Prag, 1969–1976*. Frankfurt/M.: Fischer, 1978. 253 pp.

Ra'anan, Gavriel D. *Yugoslavia after Tito: Scenarios and Implications*. Boulder, Colo.: Westview Press, 1978. 200 pp.

Rakowska-Harmstone, Teresa, and Andrew Gyorgy, eds. *Communism in Eastern Europe*. Bloomington: Indiana University Press, 1979. 338 pp.

Remington, Robin. *The International Relations of Eastern Europe: A Guide to Information Sources*. Detroit: Gale Research Co., 1978. 273 pp.

Révész, László. *Frieden durch Gewalt: Träger und Ziele der kommunistischen Friedenspolitik.* Bern: Schweizerisches Ost-Institut, 1978. 140 pp.

Riese, Hans-Peter, ed. *Since the Prague Spring.* New York: Vintage Books, 1979. 288 pp.

Rossmann, Gerhard, et al., eds. *Geschichte der Sozialistischen Einheitspartei Deutschlands. Abriss.* East Berlin: Dietz, 1978. 676 pp.

Rühmland, Ullrich, ed. *NVA-Nationale Volksarmee der DDR.* Bonn: Bonner Druck- und Verlagsgesellschaft, 1978. 304 pp.

Schneider, Eberhard. *The G.D.R.: The History, Politics, Economy, and Society of East Germany.* London: Hurst, 1978. 121 pp.

Schrenk, Martin, Cyrus Ardalan, and Nawal El Tatawy. *Yugoslavia: Self-Management Socialism and the Challenges of Development.* Baltimore: Johns Hopkins University Press, 1979. 392 pp.

Schroeder, Friedrich-Christian and Boris Meissner, eds. *Verfassungs- und Verwaltungsreformen in den sozialistischen Staaten.* West Berlin: Duncker & Humbolt, 1978. 381 pp.

Shevtsova, L. F. *Soiuznicheskie partii v politicheskoi sisteme stran sotsializma.* Moscow: Nauka, 1978. 190 pp.

Silnitský, Frantisek, et al., eds. *Communism and Eastern Europe.* New York: Karz, 1979. 242 pp.

Singer, Ladislaus. *Der ungarische Weg.* Stuttgart: Seewald Verlag, 1978. 192 pp.

Słomczyński, K., et al. *Class Structure and Social Mobility in Poland.* White Plains, N.Y.: Sharpe, 1979. 211 pp.

Sontheimer, Kurt, and Wilhelm Bleek. *Die DDR: Politik, Gesellschaft, Wirtschaft.* Hamburg: Hoffmann & Campe, 1979. 275 pp.

Teller, Hans. *Der kalte Krieg gegen die DDR.* East Berlin: Akademie Verlag, 1979. 265 pp.

Tiedtke, Stephan. *Die Warschauer Vertragsorganization.* Munich: Oldenbourg, 1978. 195 pp.

Tökés, Rudolf L., ed. *Opposition in Eastern Europe.* Baltimore: Johns Hopkins University Press, 1979. 306 pp.

Tsantis, Andreas C., and Roy Pepper. *Romania: The Industrialization of an Agrarian Economy Under Socialist Planning.* Washington, D.C.: World Bank, 1979. 707 pp.

Valenta, Jirí. *Soviet Intervention in Czechoslovakia, 1968: Anatomy of a Decision.* Baltimore: Johns Hopkins University Press, 1979. 208 pp.

Vardys, V. Stanley, and Romuald J. Misiunas, eds. *The Baltic States in Peace and War, 1917–1945.* University Park: Pennsylvania State University Press, 1978. 240 pp.

Völgyes, Iván, ed. *The Peasantry of Eastern Europe: Roots of Rural Transformation.* Elmsford, N.Y.: Pergamon Press, 1979. 192 pp.

Wiener Institute für Internationale Wirtschaftsvergleiche. *RGW in Zahlen: CMEA Data 1978.* Vienna, 1979. 535 pp.

Yugoslavia, Communist League of. *Eleventh Congress of the League of Communists of Yugoslavia.* Belgrade: Komunist, 1978. 240 pp.

WESTERN EUROPE

Adler, Alexandre, et al., eds. *L'U.R.S.S. et nous.* Paris: Editions sociales, 1978. 223 pp.

Alba, Victor. *El Partido comunista en España.* Barcelona: Planeta, 1979. 387 pp.

_____ . *Transition in Spain: From Franco to Democracy.* New Brunswick, N.J.: Transaction Books, 1978. 333 pp.

Albright, David E. *Communism and Political Systems in Western Europe.* Boulder, Colo.: Westview Press, 1979. 379 pp.

Amendola, Giorgio. *I comunisti e le elezioni europee.* Rome: Editori Riuniti, 1979. 135 pp.

_____ . *Il rinnovamento del PCI: Intervista di Renato Nicolai.* Rome: Editori Riuniti, 1978. 205 pp.

Andrieu, René. *Choses dites: 1958–1978.* Paris: Editions sociales, 1979. 508 pp.

Arango, E. Ramon. *The Spanish Political System: Franco's Legacy.* Boulder, Colo.: Westview Press, 1979. 293 pp.

Arrabal, Fernando. *Carta a los militantes comunistas españoles.* Barcelona: Actuales, 1978. 117 pp.

Baget-Bozzo, Bianni. *I Cattolici e la lettera di Berlinguer.* Florence: Vallechi, 1978. 104 pp.

Baumann, Michael (Bommi). *Bommi Baumann's Own Story of His Life as a West German Urban Guerrilla.* New York: Grove Press, 1979. 127 pp.

Benoist, Jean-Marie. *Chronique de décomposition du P.C.F.* Paris: Table ronde, 1979. 302 pp.

Bensi, Giovanni. *Mosca e l'Eurocomunismo.* Milan: La Casa di Matriona, 1978. 216 pp.

Berlinguer, Enrico, and Armando Cossutta. *Il comunisti nel governo locale.* Rome: Editori Riuniti, 1978. 111 pp.

Bettiza, Enzo. *Il comunismo europeo.* Milan: Rizzoli, 1978. 200 pp.

Bevacqua, Stefano, and Giuseppe Turani. *La svolta del 78: Il sindacato e il PCI dall'intervista di Lama alla Conferenza operaia di Napoli.* Milan: Feltrinelli, 1978. 180 pp.

Bocca, Giorgio. *Moro: Una tragedia italiana.* Milan: Bompiani, 1978. 145 pp.

Bolloten, Burnett. *The Spanish Revolution: The Left and the Struggle for Power During the Civil War.* Chapel Hill: University of North Carolina Press, 1979. 665 pp.

Bottomore, Tom, and Patrick Goode, eds. *Austro-Marxism.* New York: Oxford University Press, 1978. 316 pp.

Bournazel, Alain. *La Gauche n'aura jamais le pouvoir.* Paris: Fayolle, 1978. 247 pp.

Brown, Bernard E., ed. *Eurocommunism and Eurosocialism: The Left Confronts Modernity.* New York: Cycro Press, 1979. 408 pp.

Burles, Jean. *Le Parti communiste dans la société française.* Paris: Editions sociales, 1979. 176 pp.

Cate, Curtis. *The Ides of August: The Berlin Wall Crisis, 1961.* New York: Evans, 1978. 534 pp.

Cerroni, Umberto. *Crisi del marxismo? Intervista di Roberto Romani.* Rome: Editori Riuniti, 1978. 134 pp.

Claudin, Victor, and Francisco Herrera. *Socialistas y comunistas ante las elecciones municipales.* Madrid: Zero, 1978. 315 pp.

Close, Robert. *Europe Without Defense? 48 Hours That Could Change the Face of the World.* Elmsford, N.Y.: Pergamon Press, 1979. 250 pp.

Colorni, Giorgio. *Storie comuniste: Passato e presente di una sezione del PCI a Milano.* Milan: Feltrinelli, 1979. 267 pp.

Coverdale, John F. *The Political Transformation of Spain After Franco.* New York: Praeger, 1979. 176 pp.

Crawshaw, Nancy. *The Cyprus Revolt: An Account of the Struggle for Union with Greece.* London: Allen & Unwin, 1978. 447 pp.

Daix, Pierre. *La Crise du PCF.* Paris: Seuil, 1978. 247 pp.

_____ . *Le Futur indocile: Un Communiste dans le temps de l'incertitude.* Paris: Laffont, 1979. 239 pp.

Duhamel, Olivier, and Henry Weber, eds. *Changer le PC? Débats sur le gallocommunisme.* Paris: Presses universitaires de France, 1979. 283 pp.

Finetti, Ugo. *Il dissenso nel PCI.* Milan: Sugar, 1978. 326 pp.

Fortichiari, Bruno. *Comunismo e revisionismo in Italia: Testimonianza di un militante rivoluzionario.* Turin: Tennerello, 1978. 188 pp.

Frears, J. R., and Jean-Luc Parodi. *War Will Not Take Place: The French Parliamentary Elections, March 1978.* New York: Holmes & Meier, 1979. 149 pp.

Gintsberg, L. I. *Rabochee i kommunisticheskoe dvizhenie Germanii v bor'be protiv fashizma, 1919–1933 gg.* Moscow: Nauka, 1978. 381 pp.

Gismondi, Arturo. *Intervista sul comunismo difficile: Umberto Terracini.* Rome: Laterza, 1978. 186 pp.

Godson, Roy, and Stephen Haseler. *"Eurocommunism": Implications for East and West.* London: Macmillan, 1978. 144 pp.

Graham, Lawrence S., and Harry M. Makler. *Contemporary Portugal: The Revolution and Its Antecedents.* Austin: University of Texas Press, 1979. 401 pp.

Greece, Communist Party of. *X. [i.e., Desiatyi] s'ezd Kommunisticheskoi Partii Gretsii, 15–20 maia 1978 goda.* Moscow: Politizdat, 1979. 215 pp.

Griffith, William E. *The Ostpolitik of the Federal Republic of West Germany.* Cambridge, Mass.: MIT Press, 1978. 325 pp.

Hutter, C. M. *Eurokommunisten-Lenins treue Jünger.* Krefeld: Sinus Verlag, 1978. 176 pp.

Joll, James. *Antonio Gramsci.* New York: Viking, 1978. 160 pp.

Kapur, Harish. *"Le Nouveau communisme."* Geneva: Institut universitaire des hautes études internationales, 1978. 112 pp.

Koenig, Helmut. *Der rote Marsch auf Rom.* Stuttgart: Seewald Verlag, 1978. 364 pp.

Laurent, Paul. *Le PCF comme il est: Entretiens avec Roger Faivre.* Paris: Editions sociales, 1978. 174 pp.

Lombardo, Antonio. *Le trasformazioni del comunismo italiano.* Milan: Rizzoli, 1978. 316 pp.

Loncle, François. *Autopsie d'une rupture: La Désunion de la gauche.* Simoen, 1978. 163 pp.

Lyra, Rubens Pinto. *La Gauche en France et la construction européenne.* Paris: Librairie générale de droit et de jurisprudence, 1978. 372 pp.

McNeill, William H. *The Metamorphosis of Greece Since World War II.* Chicago: University of Chicago Press, 1978. 264 pp.

Mandel, Ernest. *La Crise 1974–1978: Les Faits, leur interprétation marxiste.* Paris: Flammarion, 1978. 226 pp.

Maravall, Jose. *Dictatorship and Political Dissent: Workers and Students in Franco's Spain.* New York: St. Martin's Press, 1978. 199 pp.

Mazzolari, Primo. *Cattolici e comunisti.* Vicenza: La Locusta, 1978. 133 pp.

Mehnert, Klaus. *Maos Erben machen's anders.* Stuttgart: Deutsche Verlags-Anstalt, 1979. 170 pp.

Mies, Herbert, and Willi Gerns. *Weg und Ziel der DKP.* Frankfurt/M.: Marxistische Blätter, 1979. 163 pp.

Mouzelis, Nicos P. *Modern Greece: Facets of Undervelopment.* New York: Holmes & Meier, 1978. 222 pp.

Negreponti-Delivani, Maria. *Analysis of Greek Economy in the Years 1960–1976.* Athens: Papazissis Publishers, 1979. 560 pp.

Occhetto, Achille, et al. *Dialogo sul movimento: I comunisti e l'universita dopo i fatti del marzo '77.* Bari: De Donato, 1978. 179 pp.

Ormea, Ferdinando. *Le origini dello stalinismo nel PCI: Storia della svolta comunista degli anni trenta.* Milan: Feltrinelli, 1978. 342 pp.

Palladino, Francesco. *Se il PCI va al governo: Intervista con Giorgio Amendola . . . e altri.* Milan: Sperling & Kupper, 1978. 191 pp.

Pallotta, Gino. *Obiettivo Moro: Un attacco al cuore dello stato.* Rome: Newton Compton, 1978. 126 pp.

Parmelin, Hélène. *Libérez les communistes!* Paris: Stock Opera et Opera Mundi, 1979. 327 pp.

Pisano, Vittorfranco S. *Contemporary Italian Terrorism: Analysis and Countermeasures.* Washington, D.C.: Library of Congress, 1979. 185 pp.

Portugal, Communist Party of. *Ensino para a democracia, democracia para o ensino.* Lisbon: Avante, 1978. 239 pp.

Rony, Jean. *Trente ans de parti: Un Communiste s'interroge.* Paris: Bourgois, 1978. 230 pp.

Royen, Christopher. *Die sowjetische Koexistenzpolitik gegenüber Westeuropa.* Baden-Baden: Nomos, 1978. 178 pp.

Rubbi, Antonio. *I partiti comunisti dell'Europa occidental.* Milan: Teti, 1978. 275 pp.

Sciascia, Leonardo. *L'Affaire Moro.* Paris: Grasset et Fasquelle, 1978. 190 pp.

Selva, Gustavo, and Eugenio Marcucci. *Il martirio di Aldo Moro: Cronaca e commenti sui 55 giorni più difficili della Repubblica.* Bologna: Cappelli, 1978. 191 pp.

Sijl, Alessandro. *Never Again Without a Rifle: The Origins of Italian Terrorism.* New York: Karz, 1979. 233 pp.

Soler Fando, Francisco. *Eurocomunismo y España.* Madrid: Prometeo, 1978. 263 pp.

Spriano, Paolo. *Intervista sulla storia del PCI.* Bari: Laterza, 1978. 236 pp.

Tamburrano, Giuseppe. *PCI e PSI nel sistema democristiano.* Bari: Laterza, 1978. 248 pp.

Tannahill, R. Neal. *The Communist Parties of Western Europe: A Comparative Study.* Westport, Conn.: Greenwood Press, 1978. 299 pp.

Tarantini, Domenico. *La democrazia totalitaria. Il Moro necessario: Potere e rivoluzione oggi in Italia.* Verona: Bertani, 1979. 165 pp.

Tökés, Rudolf L., ed. *Eurocommunism and Détente.* New York: New York University Press, 1979. 578 pp.

Willard, Claude. *Socialisme et communisme français,* rev. ed. Paris: A. Colin, 1978. 199 pp.

Winkler, Karlheinz. *Die Geldquellen der DKP.* Cologne: Edition Agrippa, 1978. 130 pp.

Zimmermann, Rüdiger. *Der Leninbund: Linke Kommunisten in der Weimarer Republik.* Düsseldorf: Droste Verlag, 1978. 307 pp.

ASIA AND THE PACIFIC

Alitto, Guy S. *Liang Shu-ming and the Chinese Dilemma of Modernity.* Berkeley: University of California Press, 1979. 396 pp.

Amnesty International. *Political Imprisonment in the People's Republic of China.* London: Amnesty International Publications, 1978. 176 pp.

Bennett, Gordon, et al. *Huadong: The Story of a Chinese People's Commune.* Boulder, Colo.: Westview Press, 1978. 197 pp.

Borrow, Davis B., Steven Chan, and John A. Kringen. *Understanding Foreign Policy Decisions: The Chinese Case.* Riverside, N.J.: Free Press, 1979. 320 pp.

Chung, Chin O. *P'yongyang Between Peking and Moscow: North Korea's Involvement in the Sino-Soviet Dispute.* University: University of Alabama Press, 1978. 230 pp.

Chung, Chong-shik, ed. *Korean Unification.* Seoul: Research Center for Peace and Unification, 1979. 392 pp.

Chung, Chong-shik, and Chong-wook Chung, eds. *Major Powers and the Peace in Korea.* Seoul: Research Center for Peace and Unification, 1978. 250 pp.

Clough, Ralph N. *Island China.* Cambridge, Mass.: Harvard University Press, 1978. 264 pp.

Cohen, Robin, Peter C. W. Gutkind, and Phyllis Brazier. *Peasants and Proletariat: The Struggles of Third World Workers.* New York: Monthly Review Press, 1979. 505 pp.

Croll, Elisabeth. *Feminism and Socialism in China.* Boston: Routledge & Kegan Paul, 1978. 363 pp.

Crook, David, and Isabel Crook. *Ten Mile Inn: Mass Movement in a Chinese Village.* New York: Pantheon Press, 1979. 291 pp.

Dashzhamts, D. *Rasprostranenie i utverzhdenie idei marksizma-leninizma v Mongolii.* Moscow: Nauka, 1978. 216 pp.

Daubier, Jean. *Les Nouveaux maîtres de la Chine.* Paris: Grasset, 1979. 287 pp.

David, Delia. *Woman-Work: Women and the Party in Revolutionary China.* New York: Oxford University Press, 1979. 256 pp.

Dengler, Dieter. *Escape from Laos.* San Rafael, Calif.: Presidio Press, 1979. 211 pp.

Fogel, Joshua A., and William T. Rowe, eds. *Perspectives on a Changing China.* Boulder, Colo.: Westview Press, 1979. 325 pp.

Gelber, Harry G. *Technology, Defense and External Relations in China, 1975–1978.* Boulder, Colo.: Westview Press, 1979. 229 pp.

Ginsburgs, George, and Carl F. Pinkele. *The Sino-Soviet Territorial Dispute, 1949–64.* New York: Praeger, 1978. 145 pp.

Harris, Nigel. *The Mandate of Heaven: Marx and Mao in Modern China.* New York: Horizon Press, 1979. 307 pp.

Hinton, Harold C., ed. *The People's Republic of China: A Handbook.* Boulder, Colo.: Westview Press, 1979. 443 pp.

Huang, Philip C. C., L. S. Bell, and K. L. Walker. *Chinese Communists and Rural Society, 1927–1934.* Berkeley, Calif.: Institute of East Asian Studies, 1978. 121 pp.

India, Communist Party of. *XI s'ezd kommunisticheskoi partii Indii: 31 Marta–7 aprelya 1978 g.* Moscow: Politizdat, 1979. 192 pp.

Kallgren, Joyce K., ed. *The People's Republic of China After Thirty Years: An Overview.* Berkeley, Calif.: Institute of East Asian Studies, 1979. 122 pp.

Kampuchea Démocratique. Ministère des affairs étrangères. *Livre noir: Faits et preuves des acts d'agression et d'annexion du Vietnam contre le Kampuchea.* Phnom Penh: Department de la presse et d'information, 1978. 112 pp.

Kang, Young-hoon, and Yong-soon Yim, eds. *Politics of Korean Reunification.* Seoul: Research Center for Peace and Unification, 1978. 250 pp.

Kim, Samuel S. *China, the United Nations, and World Order.* Princeton, N.J.: Princeton University Press, 1979. 580 pp.

Kintner, William R., and John F. Copper. *A Matter of Two Chinas.* Philadelphia: Foreign Policy Research Institute, 1979. 127 pp.

Kosaka, Masataka, ed. *Asian Security 1979.* Tokyo: Research Institute for Peace and Security, 1979. 223 pp.

Kuz'min, V. V. *Kitai v strategii amerikanskogo imperializma.* Moscow: Mezhdunarodnye otnosheniya, 1978. 272 pp.

Lee, Hong Yung. *The Politics of the Chinese Political Revolution.* Berkeley: University of California Press, 1978. 369 pp.

Lelyusin, L. P., ed. *Gosudarstvo i obshchestvo v Kitae.* Moscow: Nauka, 1978. 276 pp.

Louis, Victor. *The Coming Decline of the Chinese Empire.* New York: Times Books, 1979. 198 pp.

McMillen, Donald H. *Chinese Communist Power and Policy in Xinjiang, 1949–1977.* Boulder, Colo.: Westview Press, 1979. 373 pp.

Marr, David, ed. *Reflections from Captivity: Phan Boi Chau's Prison Notes and Ho Chi Minh's Prison Diary.* Athens: Ohio University Press, 1978. 113 pp.

Maswami, A. M. K. *Subversion in East Pakistan.* Lahore: Amir Publishers, 1979. 304 pp.

Meisner, Maurice. *Mao's China.* Riverside, N.J.: Free Press, 1979. 416 pp.

Middleton, Drew. *The Duel of the Giants: China and Russia in Asia.* New York: Scribner's, 1978. 241 pp.

Morwood, William. *Duel for the Middle Kingdom.* Edison, N.J.: Everest House, 1979. 448 pp.

Murata, Kiyoaki. *Japan: The State of the Nation.* Tokyo: Maruzen, 1979. 420 pp.

Musolf, Lloyd D., and J. Frederick Springer. *Malaysia's Parliamentary System.* Boulder, Colo.: Westview Press, 1979. 143 pp.

Onate, A. D. *Chairman Mao and the Chinese Communist Party.* Chicago, Ill.: Nelson-Hall, 1979. 289 pp.

Passin, Herbert, ed. *A Season of Voting: The Japanese Elections of 1976 and 1977.* Washington, D.C.: American Enterprise Institute, 1979. 199 pp.

Pepper, Suzanne. *Civil War in China: The Political Struggle, 1945–1949.* Berkeley: University of California Press, 1978. 472 pp.

Roshchin, S. K. *Razvitie sotsialisticheskikh proizvodstvennykh otnoshenii v MNR.* Moscow: Nauka, 1979. 160 pp.

Rupen, Robert. *How Mongolia Is Really Ruled.* Stanford, Calif.: Hoover Institution Press, 1979. 225 pp.

Schaller, Michael. *The United States and China in the 20th Century.* New York: Oxford University Press, 1979. 199 pp.

Selden, Mark, and Patti Eggleston, eds. *The People's Republic of China: A Documentary History of Revolutionary Change.* New York: Monthly Review Press, 1979. 718 pp.

Shaplen, Robert. *A Turning Wheel: Three Decades of the Asian Revolution.* New York: Random House, 1979. 397 pp.

Shichor, Yitzhak. *The Middle East in China's Foreign Policy, 1949–1977.* New York: Cambridge University Press, 1979. 272 pp.

Starr, John Bryan. *Continuing the Revolution: The Political Thought of Mao.* Princeton, N.J.: Princeton University Press, 1979. 352 pp.

Stavis, Benedict. *The Politics of Agricultural Mechanization in China.* Ithaca, N.Y.: Cornell University Press, 1978. 288 pp.

Suh, Cang-Chul. *Growth and Structural Changes in the Korean Economy, 1910–1940.* Cambridge, Mass.: Harvard University Press, 1978. 227 pp.

Teiwes, Frederick C. *Politics and Purges in China: Rectification and the Decline of Party Norms, 1950–1965.* New York: Sharpe, 1979. 700 pp.

Terrill, Ross. *The China Difference.* New York: Harper & Row, 1979. 335 pp.

Ul'yanovskiy, R. A., ed. *Komintern i vostok: Kritika kritiki.* Moscow: Nauka, 1978. 374 pp.

Voronin, S. V. *Rabochiy klass Shri Lanki.* Moscow: Nauka, 1979. 280 pp.

White, Lynn T., III. *Careers in Shanghai: The Social Guidance of Personal Energies in a Developing Chinese City, 1949–1966.* Berkeley: University of California Press, 1978. 249 pp.

Yahouda, Michael B. *China's Role in World Affairs.* New York: St. Martin's Press, 1978. 298 pp.

THE AMERICAS

Arico, José, ed. *Mariátegui y los origines del marxismo latinoamericano.* Mexico City: Siglo Veintiuno, 1978. 321 pp.

Avakumovic, Ivan. *Socialism in Canada: A Study of the CCF/NDP in Federal and Provincial Politics.* Toronto: McClelland & Stewart, 1978. 316 pp.

Bart, Philip, et al., eds. *Highlights of a Fighting History: 60 Years of the Communist Party, USA.* New York: International Publishers, 1979. 516 pp.

Belfrage, Cedric, and James Aronson. *Something to Guard: The Stormy Life of the "National Guardian," 1948–1967.* New York: Columbia University Press, 1978. 362 pp.

Blasier, Cole, and Carmelo Mesa-Lago, eds. *Cuba in the World.* Pittsburgh: University of Pittsburgh Press, 1979. 324 pp.

Castells, Manuel. *La teoría marxista de las crisis económicas y las transformaciones del capitalismo.* Mexico City: Siglo Veintiuno, 1978. 145 pp.

Chavarria, Jesus. *José Carlos Mariátegui and the Rise of Modern Peru, 1890–1930.* Albuquerque: University of New Mexico Press, 1979. 247 pp.

Colletti, Lucio, comp. *El marxismo y el "derrumbe" del capitalismo.* Mexico City: Siglo Veintiuno, 1978. 472 pp.

Cox Balmaceda, Ricardo. *La crisis democrática.* Santiago: Editorial Andres Bello, 1978. 389 pp.

Darusenkov, O. T., and B. A. Strashun, eds. *Respublika Kuba*. Moscow: Iurizdat, 1978. 320 pp.

Dominguez, Jorge I. *Cuba: Order and Revolution*. Cambridge, Mass.: Harvard University Press, 1978. 683 pp.

Espy, Richard. *Politics of the Olympic Games*. Berkeley: University of California Press, 1979. 212 pp.

Gargurevich, Juan. *La razón del joven Mariátegui: Crónica del primer diario de izquierda en el Perú*. Lima: Editorial Horizonte, 1978. 165 pp.

Klehr, Harvey. *Communist Cadre: The Social Background of the American Communist Party*. Stanford, Calif.: Hoover Institution Press, 1978. 141 pp.

Kozol, Jonathan. *Children of the Revolution: A Yankee Teacher in Cuban Schools*. New York: Delacorte Press, 1978. 245 pp.

Liebman, Arthur. *Jews and the Left*. New York: John Wiley & Sons, 1979. 676 pp.

Lopez Trujillo, Alfonso. *Hacia una sociedad nueva: Socialismo, opción cristiana?* Bogota: Ediciones Paulinas, 1978. 146 pp.

Lora, Guillermo. *¿Qué es el trotskysmo?: Bolivia y la revolución permanente*. La Paz: Ediciones el Amauta, 1978. 285 pp.

Mires, Fernando. *La revolución no es una isla: El proceso de transformación política en Cuba*. Medellín, Colombia: Hombre Nuevo, 1978. 300 pp.

Noyola, Juan F. *La economía cubana en los primeros años de la revolución*. Mexico City: Sigli Veintiuno, 1978. 279 pp.

Painter, Nell Irvin. *The Narrative of Hosea Hudson: His Life as a Negro Communist in the South*. Cambridge, Mass.: Harvard University Press, 1979. 400 pp.

Pena, Faustino. *Ensayo freudo-marxista social colombiano: Los conflictos y problemas psíquico emocionales como producto del sistema económico en que se vive*. Bogota: Herrera Hermanos, 1978. 134 pp.

Ramm, Hartmut. *The Marxism of Regis Debray*. Lawrence: Regents Press of Kansas, 1978. 240 pp.

Rodriguez, Carlos Rafael. *Cuba en el tránsito al socialismo (1959–1963): Lenin y la cuestión colonial*. Mexico City: Siglo Veintiuno, 1978. 233 pp.

Sensat, Julius. *Habermas and Marxism: An Appraisal*. Beverly Hills, Calif.: Sage, 1979. 176 pp.

Theen, Rolf H. W. *Genesis and Development of a Revolutionary*. Princeton, N.J.: Princeton University Press, 1979. 194 pp.

United States. *Directory of Cuban Officials: A Reference Aid*. Washington, D.C.: Central Intelligence Agency, 1979. 236 pp.

United States, Communist Party of. *Highlights of a Fighting History*. New York: International Publishers, 1979. 516 pp.

Walker, Walter. *The Bear at the Back Door: The Soviet Threat to the West's Lifeline in Africa*. Richmond, Eng.: Foreign Affairs Publishing Co., 1978. 246 pp.

Zarodov, Konstantin I., ed. *One Thousand Days of Revolution: CP Chile Leaders on Lessons of the Events in Chile*. Prague: Peace & Socialism, 1978. 149 pp.

Zinov'eva, R. A. *Latinskaya Amerika*. Moscow: Nauka, 1978. 168 pp.

AFRICA AND THE MIDDLE EAST

Batatu, Hanna. *The Old Social Classes and the Revolutionary Movements of Iraq*. Princeton, N.J.: Princeton University Press, 1979. 1,283 pp.

Bill, James A., and Carl Leiden. *Politics in the Middle East*. Boston: Little, Brown, 1979. 416 pp.

Djazani, Bijan. *Klassenkämpfe in Iran*. Zurich: Pinkus, 1978. 187 pp.

Eritreans for Liberation in North America. *Eritrea: Liberation or Capitulation*. New York, 1978. 114 pp.

Fokina, G. K., ed. *I. s'ezd Narodnogo dvizheniia za osvobozhdenie Angoly (MPLA)*. Moscow: Politizdat, 1978. 280 pp.

Freedman, Robert O. *World Politics and the Arab-Israeli Conflict*. Elmsford, N.Y.: Pergamon Press, 1979. 246 pp.

Gann, L. H., and Peter Duignan. *South Africa: War, Revolution, or Peace?* Stanford, Calif.: Hoover Institution Press, 1978. 85 pp.

Halliday, Fred. *Iran, Dictatorship and Development*. New York: Penguin, 1979. 348 pp.

Heikal, Mohamed. *The Rise and Fall of the Soviet Influence in the Middle East*. New York: Harper & Row, 1978. 304 pp.

Ivanov, Iu. M., and A. S. Organova. *Afrika: U istokov klassovykh bitv*. Moscow: Nauka, 1978. 214 pp.

Kaplan, Irving, ed. *Zaire: A Country Study*. Washington, D.C.: American University, Foreign Area Studies, 1978. 332 pp.

Kelidar, Abbas. *The Integration of Modern Iraq*. New York: St. Martin's Press, 1979. 200 pp.

Levin, Z. I. *Razvitie arabskoi obshchestvennoi mysli, 1917–1945*. Moscow: Nauka, 1979. 199 pp.

Marcum, John A. *The Angolan Revolution: Exile Politics and Guerrilla Warfare, Vol. 2, 1962–1976*. Cambridge, Mass.: MIT Press, 1978. 473 pp.

Miské, Ahmed-Bâba. *Front Polisario: L'Ame d'un peuple, suivi d'un entretien avec Jean Lacoutre*. Paris: Editions rupture, 1978. 383 pp.

Nyrop, Richard. *Syria: A Country Study*. Washington, D.C.: American University, 1979. 268 pp.

Pelissier, Rene. *La Colonie du Minotaure: Nationalismes et revoltes en Angola, 1926–1961*. Montamets: Pelissier, 1978. 726 pp.

Penniman, Howard R., ed. *Israel at the Polls*. Washington, D.C.: American Enterprise Institute, 1979. 334 pp.

Sahara, Democratic Republic of. *L'Escalade impérialiste contre le peuple sahraoui: Du Refus du combat par l'armée mauritanienne (opération de zouérate, 1er mai 1977) à l'engagement direct des forces d'intervention françaises (novembre-decembre 1977)*. Paris: Association des amis de la République saharouie démocratique, 1978. 146 pp.

Stookey, Robert W. *Yemen: The Politics of the Yemen Arab Republic*. Boulder, Colo.: Westview Press, 1978. 240 pp.

Toko, Gad W. *Intervention in Uganda: The Power Struggle and Social Involvement*. Pittsburgh: University of Pittsburgh, Center for International Studies, 1979. 160 pp.

Ul'yanovsky, Rostislav A. *National Liberation: Essays on Theory and Practice*. Moscow: Progress, 1978. 396 pp.

Urdang, Stephanie. *Fighting Two Colonialisms: Women in Guinea-Bissau*. New York: Monthly Review Press, 1979. 320 pp.

Warburg, Gabriel. *Islam, Nationalism and Communism in a Traditional Society: The Case of Sudan*. Totowa, N.J.: Frank Cass, 1978. 253 pp.

Zabih, Sepehr. *Iran's Revolutionary Upheaval*. San Francisco: Alchemy Books, 1979. 104 pp.

INDEX OF NAMES